Photo by Kahn

Columbia Street, looking east, Farmington, Mo.

Columbia Street in 1900 looking east. Present location of Mercantile Bank parking lot on left, Ozark Federal on right corner.

Washington Street in 1900s.

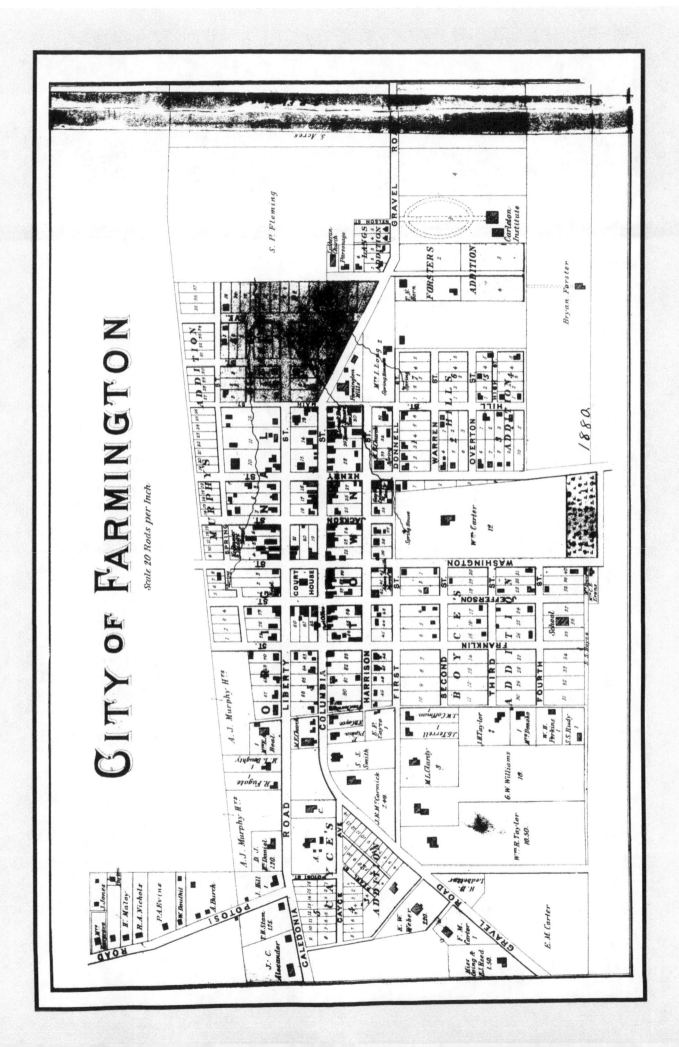

CITY OF FARMINGTON

Scale 20 Rods per Inch

FARMINGTON, MISSOURI

The First 200 Years
1798 - 1998

TURNER PUBLISHING COMPANY

TURNER PUBLISHING COMPANY
Publishers of America's History

Book Committee Chairman: Lynn Crites
Publishing Consultant: Douglas W. Sikes
Project Coordinator: John M. Jackson
Book Designer: Ina F. Morse

Copyright © 2000 Focus on Farmington
Foundation and Farmington Public Library
All rights reserved.
Publishing Rights: Turner Publishing Company

Library of Congress
Catalog Card No.: 00-102581
ISBN: 978-1-68162-494-5

Limited Edition, First Printing 2000 AD.
Additional copies may be purchased from
Turner Publishing Company and the
Farmington Public Library.

Photo: Morris Brothers Store, about 1910.

*Book cover: The seal used on the front book cover
is the official city seal of Farmington adopted
August 17, 1931.*

TABLE OF CONTENTS

DEDICATION

Clarence Edward "Pal" Wood

This book is dedicated to Clarence Edward "Pal" Wood. Pal was born on March 25, 1879, near Doe Run, MO, the son of Franklin and Rebecca Ann Wood.

Pal was a house painter by trade and an avid lover of sports, playing on the first football team for Carleton College. His hobby was collecting old pictures and newspaper articles on Farmington and its citizens. This large collection he lovingly placed in two newspaper-size scrapbooks and aptly named them "Farmingtonia." When the scrapbooks were completed, he donated them to the Farmington Public Library. Many of you may have looked at them in the library before they became so fragile.

Little did Pal know the "hobby" he began so many years ago would be the inspiration for us to compile this history book. We would like to think he would be extremely proud of us for carrying on the job he so lovingly began all those years ago. Maybe our works of love will be the inspiration for someone 50 years from now to carry on what he began.

Pal remained a bachelor and died on March 23, 1947. He is buried in Pendleton Cemetery at Doe Run, MO.

PATRON DONATIONS

The Bicentennial History Book Committee would like to thank the following people who gave so generously to make the printing of this history book possible:

Mr. and Mrs. June A. Corben
Mildred H. Eaton
Helen Giessing
Harold G. Hastings
Mrs. Alex A. Hawn
E.O. Klein

PREFACE

Bicentennial History Book Committee. Front, L-R: Committee Chairman Lynn Crites, Elma Jennings, Mary Ellen Halbrook, Jon Cozean. Rear: Terry Hall, Bonnie Coleman, Janet Douglas, Janet Beck, Jack Clay, and Mary Ruth Moon.

This book on the history of Farmington represents more than two and a half years of work by the staff of the Farmington Public Library and a committee of volunteers. To make it easier for the reader to find specific pieces of information, we have divided the book into chapters, the last of which focuses on family histories.

While the book committee is pleased with the results of its work, it must be pointed out that no single volume could contain the complete story of the city of Farmington and its residents. Often times our workers were limited by the availability of material and time to produce a thorough treatment of many topics. Because of a limitation of time and space, we chose to include in this volume reprints of selected published articles as well as original material that was submitted to us by the public. In many cases our staff had to depend on the accuracy of the information submitted to us. Thus, we cannot claim that all names, dates, places mentioned in this book are entirely accurate. To be sure, we took every precaution to avoid errors, but given our limited resources, some errors of fact and omission of information are inevitable.

Because of a shortage of space, we were forced to limit the scope of material about Farmington in this single volume. Perhaps, someday in the future, another effort may be made to expand on the work we have begun. Still, we would like to point out the Farmington Public Library contains large amounts of additional historic information about our city and its inhabitants and history. You are invited to visit the library and explore this material, which includes several thousand photos now stored on the library computer system.

We hope you enjoy this book about our favorite city.

Bicentennial History Book Committee
Janet Beck, Jack Clay, Bonnie Coleman, Jon Cozean, Lynn Crites, Janet Douglas, Mary Ellen Halbrook, Terry Hall, Elma Jennings, Mary Ruth Moon, 2000

ACKNOWLEDGMENTS

"Why don't we put together a history book?" How simple those words seemed at the time. Little did I know when I casually said them what an endeavor lay ahead for me and a group of unbelievably dedicated people.

We had our first organizational meeting in February 1998. Those present automatically became members of the Bicentennial History Book Committee and innocently embarked on two and a half years they will probably not soon forget.

To Janet Beck, Jack Clay, Jon Cozean, Janet Douglas, Mary Ellen Halbrook, Elma Jennings and Mary Ruth Moon my undying gratitude. Whether you went door-to-door selling business pages, slaved over a computer for hours writing for the book, or with red pen in hand did hours of proof reading, your words of encouragement and support were the force which kept me going.

To Bonnie Coleman and Terry Hall, two of my staff who also served on the committee many thanks. They not only worked on the history book, Bonnie typing and retyping stories, and keeping book orders straight, and Terry scanning endless stacks of photos into the computer and searching the history collection for information, all the while performing their regular library duties as well. No matter what I asked them to do, they never complained.

To the rest of the library staff: Lorraine Barnes, Mildred Eaton, Cathy Marler, Angela McClure, Fern Smallen, and Brandi Schimweg, many thanks for carrying the extra load when Bonnie, Terry and I fell behind. A special thanks to Cathy Marler for proofreading all the chapters and keeping us grammatically correct.

To Sandy Mackley, Linda Schlichter and the members of the book committee who proofread the biographies, thank you so much.

To the citizens of Farmington who rallied around and donated money when publication costs needed to be met. You came to our aid when the book committee was overwhelmed with, "What do we do now? Your unwavering support was so heartwarming and greatly appreciated.

To those people who dug through boxes of photographs in closets, attics and basements and brought them down to us so we might use them in our book. Thank you for sharing with us your most cherished treasures. A special thanks to Faye Sitzes for generously sharing with us her large photograph and history collection. To all those people the committee called for information and verification of facts, I thank you for your help.

In closing, I want to thank the families who slaved for weeks and sometimes months writing and rewriting their family history. This was very hard for many of you, emotionally as well as the actual writing of your story. Without those hours of digging through old photos and family records this book would not have become such an excellent source for family history. Your grandchildren and great-grandchildren, for generations to come, will be so glad you cared enough and took the time to write your family history.

Lynn Crites

Lynn Crites
Chairman, Bicentennial History Book Committee, 1999

FARMINGTON, MISSOURI HISTORY

FARMINGTON, MISSOURI

The town of Farmington, first known as Murphy's Settlement, has had a four-fold heritage. The first of those might be called a sort of land tenure of farming. During the Spanish occupancy of upper Louisiana, Rev. William Murphy, who had been born in Ireland and was then living on the Holston River in East Tennessee, together with three of his sons and a friend, Silas George, came to this area in 1798.

Spain was offering Spanish Land Grants to the Americans to settle the land west of the Mississippi River known as the Louisiana Territory. When they arrived by boat at Ste. Genevieve, there was no one in that settlement who could understand English. They were introduced and stayed with Mr. Madden three miles from Ste. Genevieve. The next day, using an Indian as their guide, these men came to the present site of Farmington. These five men each claimed 640 acres. On the trip back to Eastern Tennessee, Silas George died; and just one day's journey from home, Rev. William Murphy also died. His family, notwithstanding his death, came back. The sons arrived in 1800 and his widow, Sarah Barton Murphy, came later.

The Indians had proved to be a danger to the early settlers of Murphy's Settlement and in 1800 a strong log fort was built near the William Murphy claim. In 1824 the Indians were removed by the government to a tract of land in Kansas. The old fort remained intact for many years but was finally demolished.

It was not until 1801 that the first tree was felled in this settlement by David Murphy, William's son, who came out from the Gabourie Creek, near Ste. Genevieve, MO, where he had settled in 1799 with his slaves.

In 1802 he was joined by his brother, William Junior, who first settled in Illinois. Richard, another brother, also settled near his brothers in 1802.

As soon as possible, the widow Mrs. Murphy, with the remainder of her family, Isaac, Jesse, a grandson William Evans, a hired hand, and a colored woman and boy, made the journey to join her sons. They traveled down the Tennessee River, then up the Mississippi River in keel-boats, traveling only at night for their safety from Indians, to the settlement of Ste. Genevieve. On June 12, 1802, she and her family arrived at the home of her son, Richard.

The second heritage which the town of Farmington has acquired began with the arrival of Sarah Barton Murphy. Mrs. Murphy was a devout Christian and her influence was soon felt in the community. Possibly the first Protestant religious service ever held west of the Mississippi was a thanksgiving prayer meeting conducted in her home soon after her arrival. There were few problems in the early Murphy Settlement as most of the settlers were good Christians; but when a problem did arise, the disagreeing parties approached Sarah Barton Murphy for a fair and just decision which was accepted by everyone involved.

Sarah Barton Murphy donated one acre of land upon which to build a church that could be used by all denominations. A log cabin was built, 22 x 30 feet. She promised to give this church to

Sketch of Hopkins Farm previously known as the Murphy Farm. Presently owned by Scott Plummer.

Old Murphy Springhouse, on Washington Street.

the first preacher who came here and maintained the church. Mrs. Murphy, who had always been a Baptist, put religion above creed and welcomed the first Methodist circuit rider, Rev. Joseph Oglesby, who visited the settlement in 1804 and preached at her home.

Soon afterward she went among the settlement asking the parents to send their children to her house on Sundays, where she kept them all day, teaching them Bible lessons, also how to sing, read and write and gave them a good dinner. This she continued to do for some time and from this beginning grew a Sunday School which she organized and maintained until her death. The year was 1805 and this was the first Sunday School west of the Mississippi River.

Mrs. Murphy died in 1817 and was buried where the Masonic Hall is today, then later moved to the Masonic Cemetery. She lived in Murphy's Settlement only 17 years, but her influence and values live on in her descendants.

The third heritage established Farmington as the permanent seat of justice of St. Francois County. In 1821 David Murphy donated 52 acres of his farm to St. Francois County upon which to establish the county seat. This was done with

Oldest home in Farmington, David Murphy home being torn down.

the provision that he would retain two acres of town lots and one acre upon which to build the county courthouse.

As a result of this gift, Farmington was surveyed by Henry Poston, who filed the survey on February 27, 1823. The original town consisted of 24 blocks bordered by what is now Spring Street on the north, First Street on the south, Main Street on the east, and "A" Street on the west. There were 73 lots in this survey. They were about 75 feet wide, ran the entire depth of the block, and were numbered 1-73. In this deed, Mr. Murphy was to receive back his choice of lots to make up two acres. His first choice for one lot was the land where Mercantile Bank and Coldwell Bankers Real Estate is now located. The other spot he chose was the lot behind the McIntosh Building on the corner of South Jackson and Columbia Streets. This made up the two acres.

The first known ball was given in Murphy's Settlement on July 4, 1822. John D. Peers made a speech and read the Declaration of Independence. At this celebration the first political speech was made by Captain Besh, who was a candidate for Congress at that time.

Farmington was incorporated in 1836 by order of the County Court, its population was 500; 75 votes were cast, 74 for and only 1 against incorporation. The first board of trustees consisted of J.D. Peers, M.P. Cayce, Edward C. Sebastian, William Ross and Nicholas Fleming.

The fourth heritage which has been truly characteristic of this community was the early interest in education. Early education consisted of private schooling in homes and in 1803 Sarah Barton Murphy established her own private school. In 1854 the Carleton Institute was founded by Eliza A. Carleton. The original location of the school was eight miles north of Farmington, but in 1876 Miss Carleton purchased 16 acres of land within the city limits and

the institute was moved. In September 1886, the Baptists of the Franklin Association opened Farmington College, and in the same year Elmwood Seminary and Presbyterian Normal School for ladies were opened. This institution was a revival of Elmwood Academy, established in the early 1840s by Milton P. Cayce. The Farmington Public School system began about 1870 on the present site of W.L. Johns School.

A Trip To Farmington And The Lead Mines

(All we know about the author is that his name was Isaac and his account has been transcribed as it was written.)

On July 25, 1901, we left Des Arc and arrived at Farmington on the 26th. Farmington has grown wonderfully in 10 years. Its population must be near 3,000 and is the busiest place I have seen in Southeast Missouri. I visited several places; they are doing a big business. The Giessings have two mills, and one of them had an order for 10 loads of flour and was running part of every night. They grind 300 bushels of wheat daily. They bought 20 car loads of wheat from Charleston the week I was there. I did not see the host mill but I understand they are doing well. The merchants there are also doing a fine business. The Grand Leader certainly has the

right name. They carry an $18,000 stock of general merchandise, corn, hay, etc. They run two delivery wagons and their sales will reach $50,000 this year. Their home is 40 x 160 ft. besides the corn and hay houses. The members of the firm are Dave Reece and Zwart Bros., sons of the late Captain Zwart, of Ironton, MO. The next store I will mention is the Morris Bros. formerly of Des Arc. They have a splendid up-to-date house, 40x80, glass front, two-story and a large basement. They carry a $12,000 stock and buy by the car load. They get a big trade from the lead mines, and their store is crowded all the time. Their sales up to the first of August will reach $5,000. The saloons also prosper. There are five of them, and one of the saloon keepers told me they sold 150 gallons of beer daily, and there are eight or 10 other stores, all doing a fair business. There are three harness factories; they ship harnesses all over Southeast Missouri. Our merchants here buy horse collars from Farmington, as they make the best horse collars that are made.

I also visited the wagon factories. They are full of orders; Lang & Brothers shipped nine wagons the day I was there.

There are three livery stables and they seem to do a large business. I asked one of them what his stable and lot was worth; he said $1,000. I remarked to him his building was no good, and he said, "I don't charge for that, it's the lot, they are asking from $400 to $1,200 dollars for lots in this town." There are three county papers, all doing a nice business, and two banks, both doing a good business. I heard a business man say his money in the bank was paying him 25 percent a month. There are 23 lawyers and 18 doctors all doing well. There are nine churches; the Christian Church is built on modern style with raised floor and folding seats. It cost $5,000. The M.E. Church South is building one that will cost $7,000. There are also two first-class drug stores and one ice plant, but it cannot make half enough ice. The ice man told me he sold 5,890 lbs. of ice in one day while I was there. But the biggest thing in Farmington is the insane asylum which is being built and will be worth thousands of dollars to the town. They paid $100 per acre for 300 acres of land. The town has electric lights and will have an electric railroad soon. Seventeen new houses are being built. There are some good farms outside of Farmington. I was talking to some of the farmers and they said one of them raised 2,100 bushels of wheat and another 2,300.

YESTERDAY'S MAIN STREET OF FARMINGTON From the *County Advertiser*, Farmington, MO March 21, 1979

by Julia Doughty Menge

(Author is referring to present day (1999) Columbia Street as "Main Street")

Farmington, as I remember it in 1891 when I was 10 years old. I am Julia Doughty Menge, widow of the late C.H. Menge, daughter of Milton Cayce Doughty and Sara Jane Wood

Commom log house built in the area around the 1800s.

Old Murphy home, where the first County Court was held. In 1940 it was the oldest house in the city. It was later owned by Mr. J.H. Waide and still later by Mr. Tom Brown, descendants of Sarah Barton Murphy. This house ... down to make way for the Washington-Franklin School at the corner of North Washington and Murphy.

Doughty. I was born April 6, 1881, 1-1/2 miles south of Farmington at the old Doughty Homestead. My parents joined the Presbyterian Church when I was 4 years old. From that time until I married, I attended Sunday School and Church there. I was converted and joined the church at 13 years. The pastor of the church when my parents joined was the Rev. Creighton. There was one colored member of the church, Aunt Betty Green, a very devout Christian. So I was very familiar with Columbia and Liberty Streets. My father was an elder in the Presbyterian Church for many years. The following are men who served as elders with him through the years: Dr. George Williams, A.J. Leathers, General McCormack, Ellis Cayce, A.T. Nixon, George Lawson, Mr. Brantly and Ed Henderson, who is the only survivor. I also attended school in Farmington.

I will start across from the Presbyterian Church.

The brick home was owned by General McCormack, who was a devout Christian, a politician and a druggist. I will continue east on the right side of the street. The next place was the Hugh Long home; then the S.S. Smith home (a merchant); next, Dr. Horn's home; Merril Pepkins home (a lawyer).

Second block: Christian Church, a very small brick church; Doc Elgin's home (a farmer); A.J. Leathers' home (a merchant); Dr. Emmet McCormack's home (his office); the building on the corner by the Nichols family.

Third block: The Joe Weber home, a beautiful brick. He was an uncle of Judge K.C. Weber. (It stood where the Long Memorial Hall now stands). The Frank Gierse Tailor Shop, in front of the family residence in the rear; and the town hall on the second floor where all the shows and school entertainment's were held.

Fourth block: Wheeler Wade Confectionery (at site of Gas Office); next, Clarence and Emmet Morris Butcher Shop; Proughs Saloon; Rotger's Bakery run by Mr. Rotger and his son Otto, where you could buy delicious bread 5 cents per loaf, or six loaves for 25 cents. Next was Will Rotger's Harness Shop where you could buy anything to dress your horse up: harnesses, saddles, lap robes, buggy whips. Next, Dr. George William's Office, general practitioner; A.J. Leathers General Store. He sold dry goods and groceries, also ordered farm implements for his customers.

Fifth block: Old Peers Home (where Odd Fellows building now stands) that was torn away

about 1894; General McCormack Drug Store; Dr. Joe Law's office upstairs over Drug Store. He was a general practitioner. Robert Tetley Jewelry Store, residence in back and upstairs. Pelty's Cigar Store sold daily papers from a goods' box in front of the store. There was a large wooden Indian in front of the cigar store, as was the custom that marked a tobacco store, Next, Mrs. Rucker's Millinery Store, where you gave your order for your hat and did your shopping while she trimmed it; Parson Rucker's Drug Store that he tended during the week, and he preached in the county churches on Sunday.

Sixth block: George M. Wilson residence; next, an old business building that was often vacant. The Conrad Market Butcher Shop, with residence in the rear; the old Odd Fellows building, three stories. It was frame. First floor, a confectionery and baker shop; on the corner was McCown's Harness Shop. Second floor was used as a residence. Third floor was Odd Fellow and Knights of Pythias Lodge Halls.

Seventh block: Jacob Kreiger Store and residence next to it; the next was a three-story brick owned by T.P. Pigg, where the *Farmington News* was printed on the first floor. The telephone was started in the Pig Building in 1898. Next, the Heiber Hardware Store. They had toys at the Christmas season and bought junk. Next

was Lang Building, the first blacksmith shop, the wagon shop where they made wagons and the undertaking department run by Mr. Thomas and assisted by Mr. Fred Keller. They had to use four horses to pull the hearse in muddy weather.

Eighth block: Giessing Elevator Mill and Warehouse owned by John and Charles Giessing; the Long Home where there had been a tan-yard in early days. On the corner was the large home owned by John Giessing.

Ninth block: Carleton College, founded by Miss Eliza Carleton and run by the Methodist Church. There was quite a number of acres of ground. It was a boarding school. Many of our doctors, lawyers and preachers got part of their education there and a vast throng of others, teachers and farmers. Another thing of interest was the way of lighting by lamp posts with a glass box at the top, one side hinged so a kerosene lamp was put in. It had to be cleaned each day and lit at night. These were used in front of churches and some business places.

Left Side of Columbia:

First block: Starting on the left side of Columbia Street just north of the Presbyterian Church. I will start by telling of the Elmwood Seminary, a Girl's Boarding School, built about 1889. It was three stories and a basement. It was

Columbia Street looking west. Courthouse behind the trees on right, Dollar Store on left corner and Krak 'n Jack past the courthouse.

Columbia Street and Jefferson Street, Farmer's Bank, Botaniques located today.

Columbia Street in 1894.

George and Walter Morris in the Morris Brothers Store, June 30, 1921.

South Henry & First, where carwash is now located. It was the Ferd Thompson Farm Emp. Co. before, 1931 which later became Jones Machine Shop.

Mr. & Mrs. Kossuth W. Weber, Kossuth Cayce Weber and Frank Shulte Weber. On balcony, possibly M.P. Cayce Jr. About 1888 to 1890.

owned by the church. The first people to run it was Professor Wilson, wife and daughters.

Most of the scholars were from out of town. They also had day scholars. The Presbyterian Church turned it into an orphanage some years ago. The building was condemned and torn away over a year ago. Next was a house occupied by a number of different people. It was a vacant lot from there to Southern Methodist Church (as it was called at the time), it was a small frame church. Next, Dr. Smith's residence. On the corner was Lew Orten's residence (a grocery man).

Second block: Mrs. Wilson's residence (now Hugo Cozean Home), who took tin-type pictures; next, Dr. Braham's (a dentist) Office. It was moved to the country and is now a wellhouse on the William Counts Farm; Dr. Braham's residence (Cozean Funeral Home); Dr. Henry Tolman home (stood where the present site of Masonic Building is); Dr. Tolman's Office (where Christian Church is).

Third block: John Spaugh Marble Works (where Miller Funeral Home stands). On the corner, Jacobson Store where they sold dry goods and furniture.

Fourth block: Courthouse (old building).

Fifth block: (bank corner) was the Jacob Lorenze Building corner room; Cayce and Blisspringhoff Drug Store. The room just east of the Drug Store was the Post Office; Willard Rariden was Postmaster. It was a very small place. The part of the building running north from the drug store housed the family residence and Mr. Lorenze Taylor Shop. Just north of it was the Bank of Farmington. I will continue east of the Post Office on Columbia. The building (used as a pool room now) was built by Mr. Oglesby and son and was used as a grocery store. Then the Charles Borrolle Book Store where you could get new and used school books and notions and school supplies. Wiley's General Store, where they sold dry goods and groceries, was next and on the corner was Sam Gossum's Saloon.

Sixth block: Hemerly's Saloon (at site of Wood's Drug Store) was first. Next came Dr. Fugate's Office (a very small building). He doctored eyes. Peter Schmitt's Barber Shop followed and then Klein Grocery Store, the John M. Karsch Shoe Store; Bollinger's Saloon in front and family residence in back and upstairs. On the corner was S.S. Smith Dry Goods.

Seventh block: On the corner was Dalton and Marks Store, and the Dalton Boarding House stood in the yard just back of the store. Next was Isenberg home and Isenberg Harness Shop; the home of Tom Lang, who was senior member of the Lang Firm across the street. The small building on the corner was used as a little store and residence on the side. Langs ran a saw mill in the rear of their building.

Left Side of Liberty

Commencing at E.J. McKinney's home, built by M.L. Doughty, my uncle, as his home, we will start down Liberty Street. He lived there for many years and served as Postmaster a number of years. Next was the Beal Home, the home of Bert Beal Sr., and his parents. The father was a lawyer; when he died he was buried in the garden in a metallic casket. 28 years later his wife died and his body was exhumed and they were buried in the Masonic Cemetery.

Second block: The Rudy and Heidelberg Home was first. Next was the Sutt Highly residence; one place I don't remember; then the O.L. Haile residence; the Joe Bruett residence (on the corner where L.C. Mayes' Grill now stands).

Third block: Dr. Horn's residence (where cobblestone garage now stands); the Harve Highly Home (Livery stable owner) (the home now occupied by Dr. P.C. Reynierse). From there to the corner of the block was a livery stable where they kept about 20 horses and a number of buggies to haul the traveling public.

Fourth block: At present site of the St. Francois Hotel stood a family boarding house run by Mrs. Goodin. She had two sons, Morris and Horace, and a daughter, Etta. Next was Tom Taffee Milliner Store; Kingle Dry Good and Grocery Store followed and Orten and David Grocery was on the corner.

Fifth block: On corner (now occupied by Krogers), Morris Rosenthal General Store; Tom and Oscar Haile Store (at the sight of Mell's Hardware); Adam Neidert and Henry Kollmeyer Sr. had an undertaking place and blacksmith shop. Next was the Retonaz Building where they took tin-type pictures.

Sixth block: Boswell and Helber Hardware Store. The Helber home was on the side of the store. Next came the John M. Karsch residence and shoe dealer. On the corner was the Lloyd home. Mr. Lloyd hauled the mail from DeLassus in a one-horse hack. He was the grandfather of Ruffner Lloyd.

Right Side of Liberty

Commencing at the orphanage property there were no buildings on the right side of the street until you got as far downtown as the jail. An old house sat east across from the jail. Next was the Court House.

East of the Court House on the corner was Dr. Parker's Drug Store. He built the country home now owned by Arlie McClard. Just back of the drug store was a small house owned by a man by the name of Jacobie, who bought hides.

One Negro cabin stood at the sight of George Smith's Furniture Store and an old building back of Klein's Grocery Store finished out the block.

There are many things of interest in old Farmington and a few of these were the Baptist Church, a small frame building at the site of the present church; it was almost new in 1891, as the Baptists held their services in the Baptist College at the time. This was a Baptist school where many of our business people attended in their early years. It stood where the old high school now stands.

The Lutheran Church was a small frame church. The preacher did the preaching and also taught the Confirmation Class. The Catholic Church was a small church. The church was upstairs. There were two colored churches that stood where their churches now stand. The colored school was near the little church on Franklin Street. The Douglass Colored School burned and when it was rebuilt they erected it on its present site.

The Iseman Wagon Shop on South Henry was just torn away recently. Here many farm wagons were made. The Jones Machine Shop was the Herman and Herbst Blacksmith Shop, where they fixed the iron parts of the wagons. At that time there was only one public school. It stood where the W.L. Johns School now stands. There were two buildings, one four-room brick and a two-room frame. There were about 400 children attending at that time. My uncle, David Doughty, ran a planing mill. He fixed the lumber for wagon shops. There was another flour mill on North Washington owned by Henry and Dan Giessing. My brother, Job Doughty, of Strafford, MO., and brother, Walter Doughty (deceased), attended school in Farmington.

Mr. Henry Manly Sr. had a shoe shop on South Henry where he made boots and shoes to order. My uncle, David Doughty, had a carpenter shop on South Henry (where the Green's Hatchery stands) where he made window frames and did special orders for carpenters.

There were many hitching racks and posts about town and every church had its own hitching where we tied our horses while in town.

Where the county piles its lumber on South Jefferson was the livery stable where they kept 20 horses and a number of buggies. They also had a Hurdick, quite similar to a bus, only the seats run along the sides and it had a door in the end. The driver sat on the outside on the front. It was pulled by horses. The Hurdick would hold about 14 people. They also had a cab; it was more comfortable, but would only hold about six besides the driver. This livery stable was owned by William Martin, Robert Lloyd and O.J. Mayberry. They hauled passengers to DeLassus as our only mode of travel was by train. Our walks were flagstone or gravel, and our streets were crushed rock.

The first concrete walk was at the Odd Fellows Building and they called it granitoid as it was made from crushed granite instead of gravel as they use today. The Odd Fellows Building was finished in 1896. The Realty Building (where United Bank is) was finished December 1899. Adam Schmidt and Sons owned a blacksmith shop and sawmill on South Washington at the site of the Gas Building.

1826 drawing of early Farmington, by artist Charles A. Lesueur.

Columbia Street in the 1930s, now Minuteman Press on corner.

Columbia Street in the 1950s looking east.

Farmington Milestones

1798: Rev. William Murphy and an Indian guide reach Farmington.

1803: Sarah Barton Murphy, a Methodist, offers first Protestant prayer west of the Mississippi River. Holds private school in her home.

1805: Sarah Barton Murphy teaches first Sunday School west of the Mississippi River.

1817: Sarah Barton Murphy died.

1820: Farmington circuit organized by Methodists.

1822: Nathaniel Cook, first county representative to state legislature

1823: John Peers opens Farmington's first store on south side of the square.

1824: John Boyce opens Farmington's first hotel.

1826: First courthouse completed.

1832: Presbyterian Church founded. Milton P. Cayce establishes general merchandise store.

1833: Phillip Long builds Long House and his tannery.

1836: Farmington incorporated as a "village" with a population of 500.

1844: Farmington Methodist Church separates into two branches - one favoring the North and one the South.

1847: Elmwood Academy building constructed.

1849: Masonic Lodge founded.

1850: Odd Fellows Lodge founded. Second courthouse completed, cost $8,000.

1851: Plank Road started.

1853: Farmington Christian Church founded. Old Murphy spring house built. M.P. Cayce helps build town's first flour mill.

1854: Carleton College organized eight miles north of town.

1856: County's second jail constructed.

1860: Farmington's first newspaper, the *Southeast Missouri Argus* begins publication. Farmington population less than 500.

1862: Farmington population is now 600. First Catholic Mass celebrated at Thomas Lang home.

1864: Lang Undertaking Company established.

1866: Northern Methodists (Carleton) organized congregation under the name Methodist-Episcopal.

1869: St. Joseph Catholic Parish organized.

1870: First public school constructed. Present county jail constructed.

1873: St. Paul's Lutheran Church organized.

1874: M.P. Cayce builds first ice house in county. St. Paul's Lutheran School organized.

1876: Carleton Institute moved to Farmington. Southern Methodists (Murphy Long) hold first service after Civil War with 27 members.

1880: First (and only) legal hanging.

1882: First Baptist Church organized.

1883: Klein Grocery Store opens.

1884: Present Presbyterian Church built.

1885: Construction begins on third courthouse.

1886: Farmington Baptist Church established. The Bank of Farmington (town's first) incorporated. Courthouse completed, cost of $20,000.

1890: Population of Farmington grows to 1,350.

1892: First rock road built; this was Potosi Street.

1894: Opera House Hotel built.

1896: Giessing Milling Company moved to Farmington.

1897: Catholic School opened.

1902: Southern Methodists begin new building.

1903: Construction begins on State Hospital No. 4. Farmington Baptist College closes.

1904: County Infirmary built. Northern Methodists begin work on new rock building.

1908: Lutheran Church building completed.

1914: Presbyterian Orphanage opened.

1919: Potosi Street is the first concrete road in town.

1924: Long Memorial Hall constructed.

1927: Farmington High School Auditorium constructed on College Street.

1929: American Legion founded. (November): *The Press*, less than a year old, suffers tragedy when gasoline from a new linotype machine ignites and guts the newspaper's offices.

1930: (August): William Harlan, president of the Bank of Farmington, scares away would-be robbers. Ritz Theater reopens after being closed for two weeks to install the latest in sound equipment.

1931: Chamber of Commerce votes to raise money, by subscription, for the construction of a new factory for the Rice-Stix Dry Goods Company.

1932: (July): City ready to unveil its new post office billed as one of the most modern and attractive mail-handling facilities in the area. Dynamite which was somehow smuggled into the jail is blamed for a terrific explosion which temporality

allows six prisoners to enjoy a few hours of freedom.

1933: 3.2 percent beer is newly legalized. (May): Dr. E.L. Hoctor is re-appointed for a second four-year term as superintendent of Farmington State Hospital. (October): A new federal reserve bank is opened, United Bank of Farmington. It became the successor to the defunct Bank of Farmington and the Farmers Bank.

1934: (May): First Methodist Church of Farmington formally changed its name to the Carleton Memorial M.E. Church in honor of the late Eliza Carleton. State Hospital continues to grow with allocation of $1,800,000 for repairs and enlargement work. Mayor Clarence A.Tetley dies suddenly of pneumonia after short illness. Rotary Club founded.

1935: WPA begins construction on swimming pool.

1937: (July): New swimming pool opens.

1938: Measles epidemic cripples the town, reducing school attendance for a 20-year low. (July): The home of prominent attorney, Harry O. Smith, is bombed, blowing a three-foot hole in the floor of the front room. More home damage occurs when a small boulder, apparently sent flying by a dynamite blast at the city quarry, is hurtled through the side of the nearby E.K. Stevens home. (August): City Council, violating an order by Circuit Judge Taylor Smith, votes not to publish a detailed financial statement.

1939: Highway Patrol, along with the Jaycees, fingerprint all Farmington School District students. Major electrical storm causes moderate damage to the Odd Fellows Building, then the tallest structure in town. The storm brings with it a downpour of rain, two inches in 45 minutes, which ends the longest heat wave of the year.

1940: City Council voted to close down all city-run bowling alleys in order not to compete with privately-owned facilities. (September): The grandstand at Wilson Rozier Park was destroyed by fire of unknown origin. City Council voted to rebuild the structure using concrete instead of wood. (October): Civil Aeronautics Administration has chosen Farmington as site for an airport under national defense plans. October: Males between the age of 21 and 35 are asked to register for the draft. Nan Weber Garden Club founded.

1941: (April): Chamber of Commerce, in an effort to attract new industry, votes to open a subdivision and sell the lots as a method of obtaining sufficient funds for the construction of a new building for the Trimfoot Shoe Co. of St. Louis. The company indicates its willingness to transfer the operation to Farmington if it is provided with a rent-free building.

1942: Jasper E. Thomure, 20 years old, of Farmington, becomes the county's first World War II causality.
Plans are formulated for the town's first test blackout.
Elmer Brown appointed as postmaster.
(June) Bill Longson, wrestling world champion, successfully defends his title against Ray Eckert at Wilson Rozier Park.

1943: (March): Rice-Stix Shirt Factory receives the coveted Army-Navy "E" Flag.
Anthony Quinn and Gene Tierney make a brief stop in Farmington to promote the sale of war bonds.
Assembly of God Church founded.
Farmington's first Kindergarten Class organized at St. Paul's Lutheran School.

1945: (May): Local factories and mills let forth with a cascade of whistles and bells to celebrate President Truman's announcement of Allied victory in Germany.
In the Pacific, a B-29 bomber nicknamed the *City of Farmington* continues to drop tons of bombs in massive air raids on Japan. The bomber, which derived its name from Farmington's own Cecil Hulsey, the first officer, is based in the Marianas Islands.
The Chamber of Commerce, anxious to keep one of the city's largest employers, starts a drive to obtain $36,000 for construction of an addition to the Trimfoot Co. The firm, pressed for space, has already taken over the former Carleton College Building for part of its operation.
Kiwanis Club founded.

1946: (February): The St. Louis Browns of the American Baseball League announced that 125 baseball players from their many minor league baseball clubs will train in Farmington in April.
(October): An earthquake of moderate intensity shakes area, but no damage reported.
Robert F. Karsch, Westminster professor of political science and the son of Mr. and Mrs. Fred Karsch, unveiled the music to the now famous "fight song" before that year's Kansas-Missouri game. The words to the song were written by a university student.
A huge meteor roars across several midwest states.
VFW founded.

1947: The death of C.E. (Pal) Wood, a prominent Farmington citizen and chronicler of the city's history, saddens community.
(April): A passerby notices a smoldering blaze at the high school gymnasium. Lightning-damaged electrical wires are blamed for the "close call."
(August): Cecil Roberts, editor and publisher of *Farmington Press*, reveals

plans for the construction of a 1,000 watt radio station, KREI.

1948: (April): School district voters overwhelmingly approve a tax levy increase and $101,000 bond issue for the construction of a new 14-room grade school.
Cecil Roberts sells the Press Printing and Publishing Company to Art Freeman and Wally Stewart, two employees of the newspaper.
(October): Carleton College building is turned into a school building for St. Joseph's Parish.
Six prisoners in the county jail crack the concrete floor and tunnel their way to freedom.

1949: KREI-FM Radio Station will provide night broadcasting. First FM program will be a spring exhibition game between the Browns and the Cardinals.
(December): Howard Tetley Jewelers is robbed of over $5,000. (First local jewelry store robbery.)
Elks Club founded.

1950: (January): New elementary school building completed.
(February): Farmington voters overwhelmingly endorse a $250,000 bond issue for the financing of a new sewage disposal plant.
(April): Nine Farmington residents are arrested for operating their own money-raising machine, a clandestine gambling game.
North and South Methodist Churches merge.

1951: Dr. Fred A. Walker, former superintendent of Presbyterian Orphanage, returns after a stint as president of the College of the Ozarks at Clarksville, AR.
November: The city is paralyzed by a record 15-inch snowfall. The deluge destroyed five airplanes when the roof of a metal hangar collapses at the airport.

1952: (March): Tornado misses Farmington but demolishes the rural home of Mary Barnhart.
(April): Senator Robert A. Taft, Republican candidate for President, makes a brief stop in town and talks on the courthouse steps.
(June): Dedication/open house at Mineral Area Osteopathic Hospital.

1953: (September): W.L. Johns, a long-time Farmington educator, dies at the age of 81.
(November): A break in the 22-inch main pipeline of Mississippi River Fuel Corp. cuts off service to about 6,000 homes/businesses. Touches off a raging blaze that continues for two hours before workmen can cut off the flow of fuel.

1954: The Knights Football Team finally open against Flat River High School, one week after a scheduled game against Perryville High School is canceled due to word that a Perryville player contracted polio.
Freewill Baptist Church founded.

1955: September: Burglars using acetylene torches escape with undetermined amount of money from the Boswell Hardware Store and $276 from the MFA exchange.

1956: (October): Southwestern Bell Telephone Company breaks ground for a new central office building in Farmington, billed as the first step in a $500,000 program to convert the city's telephone system to dial operation.

1957: (January): Missouri State Highway Commission gives final approval for relocating Highway 67 west of Farmington.
(February): Voters in the R-7 School District reject, for the fourth time, a proposed tax levy increase which would have funded a new high school building.
(June): Bishop Eugene M. Frank, presiding Methodist Bishop of Missouri, assists in dedication for the new Memorial Methodist Church Building.
(December): A raging blaze demolishes the recently completed St. Francois Country Club. Officers of the organization immediately begin formulating plans for rebuilding the structure.

1958: (March): Voters of the R-7 School District pass a tax levy increase for the construction of a new high school.
Nazarene Church founded.

1959: The State Highway Department announces a 20-year program for making Highway 67 a full four lanes through the county.
(May): 3500 people visit the first open house at State Hospital #4 in observance of National Mental Health Week.
(August): Officials break ground at the site of the new St. Joseph Elementary School and Gymnasium.
(October): Students move into the new high school.
City voters approve a bond issue for the construction of a municipal airport.

1960: (January): Eddie Blaine, who played center and fullback for Farmington High School, plays for the University of Missouri Tigers in the Orange Bowl on New Year's Day.
Knights of Pythias founded.

1961: (January): Eddie Blaine is named to the Football Writer's Association 1961 All American Football Team on the basis of his performance at the heart of Mizzou's interior line.
(June): Farmington's new National Guard Armory, home of Company A, First Battle Group, 140th Infantry, is completed.
(September): *Farmington Press* becomes the first county newspaper to go to offset, "cold type" lithographic printing.
Lions Club founded.

1962: (August): The city's public utilities were expanded once again with the addition of a new water tower on Burks Road.

1963: (July): 4,000 to 5,000 people attend dedication ceremonies at the new city-owned airport.

1964: (March): At the Farmington High School, physicians administered doses of the Sabin polio vaccine to both children and adults.

(May): Fire guts the P.N. Hirsch Store and L&L Casuals, while damaging the Ritz Theater. Although damage to the theater was limited, the theater never re-opened.

(October): Plans for a new Farmington industry offering employment for 100 people are announced by the Matco Machine and Tool Co. of St. Louis.

1965: (July): Fire destroys six buildings near the corner of West Liberty and North Jefferson Streets. The fire apparently originated in an apartment above a liquor store at the corner.

(July): R-7 School Board officially designates Farmington High School's new football stadium as "H.C Haile Memorial Stadium."

(October): A fire in the business district left the Wulfers and Petry Furniture Co. and the E.C. Robinson Lumber Company in ruins.

(December): The city was without power for four hours after a light plane making a landing approach near the airport crashes into 34,000-volt dual feeder lines. Neither the pilot nor two passengers were seriously injured.

1967: (January): A $107,000 plan calling for the lengthening of a landing strip and widening of a runway at the airport is approved by the City Council.

(June): Construction begins on an addition to Farmington High School to include a library, additional classrooms, a band room and enlarged cafeteria. Architectural drawings of the planned 80-bed Farmington Community Hospital are released, followed a month later by the start of construction of the 51-bed Mineral Area Osteopathic Hospital.

(August): 400-500 Trimfoot Co. employees walk out on strike, the first such incident to occur during the firm's 27 years in Farmington.

1968: (September): Rumors begin flying concerning the possibility of the Biltwell Co. moving to the city and occupying the Puritan Factory Building.

St. Louis authorities apprehend four persons suspected in a $12,000 robbery (merchandise) from the Lerche Firestone Store.

1969: Archbishop John J. Carberry of St. Louis formally announces that St. Joseph Regional High School will close at the end of the school term due to financial difficulties.

(April): Farmington Community Hospital has open house.

(June): A tornado through the area takes six lives. Local hospitals treat 27 storm related injuries.

(August): Ground breaking ceremonies

for 20-acre Mineral Area Shopping Plaza to be located off Potosi Street. Three firms announce plans for moving into the new development.

(October): The City Council votes to implement a three-month trial period for one-way streets with the plan to go into effect in January 1970. Just a few weeks later the State Highway Department vetoes the plan.

Matco Machine and Tool Co. announces plans to sell machinery due to plant closing. Officials of the company attribute the firm's downfall to a damaging strike.

1970: (April): Plans announced for 191 new homes in Farmington Meadows.

(July): Jail addition expands cell capacity to 48 prisoners.

(August): Ozarks Federal Savings and Loan opens new building.

(September): Farmington enrolls 2,832 on first day of school.

(October): Chamber of Commerce establishes permanent office.

(November): Farmington city budget will total nearly one million dollars.

1971: (February): Open house is held at the new middle school.

(April): Doug Ross elected mayor of Farmington.

(September): 14,000 attend Air Show at Farmington Municipal Airport.

(November): City Ordinance creating a Parks & Recreation Department passed.

1975: (January): Senior Citizen Center opens in Farmington at 112 W. Harrison St.

(February): Million dollar Army Reserve Center to be located in Farmington.

(April): Phyllis Schnebelen is first woman to serve as Magistrate Judge.

(November): Chamber of Commerce hires first full-time manager, Jim Massie.

1976: (January): Ben Smith named citizen of the year.

(May): Encephalitis warning for the area.

(May): 258 graduate from Farmington High School.

(June): Bomb threat at Dugal's Sunday night.

1977: (January): New fire station completed.

(June): Dr. Francis R. Crouch passes away.

(September): City budget largest in history, $3,353,200.

(September): Ambulance district service begins.

1978: (March): Demolition of 1882 Farmington Milling Company on East Columbia.

(June): State Hospital celebrates 75th Anniversary.

(July): Ben-Nor apartments open.

(August): One-way streets become reality in Farmington.

1979: (March): Meals on Wheels started in Farmington.

(April): Fire at Wayside Retirement Home on Highway 00 claims 25 lives.

(April): Witten Ledbetter new mayor of Farmington.

(April): Dean Danieley Park dedicated.

1980: (August): Farmington Public Library opens new building, cost $180,000.

(October): City barn burns in one of Farmington's largest fires.

(November): Farmington becomes a third-class city.

East Ozarks Audubon Society founded.

1981: (February): Bomb threat closes Trimfoot.

(March): Dayse Baker's house, known as "Noah's Ark," was torn down as she requested.

1982: (February): School bond issue approved for new building on Fleming Street.

(June): Local airport receives $37,800 grant.

1985: Amvets founded.

1988: (January): Jon Cozean honored as Citizen of the Year for 1987.

(November): Veterans Memorial set in place at courthouse.

1990: (May): Work on Maple Valley Shopping Center begins.

1991: (September): Economic growth in Farmington skyrockets; Jack-in-the-Box; Long John Silver's; J.C. Penney's; Little Caesar's; First State Bank; Steak 'n Shake; Payless Shoes commit to Maple Valley Shopping Center.

(September): Groundbreaking held for the addition to Farmington Public Library.

1992: (July): New Farmington Police Station dedicated.

1993: (June): Eagle Lake Golf Course opens.

(November): Voters say yes to Civic Center.

1994: (March): Huffy Bicycles locates plant in Farmington

1997: (December): "First Night" at the Civic Center kicks off year-long bicentennial celebration for Farmington citizens.

1998: Little Tyke's building destroyed by fire.

1999: (June): Trimfoot Shoe Factory closes after 58 years here.

(July): Farmington begins work on Water Park next to Civic Center.

ELECTRIC POWER COMES TO FARMINGTON

A crowd of anxious Farmington residents gathered in the downtown area and near the power plant in October 1891. Workmen scurried around in preparation for an event that would alter the history of the city and its lifestyle.

At 9:00 p.m. there was a twinkling and, as one observer wrote, the "streets lighted up beautifully."

Twelve years after Thomas Edison had invented the incandescent lamp, 20 electric street lights were installed in Farmington. A power plant was constructed on Boyce Street and Perrine Road.

The Farmington Board of Alderman had granted a franchise to National Electric Manufacturing Co. of Eau Claire, WI.

The lights were not ready to be turned on at dusk and the crowd became anxious as time passed. But the reaction was one of delight when the street lamps flickered and then glowed with the artificial light.

Despite the newness of the street lamps, one writer still said, "Twenty were hardly enough for a town the size of Farmington even though they were judiciously distributed."

Farmington's First Electric Lights

From the *Daily Journal*, April 24, 1987 (originally from *Times*, Oct. 29, 1891)

Last Saturday night Farmington took a forward stride in the use of modern appliances, and for the first time in its history its principal streets were lit up after nightfall so that people could see where they were going, barring of course the friendly beams of old Lunar as that luminary made its accustomed rounds. As our readers are aware, the Board of Aldermen a short time ago granted a franchise to the National Electric Manufacturing Co. of Eau Claire, WI and contracted for twenty 32-candle power electric street lights. The franchise was bought by W.L. Hockaday, W.F. Carter, August Thomsen and Mrs. Jennie T. Forster; and the necessary machinery was furnished and put up for them by the National Electric Manufacturing Company. The work of putting up the plant has been pushed right along from the start, and last Saturday night the street lights were turned on for the first time.

When night overtook the workmen Saturday, everything was not quite in readiness, and it took them a couple of hours to finish up and adjust the wires to the dynamo. During this time a curious and impatient crowd of men and boys had gathered around the power house and in the engine and dynamo room, eager to see the first start, while others were watching the street lights at various points to catch the first flash of light. Mr. Bailey, the genial, wide-awake agent of the National Electric Mfg. Co., even appeared a little anxious, and to partake of the general interest and expectancy, he wanted the first trial to be a success. In this he was gratified. It was well on towards 9 o'clock when everything was ready and in a twinkling all the lamps "were glowing. The lights were regular and steady, no flickering, and

the streets lit up beautifully and sufficiently, even on the streets where the lamps were long distances apart, to show one the way. On Sunday night the people enjoyed the novel privilege of being lit on their way to church, and many were the satisfactory expressions on all sides. The street lamps are very judiciously distributed, but 20 are hardly enough for a town the size of Farmington, and it will not be surprising if some of our citizens who live on the dark streets are knocking at the door of our Board of Aldermen soon for more light.

The business houses that have the lights put in, as far as we have heard any expressions, are pleased with the change from coal oil to electricity. It is much cleaner and less trouble, and the light is more evenly distributed. It will probably not be long before the business houses will be using electric lights, and quite a number of private residences are to have them. Elmwood Seminary will be entirely lighted by them and will also use a complete system of electric bells.

The ice factory will be run in connection with the electric lights. Mr. Thomsen, theretofore conducting that business, having associated himself, Mrs. Forster and Messrs. Hockaday and Carter, and the capacity of the ice manufacturing plant will be increased. They will also open up a coal supply yard and keep both soft and hard coal. The whole thing is to be incorporated under the State Laws, with a capital stock of $10,000.

COURTHOUSE HISTORY

David Murphy donated 52 acres of land to be used to establish a county seat and once surveyed, a town could be laid out. According to sources, this generous gift had one stipulation: if what is now the courthouse ever ceases to be used for that purpose all of the land would revert back to the Murphy family and its heirs.

According to written history, in order to fund this building project much of the 52 acres had to be sold. This selling of property still did not raise enough money; therefore, a special tax was also assessed to help generate additional funds.

The actual construction of the first court-

house was done in stages as money was available. The walls were completed; then additional money had to be raised to add the roof. It wasn't until 1826 that the interior was completed.

From the St. Louis Missouri *Republican* of April 2, 1823, the following item appears: "Notice: Will be let to the lowest bidder on May 26th next in the town of Farmington, St. Francois County, the building of a brick courthouse, 30 feet square, two stories high and one stack of chimneys. Conditions and further plan of said building will be made known on day of letting."

John Andrews, William Evans, William Alexander

Commissioners of St. Francois County, Farmington, March 17, 1823.

From the records of court proceedings, description of the inside was as such: upon entering the building one would have encountered a large six-panel folding door of plank 1/2 inch thick with 4-inch hinges and a strong bolt. Above the door was a plain circular sash window. A staircase lead up from the first floor near the north entrance three feet wide with banisters. Both floors were laid with grooved pine plank and the walls were plastered. This building was completed in 1826.

In May of 1845 the courthouse square was enclosed by a plank fence five feet high. The planks were to be of heart pine, 12 feet long, six inches broad and one inch thick. The posts were of cedar, seven feet long, eight inches in diameter and well trimmed. A stile was built at the center of each side of the square with a gate at the top. These gates were appended with weights and pulleys which would cause the gates to swing shut. Grass was sown and locust trees were planted in two uniform rows 20 feet apart around the courthouse. Not long afterwards a hitching rack was placed outside the fence and around the square.

Second Courthouse

By 1848 this courthouse was becoming too small and couldn't even hold all the court records. Therefore, in November of 1848 the County Court ordered action on the building of a new courthouse. Due to insufficient funds, the

Farmington Electric Power and Ice Plant

First courthouse, drawing by Charles A. Lesueur, 1826.

Second courthouse

Third courthouse, 1908.

Fourth courthouse

General Assembly of Missouri authorized the County Court to borrow from the road and canal fund of St. Francois County to erect a building. With these funds and additional bonds, preparations were made to tear down the original courthouse and erect a second building on the same site.

Henry H. Wright was the contractor, having made the second lowest bid. It was built with plain Grecian lines, Doric columns, high windows and shutters, two stories high and with possibly two entrances. This second courthouse

cost approximately $8,000 and was completed in 1850.

Third Courthouse

Unfortunately the second courthouse was poorly built; and as early as 1870, the need for another courthouse was apparent. William F. Story, an architect from St. Louis, examined the old building and reported to the court there was eminent danger of the walls falling down. Temporary repairs were made by placing props on

ing, but was soon returned to the condemned building, much to the criticism of the general public.

It was not until the spring of 1885 that a petition was signed by over 100 tax-paying citizens and presented to the County Court praying the court to call a special election March 21, 1885, "for the purpose of determining whether the County Court of St. Francois County shall appropriate the surplus fund now in the treasury of said county and belonging to the contingent fund thereof, and to authorize said court to levy a direct tax in addition thereof for whatever sum may be necessary, including said surplus, not to exceed $20,000, for the purpose of building a new courthouse for said county."

The voters of the county defeated the proposition to increase the indebtedness for the erection of a new courthouse. The judges of the County Court met the issue by stating that the old courthouse had been condemned as unsafe and deciding that it should be replaced. The money needed for a new building came from surplus funds over and above those used by the county for general expenses.

During the early part of the summer of 1885 the offices of the old courthouse were vacated and moved to the Carl Braun Building on the southwest corner of the public square. The county paid Mr. Braun $230 in rent for the use of this building over a period of a year.

J.B. Legg of St. Louis, was the architect and James P. Gillick, the contractor. A considerable amount of the material from the old structure was used in order to save money. Much credit for the erection of this courthouse was due to the judges of the County Court, composed of Benjamin F. Simms, Peter W. Murphy and Richard L. Sutherland.

By the fall of 1886, the third courthouse was finished at a cost of $15,000.41, which included the expenses of the special election, architect, the contractor, etc. After the purchase of the furniture, grading the grounds, building walks, and erecting an iron fence around the square, the cost was approximately $20,000. The building was constructed of brick and of a rather modern style.

Rodgers Fence Company of Springfield, OH erected, at a cost of $756.27, the iron fence which surrounded the entire square. A sidewalk was built around the courthouse. It was made from solid flagstone four inches thick. Curbing was placed next to the fence and on March 9, 1887, a janitor was hired to take charge of the courthouse and to prevent children from playing on the lawn as well as to keep stock off the grass. Several years later the fence was removed. Part of it now surrounds a small courtyard at Mineral Area Regional Medical Center.

Fourth And Last Courthouse

The first concerted action to erect the present courthouse was launched by the Farmington Chamber of Commerce in the spring of 1925. It was not until May 8, 1925, that a general mass meeting of the citizens and taxpayers of the county was called for Farmington on May 19 of that year. After much discussion of the matter they voted at this meeting in favor of bonding the county for $250,000 for the erection of a new courthouse. Petitions were signed by the voters, signatures verified, and a special election was set for August 11, 1925. The election was held and the proposition for a new courthouse passed with more than the two-thirds majority needed.

During the fall and winter the architect, Norman B. Howard, assisted by M.C. Finley, drew up plans and specifications after many conferences with the court, composed of Judges J.H. Orten, Lee Hise, and W.E. Boyd, and the commissioners.

During the last week of January 1926, the county officials moved into the Carleton College Building, which was vacant at that time, and there the county records were guarded by a special night watchman. The old courthouse building was sold to the State Hospital and torn down soon after it was vacated.

On May 14, 1926, the contract was awarded to the McCarthy Brothers Construction Company of St. Louis, as they had the lowest bid of $217,172. Construction was started immediately and the building completed by the latter part of August 1927.

This splendid new courthouse was designed from the Roman Corinthian style. Exterior walls are constructed of Carthage and Gray Bedford stone. The four entrances to the building are so made as to enable all business property on the square to face the front of the courthouse, thus giving equal importance to the value of property on the public square.

The courthouse has marble floors, ornamental interior design and marble stairways with wrought iron balusters. The original oak woodwork is still intact. William H. Hunt, a longtime resident of Farmington, contracted in 1926 for the installation of four large Seth Thomas electric clocks, one on each front of the building; they remain as a memorial to Mr. Hunt.

A dedication program officially opening the courthouse was held on Thursday, October 13, 1927, at 2:00 p.m.

CIRCUIT COURT

On April 1, 1822, Judge Nathaniel B. Tucker of St. Charles County organized the circuit court of St. Francois County and it was attached to the northern circuit. At this first meeting there was no business brought before the court. The list of possible jurymen were: Archibald McHenry, John Baker, David F.

Grand Jury 1889

Jail in 1909, built in 1870 at a cost of $11,000.

Marks, George Estes, Hardy McCormick, Thomas George, William Spradley, Isaac Murphy, George Taylor, William Gillespie, Dubart Murphy, James Cunningham, Isaac Mitchell, Jesse McFarland, Lemuel Holstead, John Burnham, Eleazer Clay, Samuel Kincaid, Vincent Simpson and Leroy Matkins. There was no court held the following term and Judge Tucker omitted this county from his circuit.

The next circuit court in St. Francois County was held during August 1823. Judge Alexander Stuart was present and presided. There was some business this time. John Bequette was indicted by the Grand Jury for selling liquor without a business license. William, a Negro owned by Jesse Blackwell, had trouble with a slave belonging to James Kerr. Kerr's Negro, Shadrack, had received a fatal wound and William was indicted for murder.

One of the first important cases tried in the circuit court was during July 1825 under the term of Judge Nathaniel D. Cook. John Patterson, a

noted bully, had picked a quarrel with James Johnston, who was a small, quiet man. Patterson, after getting into a fight with Johnston, beat him to death. Patterson was indicted, tried and sentenced to be hanged on August 31, 1825, but some of his friends broke into the log jail, released him, and he was never captured.

Before any permanent courthouse was built the first few sessions of the courts were held in the old log Methodist Church erected on the site of the present Masonic Cemetery. For several years this church was the only building of any size which would hold a large group of people.

JAILS

In 1824, while the first courthouse was under construction, a jail was also being built. This structure was two stories high, made of logs over a dungeon three logs thick. In 1856, a second jail was built as the original one was badly burned in an attempted jailbreak. In 1870, a third jail was built under the supervision of Messrs. Carter and Walker. This same structure stands today. It is no longer used as a jail and plans are being formulated to turn it into a museum.

ST. FRANCOIS COUNTY SHERIFFS AND TAX COLLECTORS

1822-1823	Michael Hart
1823-1824	James Matkin
1825-1826	Charles Hart
1827-1828	Corbin Alexander
1829-1830	Thomas Madison
1830-1831	John Cornell
1831-1832	John Kennedy
1833-1834	Isaac Mitchell Jr.
1834-1835	Henry Hunt
1836-1838	Andrew K. Harris
1839-1840	H. Hibbits
1841-1842	Milton P. Cayce
1843-1846	Charles Meyer
1847-1848	Edwin C. Sebastian
1849-1850	Samuel S. Boyce
1851-1854	Elisha Arnold
1855-1858	Elisha Matkin
1859-1860	F.B. Matkin
1861-1864	Thomas S. McMullin
1865-1865	J.L. Resinger (Resigned)
1865-1866	Rufus Alexander
1867-1871	Franklin Murphy
1871-1875	Laken D. Walker
1875-1877	John B. Highley

Sheriff's and collector's offices were separated at election of 1876.

St. Francois County Sheriffs

1877-1880	Thomas S. McMullin (Died in 1880)
1880-	Laken D. Walker (Appointed)

1880-	John B. Benham (Died on December 18,1880)
1880-1885	Zachariah P. Cole
1885-1889	Peter Benham
1889-1891	Mark L. Creegan
1891-1895	Joseph H. Perkins
1895-1899	Willard B. Rariden
1899-1903	Jefferson D. Highley
1903-1905	Henderson M. Murphy
1905-1909	James J. Croke
1909-1913	William London
1913-1917	Joseph C. Williams
1917-1921	Charles B. Adams
1921-1925	John G. Hunt
1925-1929	H.B. (Bud) Watts
1929-1929	William (Bill) London (Shot in Fall 1929)
1929-1929	John T. Smith (Appointed)
1929-1932	Roy E. Presnell (Won special election 1929)
1932-1936	Roy E. Presnell
1936-1940	A.A. Bayles
1940-1944	Arthur "Bing" Miller
1944-1948	Herman Heck
1948-1952	Dewey Smallen
1952-1956	Clay H. Mullins
1956-1960	Clay H. Mullins
1960-1964	Clay H. Mullins (retired because of bad heart)
1963-1963	Lloyd Pinkston (appointed October 1963 to November 1963)
1963-1964	Leslie (Buck) Jones (appointed to serve out Mullins' term)
1964-1968	Kenneth Buckley
1968-1972	Kenneth Buckley
1972-1976	Kenneth Buckley (removed from office February 1976)
Feb-1976	James D. Hickman (appointed to serve out Buckley term)
1976-1980	James D. Hickman

1980-1984	Kenneth Buckley
1984-1988	Kenneth Buckley
1988-1992	Jack Cade
1992-1996	Daniel R. Bullock
1996-2000	Daniel R. Bullock

GOVERNMENT

The U.S. had a well-developed governmental system for its territories by the time Louisiana was added in 1804. Under federal regulations territorial governors were appointed by the President.

In 1804 the Louisiana Purchase was divided by two sections, the area south of the 33rd Parallel was called Territory of Orleans. North of the 33rd Parallel the region was known as the District of Louisiana. The District of Louisiana was assigned as part of the Territory of Indiana, the capitol of which was Vincennes. The people complained they had no voice in the government because the officials were too far away.

In 1805 U.S. Congress declared that the District of Louisiana should be renamed the Territory of Louisiana with the capitol in St. Louis.

Seven years later, in 1812, Congress raised Missouri to the rank of a second-class territory. The people of a region in this rank could vote and take part in their own government.

For the first time, citizens elected representatives, one for each 500 free white male inhabitants, for a two-year term to the territorial House of Representatives. They also chose a non-voting delegate to the U.S. House of Representatives. The nine members of the Upper House, the Legislative Council, were selected by the President from a list of 18 nominees suggested by the lower house.

It was at this time that the name of Missouri was officially associated with the area. The name of the area formerly known as the Territory of Louisiana was changed to the Territory

Thomas McMullin

Joseph Carrol Williams

William Rariden

Old Weber Hotel, now where Long Memorial hall stands.

Long Memorial Hall

of Missouri. Missouri was then admitted to the Union in 1821.

In 1812 David Barton and brother, Joshua, in 1814, came to St. Louis to practice law. The Bartons originally came from Tennessee and were the sons of a Baptist preacher, Rev. Isaac Barton.

David Barton, shortly after his arrival in the territory, was appointed circuit judge but soon resigned and began practicing law on the St. Louis circuit. When the constitutional convention met in 1820 he was unanimously elected presiding officer. After Missouri was admitted to the Union he was elected the first U.S. Senator from Missouri by acclamation.

After his retirement from the Senate in 1830 he moved to Cooper County, where he was elected to the State Senate in 1834-35. He died Sept. 28, 1837. David was a brother to Mrs. Sarah Barton Murphy, widow of Rev. William Murphy.

Isaac Barton, the third brother of Mrs. Murphy, also came to St. Louis, where he acted as deputy sheriff and was appointed clerk of the U.S. District Court by Judge Peck.

When Missouri was admitted to the Union in 1821, there were only eight counties in southeast Missouri; but on December 9, 1821, a bill became law for the creation of a new county to be known as St. Francois, so named for the river of the same name which runs almost throughout the entire county. The new county was made from parts of three other counties already established—Ste. Genevieve, Jefferson and Washington. St. Francois County is 410 square miles of land.

Alexander McNair, the first Governor of Missouri, appointed James Austin as presiding judge. George McGahan and James W. Smith as the County Court. They held their first meeting in the newly organized county on February 25, 1822 at the home of Jesse Murphy, original home of Sarah Barton Murphy. The Jesse Murphy house possibly stood on the property owned by J.C. Whitworth on McIlvane Street, overlooking the old Carter Spring.

Charley Hart was named the first sheriff. John D. Peers was selected by the court as its clerk and later commissioned by the governor. Mr. Peers appointed Corbin Alexander as deputy clerk of both courts. The County Court adjourned to meet at the home of David Murphy and was used for some time as a temporary seat of justice. This building was located where the present Washington/Franklin School is located on Washington Street across from Liberty Square.

David Murphy, a member of the First General Assembly of Missouri, donated 52 acres of his farm to St. Francois County upon which to establish the county seat. This was done with the provision that he would retain two acres of town lots and one acre upon which to build the county courthouse. The other lots were sold to finance the construction of the courthouse. This original settlement consisted of 24 city blocks bordered by what is now Spring Street on the north, First Street on the south, Main Street on the east, and "A" Street on the west. There were 73 lots in the survey. They were about 75 feet wide, running the entire length of the block and were numbered 1-73. In this deed, Mr. Murphy was to receive back his choice of lots to make up two acres. His first choice for one lot was the land where Mercantile Bank and Coldwell Bankers Real Estate is now located. The other spot he chose was the lot behind the McIntosh Building on the corner of South Jackson and Columbia Streets. This made up the two acres.

Farmington was incorporated in 1836 by order of the County Court. The first board of trustees consisted of J.D. Peers, M.P. Cayce, Edward C. Sebastian, William Ross, and Nicholas Fleming. The population of Farmington in 1836 was 500. On November 14, 1856, Farmington was organized as a village. The people living in Farmington in 1860 still numbered a little less than 500, but by the turn of the century the population had more than doubled. In 1879 it became a city of the Fourth Class and in 1981 a city of the Third Class.

On August 17, 1931, an ordinance in relation to the common seal of the City of Farmington was approved by the Board of Aldermen and signed by Mayor C.A. Tetley, designating that, "The seal of the city of Farmington shall be in a circular form, one and seven-eighths inches in diameter, with a device of a plow, the sun, and a sheaf of wheat engraved thereon, and surrounded by the words, 'Corporation - city of Farmington, Missouri - Seal,' engraved in Roman capitals upon the face thereof; and the same is hereby declared to be adopted as the seal of the city of Farmington." (This is the same seal used on the front of this history book.)

Farmington's municipal government derives its authority from the State Constitution and Enabling Acts. The governing body, consisting of a mayor and eight councilmen, is elected on a non-partisan ballot. City elections are held annually in April. The mayor serves four years, and each councilman serves a two-year term. Four councilmen, one from each ward, are elected each year.

The City Council meets the first Thursday and third Monday of each month, with the mayor presiding. These meetings are open to the public. All city appointments are made by the mayor, with the approval of the Council.

Farmington has four voting precincts. Any born or naturalized citizen who has attained the age of 18 years may vote in city elections. There is no length of residency requirement for voters, but registration must be completed at least 21 days prior to an election for the privilege of voting in that election.

Today the original 52 acres has grown to 5,440 acres with annexations adding an average of 134 acres per year. Originally covering little more than one-quarter square mile, the city now includes 8.5 square miles.

Mayors Of Farmington

Alvin Rucker was appointed the first mayor of Farmington (date unknown).

1879-1883	John A. Weber (was first elected mayor)
1883-1891	Ed Zeller
1891-1893	George Herzog
1893-1899	Peter Schmitt
1899-	Kossuth W. Weber (died while in office shortly after elected)
1899-1905	George M. Wilson
1905-1907	John Burks
1907-1909	George M. Wilson
1909-1911	W.R. Taylor
1911-1913	G.M. Wilson
1913-1915	Barton H. Boyer
1915-1917	E.J. McKinney
1917-1918	Charles B. Giessing
1919-1934	Clarence Tetley
1934-1939	B.T. Gentges
1939-1947	Shelton T. Horn
1947-1953	James C. Morris
1953-1959	Orville Woodard
1959-1961	Fred Revoir
1961-1965	Orville Woodard
1965-1971	Walter K. Giessing
1971-1973	Douglas K. Ross
1973-1977	Floyd Hager
1977-1979	Witten Ledbetter (died in office)
1979-1981	Floyd Hager (finished Witten Ledbetter term)
1981-1989	Ron Stevens
1989-1993	Mike O'Brien
1993-1997	Gay Wilkinson
1997-present	Kevin Engler

Current City Officials

Mayor: Kevin Engler
Councilmen:
Ward 1 Larry Forsythe, Joe Straughan
Ward 2 Mark Dotson, Charles Rorex
Ward 3 Dan Combs Jr., Betty Forsythe
Ward 4 Tom Burcham, Clarann Harrington
City Administrator, Jim Dismuke
Assistant City Administrator, Randy Holdman
City Clerk, Phyllis Hartrup
Assistant City Clerk/City Collector, Susie Miller
City Counselor, Gary Wagner
Municipal Court Judge, Ed Pultz
City Attorney, Tom Ray
Municipal Court Clerk, Lottie Trotter
Management Information Specialist, Rodney Worley

Building Inspector, Jason Gilliam
City Engineer, Kevin Tinker
Civic Center Director, Bill Towler
Electric Superintendent, Ron Sheppard
Fire Department Chief, Phil Johnson
Inventory Control Officer, Lin SanSoucie
Maintenance Supervisor, Steve Harris
Parks & Recreation Director, Bud Norman
Chief of Police, Rick Baker
Public Library Director, Lynn Crites
Public Works Director, Gary Noel
Street Supervisor, Terry Ferguson

FARMINGTON FIRE DEPARTMENT

The official date establishing the Farmington Fire Department is unclear. Several dates have been found, one from a letter written to N.D. Cayce, notifying him of his appointment by the city council as Chief of the Fire Department. This letter was written by J. Frank Foley, City Clerk, and dated June 13, 1879.

Other accounts have the department being

Mayor Peter Schmitt

Mayor Shelton Horn

Mayor Ed Zeller

Mayor George Herzog

Mayor Kossuth Weber

Farmington Fire Department

Fire at P.N. Hirsch in 1965.

Fire Truck

Fire Department staff in 1976; Driver-Ed Mackley; Clockwise: Dave Isabel; Don Giessing. John Pigg and Pete Wiley.

organized in 1884 with Ed Helber as chief; Charles C. Giessing Sr., first assistant; Henry Reuter, treasurer and J.F. Karsch, secretary.

In the August 20, 1884 *Farmington News*, the above men composing this company "do not expect anything for their services, but they do expect that the citizens of the town will encourage them in their good work and that the Board of Aldermen will furnish them with some of the necessary articles needed in fighting fires, such as ladders, buckets, etc."

The first real piece of firefighting equipment was purchased in May of 1894. A "fire engine" or mounted force pump was bought by the citizens of the east end of town (east of the courthouse). This "fire engine" on wheels contained a hose that could be dropped down a well and water pumped directly into the tank, which held about a barrel of water. Once the tank was full, it was pulled by men or horses, whichever was available, to the fire. This "fire engine" cost the fine citizens of the east end of town $180. In the same August 20, 1884 newspaper account as quoted above it says, "It is not amiss to remind the citizens living west of the courthouse of the wisdom of the east end of town in buying a mounted force pump or engine to be used in case of a fire. With two such pumps and a fire company otherwise equipped with ladders, hooks, and buckets, the town would be tolerably well fixed for putting out fires." Those living west of the courthouse must have heeded this advice because in the October 24, 1895, *Farmington Times*, mention was made of "a house or shed in which to keep the portable fire pump bought by the citizens living on the west side of the Courthouse is to be put at the rear of the Christian Church."

This engine seemed to meet the citizens' needs until September of 1917. In the local paper citizens began to voice their concern of the time wasted while trying to find either horses or enough men to pull the fire wagon. They felt a town the size of Farmington should own a motorized fire truck. They also wanted the town to look into a more efficient way to notify fellow firefighters (volunteers) of the location of the fire, instead of having to go out into the street and see which direction everyone was running and follow them.

The original firehouse was located at the corner of Franklin and Harrison Streets. This contained a couple of offices and living quarters for the dispatchers. (Today the Parks and Recreation Department, City Engineer and Building Inspector use that building.)

The city, experiencing growing pains, saw the need for a larger firehouse in which to store the department's much needed fire equipment. The City Council authorized the money for this building project, and in late 1976 the department moved to its new location. The department was still operating on a volunteer basis with the Fire Chief and Assistant Fire Chief the only full-time positions. Fire Chief Phil Johnson, planning for the continued growth of Farmington, incorporated into the Fire Department budget money to pay for Farmington's first ladder truck. This was done over a several-year period. With great pomp and circumstance this new truck finally arrived in Farmington in the summer of 1998.

As Farmington continued to grow (answering 1,275 calls in 1998) the need for a full-time staff became evident, and in July 1999 seven additional full-time staff were hired. Firefighters work a 24-hour shift from 6:00 a.m.-6:00 a.m. answering calls from car wrecks, medical calls and the obvious fire calls. All firefighters must take specialized training in all areas of firefighting, hazardous materials, search and rescue and arson training. Even the volunteer firefighters must be state certified.

Fire Chiefs have been:

N.D. Cayce - 1879
Ed Helber - 1884
Ed Mackley
Bob Oder
Phil Johnson - present

FARMINGTON POLICE DEPARTMENT

The Farmington Police Department had several different locations in City Hall which served as their offices. The first official known office was located in the first room to the left after entering the double doors at City Hall, about where the elevator is today. This office was later used by the city collector. They shared this office with the judge. The department then went to a small room in the basement next to the coal room and then later moved across the basement to another room.

During the 1940s there wasn't really a police department, but a day marshal and a night marshal. Some of the marshals were: Ed Chamberlain, George Sutherland, Horace Mullersman (day), and Mortimer Moore (night). These men walked the streets of Farmington, not having a car due to the war.

In March 1950, Farmington had its first new police cruiser, a black Nash, sold to them by Lee Wichman. In talking to one retired police officer today, he said of that Nash, "It looked like an upside down bathtub."

In 1954 the department consisted of four police officers, including the chief and a relief man. These men had no prior police training; they were just sworn in, given a gun and told to go work. Willard Dalton was hired as the relief man. They didn't have car radios, so their means of receiving calls was unique. At the intersection of Washington and Columbia Streets a red light was suspended. When a citizen called for the police, the telephone operator would flip a switch, which would turn on the red light. The officer patrolling the streets would see the light burning and contact the operator to receive the call. A second light was later hung at the intersection of Karsch and Washington Streets.

Also in 1954 the department received a newer vehicle. A black 1953 Chevrolet Bel Air, with a red light on the roof and a siren on the front fender.

The department made a third move, to an office in the building which housed the Fire Department. The fire department had radio dispatchers who lived in a three-room apartment on the east end of the building. These shared quarters were the next office for the Police Department. The Department of Public Works at the corner of Franklin and Harrison Streets was the original firehouse and then combination firehouse/police station.

In 1958 the city bought a large supply of radios to mount in the city trucks and police cars. These were dual radios, which meant you could also hear the sheriff calls. The calls were still dispatched from the Fire Department.

In 1959 the Missouri Legislature appropriated monies to the Missouri State Highway Patrol to provide training for the police officers of small towns such as Farmington. In the fall of 1959 Willard Dalton was the first Farmington police officer to attend the Missouri Highway Patrol Academy and receive training.

In 1959 a new police cruiser was purchased, a 1959 light green and white Edsel. Lee Wichman ordered the car for the department. Willard Dalton rode with a salesman to Mt. Vernon, IL to pick up the new cruiser.

During the 1960s the Police Department grew in number to six police officers. They included Chief Edward Saling, officers Leslie "Buck" Jones, Willard Dalton, Ted Shelton, Walter Ellis, and Floyd Lenz. At this same time a second police car was added. Both vehicles were equipped with two-way radios, allowing the officers to keep in touch with activities in the community. Transistor-type radios were also carried by some of the police officers.

In 1970s the Farmington Police Department had grown to eight officers and the need for more space became evident. On completion of the new firehouse, the Police Department was able to expand their offices into the existing building. This allowed for much needed office space and a separate dispatch office. Both police and fire calls were handled by the department.

In 1992 a million dollar bond issue was passed by the citizens of Farmington and the new police station was constructed on Ste. Genevieve Avenue. The Police Department has grown to include the chief, one lieutenant, three sergeants, three corporals, 10 road officers, an animal control officer, two school reserve officers, records clerk, six dispatchers, a three-man detective bureau, secretary, and a computer operator; quite a change from a day marshal and a night marshal.

The position of police chief was originally an elected office and they were called town marshals. Once the marshal was elected, the City Council would then appoint that person as po-

George Sutherland, Night Marshall and Justice of the Peace for more than 15 years.

Police Department in 1960; Buck Jones, Willard Dalton, Don Francis, Ed Wann, Floyd Lenz, Cecil Gore, and Walter Ellis.

Downtown Farmington in 1930, note the hanging light, which signaled the town marshals when there was a call.

Nash police car and officers, 1948.

23

Former Police Department Headquarters, now Public Works.

Present Police Department Headquarters.

lice chief. This election of the police chief was continued until 1977. Chief Walter Ellis was the last elected town marshal/police chief. Beginning in 1977 the police chief was, and still is, appointed by the mayor and City Council.

Town Marshals/Police Chiefs

George Sutherland
Ed Chamberlain
Horace Mullersman
Mortimer Moore
Sam Murray, 1954
Ed Saling, 1957-1971 (died in office)
Leslie (Buck) Jones, 1971-1975, 1977-(died in office)
Willard Dalton, 1975-1977
Walter Ellis, June 1977-1985
Roland Trautman, 1985-1989
Bob Oder, 1989-1993
Danny Dailey, 1994-1998
Rick Baker, 1998-to date

FARMINGTON PUBLIC LIBRARY

On May 12, 1915, at the home of Mrs. Marbury the United Daughters of the Confederacy, under the leadership of president, Mrs. G.E. Scrutchfield, laid the groundwork for the establishment of the Farmington Public Library. The library suggestion was enthusiastically received and all civic organizations were asked to participate in fund-raising projects to help with this movement.

The United Daughters of the Confederacy were given the job of finding a suitable location for the library. A committee consisting of Mrs. Robert Tetley, Mrs. Marbury, and Mrs. Laakman, reported the Tetley Building was vacant and well suited for a library. Mrs. Tetley offered her building for $25 a month and she would give $10 a month for support. The Board of Education came to the committee and offered a room at the high school free of charge.

A committee of men was formed to help the ladies make a selection. They include Clint Denman, Mr. Marbury, and Prof. W.L. Johns. Until a way of financing the building downtown was found, it was decided the rooms at the high school would be the location of the library. A Book Social was held, invitations sent out and every guest was asked to bring a book. From this social, 126 books were received. With this

Library opening on Aug. 27, 1980, Ernie Aubuchon, Ron Stevens, George Shaw, Fred Barnes, Mayor Floyd Hager, Architect Bill Reepe, Librarian Laura Massie, Mary Durst, Mit Landrum, Peggy Kellogg, Rita Belseme, Ed Bradley and Anne Ledbetter.

Library when it was located in Long Memorial Hall.

collection of "new" books the library opened its doors on October 1, 1915.

The location of the library so far from town caused some discontent among a few of the members of the United Daughters of the Confederacy. To best determine how the citizens felt, several calling committees went door to door while the mayor canvassed the business section trying to determine the best location for the library. After an excellent response from everyone it was decided to move the library to the Tetley Building. A meeting of the library trustees was held on April 20, 1916, and the following officers were elected: Mrs. E.G. Scrutchfield,

president; Prof. W.J. Johns, 1st vice-president; Mrs. C.O. Nelson, 2nd vice-president; Clyde Morsey, secretary; Barney Pelty, treasurer; Mrs. M.P. Cayce, supervisor. The secretary was authorized to have the books and furniture moved from the high school, the rent for the Tetley Building to be paid on the first of the month and the official opening date of the library was set for May 1, 1916.

On April 18, 1916, a decree issued to incorporate the Farmington Public Library was signed by John A. Knowles, Clerk of the Circuit Court. It was filed in the Recorder of Deeds on February 2, 1917, by H.M. O'Bannon, Recorder.

In July 1920 the library moved into a room at the Farmer's Bank Building and there the library remained until the completion of Long Memorial Hall in 1925. Two rooms were designated for the use of the library in Long Memorial Hall, which was built as a tribute to William Dubart Long, a pioneer of Farmington.

When the building was nearly completed, a fire delayed the formal dedication, which did take place October 31, 1924. These two rooms housed the Farmington Public Library from October 1924 until its move to 108 W. Harrison St. in August 1980.

In 1977 a proposal for a new library was presented to the City Council. From a dedicated group of Friends of the Library, members of the Library Board, and a committed librarian, a final plan for a new facility took shape. The city allocated an amount for actual construction and architect's fees, and the planning and steering committee began a fund-raising campaign to furnish the building.

The present building housing the Farmington Public Library officially opened to the public in August 1980. The library is dedicated to the memory of Witten H. Ledbetter, devoted Friend of the Library, skillful journalist and respected mayor of Farmington. One of the most eye-catching parts of the library is, in fact, an original design conceived by Mayor Ledbetter. Painted by Mike Chomyk, the large mural overlooks the quiet reading room and depicts early Farmington history. This mural was donated by Anne Ledbetter as a memorial

Helen Giessing admiring the Tabor Traveling Library.

Farmington Public Library

to her husband and dedicated not long after the library opened. At the opposite end of the library is a second mural, also painted by Mike Chomyk, which covers different scenes and characters from children's literature.

In 1990 Dr. Clifton R. Bell, a staunch supporter of the library for many years and an active member of the Library Board, advised his fellow board members they should be making plans for the future of the library and its ability to meet the needs of this fast-growing community. During that year Dr. Bell, serving as chairman of the Special Needs Committee, consisting of library board members, surveyed the patrons and general public, asking them if there were to be an expansion to the library in the future, what exactly would they like added to the current facility.

Dr. Bell compiled the data from this survey and made a presentation to the City Council, asking them for financial backing to expand the current facility. With the backing of the City Council, plus a generous donation from the estate of Dorothy H. Trigg in memory of her sister, Lottie M. Huff, who was a past library supporter and board member, the possibility of enlarging the library was well on its way.

Librarian Lynn Crites applied for a Library Services and Construction Act Building Grant in late 1991. Notification that the library had been awarded a grant came in late spring, with the ground breaking for the expansion held in September 1991.

Construction was completed by March 1, 1992, and the official ribbon cutting and Open House was held on April 5, 1992, with approximately 300 people attending. An additional 4,000 square feet was added, which included space for an enlarged children's area, separate genealogy room, quiet reading room, meeting rooms in the lower level, a handicapped entrance and much needed storage space. This brought the total square footage of the building to 8,000, plus an additional parking area.

During this expansion the library was only closed five working days while carpet was laid throughout the building. The rest of the time understanding patrons and staff walked around workmen, stacks of books, and plaster dust. Restoring the collection of books to the shelves after carpet was laid was a massive job, with the staff being helped by the Farmington High School Honor Society.

Some of the early librarians from the beginning of the library were: Miss Nettie Rudy, Mrs. Jennie Rottger, Jessalyn Counts, Miss Georgania Lutz, Miss Ruth Sutton, Miss Esther Wilson, and Mrs. Myra Dobbins Byington. Recent librarians have been Helen Giessing, Marjorie Dunaway, Laura Massie, Linda Orzcl, Candace Walter, Melanie Bullard (1985-1988) and Lynn Crites (1988-present).

The Farmington Public Library has grown from "reading rooms" to its own building of 8,000 square feet; from a book collection of 126 in 1915 to a collection of more than 34,000 volumes; a beginning membership of 200 in 1916 to its current 13,219 members.

The continued growth of the library is apparent and long-range planning has already begun to meet the patrons' needs into the next millennium.

DeLassus History

The town of DeLassus received its name from Colonel Charles DeHault DeLassus. The tract of land, a Spanish land grant, was almost 7,000 acres in size and awarded to Colonel Charles DeHault DeLassus by the King of Spain. Colonel DeLassus also received many other grants of land.

Colonel Charles DeHault DeLassus was the last Spanish Governor of the Louisiana Territory. He represented Spain and France when the Louisiana Territory was transferred to the United States in St. Louis in 1803. He signed and handed over the necessary documents for the transfer.

Rainault, a French Canadian, discovered lead on this tract in 1745. There were people other than Indians in this area several years before Murphy's Settlement was established. It is believed there was a fort somewhere on this tract at one time and also that lead from here was used by the colonists in fighting during the American Revolution. This tract extended well up into what is now the city of Farmington, as is evidenced by land records.

Camille DeLassus was a brother to Colonel Charles DeHault DeLassus and was a geologist. He was very active in this area at one time.

Augusta DeLassus was a son of Colonel Charles DeHault DeLassus and came here to live in 1869.

Placide DeLassus was a son of Augusta. When he was 10 years old, his mother took him to live with her in France for four years. There he received some education and was schooled in the ways of a French nobleman. The DeLassus family was considered among the nobility class in France. Placide was the last member of the family to live in DeLassus.

When the railroad wanted to come through Farmington sometime in the late 1860s, the citizens of Farmington decided "no." Therefore, the DeLassus family invited the railroad to come through DeLassus, which it did. The railroad was an important link to the rest of the county, being a faster means of travel to and from other towns and cities. The railroad helped improve the growth of the area. It was a means of shipping in much needed supplies and shipping out lead, local products and livestock. The late Dr. Dillard, veterinarian, once loaded mules on the railroad and shipped them to North Carolina, where they were used on the tobacco farms.

Many brave young men from the county boarded the train at DeLassus on the first leg of their journey to fight for their country in World War I.

At one time a street car ran from DeLassus into Farmington and back.

When people wanted to catch the train in DeLassus, one livery stable owner boasted that he had horses that would haul passengers from Ste. Genevieve to DeLassus by way of horse and buggy in less than six hours.

At one time there was the railroad depot, two stores, a few small businesses, a school, and the Methodist Church. Many people chose the hotel at DeLassus when they wanted to have

Depot in DeLassus, 1894.

DeLassus Hotel after the cyclone went through in 1912.

DeLassus baseball team, 1932.

a gathering, meeting or a party. It had 25 rooms, including a grand ballroom with hanging chandeliers imported from France.

Colonel Charles DeHault DeLassus spent his last years in New Orleans. He wrote in his diary that he was born in France and served the Spanish Government for 30 years. He was proud to call himself a citizen of the United States and that there was a town in Missouri named DeLassus. *Submitted by: Quentin DeLassus, great-great-grandson of Camille DeLassus, brother of Colonel Charles DeHault DeLassus.*

BRIEF HISTORY OF LITTLE DOE RUN CREEK

by Fred Lesh

The site of the bridge crossing of Little Doe Run Creek on what is now Highway W is rich in both natural and man-made history. For many years this crossing was on a well-defined Indian hunting trail and game path. It was used by the abundance of wild game, especially deer, who roamed the meadow valleys to St. Francois River, Little and Big Doe Run Creeks. Hunters and early travelers from Ste. Genevieve found deer here in such great numbers they called the two creeks "deer runs" or deer creeks. The names were later changed to Doe Run because of the many doe deer always present. From the little creek the town of Doe Run derived its name.

Little Doe Run Creek is fed by many small springs in and around the town; hence it was a logical location for adventurous frontiersmen to settle. The exact date for the settlement is not known but it was an established village before 1825, as the Pendleton Church was built a short distance below the present crossing in the year 1825. According to reliable oral records there was a narrow wooden bridge at the present site in use prior to that date. Other replacements were in use until 1851. At this time the historic Plank Road Bridge utilized this same site until 1903. Somewhere around this period, maintenance was done by Doe Run Lead Company, who also maintained a foot bridge along the north side of the regular span. This pedestrian bridge was used until the 1930s, when it was destroyed by flood and was never replaced.

In 1911 the crossing and road were maintained by St. Francois County. During the 1940s what is now Highway W became the property of the Missouri Highway Department.

Becoming an important rest stop on the Old Plank Road during the early development of Missouri's iron mining industry was not to be the little creek's only claim to history. The discovery of surface lead along her banks during the 1800s was to plunge her into the forefront of Missouri's fast-growing lead mining industry.

The little creek, by use of dams above and below the bridge site, was to play the very important role of supplying the necessary water used in the lead processing mill in the town of Doe Run during the town's boom years from 1880 to 1911.

SUMMATION: For nearly two centuries Little Doe Run Creek has played an important role in transportation and development of two of Missouri's major industries, iron and lead. The present bridge site is one of the oldest in this area. Being responsible for the name of the town that is situated along her banks and the many now-fading memories of her glory days is a part of her heritage.

The Howell House, built by John D. Tabor in 1836.

First building in Doe Run.

DOE RUN, MISSOURI

Doe Run is an unincorporated community located in south-central St. Francois County at the intersection of Highways W and B. Highway W enters the town from the southwest and continues to the northeast to Farmington. In town it is called Main Street. Highway B, Maple Street, begins at W in the center of town and runs due north. Doe Run is located about five miles southwest of Farmington.

The name of Doe Run was derived from the creek of the same name. This stream is thought to have derived its name from the female deer which roamed that part of the country. Settlements were made here in the early part of the 19th Century.

Among the early settlers were Eliaser Clay, William Reed, Isaac Welbourn and several of his grown sons, Wilson T. Barry, James Ritter, James Halbert the Baptist minister, and John Sherrill.

Very little is known of Doe Run before the year of 1880. At that time it was an unincorpo-

Downtown Main Street in Doe Run looking east.

Main Street in Doe Run looking east.

rated village and its site was pasture land and orchards. In about 1885, Wash Merryman, who lived in the vicinity, discovered particles of lead along the roadside where the water had washed the soil away. Further investigation proved that more of this gray substance could be found beneath the surface and our knowledge of modern Doe Run dates from this time.

The first house was built in Doe Run on February 15, 1887, at the beginning of the lead boom, and one year later there were 108 houses with 1,000 inhabitants.

Judge William R. Taylor, who had purchased some land in the vicinity of Doe Run, put down a shaft and struck some disseminated ore; in 1895 the Doe Run Lead Company was formed, having bought the land from Judge Taylor. Four shafts were sunk and ore was produced from these shafts continuously until 1897.

By 1900 the large lead mining operation had caused a boom in Doe Run and businesses began to open. Some of those were the Antoine Department Store, an opera house, blacksmith shop, hotel, lodge hall and even a bowling alley.

In 1911 the town of Doe Run was surveyed. The survey was filed by R.R.S. Parsons, the vice-president of the mining company. The town contained 59 blocks.

The Mississippi River and Bonne Terre Railroad ran on the east side to town. The train not only transported the lead ore out but carried passengers to the neighboring towns.

The town of Doe Run was virtually owned by the Doe Run Lead Company and this boosted the town's economy greatly until around 1916. By 1916 the production at the Doe Run Mine began to dwindle. The lead company's interests were moved to Rivermines and the Doe Run Mine closed. In the 1940s, when the mines shut down completely, several of the workers' homes were physically moved to Elvins.

Doe Run sported several businesses: Bennett's Grocery Store, run by Mag and Ruth Bennett. This store was located on the east side of Doe Run Creek next to the Masonic Lodge. In the 1940s school kids would come there to eat lunch. As many as five kids could buy cheese and drink (crackers were free from the barrel), all for 25 cents. This store later became Cozean Funeral Home. F.P. Graves had his extensive museum collection in this building.

In the 1930s on Highway W, Jack Sergent's Garage/Gas Station did business, and bread could be bought for five cents a loaf.

Lesh's Grocery Store (originally Fleming's), was another prosperous business selling food items and yard goods. In the late 1960s it became a hardware store. This store was located where the present Plantation House Restaurant stands today.

Iahn's Grocery in the 1930s went through several different owners. The grocery store originally began as a feed store, selling eggs on the side. Customers began asking them to carry other grocery items for convenience: bread, milk, etc., which they did, eventually ending up carrying more grocery items than feed!

Ralph and Gladys Edwards bought the store from the Iahns, living in the back rooms and raising their two girls there.

Jay and Elva Lacey bought the store from the Edwards in the 1950s. In 1970 Dale and Jane

F.P. Graves home in Doe Run.

Doe Run Junction Redbirds, 1905.

Doe Run Depot, 1890 - 1910.

Doe Run Lead Company Machine Shop, 1905.

Mund family, builder of the Church of God church.

Original drawing of the Presbyterian or Church of God built by Fredrick Mund, 1894.

An ice-cream shop called Dairy Queen (but not the famous one of today) was in operation in the 1950s. It was owned and run by Shortie and Della Williams.

Doe Run had one school and one school bus. The bus made three trips each morning bringing kids to school and taking them home again in the evening. The janitor, Mr. Quincy Bannister, would allow those arriving on the first trip to go into the basement to play and stay warm. He would pay those having to stay late waiting for the bus a nickel to turn up the chairs in the classrooms so he could sweep. When Mr. Bannister left, John Cromer took over his job.

Several beauty shops were located in private homes: Edith Huff, Frankie Hahn, Frances Zolman and Doris King. Bill's Barber Shop, owned by Bill O'Farrell in the 1950s, was next to Wichman's Garage/Grocery Store.

Churches today in Doe Run are Methodist, First Baptist, Pendleton Baptist, Assembly of God, Church of God and Emanuel Baptist. A Catholic Church once stood where the Masonic Lodge is today.

At its peak, the town of Doe Run had as many as 1,000 citizens and was considered one of the most rapidly growing towns in Missouri. Today, Doe Run is a small, quaint town with family-owned businesses and a past rich in history.

Much of the information for this story was taken from the personal reminiscences of Sally Weiss Barnhouse and Jane Weiss Bess.

HISTORY OF KNOB LICK, MISSOURI

About 1830 early settlers began homesteading land in the southeastern corner of St. Francois County. In this area was a knoll of the St. Francois mountains which was called the "knob." At the foot of the knoll was soil which was very salty and deer came there to lick the salt. Thus the village was named Knob Lick, first as one word, later as two words. Knob Lick is located just off Highway 67 South, on Highway DD, approximately seven miles from Farmington.

Knob Lick was surveyed in 1869 by William McDowell. The town included 11 blocks situated on the west side of the railroad. The railroad was part of the Belmont Branch of the Iron Mountain Line.

The discovery of valuable granite deposits in the nearby community of Syenite brought many stone cutters to Knob Lick from eastern states. A quarry was opened and named for its owners, William Milne and James Gordon, both natives of Scotland. The granite was cut into paving blocks, much of it shipped via the railroad to St. Louis to be used on the streets there. At one time several hundred people resided in this thriving town which had several grocery stores, a drug store, two large hotels, etc.

The first school was made of logs; a later one, built in 1914, was constructed of those famous granite blocks. The school building and several granite block homes in the area still stand as testimonials of the durability of granite.

The first church building (the present Bap-

Bess bought the store from the Laceys. For three years the store was owned by Don and Peggy Nye; then ownership returned to Dale and Jane Bess.

In 1982 Ted and Sally Barnhouse bought the store and in 1994 the grocery store closed its doors for good. It stood approximately in the parking lot of Plantation House Restaurant. Besides the grocery store Sally Barnhouse also ran an upholstery shop. The current home of Sally Barnhouse is over 100 years old and thought to be the oldest house still standing in Doe Run.

On the site of the firehouse today, a cafe once stood, which was a local hang-out for the young people during the 1950s.

On the west side of town, Mom and Pop Flanery owned and ran a family tavern which, according to local folks, had the best hamburgers in town. The east side of town also had a tavern run by Red and Virgie Becker, which people say had some pretty hot pinochle games played during the day. This later became an antique shop run by Jean Hampton in the late 1970s.

Jess LeGrande was the provider of electricity to the townspeople, owning his own electric company. Doe Run Monument Co., originally owned by Mr. LeGrande, is also where he lived. Shortie Williams later bought the business.

Knob Lick Granite Crusher, 1900.

Knob Lick Depot

tist Church) was constructed about 1880. Other churches built later and still in operation are the Church of God and the Assembly of God. One general store and the post office now make up the business district. The population in 1999 is approximately 100 people. Although smaller in size than in previous years, this village remains a place of good neighbors and caring people who are proud of their heritage and Knob Lick's place in the history of St. Francois County. *Submitted by Delores Plummer*

LIBERTYVILLE

The Community of Libertyville includes what has been known since 1799 as Cook's Settlement. In 1799 Nathaniel Cook, a native Kentuckian, was attracted to the area by its natural beauty, fertile soil, many fine springs, and the forest of choice hardwood timber. His was the third permanent settlement in what is now known as St. Francois County and, according to available information, was located approximately 3/4 miles west of what is now Libertyville.

An original abstract of the Jerry and Kay Miller Farm (previously owned by Henry Detring) shows that Zeno Trudeau surveyed and claimed that parcel of land in 1797, but he did not settle there.

The town of Libertyville was founded early in the history of this period. Some of the very earliest settlers (1810-1812) included families of McFarland, Harris, Tillman, Simpson, Kinkead, Faust, Sebastian, Presnell, Hughes, Clark, Smith, Moran, Blanks, Needham, Shaw, Moore, Crow, and Farmer. They have been described as people of more than ordinary intelligence, frugal, and ambitious.

One of the earliest of these settlers was Captain Samuel Kinkead, who came to the area with his "stolen" wife, his horse, rifle, dog, fry pan (and some say a quarter), and claimed the land on which the town of Libertyville now stands. His arrival date is established as 1810, the year Samuel and his wife, Lettice, were married. They first camped in the field just north of what is now the Ralph Detring residence. It is believed they then located their home on a small knoll just to the east of that camp on the existing Kinkead farm.

Apparently, very few school records were

Rydeen General Store, children in front unknown.

maintained throughout the 19th Century in Libertyville. However, according to available information, it is believed that formal education was present in Libertyville in approximately 1812. Records indicate a log building was erected and a school begun prior to 1820. It is also believed that "Circuit Riders," probably of the Baptist faith, held religious services in that log schoolhouse and that a Baptist Church existed in the community prior to the organization of the Christian Church. There are no known records available to confirm this. This is significant in that even in that early period of the community there was a large number of early settlers, and they believed in education and religion.

Goodspeed's *History of Southeast Missouri* states that in 1822, the Reverend William McMurtry organized a Christian Church in an "existing log schoolhouse, at what is known as Libertyville." The first officers of that church were Samuel Kinkead and E.C. Sebastian as elders and Zeno T. Blanks and Andrew Kinkead as deacons. From available records, a discrepancy of approximately 16 years exists in the organization date of the Libertyville Christian Church.

A survey of Libertyville by Zebulon Murphy in 1840 revealed there were four irregular blocks. The principal street was called "Second" and ran northeast and southeast, dividing the town. Since no county records were available regarding street names in Libertyville, it was decided to rename the streets. The three streets formed a triangle; entering Libertyville from the north where the streets forked, the street to the right was renamed "Main Street" (now Wesley Chapel Road), and the one to the left was renamed "Elm Street" (now Old Jackson Road). The streets were joined by one that formed the base to the triangle and was renamed "Lindbergh" (now State Road DD). "Main Street" was "The Hay Road," and believed to have been a part of the original U.S. Highway 61. "Elm Street" was the "Farmington to Jackson Road," and "Lindbergh" was the "St. Mary to Ironton Road."

On November 24, 1843, Samuel and Lettice Kinkead deeded to the citizens of Liberty Township (for the sum of one dollar) the land on which the log schoolhouse/church and cemetery existed, "To be continually and forever held by them and their successors for the use and purpose of a public burying ground, a schoolhouse for the benefit of said township, and also for the purpose of a building thereon, a House of Public Worship, generally termed a meeting house..." The original trustees were Zeno T. Blanks, Edwin C. Sebastian, and James C. Smith.

In July 1846 the Libertyville Post Office was originally established as "Kinkead" in St. Francois County with Samuel Kinkead as the first postmaster. The Post Office name was changed to "Locust Ridge" on March 19, 1857, to "Liberty Meeting House" on December 23, 1862, and to "Libertyville" on February 18, 1863. The Post Office existed as "Libertyville" until December 15, 1919, when Libertyville became a rural route of the Farmington Post Office.

Although the community was largely Southern in loyalty, there apparently were the same divisions in the political arena as existed in other border states. In the 1860s a troop of Union soldiers (presumably en route to the Battle of Fredericktown, MO) stopped in Libertyville to rest and to secure food and water for themselves and their animals. After watering their horses, they tied them beneath the large tree near the cemetery and church and then went to the mill for grain. The mill, located in the field to the west of the church, was operated by Mike DeGuire. Fearful the soldiers would confiscate all the grain and that the community would suffer, Mr. DeGuire slowed the mill to its very slowest speed. When questioned by the soldiers, he told them there was not a sufficient amount of water running to grind the corn at a faster rate. The soldiers, apparently tired of waiting and uninformed about the operation of a steam, saw, flour and grist mill, journeyed on. Mr. DeGuire was praised by the citizenry for his loyalty to the community.

In 1871 Washington Hughes began publication of the *New Era* newspaper in Libertyville but soon moved to Farmington and continued publication of that newspaper until 1876 when he sold it to George Harrington and moved to Marble Hill, MO.

In 1872 Libertyville had grown to one of the larger towns of the area with a number of different business enterprises established. There was the steam, saw, flour and grist mill; a tannery; newspaper; two blacksmith shops; two general stores; two wagon shops; two shoe shops; one saddle and harness shop; one drug store; two physician offices; two hotels; two saloons; the existing church (and another under construction, possibly a Methodist Church); and an "academy."

Professional medical treatment was available early in the history of Libertyville. Dr. John C. Farmer, who was also a minister of the Gospel, practiced medicine in Libertyville in the 1850s, preceding a number of different physicians during the 1870s.

A St. Francois County "Record of Physicians" lists Dr. T.A. Winn practicing medicine in Libertyville in 1874 after purchasing the practice from Dr. Farmer. A graduate of the Keokuk (Iowa) Medical College, Dr. William Madison practiced in Libertyville in 1875. In George S. Kinkead's Justice of the Peace Record, a court settlement (for a bill due) was recorded in the favor of Dr. A. Rudy on March 9, 1877. In 1889 the county record shows Dr. George Martin Rutledge, a graduate of the College of Physicians and Surgeons in Keokuk, was a practicing physician in Libertyville. In 1890 Dr. William E. Presnell, an 1889 graduate of the St. Louis College of Physicians and Surgeons, had established a practice in Libertyville and in 1892 Dr. Edwin C. Sebastian Jr. also entered practice of medicine in Libertyville.

Justice of the Peace records revealed that jury pay in 1875 was 50 cents per juror per trial. An assault case tried that year yielded a guilty verdict with a judgment of one dollar, plus court costs of 70 cents. Constable William Moore received a fee of 35 cents for serving the summons associated with that case.

When the railroad failed to build a spur into the town of Libertyville, most of the established businesses relocated. The mill moved to Fredericktown, but very little is known about what happened to the others. Kinkead family records do show that one of the hotels was still in operation by Fannie Kinkead, widow of George S. Kinkead, from 1886 into the early 1890s. This hotel was located on the Farmington Jackson Road (Elm Street), which continued to be a main connecting thoroughfare into Southeast Missouri. Traveling salesmen were frequent customers of the hotel, and it is believed a few local boarders were also present.

Throughout the years, the Libertyville School was a vital part of the community. Prior to consolidation into the Farmington School District in 1994, it was believed to be the oldest, still active, public school in the state of Missouri.

According to the 1935 *Libertyville Fair Book*, the first Libertyville Fair was organized and held in 1931 at the school. This fair was held for the purpose of providing a public occasion at which members of the newly-founded Baby Beef 4-H Club could exhibit their calves.

Old Williams home, built entirely by slaves, note Civil War soldier standing in front of the fir tree.

Libertyville Baseball team, 1901.

The first members of this club were Donald Detring, Wayman Crow, William Graham, Charles and Edward Mullersman, William Detring and Clark Kinkead. Two associate members that year were Edgar Detring and Norman Detring. The leader was Mr. H.W. Crow. In 1932 their leader was Mr. P.A. Cashion, and it was that same year when the 4-H Clothing Club was organized and boasted a total of 16 members. With the loyal backing of the entire community, the Libertyville Fair continued through 1935 and was the only fair in St. Francois County. The Libertyville 4-H Club has continued to be quite active throughout the years.

It was during this period of time (mid-1930s) that the basement of the school was hand-dug by members of the WPA. Dirt was hauled by wheelbarrows from beneath the school to the ballfield, and upon completion the ballfield was also leveled and smoothed. This school building was constructed in the mid-1920s.

In 1936 or 1937 electricity entered the community via lines installed by the Union Electric Company. Prior to that, electricity had been furnished to the school and the church by Mr. Jess Mills, who operated the Libertyville Store. Mr. Mills owned a Delco Light Plant and each day would start it for light for the Mills home, the store, and the school and church.

The Libertyville Store, which was located on the main floor of the Masonic Lodge Hall, was an established business in the Libertyville Community for more than 100 years. For many years, "The Store" had the only telephone in the community and was the site of many varied and heated political debates among the locals. It was a general meeting place to discuss current events; it was the high school bus stop, the July 4th fireworks display site, and the site of many lunchtime sandwiches, and even hot lunches, at one time. On September 20, 1978, "The Store's" last owner, Mrs. Ruby Kiepe, closed the door for the last time. Mrs. Kiepe had operated "The Store" on two separate occasions, the first time opening for business in 1954 for approximately three years, selling the business, then reopening around 1966. Other previously known owners of "The Store" included Jeff Sourness, a Mr. Abernathy, Jess Mills, Tom Bequeath, Valve Williams, Carl Kiepe, Chalmer Sandlin, Hubert Simpson, Norman Watts and Darrell Green.

In 1974 the Cook's Settlement Restoration Society incorporated as a not-for-profit organization to restore the old church building, the cornerstone of which is dated 1858. The building is now utilized, as was the original owner's intent, for a community meeting house and is governed by a Board of Directors. With the approval of this Board of Directors, Libertyville

Masonic Hall at Libertyville.

Community gatherings and family reunions are held there, and the Libertyville 4-H Club meets in the building on a regular basis.

Two churches (the Libertyville Christian Church and the Libertyville United Methodist Church) remain active in the community, as does the Masonic Lodge. According to available information, the brethren of St. Francois Lodge No. 234 at Libertyville, MO, held their first meeting on June 23, 1863. The Lodge was then chartered by the Grand Lodge of the State of Missouri on May 26, 1864. Records do not indicate where Lodge meetings were held prior to the completion of the Lodge Hall which was erected in 1865-66 on property donated by Samuel Kinkead. This building, dedicated on September 1, 1866, remains in use to date with many of the original furnishings.

The Libertyville School building, vacated in 1994 when the school was incorporated into the Farmington School District, is now a private home. At the closing of the school, a reunion was held on the grounds of the school and old church building with more than 350 former students in attendance.

We are very fortunate our forefathers came to this area bringing with them dreams and determination. For more than 180 years our community has remained strong and many close, lifelong friendships are sustained with special memories in our hearts.
Submitted by Pat Kinkead and Nancy Detring
The Libertyville School/History Book
Copyright, 1994

ST. FRANCOIS LODGE 234 AF&AM

According to available information, the brethren of St. Francois Lodge No. 234 at Libertyville, MO, held their first meeting on June 23, 1863. The Lodge was then chartered by the Grand Lodge of the State of Missouri on May 26, 1864.

Records do not indicate where Lodge meetings were held prior to the completion of the new Lodge Hall. The present building was erected in 1865-66 on property donated to the Lodge by Samuel Kinkead. This building, dedicated on September 1, 1866, remains in use to date with many of the original furnishings.

An example of an exemplary lodge member is Vincent Kinkead, a 1938 graduate of the Libertyville School. Mr. Kinkead served as the 141st Grand Master of Masons in Missouri in 1986-87. At that time, there were 90,000 Missouri Masons. Mr. Kinkead was one of a very small number of farmers to ever serve as Grand Master. Most Missouri Grand Masters are attorneys, businessmen, and politicians, including governors and President Harry S. Truman.

Mr. Kinkead is presently serving his third three-year term as Executive Commissioner for The Masonic Service Association of Silver Spring, MD. He is one of six commissioners and represents the Masons in eight midwest states.

RELIGION

Rev. C. E. Hickok, Presbyterian Minister, 1912.

Rev. Rufner, Presbyterian Minister.

Top row: Simon J. Hensley, J. P. Zolman, Grant Evans. Front row: John Doss, Oscar L. Haile, Rev. Bright, John McCarthy, Oliver J. Mayberry, 1912.

Zinprodt, Baptist Minister, 1930.

Rev. O. L. Cunningham, Baptist Minister, 1915.

Rev. Carter Martin, Baptist Minister.

RELIGION

The religious life in early Farmington dates back to the early 1800s when circuit riders were visiting the settlements periodically. In 1804 Rev. James Oglesby preached the first Methodist sermon in a log cabin erected by local settlers. The cabin/church was built on land donated by Sarah Barton Murphy.

In 1805 Sarah Barton Murphy organized and taught the first Sunday School west of the Mississippi River. The school and church were located on her land claim. Today, some of that claim is Farmington's Masonic Cemetery. A stone marker, which identifies the site where her log cabin stood, is lasting tribute to the time, effort, land and money she donated to build the first church in Farmington. The monument, erected by her great-grandson, Hugh Long, is about 7 feet high and is located in the northeast corner of the Masonic Cemetery, marking the spot where the church stood. On this obelisk are these words, "On this spot, the first Sunday School west of the Mississippi River was organized and taught by Sarah Barton Murphy, in the year 1805, in the log meeting-house which was the first Protestant Church west of the Mississippi River."

Sarah Barton Murphy had a strong Baptist heritage. She desired organized church religious worship services by a man of the cloth and vowed to give the church building to the first preacher who would stay here and take over the church. Rev. James Ogelsby, a Methodist circuit rider, fulfilled this promise. This is how the Murphys became Methodist and not Baptist. When the new Methodist Church was built, it was named the Murphy-Long Methodist Church.

It is undocumented, but it is believed that Farmington has the oldest ongoing Methodist organization west of the Mississippi River.

Area Churches Boast Long Tradition

Churches have always played an important role in settlement and growth of Farmington and surrounding area.

One of the first congregations to be organized in the county was the Christian Church at Libertyville. It was established in May of 1822 by the Rev. William McMurtry. A carpenter by trade, McMurtry had come from his native state of Virginia to Madison County before organizing the church in a log cabin at Libertyville. Its first officers were Samuel L. Kinkead and E.C. Sebastian, elders; Zeno T. Blanks and Andrew Kinkead, deacons. A frame structure was built in 1844 but it was destroyed by fire a few years later. In 1858 a brick structure, which still stands, was built. By 1888 membership had increased to 120. The congregation, which erected a new building in 1961, continues to thrive today.

The Pendleton United Baptist Church at Doe Run traces its beginnings to 1825, when it was formed with the help of the Baptist Church at Belleview. The name Pendleton belongs to an individual from South Carolina who was active in organizing the church. The name was also given to the municipal township in which the church is located. The Pendleton Church has grown and prospered over the years. In 1964 the congregation erected a new building, which was expanded in 1991 to meet the growing needs of the church.

The Three Rivers Baptist Church was organized on May 7, 1832, by Elder James Cundiff. Other founding members were William E. Edwards and wife, Polly Edwards; Z.B. Jennings and wife, Johanna; Margaret Davis, Fanny Wyatt, and Robert H. Wyatt. Services were held at the homes of members until a frame church building was erected around 1840. However, the building was destroyed by fire several years later. A new brick structure was erected in 1850, and it was replaced by another brick building in 1899. In 1937 work was begun on a granite church, which was located near the site of the 1899 structure. The Three Rivers Baptist Church has continued to grow and serve the needs of the people of the community and surrounding area.

Pendleton United Baptist Church at Doe Run.

Three Rivers Baptist Church, 1932.

Libertyville Christian Church

The History Of The Farmington Christian Church

The Farmington Christian Church is a part of that religious group known as the Disciples of Christ. During the period between 1804 and 1832, Barton W. Stone, Thomas Campbell, Alexander Campbell and others dreamed dreams and saw visions of a united church upon the basis of the Bible and the Bible alone. They affirmed that people should discard human creeds, use the New Testament as the rule of faith and practice, wear New Testament names, and practice the doctrines of Christ in the apostolic way. At first they preached these ideas in Presbyterian and Baptist churches and won many adherents. Churches where these teachings were accepted gradually left the Presbyterians and Baptists, and in 1832 they chose to be called Disciples of Christ. They held that any scriptural name for the church would be right, but the names most used are Christian Church and Church of Christ. It is estimated that in 1832 these people numbered between 20,000 and 30,000, and from that date they multiplied rapidly.

The Disciples originated in Pennsylvania and Kentucky, but many of their converts became a part of a tide of emigration moving west. When they located in new communities, the zealous ones set about to convert their neighbors to the "apostolic faith." Many laymen started new churches and sent back east for preachers to come west and help them.

The early settlers of Southeast Missouri were for the most part Roman Catholics, but soon Disciples from Kentucky and points farther east moved in. They were aflame with the missionary spirit and began at once to make converts and build churches. The first Christian Church in St. Francois County was at Libertyville, and the date generally given is May 17, 1822.

Pastor S.S. Church, of St. Louis, came into St. Francois County in 1855 and held meetings at Farmington, Libertyville and Fredericktown, which resulted in 140 additions in all. Thus, a small church was organized in Farmington. In 1857 a reporter stated that the Farmington Church had about 20 members and added that there were some intelligent, zealous and worthy brethren among them. They, with help from outside, built a capacious and commodious house of worship, with a large room in the basement for a school room and two small rooms for recitation and Bible classes.

This church was built on a lot south of Harrison and east of South Henry Street and was leased to the Farmington Academy, which held school in it on week days.

The church owed $546.39 for building materials and, being unable to pay, the mortgage was foreclosed and the property sold at the courthouse door, November 14, 1860, and Stephen E. Douthit bid it in at $50. Whether the church worshipped in the building while Mr. Douthit owned it is not known. Soon after his death, June 4, 1867, the property was sold to the Farmington Academy, and no more is known of the Christian Church until 1875.

On July 8, 1875, the property of the M.E. Church South at the southeast corner of Harrison and Jefferson Streets was sold for debt at the south door of the Court House, and Thomas E. Douthit bought it for $300, hoping a Christian Church might be reorganized. That year the Missouri Christian Missionary Society sent Evangelist H.F. Davis into Southeast Missouri to help the churches. The Disciples in and near Farmington were assembled in the above-mentioned building and organized with 42 members into a congregation September 4, 1875.

The church grew with the years, and on January 15, 1885, the Christian Church, for the sum of $800, bought the Presbyterian Church at the southeast corner of West Columbia and South A Streets. It is understood that the Presbyterians accepted the old Christian Church property as part payment. Later the church purchased the lot lying between this property and Harrison Street. The above mentioned building was completed under the direction of Pastor A.M. Harral. Pastor Robert M. Talbert began his ministry there and the building was dedicated, free from debt, on April 7, 1901. During the pastorate of Edward J. Owers, August 17, 1905, this Christian Church was incorporated by the circuit court. About 1907, a parsonage was built on the lot that had been purchased behind the church. The owner's family was first to occupy it.

Rev. J.M. Bailey died December 11, 1938, after a long ministry to this congregation. By September 1939 Rev. Talbert conducted a dedication service of the stained-glass window, which had been installed by the Century Art Glass Company of St. Louis and sponsored by the Women's Council of the local Christian Church.

During the ministry of C.R. Piety, the need of a constitution and by-laws for the church was discussed. On February 2, 1948, a committee was chosen to write the document. The work was read before the Church Board and approved. A potluck supper was held February 19, 1948, and the Constitution and By-Laws were read and adopted by a unanimous vote. In compliance with the same, the church elected officers and reorganized in fine spirit.

On October 9, 1950, the Christian Church (Disciples of Christ) bought the church building at 201 West Columbia from the Carleton Methodist Church for $25,000, agreeing to make three payments, one third of the sale price per year. In addition, the Methodists allowed the Christian Church $19,500 for the "little brick church" on the corner of West Columbia and A Streets. The Methodists had a pipe organ and the Christian Church had a Hammond organ. The pipe organ needed repair; the Christian Church did not want it. They wanted to keep the Hammond, and did, selling the pipe organ for $850.00 to Kilgen Organ Company in St. Louis, who moved it. Of course there was no baptistery, so one had to be built. The minister that was present when the transformation to the present building was completed was Rev. Gordon Miller.

The names of many of the early ministers are unknown. Following are those known: Burr, W.H. Hale, T.P. Read, Underwood, R.W. Love, J.L. Stephenson, A.M. Harral, Robert M. Talbert, Hillman, Edward J. Owers, J.M. Bailey, Wallace, Marion Frank, J.W. Moody, Virgil P. Glass, Jack Malia, Chauncey R. Piety, Gordon Miller, Beard, J.C. Stevenson, Walter Simpson, Fred Langsdale, Harry Robinson, Leon Berry, Alan Cole, Kenneth Hull and Dale Berck.

Farmington Christian Church, 1885-1950.

Farmington Christian Church, 1950 to present.

First Assembly of God Church

In May 1943 the Rev. J.W. Allen family loaded their belongings onto a truck and started for Farmington, MO to begin an Assemblies of God Church. During WWII times were hard. Gas was rationed and there were many shortages. The decision to move to Farmington was made by faith. They realized the future would be difficult but they believed God would provide.

Rev. Allen wanted to hold meetings in Farmington but facilities were not available. The Southern Missouri District of the Assemblies of God provided Rev. Allen with a tent until other arrangements could be made. The tent was set up on the lots where the Kawasaki Dealership and the Lodge are now located (104 S. Washington Street). This was only two blocks east of where the basement of the church was later built. In mid to late July of 1943, the first revival services were conducted.

August 15, 1943, while still holding services in the tent, a Sunday School was organized with eight members (Rev. Allen and his wife, Ruth Allen; daughter, Deloris Allen; son, Bud Allen; Fielding Hambrick; Minerva Hambrick; Emmett Mullinax and Minnie Mullinax).

August 23, 1943, the Southern Missouri District purchased 67 feet off the corner of lot 46, which was at the northwest corner of First and Franklin Streets. This was to be the new home for the First Assembly of God Church. The church property had to be cleared before building. There was an old shed standing that had been used for storage of funeral home supplies and possibly a horse-drawn hearse. A work day was then planned and several of the ministers from the Section came to help clear the property. Tom Gibson owned a team of mules and a scoop. When he could, he helped Rev. Allen in digging the basement. There were still the corners as well as much other digging to be done by hand. On occasion people passing by would see Rev. Allen working alone, lifting beams, and stopped and helped him.

December 5, 1943, the first services were held in the basement with 18 present in Sunday School. God blessed and the church continued to grow. The main auditorium was built and dedicated on September 14, 1947. On November 4, 1948, an application was made for affiliation with the General Council of the Assemblies of God in Springfield. On January 5, 1949, the church became a General Council church.

In 1954 a 20' x 50' addition was built with a full basement. In 1961 a second addition was added and the outside of the building was bricked.

After more than 25 years as pastor at First Assembly of God, Rev. J.W. Allen retired in March of 1969. He went to be with the Lord in 1985. Ruth Allen, his wife, lives at Ashbrook Manor and still makes First Assembly her church home when she is able to attend.

On January 20, 1969, Rev. Hugh Cerutti, current pastor, sent a resume to the Farmington Church even though he was told there wasn't any use to pursue the Farmington Church, that someone was coming and they were sure they would be elected. After two months had passed, Rev. Cerutti was contacted to be a candidate for the First Assembly of God Church in Farmington. He was then elected pastor on Sunday night, March 16, 1969. Rev. Hugh Cerutti, his wife, Mildred, and five children loaded their belongings and arrived in Farmington on March 31, 1969.

Seven and a third acres, 2/10 miles north of Farmington on D Highway, was purchased on August 16, 1972, for a new church facility. A ground breaking ceremony was held on October 31, 1976. After over two years of much prayer and hard labor, the major part of which was donated, the congregation moved to the new church. March 26, 1978, saw the rejoicing congregation of First Assembly in the Fellowship Hall for Easter Sunday morning services. Less than two months later the sanctuary was completed. On May 14, 1978, Mother's Day, the first service was held in the sanctuary. The church was dedicated on November 19, 1978. Additional acreage with a brick house just south of the church was purchased in 1994, bringing the total acreage to just under twelve acres.

The Lord has truly blessed. After 55 years the church has had only two senior pastors. Rev. Hugh Cerutti is the current pastor. Rev. Joseph Kochis joined the staff as associate pastor in 1992, and Andrew Massey joined the staff as youth pastor in 1998.

First Assembly of God Church.

First Assembly of God Church, dedicated Nov. 19, 1978.

First Baptist Church Of Farmington

The First Baptist Church of Farmington was organized as a mission of the Three Rivers Baptist Church on March 18, 1882. One of the organizing elders, Reverend James G. Hardy, served as the first pastor of the new church.

Saturday before the second Sunday, became the regular meeting time for the church. They first met in the Christian Church, then in the Methodist Churches and finally in the Farmington Baptist Church Chapel. By 1888, just six years after its founding, the membership totaled 57. They had no home of their own for 11 years.

In 1892 a building committee was appointed and their first church home became a frame structure located on the corner of West College and North Franklin Streets. By the turn of the century, the church had over 300 members. Consequently, a larger building was needed. In 1907 another building committee was formed. The panic of 1907 hindered finances but the building fund still managed to grow. The new brick building was built on the same site as the frame building and was completed in 1910. The building was not dedicated until 1917 as that was when the church was paid for. Reverend O.H.L. Cunningham was the pastor when the building was dedicated.

The first educational building was constructed and completed in 1949 when enrollment in Sunday School was 360 and church membership was 534. Reverend Ray Stone was the pastor. A new educational building was constructed and dedicated in 1962. Reverend J. Loren Jolly was pastor when this building was dedicated.

Due to the growth in attendance, which required two morning services during the ministry of the Rev. J. Loren Jolly, a new sanctuary was built and dedicated in 1973. The new sanctuary was built on the corner of West College and North A Streets. This new sanctuary would seat 700 people. Church membership was approximately 1,600 at this time.

Dr. William C. Miller became the pastor in March of 1986. The church membership was still growing and again two morning worship services were held to accommodate the members. Additional space was needed for the growing membership. A new wing was completed in 1989. This addition contains classrooms, a suite of offices, a library, a new kitchen and fellowship hall, which will seat 500 people.

Other staff members include: the Reverend John W. Jackson, who has now served as Minister of Music for 27 years; Reverend Rocky Good, Minister of Education; Reverend Russell Walje, Minister of Youth/Students; Marilyn Watts, Secretary to the Pastor; Karen Moore, Church Secretary; and Reverend J. Loren Jolly, Pastor Emeritus.

First Baptist continues to be one of the leading churches in the state in Mission support and involvement. Twenty-six percent of the present budget goes to Missions. Now the largest Baptist Church in the Mineral area, with a membership totaling 1,837, the church continues to grow with a mounting spirit of revival.

First Baptist Church of Farmington, 1973 to present.

S

First Baptist Church of Farmington, completed 1910. Educational building to left competed in 1962.

1893 First Baptist Church of Farmington.

Farmington First Church Of The Nazarene
801 N. Middle Street
Farmington, MO

On August 12, 1958, eight people met at the home of Paul Richardson at 406 C Street in Farmington, MO, for the purpose of organizing the Church of the Nazarene. Those present were Paul Richardson, Eula Richardson, James Richardson, Mary Richardson, Dean Groseclose, Opal Groseclose, Dean Groseclose Jr., and Dora Ransom. Dr. E.D. Simpson, District Superintendent of the Missouri District Churches of the Nazarene, officiated at the organization and welcomed all said members into the church. Paul Richardson was appointed to serve as the first pastor of the new church, and Opal Groseclose was appointed as church secretary. The organizational meeting was closed with a time of prayer and singing of the chorus, *Till Jesus Comes*.

Work had already begun on April 22, 1958, on a new church building under the direction of Paul Richardson. The completed building was dedicated to the glory of God on Sunday afternoon, September 14, 1958, by District Superintendent Dr. E.D. Simpson. In 1991, a major building project more than doubled the size of the original facility with the addition of a new sanctuary, classrooms, and administrative offices.

The church has had nine ministers in its history to this present time. These were Paul Richardson (1958-69), Max Downs (1969-73), David Worcester (1973-75), Clinton Wasson (1975-79), Michael Suits (1980-83), Bill Burke (1984-89), Van Williams Jr., (1989-93), Bill Bland (1993-95), and Mel Skeen (1995-present).

The Farmington First Church of the Nazarene is proud to serve and be a part of such a wonderful community!

Congregation of Farmington First Church of the Nazarene, 1958.

Farmington First Church of the Nazarene.

A Brief History Of The First Free Will Baptist Church
Farmington, MO
1952-1998

The original building where the First Free Will Baptist Church of Farmington is located at Clay and W. Columbia Streets was constructed in 1881 by the Methodist denomination and has a rich history behind it. On September 13, 1901, the cornerstone was laid to build a new building. The large stained-glass windows on the north side of the building were given by Mrs. Sarah Murphy's grandson, W.D. Long. In 1909 a pipe organ was donated by Mrs. Jane Bisby, daughter of Mrs. Isabella Long.

Rev. Damon Dodd, from the Home Missions Department of the National Association of Free Will Baptists, came to Farmington in September 1952 to hold a two-week revival with the intent of establishing a church in the city of Farmington. On the last night of the revival the church was organized with Rev. Dodd as the pastor and Clyde Gross as the first deacon.

The Free Will Baptists purchased the church property on Clay and W. Columbia Street from the Methodists in September 1954. The original sanctuary is still in use with some changes by reconstruction. A balcony that seats approximately 200 was added in 1983. The platform was extended to seat the choir and make room for a grand piano; plus a baptistery was added. The pipe organ that was originally donated by Mrs. Jane Bisby is still in use each week.

Some of the men that have served as pastors of the church since it was established have been: Rev. James Barker, Rev. Everett Hellard, Rev. Robert King, Rev. William Evans, Rev. James McAllister, Rev. Timothy Eaton and the present pastor, Rev. Roger L. Hogan. Rev. Hogan was saved and baptized in the church in 1976. He has been serving as pastor of the church since August 21, 1989. Under his leadership the church has experienced a renewed sensitivity for the lost.

Under the ministry of Rev. James McAllister the church building was enlarged to its present size. Two building programs more than tripled the size of the church building. The church was the location of the Farmington Christian Academy from August 1977-May 1988. Recently, a remodeling project was completed on the gymnasium building. The renovation includes a new kitchen facility as well as accessibility for the disabled.

The Farmington First Free Will Baptist Church has come a long way since that tent revival in 1952. The church now averages well over 300 in attendance. It employs a full-time staff of three pastors: The Rev. Roger L. Hogan, senior pastor; Rev. David E. Bates, associate pastor; and Rev. Steven L. Loveless, youth minister.

Every Sunday the bus ministry brings in boys and girls from all around the area to hear the Good News of the Gospel of Jesus Christ. Only eternity will reveal the impact that this church has had on hundreds of people all over the world. The church has an adult worship service, teen worship service and five children's churches that instruct the children on their level of understanding. We also provide a well-rounded program of worship in music and have an active mission's program as well as a very active senior citizens program.

You are invited to come and worship with us each week.

First Free Will Baptist Church, June 1998. Pipe organ donated by Jane Bisby in 1909, daughter of Isabella Long.

First Free Will Baptist Church, June 1998. Stained glass windows on north side of sanctuary donated to church by W.D. Long, grandson of Mrs. Sarah Murphy.

Front entrance of First Free Will Baptist Church.

Memorial United Methodist Church

The Methodist Church in Missouri celebrated its Bicentennial Year in 1998, honoring the first Methodist religious service west of the Mississippi River conducted by John Clark. The time was late summer of 1798. The place was present-day Herculaneum, at Bates' Rock, near the mouth of Joachim Creek. The event is commemorated by a window in the Herculaneum Methodist Church. John Wesley had been in his grave only six years. Clark had heard him preach in Old Foundry, London, and had known him. The Methodist Episcopal Church in America had been organized only 14 years. With John Clark's sermon, Methodism had reached the farthest western rim of the American frontier. Thus begins the rich history of Methodism in this region of Missouri and particularly in Farmington.

The religious life of Farmington and St. Francois County dates back to the year 1801, only three years after the first service at Herculaneum, when Sarah Barton Murphy, widow of Rev. William Murphy (a Baptist minister), came from Tennessee to take up the land granted to her husband in the vicinity where Farmington stands today. As soon as Sarah Barton Murphy had settled with her family, she called in other settlers to her home and held a prayer service of thanksgiving. This was the first religious service held in the county and the first Protestant religious meeting held in Murphy's Settlement, now Farmington.

All the settlers were either members of or inclined to the Baptist Church; but having been deprived of their pastor by the death of Rev. William Murphy, and being for several years without the public services of the Christian ministry, and the Methodist preachers being the first to visit them, they connected themselves with the Methodist Church, where most of their descendants remain, firm and steadfast to this day. The first sermon preached by a Protestant in this part of the country was preached in the house of Mrs. Sarah Murphy and said to have been preached by Joseph Oglesby in 1804. Sarah Barton Murphy gave the land and erected a log church house, which was not only the first in the county but also the first west of the Mississippi. This old log church stood where the Masonic Cemetery is now, marked by a obelisk on the Carter Street side of the cemetery.

It was about 1820 when a Methodist Episcopal Church was organized here and a frame building was constructed on the southeast corner of Jefferson and Harrison Streets; but like all churches in those days, its life was feeble. In 1844 when the Methodist Episcopal Church divided, the Farmington Methodist Church became the Methodist Episcopal Church South. Soon the Civil War came and this pioneer church suffered grievously, as did so many southern churches during this period of disorganization and bitter times. During the years of 1861 to 1876 this church building stood empty, the body having become disorganized. In the year 1876, the Rev. J. H. Headlee came to Farmington and reorganized the church with 27 members. From its reorganization, however, this church thrived and showed the vigorous life of

pioneer days. They continued to worship in their old frame building until the year 1881 when the building was sold to the Christian Church. Work was commenced on a brick church building on the corner of Columbia and Clay streets in 1881 and completed the following year. This church building stood until 1901 when the old structure was torn down and a new church was erected which was occupied until 1952.

In 1865 Miss Eliza Ann Carleton wrote to the Bishop of the Rock River Conference in Illinois, asking for help in organizing a Methodist Episcopal Church in this area. In the fall of 1865, the Rev. M. Lorin, a presiding elder of the old Missouri-Arkansas Conference of the Methodist Episcopal Church, came this way. Rev. Lorin had arrived at Potosi and there, in the course of time, met the three ministers who came here in 1866 in response to Miss Carleton's request: the Revs. N.J. Giddings, Henry Threfall, and J.H. Denman. Hearing of the Carleton Institute located a few miles north of Farmington, they came on foot to the school. There the presiding elder organized the Farmington Circuit of the Methodist Episcopal Church with six members of whom Miss Eliza Ann Carleton, of sacred memory, was one of the first. Rev. N.J. Giddings was appointed as the first pastor and took up his work on a circuit that embraced St. Francois and St. Genevieve Counties, and parts of Madison, Iron, Washington and Jefferson.

In 1868 the circuit was divided and Rev. W.A. Boucher was appointed to the Farmington Circuit and Rev. Giddings was sent to the St. Genevieve Circuit. It was during the pastorate of Rev. W.A. Boucher in 1868 that the Methodist Episcopal Church denomination at Farmington bought an old brick church, then owned by William R. Taylor. The old brick church located on the corner of Harrison and Henry Streets was used until November 1904 when the beautiful stone structure on the corner of Columbia and Franklin Streets was dedicated to the worship of Almighty God. The Copenhagen German Methodist Episcopal congregation merged with the Farmington Methodist Episcopal Church in 1917, a trend to be followed later by other area Methodist Churches.

In 1939 the Methodist Episcopal, Methodist Episcopal South, and the Protestant Methodist Churches, meeting in Kansas City, MO, voted to unite nationally and worldwide. In 1950 the two local Methodist congregations, with churches just two blocks apart, also voted for unification. Under the leadership of the Reverend Elbert C. Cole, the two separated congregations grew into one, drawing strength from one another. During the same year the DeLassus Church joined with the merged Memorial Methodist Church. Salem Church, north of Farmington, joined with Memorial Methodist Church in 1960, and in 1965, St. Paul's Church joined the congregation. The name 'United' was added in 1968 when the denomination's name was changed.

The first phase of the present Methodist building to be located on North Street, which included the sanctuary and education department, was completed in late 1954 and dedicated shortly thereafter. In 1957 the church was debt-free and dedicated as a house of prayer for all people. The second phase of the church's building program, including the fellowship hall, was completed in 1962. The church structure in the 1980s consisted of the sanctuary wing, an educational wing and a fellowship hall, which included the kitchen and provided Christian education and religious services for approximately 1,200 members. The fellowship hall has a partial basement where the Boy Scouts meet each week. There is a modern and beautiful parsonage on the well-landscaped grounds of the church built through the generosity of Miss Bertha Watts.

A new entrance office and classroom wing was approved for construction in 1998 with renovation of the sanctuary to be made during the construction period. The present pastor (1999) of Memorial United Methodist Church is Dr. David Webster, who succeeded Rev. James Powell. By the first of the year (1999), the church is holding three Sunday Morning worship services, two traditional services (8:15 a.m. and 10:45 a.m.) and a contemporary service (9:30 a.m.) with audio and visual aids to complement the three services. Sunday School classes are held concurrently with each of the three services.

Memorial United Methodist Church

Presbyterian Church

In 1826 the Presbyterian and Congregation churches organized the American Home Mission Society to evangelize the New West. In 1830 one of its missionaries, the Rev. Mr. J.M. Sadd, came to Farmington from St. Michaels in Fredericktown at the invitation of several leading citizens. Rev. and Mrs. Sadd rented a two-room log cabin at the southwest corner of the Courthouse Square. Their home also served as Sunday School, prayer-meeting hall, and weekday school room. Mrs. Corrina G. Sadd kept school, taught Sunday School, led prayer meetings, and cared for their home while Mr. Sadd gave himself totally to his missionary labors. He preached in the Circuit Courtroom in the brick courthouse when in Farmington. Mr. Sadd traveled far afield organizing the Whitewater Church in Bollinger County at nearly the same time the one in Farmington was. With the assistance of Rev. Thomas Donnell of the Belleview Church located in Caledonia, the Farmington Presbyterian Church was organized in the spring of 1832.

Rev. Sadd moved to Scott County in 1835, leaving 29 members with Rev. Donnell. During 1836 a brick building was constructed at the corner of Columbia and A streets.

In March 1833, Mr. And Mrs. M.P. Cayce were received by letter from the St. Charles Church; being an elder, he was added to the session. In 1847 Mr. Cayce founded Elmwood School at the present site of the Presbyterian Children's Home of Missouri.

During May 1865, the Rev. Mr. George W. Harlan entered the life of this church. Mr. Harlan led the congregation through some terribly troubled times with the unfailing support of Ruling Elder M.P. Cayce, who for many years was the only ruling elder of the congregation.

During 1867, the church building was rebuilt. Everything was replaced except the walls and part of the floor. Mr. M.P. Cayce paid most of the cost.

In October 1875, hymn books were purchased for use in worship, and the choir was first organized. In 1878 the Ladies Missionary Society was organized with eight members.

In 1884 the church house was sold to the Christian Church, and later sold to the Church of Christ. The property at Columbia and Cayce was acquired, and the present sanctuary was constructed. Originally, the sanctuary was limited to the area of short pews and the Sunday School was held behind folding doors in the area where the long pews are. This building cost $7,000.

On April 17, 1888, Ruling Elder M.P. Cayce was called from his labors. For over half a century Mr. Cayce had led the church, being for some time the only elder. He never faltered in his vision. An example is that Sunday School never failed to be held, even during the dislocations of the Civil War and reconstruction.

Rev. James A. Creighton was instrumental in the organization of Elmwood Seminary under the care of the Potosi and St. Louis Presbyteries. Under their care a large brick building was built in 1889. When the Elmwood Seminary closed in 1913, the Presbyterian Orphanage of Missouri (as the Children's Home was first known) was opened on the seminary campus.

During 1903 the church house was renovated and a new organ was installed.

During 1924, planning began for an educational building, space being terribly deficient. Much planning and lengthy money-raising ensued. In 1927, the annex was constructed at a cost of $25,000.

In 1951 the property known as the Harston-McKinney house was purchased for $10,500 to be used for educational space.

In 1954 the Rev. Mr. H. Bovard Cox III became pastor. During 1955, a major church repair program was undertaken, in sum of $35,060. In this reconstruction, the area at the rear of the sanctuary was pewed, in addition to many expensive repairs to the fabric of the buildings. At this time a gift in honor of Mrs. Francis Flowers Klein, plus a small organ fund, made possible the installation of the present organ.

In 1960 the Rev. Edwin R. Short became pastor. During 1961 the new educational building was constructed, fulfilling a long-term need for additional space. The cost of this building exceeded $100,000.

In 1962 the first units of Farmington Home Life were opened.

Mrs. L.B. Coghill and Mrs. E.L. Horton were elected to the diaconate in 1969, becoming the first women elected deacons. Mrs. Roy Berghaus Sr. and Mrs. L.H. Bohling were elected to the session in 1970, becoming the first women elders. These deacons and elders have made unique and wonderful contributions to the life of these bodies since that time.

During 1972 the sanctuary and old educational building were air-conditioned and in 1978 a pre-school program known as "The Window Tree" was begun.

A new model of ministry was begun in the church with the installation of husband and wife, Hart and Cheryl Edmonds, as pastors in March 1992.

The first Presbyterian Church. It was later the Christian Church. Built in 1831, torn down in 1900.

The Presbyterian Church

History of St. Joseph Catholic Church

The first Mass celebrated in Farmington was in the home of Mr. and Mrs. Thomas Lang at 223 East Columbia Street in 1862. Fifteen people attended the service. At that time, the population of Farmington was only 600. It was not until 1869 that the first church, a frame structure, was built under the direction of Father Daley, pastor of the church at French Village. The frame church cost $600 and seated 80 people. The site on which the church was built was the gift of Mr. and Mrs. John F. Bush. Mr. Bush was a Missouri State Senator, elected in 1862.

Under the pastorate of Father Joseph A. Collins, pastor from October 1907 through November 1914, our present beautiful church was built on the site of the first church. The church was dedicated on October 13, 1912, by Archbishop Glennon, bishop of the Archdiocese of Saint Louis. The contractor was a parishioner, John McCarthy, later known as the McCarthy Brothers Construction Company. They also built our present St. Francois County Courthouse in 1927.

The first rectory (parish house) was built in 1890, and our first resident pastor was Father Henry J. Shaw (1890-1892). The canonical establishment of St. Joseph as a Roman Catholic parish of the Archdiocese of St. Louis was July 27, 1890. The rectory was a two-story frame building and was in use until the present rectory was built in 1969 under the pastorate of Father Jerome Buchheit.

The parish of Saint Joseph has been served by 23 pastors since July 1890 and 18 associate pastors since 1940. Our present pastor, Father Eugene Robertson, came to Saint Joseph's in December 1995; Father Tomas Wissler, our current associate pastor, came to Saint Joseph's in June 1995. Our parish family consists of 770 families (about 2,100 people). We are currently in the midst of a renovation to the front access of our church. Our strategic pastoral plan for the future consists of additions to the school and church, and the construction of a multi-purpose building for meeting and educational purposes.

Our work may be summed up in our parish mission statement:

"We are called by Our Lord Jesus Christ, to be His church and live His gospel. We strive to fulfill our baptismal calling by prayer, worship, teaching and sharing our faith, and serving others. Guided by the Holy Spirit and through our Patron Saint St. Joseph, we commit ourselves to the responsible stewardship of all God's gifts."

St. Joseph Roman Catholic Church has been proud to be a part of the history of Farmington, Mo. We commit ourselves to be a vital and viable part of its journey into the future.

St. Joseph Catholic School

St. Joseph Catholic School was established in 1897 by then pastor Fr. James Toomey (1897-1906). He taught the students himself because the parish was unable to compensate teachers. In 1903 two Dominican Sisters from New York came to teach at St. Joseph. They left after two years, and Fr. Toomey once again taught the students, which numbered about 100.

Fr. Bernard Stolte (1906-1907), secured the services of two lay teachers from St. Louis. Fr. Joseph Collins (1907-1914) secured the services of the Ursuline Sisters to teach. The Ursulines remained at St. Joseph until the spring of 1915. Misses Genevieve Huss, Effie Lawrence and Willa Ryan taught the students during the 1915-1916 school year.

The school was closed for one year (1916-

The first St. Joseph's Church and rectory.

Cornerstone laying, April 28, 1912, for the present church.

1917) because there were so few students enrolled. In 1918 Fr. John Ryan (1918-1922) secured the services of the Loretto Sisters and reopened the school. The Loretto Sisters taught at St. Joseph until the spring of 1924. The school was closed again for the 1924-1925 school year. Fr. Francis Skaer (1924-1934) obtained the services of the School Sisters of Notre Dame, who began teaching in September 1925. This religious order of sisters taught at St. Joseph until May of 1987.

Fr. Edward O'Toole (1934-1938) was re-

Rev. Henry J. Shaw, the first resident pastor.

sponsible for purchasing lots along Ste. Genevieve Avenue for a new school. Fr. Robert McKeon (1939-1949) was responsible for the purchase of the Carleton College Building at 606 Overton. The elementary school, which until then had been in the convent building located on the north side of the church, was transferred to the Carleton College Building. The school was expanded to include high school. The first high school graduation was held on June 1, 1952.

During the pastorate of Fr. Joseph Gottwald (1949-1960), the present grade school building at 501 Ste. Genevieve Avenue was erected. The new school was dedicated on October 2, 1960.

Because of the high cost of education, the decision was made to close the high school. The last graduation was held in 1969. The closing of the high school, however, provided the opportunity for the elementary school to have separate rooms for each class.

During Fr. Thomas Albrecht's pastorate (1974-1977), the Carleton College Building was sold. Classes were moved to the school building on Ste. Genevieve Avenue and the convent building. Fr. Donald Rau (1977-1978), seeing that the convent building was unusable for holding classes, moved the seventh grade to the grade school cafeteria, and the eighth grade to the rectory basement. Fr. Rau then obtained permission to add two rooms to the grade school. In 1978 a new roof was placed on the grade school and ground-breaking for a new school addition took place. The old convent building was demolished in July 1979. Classes began in the new school addition during the 1979-1980 school year.

While Fr. John McEntee was pastor (1981-1991), the school cafeteria was enlarged and two multi-purpose rooms were added to the school. The Carleton Street entrance was remodeled to include a vestibule with entrances to the cafeteria, kitchen, and gymnasium. This latest addition was dedicated on March 6, 1988.

Ten years later, and through two more pastors, Fr. John Ghio (1991-1995) and Fr. Eugene Robertson (current pastor), St. Joseph Catholic School is thriving. The school is accredited and presently serves 168 children in kindergarten through grade eight. The 10-member faculty and principal are degreed and certified by the state of Missouri and have an average of 18 years of teaching experience. The student-teacher ratio is 18 to 1. St. Joseph School is also served by a Coordinator of Religious Education, a full-time secretary and teacher's aide, part-time physical education and music teachers, and a part-time librarian.

The curriculum consists of religious education, reading, English, spelling, mathematics, science, social studies, music, and physical education. A new computer lab provided computer education for all grades. The curriculum is enhanced by a variety of enrichment and Christian service opportunities, Student Council, DARE program, sacred liturgy and prayer, speech team, and various athletic teams.

The mission of St. Joseph Catholic School is "to provide an academically challenging education that lays the foundation for students' future successes, based on the proclamation of Jesus Christ as Teacher and Lord."

St. Joseph Catholic Church

The first St. Joseph Catholic School, erected in 1900.

St. Joseph Catholic School.

St. Paul Lutheran Church Farmington, MO

St. Paul Lutheran Church was organized November 16, 1873. However, Lutheran services had been conducted in the area as early as 1858 or 1859. During those years, pastors from Pilot Knob traveled to Farmington to conduct services in the Copenhagen Community south of Farmington.

From 1871 to 1874, Pastor Besel of Gordonville, MO made the trip, 12 miles by wagon and 60 miles by train, to preach here once a month. When the Copenhagen School burned November 13, 1873, nine families banded together and chartered St. Paul. The first church building was erected at a cost of $2,800 and stood on one acre (purchased for $175) at the south corner of Carleton and Columbia streets. Our first full-time pastor was C.F. Obermeyer and he was installed in August 1874. Fourteen pastors have served the congregation in its first 125 years. Membership has grown to over 1000 baptized souls.

The present church building on the north corner of Carleton and Columbia streets was completed in 1908 and renovated in 1949. An addition was attached to the north side of the church in 1987 and the sanctuary was redecorated in 1988.

The church offices are currently located in the old church parsonage located directly behind the church at 609 East Columbia Street.

Our school was opened in 1874 with 19 students enrolled. Today our enrollment exceeds 200. In the fall of 1998, we began classes in our new school building with a total of 14 classrooms, a gymnasium, kitchen and offices.

The current St Paul's Lutheran Church

The first St. Paul's Lutheran Church dedicated May 23, 1875.

Interior of Lutheran Church, Farmington, MO.

Churches Of The Area

All Saints Episcopal Church
Assembly of God
Chestnut Ridge Baptist Church
Church of Christ
Church of Jesus Christ of Latter-Day Saints
Church of the Open Bible
Community Christian Church

Emmanuel Baptist Church
Farmington Christian Church, Disciples of Christ
Farmington Church of the Nazarene
Farmington Presbyterian Church
First Baptist Church
First Church of God
First Free Will Baptist Church
Genevieve Baptist Church
Kingdom Hall of Jehovah's Witnesses

Memorial United Methodist Church
New Life Fellowship Baptist Church
New Horizons Pentecostal Church of God
Pleasant Hill United Baptist Church
St. Joseph Catholic Church
St. Paul Lutheran Church
Solid Rock Fellowship
Sunny View Church of Christ
Unity Christ Center
Word of Life

EDUCATION

South Ward School in 1912,
where W. I. Johns is today.

1927
Sophomore Class-Farmington High
Guth Photo.

EDUCATION

In 1805 Sarah Barton Murphy set up the first day school in Murphy's Settlement. Before the beginning of the public school system, private educational institutions provided educational opportunities for young people. These predecessors to public education, Carleton College-1859, Moothart Baptist College-1886, and Elmwood Seminary-1847, caused the city of Farmington to be nicknamed "Little Athens." Farmington was also home to the headquarters of the Moothart Commercial Colleges. Jackson Military Academy was located in the area, along with Sterling Academy, which began in Cook Settlement in 1862. (Cook Settlement was begun in 1800 by Nathaniel Cook who received the land in the southeastern part of the county by Spanish grant. Cook was joined by James Caldwell, William Holmes, Jesse Blackwell, James Davis and Elliot Jackson. The settlement became one of the most prosperous in the new territory. Cook Settlement was the beginning of Liberty Township.) Farmington, with a population of 600, was also home to the Farmington Academy, which offered a 20-week course and advertised that "the principal will give his individual efforts to promote the healthful exercise and expansion of the physical, mental and moral powers of his pupil."

On June 13, 1812, the United States Congress passed legislation that common fields and commons in accordance with rights established by residence or cultivation before 1803, and lands not rightfuly owned by any private individual, or held as commons, shall be reserved for the support of schools. Although Missouri joined the Union in 1821, it was not until 1853 that State tax money was provided for public schools. At that time one-fourth of the state revenue was to be used for public education and in 1887 it was increased to one-third.

There are records of public schools in our area as early as 1856: John S. Levering taught in District Number 1 School Township 8 in 1856 and A. Jacobi taught in Township Number 7 District No. 3 in 1859. In 1843 Samuel Kinkead and his wife, Lettice, donated land in Libertyville for a school, a meeting house for public worship, and a burial ground; but the date the school began is unknown.

Today's educational needs are met by Farmington R-7 School District, UNITEC Career Center, numerous parochial schools, and Mineral Area College.

Baptist College

Farmington Baptist College, a co-educational academy, was opened in Farmington in 1883. In 1886 a two-story brick building was erected on 10 acres of land bought by J.S. Gashwiler from William P. and Margaret Doss for $750. The campus was located on the new electric railroad line one and one-half blocks from the public square. Farmington High School was later erected on this same piece of land. Because Mr. Gashwiler became heavily in debt, the Franklin Baptist Association, which had been established as the old Three Rivers Baptist Church in about 1832, purchased and operated the school. Professor E.J. Jennings, a native of the county, was the first president and instructor; he served for 15 years. During its heyday the college had an average enrollment of 100 students. The faculty in 1891-1892 were as follows:

Professor E.J. Jennings-President (Latin, Philosophy, English); Professor James W. Campbell (Greek, Mathematics); Charles R. Pratte (Natural Science); and Mrs. E.J. Jennings (Music).

Fire destroyed the main building on February 22, 1894. The school continued in the nearby Baptist Church until a brick building was erected in 1896. On August 23, 1902, the association transferred the property to the following trustees: W.A. Cloud, W.T. Haile, L.T. Hunt, C.T. Tullock, T.E. Gideon, George J. Reeves, R.A. Morris, George Steele, Mrs. Martha Brannon, Thomas Horton, O.J. Mayberry, and G.W. Scoggins.

Due to continued financial problems the college was advertised April 25, 1903, as follows: "Farmington Baptist College for sale. Large 7-room brick school house, also 8-room frame house with dormitory and stable. Situated on new Electric Railroad line, 1-1/2 blocks north of Public Square, containing 10 acres of fine land. Can be laid off in town lots. Splendid site for hospital." And so the college was sold and became the Baptist Sanitarium.

Baptist College in 1896.

Carleton College

In April 1854 Carleton College was opened in a log cabin near Big River Mills about eight miles north of Farmington, MO by Eliza Ann Carleton. Miss Carleton wanted to offer, under Christian leadership, the same course of study as the best colleges to the young people of Southern Missouri. Courses offered were Latin, Greek, French, English, German, mathematics, science, music, history, and botany. Miss Carleton received two dollars in cash and three dollars in trade for each student. In 1885 Miss Carleton gave the school to the St. Louis Conference of the Methodist Episcopal Church, which continued to operate it as non-sectarian. The "Act to Incorporate Carleton Institute with University Privileges" was approved by the Missouri Legislature March 4, 1859. The school was in existence for 24 years before moving to Farmington.

Miss Carleton bought 16 acres of land within the city limits of Farmington and in 1878 the college opened in a four-story brick building which had been erected on the campus. In 1884 a four-story second building was added as the gift of Miss Carleton's uncle, Henry Carleton, and a two-story brick building served as the president's residence. The 16-acre campus faced Ste. Genevieve Avenue where the home of Dr. and Mrs. F.R. Crouch is today (714 Ste. Genevieve Avenue). Science Hall, containing an auditorium, literary society halls, library, and classrooms, was added to the campus at a cost of $30,000. The funds were raised through a campaign which added $10,000 to the building fund. The citizens of Farmington had contributed $17,000 the year before. At some point in time one of the existing buildings was converted to a dormitory for young women. Enrollment approached 250 students. The Carleton College Yellow Stockings of 1896 appears to be the earliest football team in the area according to "Pal" Wood's scrapbook.

In 1904-1905 the tuition fees were $14 for the fall term and $12 for the winter and spring terms. Musical instruments could be rented for $3 to $4, elocution lessons were offered at $5 per term, room and board was $2 per week, and meals were 15 cents.

The college served St. Francois County for a total of 62 years: 24 years north of Farmington and 38 years in Farmington. The last graduating class was June 1916.

Eliza Ann Carleton was born in Virginia in 1826. After moving to Missouri in 1843 she taught school in District 31 at Hickory Cabin School House in Perry Township. She attended Arcadia College (later Marvin College) and received a master of arts degree. When her intended husband died, she gave up her plans to go to China as a missionary. Instead, at the age of 28, she resolved to establish a college. Never weighing more than 100 pounds, Miss Carleton served the school as president, taught classes, acted as matron, supervised the college farm, which produced vegetables, milk and eggs for the student boarders, and acted as pastor, frequently conducting services. Miss Carleton died September 17, 1915, at the age of 89. A monument was erected in memory of Eliza Ann Carleton June 14, 1918, at the Masonic Cemetery in Farmington, MO. Mrs. Winifred Carleton Watkins and Dr. C. E. Carleton are descendants of Eliza Ann Carleton's family on their father's side.

Elmwood Seminary

Elmwood Academy, the earliest academy in Farmington, was constructed in 1847 for the children of M.P. Cayce and other children in the neighborhood. This academy, located on the site opposite the Presbyterian Church, was the forerunner of the Elmwood Seminary for Young Women and Presbyterian Normal School. Elmwood Seminary was established in 1885 under the care and ownership of the Presbyterian Church, represented by Potosi and St. Louis

Log cabin in which the first Carleton College was started in 1854.

Drawing of Carleton College campus, circa 1906.

Carleton College Class of 1899.

Elmwood Seminary, 1913.

Presbyteries. Although denominational, it was non-sectarian. Students were offered two years of college work in addition to a four-year academic course. The four or five-acre campus was located in a grove of large trees. In 1890 a new building was constructed at a cost of $20,000; and in 1908 the school became fully accredited with the State University. Students came from as far away as Texas and California. The school closed its doors in 1914. Today the Presbyterian Home for Children is located on the Elmwood Seminary campus.

Farmington Public Schools

Even though there is evidence that public schools began in our area as early as 1856, local newspapers report that the first public school opened in Farmington in 1870. The school building was a large, two-story, frame building and housed all of the white student population. The building was located on the grounds where the W.L. Johns Grade School (bordered by Jefferson, Franklin, Fourth, and Boyce Streets) was later built. When the original building was destroyed by fire in 1884, South Ward School, a large two-story brick building, was built on the same grounds. The building had four extra large rooms; the grades used the downstairs and the high school used the upstairs. The Class of 1896, numbering nine members, was the first to graduate from Farmington High School.

Around 1900 another grade school was built on the site where Liberty Hall is today (across from Washington Elementary School on Washington Street). The two-story brick building was known as North Ward School; the name was later changed to the Annie Lloyd School. Four teachers taught grades one through eight. Upon completion of eighth grade the students would attend high school at the South Ward. The Negro students attended Douglas School, located at the west end of town. Miss Dayse Baker taught at the Douglas School from 1901 to 1952.

The smallest graduating class was in 1908, two boys and one girl. Commencement was held in the public hall over the City Drug Store (where Ozark Federal Savings and Loan now stands). The upper floor was known as the opera house and plays were given there after the Braun Hall discontinued their public hall.

Due to the deterioration of the original school, classes were moved to the old Baptist College in 1909, and during the summer of 1910 work began on the new $50,000 building which would house the high school. The building was heated and cooled by a "fan system" which kept

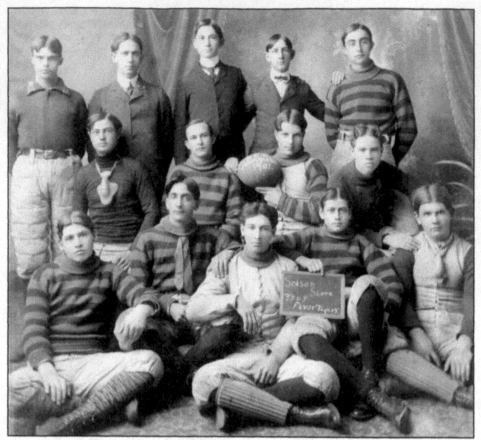

Carleton College fooball team, 1901.

Farmington's first public school, built about 1870.

all the rooms and halls supplied with fresh air at the desired temperature. The study hall/auditorium combination seated 400 for public gatherings and 150 students at single desks for regular school work. There was a gymnasium, library, two science rooms, two offices and 16 other rooms. The building opened on March 10, 1911, and the Class of 1912 (10 students) was the first to graduate from the new building. The teachers

employed were normal, college or university graduates. Twenty units of credit were offered at the high school, which was fully accredited by the State University.

Professor W.L. Johns became the superintendent of the Farmington Schools in 1915. He was credited with being instrumental in the growth and development of an education program that was one of the finest in the area. The school building located at 510 South Franklin is named after him. In 1921, Professor H.C. Haile became principal and athletic coach at the high school. Farmington's reputation for excellence in education and athletics began under his guidance. Today's football stadium is named after him.

A gymnasium, now known as Truman Auditorium, was financed by a bond issue passed by the voters in 1927. The $60,000 building was constructed by the McCarthy Construction Co. The auditorium, which could seat 865 people, had a large stage which could be separated from the gymnasium by a sound-proof door. Truman Auditorium still serves the public schools and is still the only true auditorium in Farmington today.

A fire caused extensive damage to the high school on February 2, 1934, and the school had to be rebuilt. High school classes were held in the old Carleton College building during reconstruction. The rebuilding, which included the addition of a small building to house the Manual Arts Department, was done at a total cost of $51,000. Florence Bone, retired Farmington teacher and former school board member, was a member of the 1934 class. Mrs. Bone saved a newspaper article from that year that gives this account of the fire: "Mr. Parker, the janitor of the High School, smelled smoke while opening the doors of the class rooms to aid heat circulation. Reaching the third floor, he found the ceiling of the northwest room, Mr. Talbert's citizenship room, already in flames. Despite the aid of the Flat River Fire Department the fire could not be gotten under control until the third and second floors were completely wrecked." "I remember that day," said Florence Bone. "I was on my way to school and when I walked up the street and saw it, I just started crying. It's funny because when you are a kid you say you wouldn't care if your school burned to the ground but when it happens, it's really sad. There are a lot of memories in that old building." The February 28, 1934, school newspaper, *Junior Journal*, reported, "Students, teachers and townspeople helped to carry books, chairs, files and pictures from the burning building. Many worked for days after the fire and helped to salvage and move many hundreds of dollars worth of valuable books and equipment. Even the paddle from Miss Geissing's room was rescued after a short search for that indispensable article."

The February 9, 1934, *Farmington News* reports that the board of managers of the Carleton College property offered the use of Science Hall to the District. The Board of Education accepted and began preparing Science Hall for the occupancy by the high school and grades 6, 7 and 8. Supt. Johns and Rolla Cozean, president of the Board of Education, went to St. Louis and bought 216 tablet arm chairs, six teachers' desks and chairs, several dictionaries, and some smaller items of equipment. Local plumbers and CWA workers worked all week in order for school to resume on Monday, February 12, 1934. The Board of Education decided to furnish all textbooks at wholesale costs (Students were required to buy textbooks at that time. Today, students are no longer charged for their books.) A poem written by Eleanor Zimmer and published in the junior class paper chronicles the fire:

Quarterly Report of Scholl Taught In Elmwood Academy In District Number I School Township 8, St Francois County MO. For the term commencing Sept. 1st and ending Nov., 20, 1856.. By John S. Levering.

Students Name	Age	Students Name	Age
Wm. Covington	13	John Boyce	7
Callard Arnold *	12	Dudley Boyce	5
Wm. Pim	12	Henry Clay	13
John Pim	9	Robert Clay	7
Wm. Bynam	14	Wm. Clay	10
Fana Bynam f	13	J.C. Alexander	7
R.A. Elkins	12	Ernst Weber	7
Mary E. Elkins f	9	Adam Weber	6
Rebecca Elkins f	7	Jacob Helber	6
T.P. Sargent *	15	Catherine Myers f	11
Martha White f	6	Thomas Williams	12
Mary P. White f	12	J.D. Peers	10
Elizabeth White f	13	Clarence Reed *	8
E. Kinkead	10	Payton Reed *	9
Sophina Kinkead f	8	J.W. Brady	9
Geo. Stratton	7	P.D. Brady	7
Augustus Stratton	9	Anna Green f *	6
F.M. McFarland	9	C.A. Stratton f	8
Charles McFarland	6	James Gulpine	6
Valentine Rucker	8	Jane Gulpine f	8
Wm. Myers	20	Frank Villar *	7
John Alexander	8	Ben Villar *	15
George Williams	15	Wm.A. Meridith *	22
Charles Hart	14	Annita McFarland f	11
Wm. Boyce	11	Emma McFarland f	8
Lawson Farley *		Wm. Murphy *	16
Susan M. Pim f	5	Mary L. Wilson f	8
Prudence Doughty	12		

Those marked with f are female. Those marked with * are out of district and not entitled to Public Funds

Subjects Taught: Orthography, Reading, Writing, Arithmetic, Geography, Grammar, Philosophy, Algebra, Book Keeping

Books Used: Webster's Elementary Speller, Webster's Dictionary, McGuffeys 1st, 2nd, 3rd, 4th, Readers, Sanders 3rd Reader, Farleys Arithmetic, Smiths Geography, Pinkhams Grammar, Comstocks Philosophy, Daives Algebra, Duffs Bookkeeping, Farleys Primary Geography, Davises Primary Arithmetic

The high school damaged by fire, Feb. 2, 1934.

North Ward School, Miss Nellie Halter, teacher. **First row:** *Paul Nations, Floyd Halter, Allan Burks, ? Ebrecht, Francis (Dick) Fuhrmeister, John Davis, John A. Sprott, Eugene Karsch, Carson Morris.* **Second row:** *Paul Coffer, Clyde McClintock, Roy Adams, William Huff, Florence Mitchell, Martha Raines, Bunny Smith, Dorris Swink.* **Third row:** *Emory Kreiger, unidentified, Corbin Davis, Henry Hunt, unidentified, Florence Tetley, unidentified, Maud Hawn, Lee Maynard.* **Fourth row:** *Geraldine Burks, Alma Maynard, Opal Watts, Laura Cleve, Cloud Cole, Bryan Cunningham, unidentified.* **Fifth row:** *unidentified, Clarence Tucker, unidentified, Roy Dobbins, Miss Nellie Halter, unidentified, Mattie Cunningham, Horace Eaton, Laura Stiksel.*

High school football team, 1916.

"Loud and clear came the summons
Calling the people one and all
For our dear old high school was burning
That had stood so stately and tall.
At last the flames were extinguished
And the people went on their way
But they will remember what they had
    witnessed
For many and many a day.
Co-operation was gladly given
By the people one and all
And Monday we resumed our studies
In the Carleton Science Hall.
But we know our high school is lonesome

And is patiently waiting the day
When She is rebuilt and completed
And we have come back to stay."

One week after the fire Mrs. Florence Bone and the other 55 seniors finished their classes in Carleton College. Mrs. Bone said, "We joked about being the only class who graduated from college before graduating from high school."

A newspaper article from July 22, 1935 announced that the new high school building would be open for public tours by Superintendent W.L. Johns and other school representatives. The building served the high school population

until the new high school was built in 1959 and then became the junior high school in 1962. The building was torn down in 1985.

The present high school was erected in 1959 and the Class of 1960 was the first to graduate from the new building. Since then, the high school has been expanded a number of times: 1961-business wing; 1967-library, cafeteria, industrial arts addition; 1967-Ag building; 1972-addition to dressing rooms; 1973-west wing addition; 1990-completion of Vo-Ag/industrial technology addition; 1991-92-PAYS building; 1992-93-Black Knight TV Studio; 1993-renovation of 1973 west wing addition; 1993-94-science/language arts wing; 1994-95, music wing; 1995-96, new entryway, lobby and restrooms. In 1959-60 the high school served around 400 students; today there are 1,200 students at the high school. Principals of Farmington High School have included: O.C. Lynch (1911), H.C. Haile (1921), Joe Tolson (1949), Larry Ackley (1969), Jim Dinwiddie (1976), Charles Carleton (1983); David Cramp (1991); and Dave Waters (1994). Dr. Waters has just been named Missouri's Principal of the Year.

Elementary buildings are Washington-1948, Franklin-1953, Jefferson-1965, Truman-1971, W.L. Johns-1941 (the new South Ward building was built in 1941 as a WPA project and was later named W.L. Johns), and Lincoln-1994. The middle school was begun in 1982 and was ready for occupation in 1984-85. The elementary buildings have had numerous additions and are extremely overcrowded at this time.

Many schools existed in the rural area and chose to annex to Farmington R-VII: Oak Hill, Sugar Grove, Valley Forge, and DeLassus became a part of the Farmington District in 1953. Chestnut Ridge followed in 1965. In 1966-67 the Doe Run School District joined with Farmington. The school buildings in Doe Run were used as an elementary campus until the buildings were sold in 1984. Busiek School and Crossroads School reorganized with Farmington R-7 in 1974. The Crossroads property was sold in 1975 and the Busiek property was sold in 1984. Knob Lick School was annexed in the 1991-92 school year and the property was sold in December 1991. Libertyville joined Farmington in 1994-95. That property was also sold.

Farmington public schools have won many honors over the years: Farmington High School was selected as a Blue Ribbon School of Excellence in 1992-93 and again in 1997-98 by the U.S. Department of Education. The Farmington Middle School was selected as a Gold Star School in 1996-97.

A profile of the Farmington R-7 School District prepared by school officials for the Southeast Missouri Regional Planning and Economic Development Commission gives a snapshot of the district as of 1999.

Farmington R-7 School District

The Farmington School District consists of approximately 320 square miles in the city and surrounding rural area. The district serves approximately 3,600 students in grades K-12. The

1901-10 St. Francois County

School Dist #	Name of School	School Dist #	Name of School
1	Rouggley	35	Sugar Grove
2	Valles-Mines	36	Valley Forge
3	Blackwell	37	Clearview
4	Primrose	38	Unity
5	Bismarck = C-3	39	Coppenhagen
6	Coonville	40	DeLassus
7	Elvins	41	Flannery
8	Mosteller	42	Stone
9	Hall - in Marion	43	Stonny Point - Washington Co.
10	French Village	44	Dent - Iron #8
11	Carrow - in Marion	45	Iron Mountain
12	Bonne Terre	46	Hilderbright
13	Sink Hole - in Marion	47	Cartee
14	Scott	48	Independence
15	Patterson	49	Fairview
16	Lambeth	50	Libertyville - 02
17	Pleasant Mound	51	Possum Hollow
18	Germania	52	Knob Lick - 01
19	Hunt - in Perry	53	Webb - in Liberty
20	Murrill - in Perry	54	O'Bannon
21	Doe Run	55	Syenite - in Liberty
22	Big River Mills	56	Middlebrook - in Iron
23	Cedar Falls	57	King
14	Farmington	58	Burch
25	Jennings	59	Cross Roads
26	Barton	60	Rock Creek
27	Esther	61	Flat River
28	Clay - in C-4	62	Rockwell
29	Desloge	63	Leadwood
30	Walnut Grove - in Randolph	C1	Knob Lick
31	Randolph	C2	Libertyville
32	Gumbo	C3	Bismarck
33	Loughboro	C4	Frank Clay
34	Oak Hill	64	Koester

First kindergarten class in Farmington. Miss Rickus Class at W. L. Johns. First row: Mary Sue Stockenberg, unidentified, Karen Griffen, unidentified, Marilyn Cowley, John London, Vickie Havenier, Joan Ellen Williams, Billy Wilkerson, Eva Jane Harrington, Glenda Hopkins, _____ Shannon. Second row: unidentified, Jimmy Cleveland, Ken Akers, Jim Marty, unidentified, Charles Dickey, Roy Clark, Larry Smith.

District is fully accredited. There are nine different school buildings, including an early childhood center, one kindergarten center, three elementary schools, one middle school, one high school, an alternative school, an at-risk school and a juvenile detention school.

W.L. Johns Early Childhood Center: The Center is located on a three-acre tract at 510 South Franklin Street. The one-story facility was constructed in 1940. The facility presently serves preschool programs and Caring Communities.

Truman Kindergarten Center: The Center is located at 209 West College Street. The one-story brick building was constructed on a two-acre site in 1970. It was built for a sixth grade facility and was located adjacent to the middle school, which later moved to a new campus. The facility now serves approximately 240 kindergarten students and it has a faculty/support staff of 38.

Washington-Franklin Elementary School: The original Washington building is a two-story brick structure at 509 North Washington Street that was built in 1948 on a four-acre site. The original Franklin building is a one-story brick structure at 103 Murphy Street that was built in 1953 on a two-acre tract. The Washington and Franklin buildings were connected in 1993 with an addition that includes office space and a multi-purpose room. This facility serves grades one through four with an enrollment of approximately 540 students and a faculty/support staff of 57.

Jefferson Elementary School: The school is located at 9 Summit Drive just off Route D in the northern portion of the city. The facility is a one-story brick building and was constructed on a 10-acre site in 1965 with additions in 1967, 1989, and 1993. The facility serves grades one through four with an enrollment of approximately 550 students and a faculty/support staff of 54.

Lincoln Intermediate Center: The Center is located at 708 S. Fleming next to Farmington Middle School and is a one-story brick building constructed in 1994 on a 13-acre tract. The facility serves grades five and six with an enrollment of 560 and a faculty/support staff of 58.

Farmington Middle School: The School is located at 506 South Fleming and is a one-story brick building constructed in 1983 on a 10-acre tract. The facility serves grades seven and eight with an enrollment of approximately 570 students and a faculty/support staff of 66.

Farmington High School: The high school is located at One Black Knight Drive on a 38-acre tract. The brick structure was built in 1959 and has had several additions. The facility serves students in grades 9 through 12 with an enrollment of approximately 1,200 and a faculty/support staff of 115.

PAYS: In 1991 a building was constructed adjacent to the high school to provide housing for Project Assisting Youth Success, an alternative education program for at-risk students. The three major components of the program are academics, work study, and day care for parenting teens.

Black Knight TV: A building adjacent to the high school serves as a studio for Black

FARMINGTON R-7 SCHOOL DISTRICT
BOARD MEMBER INFORMATION BEGINNING 1891
(Compiled from Minutes)

SECRETARY (NOT ELECTED)

	DATE STARTED	DATE LEFT	YEARS SERVED
CAYCE, J. P.	1908	1944	36
ZEIBA, FRANK	1944	1979	35
MERSEAL, RUTH	1979	1987	8
FRANCIS, CAROL	1987		

ELECTED FOR THREE YEAR TERMS UNLESS INDICATED BY NUMBER IN ( )

	YRS SERVED	ELECTED
ALEXANDER, J. F.	3	1897
BEABOUT, WILLIAM	3	1980
BLAIR, WILLIAM	3	1976
BOATRIGHT, DR. KEVIN	3	1992
BONE, FLORENCE	9	1985, 1988, 1991
BOYER, JIM E.	9.75	1977, APPOINTED 6-80 TO FILL UNEXP TERM (UNTIL 4-81) OF JERRY OWEN WHO RESIGNED, 1984, 1987
BURKS, J. N.	3	1899
BURKS, JERRY B.	6	1914, 1917
BURKS, JOHN T.	2	1908 (RESIGNED 3-1910)
BYINGTON, SAMUEL	3	1904
CAYCE, M. P.	3	1896
COLSON, DAVID L.	12	1965, 1968, 1971, 1974
COX, ROBERT	12	1966, 1969, 1972, 1975
COZEAN, C. H. "HUGO"	30	1950, 1953, 1956, 1959, 1962, 1965, 1968, 1971, 1974, 1977
COZEAN, ROLLA	11	1923, 1926, 1929, 1932 (RESIGNED 4-34)
CROUCH, DR. F. R.	3.5	1956, 1961-RESIGNED 10-61
DOBBINS, JAMES		1891 (FINAL YEAR-NO RECORDS PRIOR TO 1891)
DOBBINS, HARRY	3	1913
DUGAL, LEO	7.75	APPOINTED 6-58 TO FILL UNEXP TERM (UNTIL 4-59) OF DR. NEWMAN WHO RESIGNED, 1959 (1), 1960, 1963
EVANS, LLEWELLYN		1891 (FINAL YEAR-NO RECORDS PRIOR TO 1891)
FITZ, THOMAS P.	8	1959, 1962, 1965 (2-REORGANIZATION)
GAMBLE, CAROL	12	1984, 1987, 1990, (MSBA PRESIDENT-1991), 1993
GEISSING, JOHN	3	1892
GIESSING, CHARLES	15	1895, 1898, 1904, 1907, 1910
GIESSING, JOHN E.	8	1930, 1933, 1936 (DECEASED IN 1938 WHILE BOARD PRESIDENT)
GRAVES, DR. JOHN B.	11	1919 (2), 1921, 1924, 1927
HARRINGTON, SHIRLEY	3	1980
HAW, DR. J. L.	6	1892, 1899
HERMAN, HARRY	9	1895, 1898, 1901
HIGHLEY, FRANK, JR.	9	1941, 1944, 1947, 1950 (DIED IN ACCIDENT 5-50)
HOFFMAN, W. L.	7	APPOINTED 4-1934 TO FILL UNEXP TERM OF ROLLA COZEAN WHO RESIGNED, 1935, 1938
HORTON, DR. E. L.	18	1930, 1933, 1936, 1939, 1942, 1945
HUCKSTEP, DR. ROBERT A.	15	1964, 1967, 1970, 1973, 1976
HUTSON, KEITH	—	1999
JAMES, LEA ANN	3	1996
JENNINGS, ELMA L.	6	1978, 1981 (1ST FEMALE R-7 BOARD MEMBER)
KARSCH, FRED M.	14.5	1913, 1916, 1919, 1922, 1925 (RESIGNED 10-1927)
KARSCH, J. M.	9	1891 (NO RECORDS PRIOR TO 1891) 1894, 1897
KLEIN, J. E.	15	1900, 1906, 1909, 1912, 1920
KNAUS, A. C.	3	1901
KOCH, DAVE	3	1983
LANG, THOMAS		1891 (FINAL YEAR-NO RECORDS PRIOR TO 1891)
LEWIS, ROBERT D.	12	1960, 1963, 1966, 1969
LONDON, WILLIAM	6	1924, 1927
MARBURY, B. H.	3	1920
MARKS, J. A.	3	1896
MARTIN, WILLIAM C.	12.5	APPOINTED 10-61 TO FILL UNEXP TERM OF DR. F. R. CROUCH WHO RESIGNED, 1962 (2), 1964 (1-REORGANIZATION '65), 1967, 1970, 1973
MAYBERRY, O. J.	6	1902, 1905
MCCORMICK, E. C.	6	1900, 1903
MCKINNEY, E. J.	4	1910 (1), 1911
MILLER, BERL J.	12	1948, 1951, 1954, 1957
MILLER, JOHN H.	24	1934, 1937, 1940, 1943, 1946, 1949, 1952, 1955
MITCHELL, J. D.	3	1915
MURRILL, JOHN	6	1908, 1911
NEIDERT, ADAM	3	1893
NEWMAN, DR. PAUL	10	1948, 1951, 1954, 1957 (RESIGNED 6-58)
OWEN, JERRY L.	1	1979, RESIGNED 5-80
PAUTZ, DR. DUDLEY D.	6	1978, 1981
PRATT, JESSIE	1	1892 (1)
PULTZ, ED	—	1995, 1998
RAINS, RANDY		1999
RARIDEN, W. B.	21	1903, 1906, 1909, 1912, 1915, 1918, 1921
REVOIR, F. L.	12	1938, 1941, 1944, 1947
RHODES, DR. ROD	3	1993
ROBERTS, CECIL W.	6	1937, 1940, 1943
ROBINSON, DR. DENNIS D.	—	1994, 1997
SATTERTHWAITE, BOB	5	1986 (2), 1988
SCHMIDT (SMITH) PETER	5	1891 (NO RECORDS PRIOR TO 1891), 1893
SEBASTIAN, LARRY	—	1990, 1993, 1996, 1999
SHEETS, HERBERT R.	6	1979, 1982
SHERRILL, MIKE	—	1995, 1998
SHORT, RONALD D.	18	1981 (1), 1982, 1986, 1989, 1992, 1996
SMITH, O. A.	6	1914, 1917
SMITH, TAYLOR	6.5	APPT 10-1927 TO FILL UNEXP TERM OF FRED KARSCH WHO RESIGNED, 1928, 1931
STANFIELD, DR. L. M.	18	1946, 1949, 1952, 1955, 1958, 1961
STOVER, WARREN C.	2.75	APPOINTED 6-50 TO FILL UNEXP TERM OF FRANK HIGHLEY, 1951 (2), 1953 (1 MO-LOST IN SPECIAL REORGANIZATION ELECTION 4-30-53)
STRAUGHAN, ELLIOTT	6	1953, 1956
STRAUGHAN, R. R. "RUSTY"	9	1983, 1986, 1989
SULLIVAN, JERRY	—	1991, 1994, 1997
TAYLOR, R. P.	6	1907, 1910
TETLEY, ROBERT	3	1891 (NO RECORDS PRIOR TO 1891)
WATKINS, DR. GEORGE L.	15	1923, 1926, 1929, 1932, 1935
WELLS, L. O.	1	1918 (DIED 4-1919)
WHITE, C. Y.	10	1938 (1), 1939, 1942, 1945
WILLIAMS, GEORGE K.	21	1916, 1919, 1922, 1925, 1928, 1931, 1934
WRIGHT, JIM	.75	1985 (RESIGNED 1-86)
WYATT, JOHN	6	1972, 1975
YOUNG, W. H.	6	1902, 1905
ZELLER, EDWARD	3	1894

Knight Television. Black Knight TV is an innovative technology program for high school students. The local cablevision company provides a cable channel for the school district to air school and community events to cable viewers.

Truman Auditorium, Reading Literacy Center, Senior Citizens Facility: These buildings are located adjacent to the Truman Kindergarten Center on a four-acre site. (These buildings served middle school students prior to the construction of a new middle school on Fleming Street in 1984.)

Truman Auditorium/Gymnasium is used extensively, not only by the school district, but also by the Farmington Community for various activities/events.

The senior citizens facility is located in the same building as the Reading Literacy Center and is described elsewhere.

Midwest Learning Center: Midwest Learning Center is an alternative school operated in cooperation with Presbyterian Children's Services.

School Bus Transportation: All pupils living one mile or more from their attendance center are eligible for school bus transportation. Approximately 42 percent of the total student enrollment use school bus transportation and approximately 16 percent of the students using school bus transportation reside within the city limits. During the 1998-99 school year an average of 1,551 students rode the bus each day.

FARMINGTON R-7 SCHOOL DISTRICT
SUPERINTENDENT HISTORY

	DATE STARTED	DATE LEFT	YEARS SERVED
S. T. GRISHAM, PRIN.	1891	1896	5 YEARS
A. H. AKERS, PRIN.	1896	1898	2 YEARS
MRS. WM GIESSING, PRIN.	1898	1899	1 YEAR
MRS. R.N. GIESSING, PRIN.	1899	1900	1 YEAR
NATIONS, G. O., PRIN.	1900	1902	2 YEARS
NATIONS, G. O.	1902	1903	1 YEAR
HELMS, JAMES R.	1903	1904	1 YEAR
DUNLAP, J. W.	1904	1907	3 YEARS
LYNCH, O. C.	1907	1914	7 YEARS
JOHN, W. L.	1914	1946	32 YEARS
BELL, DR. CLIFTON E.	1946	AUGUST 1958	12 YEARS
NEWELL, P. J., JR.	AUGUST 1958	FEBRUARY 1965	7 YEARS
HENRY, DR. B. RAY	MARCH 1965	JUNE 1970	5 YEARS
PARKS, RALPH E.	JULY 1970	JUNE 1979	9 YEARS
ORTH, DR. LEE J.	JULY 1979	JUNE 1980	1 YEAR
ROREX, DR. CHARLES E.	JULY 1980	JUNE 1986	6 YEARS
WEBB, DR. ROBERT	JULY 1986	JUNE 1998	12 YEARS
CRAMP, DR. DAVID	JULY 1998		

* In 1902 the title was changed from Principal to Superintendent.

Board on Education for 1912.

Student Growth: Student growth is the foremost concern of Farmington School District. A new elementary school and additions to current buildings are needed. Voters turned down an $8.3 million bond issue by a narrow margin on April 6, 1999.

Report made to the board of trustees of Township No. 7 District No. 3. Mr. L. Hopkins, Mr. H. Meier and Mr. J. Jones, on the Public School taught by A. Jacobi, teacher, from the 5th of September to the 5th of December, A-D. 1859

Name	Age	Progress	Behavior	Reader	Arithmetic
G. Rickus	10	satisfactory	satisfactory	4th reader	Multiplication
J. Rickus	8	" "	" "	2nd reader	Addition
J. Mason	13	" "	" "	3rd reader	Multiplication
M. Landrum	8	" "	" "	2nd reader	Addition
H. Kohlmeier	11	" "	" "	3rd reader	Multiplication
H. Kleinschmidt	11	" "	" "	4th reader	
W. Meier	6	" "	" "	spelling book	
J. Ehbrecht	9	" "	" "	2nd reader	
F. Ehbrecht	7	" "	" "	spelling book	
M. Doughty		middling	middling	4th reader	Multiplication
J. Doughty		satisfactory	middling	2nd reader	Addition
M. Jones			satisfactory	4th reader	
C. Miller	10	satisfactory	satisfactory	4th reader	Multiplication
H. Meier	7	" "	" "	1st reader	Addition
L. Meier	9	" "	" "	1st reader	Addition
C. Jones		" "	" "	3rd reader	Addition
M. Mason	11	middling	" "	3rd reader	Multiplication
E. Mell	5		" "	spelling book	
M. Ward	7	satisfactory	" "	spelling book	
F. Zimmer	7	" "	" "	spelling book	
M. Zimmer	9	" "	" "	1st reader	Addition
M. Hopkins	6	" "	" "	spelling book	
E. Hopkins	8	middling	" "	2nd reader	
A. Hopkins	12	satisfactory	" "	4th reader	Multiplication
M. Kleinschmidt	7	" "	" "	2nd reader	Addition
H. Walker	8	" "	" "	spelling book	Addition
J. Kuocher	11	" "	" "	4th reader	Multiplication
H. Kuocher	10	" "	" "	4th reader	Multiplication
Ph. Mason	11	" "	" "	3rd reader	Multiplication
Th. McClintock		middling	a bad boy who		

quitted my school because during my absence he had a fight with H. Kohlmeier, teased the girls and was afraid of punishment

Name	Age	Progress	Behavior	Reader	Arithmetic
J. McClintock	17	satisfactory	satisfactory	1st reader	Addition
F. McClintock	9	" "	" "	2nd reader	
J. Beck	6	" "	" "	Spelling book	Addition
L Beck	10	" "	" "	1st reader	Addition
R. Beck	8	" "	" "	Spelling book	Addition

The 30th of November I received 44.00 School Fund from Mr. F. Rickus the president of the board. As textbooks in reading I used the first, second, third and fourth reader of McGuffey. The spelling I used Websters spelling book. The whole school learned writing, the classes of the third and fourth reader wrote on paper, and the other children on their slates. I tried to teach Geography and English Grammar, but the school being chiefly composed of smaller children, was not advanced enough to comprehend those branches. During the next term the third and fourth reader class should be instructed in these studies. In Arithmetic I used no textbook, that department being always neglected by the late teachers. When I commenced teaching I had one scholar who knew the multiplication table, and of the rest scarcely three could give me the result of the most simple addition. I formed two classes in Arithmetic, the first one is now practicing Multiplication, the rule of three in its plainest application and proportions of the first degree. The second class is studying Addition. I used Thieme Dictionary a work published in 1854 to guide my pronunciation, it is compiled from Walker, Webster and Flugel, and gives the most elegant and approved accent.

I could not pass in silence over the fact that during the month of October, many books and copy books, the property of my pupils have been spoiled and cut in pieces in the schoolhouse, the perpetrators of which misdemeanor I could not catch. I do not know the cause of this infamous act, but I wish to direct the attention of your honorable board to it.

Respectfully Yours

A. Jacobi

Public School Traditions
How The Knights Got Their Black And Gold Colors

(From Sports Chat *by H.C. (Hap) Haile, Oct. 27, 1960)*

The colors changed to black and gold in 1915 and the 65 or so students in high school didn't even get to vote on the issue. According to Hap Haile the junior class colors were black and gold and most of the football players that year were juniors. In those days the football players furnished all of their equipment, including the football. So the football players bought black sweaters with gold striped sleeves. Then the pennant fever hit and pennants were ordered with a black background and Farmington High School in gold. The colors continued on the pennants and the colors today are still black and gold. (Previously, the colors had been ruby red and silver gray because the boys had bought gray sweaters with a red letter F.)

How FHS Got The Knights Name And Insignia

(From Sports Chat *by H.C. (Hap) Haile, Oct. 27, 1960)*

Hap Haile reported in his *Sports Chat* that before the Mineral Area Conference was organized, Farmington was one of the "independent" schools and scheduled games far and near from St. Louis to the Bootheel. The newspaper write-ups before and after the games referred to the Farmington team as "the miners," "boys from the Lead Belt," "from the foothills of the Ozarks," etc. We felt we were in need of a name and insignia. Hap Haile suggested the name "Tigers" to Supt. W. L. Johns since the school colors were black and gold. Supt. Johns said it seemed as though every football player from Missouri University who went out into the high school coaching field wanted to name his team "Tigers." Supt. Johns said there were enough tigers in Missouri to fill a jungle. So the tiger idea was dropped.

Then Mrs. Essie Yount Newman, who had been sponsor of the school paper since its in-

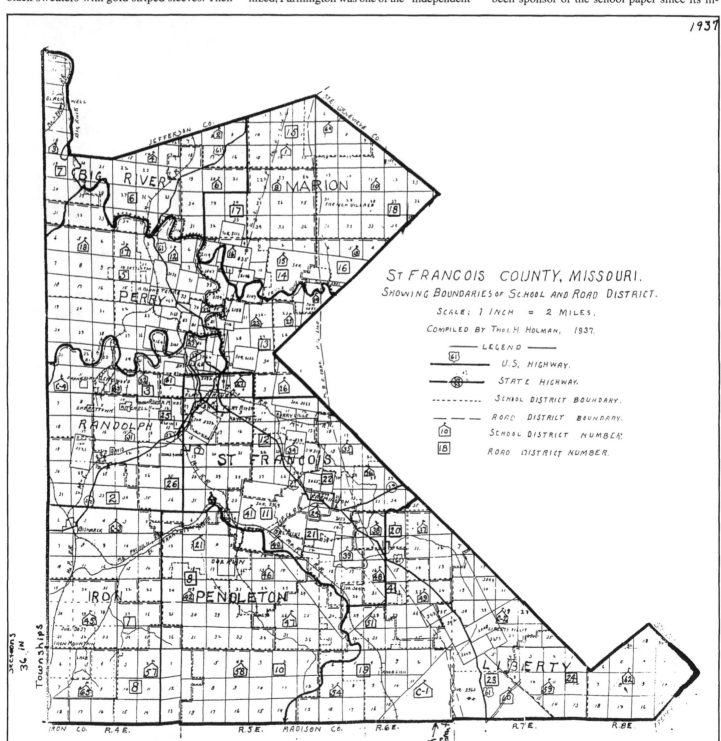

fancy, became very interested in an emblem. She and her staff arrived at the name of "Knights" and suggested that it be adopted as our name and a school artist designed the Knight in full armor. It brought out some comments such as: "too sissy" and "Alphonse and Gaston." The pep squad's platform was that it was an excellent word to use in school yells as it rhymed with "right, might, and fight" and "life is not so short that there is not time for courtesy." It was put to a vote before the student body and "KNIGHTS" won two-thirds of the votes so, outfitted in armor, he was given a spear and put on a horse and has ridden high, wide and handsome for the past 30 years. The election date was November 6, 1930. The Farmington High News became *Knight Life*.

Mrs. Essie Yount Newman responded to Hap Haile's October column with additional information. *(Sports Chats* by H.C. (Hap) Haile, November 24, 1960).

Students of Farmington Public School, 1888. Left to right, back row: Laura Morris, Mary Asbury, Rosa Burke, Kathleen Weber, Eva Cragen, Joyce Conway, Susie Hartshorn. Front row: Lessie Retornez, Daisy Rickard, Julia Doughty, Minnie Hemerle, Emma Prough, Emma Lorenz, Mary Braun. In front, John Neidert.

Mrs. Newsman's English Class, in which most of the 1930 undefeated football team were members, got the "Knights" idea when studying Tennyson's *Idylls of the King*. Most of the team members and all the members of the *Farmington High News* staff were in favor of it and it was put to a vote of the student body and it passed by a two-thirds majority.

Mrs. Newman also remembers that it was Anna Mae Sides. who, with her artistic ability, "designed" the Knight and put him on a horse holding his spear. We have been asked how the "opposition" accepted the insignia. There was a certain amount of bantering, but not too serious, and some of the first ones to wear a Knight head insignia on the arms of their sweaters were the ones who opposed it.

Sporting goods companies had a large amount of emblems in stock: Pirates, Tigers, Black Cats, Mustangs, Bears, Dragons, etc. The nearest they had to the Knight was a Trojan. So the Knight head had to be designed especially for FHS.

When the *FHS News* became *Knight Life*, some of the solicitors for subscribers had some explaining to do. "What did you say? Subscribe for 'night life!' Do we have to pay for that now too? ...thought the kids had too much 'night life' already!"

The schools in the district are still home of the Knights. The middle school students are the Squires, the students in the gifted program are Pages, the band is the Black Knight Marching Band, and the parents who help with the band's performances are the Knight Shift.

Farmington High School Senior Doors

Ask anyone who attended the high school on College Street and they will probably remember the "Senior Doors." In those days everyone had a study hall so all were well acquainted with the third floor study hall. There was a single door at each end of the study hall as well as the Senior Doors in the center. Underclassmen were not allowed to walk through those wooden, double doors designated as Senior Doors. We lived in fear that somehow we would be pushed through the Senior Doors as we passed and would be marred for life (if we were allowed to live). Occasionally an underclassman would test the system and walk through the doors; the punishment was to apologize to the senior class at an all-school assembly.

Becoming a senior and walking through the Senior Doors was a milestone for the FHS students. This tradition came to an end with the Class of 1960 when the high school moved to the new building.

Farmington High School Carnival And Senior Trip

In order to help finance the Senior Trip, a school carnival was held each fall. Businesses donated food items and parents donated canned goods and bakery items. Students were busy gathering everything and anything that might

be sold or consumed at the carnival: walnuts, pumpkins, crafts, and knickknacks. Competition was keen and often underhanded because points were given to each class for the items they brought in. Points were assigned to items according to their dollar value or how great the need for the item at the Carnival Country Store, the Carnival Dinner, or other booths. Points were also awarded for class participation in carnival activities, having the winning class float in the parade, and for money spent at the carnival by those attending. The class that accumulated the highest point total crowned their candidates as Carnival King and Queen.

The Carnival/Senior Trip tradition came to an end with the move to the new high school. The Class of 1961 had earned the bulk of their senior trip money during the carnival held during the fall of their junior year. There was no carnival in the fall of 1960; the last senior trip was taken by the Class of 1961 in the Spring of 1961.

Farmington High School Homecoming

With the move to the new high school, the homecoming tradition began. The first fall in the new building, 1960, saw the beginning of the tradition that is still the fall highlight of the school calendar. Homecoming weekend means a parade, a football game, crowning a Homecoming Queen, a dance and numerous alumni activities. A number of classes schedule their class reunions for Homecoming Weekend. The first Homecoming Queen of Farmington High School was Mary Ann Rickus Klepzig, Class of 1961.

Moothart College

(Reorganized as Ozark Business College, Inc., 1917)

George Washington Moothart, an Illinois native, organized a chain of business colleges, the first being in Desoto, MO in 1899. He later opened additional schools in Cape Girardeau, Bonne Terre, Dexter, Kennett, and Farmington. At one time small branches were opened in Flat River and Bismarck but were later moved to Farmington, which became the headquarters in 1904. Mr. Moothart placed his schools in small towns because he believed the high cost of living kept many students from attending urban institutions and also that the moral environment was higher in smaller communities.

The Farmington branch, located upstairs over what was then the *Farmington News* (southwest corner of Columbia and Jackson Streets), was made possible by Mr. Moothart, president, as well as sponsors and shareholders: L.M. Miller and John Doughty of Farmington, I.E. Butler of Cape Girardeau, and C.P. Cooley of Ste. Genevieve. Students were trained in accounting, bookkeeping, stenography, and secretarial duties.

After several years of growth, the college was moved to the IOOF Lodge building at the southeast corner of Columbia and Washington Streets. The college used the entire second floor of the lodge building. In 1914 Mr. George A. Miller became the principal and general manager. In 1917 the college was reorganized as the Ozark Business College, Inc. Additional sponsors were Francis F. Benham, Taylor Smith Sr., Charles F. Porter, Judge Kossuth Weber and Edward C. Revoir, who all served as shareholders and on the board of directors.

During these early years no local schools or colleges offered these subjects. The college preferred high school graduates as students but also accepted eighth grade graduates and sometimes younger in special cases. Because elec-

tric typewriters and computers hadn't been invented, manual typewriters were the only equipment available. Gregg shorthand, touch typing, double-entry bookkeeping and accounting were taught. Each and all courses included spelling, business English, penmanship, arithmetic, computations, business efficiency, business law, personality, and salesmanship with special emphasis on how to sell yourself and your capabilities. Emphasis was placed on accuracy and satisfactory completion of work instead of speed.

During the years of World War I enrollment doubled and then tripled. Although there weren't enough classrooms, desks, or equipment, no students were turned away. The demand for graduates with business skills brought the enrollment to 240 students. Miss Ora Klepsattle of Desloge, as well as the Lawrence sisters, served as instructors. Roy A. Miller, Harry P. Miller, Hazel F. Miller, Lois A. Miller, Ralph E. Miller, and Cecil G. Miller, sons and daughters of Mr. L.M. Miller, also became instructors. Some of the students were Paul J. Clay, Eddie Effrein, Dewey Kocher, O. Richardson, John Patterson, Norman Watts Jr. Cecilia Best, the Herbst girls, Irl Beatty, Marie Beatty, Beulah Beatty, Zilla Cunningham, George Shinn, Tom Horton, Amy Wells, Wyman Buckner, Floyd Buckley, Clarence Carver, Lucius Antoinne, Geraldine Perkins, Lillian Mayberry, Virgie Patterson, Elmer Kerlagon, Gertrude Watts, Daisy and Bessie Boyd, Lawrence Tesreau, Joy Kite, Mildred Huff, Marie McMahon, and Aleta Kollmeyer as well as many others. Most of the students were from Southeast Missouri but some came from St. Louis, Illinois; Arkansas; Texas; and Oklahoma as well as other locations.

In the early 1920s high schools and colleges began teaching shorthand, typing, bookkeeping, accounting and related subjects, causing enrollments to decrease. In 1928 Mr. George A. Miller, president and general manager, moved to St. Louis. Miss Effie Lawrence continued the operation of the college until it was closed in the late 1930s.

Moothart College had a football team in 1906.

Presbyterian Orphanage

Several ministers of the Potosi Presbytery became touched by the plight of homeless children of the "lead belt." Because of mining accidents, there were always orphaned children and never enough homes for them. The Orphanage began in 1914 when the Potosi Presbytery acquired the Elmwood Seminary by paying off the $12,000 debt. The property included a large brick building, a house, and a slave cabin. The purchase of the property along with repairs and furnishings were made possible by a $15,000 gift from Mrs. James Butler of St. Louis. The converted school building was named Butler Hall in her honor. Rev. O.E. Sutherland was the first superintendent. The first supervisor was Miss Nettie Ward and the first two children to enter were Elbert and Hazel Kyle, ages 6 and 4 (May 15, 1915). The Potosi Presbytery and The Synod of Missouri (Presbyterian Church, U.S.) struggled to provide support until 1917.

In 1917 the Synod of Missouri (The United Presbyterian Church in the USA) joined in sponsorship and the orphanage became the Presbyterian Orphanage of Missouri, the only Presbyterian child-care facility in the nation directly related to both the northern and the southern Presbyterian churches. It continued to be so until the reunion of the two church bodies in 1984.

In 1919 the Reverend William S. Stinson assumed duties as superintendent of the orphanage. Rev. Stinson was accompanied by his wife and their three children. Rev. Stinson was the eldest child in a fatherless family of six and had worked at an early age to support his mother and five sisters. Under his supervision the orphanage began serving children who were not necessarily orphans but who could not be properly cared for at their natural homes. Butler Hall was the home of 115 children. The kitchen and laundry were in the basement. The reception room, study hall, dining room and three rooms for workers were on the first floor. When the weather was bad, the only places to play were the hall or study hall if it was not in use.

One of the assets of the orphanage was a printing press. During the early years the press enabled the orphanage to publish a newsletter on a regular basis. The newsletter's name changed with the times from *Elmwood Home News* to *the Elmwood Quarterly* and then to *The Orphan's Messenger*. These publications contained the antiquated typefaces of the old lead press, a beautifully dated writing style and historic photographs. The newsletter later evolved into *The Children's Voice* and ultimately, *The Bridge*. For a time the press, operated by some of the boys at the orphanage, helped to earn income for the home but eventually lost money and was sold.

After the death of Mr. Stinson in 1930, Mrs. Stinson assumed the role of superintendent. When she resigned in 1939, she was succeeded by the Reverend Peter W. Fischer of St. Louis.

A gift of Peters Shoe Company stock, valued at $15,000, was made by the family of F.H. Peters in 1932. This gift served as the nucleus of a building fund, and by 1939 the orphanage had received sufficient additional funds to proceed with the construction of the administration building, which was completed in March of 1940.

Until 1943 the home farmed a rented eight-acre tract on the west limits of Farmington. The cows were driven in to the campus for milking. The boys gardened a portion of the campus. Mr. Earl Woodard, a former resident, remembers this period: "I remember we had about four acres to garden at the orphanage. We learned a lot about gardening because we ate what we grew and we canned a lot of it. It was funny now that I think about it because we drove the cows in for milking through town (or part of the town). I remember stealing eggs, too, from where the orphanage kept its supplies; and when it was our turn to feed the fire in the furnace, we'd put them in a can full of water and place them on top of the furnace to boil. The lady who was in charge of us was big and was strict. She came down one time when we had the eggs on top of the furnace to boil. We were scared to death, but apparently she couldn't see very well

President Moothart of Moothart College.

Presbyterian Home for Children in 1914.

because she didn't say anything. She just walked away."

Through gifts donated by Mr. Joseph Sunnen of St. Louis, the home undertook the purchase of an 85-acre farm on June 9, 1942, to raise food for the children. *The Orphan's Messenger*, September 1942, reports:

"After a thorough investigation of the facts concerning costs of produce, meat and dairy feed we found it would be a paying proposition to own a farm. The small rented acreage which we worked netted a worthwhile profit. The farm committee looked at several farms and had the opinion of the Doane Agricultural Service to verify its findings. They settled on the Kosky farm a little less than two miles from the Orphanage on the northeastern edge of the town. It consists of 85.9 acres, quite level, all of which are under cultivation and pasture. The 25 acres of pasture are sufficient for our herd and is well watered by a spring. The cultivated land has not been abused and is quite productive. The orchard consists of 75 fruit trees and a grape vineyard that last year produced 2,000 pounds of grapes.

"The buildings consist of one six-room house in perfect condition; a barn large enough for a dairy herd of 21 cows, 4 horses and a winter feed shed with a loft that will hold 50 tons of hay. The barn will need a new roof and a cement floor for the dairy side as a sanitary measure. Work on this has already begun. There is a tool shed, hog house, corn crib, brooder house, chicken house, smoke house—all of which are in serviceable condition, and need only minor repairs. There is a good cistern, a deep well and spring house, electric light and telephone line. The roads to the farm are gravel but always open.

"We were too late to get the crop, but the fruit was donated to us. Fourteen bushels of grapes and seven bushels of pears were gath-

ered at the time of this writing. Mr. Lewis Asher, our farmer, has moved into the house and the dairy herd and pigs will be moved as soon as the barn is ready.

"We purchased some farm machinery and two horses at the sale of assets. The land cost about $60 an acre. This is unusually low for land as good and so well located. The mortgage can be taken up any time we have the money on hand. This will save the interest as well as release the principal for the government war needs."

Lewis Asher, farm manager for 36 years, wrote: "Sammy, the bull calf, is the latest addition to our farm. He was sent to us as a special gift of Mr. and Mrs. Barron of Poplar Bluff and their son, Robert. He is a registered Jersey and will replace Hercules, of whom we now have several heifers. We are going to build a hen house to house 150 hens. (The poultry operation eventually housed 20,000 hens.) We butchered nine hogs this fall. Most of the meat is already eaten. We have eight shoats that will be ready soon and 12 little pigs in two litters. Among our Christmas gifts was one of $2,000 from Mr. and Mrs. Joseph Sunnen to be placed in the Building and Farm Fund. We are using it with the $4,000 sent by the Sunnens before to pay for the greater part of the farm, and the farm will be named the 'Joseph Sunnen Farm.'" (The lake on the farm bears Lewis Asher's name.)

Carl Harris, a graduate of the University of Wisconsin Agricultural School and a Metropolitan Life Insurance Company employee, who renovated and sold foreclosed farms, arranged for the purchase of the neighboring 120-acre Giessing farm. The farm began a hog-raising program so that the boys could learn scientific farming and help to solve the problem of feeding the residents of the home. Six registered cows, which ultimately led to a sizable herd, were purchased.

During the next couple of years the older boys of the home moved to the farm. Two log cottages where built: Harris Cottage, named in honor of Carl Harris, who was then board chairman and who continued to improve the farm program, and St. Francois Cottage, named in recognition of local citizens who supported the home.

In 1944 the Ringling Brothers' Circus fire at Hartford, CT, shocked the world. Warnings that, "It can happen here," resulted in inspection of the premises and Butler Hall was condemned. A new sleeping wing for small boys

was built on the north of the administration building and another for girls on the south. These two new wings, dedicated in 1936, provided fireproof quarters for all the small children.

In 1945 Rev. Fischer left to rejoin the ministry and Rev. Fred A. Walker came from a pastorate in Dallas, TX to become the fifth superintendent. Rev. Walker left the position for six years to accept the presidency of his alma mater, the University of the Ozarks, in Arkansas. Rev. William M. Griffin replaced him as superintendent during those six years. Rev. Griffin made many improvements to the farm program. He also helped displaced persons find homes during the war (Kono family).

In 1950 the Women's Association of the West Presbyterian Church of St. Louis donated a "merry-go-round swing" to the orphanage. In that same year Pevely Dairy donated $4,000 toward the cost of a new dairy barn.

In 1951 Superintendent Fred Walker returned to supervise the orphanage. Dearing Hall, housing for young girls, was near completion. In 1954 Harlan Hall, which housed boys 11-13 years of age, was dedicated. Mr. B.H. Jennings donated 10 acres of land on the Castor River in Madison County near Marquand, MO in 1957. Two log cabins from the farm were moved there, other recreational buildings and facilities were added, and Camp Jennings opened as a country retreat for the children. In 1958 three cottages on the farm campus were dedicated: Green Cottage, in honor of Mr. and Mrs. A.P. Green of Mexico, MO; Harris cottage, in honor of Carl E. Harris of St. Louis; and Lothrop Cottage, in honor of Grafton Lothrop of St. Louis. In 1967 an activity building/gymnasium was built on the farm campus. The building included a gymnasium, woodworking and handicraft shops, a study hall/meeting room, dressing rooms, and showers.

In 1968, after 20 years of service to the home, Rev. Fred Walker retired. He founded Home Life for the elderly, a retirement center in Farmington and predecessor of what is now Presbyterian Manors of Missouri.

The Rev. Gordon Monk directed the home from 1968 to 1969. Major changes in federal and state laws governing child care, labor, health, fund raising and fire safety codes caused a sharp increase in operating costs and a marked change in the number and kinds of clients served during the late 1960s. These changes would eventually lead to the end of the farm's operation.

Harold Showalter became the executive director in 1970. Child care at the home was increasingly focused toward the adolescent child. The first on-grounds classroom program began. In 1977 a family counseling office was established and in 1978 the Cayce Cottage was rebuilt to replace the old Cayce family residence and one of two cottages lost to fire in 1974 and 1976.

(Information taken from pamphlet published by the Presbyterian Children's Services, Inc. in 1989)

TRANSPORTATION

A Day on the Plank Road...Circa Y2K

by Douglas K. Ross, DDS, MAGD

Today is a very special day for you! It's a warm clear spring morning after a terrible and frightening over-night storm that's now passed and hangs over the eastern horizon. The sun is beginning to cast its powerful rays over that storm system as crimson purple, burnt orange and ruby red in the eastern sky as you walk to your automobile. The air is pure and fresh and you are excited to be alive to take it all in. You even look heavenward and say a respectful prayer of thanksgiving for being able to enjoy it all and that your family is safely asleep inside your home.

Your windows are down as you drive slowly west on Missouri Route W. You are on a special trip back in time, a time when your hometown was but a wisp of the bustling fine small city it has become today. As you pass the tall and commanding city water tower, pull over and park. It's early on a Saturday and there's absolutely no one else on the road yet, so it's safe to walk to the middle of the roadway. You're standing in the middle of a toll gate for the Plank Road- Get out your change to pay the toll. You will probably have to pay the maximum fee of 25 cents since your conveyance is about the same size as a wagon and team.

It is 1853! There were seven such "tollgates" in all, from Iron Mountain and Pilot Knob to Weingarten and Ste. Genevieve. The company was called the Ste. Genevieve, Iron Mountain and Pilot Knob Plank Road Company. Those in charge of the project were James Kirkwood, William Singleton, and Joseph Miller. Each one was an engineer and all became famous, gaining national reputations as builders of roads and railroads later on in the century. Plank roads were commonly called "the farmers railroads" and were first built in Russia, then in Canada and New York. The first plank road in Missouri was the 10-mile-long New Madrid and Stoddard Plank Road. The last one in Missouri was the Providence Plank Road in Boone County. Our plank road was the longest ever built in the United States! It was 42 miles long and handled one-lane traffic with east travel given the right-of-way. Turn-outs were provided. Total trips took five days! The total cost was $200,000 shares of stock sold to investors for $50 each. In 1857 the company went out of business due to the building of the St. Louis and Iron Mountain Railroad. St. Francois County continued to maintain the road as a public road. Today the route is Missouri Route 32 from Ste. Genevieve to Farmington and Missouri Route W to Iron Mountain; the Pilot Knob "spur" is Missouri Route V.

But hey! Enough of these basic details! There's more important things for you today.

You've paid your toll. Get back in your car and continue back in time on your trip of memories and have some fun. Be careful as you go through DeLassus (dell-a-sue) and cross the St. Francis River on your way to Rock Springs. Drive slowly and you just may see several wild

Rosenstingle in front of the courthouse, note town pump in right background

Last run on the Plank Road, at tollgate.

deer feeding in the fields on both sides of the road. They'll probably leap right in front of you. Don't hit any. They've never seen a vehicle such as the one you are driving! As you round the turn in the road, pull off to the left. That big rock is Rock Springs. Park and get out.

The sun has followed you closely on your journey today. Its warm rays are tweaking the skies overhead now to lighten your way. It's a good thing too because you must be very careful where you step. Rock Springs is one of those "turn-outs" I told you about earlier. There are buckets and buckets of "souvenirs" from all the horses, oxen and mules stopped here waiting on passing traffic. Which reminds me, there's a fully loaded wagon from Ste. Genevieve coming down West Columbia Street now and headed this way. They will be stopping here, since there's another loaded one from Iron Mountain now in Doe Run headed east with the right-of-way.

Listen to all those frogs croaking, celebrating that big rain last night. The crows are cawing loudly over in the corn field to the north and just a bit further the small-mouth bass are surely jumping with joy and gorging themselves on all the bugs and larva that have washed into their

feeding spots. Now is a good time for you to inspect the Plank Road personally, while you can kneel on the road itself and not fear getting stepped on. Look closely at those 2-inch thick, 8-foot long planks laid cross-ways on the three rows of long timber sills placed in staggered patterns. Don't waste this opportunity to actually run your fingers across the heads of the four-sided iron nails holding it all together. Can you imagine how many there are in all the 42 miles of the road and how long it took the many men driving them to build it - not to forget the men who labored long and hard in hot and dusty forges to make each one by hand and to cut into the timbers and planks in the sawmills throughout the area. Uh oh, the wagon from the east is here.

Isn't that a fine looking pair of working animals drawing that forerunner of the "18 wheelers" we see today. Go over and see what's aboard; a piano from New York, a barrel of sugar from Cuba, two sacks of coffee from Brazil, 29 bolts of fabric from Massachusetts, mining tools from Pennsylvania, four boxes of books from Illinois and a cask of whiskey from Kentucky. Walk around to the other side and see the rest;

boots from Ohio, assorted wines from France, rifles from New York, china from England, candy and canned fruits from New Orleans and a carton of paper from Indiana. These days we see all kinds of goods going by to Iron Mountain and that big warehouse and mercantile operation down in Ironton. The wagon from Iron Mountain is just about here. Look, it's full of iron ore for the furnace at Valley Forge to make into "blooms" to take on to Ste. Genevieve for shipment on the Mississippi. There won't be another wagon from the west for awhile so you can drive on now. Later there will be wagons of granite, marble, lead, cobalt, nickel and a mix of agricultural products. This is indeed a busy road of commerce! No wonder the railroad wanted to cut in on it!

As the road winds up Chalk Hill and into Doe Run, you may just decide to jump back into the present just long enough to stop at the Plantation Restaurant for some breakfast. You may even see me there having my breakfast and reading the newspaper. I'll be at my favorite table, the third from the corner on the roadside of the room. Join me until you're ready to go back to 1853. I'm probably having my favorite of "two over-easy, ham, hash browns, biscuits, grapefruit juice, coffee and ice water."

Stono Mountain looms in the west. You'll see some radio transmission towers now but in those days radio was not on anyone's mind yet. As you wind down the road you will go through Haggai (hog eye) and then on to Iron Mountain, at one time a community of 4,000 people when the mine was at its peak. Iron Mountain began in 1797 when Spain gifted Joseph Pratt 20,000 arpends of land to say thank you for helping with the local Indians. There was an actual mountain of almost pure iron ore there on the surface for the picking. The operation continued until 1959.

An aggregate business continues today in the form of "trap-rock" and the rock is shipped world-wide. Spend all day if you want. Look at all the history and talk to the people. I grew up there myself so it is indeed dear to my heart, but you really need to get going back. Come back later some other day to see the unique dam at Iron Mountain Lake built in 1847, the "reservoir" on top of the mountain and the old "pipeline route.Ö See if you can snag a tour of the old mining area and all the "cuts," and where the Union Army camped prior to the Battle of Pilot Knob. Be sure and see where the old race track was and where the famous Iron Mountain Hotel stood. My grandfather, T.L. Ross, ran it for the mining company but Grandmother Nellie did most of the work. I think my mother, Ethel, worked in the kitchen and the laundry as well as in the grocery store next door with my dad, J.G.

This time, after you've passed through Haggai, turn off on Missouri Route V. This part of the road system wasn't planked. It was only a wagon track path of two ruts cut into the turf. That's what it still was in 1948 when I used to sometimes ride early in the morning on a little school bus with Roy Bay, principal of the school, to pick up students as far as the Iron County Line. Go as far as King School Road and turn around to continue your trip.

The Plank Road was the Columbia Street we know today with the many fine homes and stately trees, some almost as old today as the history we're enjoying now with this story. Go to the library sometime and read all about the "electric railroad" that used to ply the center of the street and its route through town. Note it was clean electric, not smelly and dirty steam from coal. This is the street I fell in love with when I was 8 years old (1946) and decided this was where I was going to live when I grew up. I hadn't a clue what I would be doing to earn a living but I knew this was the place to do whatever I'd be doing. Nineteen years later that dream came true and for the past 34 more it's a dream in motion. Only God knows how many more are planned.

As you drive through downtown, try to ignore the paving and let your imagination soar. You're on a wooden plank road! Let yourself feel the bumps and joints. Have fun! Once you cross Henry Street, look to the left and you'll see my dental office. It's been there since 1965 and my plan is to keep working until 2015. We'll see, won't we. I don't have a clue what was there in 1853 but it was probably some type of store or shop just bustling with activity.

The Main Street crossing sees a slight change in direction to Ste. Genevieve Avenue. Continue on to the junction of Missouri Route 00, 32, and W. Your route now is purely on MO 32. Exactly one mile, 5536 Highway 32 East, pull into the driveway of the Southeast Missouri Treatment Center and stop just short of the quaint white house standing there. It dates back to the days of the Plank Road. The Huss family lived there. The last of the family, Miss Genevieve Huss, was indeed a dear. She loved history, was vivacious, and was a true community spirit. A professional educator in the local school system, she was the local authority on the Plank Road during her lifetime. She was instrumental in the construction of the granite rock pile monument

First automobile, Judge Taylor.

Trolley car in front of the third courthouse.

and the sign standing today. Hopefully someone will have replaced the rotting boards I noticed on my last trip by there. It's exactly 0.3 miles on toward Ste. Genevieve.

Pull in and park at the monument. Look straight ahead, past the home built there, kinda down their driveway. That's the route of the old Plank Road, just an old country pathway but one so rich in history and memories. As your eyes focus on the other buildings at the bottom of the run, you are looking at what was Valley Forge. The road turned sharply to the left and crossed Wolf Creek on a well-constructed bridge that stood for many years, well after the roadway was replaced and relocated in today's location. Virginia Lee (Schneider) Meyer lived by the bridge and, in 1939, painted an oil painting of her memories of the bridge. The painting is in the possession of Mary Meyer, now living in Terre Haute, IN. You can see a color photograph of it at the library. If you're really adventurous, drive on exactly 0.6 miles. Having now crossed Wolf Creek, pull off and park on the shoulder of the road. Get out and check the name on the mailbox and write it down. Sometime next week, call the property owner and tell him I've suggested you call. Ask for permission to enter on private property to see the large stone bridge abutments still standing robustly in the creek banks. There you can let your imagination fly again. See the smoke coming from the forges. Hear all the activity of the small community that rested in this grove of trees and the meadows of the area. There was a cooper shop, a flour mill, a store, a school full of children and two rows of houses neatly maintained. Stay long enough to let the aroma of baking bread, smoke houses curing hams and bacon, and the kilns glowing with charcoal for the forges, all swirl around your head and into your nostrils. Close your eyes and continue to enjoy. You'll not soon duplicate the aura. Take it all in!

Continuing on your journey, you'll soon pass the entrance to Hawn State Park. Be sure to come back later on in the year, and visit Pickle Springs too. Just up the hill the tracks of what used to be a very busy railroad are crossed. You are now driving on what I call The Snake, a very dangerous stretch of highway with steep undulations and curves that defy every driver that tackles them, especially the large trucks and school busses. Surely someday politicians and the Missouri Department of Transportation will admit and recognize the problems and correct them, but that's another story for another time. Drive on to Zell Station; here the route to Ste. Genevieve is totally different than the original.

The roadway essentially followed the same route as the railroad does today. Go exploring and see how far you can proceed on the backroads of beautiful Ste. Genevieve County through Zell and along Gabouri Creek until you find your way into the City of Ste. Genevieve on Main Street. Be sure to stop at the Beauvais and J.B. Valle homes. History, history, history. Ste. Genevieve is a "History Town" on the Mississippi. You won't be able to duplicate an arrival at the river as you could've a century and a half ago. The Mississippi River has changed course and is much further away. Can you imagine that!!!

Well, I'll tell you this, "time traveler," I sure have enjoyed taking you on this journey. I've seen every scene as vividly as you and experienced every sensory sensation too, just as you have. Let's do it again soon. But this time, take some others along with us to share. Do we live in some great place or what? "You've got that right Vern!" As long as I live, I'll always be preaching and boasting to anyone that'll listen; Farmington is the finest small city in the state of Missouri! Thanks for coming along today. God Bless and keep you safe in His arms til we meet again. Remember to "buckle-up" and drive safely back home to your family on the Plank Road!

The Electric Railroad

One of the most important dates in Farmington's history occurred on July 24, 1904, when Thomas Lang Sr. pulled a switch and the town's new electric railroad suddenly sprang to life. With E.C. Rickard as motorman and Guy Tullock as conductor, the single-car trolley pulled out of its DeLassus Station and in six minutes had reached the Farmington city limits and made its first stop at the Presbyterian Church. The car next stopped at the post office (at the present location of Mercantile Bank) for photographs and then rumbled on towards the north end of town. The first passengers included stockholders in the railroad, businessmen, city officials, and media representatives.

Tracks soon were extended north to Esther, where the line connected with the Illinois Southern, and to Flat River, where connections were made with the Mississippi River and Bonne Terre Railroad. The south end of the tracks at DeLassus coupled with the Belmont branch of the St. Louis and Iron Mountain Railroad (later Missouri Pacific). Passengers also had access to the Frisco lines. Thanks to these links with main trunk railroads, passengers on Farmington's trolleys could make frequent daily connections with passenger trains bound for St. Louis, New Orleans, and other principal cities around the nation. In short, the St. Francois County Electric Railway Company had now put Farmington "on the map."

Until the arrival of the electric railroad, travel to and from Farmington had been difficult. Those wishing to go to St. Louis often took a stagecoach from Farmington to Ste. Genevieve, where they boarded a steamboat for the trip to St. Louis. Completion of the Plank Road from Farmington to Ste. Genevieve in 1853 made the trip only slightly more convenient. The situation improved somewhat with the construction of a new railroad three years later between Pilot Knob and St. Louis. Still, Farmington residents had to rattle along by stagecoach to Iron Mountain to board the St. Louis train.

Although the Iron Mountain Railroad was a tremendous improvement over previous methods of transportation to St. Louis, many Farmington residents wanted a more direct rail link to the rest of the world. In 1869 an attempt was made to bring a rail connection to Farmington, but the plan was dropped when city residents voted down a $30,000 bond issue needed to fund construction. Several subsequent attempts to bring the iron horse to Farmington failed until 1901 when a group of city businessmen, which included Peter Giessing, H. Sleeth, J.P. Cayce, W.R. Lang, M.L. Clardy, John Giessing, Thomas Lang, Louis Miller, W.F. Doss, A.T. Nixon, J.M. Morris, and Dr. E. C. McCormick, decided to build their own railroad. At that time the decision was made to go with electric power, which was seen as more practical than traditional steam power.

Some $125,000 was raised by Farmington residents for the project, including $57,203 for right of way for tracks. Construction began in 1902. A power house was constructed, machinery installed, and about four miles of track was laid before the line ran out of funds. In 1904 the company was taken over by new owners, and the tracks were extended to Esther. Six years later the company was in receivership and in 1912 the assets were purchased by the Mississippi River and Bonne Terre Railroad. By this time the property was valued at $366,170. The following year construction was completed on a new depot on North Washington Street, where the *Farmington Press* is now located.

In its early years the electric railroad operated on 11.8 miles of track. There were few streams to cross and the longest trestle was about 15 feet. Ballast for the tracks was chat (tailings) from the nearby lead mines. The poles used to

Breaking ground for the electric railroad in DeLassus, 1902.

St. Francois Railway opening day ceremonies 1904, south side of courthouse.

St Francois Railroad in front of the third courthouse, around 1904, note gazebo roof in background.

New diesel engine for Farmington.

Note: The image above is the St. Francois County Railroad Company pay check.

ST. FRANCOIS COUNTY RAILROAD COMPANY.

BONNE TERRE, MO. FEB 6 1919

PAY ROLL

BANK OF FARMINGTON

PAY CHECK

NO. 2925

FARMINGTON, MO.

PAY TO THE ORDER OF R. H. Wills

$ 46 80

FORTY SIX DOLLARS EIGHTY CENTS

DOLLARS.

IN FULL PAYMENT AND SATISFACTION FOR SERVICES RENDERED THE ST. FRANCOIS COUNTY RAILROAD CO. FROM JAN 16 1919 TO JAN 31 1919 INCLUSIVE

THIS CHECK IS NOT VALID UNLESS PROPERLY SIGNED AND CANNOT BE DRAWN FOR CURRENCY OR TO THE ORDER OF THE OFFICIALS ISSUING IT. NOT GOOD FOR ANY SUM EXCEEDING $200.00 DOLLARS.

hold the electric lines were about 110 feet apart and extended about 16 feet above the track. The original power station was located at what was called "electric place," which is close to the present site of the Mineral Area Regional Medical Center. Three boilers, supplied with water from an artesian well, drove two Western Electric generators that powered the trains.

In 1926 the company was purchased by 20 Farmington businessmen, who included M.P. Cayce, C.H. Giessing, G.B. Snider, F.W. Schramm, D.F. Giessing, C.E. Rozier, W.R. Lang, the P.A. Shaw estate, L.H. Williams, W.C. Fisher, the Morris Brothers, George Tetley, the C.A. Tetley estate, Harry Denman, O.J. Mayberry, B.T. Gentges, C.Y. White, E.J. Lawrence, Henry Giessing, and the Klein Grocery Co. By 1927 the rail link to Flat River and Esther had been eliminated while a new connection with the Missouri-Illinois Railroad was made at Hurryville.

By the late 1920s the railroad no longer produced its own electricity, but rather purchased power directly from the city which necessitated the construction of a new brick building near the depot where the city's alternating current was converted to direct current needed to power the trains.

While passenger service was important, especially in the early years of the trolley's operations, the railroad depended on freight service for most of its revenue. The firm's first customer was the Giessing Milling Co., which received a shipment of oats and corn. The most important client was State Hospital No. 4, which depended on the railroad for delivery of coal used at its power plant. Other important customers were the two flour mills, Schramm's Ice Plant and Coal Bins, Lang Manufacturing Co., and the

Standard and DeForest Oil companies. By the start of the Great Depression the railroad was handling up to 75,000 tons of freight a year and employed about 12 persons to run the line.

Before automobiles cut into passenger service by the early 1920s, there were as many as four trolleys making up to 20 trips per day between DeLassus and Flat River. The first train to Flat River pulled out at 6:15 in the morning and the last at 10:48 p.m. Trips were scheduled so that passengers could make timely connections with steam-driven passenger trains that stopped at Flat River and DeLassus. As an example, a passenger could leave St. Louis at 8:02 a.m. on the Mississippi River and Bonne Terre Railroad, transfer at Flat River, and arrive in Farmington on the trolley three hours and 56 minutes later. The roundtrip fare for this trip was $3.45.

To assure trains ran on time, all crew members were required to used certified railroad watches. Generally the trains ran within three minutes of scheduled times. In the early days the cost of a ticket from DeLassus to Flat River was 30 cents. One of the most popular destinations for passengers was Woodland Park, a large picnic area located near what is now Eagle Lake Golf Course, which boasted a baseball field and picnic facilities. A round-trip ticket to the park was 15 cents.

In later years passenger service was discontinued and the line concentrated on its freight service. By the early 1950s the electric trains were replaced with several second-hand diesel switch engines. However, with the decline of the flour mills and the use of coal, the railroad was no longer profitable. Indeed, during its last decade of operation beginning in 1947, the railroad reported a profit in just one year, 1951, when

it cleared a grand total of $147. That same year, the total passenger revenue of the line was just $1.75.

As the line was preparing to close, the railroad basked in one last bit of glory. The Farmington Homecoming in July 1957 featured a 50-cent ride on "the last train to DeLassus" - a flat car pulled by a diesel from the festivities at Long Park to DeLassus. Those who made the trip were the last passengers ever to buy tickets from the St. Francois County Railroad Co. The last blast of the train's lonesome whistle was heard on November 15, 1957.

Officers of the line at the time included President Dr. L.M. Stanfield, who owned 69 of the 250 outstanding shares of stock; Vice President J.O. Swink, a lawyer and circuit judge, who was also the line's part-time engineer; and Secretary M.P. Giessing. Other board members were C.H. Giessing, B.T. Gentges, Arlie McClard, all of Farmington, and Dr. W.A. Rohlfing of Flat River. Other key personnel included Paul Rickus, engineer, and Emmett Welch, fireman.

The old depot was later torn down to make way for Heck's IGA Store on North Washington. Most of the track was pulled up and sold for scrap. However, at various points around town a few pieces of track remain covered by asphalt and one old bridge still stands just north of town, all in silent testimony to an electric railroad that had been called "Farmington's greatest enterprise."

While the electric railroad is best remembered today, Farmington was also served for a brief time by a steam railroad. The brainchild of railroad developer, Louis Houck, the system was begun in 1894 and ran from points south of Cape Girardeau, north through the counties of Perry, Ste. Genevieve, and St. Francois. In 1912 it reached Farmington, which was the northern end of the line. Its Farmington depot was constructed on East College just east of the present Church of God on East College street.

Unfortunately, the railroad was plagued with problems. The rails were poorly constructed and the trains constantly jumped the track. Saline Creek frequently overran its banks, covering the track with mud. Its timetable was a joke and of little use to travelers and shippers. Once sparks from the engine burned a trestle near Farmington, holding up the train for about two weeks. In 1917 steam trains were abandoned and a motor car was operated on the rails for several years to serve farmers along the route. The company went into receivership in 1927. While the railroad's erratic service drove away many customers, the largest factor in the failure of the Houck Railroad was the rapid development of motor transportation in this section of the state in the late teens and early 1920s.

FARMINGTON AVIATION CORPORATION

The Farmington Aviation Corporation was formed in the spring of 1946 as a privately-owned airfield by Harry Peterson who owned the land, and Claude Lovitt and Fred Auchter, who jointly managed the field. Besides these three men, the field had active personnel of Dorthea (Mrs. Fred) Auchter as bookkeeper and Graham Bell and Otto Sharp, both as helpers and maintenance men.

Harry Peterson was from Flat River and owner of the Pepsi Cola Bottling Company. Claude Lovitt was in the Naval Air Service during World War II and came to the area with his wife, Toddy, from Florida.

Fred Auchter and his wife, Dorthea, came to the area from Wichita, KS, where he had been an employee of the Boeing Aircraft Company. Auchter was an instructor from 1941 to 1943 at the National Defense Training School in Flat River, where local residents were trained to work in defense factories.

The field was a part of a 200-acre farm owned by Peterson at the east edge of Farmington bounded by Ste. Genevieve Avenue and 00 Highway. Several homes and three businesses, Lees' Tom-Boy Store, Farmington Frozen Food Locker Plant and Ozark Village Cafe, Service Station and Cabins, were also located on the tract.

Of the 120 acres comprising the field 53 acres were used for the runways, all of which were heavily sodded to provide a good landing cushion. There were three designated runways, a north-south of 2,400 feet; an east-west of 2,600 feet and a northwest-southeast of 3,200 feet. All of the runways were 300 feet wide and used by both single and twin engine planes.

The field was equipped with lights along the runways in 1949 and a directional beacon. A large hangar, 96 X 93 feet, was built that could house 22 light aircraft. Seventeen planes were kept permanently at the hangar, seven of which belonged to the Farmington Aviation Corporation. The field also boasted refueling pumps, office and repair shops.

One of the most outstanding features of the airfield was the Civil Aeronautics Administration Communication's Station located at the field. This was the only CAA station located on a privately owned and operated airfield.

Since this was immediately following World War II, many of the returning servicemen were taking flight lessons on the GI Bill. Both Lovitt and Auchter were qualified by the CAA to give flying instructions and to issue private and commercial pilots licenses. Lovitt held a rating from the CAA as a flight examiner and Auchter as a maintenance inspector.

Flyers from all over the country used the field during its operation. The registration book kept at the field showed pilots in from Boston, MA; California; Oregon; Florida and many other states. It was estimated that during the early 1950s as many as 200 planes a month stopped at the airport.

The field also hosted an annual fly-in with visitors coming from many parts of Missouri, Arkansas, Illinois, and Oklahoma. While the visitors were here, they would be taken on tours of the community and many elected to stay overnight at the Ozark Village Complex.

Auchter and Lovitt operated the airport as partners for several years until Lovitt disposed of his interest and Auchter continued the operation alone until his death in July of 1956.

After Auchter's death, Peterson brought in other managers to run the field, but it never again had the same spark and enterprising atmosphere as was there in the early part of its operation under the guidance of Lovitt and Auchter.

In 1956 Peterson offered to turn the field over to the City of Farmington to become a municipal airport for a good-faith-fee of $1. The offer was rejected by the city and the field eventually was closed and the CAA Station moved to Cape Girardeau.

The Farmington Aviation Corporation moved Farmington from the barnstorming era into the modern air age and was an asset to the entire area by making it attractive to companies who were looking for building sites in progressive communities with modern transportation facilities.

Peterson, Auchter and Lovitt were men who loved the spirit and excitement of flying and saw it as the future. They were the pioneers of commercial flight in St. Francois County and should be remembered with gratitude.

Farmington Airport Show in 1933, Rolla Williams manager of Roseland Theater.

Aerial view of the airport in 1946, located behind Ozark Village, where the Sports Complex is today.

Fred Auchter, manager of Farmington Airport, checks out the propellor, while unidentified mechanic looks on in 1946.

MEDICAL HISTORY OF THE COMMUNITY

Dr. August Franklin Eugas

August Franklin Eugas was born at Yount, MO on October 9, 1866. He was the son of William and Dora Heitman Eugas. He had three brothers, Tom, Charles and Henry, and two sisters, Catherine and Emma. He graduated from Barnes Medical College in 1904 and located at Libertyville in this county. Later he moved to Doe Run, where on October 11, 1911, he was united in marriage to Catherine Smith. To this union was born three children.

Dr. Eugas moved to Farmington in 1913. He had enjoyed a large practice at Doe Run and Libertyville, much of which he retained after coming here and to which was added other practice until he soon became one of our busiest, as well as best-loved physicians. He was of a quiet, unassuming disposition, one who readily made friends and uniformly kept them.

Dr. Eugas died December 20, 1920, at the age of 54 years. He is buried in Yount, MO. At the time of his death, his mother was still living, but his father had passed away 10 years earlier. He was a member of the Methodist Church at Doe Run and of the Masonic and Odd Fellow fraternities. He was a noble husband and father, as a well as a true friend.

Dr. Emil Herwig

Dr. Emil Herwig was born in 1862 somewhere in the eastern United States. He was married and lived in Johnstown, PA. In the Great Johnston Flood of 1889, he saw his wife floating down the waters on a rooftop. Over 2,000 people died in this flood.

Sometime after, he moved to DeLassus and opened a medical practice in Farmington. His

Doctors and businessmen of Farmington in 1894, Columbia Street. Senator M.R. Smith, Mr. Philip Cole, Mr. John Wescoat, Dr. George Williams, Dr. A.J. Smith (brother of M.R. Smith). Photo taken in front of Dr. Williams offices. Old Rotger building on the right.

office was located upstairs in the old Farmer's Bank Building, which is now the Roberts Building. He married for the second time. His wife was Genevieve Murphy, daughter of Franklin Murphy. She was also a great aunt of Gene Cole of Farmington. Mr. Cole says that his great uncle, Emil Herwig, was a "gruff" and colorful character and small in stature. He owned a touring car but could not drive. He would hire someone to drive him to Farmington to work. If he could not locate a driver or if he felt like it, he would walk to Farmington. His name was a German name of nobility. Mr. Cole said that he was a good doctor to see if one had pneumonia.

The Knights of Pythias Lodge was named Herwig-Hunt Lodge. Mr. Cole was related to both men.

Dr. Herwig and Genevieve had one daughter, Wilhelmina. She married Braddell Jesse, the son of Dr. Rutherford Jesse for whom Jesse Hall at the University of Missouri is named.

Dr. Herwig died in 1955, Genevieve died in 1942 and Wilhelmina in 1995.

Dr. George Lancaster Watkins

Dr. George Lancaster Watkins was born at Clinton, MO on May 18, 1888. His parents were Dr. Charles Henderson Watkins and Ella Dozier Watkins. He moved with his family to Joplin, MO in 1900, where he lived until he entered Washington University School of Medicine in 1907.

He received his M.D. degree from this University in 1912, following which he interned at Mullanphy Hospital in St. Louis, MO and at the Bonne Terre Hospital in Bonne Terre, MO. He moved to Farmington in 1914, where he entered medical practice.

On April 2, 1914, he married Miss Genevieve Keith, daughter of Mr. and Mrs. Hugh L. Keith, of St. Louis. To this union four children were born, Josephine, George, Warren, and Tommie.

On May 8, 1917, Dr. Watkins was commissioned first lieutenant of the Medical Corps of the United States Army and assigned to ser-

vice in the British Expeditionary Forces. He was later transferred to the 15th United States Cavalry, where he remained until the signing of the Armistice. He was discharged from service on January 19, 1919. From this time he was engaged actively in the practice of medicine in this community.

During these years of practice, Dr. Watkins was a member of the staff of The Bonne Terre Hospital and in recent years surgery consultant at the State Hospital No. 4. His life's ambition was the establishment of the Medical Clinic in Farmington and this came to be in August of 1948.

Dr. Watkins passed away on December 25, 1954. Not only Farmington, but the entire area for miles around, sustained a deep loss at his passing. Few local citizens were any better known or loved by any more people than Dr. Watkins. For 40 years he had been the "family doctor" in hundreds of homes in this area. He was not only a good doctor but an outstanding citizen

The Medical Arts Clinic, which was built in 1948 and since enlarged, will be an everlasting monument to his foresightedness and genuine interest in his home and community.

Baptist Sanitarium

In the 1903 minutes of the Franklin Baptist Association, the record states that the Farmington Baptist College property was sold August 7, 1903, for the purpose of establishing a sanitarium. The property was sold for $10,000.

On September 1, 1903, the building became the Baptist Sanitarium. It was to be conducted by a Board of Trustees with Dr. M.H. Topping of Farmington as chief surgeon and Dr. W.H. Mayfield of St. Louis as chief consulting surgeon.

Dr. Topping was qualified to occupy the position of chief surgeon. He was a graduate of Louisville Medical College and the Illinois School of Electro-Therapeutics. He had practiced in St. Francois County and was well and favorably known. Dr. Topping was also president of the institution. He had acquired a na-

Dr. George L. Watkins

tional reputation for his success in sanitarium work. As with all his other sanitariums, success has crowned his efforts; so has this one been eminently successful and been alike paying to the management and profitable to the patrons. Dr. Mayfield has not lost a single case among these patients who have come to this institution for operation and treatment. The sanitarium stands on four acres of beautifully located ground on the electric railroad within two blocks of the courthouse. The main building can accommodate 30 patients and has private and public wards, electric lights, furnace heat, perfect sewerage, bathrooms on each floor, shower baths, hot and cold water and every modern convenience known to sanitarium science. It has hot air apparatus for treatment of rheumatism and abdominal troubles and all the best appliances, which accompany the operating table and to assist the surgeon in his work. There is a force of four trained nurses. The institution is under the business management of Mary K. Rose, a business college student of several years' experience, in charge of the sanitarium and to her energy and ability is the popularity of the establishment largely due.

By resolution of the incorporators every registered physician in St. Francois County and southeast Missouri is asked to participate in the work and invited to bring their patients for nursing and sanitarium care. The sanitarium is open to all doctors; the management is thoroughly imbued with the spirit of treating all physicians kindly and alike and extends to them a cordial invitation to visit the institution.

The Farmington Sanitarium still existed in 1904, when it treated 125 patients. Thereafter, it was no longer mentioned in the minutes of the Association.

The streets bordering this property were: West College; North "A" and North Franklin.

On August 7, 1909, financial problems led to the sheriff's sale at the courthouse door. R.B. Winters bought the property for $50. The property was then sold to Robert Tyzzer, who sold it to the School District of Farmington on December 9, 1909.

The brick building was used as a gymnasium and possibly for a few other classes. A new high school building was built at the College Street location in 1912. This further lessened the need for the Sanitarium building. When the high school added its gymnasium building in 1927, the Sanitarium building was doomed. Soon after it was demolished and turned into an area for track and a football field for the high school. This would be the area that is located just north of the present Senior Citizen's Center. I can remember when the brick building, Washington School, was built in the late 1940s and then the three-story building was used exclusively for a high school. When a new high school was completed in 1960, at 1 Black Knight Drive, the building was used as a middle school for grades 7 and 8. The building had served its usefulness, but was structurally unsound. A new middle school was constructed. Demolition of the building began in 1985. Today it is a parking lot.

Researched and compiled by Elma Overall Jennings for a videotape on the *History of Farmington* produced in 1989.

A HISTORY OF THE MEDICAL ARTS CLINIC

Dr. George Lancaster Watkins was a general practitioner of unusual talent and boundless energy who, over a period of approximately 24 years, had built up an extremely large practice in St. Francois and surrounding counties of southeast Missouri. He started as a partner of a Dr. Downing, with whom he was associated from 1914 to 1917, when Dr. Watkins entered the Army for the duration of World War I. In his wartime service, Dr. Watkins was assigned to the British Army where he served as a battalion surgeon until subsequent reassignment to the Army of the United States. After discharge, he returned to Farmington and conducted a solo medical practice here from 1919 until August 18, 1938, when he was joined by F.R. Crouch, M.D., who worked with him for the next three and one-half years. The cold hard facts of the clinic's start and growth will be interrupted here as I (F.R. Crouch, M.D.) make an effort to portray what rural Missouri practice was like in those days.

Much can be recalled, and perhaps an entire book could be written about the early days of my own practice in St. Francois and surrounding counties. Dr. Watkins was an extremely skillful doctor, both in the realms of technical ability and of rapport with patients. I don't believe there would be many now or even then who would argue either point. On the other hand, he set a standard of quality and quantity of work which was difficult for an ordinary mortal to match, and there was the constant feeling that competition was the order of the day, in spite of the fact that there was more work than two busy doctors could do adequately. There was a constant emphasis on how busy one could be, how long one could go without sleep and even on how much could be recorded on the ledger as a measure of work done. This shaky start on August 18, 1938, was made all the more fragile by the fact that Dr. Watkins finally yielded to a severe hepatitis and diabetes mellitus on the following day. When, on August 19, I returned from my first all night vigil on a home delivery, in a part of Ste. Genevieve County where the conveniences of electricity and the telephone had not yet been realized, it was to find my new associate desperately ill with diabetic acidosis as above, and I took him in his car to St. Louis where his old friend, Dr. Walter Baumgarten, cared for him for the following month at St. Luke's Hospital.

In those four weeks, and in fact for many thereafter, I was "the new young doctor" and was avoided as much as possible by all who thought they might survive until "the old doctor" returned. Those who were forced to accept my services almost always had to have the same medicine as that given by my predecessor for "the same thing." Since the keeping of records was not Dr. Watkins' strongest point, I had to consult the pharmacists (Edward O. Klein and Ralph Dillard at Laakman's, Ellis Lawrence and Yancey White at City Drug Store, Tom Foulon at Foulon's Drug, Travis-Robinson at Robinson's Drug, Mert Green in Desloge and Henry Carrow at West End in Bonne Terre) to learn some of the many special concoctions that the good doctor had used over the years and which had met

Dr. F. R. Crouch, M.D.

with such apparent success. Since Sulfanilamide, which marked the beginning of the era of antibiotics, had been put on the market in 1936 or thereabouts, and I was not to learn of the potential of its successors, including penicillin and its many derivatives and relations, until the war years, therapy in general was in a primitive state.

Our office was in the back of what was then the Ozark Building, the first floor, which we shared with what was then the embryonic Ozarks Federal Building and Loan Association. Many procedures which are now considered strictly hospital ones were of necessity done in the office, these ranging from T&A's, emergency D&C's, the treatment of minor fractures (x-rays usually, if at all, by Dr. Jones E. Klein, the new dentist who had his office upstairs in the same building) the opening of abscesses and even one instance of bone curettage and casting of acute osteomyelitis of the fibula. These all were done after the return of Dr. Watkins, and my role was generally that of anesthetist or muscle man, depending on the success of the anesthesia given by me.

One has to realize that the onset of this practice and clinic was at a time of economic distress known then as "The Great Depression." People had little money, sickness and accident insurance was non-existent and a doctor's collection rate was scandalously, or at least distressingly, very low. Hospitalization was truly an emergency affair. In my chosen field of special interest, obstetrics, where the patients were young and usually quite poor, it was considered a luxury to be able to deliver a hospital baby in good light, warm surroundings, using sterile techniques, with adequate help, anesthesia, and excellent post partum care for mother and newborn care for baby. Much more often, in the three and one-half years of practice preceding my Army service, there were long nights and days of labor at patient's homes with improvisations of lighting, anesthesia and general care that are almost unheard of nowadays. The big "OB Bag" contained a Kelly pad, forceps, instruments for a craniotomy, a stove-top sterilizer and countless other objects and medications which are in modern practice relegated mostly to medical museums. A "portable" OB table proved to be so heavy and cumbersome that it was relegated to a spot in the trunk of the car and the old system of an ironing board to give a firm surface on the edge of the bed, two chairs for the mother's feet and a Kelly pad draining into a pail (hopefully clean and strategically placed) was used. With the only hard pavement roads being US 61-67, and all others in St. Francois County being river gravel or chat, and most in Ste. Genevieve County having no surface whatsoever until the environs of the county seat were reached, one soon learned the places which could and could not be reached by "ordinary" transportation. Thus an occasional call had to be finished by team and hay rig, and many, especially in the Avon, Coffman and Clearwater communities, by generous neighbors or concerned relatives who kept old large-wheeled vehicles for such purposes. J.C. Harter was one of these especially concerned and well-equipped neighbors, nor will I ever forget the late Ralph Winebarger and his big red cattle truck which served so well when the Greasy Creek and Little Saline were bank and floorboard high on many a night when Grandma's asthma was "giving her fits."

Each incident mentioned calls to mind many others, but this general picture should be quite clear, leaving plenty to the memories of the older generation, and perhaps bringing into focus more insight and understanding by the younger.

At this point I shall return to a more objective format and relegate the first person to its proper place in a historical narrative.

Dr. Crouch was away for about four years during World War II, with Washington University's 21st General Hospital, and for postgraduate training after its ending. Dr. Watkins managed to hold the practice together during the war years and with the return of Dr. Crouch in 1946 and of his son, Dr. George Linn Watkins, who returned from Navy service in 1947, the nucleus of the clinic was established. The younger Dr. Watkins did general practice until 1950, when he left to complete his surgery Board qualifications. Meantime, the Medical Arts Building was completed and the younger Dr. Watkins returned to join the partnership permanently and to do general surgery exclusively in 1952.

With the coming of C.E. Carleton, M.D., after six years of service in the U.S. Navy, in 1953, the partnership was officially named the Medical Arts Clinic. Continued growth of the practice brought Dr. A.G. Karraker into the group in 1954. On December 25, 1954, the elder Dr. Watkins died at age 65. This intensified the need for new men and it was at the height of this campaign for recruits on January 21, 1955, that Dr. Crouch received a cerebral concussion and fractured femur in an automobile accident. Dr. R.A. Huckstep was then found working in a VA hospital in Texas and he joined the group in June 1955. Dr. Crouch returned to limited activity in June, full activity in September and no new permanent additions were made until Dr. Chastain joined the group in June 1959. Dr. Chastain's training was largely for general practice, but his special interest was pediatrics and he continued to do pediatrics primarily. The increased surgi-

cal load brought the addition of another board surgeon, G.A. Oliver, M.D., in 1960. Dr. Tom R. Burcham was recruited in 1963 to help handle the increased family practice responsibilities, and with the building of the new Farmington Community Hospital, and the aging of the original partners, the clinic's need for doctors continued to increase.

Not mentioned in the foregoing account are four doctors who came for shorter periods and left for greener pastures: the late H. Stanton Knotts, M.D., who did general practice long enough to return for more surgical training; the late Tommy K. Watkins, M.D., who did pediatrics, but left to return to the U.S. Navy and specialty training in radiology; Paul J. Roesler, M.D., who practiced two years, was drafted into the Army, then trained in radiology; and James J. Stout, M.D., who did internal medicine for two years, then left to do solo practice in Albuquerque, NM. Of this group, Dr. Knotts became a surgeon and practiced in Indiana until his untimely death. Dr. Tommy K. Watkins completed his radiology training and was serving with distinction in the U.S. Navy in Japan, when he developed a brain tumor and died in San Diego in the spring of 1969. Dr. Roesler is a senior diagnostic radiologist at the Glockner-Penrose Clinic in Colorado Springs, CO. Dr. Stout, at last report, was still practicing as a cardiologist and internist in Albuquerque.

Meantime, the Medical Arts Clinic has continued to grow, acquiring Dr. Juan Cancelada, who, since joining the group, has qualified for the American Board of Obstetrics and Gynecology and been accepted as a Fellow of the American College of Obstetrics and Gynecology.

Dr. Dennis Dierker joined the group in August 1971 to give some relief to the overworked Family Practice Section.

Dr. Crouch's health problems led to the acquiring of Dr. George W. Dent in January 1971. Dr. Dent is a specialist in obstetrics and gynecology. He came to the clinic soon after his discharge from the Army where he had served in Germany following medical school internship and residency at St. Louis University Medical Center. Dr. Dent is a native of Salem, Dent County, MO.

The impending departure of Dr. George Watkins led to the need of another surgeon, and the clinic was fortunate to obtain the service of Dr. Robert Hoye in September 1972. He is a product of the St. Louis University School of Medicine and for 14 years he was employed by U.S. Public Health, National Institutes of Health, where he became deputy chief of surgery of the National Cancer Institute at Bethesda, MD. He and his nurse-wife, the former Shirley Melcher of Weingarten, have recently moved into their new semi-rural home with their three children.

Medical schools represented in the group are as follows:

Doctors Watkins, Crouch, Carleton, Oliver and Huckstep are graduates of Washington University. Dr. Karraker is a graduate of the University of Illinois. Dr. Chastain is a graduate of Columbia University School of Medicine in New York. Doctors Burcham, Dent and Hoye are products of the St. Louis University School of Medicine. Dr. Cancelada obtained his M.D. at the National University of Mexico in Mexico

City but received his postgraduate training and qualified for his board at hospitals affiliated with Washington University in St. Louis. Dr. Dennis Dierker, a graduate of the University of Missouri-Columbia Medical School, came to the clinic after several years of practice in Lebanon, MO. Dr. Burcham had practiced in Doniphan, MO, before joining the group.

The presence of this number of doctors in a single group in a town of Farmington's size is the result of many years of recruiting. The Medical Arts Clinic Group is the nucleus of the staff for the Farmington Community Hospital, along with two other family physicians from Desloge and the two osteopathic physicians of the Farmington Clinic.

In 1973 for reasons of health, Dr. Crouch resigned from the clinic and this was followed by the resignation of Dr. George Watkins in January 1974. These doctors retain an emeritus status in the clinic.

Two large major additions, as well as several minor ones have been made to the clinic building. If current plans for more personnel, who are badly needed in the area, come to pass, continued growth in the physical plant is contemplated.

Strict adherence to the highest standards of medical practice has been a long-standing principle. Communication, consultation and every effort to keep the best interests of the people at heart have enabled the clinic to function as a unit with the doctors teaming together to produce that ideal service. This involves regular staff meetings both of clinic and hospital. It also involves compulsory postgraduate study and activities for all, a rule which was unique to this group at the time of its inception in 1953. Another unique feature is compulsory vacations, things that were so unique in the early days that they had to be taken unannounced or clandestinely.

Since the above summary was written, the clinic has been fortunate to have Dr. Walter C. Gray join on a part-time basis in family practice and Dr. Darrell Griffin, a trained pediatrician. Dr. Griffin's medical school was the University of Missouri at Columbia and he has joined the group to provide definitive care particularly in the relatively new field of neonatology, as well as in general pediatrics.

As the community, clinic and hospital grow together, so have been developed almost miraculous technical tools which will need more and more trained people, more and more doctors, and hopefully will come the day when Farmington reaches the stature of a recognized medical center.

ST. FRANCOIS COUNTY POOR FARM

By virtue of a law passed in the state of Missouri in the year 1879, the various counties of the state were authorized to provide for the "support of the poor." Those included the aged, infirm, lame, blind and sick. The laws provided that the county court in each county should be responsible for enforcement of this law and furthermore the court may purchase or lease any quantity of land not to exceed 320 acres, erect a

The buildings at the old County Farm, re-covered and re-painted. Township 35 Southeast of Farmington, five or six miles, built 1881.

building to house the people and appoint a superintendent. Provisions were made for either running these institutions from funds taken from the county treasury or else by contract or lease to the superintendent.

St. Francois County acted accordingly and in March 1881 purchased 320 acres of land for $3,000 from James W. Coffman. This land was located in Township 35, about six miles southeast of Farmington in the vicinity of Knob Lick.

A special term of the county court was held during March of 1881. The contract for erecting a building on the Poor Farm was let to Messrs. Morgan and Miller at a cost of $1,000. Tillman Justice was the first superintendent of the farm and his contract lasted six months. He contracted to give the county one-third of the crop and receive $6 a month for the care of each person at the Poor Farm. Mr. Justice began his duties by clearing six and one-half acres of land which would later be used for cultivation and fencing in part of the tract. A smoke house was built in November of that year at a cost of $26.75 and a large crop of wheat was sown. The laborers used on these various projects received $1 per day in wages.

The second year the county court changed its policy and proposed to lease the Poor Farm rent free, together with the growing crop of wheat, to the highest bidder who would agree to keep the paupers for the least money per head.

The policy for contracting with a superintendent to be in charge of the Poor Farm varied from time to time. In 1898 John W. Mitchell was superintendent, having signed a contract for three years. He was to provide all clothing, food, sleeping quarters, medical care, burial facilities, in addition to the maintenance of fences and the care of the fruit trees. Around 1904 the 320 acres, including all houses, were purchased by R.P. and W.R. Taylor for $5,200, with J.A. Lawrence being the agent in this transaction. The land where the Poor Farm had been located was later sold to Ed Klein.

Jacob Blum was probably the first person coming to the Poor Farm on April 9, 1881. Later came Joseph Bartell, Thomas Easter, Mary E. Crenshaw and Fred Willen. By the spring of 1882 there were a total of 14 being cared for by the county.

The Poor Farm lasted for over 20 years, but in 1904 the policy of the county court was changed. The land occupied by the Poor Farm was sold and a modern infirmary was constructed at a cost of $12,000. It was located on a 21-acres tract of land one mile north of Farmington. The architect was H.H. Hoheschield and the contrac-

tor T.H. Glover with a low bid of $6,350. Today this is the site of Mineral Area Regional Medical Center.

After the completion of the building 10 applicants were made for the position of superintendent of the new County Infirmary. George M. Fraser was given the position at $25 a month, together with the living expenses for his family, which included his wife and three children. Mr. Fraser's position began in January 1905.

In 1935 there were 24 living at the infirmary, seven women and 17 men. Their ages ranged from 30 to 78. One man was there for 16 years and another for 13. These people were supplied with sufficient reading matter which consisted of magazines and two daily papers. The radio was the main form of entertainment and two loud speakers were placed at either end of the building and during the summer months the broadcasting of the ballgames could be heard throughout the halls.

There was a truck farm of considerable size and a large grape arbor which yielded 800 pounds of grapes in 1934. They also had 100 chickens and three cows.

The County Infirmary continued to serve many people in need over the years, but in 1950 the Infirmary went on the auction block and was sold for $17,500.

Mineral Area Osteopathic Hospital

In The Beginning

It was fall of 1950 when four osteopathic physicians practicing in this area learned that the County Infirmary (also called the Poor Farm) was going on the auction block. Dr. L.M. Stanfield, Dr. W.D. Morris, Dr. P.C. Reynierse and Dr. W.A. Rohlfing decided to try and buy the building and 12 acres and turn it into a general hospital.

During the auction there were other interested parties there to bid but upon learning of these good doctors' intentions, the other bidders backed off and the auctioneer hit his gavel one last time, giving ownership to these four doctors for a total of $17,500. The doctors were then on their way to building a much-needed hospital and they invited other area osteopathic physicians to join them. A non-profit corpora-tion was formed in February 1951 and included Dr. C.E. Owen, Dr. E.W. Lake and Dr. E.W. Delezene. Although a Reconstruction Finance Corporation loan was approved, the doctors decided to refuse the loan in order to operate the hospital on a non-profit basis. Accepting the loan would have meant the hospital would have been a for-profit operation under the supervision and requirements of the federal government.

Architect Joseph Bangert was employed March 14, 1951, to plan the new hospital, the only hospital available to patients of osteopathic physicians in a 75-mile radius. Orville King, contractor, was employed in June 1951. The first hospital board named was Dr. L.M. Stanfield, president; Dr. C.E. Owen, vice-president; Dr. W.A. Rohlfing, treasurer; and Dr. P.C. Reynierse, secretary; Dr. W.D. Morris, Dr. E.W. Delezene and Dr. E.W. Lake were members of the board.

The new hospital was planned to include areas for surgery, obstetrical, x-ray, and 30 patient beds. All patient rooms were on the first floor with business offices and intern offices on the second floor. The hospital grounds were beautiful with large maple trees and an iron fence which once surrounded the County Court House. The total cost of the new hospital called Mineral Area Osteopathic Hospital was $125,000. It open its doors June 1952.

Joining the first medical staff along with the founding physicians were Dr. J.L. Margreiter Jr., Dr. George W. Johnson, Dr. K.P. Wheeler and Dr. Paul Edgar. Miss Myrna Hoyt was superintendent of nursing; Louis Clayton was lab tech and Monroe Stewart was business manager.

Other staff included Marcia Lee Harter, bookkeeping; Lorelie Wunning, receptionist; Mrs. A.W. Wunning, first cook, Mrs. Mary Crawford, assistant cook, Mrs. Rosalie Barnhouse, housekeeper.

The nursing department included, along with Miss Hoyt, Elizabeth Doyle, RN; Edith Mercer, PN; Golda Saling, PN; Mamie Hutson, PN; and nurse aids: Shirley Smith, Dorothy Jenkerson, Laverne Voyles, Velva Hillman, Ruth Watts, Mary Ann Dugal and Rose Shinn.

Monthly payroll for the 35 employees was $5,000.

Mineral Area Osteopathic Hospital became the 52nd osteopathic hospital in Missouri. In 1987 the hospital's name was changed to Mineral Area Regional Medical Center.

St. Francois County Infirmary, became Osteopathic hospital in early 1950s.

A Hospital Is Born

It was June 17, 1952. The Lead Belt Area was experiencing a heat wave, and before the day ended thermometers would reach 104 degrees. Staff members at the new Mineral Area Osteopathic Hospital opened windows and turned on fans to make their first patients as comfortable as possible. Despite the heat there was an air of excitement; Farmington's first acute care, not-for-profit hospital was open for business.

Mrs. Helen Pratt of Richwoods, one of two expectant mothers, remembers that day well. She said, "Dr. Owen was my doctor (C.E. Owen, D.O.). The other mother-to-be was Dr. Stanfield's patient (L.M. Stanfield, D.O.). Both doctors spent most of the day at the hospital, each hoping to deliver the first child.

Thanks to Mineral Area Staff members, who went out and talked to Farmington area merchants, there were lots of presents for the first baby and the family. Because Mrs. Pratt's son, Ed, was the first baby born at the new hospital, the Pratt family became the recipients of those gifts. Included were meals in area restaurants, free gasoline, flowers, all kinds of baby gifts, a trip to the beauty shop for mom and a free ride home to Richwoods, compliments of a Desloge ambulance service.

Remembering the first day at the hospital, Mrs. Pratt says, "Myrna Hoyt was the nurse in charge and she kept things going like clock work. In fact, all of the hospital employees were nice and really excited about what they were doing."

*Reprinted from The Independent Journal. Thursday, June 18, 1987.

Present Mineral Area Regional Medical Center.

PARKLAND HEALTH CENTER AND BJC-MG

History Of The Medical Arts Clinic Building

Dr. George Lancaster Watkins began a solo practice in Farmington in 1914 that was interrupted by World War I Army service as battalion surgeon assigned to the British army for a period of time until the U.S. Army needed his talents. He was welcomed home in 1919. Joined by Dr. F.R. Crouch in 1938, their practice grew with the personalities and talents of rural physicians, who took pride in having a healthy constitution and the ability to require little sleep. Hospitalization was for emergencies only, with most infant deliveries at home with less than adequate facilities, poor lighting and little anesthesia on a portable table. The rural roads were often difficult to travel on, consisting of river gravel or chat, until the county seat was reached. Often a team of horses and a hay rig had to assist the physicians on their efforts to care for patients, especially in the Coffman, Avon and Clearwater areas.

With the addition of Dr. George Linn Watkins after naval Sservice in the Pacific Theater in World War II in 1946, the nucleus of the Medical Arts Clinic was completed.

Plans begun in 1947 to build a modern medical officer were completed in 1948. Designed by Denecke and Denecke of Fredericktown, it was constructed by the Walter Brockmiller Construction Company of Farmington. Several remodelings have been necessitated with the addition of the following: Dr. C.E. Carleton, 1953; Dr. A.G. Karraker, 1954; Dr. Robert A. Huckstep, 1955; Dr. C.W. Chastain, 1959; Dr. George A. Oliver, 1960; and Dr. Tom R. Burcham, 1963. Practicing with the clinic for short times were Doctors H. Stanton Knotts, Tom Watkins, Roseler and Stout. Joining in the 1970s were Doctors Juan Cancelada, Dennis Dierker, Robert Hoye, Walter Gray and Darrell Griffin. The clinic has continued to add medical staff.

A life's goal of the Farmington physicians was to be able to hospitalize their patients locally, avoiding the extra time required to drive to either Bonne Terre, Fredericktown or Ironton for hospital facilities. The time, effort, energy and fiscal challenges were monumental. Together with all mentioned on the original bronze plaque commemorating the dedication of Farmington Community Hospital, June 22, 1969, are the hundreds of unnamed citizens who generously gave donations and memorials ranging from $5 to $1,200. Many hospital rooms were partially or totally furnished by grateful families. Community support through purchasing bonds was also important for this private hospital.

Parkland Health Center

Parkland Health Center was originally known in our community as Farmington Community Hospital. The outcome of a group of civic-minded business and community leaders, the doors of the now 130-bed hospital opened April 16, 1969, to serve the citizens of St. Francois and surrounding counties. Before this time, local physicians had to travel to Bonne Terre Hospital or Madison Memorial Hospital in Fredericktown to provide in-patient care.

Members of the original governing body were Harry Lee Denman Jr.; George Watkins, MD; George Oliver, MD; John Jack Hirsch; Vernon Giessing; Don Mell; Stuart Landrum Sr.; David Colson; Lacy Coghill; J.B. Reinhart Sr.; and Robert Boswell. Taylor Smith was the hospital's attorney and N.C. Watkins, auditor.

Original medical staff members were J.A. Armantrout, DO; T.R. Burcham, MD; C.E. Carlton, MD; C.W. Chastain, MD; F.R. Crouch, MD; R.A. Huckstep, MD; A.G. Karracker, MD; D.A. McFadden, DO; G.A. Oliver, MD; and G.L. Watkins, MD.

Other physicians who served our community through their association with the health center include Juan Cancelada, MD; George W. Dent, MD; Dennis Dierker, MD; Dr. Robert Hoye, MD; the late Walter Gray, MD; and Darrell Griffin, MD.

William D. Blair of Farmington faithfully served as administrator of the hospital for more than 25 years, beginning in 1970. Bill continues to serve the hospital as a volunteer since his retirement in 1996.

Mrs. Gene Lockridge, RN, served as director of nursing service until 1993. Mrs. Lockridge also served as interim administrator when Joe Durham left in 1969 until William Blair was hired in 1970.

In 1992 Farmington Community merged with Bonne Terre Hospital and Christian Health Services to form Parkland Health Center. A second merger occurred in June 1993 when Christian Health Services merged with the BJC Health

Parkland Health Center

Farmington Community Hospital dedication, May 1969. Left, Dr. Carleton, and Dr. Crouch.

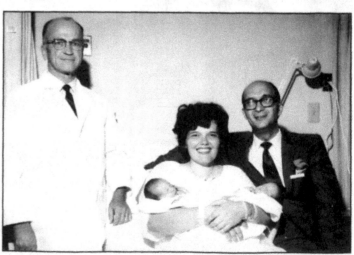

First babies born (twins) at Farmington Community Hospital, 1969.

System. As a member of the BJC Health System, Parkland is a member of a 24,000-employee health system that includes Barnes-Jewish Hospital, Barnes-Jewish West County, Barnes-Jewish St. Peters, Christian Northeast-Northwest, St. Louis Children's Hospital and Missouri Baptist Medical Center in St. Louis, MO; Alton Memorial Hospital, Fayette County Hospital and Clay County Hospitals in Illinois, Missouri Baptist Medical Center in Sullivan, MO and Boone County Hospital Center in Columbia, MO in addition to several nursing homes in Missouri.

Mr. Richard L. Conklin became president of Parkland Health Center in 1996. Rick, a very civic-minded gentleman, diligently works to carry out the mission of the Health System, "to improve the health of the community and people we serve." Other members of administration are Mr. Tom P. Karl, vice-president, Finance; Mrs. Kathy Hight, director, Patient Care Services; Mrs. Carol Coulter, director, Risk And Quality; and Mrs. Sheri Graham, director, Human Resources and Administrative Services.

Since the merger with the BJC Health System, the health center has grown to more than three times its original size and employs 435 local citizens. Expanded services to community include Home Health, Intensive Care, 24-hour Emergency, Obstetrics, Pediatrics, Sleep Disorder Lab, Oncology, Outpatient Renal Dialysis, Physical Therapy, General and Geriatric Medical Care, Surgical Services, Cardiac and Pulmonary Rehab, Industrial Wellness, Specialty Clinics, After Hour Physician Services, Community Education and Ancillary Services. In the fall of 1999, a free-standing Surgery Center located directly behind Parkland Health Center in Farmington will be open for service.

The employees of Parkland Health Center care about our community and reflect their pride as they play an active role in the local Caring Communities Organization; the Family Violence Council; A+ School to Work Programs; Chamber of Commerce Memberships throughout St. Francois County; The Farmington Training Institute; Heart, Cancer and March of Dimes fund raisers; school to work programs; and various other civic organizations. Parkland also provides a learning atmosphere for medical students and students enrolled in radiology, physical therapy, respiratory and nursing programs through Southeast Missouri State University, Mineral Area College, Sanford Brown College, Maryville College and St. Louis Community College.

Parkland is very proud and thankful of its volunteer auxiliary services. With over 125 members in this volunteer service, meals on wheels are delivered Monday through Friday to those who are unable to prepare their own meals. Our ambassadors assist patients to their destinations on a daily basis and our volunteer gift shop workers provide fresh flowers, gifts, sandwiches, coffee and snacks to the many visitors who enter our doors each day.

As a proud

member of the Farmington Community since 1969, we want our citizens to know that at Parkland Health Center "Our Family Cares About Your Family!"

A Brief History Of Southeast Missouri Mental Health Center

The 40th General Assembly in 1899 authorized the establishment of State Hospital No. 4 in southeast Missouri and appropriated $150,000 for the purchase of a site and erection of buildings. A Board of Commissioners was appointed and traveled towns of southeast Missouri before deciding upon a location near Farmington. The Commission also visited in-

State Hospital # 4

Grounds of the State Hospital #4 in 1911.

State Hospital Cemetery

stitutions in different states and finally decided to adopt what was known as "The Cottage Plan." The first five cottages were named after the men on the commission, Allen, Buchanan, Clay, Berry and Rigg, but in 1903 the names were changed to honor the five governors from 1896 to 1916, Stephens, Dockery, Hadley, Major and Gardner.

Three hundred twenty-six and a half acres of land were purchased at a cost of $20,000. The state paid $13,889.90 and the citizens paid $6,100.10. The assembly of 1901 appropriated $120,000 for additional buildings and equipment. During 1901 and 1902 five cottages for patients were constructed as well as a dining room, kitchen, powerhouse, barns, laundry, ice plant, the Administration Building, Hall Building, superintendent's residence, the Harrison Building, and the Folk Building which housed amusements and a dormitory for employees.

In January 1903 Dr. William Hall, superintendent, admitted the first seven patients. By 1904 there were 332 patients in the institution. Salaries for attendants ranged from $18 per month to $27 for a twelve-hour day. There is an undocumented story that in 1903 gray squirrels were brought to the hospital to entertain the patients and that this was the first time they were introduced to Missouri.

Buildings and cottages continued to be added to the facility. The campus included barber shop, drug store, post office, bowling alley, etc. The hospital made their own mattresses, grew their own food, had a dairy, cannery, greenhouse, power plant and grave yard. They were a self-contained community. During the early years patients who were able worked to help maintain the facility.

In the years before telephones there was a large bell sitting outside the Administration Building that was used to summon staff by designating a certain number of rings for various persons. This bell was moved when the facility vacated the old grounds and now sits beneath the flag at the new mental health center .

In 1924 one of the treatments was hydrotherapy, which was followed by lobotomies in 1940. Electro-shock therapy was introduced in 1942. The last lobotomy was performed June 16, 1943. Records show a total of 200 lobotomies were performed in Farmington with a mortality rate of 2%.

By 1930 there were 1,080 patients in the institution and Dr. Hoctor was hired as superintendent. Dr. Hoctor became well respected in southeast Missouri and beyond as a gifted and caring psychiatrist. He dedicated his life to the hospital and after he retired in 1978 he lived on the hospital grounds until his death.

In the 1950s patients in music therapy had a radio show which was broadcast from the hospital grounds through the local radio station. In

that year the average daily census peaked at 1,989 in 1960, and a school was added in 1960 with fully certified teachers.

Beginning in the mid-1960s there was a steady decline in population due to new and improved treatment programs, increased treatment staff, new drugs and placement in the community foster homes and boarding/nursing homes. In 1977 the average daily census was 525. As years progressed, the number of clients placed in the community and under the supervision of the hospital was near 1,000.

In 1984 the Missouri General Assembly approved the conversion of most of the hospital into a medium-security prison and most of the buildings and grounds were transferred to the Department of Corrections. A new 210-bed mental health center was built and in July 1987 Southeast Missouri Mental Health Center opened and the name Farmington State Hospital No. 4 no longer existed as such. The facility was reduced to 127 acres, one central building and five group homes along with three of its original buildings.

In 1999 the mental health center's average length of stay is seven days or less and many clients are treated and released within 23 hours. This is contributed primarily to the continued advances in medicines and treatment along with improved systems of follow-up care. The mental health center provides services to 31 counties in southeast Missouri and follow-up services are contracted by the Department of Mental Health from agencies nearby or in the clients local communities.

The future looks bright and secure for the facility as they now have two major treatment programs interfacing with the Department of Corrections and the 1999 General Assembly appropriated $7.7 million for a 66-bed addition to house forensic clients.

DR. EMMETT F. HOCTOR

Emmett Francis Hoctor was born August 22, 1896, in Omaha, NE, the son of Thomas and Pauline Paulson Hoctor.

Dr. Hoctor was the superintendent of the Farmington State Hospital No. 4 for 41 years, beginning in 1925. On many occasions he told the story of his arrival at Farmington in 1925. He approached a group of patients in the hospital yard and announced with a smile he was the new superintendent. One of the men eyed him disdainfully and remarked to the others, "That's who I thought I was when they first sent me here."

When he came to Farmington in 1925, he had intended to stay only a couple of years before establishing his own practice in St. Louis. He never got around to leaving. Throughout the years he turned down numerous offers to remain

Dr. Emmett F. Hoctor

in Farmington. He worked almost constantly, lived austerely and never married.

In 1963 Dr. Hoctor asked to be relieved as superintendent. He didn't want to leave the hospital; he just wanted more time to treat patients. State officials made him director of an outpatient clinic in a new building named in his honor. He spent his time between seeing patients in that facility and in clinics in small southeast Missouri towns. He retired as director of Outpatient Clinics in 1977.

In 1966, Dr. Hoctor received the Knight of St. Gregory Award, the highest honor given to a Catholic layman bestowed by the Pope. He was a Jesuit-educated graduate of Creighton University Medical School in Omaha, NE, where he received the Alpha Sigma Nu Award, which is a Jesuit honor given to the top student of the class.

Dr. Hoctor was the recipient of numerous honors not only from his church but from the American Psychiatric Institute. He also received Presidential Citations from Presidents Nixon and Ford.

He spent his entire career at the Farmington State Hospital. A book about Dr. Hoctor, *Let Me Not Be Mad Sweet Heaven*, was published in 1977 by John Stewart, a former minister who called Dr. Hoctor "one of the greatest humanitarians I had the privilege to meet in my lifetime."

Dr. Hoctor was a member of the St. Joseph Catholic Church and served in World War I.

He died on May 3, 1986, and was buried in Cavalry Cemetery in Omaha, NE.

RECREATION AND ACTIVITIES

Fairgrounds – Parks 1870s to early 1900s

There has always been a need for a community to have a place for citizens to gather for different kinds of outdoor events. Fairs were popular places for people to gather for entertainment, visiting friends and neighbors and for farmers, stockmen and manufacturers to show off their produce and products.

This need was addressed in the early 1870s by a group of county residents, when they formed the St. Francois County Agricultural and Mechanical Association. The land for the fairgrounds was purchased from the Alexander family, consisting of 20 acres located as part of Survey 2969 on the north side of the gravel road (now west Columbia Street on Highway W). We found in the *Farmington Times* dated March 4, 1872, an advertisement for lumbermen to bid for furnishing material which was to be delivered at DeLassus Station of the Iron Mountain Railroad or to the fairgrounds located on the gravel road half mile west of Farmington. These bids were for material, oak and pine lumber for five separate buildings: a floral hall 35 x 80 feet, a ladies room 16 x 32 feet, a pagoda (dimensions not given), office octagon shape of 16 feet, amphitheater (dimensions not listed), delivery of which to be made starting May 15, 1872.

From a program of the 1891 fair we find an invitation for all to attend and compete in the activities. The directors at this time were Thomas Lang, N.J. Counts, A. Parkhurst, Flem Dent, J.C. Alexander, Sam Fleming, James Highley, C.P. Clark, and Phil Gruner. A register of subscribers who had stock in the association was kept and includes names of businessmen, farmers and stockmen from all areas of the county.

Events at the 1891 fair featured many classes of livestock: horses, cattle, sheep, hogs, poultry, etc. Some of the classes we probably would not find in our fairs today would be for "Best Five Pound Hand Tobacco" and "Best Display Homemade Boots and Shoes." These early fairs also had competition for manufacture of farm wagons, buggies, plows, etc. Farmington in those days had several farm implement manufacturing companies, as well as blacksmiths who needed to display their wares.

It would appear that horse racing and wagering on races was very popular at these fairs. From a September 1, 1887, issue of the *Farmington Times*, a reporter tells of a race between two colts, one owned by Mr. Hunt was named Blue X and ridden by Duck Mitchell. The other colt named Spot was owned by Mr. Bray and ridden by Cayce. Spot was declared the winner by six inches. This article also named Aaron Cole, Milton Covington, and a Mr. Westover as being on the grounds with their fine racing colts.

Some of these early fairs ran for as many as five days. Imagine the excitement of such an event, with people from around the county traveling to the fair in wagons, buggies and on horseback to attend and visit with friends.

The setting is Wilson-Rozier Ballpark in the 1940s where these players were part of the team that played against the Farmington Blues. Left to right: Larry (Yogi) Berra, Chuck Deering, Joe Garagiola, Pete Reeser and Red Schoendienst. Note: Berra signed the photo "Larry Berra." Joe Garagiola was still with the Columbus, Ohio farm club. Photo provided by Reg Spence.

Tennis courts at Carleton College.

This fairground probably lasted until the early 1900s, but in 1909 we find a new association being formed called the Southeast Missouri Fair Association. They filed articles of incorporation in July 1909. This group purchased 31 acres from J.J. Butterfield, north of Farmington on the St. Louis Road and also entered into an agreement with Butterfield for the use of a water system. Mr. E.E. Swink was president of the association.

We can be pretty sure this fair was a success. There are some old pictures of horse racing and automobile racing at this fair, plus the usual classes of produce and homemade products. This fairground was damaged by a tornado on April 13, 1912. It was located where the Jefferson Elementary School is today on north Washington Street.

Later the fair was moved to the Wilson Rozier Park in Farmington and then to the present fairgrounds located between Farmington and Park Hills on Highway 67. The fair has been a popular event in the county for well over 100 years. It is a tribute to the many civic-minded men and women who have given their time and talents to make it a success.

Woodland Park

In the early 1900s another spot of fun and games for local folks would have been Woodland Park. The builders of the St. Francois County Electric Railway established this park mid-way between Farmington and Flat River for the free use of its patrons. The railway's service to Flat River was completed in late 1904. This park consisted of several acres of tree-covered land ideal for a park. They built a fine baseball park, a large dancing pavilion, swings, seesaws and other recreational facilities. The entire park was lighted by arc lights. This was a favorite place for family outings and picnics. The fare was 10 cents one way or 15 cents round trip from either Farmington or Flat River.

St. Francois Country Club

The St. Francois Country Club was located in the DeLassus area west of Farmington along and north of the St. Francois River. It was on a 63-acre tract of which about 12 acres was wooded, with the remaining land being used for a golf course. The club was started in 1922 by private individuals who operated the club until 1927. At that time the club property was purchased by a group of local people and incorporated as the St. Francois Country Club. The officers were Taylor Smith, George W. Morris, William M. Harlan, George C. Whaley, and H.O. Smith. Besides the nine-hole golf course, the club has a small clubhouse, with very attractive grounds, tennis courts, picnic grounds and a swimming pool in the river. Plans were made for enlarging the usefulness of the club from a community standpoint. It was proposed to establish a membership fee at a very small cost for people not interested in golf. Thereby this would provide income to improve the swimming pool, tennis courts, picnic grounds and clubhouse, so the club could become a recreation center for the entire community.

Clardy's Grove

Clardy's Grove was located on Highway W west of Farmington and was used many years for holiday picnics on July 4th and Labor Day, etc. The local Farm Bureau Store held picnics there for several years. Also horse shows were held at this location. The name Clardy's Grove came from the name of the owner of the property, Mr. Martin L. Clardy who was an attorney as well as head legal council for the Missouri Pacific Railroad. He also practiced law in the local courts. His large country home still stands just west of the Highway 67 and W overpass. The grove of trees where the picnics were held was on the south side of Highway W about where the overpass is located today.

Iron Mountain Fishing Club Of Farmington

Iron Mountain Lake has long been a place of recreation for fishing, swimming and boating. This lake was built in the mid 1800s by the American Iron Mountain Company, for the purpose of establishing a water supply for hydro mining. It was said to be at that time the largest man-made lake west of the Mississippi River. There was an early 1900s club incorporated as the Iron Mountain Fishing Club of Farmington, MO. In the corporate papers it says the object of the club was to encourage debating, reading and literature, also to avail themselves of the Missouri State Fisheries and the building of a clubhouse at the Iron Mountain Lake. Eligibility was men of good moral conduct with the membership not to exceed 250 members. Membership fee was $20 plus $5 annual dues. Names of some of the members on the corporation pa-

Clardy home on Highway W.

Clover Club in 1947, old Corral Drive-In location.

pers were G.B. William's, Benjamin Bisch, Henry Tetley, C.R. Fleming, M.P. Cayce, J.B. Smith, W.L. Hensley, and W.M. Harlan, plus many others.

The Clover Club

The Clover Club was located on the Old Highway 67 half way between Flat River (Park Hills) and Farmington. Shortly after its completion, a drive-in movie was built next to the club.

The Clover Club was the social spot of the area; when it was built in 1947, this area had no country clubs, Elks Lodges or VFW Posts to go to for socials and entertainment.

The Clover Club was built in 1947 by Irvin (Greasy) Greif, his wife, Katy, and a co-partner, Carl Moranville. The Greifs became the sole owner of the club in the early 1950s.

The Clover Club seated 375 people and had the largest dance floor between St. Louis, where the dance boat, Admiral, cruised the Mississippi River and East Cape Girardeau, where the Purple Crackle attracted fans from a three-state area.

Mr. and Mrs. Greif (known as Katy and Greasy) offered live music on Wednesday and Saturday evenings year round. They provided many of the "Big Band Sound."

The cover charge was $2 per person and the men must wear a tie and jacket. The doors opened at 12:00 noon and were open until 12:00 midnight, except on Saturday night when they could remain open until 1:00 a.m.

Later during the years between 1953 and 1956 the Greif's twin boys, Bill and Bob, started a barbeque business during the summer in order to help pay for their college.

In 1956 Greasy and Katy decided that the long hours and six days a week was enough.

They converted the Clover Club into Suburban Furniture, Inc. This furniture store burned to the ground on December 9, 1960. Suburban Furniture was back in business on February 1, 1961 and operated until May 1, 1982.

Edwards & Plumlee Theaters

It's hard to imagine that moving pictures have been around for only a relatively short time, having first appeared in the 1920s without sound. These were called "Flicker Flash Backs" and practically every small town in America had one or more of these movie houses.

During World War II movie attendance reached an all time high. But following the war, and with the advent of television, movies began to lose their audience. This forced many small theaters to close their doors.

During this time in 1947, Tom Edwards of Eldon, MO and Harold Harriss bought the Lead Belt chain of theaters from George Karsch. The chain consisted of eight movie houses: the Ritz in Farmington, the Roseland in Flat River; Oden in Bonne Terre; Regal in Elvins; Grand in Desloge; Roxy in Leadwood; Ozark in Bismarck; and State in Ironton. To these were added Tom's & Ozark in Eldon and Oak Grove in Colony.

Tom Edwards moved to Farmington that same year with his wife, Connie, daughter, Jodie, and son, Tom, who had been a pilot in World War II and was completing his education at Missouri University.

A few years later, Frank L. Plumlee bought out Harriss and the theaters became known as Edwards and Plumlee. During the ownership and skillful marketing practices of these two forward-looking men, Tom Edwards and Frank Plumlee, the theaters began to make improvements.

Both of the men were strong supporters of the community and involved in the Chamber of Commerce, Kiwanis and other organizations. Tom Edwards was well-known for his appearances in the annual Kiwanis Variety Show.

In 1949 Edwards and Plumlee constructed one of the first drive-in theaters in Missouri, the Corral Drive-in on then Highway 67 midway between Farmington and Flat River. The Corral became a pattern for many other drive-in theaters in other states. The drive-in proved to be extremely popular with families as they could load up the kids, refreshments, family pet and attend the movies in the comfort and privacy of their own vehicle. On many warm evenings, the ramps would be dotted with lawn chairs and blankets as families took the opportunity to visit and enjoy the night-time breezes.

In May of 1964 fire heavily damaged the Ritz in Farmington and the theater was closed and never re-opened. In 1965 the Roseland in Flat River was renovated and air conditioning added.

Eventually, Tom and Connie returned to Eldon, MO and their son, Tom and his wife, Nedra, took over the operation until the theaters were sold.

Jodie Edwards Needy, now of Columbia, MO, was in the eighth grade when her family moved to Farmington. She recalls "it was an absolutely perfect place to grow up. I have only wonderful memories of Farmington."

Corral Drive-In

The Corral Drive-In opened the summer of 1949. The drive-in, located on 13 acres on Old Highway 67, sported two screens (second screen added in 1978), 500 speaker posts and a concession stand.

David Jennings ran the drive-in from 1963 until it closed in the fall of 1983. He began working in the theater business in the mid-40s: projectionist at the Flat River Roseland Theater, managed theaters in Bonne Terre and Flat River and maintained the sound and projection in the nine theaters in the local circuit.

According to Jennings, the drive-in was really begun in 1948 by a well-driller named Bates. Bates drilled a well and poured the foundation for the snack bar. Edwards and Plumlee bought the land from him and Bates used the money to begin the Starlight Drive-In in Cape Girardeau. The original drive-in, located on nine acres, had a single screen 40 feet wide and 30 feet high. When Cinemascope arrived, a 10-foot section was added to the top and the width was doubled. The drive-in could handle 500 cars. The drive-in got its name when the public was asked to vote on a list of possible names. The "Corral" took on a western theme with a giant chuck wagon sign at the entrance and a concession stand called the chuck-bar. Kerosotes bought the drive-in in 1975, eventually adding four more acres for an additional screen and speaker posts for 500 more cars.

The Corral always hosted a huge fireworks display on July 4. The theater was filled and cars would be parked on the surrounding country roads and on Highway 67 as far as you could see. According to Jennings, "We'd set off the world's largest aerial bomb. It was built in Hong Kong. It was shot out of a 12-inch pipe buried four feet in the ground. It showered the whole area. One was all we could afford. It took three guys to set everything off."

There were double features every night at the Corral and triple features on Saturdays. There were three movie changes per week in the early years. If you visited the Corral, you can probably remember getting your windshield washed as you entered. In the winter you would receive a coupon for a free gallon of gasoline (to heat the car) when you purchased five gallons at a local station. The summer nights were always warm, filled with stars and lightning bugs. No matter the season, you could stuff yourself with hot dogs, dill pickles, popcorn and candy from the chuck-bar. The prices were low so people didn't need to bring snacks from home. Jennings said "We had grassy ramps. Not much of a mosquito problem and grassy ramps for people to put blankets on." Most of the city drive-ins had asphalt ramps and also had to spray for mosquitoes.

"Like all drive-ins, the Corral had its share of sneakers-in. Oh yes! Over the fence (six feet high), under the fence, driving in through the exit with their lights off. They'd come across the field in the back and crawl under the barb wire." Albert Lowry, an employee, would lay in the field and then pop up and catch them. He would escort them to the ticket booth to buy a ticket. Jennings said customers would warn him at the ticket booth of cars down the road loading kids into trunks. "We noticed a lot of cars with heavy rear ends."

The first concession stand, located near the original screen, was gutted by a burglary fol-lowed by a fire in the mid-70s. The second concession stand was centrally located between the two screens. The Corral was one of the first drive-ins to have self-service concessions. There was a continuous stream of people through the stand, "it was like an intermission that never ended."

Everything happened at the Corral. In later years there was crime: burglaries, armed robberies and fights. One night two people were shot in their car. Another night a woman gave birth to a baby outside the entrance. Jennings assisted the delivery by holding the flashlight.

When Eastman Kodak invented a process so that movies could be filmed in natural light, the prints were darker and the automated projectors couldn't cast enough light to send the image to the screen. VCRs were also a part of the social change that led to the downfall of drive-ins.

The Corral Drive-In closed in the fall of 1983.

Sources:

Obert, Jim. *Glory Days of Corral Drive-In Recalled.* Press Leader. Farmington, Missouri. Tuesday, July 13, 1992.

Obert, Jim. *The Corral Drive-In—Never a Dull Night.* Press Leader. Farmington, Missouri. Thursday, July 16, 1992.

Farmington Civic Center

The need for a community center to meet the recreational and cultural needs of the citizens of Farmington had been expressed over a period of several years. The limited population and consequent lack of funding were the main

Corral Drive-In in 1946.

Farmington Civic Center

reasons for these ideas and proposals not being acted upon.

By the 1990s Farmington had experienced a large growth in population, commerce and resources and the idea for a community center was revived. In 1992 an organized effort was begun to make this idea a reality and prominent among those involved was Kevin Engler.

In January 1993 Farmington Mayor Michael O'Brien appointed an ad hoc committee of citizens and city officials to assess the interest of the citizens of Farmington. The committee members were: Bud Norman, director of the Parks and Recreation Department, Clifton Bell, Mary Ruth Moon, Irvin Rudasill, Kelly Legan, Amy Mell, Harry "Chip" Peterson, the Reverend Bill Miller, Jerry Sullivan and Lisa West. The committee was chaired by city councilman Jim Kellogg.

The committee met throughout January and February, developing a form and a procedure to conduct a random telephone survey of Farmington residents. A provision was also made for a written survey available to residents not contacted by telephone.

The telephone survey was conducted by committee members between February 22 and March 1, totaling 334 telephone contacts. The results showed a positive response of 92% favoring a community center with 97% willing to pay a reasonable user fee to help maintain the facility.

On March 15, 1995, the mayor and city council accepted the unanimous recommendation of the ad hoc committee that the concept of a community center be pursued.

Three committees were formed among city council members for further planning. These were Facilities, chaired by David Holman; Location, chaired by Kevin Berry; and Finance, chaired by Jim Kellogg.

After these areas were assessed, reports were presented to the full council in July. The recreational and community components of the center were decided upon, the location of the proposed building on Liberty Streets and Black Knight Drive was adopted and the funding mechanism of asking the citizens to approve a 1/2 cent sales tax to fund capital improvements was approved. The election concerning the sales tax was placed on the ballot for November 2, 1993.

After the measure was approved by a large majority of the voters, planning continued under a special appointed committee of city council members consisting of David Holman, Lindell Kennon, and Jim Kellogg.

During 1994 Hastings and Chivetta was selected as the architectural firm for center design, Brockmiller Construction Company was awarded the contract for construction of the building, and Mr. Bill Towler was hired as community civic center director.

In 1995 while construction continued, work was completed on developing a policy manual, finalizing membership fees, developing program activities and hiring staff for the center. A community center newsletter, initiated by Director Bill Towler, kept citizens informed on the center's progress. Council members toured the facility at the various stages of construction.

After the community civic center officially opened on December 28, 1995, the response from the community was overwhelmingly positive. In his report to the city council on January 14, 1996, Director Bill Towler reported that there were already 611 members using the facility.

Today the facility plays host throughout the year to local and regional sporting events, concerts, exhibitor shows and family events. Membership has grown to 1,800. In the summer of 1999, construction will begin on an outdoor water park with a completion date in the spring of 2000.

Farmington Parks and Recreation

Farmington has nine city parks all of which are maintained by the City Parks and Recreation Department.

The earliest land destined for a park was on the site of the original Long House built in 1833 by the late Phillip Graham Long and his wife, Isabella Murphy Long (of the original Murphy family). Originally the house of log construction contained one room but was extended to three units, each with its own stairway and then a kitchen as the family grew. Later the en-

Bowling team of 1903.

1893 baseball team.

Old Farmington Band, no date.

Public swimming pool, Farmington.

Wilson - Rozier Park

The first editorial about a need for a ball field was in the January 1922 issue of the *Farmington Times*. In 1935 a portion of land was acquired by the city on Perrine Road from Sylvester Rozier for $700. It was known as the Athletic Field. A grandstand was built in 1936-37 by the W.P.A. The city added another portion that is the current park. Total purchase price was $2,100. It became known as Wilson-Rozier Park, named after Sylvester Rozier, who had married May Wilson, daughter of G.W. Wilson.

The park then was a grand ball field, seating 1200. In 1937 it was a well-lighted ball field. On September 3, 1940, fire destroyed a large portion of the grandstand, causing $10,000 in damage. The city carried only $3,000 in insurance, so it asked for additional funds and the grandstand was rebuilt with the help of the W.P.A. A refreshment stand was added later. It was thought to be the most modern ball park in southeast Missouri. Later, lighted tennis courts were added, along with paved drives, covered pavilions with picnic tables, cooking facilities and restrooms. Roller hockey and skating is allowed on designated tennis courts.

One of the shelters with a covered fireplace at one end was erected by the Twenty-Five Gardeners Club and the Rotary Club. It was dedicated in 1967 by Rotarian George Shaw, past president of the Club, in the memory of Jess Stewart and his son, David, who lost their lives in a fire. A bronze plaque donated by Ozark Steel Fabricators, inscribed "The Stewart Memorial Shelter." was placed on the shelter. Material and work on the shelter was donated by friends of Jess Stewart and his son. Mr. Stewart was the publisher of *The Farmington Press*.

Some time in the 1940s the Farmington Blues baseball team, a semi-pro club, challenged a team containing such professionals as Yogi Berra, Chuck Deering, Joe Garagiola, Pete Resser and Red Schoendienst.

In the 1950s the city obtained a portion of land from John Goetz on Middle Street. It was part of the original Karsch tract and was called Harlan Park. According to neighbors it was named for a little boy who lived nearby. The park also adjoins Harlan Street on one side. It has a playground and picnic equipment.

Another portion of land at the corner of Trimfoot and Morris Streets was acquired for a park and it is called Trimfoot Park, after the Trimfoot Shoe Company located nearby. It also has playground and picnic facilities.

In the 1960s the Junior Chamber of Commerce provided a spacious park on land next to the airport, on Perrine Street, with covered pavilion and picnic tables.

The Dean Danieley Park, off Hollyhock Lane, was dedicated to the memory of Dean Danieley, past president of Farmington Optimist Club, on land donated by Cooper Oil Co. and sponsored by the Optimist Club in January 1977. It has restrooms, a covered pavilion, playground equipment, picnic facilities and wooded trails for leisure nature walks.

About 1981 an Industrial Park was created southwest of Highway 67 and Highway W by the Industrial Development Authority. It was renovated and the City Lake formed and stocked with several kinds of fish by the Missouri Department of Conservation. In 1985 it was

tire structure was clapboard covered. In time the house passed to a daughter, Mrs. G.H. Bisby (Jennie Long), who in 1927 willed it and surrounding land to the city of Farmington. After the city acquired the property it was used as a residence for the City Park Superintendent and during World War II as a day nursery for children of employed mothers of a local manufacturing company.

In 1935 a public swimming pool was started by the W.P.A. for $17,993, with a wading pool for small children added later. The pool opened on July 4, 1937, at 1:00 p.m.. The hours were 9:00 a.m. - 10:00 p.m. everyday. Cost was 10 cents for children and 15 cents for adults. Attendants were on hand in the dressing rooms to assist swimmers.

In the spring of 1951, the city decreed to raze the house. The Monday Club, a Federated Women's Club, protested and in the spring of 1952 offered to lease the house from the city until it could be determined how it could be saved as a place of historic interest.

Recently a large gazebo was built and today "Summer Concerts In the Park" provide entertainment throughout the summer.

Toward the front of the park, on Ste. Genevieve Avenue, is a pyramid of stones marking the spot where Phillip Long had his tannery. This marker was erected in the early 1920s with descendants of the Murphy and Long families each laying a stone. This park is known as Long Park and occasional tours are given of the historic Long House.

Hunting group

Ritz Theatre, c. 1930s. South side of courthouse on Columbia Street.

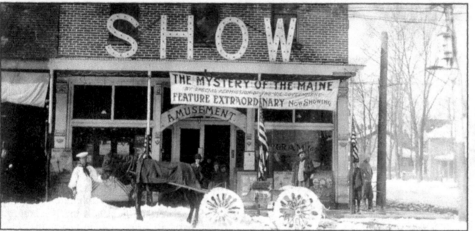

Brown Theater, corner of Jefferson and Liberty, now 214 Package Store.

The O'Sullivan sisters enjoy a relaxing moment.

opened to fishing. In 1987 a "Wiggle & Giggle" fishing contest was started for children of pre-school to 14 years of age. In 1989 under an agreement with the Department of Conservation, the Community Assistance Program was formed. At that time the program was set up so the city maintained the grounds and the Department of Conservation provided a fishing jetty, bathrooms and parking area. Also at that time the Department of Conservation officially began stocking the lake on an annual basis and provided guidelines regarding fishing regulations and use of the facility.

Three soccer fields were built nearby in 1995, all in use today.

About 1991 the Sports Complex off Ste. Genevieve Avenue was built. It features four lighted baseball/softball fields, with a playground area added later.

In 1998 Bicentennial Park, on the corner of West Columbia and First Streets, was developed by the city of Farmington, Chamber of Commerce and the Focus on Farmington Foundation, in cooperation with the Bicentennial Committee, the Missouri Department of Conservation, the Wal-Mart Foundation and many other private donors, both corporate and individual. Ornamental trees and flowers are planted among walks, and a fountain is to be placed in the center.

At present, a new park in the southern region of Farmington, near the East Industrial Park, is in early development. It is approximately 77 acres in size and includes the existing F.R. Crouch Bird Sanctuary. It will have walking/biking trails, athletic fields, picnic areas and traditional playgrounds.

The present Park and Recreation Department of Farmington consists of Bud Norman, director; Kevin Amonette, foreman; Tina Whaley, recreation programmer; Kevin Cross and Robert Sullivan. About 60 part-time employees are hired annually to assist the Parks and Recreation Department in providing its year-round recreational program for children, youth and adults.

Drummer's Convention sketch 1912.

BUSINESSES
AND
ORGANIZATIONS

(Pink) McCarver, Corb Huddleston, Horace Trautman and Clarence E. Morris in McCarver Saloon in 1895, became Carver Cafe then Capital Cafe, now home of Farmington Martial Arts.

FARMINGTON BUSINESS AND PROFESSIONAL WOMEN'S ORGANIZATION
Organized March 1930

Club Motto: Better Business Women For a
               Better Business World
Club Colors: Green and White - adopted 1937
Club Flower: Rose

    Federation Objectives: To elevate the standards for women in business and the professions; To promote the interests of business and professional women; To bring about a spirit of cooperation among business and professional women of the United States; To extend opportunities to business and profession women through education along lines of industrial, scientific and vocational activities.

Charter Members

Beulah Beatty	May Blaylock
Bessie Brady	Grace Bray
Jennie Carver	Ella Darnell
Myra Dobbins	Viola E. Fohrell
Mae Garner	Naomi Garner
Ruth Garner	Cecilia Gentges
Amanda Giessing	Marcia Lee Harter
Mrs. E.C. Holler	Mrs. Bertha Hughes
Mrs. L.M. Laakman	Effie C. Lawrence
Beulah Lindsey	Olla Lindsey
Geraldine McFarland	Mildred Meyer
Roberta Meyer	Blanche Moore
Edna Revoir	Frieda Revoir
Mary H. Roberts	Esther Rudloff
Nora Williams	

Past Presidents

Cecilia Gentges	1930-1932
Beulah Beatty	1934-1935
Genevieve Lang	1936-1937
Lulu Laakman	1940-1941
Cecile Politte	1944-1945
Amanda Giessing	1946-1947
Lodean Jenkins	1949-1950
Helen Meyer	1952-1953
Neta Schnieder	1954-1956
Leraun Baughn	1958-1960
Lodean Dugal	1962-1963
Isabelle Dixon	1965-1966
Lucille Ford	1967-1968
Fame Flippin	1970-1971
Beverly Hovis	1972-1974
Nora Williams	1932-1933
Naomi Garner	1935-1936
Marie Beatty	1939-1940
Bernice Coley	1942-1944
Lulu Laakman	1945-1946
Esther Rudloff	1947-1949
Clara Underwood	1950-1952
Helen Corken	1953-1954
Opal Wright	1956-1958
Fanny Knowles	1960-1962
Ruby Beard	1963-1965
Genevieve Lang	1966-1967
Nell Marie Cleve	1968-1970
Dr. Lois Ward	1971-1972
Dorothy Smith	1974-1975
Mary Ruth Moon	1975-1977

Fame Flippin	1979-1980
Pat Pigg	1982-1983
Moretta Davis	1984-1985
Linda Ray Showalter	1986-1987
Mary Ruth Moon	1988-1989
Kerry Glore	1990-1992
Sue Evans	1993-1994
Carol Faircloth	1995-1996
Peggy Ropelle	1997-1998
Helen Lent Baker	1977-1979
Karene Ray Hunt	1980-1982
Dorothy Smith	1983-1984
JoAnn Harrington	1985-1986
Delores Plummer	1987-1988
Ann Taylor	1989-1990
Cara Detring	1992-1993
Pamela Hart	1994-1995
Eileen McClanahan	1996-1997
Shelley Busch	1998-1999

Past Woman of the Year

Gloria Doss	Opal Wright
Cecilia Gentges	Marie Stewart
Dr. Lois Ward	Nell Marie Cleve
Lucille Ford	Dr. Norma Farmer
Beulah Garner	Dorothy Hunt
Nancy O'Neal	Bea Mayes
Genevieve Jones	Roberta McCreary
Letty Burris	Nora Merseal
Dorothy Smith	Esther Wilt
Margaret Clark	Karene Kay Hunt
Ann Taylor	Vesta Halter
Kerry Glore	Mary Ruth Moon
Delores Plummer	Sue Evans
Peggy Ropelle	Carol Faircloth
Pamela Hart	Mickie McClanahan
Eileen McClanahan	

Club Collect

Keep us, O God, from pettiness; let us be large in thought, in word, in deed. Let us be done with fault-finding and leave off self-seeking. May we put away all pretense and meet each other face to face without self-pity and without prejudice. May we never be hasty in judgement and always generous. Let us take time for all things; make us to grow calm, serene, gentle. Teach us to put into action our better impulses, straightforward and unafraid. Grant that we may realize it is the little things that create differences, that in the big things of life we are at one. And may we strive to touch and to know the great common human heart of us all, and O Lord God, let us forget not to be kind! Mary Stewart

Emblem Benediction

This Emblem binds us all in one great sisterhood. It bids us hear our conscious call for nobler womanhood. God guide us when we wear this Emblem o'er heart, and keep us true and always fair, God bless us as we part.

History

The Farmington Business and Professional Women's Organization began in 1930, with the first charter meeting being held at the St. Francois Hotel, formerly on Liberty Street. Twenty-seven members were chartered that first year and were

Cecilia Gentges

led by the first president, Cecilia Gentges, who currently resides in the Kansas City area.

The first charter was presented to the organization by Margaret Hickey of Miss Hickey's Secretarial School in St. Louis. Of the original membership, Roberta McCreary remained an active member until 1996 and Beulah Garner is the only remaining charter member of the Farmington LO. When the club was first organized, the membership was limited to 30 women. There was usually a waiting list. This has changed through the years with the membership being open to working women for a number of years. Within the past few years this has changed to an open membership to women and men who support the goals and objectives of BPW.

BPW has always been active in the community with various service projects. In the early 70s, the Farmington LO chaired a sidewalk survey for the city. They were involved in early, yet defeated, efforts to get a civic center in Farmington; in the mid-80s they, along with the Flat River BPW, started the day care at Mineral Area College; they have held three (3) Working Women's Affairs on the campus of MAC with such guest speakers as the late Mary Phelan of KMOV-TV, Dr. Debbye Turner, former Miss America, and Mrs. Betty Hearns, a former first lady of Missouri. In 1998 they actively supported a state-wide project, Operation Sweatsuit. The Farmington LO sends a representative to Girl's State each year and offers a scholarship to Mineral Area College.

In 1970 the LO began to recognize a woman in the community for her various activities and dedication to BPW. Opal Wright was the first recipient of this award and it has continued on through 1998. Another award they present is the "Employer of the Year" award. This goes to an employer who recognized the needs of their female employees and offers various programs/benefits for them.

The Farmington BPW has been active not only locally but has supported the district, state and national activities as well. Several members through the years have attended state and national conventions,

The monthly meeting is held at Plank Road Inn, 3rd Monday, at 6:00 p.m. Current membership is at 46.

FARMINGTON CHAMBER OF COMMERCE

Though the exact date om which the Chamber began as an organization is not known, records suggest that the Farmington Chamber of Commerce existed at least as early as 1926. Based in part on a need to attract significant industry to town, the Chamber was incorporated as a 501(c)6 organization in the state of Missouri on July 2, 1941.

The Chamber's first "office" was no more than a chair and a desk inside Stuart Landrum's insurance agency. Later, the Chamber occupied its first dedicated office at 2 W. Liberty Street. The Chamber then moved for a short period to a small corner office on the corner of N. Washington Street and Spring Street. Late in 1991 property and a building became available at 302 N. Washington (on the corner of Washington Street and College Street). The Chamber purchased this lot and the 1,000 square foot house on it from an auction on the courthouse steps. The building was renovated to provide space for a lobby/front office, director's office, meeting room and a kitchenette. The Chamber operated from this facility, which it had outgrown, until 1999. Plans call for the removal of the current building and the construction of a new facility on the original lot.

As the number of Chamber businesses and projects grew, managing the activities of the Chamber became a task beyond the ability of the volunteer president and board. Early staff members of the Chamber of Commerce included Mary Lee Hibbits, Harry Sailor, Sandy Groves, Jim Massie, Janet Douglas, Jack Masters, and Glenna Ratliff. Glenna served as the Chamber secretary for 15 years from 1977-

1992. In 1992, through a cooperative partnership with the city of Farmington, the Chamber hired its first full-time professional staff person, Laura Long. Under her direction, membership in the organization approximately doubled, allowing the Chamber more financial latitude to make the full-time professional position a permanent one. Laura (Kerr) Nicholson assumed the position of executive director of the Chamber in July 1995 and moved the organization to a new level of communications, technology and business services.

The mission of the Chamber is to take a leadership role in improving the economic environment and enhancing the quality of life of the Farmington area through the development and achievement of both short and long-term goals. This mission statement, substantially unchanged for nearly 60 years, has provided a backdrop for the Chamber's activities.

The acquisition of the Trimfoot Shoe Co., spearheaded by the Chamber, involved a unique land deal in which many individual citizens purchased parts of the plant site. Later in the 1950s, the Chamber successfully pushed for the development of Karsch Blvd. This development made a tremendous difference in the future of the community, allowing millions of dollars to be earned, spent, and sold along this short strip of road. The Chamber worked on many projects in the 60s and 70s. Among the most prominent are the Wabash Semi-Conductor Plant, the Puritan Shirt Factory, Matco and the Biltwell Plant. In 1979 the Chamber was the prime mover in the legislation to purchase the industrial park land from the state. In that same year the Chamber urged the city to hire a full-time, professional economic development specialist. The Chamber began its efforts on the acquisition of the prison and the expansion of the State Hospital (Southeast Mis-

souri Mental Health Center) in the mid-80s. These institutions, combined with the strong medical and educational systems, have made the local economy virtually "depression-proof" with their steady source of jobs and revenue. The Chamber's activities in the 90s could be best summed up by the word "partnership." A partnership between the Chamber and the city helped to attract another major industry, Huffy Bicycles, to Farmington. Similar partnerships have led to the creation of a new community park, initial development of a bicycle trail and concerted efforts to prepare for the future of this growing community.

Perhaps one of the most endearing traditions of the Chamber of Commerce is Country Days, a community promotion that began in 1978 on the suggestion of the Chamber's Retail Committee. Through the years, Country Days has grown to become one of the most popular festivals in the area, attracting thousands of visitors and featuring award-winning musical artists. Featured artists at Country Days have included The Oak Ridge Boys, Sawyer Brown, Dolly Parton, Aaron Tippin, Patty Loveless and Diamond Rio. Part of the success of this Farmington tradition must be credited to the leadership of the general chair (and co-founder) of the event, Willa Dean Meyer. Under Willa Dean's watchful eye, Country Days has grown and changed with the times while keeping its strong sense of history and tradition.

In 1995 the Chamber received word that its request for the formation of a charitable "sister" organization was tentatively approved by the IRS for a three year advanced ruling period. With this announcement, the Focus on Farmington Foundation began its work in the community. The Foundation, a charitable organization under section 501(c)3 of the IRS code, is organized to create opportunities that enhance the quality of life and preserve the traditions of the Farmington community. Projects of the Foundation have included funding equipment and scholarships for needy children to the Farmington Community Civic Center, providing funding for the development of Bicentennial Park, for the creation of a bike trail through Farmington and for the establishment of a transportation museum. The Focus on Farmington Foundation received word in May 1999 that it had received its official, permanent designation as a charitable organization.

Through the years no private organization has had a greater impact on the history and the quality of life in Farmington than the Chamber of Commerce. Much of the growth of the Farmington community can be attributed to the fact that the Chamber of Commerce has been blessed with an enthusiastic, forward-thinking group of volunteers who recognize that a strong community does not "just happen;" it must be created.

Farmington Chamber of Commerce

Kiwanis Club of Farmington

The first Kiwanis Club in St. Francois County, MO was founded on July 30, 1945, and held its first meeting on August 8, 1945. There were 30 members when the club held its Charter Night Dinner on September 19, 1945, at the Long Memorial Hall. Sponsors of the club were the Kiwanis Clubs of Sikeston and Cape Girardeau.

First officers were Berl J. Miller, president; the Rev. William T. Magill, vice-president; B.E. Caruthers, secretary; James J, Politte, treasurer. The first directors were: D.C. Curtis, Charles M. Kelley, Arlie McClard, the Rev. Fr. Robert E. McKeon, J.O. Swink, and B.F. Walther.

The club's 10th anniversary dinner was October 18, 1955, at the Memorial Methodist Church when Albert Karsch was president. The 20th anniversary dinner was on December 28, 1965, at the church when Harold Clark, president, was completing the unexpired term of Supt. P.J. Newell. The 25th silver anniversary dinner was held September 2, 1970, at the Empire Club during the presidency of Vinton G. Johnson. The Kiwanians held their 30th anniversary under Robert W. Dugal, president, on July 30, 1975, at the Bridlewood Club (formerly the Empire). The 35th anniversary was held on October 1, 1980, in the banquet room of Kentucky Fried Chicken in Leadington, MO. George H. Treaster was the incoming president. The 40th anniversary in 1985 was held at Plank Road Inn with R.G. Robinson Jr. as president. The 50th anniversary dinner was held on 1995 at Anderson's, Gene Denman was president.

Early fund raising activities for aiding underprivileged children in the community have included pancake days, variety shows, basketball tournaments, sale of peanut brittle, peanuts, popcorn, zip code directories, Christmas trees and gum machines in local stores. Variety shows, gum machines and the selling of peanuts, popcorn and zip code directories have given way to Ravioli Day, Radio Days and an annual golf tournament as a way of fund raising. Kiwanians still flip pancakes and sell Christmas trees once a year and talk of reviving the much loved and still talked about variety show.

Years ago the club bought telebinocular and audiometer machines for use in the schools and has given hospital equipment to Farmington Community Hospital (Parkland Health Center), the Mineral Area Osteopathic Hospital (MARMC) and funding for equipment at the University of Missouri Medical Center. The club erected a picnic shelter at Wilson-Rozier Park in 1955 and later donated $2,000 for a third tennis court at the same park.

Prizes were once awarded to boys growing the most bushels of corn to the acre and shoats given to the 4-H club and to the Future Farmers of America. The club began the first summer playground program at the county seat and paid all its expenses for several years.

Today the club awards scholarships to Mineral Area College, sends two high school students to Boys and Girls State, donates to Children's Haven, sponsors a student to HOBY (Hugh O'Brien Youth), pays the expenses for two campers at Kiwanis' Camp Wyman, sponsors Farmington's Wiggle 'n Giggle Fishing Day, and when needed helps with expenses of the Key Club at the Farmington High School. The local club also supports the International Kiwanis Club Worldwide Service Project, in the hope of abolishing iodine deficiency disorder worldwide. These are just a few individuals, groups and events which the Farmington Kiwanis Club sponsors today.

Current officers for the 1998/99 year are: Lynn Crites, president; Dennis Scanga, president elect; Marvin Hahn, vice-president; Keith Bishop, treasurer; Floyd Becker, secretary; Tim Hankins, immediate past president.

Board Members are Dan Combs, Laura Nicholson, Tony Miano, Don Pierson, Cary Flanagan, Mark Griggs and Jeffrey Allison.

Tom Fitz as Groucho

Kiwanis Review

St. Francois, MO Lodge #48 IOOF

St. Francois Lodge #48, IOOF, Farmington, was instituted on October 7, 1850. Lodge met over J.D. Peer's Store. His son, born September 2, 1825, was the first Noble Grand and is buried in the Masonic Cemetery. The lodge met at 6 1/2 o'clock (not 6:30 p.m.). In 1867 the Lodge moved to a building diagonally across the street from the First State Bank. In the early days there weren't many banks and the lodge made loans to members and others also. In 1893 they purchased the old J.D. Peers home, located where the Ozark Federal Savings and Loan is now, for $5,000. A three-story building was erected for $13,500 in 1894. City Drug Store occupied the corner; next to it was a Variety Store. Over the years it had many tenants. Beginning in 1903; the second floor was occupied for many years by the Ozark Business University (The Moothart School). Later it housed a movie theater, the Missouri National Guard in the 1930s, the Elks Lodge, the Knights of Pythias Lodge and a Boy Scout Troop. The IOOF Lodge met and conducted their business on the third floor. On March 27, 1861, the Odd Fellow Cemetery was purchased from Mr. and Mrs. Dale Evans for $37.50. Farmington Rebekah Lodge No. 407 was instituted on January 16, 1904, and meets in the lodge. The following Liberty lodges have consolidated with St. Francois Lodge No. 48: Libertyville, Knob Lick, Doe Run, DeSoto, Yount and Bonne Terre. In 1962 the lodge building was sold to Ozarks Federal Savings and Loan. The lodge moved in 1966 to the present building at 110 South Washington (previously the National Guard Armory). Currently it is the meeting place for other branches of the Order: Encampment, Ladies Encampment Auxiliary, Patriarchs Militant and Ladies Auxiliaries Patriarchs Militant.

Some Odd Fellow projects and benefits are as follows: largest non-corporate contributor to the Arthritis Foundation, funds a chair at John Hopkins Visual Research Center in Baltimore, has sent youth to the United Nations Pilgrimage for Youth for 50 years, has provided financial support to help some older members remain in their homes. The oldest project, the Education Foundation, the IOOF maintains is the International Peace Garden on the border of North Dakota and Canada; IOOF is a family fraternity whose motto is Friendship, Love and Truth and its Objective is to improve and elevate the Character of Mankind. Odd Fellows are active in 24 countries.

History of Sarah Barton Murphy Chapter, DAR

The National Society, Daughters of the American Revolution, was founded in 1891 in Washington D.C. with the motto "God, Home and Country." They were dedicated to keeping alive the memory of the soldiers and patriots who fought for the freedom of our country from England during the American Revolution. President Benjamin Harrison's wife served as the first president general and lent prestige and credibility to the new organization.

Odd Fellows Building

The Sarah Barton Murphy Chapter, Daughters of the American Revolution, was organized in Farmington March 11, 1914, with 23 charter members. Through the years the chapter has been active in civic affairs, trying to carry out the objectives of the National Society: Historic, Educational and Patriotic.

The Sarah Barton Murphy Chapter was named after Reverend William Murphy's second wife, who after her husband's death, followed her sons to the newly established village known then as "Murphy's Settlement." She was a great help and inspiration to the fledgling community, serving as Sunday School teacher, judge and sometime mediator to the surrounding area. The new chapter felt it was a fitting tribute to give the new chapter the name of Sarah Barton Murphy.

In 1915 Sarah Barton Murphy Chapter marked the graves of three Revolutionary War soldiers buried in St. Francois County—William and Joseph Murphy (sons of Reverend William Murphy and his first wife, Martha Hedges) and James Cunningham. In 1916 on Flag Day, they marked the grave of Revolutionary War soldier, James Caldwell. In the ensuing years James Cunningham's grave has been lost. James Caldwell's remains were removed from his burial place inside the city to Parkview Cemetery northeast of Farmington. Joseph Murphy's remains were removed in the 1930s from his burial place on the old Bressie farm near Flat River, MO, to the Masonic Cemetery next to the grave of his half-brother, David Murphy. William Murphy rests in the small Murphy Cemetery southeast of Farmington.

In October 1992 Sarah Barton Murphy Chapter rededicated the grave of Sarah Smith Stringer, Missouri's only REAL daughter. A Real daughter of the DAR is the child of a revolutionary War soldier. Sarah was born in 1821 and died in 1915, just one year after becoming a DAR member. She is buried in Bismarck, MO.

Sarah Barton Murphy Chapter has always believed that the key to the future of our country is education. They have helped support the DAR public and private schools, helped foster the doctrine of good citizenship in our students, worked to erase illiteracy in our adults, encouraged Americanization of our newest citizens and encouraged patriotism in all.

The chapter has grown steadily through the years because of two basic principles: Accomplishment and Service. Sarah Barton Murphy Chapter can look back over 84 years of service to the Farmington area and to the nation. They have tried to make a "lasting difference." When the National Society, Daughters of the American Revolution calls on its chapters to do the seemingly impossible, Sarah Barton Murphy Chapter rises to the challenge. *Written by Mrs. William (Irene) Murdick.*

FARMINGTON LIONS CLUB

The Farmington Lions Club was chartered in 1962 under the leadership of Don Sanders. Since that time we have had 37 presidents to lead this club:

1961-62	Don Sanders
1962-63	John Whitworth
1963-64	Paul Dugal
1964-65	Walter Giessing
1965-66	P.C. Reynierse
1966-67	W. Cannon Kinard
1967-68	Don Alexander
1968-69	Ernie Jones
1969-70	Gene Thompson
1970-71	Maurice Harrington
1971-72	John Wyatt
1972-73	Ralph Parks
1973-74	Danny Alcorn
1974-75	Ross McCarley
1975-76	Marvin Dobbs
1976-77	John Martin
1977-78	William Allen
1978-79	J.L. Seal
1979-80	John Crouch
1980-81	Marshall James
1981-82	Dave Gillispie
1982-83	Lee Roy Nichols
1983-84	Dr. Charles Rore
1984-85	Jim Dow
1985-86	John Wyatt
1986-87	Kevin Cook
1987-88	David Braun
1988-89	Dr Dennis Suhrzski
1989-90	Dr. Evan Williams
1990-91	Steve Marler
1991-92	Chuck Deleal
1992-93	Kevin Engler
1993-94	Tom Hampton
1994-95	David Holman
1995-96	Tom Hill
1996-97	Bill Eaton
1997-98	Guy Roberts
1998-99	John Ratliff
1999-00	John Denkler

Our Lions Club has a current membership of 44 members, who meet weekly at Plank Road Inn for a breakfast meeting starting at 7:00 a.m. each Tuesday.

Service Activities

•Sight First: Lions Conquering blindness. Its aim is nothing less than the elimination of preventable and reversible blindness around the world.

•Lions Youth Outreach: Changing tomorrow today. Its objective is to help young people develop essential life and citizenship skills such as sound judgment, self discipline, acceptance of responsibility, ability to communicate with various age groups, ability to get along with others, critical decision-making ability with regard to drugs and alcohol and a desire to serve others.

•Hearing and Speech Action And Work With The Deaf
  •Environmental Services
  •The Leo Club program
  •Youth Exchange
  •International Relations

Lions RECYCLE For Sight

Cans, bottles, paper. Recycling has become a routine part of our lives. But there is another item you can recycle that can benefit someone living in a developing country. **Recycle your used eyeglasses.**

Millions of people have little chance for receiving the eye care they need. By donating your old eyeglasses and sunglasses you can help improve a person's vision and possibly change their life. Join your local Lions in their Recycle For Sight effort by bringing your old glasses to:

For more information, contact:

We Serve

FARMINGTON ROTARY CLUB

The Farmington Rotary Club traces its beginnings to the cold dark days of the Great Depression when 23 community leaders of the town gathered together in February 1934 to form the city's first service club. Charter members were: R.L. Boswell, W.T. Coghill, C.M. Dearing, Edward B. Effrein, Arnold A. Gieringer, C.C. Gower, Marcus Kirkland, H.W. Manley, John A. Neidert, Raymond S. Roberts, L.K. Rosser, Floyd Eugene Carroll, Frank Q. Crockett, Harry Denman, J.M. Foxx, Theodore J. Giessing, W.L. Johns, E.J. McKinney Jr., J.H. Miller, John M. Roberts, John B. Robinson, C.C. Schuttler, and Dr. Lee M. Stanfield.

The guiding force behind the new club was Dr. Lee M. Stanfield, a former Rotarian from Ferry, OK, and a native of St. Francois County. He was assisted by C.C. Gower, Marcus Kirkland and Harry Denman. The first officers were: Frank Q. Crockett, president; Marcus Kirkland, vice president; C.C. Gower, secretary; Dr. Lee M. Stanfield, program chairman; and Theodore J, Giessing, director.

The charter, No. 3653, was presented to the club on March 9, 1934, at a special ceremony held at the Lutheran School Hall. The principal speaker of the evening was past district governor, William H. Barnes of Clayton. Rotarians from Fredericktown served as the sponsoring club and their president, N.W. Parkin, acted as master of ceremonies.

Despite the winter snow and stormy weather that evening, 175 persons attended the festivities, including 106 Rotarians and their wives from nine neighboring cities. The new club flourished from the very beginning, boasting a total of 34 members at the end of its first year.

Since its founding, a number of Rotarians have been highly active in the activities of Rotary and Rotary International. One of the most outstanding was Lawrence M. Burns (1900-1981).

Larry served as club president in 1960-1961; district governor in 1961-1962, and club secretary 1970-1973. He started the *Kernel* bulletin in 1967 and continued as its editor and publisher until 1979. He was a strong backer of the Rotary Foundation, which is involved in many activities on an international level. Under his leadership, Jon Cozean, a Rotarian since 1984, was named a Rotary Fellow in 1960 to receive a scholarship to study a full year in Ecuador in 1961-1962. In 1978 Larry was the first member of the Farmington club to be named a Paul Harris Fellow, which is a high honor for Rotarians worldwide.

Other outstanding Rotarians who were highly active in the club over the years include: Bill Dicus, Dr. Fred A. Walker, Wayne R. Sheets, Drexel Chapman, Timon I. Romburg, Paul Lober, Ted Westmeyer, Allen Hensley, Frank Zieba, Gregory Westover and Ben Lewis. Dr. Emmett F. Hoctor, long-time superintendent of the old State Hospital No. 4, was an honorary member of the club.

The Farmington club has been involved in many activities over the years to further the goals of Rotary. From the beginning the club has frequently attended inter-city meetings with other area Rotary Clubs, including those at Bonne

Rotary Club 1944-45

Rotarian Larry Burns

Terre, Fredericktown, Ste. Genevieve, Ironton, Flat River (Park Hills), Jackson and Cape Girardeau. The Farmington Rotary Club has also participated in joint activities with other area service clubs as well. For example, in 1955 the club helped to celebrate the Golden Anniversary of Rotary International by hosting a dinner for members of the Farmington Kiwanis Club. Each guest at the dinner was presented with a golden copy of The Rotarian. Later in that year a number of members and their wives traveled to Chicago, the birthplace of Rotary, to join with 200,000 other Rotarians from around the world in celebrating the founding of the first club.

A major feature of the Farmington Club has been sponsorship of the annual Rotary auction. Now in its 47th year, this fund raiser helps support the various activities that the club sponsors each year, including a scholarship for a needy student from Farmington High School to attend

Mineral Area College, awards for winners in the 4-H competition at the county fair and numerous other activities. In addition, the club has also supported numerous programs sponsored by Rotary International. Several years ago the Farmington Club raised $5,000 to help fund a multi-million dollar program called "Polio Plus" to help eradicate polio and other diseases from the world. Run in conjunction with the World Health Organization, the program helped immunize millions of children in Third World countries against these widespread diseases. In addition, the Farmington Club has been involved with many exchanges of students and businessmen and women from all parts of the world. These programs have helped to promote international understanding and cooperation.

Present officers of the Farmington Rotary Club are Harold Hastings, president, Ed Perez, vice president, and Don Gann, secretary.

Business Licenses Issued In Farmington, MO, 1859

P.H. Gooch	Dram Shop License
John A. Weber	Merchants License
John A. Weber	Billard Table License
Robert D. Clay	Merchants License
M.P. Cayce	Merchants License
John B. Fleming	Dram Shop License
Douthit & Son	Merchants License
L.K. Peers	Merchants License
J.J. Helber & Co.	Merchants License
Ross Jelkyl	Merchants License
J.J. Brady	Merchants License

Businesses Before 1900

Information taken from letterheads, receipts etc.

Milling Companies

Cayce and Weber	Farmington Flouring Mills
S.S. BOYCE	Farmington Flouring Mills S.S. Boyce and I.H. Rodehaver
Giessing and Brother	Farmington Roller Mills
Giessing Milling Co.	Regulator Roller Mills
Morris Rosenthal	St. Francois County Roller Mills
F. Reuter and Son	St. Francois County Roller Mills

Blacksmiths and Wagon Manufacturing

Hermann and Herbst	General Blacksmiths
Adam Schmitt	Blacksmith and Wagon Maker
Gay and Iseman	Blacksmith and Wagon Maker
Kollmeyer and Neidert	Blacksmith Wagon Maker and Undertaker
Lang and Brother	Wagons, Carriages, Plows and Lumber

General Merchandise

Boyd Merchantile Co.	Gen. Mdse., Hay Grain and Produce
M.P. Cayce and Son	Gen. Mdse
J.A. Weber and Sons	Gen. Mdse. Dry Goods, Notions, Liquors
Smith and Terell	Groceries, Clothing, Shoes, Hardware, Notions Gen. Mdse.
Morris Rosenthal	General Mdse.
Falk and Rosenthal	Groceries, Dry Goods, Shoes, Clothing
George Eisenberg	Saddlery, Hides, Wool, and Tallow
Simon Jacobson	Groceries, Clothing, Shoes
Miss S.E. Baxter	Millenary and Fancy Goods
A. Kugel	General Mdse.
A.J. Leathers	General Mdse.
Conrad Markert	Butcher and Curer
A. Retornaz	Hardware, Stoves, Tinware, Roofing, Paints

John Iseman	Lumber, Shingles, Building Material
S.S. Smith and Sons	Hatters and Furnishers
Haile Brothers & Martin	General Mdse. Clothing
Valentine C. Peers & Co.	General Mdse.

Businesses in Farmington 1900-1920s

Mayberry & Highley	Star Livery And Feed Stable
Coffman Brothers	Livery And Feed Stable
Perry B. McCormack	City Livery Feed And Sale Stable
Mayberry Byington And Tullock	City Livery Stable
Clarence W. Young	Livery And Feed Stable
T.W. Woodard	Livery Feed And Sale Stable
Tetley Klein Lumber Co.	Lumber, Hardware, Paints, Etc.
D. J. Doughty	Hardware, Sash, Doors, Paint, Etc.
Charles Hilliker & Son	House, Sign & Decorative Painter
Harry Dobbins	Tinner
Thompson And Russell	Plumbing And Heating Contractor
McCarthy	Lumber And Construction Co.
Wesley Pratt	Painter And Decorator
A.H. Hemmelgarn	Gen. Contractor, Builder, Concrete Work
Farmington Merchantile Co.	Gen. Merchandise
George Herzog	Boots And Shoes
Fisher Merchantile Co.	Gen. Merchandise
Henderson Merchantile Co.	Gen. Merchandise
John M. Karsch	Boots And Shoes
McCormick Sprott & Co.	Gen Merchandise
Maude F. Highley	Millenery, Stylish Hats, Novelties
Cole And Nixon Merchantile Co.	Gen. Merchandise
City Drug Store	Drugs, Novelties, Etc.
McCormick Drug Co.	Manufacturers of Pharmaceuticals
E.M. Lackman	Drugs, Medicines, Paint, Glass, Etc.
Morris Brothers	General Merchandise
W.R. Watts	Contractor And Builder
Grand Leader Merchantile Co.	General Merchandise

Some Of The Businesses In 1925

Editor's Note: The following business descriptions taken from the book "Message to the Homemaker."

Farmer's Bank

The bank was organized in 1904. It occupies the ground floor of its own substantial brick building which is situated on the southwest corner of the square.

OFFICERS: P.A. Shaw, president; G.B. Snider, active vice-president; W.C. Fischer, vice-president; L.H. William's, cashier.

DIRECTORS: Wm. C. Fischer, F.W. Schramm, Wm. London, G.B. Snider, C.B. Denman, P.A. Shaw, L.H. William's.

Farmington Milling Company

This mill was established many years ago and has almost always filled every need of the public in its town and field. The present owners assumed control in 1882. The leading brands of flour are; Farmilco, Golden Rod, Soft Wheat and Stag. John Giessing, president; J.E. Giessing, vice-president; and C.H. Giessing, secretary and treasurer.

Klein Grocer Company

This firm opened its doors for business in 1880. It has always followed the policy of handling the best groceries and selling same at rock-bottom prices. They carry an immense stock of staple and fancy groceries, fruits, vegetables and produce and furnish prompt and reliable service at all times. Goods are delivered to any part of the city. This business is located on East Columbia Street and under the efficient management of H.W. Manley.

Bank Of Farmington

The Bank of Farmington opened its doors for business in 1886 and is the oldest bank in the county. It is located on the southeast corner

Farmington Milling truck

Cayce and Son, first large department store.

Klein's Grocery, outside.

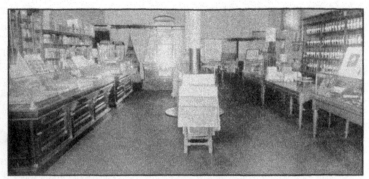

Inside City Drug Store, 1904.

Klein's Grocery changing hands to Dugal's.

Thomas Lang, founder of Lang Brothers Wagonmakers.

Drawing of Lang & Brothers, Columbia Street and Main Street.

of the public square. It is equipped with fire-and-burglar proof safe and vault, fire and burglar insurance is carried and depositors' money is otherwise fully protected from loss through any cause whatsoever. The officers are: H.W. Harlan,president; W.R. Lang, vice-president; M.P. Cayce, cashier; S.F. Isenman, asst. cashier. The directors are as followers: W.R. Lang, K.C. Weber, W.M. Harlan, Peter Giessing, M.P. Cayce, W.F. Doss and J.E. Klein.

Lang & Brother Manufacturing And Mercantile Company

Located on East Columbia Street it was back in 1865 when this enterprise was started in a small way. It has grown gradually, but steadily keeping even pace with the progress of the community and is today recognized as one of the greatest industries in the county. This enterprise is devoted to the manufacture of the famous Lang wagons and farm imple-

ments, also doors, window frames and truck bodies. They also do an extensive business in the sale of lumber and building material. This company was incorporated in 1903 and has a capital stock of $100,000. W.R. Lang is secretary and manager.

Karsch's Shoe Store

One of Farmington's oldest businesses was the boot and shoe factory of John Michael Karsch who was born in Germany in 1846. After coming to the county-seat as a young boy, he later became an apprentice shoemaker at Valley Forge, east of Farmington. In 1871 he purchased the shoe shop of Mike Bieser and began his own business on the site west of Dugal's. In 1883 he built a brick building to the east of Dugal's. After Karsch's death in 1901, his business was carried on for years as a retail shoe store by four of his eight sons. In 1974 the two buildings burned on October 4, 1974, and were rebuilt by Mr. and Mrs. Leo Dugal.

City Drug Store

The people of Farmington demand the best of everything and so far as their wants in the line of drugs and allied specialties is concerned, the City Drug Store, located on the southeast corner of the square, meets every requirement in its large and growing field. The business was first started in a small frame building which was located where the Bank of Farmington now stands, and was moved to its present location in 1894. The store is a model of neatness, good taste and convenience and the stock carried is the largest in the city. E.J. Lawrence and C.Y. White are the owners of this business.

Giessing Milling Company

They are manufacturers of high grade winter wheat flour which is sold locally and shipped to other sections of the country. Two of their special and celebrated brands are "Pearl" a self-rising flour and "Giessing's High Patent," both of these brands have been on the market for years. This industry is located at the corner of East College and North Washington Streets. It is one of the pioneer industries of the country, having been in operation since 1860. Officers are: Peter Giessing, president; Henry Giessing, vice-president; and D.F. Giessing, secretary and treasurer.

Robert Tetley Jewelry Company

This business was established by the late Robert Tetley back in 1868 and has long been a leader in its line of jewelry. It is owned by the estate of Mr. Tetley and managed by his son G.A. Tetley. The store carries a full line of diamonds, watches, clocks, silverware, sewing machines, and attachments, musical instruments, etc. They also maintain a well-equipped watch, clock, and jewelry repair department under the personal supervision of Mr. Tetley.

Helber Hardware Store

One of the pioneer retail houses of the city, this business was established more than 50 years ago, and three years ago it passed into the hands of C.E. Carlton. This store carries a well selected line of staple hardware, furniture, stoves, sporting goods, toys, crockery and household necessities. The business is housed in a brick building located at 218 East Columbia Street.

Gierse's Cleaning Works

Many of the most careful dressers of Farmington have their clothes cleaned and pressed by Gierse's Cleaning Works. Located on West Columbia Street this firm has been in operation since 1882. They do dry, chemical and steam cleaning; pressing and repairing, and high grade tailoring. They recently installed a new odorless, continuous flow clarifier which puts clothing to be cleaned through 20 baths of clean, fresh naphtha before they call it cleaned. The active head of this firm is Fred J. Gierse.

Fitz Chevrolet Company - 1939

Among the greatest motor sales and service firms in the Lead Belt is the Fitz Chevrolet Company, dealers in the world famous Chevrolet six automobiles, genuine Chevrolet parts, accessories, tires, batteries, etc., with well-equipped service department in connection. Most automobiles are sold, but the new 1939 Chevrolet is bought. It represents a combination of beauty, utility and speed and long life not commonly found in cars selling at anything near its price. This firm has some exceptional bargains in good used cars; they are offered at low prices and on favorable terms. Another feature of the concern is a modern service department with factory-trained

Bank of Farmington on Washington Street faces west and the court house, 1897.

Karsch's Shoe Store 1883.

Inside the Farmington Bank.

Giessing and Brothers Mill

Helber Hardware

Giessing Milling Company

mechanics of the highest ability. The active head of this firm is C.S. Fitz, who purchased the business in 1936. He is one of the most alert and progressive men that Farmington has ever had. He has a reputation for honesty and fair dealing and being among the first to lend his support to measures to benefit the community.

Farmington Laundry 1939

This is one of our pioneer industries, having been incorporated in 1908, and has been

Gierse's Cleaners delivery wagon.

under the present ownership since 1914. It is without doubt one of the largest, most modernly equipped and most efficiently conducted laundries to be found anywhere in the smaller cities of Missouri. The business is housed in a brick structure which is adapted for the purpose it was intended. This laundry not only serves the city of Farmington, but draws business from the Lead Belt, having a fleet of trucks which cover Bismarck, Flat River, Desloge, Ironton, St. Genevieve, Bonne Terre, Crystal City and Festus. The Farmington Laundry furnishes employment to about 25 employees and its payroll is important to the local economy. The president and manager of the laundry is B.T. Gentges, a man of business ability and high integrity and always ready to support projects for the benefit of his home city.

The *Missouri Argus* And Other Interesting Old Newspapers

The *Missouri Argus* was only four pages in length and all printed at home. The page size was 12 1/2 x 18 1/2 inches and the paper used was of full-rag content. The paper contained quite a lot of reading matter, but not a line of

local news excepting that which was contained in the advertisements of which there were surprisingly large numbers. There were no local news items, no births, no marriages, no deaths and not even on the Civil War in so far as one could determine by the reading matter content of the paper unless it would be deducted from a reading of President Lincoln's Emancipation Proclamation. The paper's reading matter contained such things as a column-long poem entitled *Red Hot Lines on an Old School House* and stories *on Interesting Discoveries of Pompeii, The Emancipation Proclamation*, and the Minutes of the Third Annual Meeting of the Missouri Association of United Baptists held at Mt. Pleasant Church in Iron County, on October 10, 1862.

The printing office of the *Argus* was located on the east side of the public square one door north of the Farmington Hotel. The hotel was on the corner where the Reality Building now stands and was a combination log and frame house. Mercantile Bank's parking lot now occupies this space. The paper was published every Thursday by J.H. Brady with Hoe H. Brady and Val C. Rucker as compositors. The subscription rates announced were $1 per

Frank Gierse Merchant Tailor. Father, Frank Gierse; Mother, Mathilda Gierse; Children, Charles and Fred; Tailors, Joe Rimmelin, Henry Springmeyer, Charley Reuter and George Cleve.

P.T. Pigg

Farmington Laundry 1908.

Farmington Laundry, now Mid-State Laundry.

year if paid in advance, or $1.50 if paid at the end of six months and $2 if paid at the end of the year. Advertising rates were .50 an inch with a graduated reduction for repeat insertions.

The *Southeast Missouri Argus* was established by Nichol, Crowell and Shuck. This paper was published in 1860 and from accounts given in the book, *History of Missouri*, this paper was still active in 1880. In 1889 the paper was renamed *The Herald* and in 1892 it was moved to DeSoto.

The *New Era* newspaper. which began publication at Libertyville, was removed to Farmington in 1876 and to Marble Hill in 1876.

In 1872 *The Times* was started by C.E. Ware

Bill Hall's Station

Late 1880s, shipping out an order of wagons to Mississippi County, Missouri.

St. Francois Hotel

Laakman's Drug Store

Burnett Meat Market, 1925, location unknown.

Lloyd & Mayberry Stables in 1897, located behind Braun Hotel, corner of Jefferson and Harrison, now parking lot across from the Fire Station.

Braun Hotel, corner of Columbia and Jefferson St.

and J. Rodehaver. It was later published by Theodore D. Fisher.

The News was established in 1883 by P.T. Pigg and *The Herald* was established in 1886 by Isaac Rodehaver.

Tetley Jewelry Store

By 1911 the only newspapers listed in the Missouri Blue Book were *The Farmington Times* published weekly by Times Printing Company, *The Farmington News*, published weekly by Harry & Clint Denman and *The St. Francois County Republican* published by T.P. Pigg.

Tetley Jewelry Store

In 1852 John and Elizabeth Babbington Tetley and family left their native home at Derbyshire, England and came to Boston, MA. Their parents returned to England but six of their children, three boys and three girls, remained in the United States. The three sons, George, John and Robert, came west to Washington County, MO. John and Robert came to Farmington about 1862, where they met and married daughters of William J. Gay.

The Gay family, William T. and his wife Selina Down and four children, left Devonshire,

England and immigrated to America in 1852, taking passage to Liverpool, landing in New York after a long and dangerous ocean voyage. From there they went to Belevue, OH where Mrs. Gay's sister lived. After nine years they came to St. Francois County, where he purchased a farm. The father followed his trade making wagons, buggies, plows, grain cradles and all types of farming implements. In 1871 he became the partner of Isenman and from that time this partnership was known as Gay & Isenman.

In May 1880 their business was completely destroyed by fire with no insurance and a loss of about $6,000. They rebuilt and continued until the death of William T. Gay in February 1884. William T. and Sam, the two sons, followed their father's trade and began a wagon-making business at Ironton. Sam's son, Dr. Roger Gay, and his two grandsons, Dr. Le Pettit Gay and Dr. George Gay, became well-known physicians in Missouri.

John Tetley also known as Jack, married Martha Gay and settled on a farm south of Farmington. Their lovely farm home was located at the intersection of Highways H and AA. During the time that Sam Hildebrand was so active, it was not unusual for the Jack Tetleys to find his horse in their barn and one of theirs gone, the cot on the porch had been used, food from the kitchen gone and a piece of money on the table. The Tetleys never did see Sam.

Jack and Martha Tetley were the parents of three girls and two boys. Many of their descendants still live in the community today.

Robert T. Tetley married Ann Gay in 1867. Soon after their marriage, they built the Tetley Jewelry Store building, which was also the birthplace and home of all their children. At the death of Robert Tetley, his son, George, continued to operate the jewelry store until his death in 1946. The business was sold; but the grandson, Howard Tetley, opened his jewelry store down the street on east Columbia. There has been a Tetley Jewelry Store in Farmington from 1869 to 1977 when Howard sold his store to William Krekeler.

Henry, the oldest son, was a watchmaker and worked in the store with his father and brother, George. Sam and his brother-in-law, Emil Klein husband of Elizabeth, operated the Tetley-Klein Lumber Company for 30 years until the death of Mr. Tetley.

Elizabeth married Emil Klein, one of the two brothers who founded Klein Grocery Store, now Dugal's. William moved to St. Louis where he was a jewelry salesman. Clarence, the youngest son, was a dentist and at the time of his death, had been a well-known mayor of Farmington. He was instrumental in bringing the Rice-Stix factory to Farmington.

By Ann Caroline Tetley, article from the *Evening Press,* March 19, 1979

Neidert Undertaking Company

Adam Neidert, who founded the A. Neidert Undertaking Company, was among the earliest regularly licensed embalmers in the

Inside Tetley Jewelry Store.

Telephone company, 1902.

Thought to be one of the first businesses in Farmington, Rottger City Bakery and Confectionery as it was being torn down. Believed to be located across from the court house where the Black Crow is today.

Opening day ceremonies for Liberty Loan held on the courthouse lawn with the gazebo in the background.

state of Missouri, entering the business under license in 1895. The original structure in which the business began was located on Spring Street. The business was moved to Columbia and Franklin Street in 1897. The original structure was one story.

John A. Neidert, after childhood and young manhood spent in close association with his father, Adam Neidert, joined the business in 1913. In 1915 the original building at the present location was remodeled, modernized and made into a two-story structure of brick. With the advancing age of Adam Neidert, more of the management of the business was assumed by John A. Neidert, until, in 1919, sole ownership was acquired by John and the name changed to Neidert Undertaking Company.

In 1940 Berl J. Miller bought the funeral home from John A. Neidert. Mr. Miller, originally from Perryville, bought one-quarter of the business in 1939. When Mr. Neidert decided to retire from business, Mr. Miller was given first chance to buy out his share and quickly agreed to do so. With the new ownership Mr. Miller made some changes to his funeral home. Tearing down the front porch and painting the entire building white were two major changes. He also converted the front office into a reception room and made several minor changes as well.

Mr. Neidert and his family moved into the residence at 311 West College, where Mr. Miller and his family had been living. The latter and his family moved into the apartment on the second floor of the funeral home.

Berl Miller and his wife, Juanita, remained the owners and operators of Miller Funeral Home until 1978 when he sold the business to David Taylor, a former employee of the funeral home. Mr. Miller retired from the funeral business after 45 years, but remained in an advisory capacity.

CAMELOT NURSING CENTER

Camelot Nursing Center was founded in 1981 by three business partners: Lee Mitchem, Kelso Ballantyne and Robert Huckstep.

Dr. Robert Huckstep took an active part in Camelot throughout the years as medical director until he passed away in November of 1992. He moved to this area in spring of 1955

Camelot Nursing Home

and opened up a private practice in June. He was married to Mary Huckstep for 48 years and they have three children: David Robert, Carol Sue and Stephan Charles. Dr. Huckstep took an active roll in our community and belonged to several organizations: AMA, American Medical Association, Internal Medicine, Farmington School Board, Board of Trustees at Mineral Area College and Kiwanis. Dr. Huckstep retired from private practice in 1984. During his retirement he worked at the state hospital for a while.

Camelot's executive director, Barbara Boyd, has been with Camelot for 16-1/2 years. She is married to George Boyd, who is currently juvenile officer 24th Judicial Circuit. Their daughter, Barbara is married and lives in Cape Girardeau with husband and two children. Their son, Brian, is currently attending Mineral Area College. Their son, Mike is attending Farmington High School. Barbara also held the position as Director of Nurses. She has been in the Farmington area for 40 years. She graduated from Mineral Area College RN with an associate degree and was also in the Mineral Area College LPN program.

Camelot is dedicated to meeting the needs of the community. Over the years we have expanded to include a complete therapy unit.

Dr. Robert Huckstep, began Camelot Nursing Home.

Camelot is there for short-term stays as well as long term plans and we take great pride in our longevity of staff members.

COZEAN FUNERAL HOME

Cozean Funeral Home is one of the oldest mortuary establishments in Missouri. Organized in 1864 by Thomas Lang, one of Farmington's outstanding leaders during the 19th century, the firm was a sideline of Lang's better known wagon manufacturing business. During the firm's early history, Lang largely assisted area families by providing embalming services and caskets manufactured at his wagon plant.

As Farmington continued to grow, Lang decided to inaugurate the region's first full-service funeral home in 1889. Lang died in 1903, but the family continued to operate the funeral business. In 1912 the mortuary was moved from the wagon works to the new Tetley Building on Columbia Street. Two years later the firm was sold to Henry Rinke, a pioneer embalmer and community leader at Flat River. In 1916 Rinke sold Farmington Undertaking Co. to his daughter and son-in-law, Elva and Rolla Cozean. In 1930 the firm expanded its operation when it was moved to a large graceful dwelling on North Washington Street. During the 1930s and 1940s, a mainstay of the firm was Elva Cozean, who often coordinated the many aspects of the firm's operations.

The need for additional space prompted the business to move in 1940 to its present location on West Columbia Street. In 1943 ownership of the firm passed to Charles Hugo Cozean, who continued to expand the business and its facility over the next 40 years. During his years with the firm Hugo served as president of the Southeast Missouri Funeral Directors Association and later as chairman of the State Board of Funeral Directors and Embalmers. Following his death in 1982, the business has been operated by his son, Jon, who represents the fourth generation of the family's commitment to Farmington Undertaking Company. During 1993-1994 the firm's building was remodeled and enlarged, making it the largest funeral facility in this part of the state.

Over the years the firm has been known for innovation. It introduced the area's first motor driven hearse and later the first Cadillac hearse. It was the first area funeral home to use air conditioning, electronic organs and computers. For more than 40 years beginning in 1925, the firm employed Nellie Harter, the first female embalmer in southeast Missouri and one of the first to be licensed in the state. In 1992 Cozean Funeral Home was elected to membership in the International Order of the Golden Rule, an organization of leading independent funeral homes in the United States and abroad. The firm has also been actively involved with the Associated Funeral Directors Association, an international organization serving selected funeral homes, for more than half a century. Every three years the firm participates in the Civil War re-enactment at Pilot Knob. where its unique 1844 horse-drawn hearse is displayed while staff members, dressed in authentic period clothes, give lectures on funeral practices in the mid-1800s. For the past five years Jon Cozean has represented southeast Missouri on the board of directors of the Missouri Funeral Directors Association. In 1997 Cozean Funeral Home was recognized for its long tradition of service in the area with a special "tradition and progress" award by the Farmington Chamber of Commerce.

Cozean Funeral Home as it appeared between 1940 and 1956.

The first Cadillac hearse in St. Francois county was a 1941 model shown in front of the Cozean Funeral Home in 1947.

Jeff Allison (left) and Jon Cozean participated in the Civil War Re-enactment at Pilot Knob.

Rolla Cozean (left) and Alvin Hood are seen with this 1923 Model Gardner. the first new hearse purchased by a funeral home in St. Francois County.

CROUCH, FARLEY & HEURING, PC
Certified Public Accountants

John R. Crouch founded our firm in 1975. The firm name was John R. Crouch, CPA. In 1980 the firm was incorporated as John R. Crouch CPA, Inc. Marion R. Farley became a shareholder in the firm in 1987 and the name was changed to Crouch & Farley, PC. In 1998 Terry L. Heuring became a shareholder and the firm name was changed to Crouch, Farley & Heuring, PC. The firm is presently one of the largest CPA firms in southeast Missouri, employing 15 people.

When John Crouch founded the firm, it was located on the second floor of the old United Bank (later Mercantile Bank) building at the corner of Columbia and Washington Streets. That building was torn down in 1990. The office had two rooms and was rented for $60 a month. The Bank allowed Crouch to use its copy machine and some of its other facilities. At the start Crouch performed all work and had no employees. After two months, Crouch hired the first employee. In 1978 Crouch built a new office building at the firm's

present location at 119 N. Henry Street. Additions to this building have been constructed three times. In 1982 a second wing was added. In 1984 the second floor was converted into office space. In 1999 the building was doubled in size with another wing. The present building is 5,300 square feet.

The firm has a history of innovation. It purchased a Wang Word Processor about 1979. This was one of the first word processors in Farmington. In 1981 the firm purchased a Radio Shack Model 12 microcomputer, one of the first microcomputers in business use in our area. In 1982 the firm became the first firm in our region to have a voluntary peer review of its accounting practice. The firm is a charter member of the "private company practice section" (PCPS) of the American Institute of CPAs. The PCPS is devoted to the quality practice of accounting and is largely responsible for mandatory peer reviews and continuing professional education that are now universal throughout the profession.

Crouch, Farley & Heuring, PC has been oriented to quality from the very first day it was in existence. The first aspect of this quality has been accomplished by providing the very best accounting and tax library possible. The second aspect of this quality has been the

extensive continuing education that all members of the firm receive each year. The third aspect is the required review and checking procedure that is applied to every piece of work produced by the office.

The quality work orientation, combined with sound business practices, will help assure many years of future service to Farmington and the surrounding region.

L-R, May 1998. John R. Crouch, Tammy Homan, Amber Cook, Barbara Halter, Terry Heuring, Jennifer Saddler, Mike O'Shea, Anita Stricklin, Susan Freed, Laurie Sundhausen, Dena Ridings, Sharon Amsden, Marion R. Farley

Don Danieley Agency American Family Insurance

Donald P. Danieley was working with his father on the family farm in Ste. Genevieve County near Coffman, MO when he graduated from Ste. Genevieve High School in 1949. Don also worked as a farm operator on a farm owned by a St. Louis man.

On September 19, 1952, Don married Maxine Andriano in Farmington, MO. After their marriage Don continued to farm and was appointed to the board of directors for the Ste. Genevieve County Farm Bureau. It was through this association that Don became aware of insurance agency opportunities in both Ste. Genevieve and St. Francois counties. He pursued this opportunity and in late 1955 became the agency manager of St. Francois County Farm Bureau Insurance, selling his assets in the farming operation.

Don worked with Farm Bureau Insurance for the next two years. In 1957 the Donald P. Danieley Insurance Agency became the Farmington representative for the Farmer's Mutual Insurance Company, which later changed its company name to the American Family Insurance Group.

In January 1960 Don was promoted to district sales manager. Dean Danieley, brother of Don, was hired to run the local business, which he did from his office in the Ozarks Federal Savings and Loan building.

With the untimely death of Dean in 1971, Don returned to the Farmington agency in January of 1972 and relocated the business at 2 S. Jackson St. behind the Post Office. Another move came in 1978, when the business claimed the site of Dandy's Ice Cream Parlor at 313 Ste. Genevieve Avenue, an enterprise operated by Don's wife, Maxine, Marcia and Diane from 1975 to 1978.

During his insurance career Don won the American Family Insurance "All-Star Award," the top honor given by American Family Insurance Group. State Director Pete Walton noted, "You are an excellent example of true professionalism in your American Family career."

Don retired after 42 years in the insurance profession. Upon his retirement, American Family, after considering Farmington's continued growth, encouraged the development of a second office in town offering automobile, homeowner, business, health and life insurance.

Marcia Danieley, having worked for her father, Don, doing filing and miscellaneous clerical duties since the age of 12, obtained her insurance license while a junior in high school. After attending Murray State University in Ken-

tucky, Marcia worked as a broker in Houston, TX and then in St. Louis. In 1985 she moved back to Farmington to work as an assistant agent for her father. In 1991 Marcia started her own agency with American Family at the same 313 Ste. Genevieve Ave. location. David Danieley worked for his father's agency during his high school years. He graduated from ITT Technical Institute in 1991 and returned to Farmington and resumed working for Don. David became a part-time agent for American Family Insurance Company in July 1996. When Don retired in November 1996, David became a full-time agent with his own American Family agency on the corner of Washington St. and Karsch Blvd.

Don is enjoying his retirement, as he has a variety of interests and property to manage.

Dandy's Ice Cream Parlor which became the home of the American Family Insurance.

Marcia Pease's American Family Insurance agency.

David Danieley's American Family Insurance agency.

Donald Danieley

Marcia Danieley Pease

David Danieley

EARTH MOTHER HEALTH FOODS

Earth Mother Health Foods in Farmington is far more than just a business to owner, Marylee Visnovske. It is a part of her heritage, a mission from God and a labor of love.

Marylee purchased a small health food store business in downtown Farmington in 1991, changed the name to Earth Mother Health Foods and moved it to 202 West Karsch Blvd. in 1993. Her husband Bill retired from River Cement and joined her in the store in 1995.

The knowledge and love of herbal medicine was passed down to Marylee from her great-great-grandfather, ByBrva Lilburn Cahow, an American Indian living in Monroe County, IL at the time of his daughter's birth. Mary Cahow, her great-grandmother, married Isaac Bettis. Their daughter, Florence Lee Ann Bettis, was Marylee's grandmother. Florence's brother, Bill, became a licensed medical doctor. Bill and his mother practiced both kinds of medicine together recognizing the value in both types of medicine. Florence Lee Ann Bettis married John Magre and one of their children was Marylee's mother, Muriel. Muriel was born on Calico Island across the Mississippi River from Crystal City, MO. The families sort of lived and carried their herbs back and forth across the mighty Mississippi, as Muriel still refers to it on her weekly visits. Muriel is the last one of her generation living, her memory is failing her, but she still remembers life on the river, calls herself a "River Rat" and can tell you exactly the proper way to pull a boat across the river by reading the flow of the water. Florence Magre's home was also a kind of birthing clinic giving birth to Marylee and almost all of her 12 cousins as well as her sister, June Ann. She was the last one born at 900 Mississippi Ave. Crystal City, MO.

Muriel's oldest brother, Uncle Johnny Magre, was Marylee's teacher of herbs as well as her Grandmother Florence. Florence and Johnny had been taught by Mary Cahow and passed the herbal wand on to Marylee, who was named after all of her grandmothers and great-grandmothers. Marylee married Bill Visnovske in 1961. They have three children. Their daughter Vicke and granddaughter, Damiana, reside in Farmington. Vicke is a high school art teacher at K-14 in Washington County. Vicke, keeping with the trend, also had a midwife for Damiana's birth.

Eddie resides in up-state New York working as a Rescue Ranger in the mountains. He is an accomplished rock/mountain climber. His latest climbs can always be viewed at Earth Mother. The most recent was the Amadablam in the Himalayas near Mt. Everest. His fiancé, Barbara, is a ranger and teacher of nature in the mountains.

Wm. (Leroy) and wife Sara, live in Florida. Leroy is employed by FEMA and Sara is an occupational therapist. Leroy is a runner and Sara joins him in cycling. Earth Mother sends boxes regularly to New York and Florida. The Visnovske children are all into vitamins and herbal medicine. They grew up on all organic food from their Dad's garden. Once you taste organic food, that's what you want; there is a difference.

Marylee feels she has passed that wand of herbal medicine on to her children and now is teaching her granddaughter, Damiana. She recently took Damiana to visit the grave of the old medicine woman, Mary Cahow Bettis, and Damiana named the wild herbs growing on her grave. She also gives pretend echinacea to her baby dolls, so the herbal wand will continue to be passed on.

Marylee and Bill now have a full-time helper at the store, Rick Steinc. He was hired as manager and is a very caring person that all the customers adore. The theme at Earth Mothers says it all on the sign as you are leaving the store (THANK YOU FOR LETTING US CARE).

Marylee and Bill Visnovske

Earth Mother Health Foods

EDWARD JONES

Edward Jones got its start more than a century ago, in 1871, as the bond house of Whitaker & Co. In 1922, Edward D. Jones Sr. founded the financial services firm that bears his name, and in 1943 Jones merged with Whitaker.

Until the 1950s, Edward Jones was typical of most New York Stock Exchange firms. In the 40s and 50s, the representatives from Edward Jones were called "TNT" brokers, because they traveled the countryside surrounding the company's office in St. Louis from Tuesday until Thursday looking for business.

In 1948 Edward D. "Ted" Jones Jr., son of the founder, returned to work in the family business after studying agriculture at the University of Missouri and a stint on Wall Street. While working his territory in rural Missouri and Illinois, he began experimenting with the concept of locating offices in communities outside St. Louis. In 1955, he hired a representative for Mexico, MO; and with the opening of this first branch office, a new era began.

In the past 40 years, Jones has brought Wall Street to Main Street in communities across the country. Jones' one-person office strategy runs counter to that of virtually every other major securities firm in the United States and has helped fuel remarkable growth for the company. Revenues have grown from $16 million in 1977 to an estimated $1.4 billion at year-end 1998. With more that 4,000 branch offices in 50 states, Jones growth has been extraordinary; in 1980, the number of Jones offices totaled 304.

In 1994 the firm's Canadian affiliate, Edward Jones Canada, opened its first office. Today, there are nearly 200 Canadian offices, including 25 in the Toronto area. In 1997 Edward Jones expanded its international presence by opening offices in the United Kingdom through the firm's affiliate, Edward Jones Limited.

Edward Jones intends to remain a leader in the industry by continuing to offer investments tailored to the needs of individual investors. According to John W. Bachmann, managing principal, the firm is training more than 150 additional investment representatives each month to work in one-person branches located in both large suburban and rural communities across the country.

Our local office here in Farmington opened in 1979. Kevin Engler has been the investment representative in the office since 1986. As the community has grown, Edward Jones, along with Kevin, saw the need for an additional investment representative office. John Brown accepted the position and started serving clients in 1998.

1998 brought the Centennial for Farmington and we at Edward Jones are proud to be one of the few firms that existed when the town of Farmington was founded. Both Kevin and John look forward to serving the ever-growing community well into the next century.

Southeast Missouri Telephone Station, 1932, which is now Edward Jones.

Present location before remodeling.

Present location.

Farmington Presbyterian Manor
A Christian Vision Of Retirement Living

Farmington Presbyterian Manor, established in 1962, was originally developed under the auspices of the Presbyterian Synods of Missouri but came under the Synod of Mid-America with the regional 'synods in 1973. The program was originally called "Presbyterian Homelife"

The first of three Missouri Manors, Farmington Presbyterian Manor was the result of the leadership of Dr. Fred Walker, superintendent of the Presbyterian Home for Children, with the support of Grafton Lothrop, chairman of the executive committee of the Children's Home; and the Rev. Edwin Short, chairman of the committee on schools and homes for the Presbyterian Church.

After a series of reorganizations, by January 1990 two corporations were created: Presbyterian Manors, Inc., which owns all the Manors in Missouri and Kansas and their assets, and Presbyterian Manors of Mid-America, Inc., which provides management services for the Manors.

The first board of trustees was formed in May 1958, with Mr. Grafton Lothrop installed as the first president of the board of directors. Through the years of growth and service, the Manor has been continually supported by leaders in the community. Many familiar names from the community appear in records of past board members and those active in support of the Manor.

Groundbreaking for Presbyterian Homelife was held November 19, 1960, with ceremonies led by Dr. Fred A. Walker, Mr. Glenwood Lees and Mr. Taylor Smith, who were all leaders in the community. By June 1961, residents were being accepted for the new Presbyterian Home as construction continued. The first two residents, Mrs. Laura Waters of Farmington, MO and Mrs. B.C. Hardesty of St. Louis, MO, lived temporarily in Harlan House which was part of the Presbyterian Children's Home, while they waited for construction to be completed. The first employee for the new facility was Mrs. Edith Wilber.

There was expansion in 1964, adding health care beds to the Manor. By November 1967, some private homes were added to the Manor and at that time there were 75 residents.

Now, Farmington Presbyterian Manor is a continuing care retirement community that is home to nearly 200 people. Residents may choose from cottages, duplexes, apartments, residential care rooms or suites, or rooms in the Health Care Center which includes a 20-bed special care unit.

Community churches, individual volunteers from the community and friends and family members of residents continue to support the Manor's tradition of Christian Service.

Presbyterian Manor entrance.

Serene setting of Presbyterian Manor.

HISTORY OF FIRST STATE COMMUNITY BANK

First State Community Bank (FSCB) has been a locally-owned, community bank and a Farmington landmark since its grand opening as First State Bank of Farmington on May 9, 1954. During a time when the economy wasn't at its strongest, B.H. Jennings believed Farmington needed a locally-owned bank, so Jennings gathered enough investors to see his dream fulfilled. From that moment, First State Community Bank's history has been a success story.

With a long history of community development and civic involvement, FSCB made a name for itself as the Friendly First and has maintained a tradition of personal service and long-term customer relationships throughout the years.

Originally incorporated as First State Bank of Farmington in July 1953, the Finance Commission of Missouri approved the bank charter in November 1953, with $100,000 of common stock. The bank's first board members were B.H. Jennings (president and chairman of the board), H. Boxdorfer (vice president), C.A. Doubet (secretary), R.E. Adams, A.J. Butterfield, C.B. Denman and C.E. Rozier. When R.E. Adams resigned in November 1956, Clarence Wade joined the board and was an active board participant until 1997 when he became a director emeritus.

Although board meetings were originally held in the dining room at Ozarks Cafe, the group was able to meet in the bank lobby for the first time on June 7, 1954. The bank building, located at 201 East Columbia Street, was designed by B.H. Jennings' son, Harry F. Jennings, an architect.

The bank grew and made itself known throughout the community. In July 1956, it was necessary to hire an executive vice president for the bank, and Grover Jennings accepted the position.

B.H. Jennings saw the need for First State Bank as a community bank in Farmington and successfully operated it until he passed away in November 1963. At that time, H.F. Jennings, was elected president and chairman of the board at the January 1964, board meeting. H.F. Jennings oversaw the continued growth and progress of the bank until he retired in 1980.

William H. (Bill) Cooper, who had served on the board of directors since 1964, purchased control of the bank in 1980 and was elected chairman, the position he continues to hold today. That same year, Jack Sebastian was appointed president of the bank, (he had previously been appointed executive vice president in 1967), and he remained the president of the bank until he retired in 1994. After Sebastian retired, his son, Matt Sebastian, was appointed president of the bank in Farmington, where he remains today. It was also at this time that Greg Allen was appointed president of First State Bancshares, Inc., the holding company that owns and operates the subsidiary banks.

In July 1968, the board applied for permission to open a facility located at Karsch Boulevard and Washington Street. The new facility, opened in March 1970, was a combination drive-up and lobby facility that was open Monday through Saturday. This facility became the site for the town's first "time and temperature" sign.

As the bank's assets continued to grow, staff and supplies began to outgrow the bank building itself. The main bank located at 201 E. Columbia Street underwent two major expansions. In 1982, the building size doubled and the drive-up lanes were relocated to the east side of the building. The second expansion was completed in December 1987, when the second floor storage area was converted to office space. Since then, the bank has undergone a number of remodeling projects, moving and adding offices as necessary.

First State Bank, 1954.

1979

On March 11, 1984, First State Bancshares, Inc. (FSB) was formed as a one-bank holding company so that additional banks could be purchased. Iron County Security Bank (located on Main Street in Ironton) was purchased in 1987, and it remained a separately-chartered bank within the holding company until January 1999. The former First Federal Savings of SEMO (located on School Street in Bonne Terre) was purchased from Capital Bank in 1991, and it opened as (and remains) a branch of First State Community Bank.

As Farmington's business sector grew, the bank opened a full-service, free-standing facility in the Maple Valley Shopping Center on August 4, 1992. This facility's transactions steadily increase as the area continues its development.

Although First State Bank was well-known throughout the community, it was not the only First State Bank in Missouri. This name duplication became increasingly confusing as the holding company looked at other bank purchases. In September 1996, First State Bank of Farmington officially changed its name to First State Community Bank to set itself apart from other First State Banks in the state. The name change also reflected the bank's commitment to the communities it serves, maintaining that each location is a true community bank.

In October 1996, First State Community Bank opened a loan production office in the St. Mary branch of First Financial Bank of Ste. Genevieve County. First State Bancshares, Inc., officially purchased the St. Mary location in January 1997. Immediately following the St. Mary purchase, First State Community Bank opened a temporary banking facility in Perryville in February 1997. Construction began on a permanent location, and the Perryville Bank opened in its present location (406 North Perryville Blvd.) in January 1998.

In a continuing effort to provide a wide variety of financial products and services to customers, First State Community Bank entered into an agreement with Farmington-based Conservative Financial Services, Inc. (CFS) in June 1997 to provide investment services in the banks. Financial representatives have offices in or regularly visit every FSCB location to meet with customers, offering products and services that are not available through the bank.

First State Community Bank purchased Joachim Federal Savings & Loan in DeSoto on June 12, 1998, and on June 22, 1998, the bank officially opened its full-service Park Hills facility. First State Bancshares continued its expansion into southeast Missouri by purchasing three branches from Mercantile Bank of Southeast Missouri in Malden, Portageville and Hayti on November 20, 1998.

With the conversion of Iron County Security Bank to a First State Community Bank in January 1999, the bank has 12 banking locations in 10 towns, with current assets of about $335 million. The small community-bank started by B.H. Jennings in 1954 has grown to become the second largest banking corporation headquartered in southeast Missouri.

First State Community Bank's proud tradition of serving the local community continues as deposits fund development that customers can actually see: the new subdivision across town, the new business in the industrial park, the neighbor's remodeling project. First State Community Bank is proud to fund the projects that make the communities they serve grow and prosper. That's what a community bank is all about.

First State Community Bank employees today.

MERCANTILE BANK

The history of Farmington would not be complete without including Mercantile Bank. It has been an active part of Farmington history since January 16, 1934. The citizens of Farmington were filled with relief that the problems of the great depression were at last winding down. Our country had elected a new president who promised economic recovery and the new bank of Farmington was opening its doors for the first time that morning.

The Missouri Commissioner of Finance had effectively frozen deposits in Farmers Bank and the Bank of Farmington in 1933, with only 5% of each deposit available for withdrawal. The new United Bank of Farmington assumed some of the assets and liabilities of the two older banks and could immediately release 60% of each deposit balance. It was organized as a member bank of the Federal Reserve System; and the newly created U.S. Government Insurance plan was to insure each deposit up to $2,500. This plan was created by the Banking Act in 1933 and would become known as Federal Deposit Insurance Corporation (FDIC) under the Banking Act of 1935. The new bank was opened in the location formerly occupied by the Bank of Farmington at Columbia and Washington Streets. Employees and officers were drawn from each of the older banks. All officers and directors of the bank were well known to the people of the community, except the new cashier, Mr. Dearing who came from Palmyra, MO. He had spent the past year engaged in liquidating closed banks. President-elect was W.M. Harlan. Officers of Mercantile Commerce Bank and Trust Co. of St. Louis and the First National Bank of St. Louis were present the first week to help the new bank to get organized. The United Bank of Farmington opened with total deposits of $1,368,305. Wendell Dearing became president following W.H. Harlan.

Vernon K. Giessing replaced Wendell Dearing as president in 1965. Throughout his career with the bank he promoted the modernization of banking procedures and was farsighted in seeking additional space for future expansion. Under his guidance, the bank affiliated with Mercantile Bancorporation on March 1, 1973. The name was changed to Mercantile Bank of Farmington, February 13, 1975. That same year the bank became the first in southeast Missouri to offer its customers an automatic teller machine (Fingertip). The Leadington facility was opened in February 1978.

Rolla Gordon became president in December 1976. The era of technological revolution in banking had begun. Mercantile of Farmington installed the first two-pass fine-sort proof system in America in the fall of 1982 in order to speed up handling of the growing volume of checks. Mercantile was a forerunner in community banking with the installation of a four-lane automated drive-through bank in Farmington as well as a facility in Leadington. MESA (Mercantile Exclusive Senior Account) was the first program in the area geared especially toward those 55 and older. All these changes were conducted while maintaining a warm and caring relationship with the customers. The completion of the dream began by Mr. V.K. Giessing and brought to fruition by Rolla Gordon was the bank building which presently houses Mercantile Bank. It covers the entire block between Columbia and Washington. This beautiful, spacious facility became a reality and opened its doors to the public in October 1987.

Along with a new bank building came a new bank president. David Felske came to Mercantile from Illinois in the fall of 1987. This was only the first of many changes, along with much growth for the corporation. Mercantile of Potosi merged with Farmington and Leadington on December 28, 1990. The name then became Mercantile Bank of the Mineral Area. Thomas Jacobson became president and CEO of Mercantile Bank of St. Louis, N.A. He had a long-range vision including a well-laid out plan of growth and acquisition, as well as streamlining the organization to become the largest bank in Missouri and a power to be reckoned with nationally.

Lowell Peterson came from Minnesota in 1993 to be the president in Farmington. Banks all over the nation were in the merging, acquisition and downsizing mode, Mercantile among them. Locally, Mercantile of the Mineral Area consolidated with seven other banks in southeast Missouri, including Perryville, St. Genevieve, Dexter, Sikeston, Poplar Bluff, Cape Girardeau and Doniphan to become Mercantile Bank of Southeast Missouri. There were eight regional banks in Missouri instead of the 60 separate units. Lowell Peterson went to the Cape Girardeau branch to become president in that city in April 1998. Three of the five years Lowell Peterson was in Farmington, the bank won the Grand Slam Award, which is an award given to the highest performing bank in the entire system which consists of more than 70 units.

John A. Davis was named president of the Farmington Bank in June 1998. He is originally from Arkansas but transferred to Farmington from the Mercantile Bank of Perryville. The Mercantile of Ste. Genevieve Bank became one of the Farmington branches in the fall of 1998. On December 12, 1998, the final realization of Thomas Jacobson's long-range vision falls into place. Mercantile Banks across Missouri will join together under the name of Mercantile Bank National Association. As a result, there will be more places to bank and greater convenience than ever before.

We at Mercantile Bank are proud of our history of commitment to Farmington and the surrounding area. We look forward to a bright future of continued service to our customers. When the United Bank of Farmington opened its doors on January 16, 1934, the citizens of Farmington entered the bank in a mood of hopefulness that would soon develop into confidence that would still be growing some 65 years later. The promise of economic recovery to a nation that had been stunned by both war and a great depression was fulfilled and paved the way for a successful partnership uniting business and community. Mercantile Bank has a long history of community involvement and an impressive record of community service. The result of this teamwork is responsible for the continued growth and prospering of our communities making them better places to live and work together.

The front door of United Bank of Farmington was located at the corner of the building for many years.

Mercantile Bank

HISTORY OF THE FARMINGTON PRESS

The Press Printing and Publishing Company, publisher of *The Farmington Evening Press*, was founded in 1929 by two brothers, Cecil W. and John Roberts. The early *Press* newspaper, printed weekly, was a simple news-sheet distributed free in competition with the *Farmington News*.

For 18 years the two brothers continued in partnership as printers, newsmen and with a growing office supply division.

In 1946 the business arrangement changed; John taking the office supply portion, the beginning of the Roberts Office Supply, and Cecil continuing in the news field. Cecil became interested in radio and on May 1, 1948, sold his printing plant and newspaper to two employees, Walter M. Stewart and Arthur L. Freeman Jr. and began what is now KREI Radio.

In the meantime, Jesse Stewart with his older brother, Paul, and his father, the Rev. William Stewart, owned a printing plant and published a newspaper, *The Bulletin*, in Bonne Terre during the depression years.

On Nov. 1, 1950, Jesse bought the half interest of *The Press* owned by Wally Stewart (no relation) and for a time managed both newspapers until *The Bulletin* and another Bonne Terre newspaper, *The Star-News Register*, merged and became *The Register*, edited by Joe Stewart, Jesse's brother.

Three years later, in January 1953, Jesse bought out his partner, Art Freeman. In the 1950's publishers in the area from Perryville to Festus met numerous times to discuss the possibility of forming a central offset printing plant. While some could see the advantages of printing their newspapers in a central plant, no one wanted to get involved financially in such a new venture, as offset equipment and chemicals were still in the experimental stage.

Jesse and his wife, Marie, decided to take the plunge into offset when their old Babcock press refused to run anymore. With some homemade equipment, a new Argyle camera, a light table, a Nu-Arc plate burner and a used LB Harris automatic flat sheet press, they made the switch to offset in September 1961, not missing a single issue. The difference was immediately noticeable, especially in the pictures. *The Press* came to life.

New equipment was added as it was developed. A two unit Goss Community Press was installed in 1966. The speed of which greatly increased the job potential as well as production.

In addition to publishing the newspaper, Jesse was also circuit clerk from 1945 until his death in 1967. During that time period, he wrote probably one of the most honest and unbiased editorials ever entitled, *Throw the Rascals Out*, where he exhorted voters to turn out all of the incumbents holding county office, including himself. After his death, his widow, Marie, operated the *Press* for six years until February 1973 when she sold to Wit and Anne Ledbetter. The Ledbetters' wanted to return to their "home" stage after several years in Iowa.

The Press was being published at 1 West Liberty, a building on the northeast corner of the square at that time. The Ledbetters, after first trying to merge *The Press* and the older *Farmington News*, moved to become a bi-weekly, publishing on Mondays and Wednesdays.

The newspaper grew in number of pages and circulation over the next year and on June 4, 1974, *The Press* became the *Evening Press*, Farmington's first daily newspaper. The following year the *Evening Press* purchased the building at 119 East Columbia Street from Missouri Natural Gas and the presses and equipment were moved over one weekend.

In December of 1977 the paper was sold to Smith Newspaper, Inc. and underwent several expansions under the direction of publisher Craig Watkins. In February 1978 the size of the sheet being used to print *The Press* was cut from 34 to 30 inches, a more modern and readable size.

In July 1978, *The Press* entered the world of private postal systems when it purchased the Advertising Mail and Parcel Service from Stan Blake. The AMPS service delivered over 60,000 pieces of advertising materials each week, including *the Evening Press'* free-circulation Green Sheet.

The paper again became a locally owned and published paper when it was sold to Robert and Emily Firebaugh in October 1982. The Firebaugh's returned to publishing *The Press* as a bi-weekly on Tuesdays and Thursdays as well as the weekly free Green Sheet.

In July 1988 the paper was again sold to a newspaper conglomerate, American Publishing. The paper was renamed the *Daily Press Leader* and a daily schedule was again resumed. Joel Goodridge was the first publisher, followed by Mark Griggs who remained publisher until the *Leader* was sold to Pulitzer Community Newspapers, part of Pulitzer Publishing, in November of 1998.

Pulitzer had previously purchased the *Daily Journal* in Park Hills and the weekly *Democrat News* in Fredericktown.

The *Press* and *Journal* continued operating as two separate daily papers until November 1998 at which time they were merged into one daily paper as the *Daily Journal*, with Russ Cannon as publisher.

The Daily Press Leader, with Jon Seals as managing editor, ended its career by receiving nine awards from the Missouri Press Association, including second place in the state for General Excellence.

After the merge, a weekly Farmington supplement to the *Daily Journal* was printed on Wednesdays under the original banner of *The Farmington Press*.

Cecil W. Roberts, Editor, The Press. Photo 1928.

Farmington Printers. 1. Carl Crow, 2. Waide Nations, 3. C.S. (Sport) Reeves, 4. Will H. Lewis, 5. Edgar (Tick) Haley, 6. John Applegate, 7. Ed Barroll, 8. E.V. Conway, 9. Barton H. Boyer, 10. James C. Watson. Reeves, Barroll, Conway on the Times. *Crow, Nations, Lewis on the* Herald. *Haley, Applegate, Boyer, Watson on the* News.

Missouri Beauty Academy

With a class of 13 students, the Missouri Beauty Academy was established in September 1935 by Violet Mitchell. The location was upstairs of the Realty Building, which was the United Bank of Farmington on the corner of Washington and Columbia Streets.

In 1937 the school was moved across the street to 22 E. Columbia in the Tetley Building.

In 1945 Howard Gordon bought the business and in 1947 Gertie Rickard Hellen purchased the beauty school after being trained as a cosmetologist and instructor in 1945. Their telephone number was "#3." Rent was from month to month, no lease or contract. Mrs. Tetley, mother of Roberta and Ann Caroline, was a trusting person.

Mary Ruth Moon, daughter of Gertie, trained in 1949 and other daughter, Esta Lea Cissell, was trained in 1956. Mary Ruth bought the business in 1963. In 1967 the school was moved to 118 E. Columbia, what was the Voelith Building, Betty Phelps dress shop.

In 1973 after a fire destroyed the building, the beauty school moved to 201 S. Washington, Charles Banta building.

Mary Ruth's daughter, Debra Smith, owner of Hair It Is, was trained in 1979 and was one of the instructors. She was the third generation associated with the school.

Hundreds of students and many family members have become cosmetologists.

In 1984 the Missouri Beauty Academy was nationally accredited by NACCAS, Washington, DC.

In September 1985 a 50th anniversary was celebrated with an open house for the alumni and public. A "Yesteryear Beauty Shop" was displayed with old equipment, implements, records, pictures and history.

In July 1996 the Missouri Beauty Academy business was sold, thus, ending a family tradition of many years.

Missouri Beauty Academy

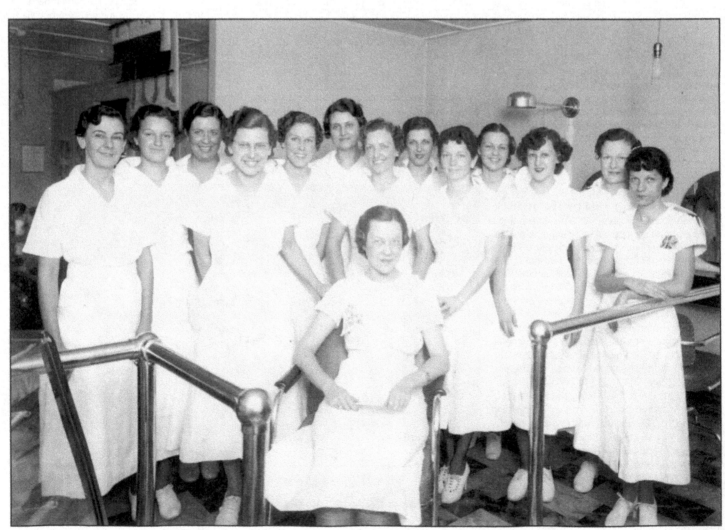

Missouri Beauty Academy Class of 1936. Mamie Beard, Beulah? Hindrich, Dorothy Doughty, Anastacia Goverau, Dolly Ayers, Dorothy Landalt, Annabelle Hindrich, Juanitta Mills, Betty Griffin, unidentified, Glenda Hopkins, Toots Welland, Emily Harston and Ethel Dannenmueller (Head Instructor).

Ozarks Federal Savings and Loan Association

The history of Ozarks Federal Savings and Loan Association began in the spring of 1930 when brothers, L.B. Coghill and W.T. Coghill, opened an office on the second floor of the Realty Building (formerly United Bank of Farmington, now Mercantile Bank). The Coghills, each having years of experience in the banking business and a keen interest in the related business of savings and loan, got together a group of young professional and business men to consider the feasibility of such a venture. The group drew up articles of incorporation, subscribed to 500 shares of stock and applied to the Department of Savings and Loan Supervision of the State of Missouri for a charter. The charter was granted and the name was to be Missouri Ozarks Savings and Loan Association. Officers and directors were chosen as follows: L.B. Coghill, president; Theodore J. Giessing, vice-president; W.T. Coghill, secretary-treasurer; Taylor Smith Sr., E.A. Herzog, Dr. R. Appleberry, R.S. Roberts and A.A. Gierringer, directors.

In 1933 the association moved from its second floor office to a first floor location on the southwest corner of W. Columbia and Jefferson Streets. This building was known as the Braun Hall and had been the post office for many years. Ozarks purchased the building for $14,000 and it was the Association's home for 37 years, during which time remodeling and enlargement of its quarters were done several times to meet the growth of the business.

Also in 1933 the Missouri Ozarks Savings and Loan was admitted to membership in the Federal Home Loan Bank System, being the first in Southeast Missouri and one of the first in the State. In 1935, the Association's name changed to Ozarks Federal Savings and Loan Association to conform to Federal regulations.

In 1970 property was acquired on the corner of E. Columbia and Washington Streets to build a new office. The new facility was officially opened in October of 1970 and was extensively remodeled in 1988.

Over the years, the Association's business was extended to other communities in need of its services, via branch offices in Fredericktown, Festus, Potosi, Ironton and Piedmont.

Ozarks Federal takes pride in being competitive in the field of savings plans and home mortgages. They have enjoyed a steady growth and continuous growth over the years, reflecting the confidence of its customers. The assets have grown from $1,257 in 1930 to over $156 million today (1998).

L.B. Coghill retired as president in 1965, succeeded by his brother, W.T. Coghill.

Bill Braun succeeded W.T. in 1968 and resigned in July of 1969. Taylor Smith Jr. was president and CEO from 1969 to his retirement in 1982. Don Effrein was then appointed president and CEO and currently holds these positions. Other officers are Verdell Sitzes, senior vice president and treasurer; Wilma Pinkley, secretary; Garland Abernathy, Craig Schnurbusch and John Higginbotham are vice-presidents; Mary Lee Hibbits, Sandra Hoehn, Mary Ann Webery, Dennis Fowler, Kenneth Chapman, Steve Effrein and Diane Dinkins are assistant vice-presidents; and Carolyn Allen, Bill Allen, Carol Bloom, Sandy Sales and Pam Vierse are assistant secretaries.

Current board of directors are Don Effrein, Verdell Sitzes, C. E. Carleton, M.D., Terry Detring, Dennis McIntosh, Clayton Osman, Dudley Pautz, D.V.M. and George Wohlschlaeger.

Through the years Ozarks Federal has gained the confidence of its customers and the loyalty of its employees. Of the 24 employees in the home office in Farmington, 16 have been with the Association for over 20 years, six over 30 and one (Wilma Pinkley) has been with Ozarks for 40 years.

Ozarks Federal looks forward to the prosperous growth of Farmington and surrounding communities and is proud to be an instrumental part of it.

Ozark Federal Savings and Loan Association

Board of Directors, left to right: L.B. Coghill, Taylor Smith, W.K. Giessing, W.T. Coghill, K.C. Weber, J.P. Cayce, C.Y. White and E. A. Herzog.

OZARK STEEL

Along many skylines, skeletons of new high rise office buildings are changing the way cities look. From Virginia to Washington State and from Chicago, IL to Houston, TX these skylines are climbing to greater heights. For the past 37 years cities have been changing. To very little knowledge of the local community, a lot of these skyline giants started right here in Farmington, MO.

In 1962 Ozark Steel began fabricating miscellaneous steel for the local mining industry. Soon after the knowledge of their presence, people began to call upon Ozark Steel to supply structural steel for local buildings such as schools, churches and stores. This gave the company an alternative to fabricating just miscellaneous steel to the mining industry, which turned out to be a good thing as mining started to be phased out in the area.

Having opened the door with local construction companies, Ozark Steel began to expand and was soon selling structural steel to general contractors outside the local area: places like Shreveport, LA and Indianapolis, IN where the demand for their product was needed.

Today, Robert, David and Gary Laut, the three sons of the founder of the company, William Laut, are still fabricating structural steel for the construction industry but on a much larger scale, providing steel for the construction of buildings like the AMA Headquarters in downtown Chicago, Sears Headquarters in Hoffman Estates, Illinois and A.G. Edwards in downtown St. Louis.

Over $20 million dollars worth of fabricated structural steel leaves Farmington, MO on average a year, destined for the skylines around the country. Ozark Steel employs over 75 men and women, helping to boost the economy for stronger growth in the area. Helping support local organizations such as the Boy Scouts and area baseball/softball organizations is a very important part of Ozark Steel. They have also contributed structural steel to local schools for bleachers and goals. These are just a few of the things Ozark Steel has been doing and will continue to do as a part of the local community of Farmington, MO.

Ozark Steel Fabricators

William Laut, the founder of Ozark Steel.

Aerial view of Ozark Steel.

Plummer's Hardware

For over 100 years the building at 101 East Liberty street in downtown Farmington has housed a hardware store. In 1890, the store was founded by Mrs. Robert (Emma) Boswell and her brother, Edward Helber. Throughout the years the business was owned by various members of the Boswell family until it was purchased in January 1974 by James S. and Delores Plummer from Mrs. Elizabeth Boswell.

At the time the Plummer's purchased Boswell Hardware, they were owners of Gambles Hardware store located exactly one street away at 101 E. Columbia Street, a business that they had owned and operated since 1969. By relocating, they expanded their business space greatly as the former Boswell building contained 21,280 square feet counting both retail and storage space. Throughout the years both the exterior and interior of this historic building has been extensively remodeled, but the family tradition of giving personal service to their customers and the stocking of hard to find items remains what Plummer's Hardware is known for in both Farmington and the surrounding area,

Where once horse collars, plow handles and cream separators were displayed, the shelves are now stocked with modern power tools, the latest in lawn and garden equipment as well as state-of-the-art merchandise in all departments. In place of the ornate wooden cash registers and handwritten receipts, computers are now used to check out customers, order stock and compile records.

In January 1991, the next generation of the Plummer family purchased the business. Scott Plummer, only son of Jim and Delores Plummer assumed ownership and continues to carry on the tradition of personal service to his customers.

Boswell Hardware Co.

PREFERRED LAND TITLE COMPANY

Preferred Land Title Company is a progressive company with a lot of history. It is a privately owned company which is a title insurance agency and provides a wide range of title related services and information about real estate to interested persons. The company has land records for St. Francois, Ste. Genevieve, Washington, Madison, and Cape Girardeau counties.

The beginning of this company was in 1906 when J. Brid Smith, O.W Bleeck, and George C. Forster formed a corporation named Smith-Bleeck-Forster Land and Abstract Company. In 1906, information about the title to land was provided in the form of an "abstract" which was a compilation of the information from all the recorded deeds, court and tax records of the county.

In 1926 the company name was changed to O.W. Bleeck Land and Abstract Company and O.W. Bleeck, Edna P. Bleeck, and J.P. Cayce were the owners. Then on July 22, 1931, the name was again changed to The St. Francois County Abstract Company with Thomas H. Holman, Wm. M. Harlan, M.P. Cayce as stockholders. Miss Alleda Kollmeyer was the corporate secretary. The company was housed at Room 11 of the Realty Building at No. 1 Columbia St. Farmington, MO. Sylvan Powell and Margaret Powell bought the shares of Wm. M. Harlan and M.P. Cayce in 1946.

In 1953 Milton and Phyllis Schnebelen bought Mr. Holman's interest in the company. Phyllis Schnebelen is the daughter of Sylvan and Margaret Powell. Milton had come home from service in the Navy and resumed his career in law and began to work in The St. Francois County Abstract Company. The office was on the second floor of the United Bank Building. In 1961, Phyllis and Milton bought out Phyllis' parents, the Powell's. From there the company was modernized and moved twice. It was moved to 111 West Liberty Street, and then to 108 W. Columbia Street, to the former Southwestern Bell Telephone Building. Then in 1973, it was moved to its present location at 12 West First Street. During the years that Milt and Phyllis ran the company, they utilized the most modern equipment available and the newest ideas to increase productivity. Milt and Phyllis pursued their law careers as well. Milt was city attorney for Farmington and Phyllis served as magistrate judge from 1975 to 1978. Their law experience provided the knowledge to bring professionalism to the title business in the area. Milt and Phyllis worked in the business until 1987 when Milt suffered a stroke. They both retired at that time.

The company changed its name again on July 12, 1993 to Preferred Land Title Company. The company has grown from its status of two employees in 1953 in one office to five offices performing title work in six counties and employing 42 people. Metro Title Insurers, Inc. is a subsidiary of Preferred Land Title Company and is located in Cape Girardeau, Mo.

Cara Detring, daughter of Milt and Phyllis, has run the company since 1987, having joined the company in 1976. Terry Detring, Cara's husband, provides the accounting and financial expertise for the company. Craig Schnebelen, Milt and Phyllis' son, manages the computer systems which gives the company a competitive edge. At one time or another, all of the family have worked in the company. Milt, Phyllis, Cara, and Craig have maintained an active role for the company in the state and national trade associations for the land title industry, Missouri Land Title Association and American Land Title Association. Milt, Phyllis, and Cara are all past presidents of Missouri Land Title Association and Pam Hart, who is vice president of the company is also a past president. The company has had two employees named as Young Title Person of the Year and three employees named as Title Person of the Year in the Missouri Land Title Association, and Milt and Cara have served on the Board of Governors and as officers of the American Land Title Association. Other long-term employees are Bonnie Weekley, Pamela J. Williams, Carel Payne, Donna Thompson, Beverly Latham, Shirley Horn, Brenda Haney, Jeanna Wells, Wanda McDaniel, Chris Stewart and Neal Hudson.

In addition to title insurance and title information services, the company provides closing services and escrow services. Preferred Land Title Company provides the most professional title services available in southeast Missouri.

St. Francois County Abstract Co.

Dr. Douglas K. Ross
Dental Office History
1965-2015

A smile is one of God's gifts to mankind; it can raise a smiling person's self-worth immensely, as well as the other person receiving that smile. It takes far fewer muscles to smile than it does to frown. A person can certainly smile without teeth, but they sure look a lot better with them. If those teeth are real solid, healthy, aligned well and sparkling clean, they work lots better too. If the gums and other supporting tissues are just as healthy, there's no reason why those God-given gifts shouldn't fully last a lifetime. This is the essence of the dental practice of Dr. Douglas K. Ross, DDS, PC. The "mission statement" is as follows: "We want you to keep your natural teeth for a lifetime of healthy chewing, smiling and enjoyment"

"Doug," as he prefers to be called, began his dental practice July 31, 1965, and the first patients were the children of Mr. Don James. Don had told Doug years earlier, when he had called on the family grocery store in Iron Mountain and knew the Farmington plan, to be sure to call him and have his family as the first day patients. So it was, and one of the dollars collected that day was framed and placed on the wall (only to be stolen a year later in a break-in robbery). Don and Doug still laugh about the irony of that day. More of Doug's history can be found in the "personal biography" section of this publication.

The office site itself in January 1965 was but a pile of cans, wire and trash on a vacant lot owned by Dr. C.H. Ketring, between the Western & Southern Insurance offices and Jennings Lumber Co. (now First State Community Bank). Doug had flown home from his duties in the U.S. Army Dental Corps in Paris, France to see the site and discuss arrangements for planning and construction details. He returned after a week at home in Iron Mountain and began drawing detailed construction plans in his dining room. The drawing board crowded the table and countless sketches hung on the walls to the chagrin of his six-month pregnant wife, Pam. Within six weeks the plans were finished and in the mail to his father, J.G. Ross, who worked closely with the future landlord on a regular basis to effect completion by July when the tour of duty would end. As with any project, there were many people involved. To name a few: the carpenters, John Eck and Chalmer "Hank" Forsythe; the plumbers, Drexel and Ted Chapman; the electrician, Cecil Rhodes. Windows and doors came from Knox Glass; most of the materials from Gifford Lumber Co.; carpet and furniture came from Suburban Furniture Co.; and the dental equipment was supplied by Midvale Dental Supply Co of St. Louis.

The actual operation of the practice started while still in Paris. Letters were sent to all the area's dentists in the five-county region introducing himself and soliciting suggestions and comments from anyone who would respond; many did with some very good advice. Dr. William Watson of DeSoto annually reminds Doug of the letter he received over three decades ago

and how he was glad to be a part of the process of a new practice in Farmington.

Help wanted ads for a "dental assistant" were run during June in the *Farmington Press, Farmington News*, and the *Daily Journal*. Over 20 responses were received and forwarded to France. Contacts were made to arrange interviews in July once the tour was completed. Mrs. Lorene Kollmeyer stood out from all the other applicants. Even though she had no experience in a dental office, except having been a patient herself, her biggest asset was that she "sure did want to learn the ropes" and she did. She soon became a Jack-of-all-trades, literally running between answering the phone, making appointments, collecting payments, keeping records, assisting at the dental chair, cleaning and sterilizing instruments and countless other things. The plan was to hire a second assistant after the first year in operation; however, the plan quickly changed and Mrs. Dorothy Thomas was employed as a chair-side assistant after only six weeks and Mrs. Kollmeyer could then concentrate on the front office which she did well.

A dental practice is no different than any other business when it comes to staffing. Employees come and employees go; some serve many years, some not as long. Surely someone will be left off the list and that's not intentional, so here's an honest effort at those who participated in patient care: Alma Hawkins, Linda Butcher, Marilyn Miller, JoAnn Vessell, Linda Treaster, Jessie Stephens, Karen Roberts, Karen Boring, Donna Freeman, Bonnie Byington, Karen Pettus, Kevin Maxwell, Tami Browers,

The office of Douglas K. Ross.

Ann Burkhart, Debbie Reynolds, Gail Moore, Shelly Sadler, Tammy Geneux, Tammy Govreau, Carla Rawlins, Beth Sutton, Heather Branham, Lynn Short, Rita Thorn, Michelle Strickland, Cheryl Dixon and we can't leave out Pam, Julie, Bradley and Jennifer Ross either. Although Kevin and Scott did also work as cleaning staff at times, as did others not listed due to space limits. Today, the staff includes administrative assistants, Marilyn Bates and Jennifer Skinner; dental assistants, Shanna Hart and Kirstin Dennis; and registered dental hygienists, Tina Gipson, Julie Roth and Sherry Cauley.

More dentists than just Dr. Ross have successfully utilized the dental office at 215 East Columbia Street - Dr. Don Oliver was first for several years, one day a week, when starting his orthodontic practice; Dr. John Jackson utilized the office in the evenings for several months when he first came to town until his office was ready several blocks away; Dr. Tom Finley used the office in the evenings for several months before moving to Desloge; and most recently, Dr. Tom LaMartina practiced there a year before deciding he really wanted to "try it on his own" several blocks away.

The office has undergone a metamorphosis since its design and construction in 1965. Several redecorations and renovations are in the history books about every six to eight years. In the early 90s a major change occurred with the addition of a 5x45' addition on the east side to provide more instrument sterilization facilities, patient records storage and business office space. A small porch-like roof was placed on the front of the building. The dental equipment and the reception room furniture have been replaced three times so far and will probably be changed again at least once more before Doug "retires." The original aquarium gave way to a bird cage, which gave way to a haven for large lovable stuffed toy animals; Garfield and Speedy Gonzales are now the "office heroes." Every four months for the past six years some other such "animal" is given away to some lucky child in the five-county area. The Japanese Garden just outside the two major treatment rooms has grown and matured tremendously since 1965. Flowers bloom from spring to fall every year and also in the planter box on the street side. There the trees planted in the sidewalk attest to Doug's love of trees n' such. In the early

60s he convinced the city council to go along with the tree-planting project, resulting in the trees on Columbia Street in the downtown area we all enjoy today. A major change occurred in the garden in the 80s when a statue of Jesus Christ replaced the one of Princess Kuan Yen - for reasons Doug will gladly and openly tell you, given the chance.

At one time a tall flag pole stood commandingly at the front of the office and a light shown at night to light the standard of our nation's pride and the very large flag waving there; but after losing a dozen such flags to vandals, the effort was abandoned; perhaps sometime again another effort will be made.

The office building itself was seriously threatened one night in the first several years of operation. Doug was returning to the office after a Jaycee meeting to finish some laboratory work and noticed smoke and flames coming from a rear window across the street at Robinson Lumber Co., where the Wohlschlaeger building stands today. He called the fire department and watched as a crowd soon developed to view the excitement. Soon the fire became intense and more serious. Doug got his water hose from the garden and stood guard by spraying his building's roof now receiving red-hot cinders blowing from across the street. Soon the Wulfers and Petrie Furniture Co. building next door was engulfed in flames and Tetley's Jewelry Store was in line for the same fate. Luckily the firemen were successful in saving the Tetley building. It was a long night. When morning arrived, two former Farmington businesses lay in total ruin, with wet ashes giving forth that odor everyone fears.

Dental Survey, a national dental magazine, published a feature story on the office with many photographs and a floor plan in 1967. Responses were received from many dentists from across the country for more information. In 1971 the office was part of a *Post Dispatch* article dealing with Doug's service as mayor of Farmington. In 1997 another article appeared in the *Missouri Dental Journal*. There's also "The Infamous Articles" in 1972; the *New York Times*, the *Grit Magazine* and the *Daily Journal*; all screaming, "Man Puts Bite into Protest." This was during the time of service as mayor a disgruntled citizen (also a patient of Dr. Ross) became so aggravated at some of the policies being espoused by Mayor Ross he decided to

take action. He rushed into the office; uttered some choice four-letter words; removed both his dentures (made in the same office two years earlier) and threw them into the waste can at the front desk and stormed out. Doug shared the story at lunch with a friend, who then told the story to a reporter who then wrote the story and put it on the UP wire service. The story was even heard on a Dallas TV news show by someone visiting from Farmington.

The ultimate "dental office story" also took place during the "mayor phase." Another disgruntled citizen did not like the "new young mayor" refusing to certify his latest subdivision until he posted the appropriate "performance bond." It seems he had never had to do that before with other mayors. He stormed into Doug's office, that was full of patients being cared for, with a .38 caliber pistol sticking out of his back pocket. He demanded his papers be signed immediately. Needless to say Doug calmly told him to get out of the office, go to City Hall, file the proper bond and as soon as the City Clerk relayed that had been done, the signature would be done. Thirty minutes later, no shots were fired, and the deed had been done as promised - all according to the LAW. Everyone gave a sigh of relief, especially Doug. He admitted later he was scared out of his wits when he saw the pistol but somehow "managed to keep his cool." Nothing like that has happened since.

Today, computers networked together to handle appointments as well as patient records, accounts, continuing preventive care and a list longer than this entire article have been in place for the past several years. Digital cameras and close-up intra-oral cameras are being used on a regular basis to help people see and better understand their smile "needs" and express their smile "wants." Other items of recent development are sophisticated ultrasonic devices, telescope glasses, a plethora of light-cured materials and other new chemicals for use in providing great smiles and improving people's well being and health.

The title at the beginning of this article mentions the year 2015. Doug will be 77 years "old" or "young," depending on lots of things between now and then and what God in His wisdom has in mind. If the answer is "Yes," Douglas Kent Ross will still be caring for patients; if the answer is something else, so be it! Surely there'll be lots of smiles in Heaven too.

The office of Douglas K. Ross, 1967.

The Japanese Garden in 1967.

DICUS DRUG

E.M. Laakman founded Laakman Drug Store in Farmington in 1901. Mr. Laakman operated the business until his death in 1928. Mr. Ralph Dillard was a pharmacist working for Mr. Laakman and the store was sold to Mr. Dillard. Mr. Dillard continued to operate the business until 1952 when it was purchased by Mr. William E. Dicus. Mr. Dicus also owned Dicus Drug located in Fredericktown, MO. Mr. Dicus and his partner, Charles Venker, then opened a drug store in Ste. Genevieve, MO, in the 1960s and a third partner, Jerry Venker became a part owner of the business. In 1971 Ronald D. Short became a part owner when Mr. William Dicus decided to retire. The three partners continued to operate the three drug stores for many years. The Fredericktown and Ste. Genevieve stores were sold when Charles and Jerry Venker retired. Mr. Ronald Short continues business at Dicus Drug, now in its 98th year of continuous service to the community.

The original Laakman Drug Store was located at the corner of Columbia and Jefferson Streets, across from the courthouse. The store had fountain service until 1966 when the store was moved to its present location at 117 E. Columbia St.

Laakman Drug Store was the first air-conditioned business in Farmington. This was due to the location of Missouri Natural Gas Co. offices, which were located upstairs over the drug store. The sign in Laakman's window read "It's Cool Inside." Tables used in Laakman's ice cream parlor are now being used in Dicus Drug.

Pharmacist Ronald Short is a graduate of Farmington High School and St. Louis College of Pharmacy.

Dicus Drugs, late 1970s.

MANLEY & KARRAKER, P.C. LAW FIRM

The law firm resulted from the original law practice of Mr. J.P. Cayce, who started it in 1904 after graduating from Princeton University. At the time of its origin, it was located in the old Realty Building, site of the present Mercantile Bank. In 1946 Robert B. Manley joined the practice, and in 1962 he and Mr. Cayce formed a partnership under the name of Cayce and Manley. This partnership continued until the death of Mr. Cayce in 1957.

Robert Manley continued the practice from 1957 as a sole practitioner until October 1983 when Kevan L. Karraker joined the practice and later became partner and the name of the firm became Manley & Karraker.

When Mercantile Bank, which became owner of the Realty Bldg., decided to tear down the building and build a new bank building, Mr. Karraker acquired vacant property at 110 S. Jefferson Street and constructed thereon a new office building where the firm of Manley & Karraker continued its practice.

In September 1988, William G. Reeves joined the firm as full partner, and the name of the firm was changed to Manley, Karraker & Reeves, P.C. Mr. Manley retired in 1996, and Mr. Reeves left the firm in November 1997, Thereafter Mr. Karraker continued the firm practice at 110 S. Jefferson Street as a sole practitioner.

The firm has been blessed through the years with having excellent staff secretaries, two of whom were Marie B. Huffman and Marilyn Pirtle, both of whom contributed immeasurably to the success of the firm.

MEDICATE PHARMACY

In 1967 in Farmington, Medicate Pharmacy began as a small retail pharmacy serving the local community with prescriptions, over-the-counter medications, and a limited selection of durable medical equipment. Founding owners were Jack and Barbara Dunning.

In 1993 Medicate Pharmacy of the Leadbelt opened in Desloge, MO and Medicate Clinic Pharmacy in Farmington was opened in 1996. The Medicate Long Term Care Pharmacy and Home Infusion Pharmacy were moved to their new location at 312 East Karsch in 1994. The warehouse facilities were also expanded at that time at the same location.

Medicate Pharmacy has expanded its service area for prescription and durable medical equipment over southeast Missouri, including both retail and long-term care nursing facilities. The retail locations and gift items and greeting card selections have been increased as well as offering a wider variety of over-the-counter products and services.

Customer oriented pharmaceutical care is very popular with our patients. Their "one-stop" health related items with free delivery and set-up of durable medical equipment are equally important.

From humble beginnings in 1967, Medicate Pharmacy has become one of the highest volume independent pharmacies in the state of Missouri. Medicate's Durable Medical Equipment department, its Home Infusion Pharmacy, and its Long Term Care Pharmacy became Joint Commission Accredited in 1998.

Medicate Pharmacy will continue to expand their business into the next century to bring the ultimate in health care to the community.

The Medicate Pharmacy Staff.

Medicate Pharmacy

FARMINGTON ANIMAL HOSPITAL

Dr. W.C. Dillard established Farmington Animal Hospital in 1930. First operating out of a local livery stable, the practice then moved to East Harrison Street on the site of what is now Dr. Fred Schaper's dental office. Dr. W.R. Sheets purchased the business in 1946. Dr. Sheets was a 1943 graduate of Michigan State University Veterinary School and served during World War II in the U.S. Army Veterinary Corps stationed in Canton, MO; the Farmington area was part of his territory. Dr. Sheets immediately began to expand the business with the help of Mrs. Florence McCoy as office manager, as well as Al Crabtree, on a part-time basis. Jack Clay joined the firm on a full-time basis in 1949. Dr. Sheets and Jack traveled a seven-county area providing veterinary services. Both Mrs. McCoy and Mr. Clay remained with the Farmington Animal Hospital until their respective retirements.

In 1951 the "new and modern" animal hospital was completed on Karsch Blvd., containing both small and large animal facilities. It was a state-of-the-art veterinary clinic in its day. An article regarding the business subsequently appeared in the *St. Louis Post Dispatch*. After moving into the new facility, Dr. Sheets began employing a succession of senior veterinary medical students on an internship basis, including Dr. Bob McNab, Dr. Al Doughty, Dr. Bill Bryson, Dr. Floyd Swanstone, Dr. Charles Counts, Dr. Joe Hooker and Dr. Dudley Pautz. Dr. Sheets was honored by his peers by being a longtime member of the Missouri State Board of Veterinarians and was later named Missouri State Veterinarian of the Year, 1963. Dr. Pautz became a full-time employee and then a partner in the firm. Drs. Sheets and Pautz operated as partners in the business until 1986 when it was sold to Dr. James McNeill.

Dr. Vicki Monnig joined the practice in late 1986. Other veterinarians employed by the practice in the following years were Dr. Marge Protheroe and Dr. Andre Oberle. In 1992 Dr.

McNeill sold the business to Dr. Monnig and her husband Joe at which time it became a small-animal practice. Dr. McNeill continued to practice at Farmington Animal Hospital until 1996, Dr. Alisa Powell from 1992-1998, and Dr. John Ragsdale from 1996-1997. Dr. Rachel Cook joined the practice in 1997, and she and Dr. Monnig currently provide quality veterinary care for their patients.

Due to an expanding business and lack of space, the original Farmington Animal Hospital on Karsch Blvd. was demolished in 1997, and a new hospital was constructed on the same site. The new building has a modern attractive appearance and includes facilities for boarding, grooming, and retail sales of premium pet foods and supplies in addition to a well-equipped, modern veterinary hospital.

LITTLE CAESAR'S PIZZA

September 1991 saw the addition of a new pizza parlor to Farmington's busy Karsch Boulevard. Entrepreneurs Dan and Betty Combs opened the popular franchise restaurant featuring Pizza! Pizza! two pizzas at one low price. For example, customers could order for carryout, two medium pizzas for only $9.99 plus tax, as well as the Family Choice Deal of one medium supreme pizza plus one medium two-topping pizza for the kids, for the low price of $11.99 plus tax.

Home delivery of menu items, pizza, pasta, salad and soft drinks, later became a popular alternative to carryout or the limited seating, eat-in counter.

Quickly achieving one of the highest Little Caesar's sales volumes in the Midwest, Dan and Betty expanded their business, adding restaurants in Desloge and Festus. Not surprisingly, future plans include opening yet another Little Caesar's restaurant.

Little Caesars Pizza

Farmington Animal Hospital

T-Rex Corporation

Craig P. Nesbit, president, and Susan J. Nesbit, vice-president, secretary-treasurer, began the T-Rex Corporation on July 31, 1972.

The business has grown from one convenience store with garage bays to the present seven convenience stores. Employing state-of-the-art technologies, the stores feature ATMs, as well as card-reading gasoline pumps.

At each T-Rex, the Nesbits are proud to offer their customers the popular Shell brand gasoline, as well as convenience foods, with emphasis on quick, convenient, one-stop shopping.

In addition to their convenience stores, the Nesbits also own two smoke shops, as well as a Blimpie's restaurant. They plan to grow to meet the demand in each of their current areas of enterprise.

T-Rex #1
Karsch & Washington
13 West Karsch
Farmington, MO 63640-2144
(573) 756-3216

T-Rex #3
519 East Main
Park Hills, MO 63601-2623
(573)431-2720

T-Rex #4
Highway 67 & 8
1609 West Columbia
Farmington, MO 63640-3514
(573) 756-7557

T-Rex #5
Highway 67 & 8
336 North State Street
Desloge, MO 63601-3052
(573) 431-2035

T-Rex # 7
Highway 61 & 32
795 Ste. Genevieve
Ste. Genevieve, MO 63670-1826
(573) 883-5728

T-Rex #8
Highway 55 & 51
2020 Lake Drive
Perryville, MO 63775-9758
(573) 547-1434

T-Rex # 9
Main & Wood
601 West Main
Fredericktown, MO 63645-1111
(573) 783-7369

Smokes To Go #2
1137 North Desloge Street
Desloge, MO 63601-3052
(573) 431-0125

The T-Rex

HOMES

History of the Long House

The original Long House was built in 1833 by Phillip Graham Long and his wife, Isabella Murphy Long (of the original Murphy family). Originally, the house of log construction contained just one room downstairs and one upstairs with enclosed stairway and fireplace. As the family grew to include 12 children, other additions were made. The first was to the south of the original with a room downstairs and room above, enclosing a "dog run" or, in present day terms, a breeze way, with a stairway to the upper low-ceilinged room. Much later, another addition was built to the north of the original, also with a room down and above with individual stairway; thus the house contained three units, each with its own stairway. Then a room was added for a kitchen as an ell to the north section.

The original and south addition were of log construction with beautiful hand-hewn logs. The third and kitchen additions were of clapboard construction. At the time of adding the north section the entire structure was clapboard covered.

In time the house passed to a daughter of the original builder, Mrs. G.H. Bisby (Jennie Long) who, in 1921, willed the house and surrounding area to the City of Farmington. It was used by nieces and great nephew as a residence until 1921. After the city acquired the property, it was used as a residence for the City Park Superintendent and during World War II as a day nursery for the children of women employed by a local manufacturing company.

In the spring of 1951, the city decreed to raze the house because of its age and uselessness. The Monday Club, a Federated Women's club numbering 25 members, protested the destruction, and in the spring of 1952 offered to lease the house from the city for a short period to enable the group to determine how it could be saved as a place of historic interest. Beginning at once, sufficient repairs were made for the safety of the building. Then began diligent work by the Monday Club to interest other clubs and civic organizations in complete restoration. A council of these organizations was formed, their support given and bids secured for the work. The city of Farmington agreed to assume one-third of the cost, the Monday Club one-third, and other interested groups the final one-third. Work was completed in late summer of 1954. To defray part of the cost, the Monday Club sponsored Farmington's first Homecoming. Other means of raising money were promoted by the various organizations and through this combined effort and help from the city, the last payment on restoration was made in 1954.

The contract did not include interior decoration other than painting the woodwork. The Monday Club began working for completion of the interior. In the summer of 1967 the south room and adjoining hall were decorated, and with gifts of beautiful parlor furniture, the house now has a complete parlor.

The center room, with its original log and chinking interior, and the north room and

Long House

Inside of Long House

kitchen are used for club meetings and entertainment. One unique feature, few people know about, is located in the downstairs north room. Hidden under the piano is a trap door which leads to a small space under the house. Stories reveal this small space was used to hide slaves during the Civil War. The north room upstairs is furnished as a lounge and the center upstairs room as a bedroom. Only one room in the house, the south upstairs room, is unfinished and at present is used for storage.

Many items of furniture have been purchased by the Monday Club and many have been donated and some loaned, all in keeping with the style of the house. Additional furnishings are still being solicited and purchased.

To those interested clubs and civic groups, the fact that this is the oldest remaining house in Farmington was the compelling force which rescued the Long House from destruction and it is now one of the few landmarks of the Old Farmington.

On the north lawn stands a granite pyramidal structure identifying the site of the first industry in Farmington, a tannery owned by Phillip Graham Long. When this marker was

At right: Location of first tannery in Farmington, established by Phillip Long. When the monument was erected, descendants of Phillip Long and Isabella Murphy gathered for the dedication. Each descendant laid a stone for this monument.

being built, a stone was placed by every remaining member of the Long Family.

Long House Furnishings

The chair in the "dog-run" is a birthing chair.
The fainting couch is from the Shaw house and was donated by Mary Ledbetter.
The hall tree has an umbrella stand.
There is a Mother-Daughter love seat in the house.

The Oak wardrobe and armoire in the upstairs bedroom are in the Rosebud design.
The rug in the parlor was put together in sections.
The stairway piano was from the old Taylor house.
The china in the "Meeting Room" is the "Tea Leaf" pattern. Abraham Lincoln also had that pattern.

History of William and Minnie Detring Home

Samuel P. Harris, of Virginia ancestry, came to Cook Settlement in 1821 from Richmond, Kentucky. He purchased hundreds and hundreds of acres of land in Liberty Township of St. Francois County. His grandson, Andrew K. Harris, inherited this farm and the pre-Civil war brick mansion house that was built around 1845. No record of how long it took to build the house is known.

The foundation is laid up of large stone blocks that were cut on the farm as seen from a full basement. The walls of the two story house are 18" thick of solid brick. There used to be a fireplace in each room. The home has been completely remodeled by the present owners, and when doing so, practice handwriting was found behind a wood fireplace mantel that was dated 1857. A brick summer kitchen stood next to the main house where food was prepared. There were at least five slave cabins on the farm at that time.

The farm remained in the Harris family until 1901 when William Detring Sr., grandfather of William A. Detring (present owner), rented the farm. The Detring family rented the farm until 1946 when the daughter of Andrew K. Harris sold the farm to William and Minnie Detring.

William and Minnie Detring's home.

Old Marion Parks homestead 1936.

Pipkin house on Columbia Street next to Butterfield's.

The turn of the century home at 604 W. Columbia St. was built by Mr. and Mrs. J. Paul Cayce. The house has a lot of curved glass, unusual arrangement of floor plans and a ball room on the third floor. This picture was taken in 1903.

Jacob Helber, 1907, corner of Ste. Genevieve Ave. and Fleming St., home of James Hrouda.

This house at 705 W. Columbia St. was built in the early 1900s as a frame structure, but in 1929 the home was bricked over. In 1932 Carlisle E. Rozier was making it his home.

George Wilson home, located where the Post Office is downtown, 1940.

George Herbst lived in this home at 311 North Jefferson St. in 1932.

Charles Cunningham built this home is 1840 across from Parkview Cemetery.

Joseph Counts home at 601 North Washington St.

This house at 503 W. Columbia was built in 1880 by the son of the first Milton P. Cayce, whose father came to St. Francois County in the early 1830s. The Cayces owned slaves, who lived in quarters behind the original house until the end of the Civil War.

The home at 628 W. Columbia St. was built in 1904 by Dr. Frank Keith when he became the first superintendent of the State Hospital. Louis Miller was the architect.

Judge William R. Taylor's home at 502 W. Columbia was built about 1863-1865 on part of the Sarah Barton Murphy survey. Mr. Taylor was the grandson of Richard Taylor, an uncle of President Zachary Taylor.

Swink home called Oak Grove, was located on Weber Road next to Maehill Care Center.

Moothart home 1912, Third St.

D. F. Giessing house, corner of Jefferson and Murphy Sts.

1932, residence of Harry Denman, Editor of the Farmington News.

Famous Sons And Daughters

Dayse F. Baker

Miss Dayse Baker was born in Clarksville, TN on September 15, 1880. She came to Farmington with her enslaved parents and attended elementary school. But because she was black, she was not allowed to attend high school in Farmington. She returned to Clarksville to live with an uncle while she completed high school. She attended Frances Rhoda College and then returned to Farmington to begin teaching at the Douglas School in 1903 at the age of 18. She was one of two teachers for 75 children, grades 1-8, in the one-room Douglas School. Miss Baker retired from the Farmington School District in 1954 after a teaching career of 52 years. In 1954 it was Miss Dayse Baker who pressed the issue of integration before the Board of Education by locking herself in the bathroom to pray.

Miss Dayse Baker wore a variety of hats: she helped raise college funds for black students, helped people who were in trouble, cared for members of her family, was a dedicated member of the United Memorial Methodist Church, and sparked hundreds of students. Miss Baker was honored by 232 friends at the Dayse Baker Testimonial Dinner in April 1973. She was honored again in 1973 at a banquet held by local civic groups. A city proclamation named April 2, 1973 as Miss Dayse Baker Day in Farmington. In addition to the honors by her fellow Farmingtonians, she received a memorial from the Missouri House of Representatives, as well as letters of recognition from U.S. Senator Stuart Symington, Secretary of State James Kirkpatrick, Governor Christopher Bond, Congressman Bill Burlison and State Treasurer James Spainhower. *The Farmington Evening Press* honored Miss Baker in 1979: "It is out of admiration and love for one of Farmington's oldest and most respected citizens

Dayse Baker, Principal of Douglas School

that the *Farmington Evening Press* wishes to dedicate its 1979 Centennial Edition to Miss Dayse Baker. Almost as old as the town itself, Miss Dayse Baker is one of its most valued citizens."

She lived in a little house on Main Street, which she called "Noah's Ark." When taking care of the "Ark" became too much for her, she moved to St. Louis to live with a nephew. When she became ill and had to be hospitalized, consent papers had to be signed for some tests. "Just put your X right there," the well-meaning nurse told Miss Dayse, realizing the slim chance that a 99-year old sick black woman could write. Miss Dayse roused through her pain and bristled with dignity as she took the pen. "X's are for people who can't write," she told the nurse as she signed. Miss Dayse Baker died October 13, 1979. In the *Farmington Press* article telling of her death, the paper says her epitaph should read:

MISS DAYSE BAKER
September 15, 1880 - October 13, 1979
"By sheer competence she proved to Farmington the idiocy of the color line."

There is some conflict as to her birth date. Her birth date is given as September 15, 1881, in several sources but her tombstone gives the 1880 date. A local newspaper article says "In September (1979) she got a congratulatory card from President Carter for what Carter had been informed was her 100th birthday. And Miss Dayse, although she was really 'only' 99 and had never, never admitted her age, became 100 and urged her family to adopt that number when referring to her.

David Barton

David Barton was Sarah Barton Murphy's nephew. His father was Isaac Barton. He was born December 10, 1783, in Tennessee. He graduated from Greeneville College, TN and entered the law office of a distinguished jurist of that state. It was from this lawyer that he received training which aided in making him one of the ablest lawyers of his day.

It was in 1809 that David and two of his brothers came to Missouri where they practiced law. One brother, Joshua, who was a United States District Attorney in St. Louis, was killed in a duel with a Thomas Rector in 1823. This tragedy deeply affected David who criticized the actors in the affair.

David settled in St. Charles to practice law. He served in the Army during the War of 1812. After the war, he moved to St. Louis where he became the Attorney General of the Territory of Missouri in 1813. He was also elected to the St. Louis circuit bench. In 1818, the Territorial Legislature was meeting in St. Louis, where he became Speaker of the House of Representatives. Then, in 1820, he was elected president of the first Constitutional Convention without opposition. He penned the constitution that was adopted by that body, which was replaced by the Drake Constitution in 1866.

It was in the first State Legislature, in 1821, he was chosen United States Senator by acclamation. Two different accounts are offered to the selection of Thomas Hart Benton as the sec-

David Barton

ond senator elected. One reads that Barton was able to convince a friend, who was sick, to send a letter voting for Benton, who won by one vote. The other account reads there was a tie between Benton and another man; and David Barton, being highly respected, was allowed to choose the second senator. David Barton served only 10 years as a member of the Senate, while Thomas Hart Benton served 30.

Barton and Benton were friends but their political views divided them. Barton was a Whig while Benton was a Jackson Democrat. In the memorable debates over the Foote Resolution, David Barton, on February 9, 1830, gave a powerful accusation and censure on his colleague, Thomas Hart Benton. Critics have pronounced it equal to Webster's reply to Hayne. Barton was the greatest orator west of the Mississippi River. He was nicknamed "Little Red."

Barton opposed the policies of Jackson and Benton. It was his part in the election of Adams in the race for the presidency in the House in 1824 which led to his political downfall in Democratic Missouri in 1830. He was defeated for re-election to the Senate. His friends secured his election to the Missouri State Senate where he served for four years.

Thomas Hart Benton wrote *Thirty Years Review* in which he made no mention of Barton except to his voting record. It is mainly for this reason that Barton has remained comparatively unknown while Benton's personality stands out conspicuously. It is sad as these two men were once very good friends.

David Barton moved to Booneville, MO, where he served as circuit judge, after retiring as state senator.

He died September 28, 1837, in Booneville where he was buried. His remains were removed to the new cemetery. Later, the remains were moved again to Walnut Grove Cemetery. A new marble shaft was placed on this site. The old monument was placed on the campus at the University of Missouri, Columbia. It was placed by the side of Thomas Jefferson's memorial at Jesse Hall. It is located on Francis Quadrangle to the west of the steps of Jesse Hall. The city

John L. Bradley

of Booneville donated the monument dedicated to David Barton to the University.

David Barton did not live in Farmington but we felt that he should be included as he was a powerful and influential man, shaping the future of Missouri and the United States. Sarah Barton Murphy was his aunt and probably had an influence on David as they did visit with one another.

John L. Bradley

John L. Bradley was the Democratic senator from the 26th District, born in Knoxville, TN June 9, 1852. He came to Missouri with his parents as a boy, 5 years of age, settling in Doe Run, MO.

He was educated in the common schools and was engaged in merchandising at Flat River. In 1877 he married Miss Julia H. Paston of St. Francois County.

He was a member of the house in the 40th and 41st General Assemblies and was first elected to the Senate in 1902 and re-elected in 1906.

His biggest interest was in labor questions, and he will always be known as the author of the *Eight-hour Law for Miners* and the *Sixteen-hour Law for Railroad Employees*.

George Washington Brooks
The Last Slave's Story

(Taken from a series of articles by Sarah Heimburger, *Daily Journal* assistant editor, published in the *Daily Journal*, Park Hills, MO, May 29, 1999 through June 2, 1999)

"FRENCH VILLAGE - The humble headstone in St. Anne's Parish cemetery reads 'George Washington Brooks, 1853-1937: Faithful in All Things.' It is a fitting epitaph for a man who stayed with the family who owned him decades after he was emancipated.

"The history and personal effects of George Washington Brooks will be preserved and displayed in the Missouri Historical Society Mu-

seum in St. Louis' Forest Park. George's pair of eyeglasses, cross pendant, his 'everyday' pocket knife and his 'good' knife' might seem like any other antiques in a glass case. But according to the museum, the value in George's former belongings come with the stories that follow:

George was born April 1, 1853, on steamboat Captain James Brooks' plantation on the Isle Au Bois in Jefferson County. When George was seven years old, Mrs. Brooks gave George to her daughter, Luella E. Brooks Au Buchon, as a wedding gift. Luella and her husband, Ferdinand F. Au Buchon, made their home in French Village. Their home can be seen a short distance from Route Y and is located next to the general store that Ferdinand ran. He bought goods in New Orleans, had them shipped to Brickey's Landing and then pulled them by ox cart to French Village. "George would accompany the Brooks family on buying trips to St. Louis. According to an account in his obituary, Mrs. Brooks would have George and his brother, Dib, carry her packages. George was almost separated from the family forever when he was snatched from the sidewalk by a thief. At that time, slave patrols had been established, and blacks were often kidnapped and literally sold down the river." The thief dropped George and he was reunited with the family. Dib met a similar fate some time later and George never saw his brother again. George had four other brothers and sisters. According to Katherine Odile McCormick Jensen, George never knew who his father was. "It used to seem to comfort him to say, 'I reckon we all had the same daddy, don't you think? All six of us, 'cept maybe Dib, who was born when my mammy belonged to the Rush Tower folks, before your folks bought her?'"

When the Civil War broke out, Ferdinand, fearing for George's safety, sent him back to the Brooks Place in Jefferson County. "The following morning, the Au Buchons found George curled up on the doorstep of their French Village home. He refused to go back, and remained in the house from then on as a paid servant.

"When he was 9 years old in 1862, word reached the Au Buchons in French Village that it became necessary to deliver $1,000 worth of gold to the Brooks Place. George volunteered to make the trip, reportedly hiding the gold in his boots. The woods were full of Guerilla soldiers, and Brooks Place was guarded against bushwhackers. He was almost mistaken for the enemy and shot, until James Brooks identified the horse George rode and ushered him in. Another time, word reached French Village that soldiers were coming. George helped Luella bury all the valuables they could; then he hid in a flour barrel until it was safe to come out. Through a notch in the barrel, he watched as the soldiers ransacked the house, throwing against the wall a ball of yarn in which he had hidden a mosaic piece of jewelry. But the men didn't find the jewelry, and the piece was purportedly passed down from generation to generation afterward, a testament as to how George had succeeded again.

"George took a dim view of emancipation. He was an unreconstructed Negro and always said Negroes never should have been freed. He had nothing but scorn for the present generation of 'upstarts', as he called them, among his race."

When Luella became an invalid, George

took care of her for the last 10 years of her life, helping raise her six children. One of those children, Florence, eventually brought George with her to Farmington. Florence was married to Dr. E. C. McCormick, son of Union Brigadier General James R. McCormick, and they lived in the McCormick house on Columbia Street.

George was a devout Catholic. Although he never learned to read or write, he could converse in German and French learned from the early settlers. In addition to George's yarn spinning about "Indian John," who reportedly distracted settlers while his comrades robbed them, George would gather calamas root for "winter sickness" as he called pneumonia, bloodroot for misery and buckeyes to ward off evil and to make a salve for sores.

George remained in Farmington to take care of the McCormick home long after family members had left. He eventually became ill and was moved to St. Louis to stay with Katherine Odile McCormick Jensen.

He died in 1937. By that time, he was so popular and so well-loved, when the St. Louis funeral home initially refused to place his body in a parlor (they were going to put him in the hall) they eventually had to give over their entire facility to him, so great was the tide of flowers and visiting dignitaries who came to pay their respects. When Brooks was carried to French Village to be buried in the family plot, the priest at St. Anne's Parish at the time wouldn't allow him to be buried in the cemetery, although descendants of the Au Buchon family who originally owned him were adamant he be included. The priest compromised but made sure the slave was buried just outside the fence surrounding the family plots. The fence has since been torn down and the cemetery has expanded greatly.

"He prospered in a modest way and saved his money," Katherine remembered to the *Post-Dispatch*, "but it didn't do him much good. In his effects were found old notes for $500, $700 and $800 he had lent to white men who never paid him back.

According to a family member "he was, in a way, even more of a natural born family member. He stayed on while the rest of the family moved away."

Eliza Carleton

In 1839 Eliza Carleton, a native of Montgomery County, VA, traveled with her father, Jacob Carleton, to a wilderness we now know as Farmington, MO. The trip was made in a covered wagon. Miss Carleton's mother had passed away 13 years earlier when Eliza was just an infant. Realizing that Eliza needed a mother, Jacob had solicited the assistance of his mother, Susannah Carleton, to raise Eliza. Susannah was to become the only mother Eliza would ever know.

The trip to Missouri was prompted by Mr. Carleton's quest for new land to farm. Mr. Carleton bought property east of Desloge. A homestead was established with Eliza assuming the household duties. She would remain devoted to her father, caring for him until his death many years later.

Miss Carleton received her early education in district schools in Virginia and later

South Bend, IN. Jacob Carleton had moved to South Bend to live with relatives after leaving Virginia and before moving to Missouri. Determined to continue her education, Miss Carleton gathered books, studying literature, math, Latin and science during her free moments. She exhibited an early dedication for learning. This devotion was to become the hallmark of her life.

Realizing that her education could not progress unless she had formal instruction, Miss Carleton applied for admission to the Arcadia College in the Arcadia Valley. At the time, the College was an all-male institution highly respected for its curriculum. Eliza pleaded for a seat. Miss Carleton was allowed admission on the condition that she maintain respectable grades. She would be shown no consideration for being a woman. Graduating before her 19th birthday, Miss Carleton led her class as valedictorian. She was awarded her MA degree from Arcadia College in 1853.

After graduation, Miss Carleton was determined to see that the children of the Mineral Area receive an opportunity for education. A very moral and religious woman, Miss Carleton felt a good education was every child's God given right. It was her belief that no child should have to suffer poverty and ignorance for lack of a school.

Miss Carleton opened a one-room, log schoolhouse in Perry Township, St. Francois County in 1845 at the age of 19. With donations from others who shared her vision and tuition of $3.00 in trade or $2.00 in cash, a family could secure a year of formal instruction for their student. More often than not, Miss Carleton accepted chickens, pigs, grain or other staples as payment for her services.

What started as a small one-room schoolhouse, grew to become the foundation stone of the Carleton Institute, founded in April 1854. Eliza named the institute in honor of her father. An act to incorporate Carleton Institute with university privileges was approved by the legislature in Jefferson City in 1859. With this act, the school became Carleton College. Miss Carleton served the college as president and instructor of English. The college would prove to become the beginning of a formal, higher education program for the young people of Farmington and surrounding communities. It remained a viable institution until its closing in 1913. The college building was reopened after WWI to serve as a center to retrain veterans of the War. After completion of this program, the building was closed until it was purchased by the Catholic Church, serving as an elementary and high school building until the early 1960s. An interesting aside was the football team fielded by Carleton College which played St. Louis University in the early part of this century. Today, Carleton Street runs north and south along a line, which once bordered the west side of the campus. Carleton Street is named in honor of the college and its founder.

At the time of Miss Carleton's death in 1916, she was so revered by the citizens of Farmington, all businesses in the city were closed on the day of the funeral, a Saturday. It was a measure of the homage the citizens of Farmington and surrounding communities paid to Miss Carleton. She was laid to rest in the Masonic Cemetery on Henry Street just to the south of downtown Farmington.

In 1898 Earl Carleton, a nephew of Eliza, arrived as a child of 9 from South Bend, IN. He was to live with his uncle and aunt, Jacob and Emma Carleton Helber. Jacob Helber was a successful hardware businessman. Jacob built and resided in the large red brick, three-story home that still stands today at the corner of Ste. Genevieve Avenue and Fleming Streets. Earl's parents sent him to Farmington to receive a good education. He attended Carleton College. After completing his education, he went to work for St. Joe Lead Company, then left to join Mr. Helber in the hardware business.

On June 23, 1915, Earl Carleton married Wilma Denman, daughter of Harry and Lou Denman. Wilma's father was a successful journalist and owner of the *Farmington News*. To this union two children were born. Winifred Louella Carleton, born Nov. 22, 1916, and Charles Earl Jr., born March 11, 1924. Winifred Carleton attended college at Southeast Missouri State in Cape Girardeau. After attending college, she accepted a position with the Trimfoot Shoe Company. Winifred remained with Trimfoot for 38 years, retiring in 1982. Winifred married Warren Watkins, son of Dr. George Lancaster Watkins, in 1943. Dr. Watkins was a prominent Farmington physician and founder of Medical Arts Clinic. In 1946, Winifred and Warren became the proud parents of a daughter whom they named Susan Jo. Susan grew up in Farmington, graduating from Farmington High School in 1963. Susan attended Williams Wood College in Fulton, MO, graduating with a BS degree in education in 1967. Susan married Mr. Chuck Hall of Boise, ID. They moved to Cleveland, OH where they raised three daughers: Jennifer, Amy and Lisa Hall. Mr. Hall became a prominent Cleveland investment banker. Sadly, Mr. Hall passed away at age 50 in 1995.

Charles Earl Carleton Jr. graduated from Farmington High School in 1941 at the age of 17. He attended Flat River Junior College where he won a Navy Scholarship to study medicine. Transferring first to Westminister College in Fulton, MO, then to Missouri University in Columbia, MO, he completed his BS degree in medical science in 1947. Charles was accepted to the Washington University School of Medicine in St. Louis. He graduated with a doctorate of medicine in 1949. Dr. Carleton served his internship and residency at St. Louis City Hospital and served a tour of military duty as a medical officer in the US Navy, earning the rank of lieutenant upon discharge in 1952.

After completion of military service, Dr. Carleton and his young family returned to his hometown of Farmington. He joined the staff of Medical Arts Clinic to begin a practice in 1953. Dr. Carleton remained a partner of Medical Arts until his retirement in 1996. During the 43 years of partnership, he served as both president of Medical Arts and later, the first Chief of Staff of Farmington Community Hospital. Dr. Carleton served as president of the Farmington Chamber of Commerce in 1965 and has served on the Board of Directors of Ozarks Federal Savings and Loan since 1974. He is currently medical director of Hospice Care Inc.

Eliza Carleton

On Sept. 7, 1945, Dr. Carleton married Martha Joan Havniear at the Carleton Memorial Methodist Church. Dr. and Mrs. Carleton became the parents of two sons, Charles Edward, born 1946, and John Richard, born 1951.

Charles graduated from Farmington High School in 1965 and later earned BS, MS and specialist degrees in educational administration from Missouri University and Southeast Missouri State University. Charles served as the sixth principal in the history of Farmington High School, a position he occupied for eight years. He later served the Farmington District as assistant administrator to the superintendent, retiring in 1998 to become assistant administrator for Mineral Area Regional Medical Center. Charles "Chuck" Carleton married Jane Barron in 1970. Jane graduated from Methodist Hospital School of Nursing, earning a degree in nursing in 1971. She currently works for Parkland Health Center as a nursing administrator.

John graduated from Missouri Military Academy in 1969 and later earned BS, MS and specialist degrees from the University of Missouri in Columbia, MO. John married Pam Gable in 1974. Pam graduated from the University of Missouri earning BS and MS degrees in special education. She teaches special education for the Warsaw School District. John has served the Warsaw School District as a teacher, and currently occupies the dual role of elementary principal and Director of Elementary Education. John also serves on the Board of Directors of the Midwest Hemophilia Association in Kansas City, MO.

Charles and Jane have two children, Carolyn, a registered nurse, and Charlie, who has aspirations to follow his grandfather as a doctor. Carolyn is married to Dr. Guy Roberts, son of Dr. and Mrs. Gerald Roberts of Farmington. John has two children, Kristin and Brian. Kristin plans to attend Missouri University to study sports medicine, while Brian hopes to become a CPA.

Throughout the history of the Carleton family, a tradition of community service has existed. Family members have dedicated themselves to serving others through business, medicine and education. From the humble beginnings of a one-room schoolhouse given root by a tiny but visionary lady, Eliza Carleton, grew a college and a family lineage which has contributed 160 years of educators, doctors, nurses and business people. Each family member, like so many other founding families, has contributed a foundation stone upon which the city has been built. Each in their own way, helped to make Farmington the city of tradition and progress for which it is recognized today.

Ethelean Cayce Proud Of Her Deep Roots

The pioneer families that lent their names to the early pages of Farmington history brought with them a spirit that in many ways is still evident in the community today.

But of their many descendants who still call Farmington home, few can match Ethelean Cayce in the many ways she exemplifies the spirit of the town's forefathers. At 74, the woman maintains girlish enthusiasm when talking at length on her family, which is one of the first black families to settle in the farming community.

It was just after the end of the Civil War that Jeter Cayce accompanied a family from Virginia when the clans moved to the west. Jeter had been property of the Cayce family prior to the War between the states and he took on the surname to accompany his status as a free man.

According to Ethelean, the settlement of her family in Farmington ended for good any connection with slavery. She remarked that during her upbringing discussion of the topic was not allowed in the Cayce household, and that's the way the woman still prefers it to be.

Shortly after crossing the Mississippi and settling in Farmington, Jeter bought a tract of land in the vicinity of First and Washington Street. Miss Cayce's modest home stands on part of the original tract.

That original $450 acquisition has been carved into several smaller parcels, one of which includes the nearby St. Francois County Abstract Co. Just behind Miss Cayce's home is the Knights of Pythias Hall, a building that formerly was the St. Paul's Methodist Church. Its congregation included many members of the city's black community during its nearly 100 year life span.

Ethelean was born in 1905 in the old Elmwood Seminary where her father, Parnell, was a custodian. The site of the seminary is now occupied by the Presbyterian Home for Children.

Looking very much unlike a woman nearing the three-quarter century mark, Ethelean spoke fondly of the domestic chores she performed in others' homes during most of her life. She spent 25 years with the Will Harlan family in Farmington and she remembers those times as if she was a part of the family she worked for.

Jeter and his 14 children would be proud of the care Ethelean has taken in preserving the family name over the last 100 years. There are photographs covering most of the wall in her home and plenty of boxes loaded with snapshots that date back to the early 1900's. But it's the attitude of having a duty to perform, so to speak, that best supports Ethelean's role as custodian of the family history.

"I've really had a full life here in Farmington," Ethelean remarked.

When asked if she was often the target of racial abuse, Ethelean would pause for a moment and respond almost defensively that her skin color really didn't prompt others to show contempt or disrespect.

"Farmington has always been good to colored people," she said in response to how she was treated by the white community. Ethelean apparently harbored no ill-will based on the events of American history, adding that she considered herself "lucky" to have been able to spend her lifetime in Farmington.

The last of the Cayces living in Farmington, Ethelean said the televised mini-series "Roots" which aired in February, "shook me up" in depicting the treatment blacks received over the years. But she was mindful to remark, "You can't blame one generation for what another generation did."

Ethelean completed an eight-grade education at the Old Frederick Douglass School on the west side of Farmington. There, she studied under Miss Dayse Baker, a figure whose name is synonymous with the education of blacks in the community.

It wasn't long after graduation, however, before Ethelean was placed by her family in a well-to-do home and began her years as a domestic servant. The experience got off to a rocky start, however.

"I just can't do it," Ethelean remembered crying to her mother after a day of scrubbing cupboards, but all she was told was, "Go back, you'll learn to like it."

Her mother's firm advice took hold with the teenager and Ethelean went on to help many families with various household chores. There are numerous pictures displayed by Ethelean of children she helped take care of over the years. Many today are mothers and fathers and they still manage to keep in contact with the woman who shared a big part of their childhood.

Marriage was not a successful endeavor, Ethelean admitted, and she said little of the three spouses in her life. Most of her words are for the sisters, brothers and parents who have shared the Cayce name. It's this love of family and job that has drawn the focus during most of Miss Cayce's years.

With the amount of energy and enthusiasm that she still breathes into the Farmington scene, Ethelean Cayce will continue to occupy a big page in Farmington history. It's people like Ethelean who continue to demonstrate the characteristics of the men and women who first settled the area.

She may well be one of the last pioneers.

Robert Forsyth

Robert Forsyth was a very gifted artist, horticulturist and a man of integrity. He lived to a ripe old age of 80 years, 8 months and 12 days. He was born in Matagarda Bay, Texas, August 25, 1852, the son of Leonard Emmet and Mary C. Lightner Forsyth. His father was born in Wheeling, WV, and was of Scotch Irish descent. His mother was born in Pittsburg, PA of Dutch Revolution stock. They married in Pittsburg and were the parents of two sons.

Ethelean Cayce

They moved from Texas to Kentucky when the children were small and then to St. Louis, where Robert started school at age 5 in the basement of the old Episcopal Church at Tenth and Pine Streets. The family lived across from the church but later moved to Eighth and Locust where the Mercantile Trust building was in 1933. His mother died while they lived there. He was 6 years old and was sent to live with her family in Pittsburg where he lived for eight years. During this time he attended Kenwood Boys School, an Episcopal School at New Brighten, PA. At the age of 15 he returned to Missouri where he lived on his father's farm in Jefferson County. He was employed at the Vulcan Iron Works in St. Louis. He married Ardelle Pipkin when he was 20. She was the sister of Merrill Pipkin formerly of Farmington. They settled in Kimmswick, where five years later his wife was claimed by death.

Robert went to Chicago where he was engaged in business and attended art school. He later was in business in Milwaukee and Cleveland. During this time he spent time in Farmington with Merrill Pipkin and he invested in a fruit farm two miles north of Farmington (Gaebe Fruit). He moved to Farmington in 1900 to manage the farm. He sold it in 1919. In 1909 he spent three weeks in the Isle of Pines investigating land for a company of Cleveland men with a view to grow citrus fruits.

On November 28, 1912, he married Elsie Cayce who lived on Columbia Street. When she died in 1930, she left the house to Robert until his death, when it was returned to the Cayce family. He was a gifted horticulturist and their yard was a sight to behold. One of the neighbors, Wilson Williams, in recent years told of their enjoyment of the fabulous scene next door of all the flowers and trees.

In Mr. Forsyth, the editor of the *News,* he found a real friend and co-laborer. Many times his work, both in story and picture, appeared in these columns. He contributed an article on the *Trees of Farmington* which was almost classic. The editor of the paper wrote the following article about Mr. Forsyth. "A prophet is not without honor save in his own country" is as true today as when it was written 2000 years ago. And in every community there are "prophets," painters, writers or philosophers, who go in and out among their familiars, and no one knows of their unusual talents or realizes they are entertaining a genius in their midst. Here in Farmington we have such a man, who is active in many occupations, but of whom very few know that his leisure hours for many years have been devoted to labor with brush and pencil, a labor of love on his part which has resulted in many canvases and sketches expressive of his talent. As a young man, Robert Forsyth spent the leisure hours of many years, first as a student, then as a student-teacher, in the Art Institute of Chicago, and as an illustrator, especially for articles about dogs and horses, in the drawing of which he has shown a special aptitude. Besides his collections of sketches of animals, he has given many chalk talks on these subjects, which were much enjoyed by young people.

Among his paintings are many of outstanding merit, his canvas of an old log cabin which stood until recently, near Old Maid Springs is beautifully executed, an old water mill in the Ozarks, Dead Man's Gulch on the winding road to Arcadia, in the full beauty of mid-summer foliage, his own home surrounded by trees in the richness of autumn coloring, are but a few of his works. He has also made several copies of the Dupuy Coat Of Arms-work that requires closest attention to nicety of detail and great delicacy of execution. Mr. Forsyth has done some portrait work, one piece in particular, a likeness of his wife, from a photograph taken when she was a young girl, being beautifully done. A piece of work which the artist himself thinks his best is a set of 12 sketches illustrating "Tears" drawings of decorative and allegorical figures, descriptive of verses of poetry which he has chosen as beautifully illustrating the subject verses of the Bible, Bryon, Scott, and other classics, for our artist is a man of marked literary talents, a reader and thinker of unusual ability.

In spite of his 80 years Mr. Forsyth is still using his brush as his favorite pastime, and just last week showed the writer a newly finished canvas of an allegorical representation of the "Journey Of Life," which appeals strongly to one's sense of the beautiful. Mr. Forsyth was born within the sound of the Gulf of Mexico, Matagardo Bay, TX, and has been an ardent lover of nature in all its manifestations. Mr. Forsythe has been an enthusiastic amateur naturalist all his life. And one outgrowth of this was the appointment in 1919 as assistant observer of the United States Weather Bureau, which office he held until his death in 1933. The following extracts are taken from a letter to J.P. Cayce from Roscoe Nunn of St. Louis, meteorologist and director of the U.S. Weather Bureau at St. Louis, dated May 13, 1933.

"Your letter of May 12, 1933, was received and I am sorry indeed to learn of the death of Robert Forsyth. Mr. Forsyth was an excellent cooperative observer for the last 15 years. He was one the most faithful and reliable of the entire corps of observers in Missouri."

Mr. Forsyth and his wife never were privileged to have children. They are buried in the Masonic Cemetery on S. Henry St. in Farmington.

Plank Road sketch done by Robert Forsyth.

B.T. Gentges

B.T Gentges was born July 10, 1875, near Quincy, IL, the son of John J. and Mary Meckes Gentges. He married Elizabeth Westhoff on November 23, 1897. To this union four children were born: Mary, Francis (deceased in childhood), Josephine, (died in infancy) and Cecelia. In 1910 Elizabeth died, leaving B.T. to raise his two girls.

In 1914 he moved to Farmington from Monroe City, MO and opened the Farmington Jet White Laundry. When he bought the laundry, it was located in the old Methodist Church building on South Henry where the Little Town Tavern is today. He soon moved the laundry to North Washington in the building later occupied by Small Engines. In 1924 he erected the building where the present laundry is today, and five years later enlarged it to its present size. In 1953 he sold the business to Robert Falast and Darrell Bay.

In 1916 he married Elsie Buckman Miles, the widow of Dr. Andrew Miles of Monroe City, MO. Mrs. Miles had two children, Tom and Velma. From the second marriage, Charles and Nancy were born.

Mr. Gentges, a civic-minded person, was one of the 18 men who took over Carleton College when the Methodist Church found it too much of a financial burden. He also joined a group of men to finance the continuous use of the old electric trolley which ran from Hurryville through Farmington to DeLassus.

In 1922 Mayor C.A. Tetley appointed him alderman of Ward I and he held this post for five terms. When Mayor Tetley died in 1934, Mayor C.H. Giessing and others insisted he run for mayor. He was re-elected twice and chose not to run for a fourth term.

Mr. Gentges was elected president of the Chamber of Commerce for the years 1931 and 1932. During that time the newspapers credited the Chamber for fostering the building of the present courthouse, paving the city's main streets, the White Way was erected and the modern sewer system was built. Through the efforts of the Chamber, Highway 61 was routed through the city, the present post office building was

B.T. Gentges

erected and Rice-Stix factory located in Farmington. While Gentges was mayor, more streets were paved and Wilson-Rozier Park and the municipal pool were built.

B.T. died at his home on January 18, 1964. He was buried in the Calvary Cemetery in Farmington, MO.

Taken from an article written for the *Evening Press*, March 19, 1979 by Willa Dean Meyer.

Harvey C. "Hap" Haile

Harvey Clinton Haile, son of Oscar and May C. Byington Haile, was born in Farmington March 5, 1896.

He was united in marriage to Agnes Vincel.

Mr. Haile was a life-long resident of Farmington and one of its most beloved and outstanding citizens. He was educated at Bradley University, Northwestern University, and Illinois University, all in Illinois.

He was a member of the First Baptist

Harvey "Hap" Haile and his daughter, Phyllis Schurter.

W. L. Johns

Marcus Kirkland

Church, the Masonic Lodge and a veteran of World War I.

Mr. Haile served as high school principal, athletic director and manual training teacher in Farmington High School for 27 years. He was also physical education director for St. Joseph High School for 10 years.

He created two annual awards for outstanding athletes: one in honor of his mother, given to the outstanding athlete in Farmington High School, and one in memory of his father, given to the outstanding athlete in St. Joseph High School.

In 1964 Mr. Haile received the state award for his work in the President Kennedy Physical Fitness Program. The plaque was awarded to him in ceremonies at Sedalia, MO.

The football field at Farmington High School is named after "Hap" Haile.

"Hap" Haile died on July 1, 1966, after being struck by a car, while he was crossing Highway 67. He was buried on July 4, 1966, in the Masonic Cemetery in Farmington.

W.L. Johns

W.L. Johns was born at Grubville, Jefferson County, MO, the son of William A. and Mary Sullins Johns. He was married to Miss Emma Belle Cole of Blackwell, MO in November 1897. They were the parents of two sons, Delos Cole Johns and Burdette T. Johns.

His service to the cause of education until he retired from active duties in 1946 extended over a period of 51 years. As a young man, he first began as a teacher in the rural schools of Jefferson County. Later he taught for a time in the public schools at DeSoto, until coming to Flat River in 1905 as superintendent of the Flat River schools.

In 1914 he accepted the position as superintendent of the Farmington Public School System and remained in this capacity for 32 years. In the spring of 1946, he announced to the school board his intention to retire from active service.

Through all the many years of his school service, Mr. Johns found time to take an active part in all of the civic and religious affairs of the community. He was a long-time and most active member of the Farmington Chamber of Commerce, a charter member of the Rotary Club and served one term as president of the club. He was a devout and active member of the Baptist Church and devoted much of his time and energy to the work of his church.

Mr. Johns passed away on September 2, 1953, following a lingering illness. He was buried in Parkview Cemetery in Farmington, MO.

Marcus Kirkland

Marcus Kirkland was born near Downing, MO in Schuyler County on October 27, 1888, the son of Mr. and Mrs. Charles H. Kirkland. He attended grade and high school at Downing, and at his graduation delivered the salutatory address.

Mr. Kirkland went to Flat River in 1915 and at that time was affiliated with his brother, John, in the furniture business. Before going to Flat River he was a salesman for "Heinz 57 Varieties."

In 1917 he volunteered for the army and served two years, one of these in France. He was made a sergeant and served in the Medical Corps. After being discharged in 1919 he returned to Flat River.

On June 26, 1919, he was married to Minnie White of Fredericktown, MO.

He bought a variety store in Flat River in 1923 and operated that store until he came to Farmington in January 1930 as owner of the Ben Franklin Store and later in the year moved to Farmington.

The untiring efforts of Marcus, along with Dr. L.M. Stanfield, C.C. Gower, and Harry Denman, resulted in the birth of the Farmington Rotary Club. It was chartered February 16, 1934, and he served as president during its second year.

He had a perfect attendance record of 27 years. A little sidelight on this marvelous record was that Marcus was forced to spend 14 days in a hospital in 1955, but believe it or not, he continued right on with his perfect attendance record.

He was a member of Farmington Lodge No. 132 AF&AM, Eastern Star Chapter, past president of the Farmington Chamber of Commerce, a member of the board of trustees of Mineral Area Osteopathic Hospital, and served a few months as acting administrator. He was a charter member and past commander of Coleman-Frazer American Legion Post, Flat River. He transferred to LePere-McAlister Post in Farmington and had 45 years continuous membership.

He sold the Ben Franklin Store in October 1947 and retired soon after.

Mr. Kirkland spent many hours in research, which resulted in his writing a very interesting history of Farmington.

He died on August 7, 1964, in Stuttgart, AR and was buried in Parkview Cemetery.

Tim Lollar From Farmington To The Major Leagues

My family and I moved from St. Louis to Farmington after my second grade year, and that was my first opportunity to play organized baseball. The Khoury Leagues, Atom, Bantam, Midget, and Juvenile were divided by age groups and were played at different parks throughout the city. I remember playing many games at what used to be the Farmington Junior High School field behind Gib Cresswell's house. During those early years we also played at the field by the Elk's Club. Once we were old enough for Midget League, we got to play at Wilson-Rozier Park. I still believe that is one of the biggest fields I have ever played on. For me, late spring was almost like Christmas. I couldn't wait to see the sports section of the *Farmington Press* to find out which team I was on.

The next competitive level for me was the

Tim Lollar

Babe Ruth League. We competed with teams from all the surrounding communities in hopes of reaching the playoffs and then the "World Series." Our teams never made it, but it wasn't for lack of effort. Jim Boyer put in many hours with us practicing and trying to hone our skills

After I turned 16, I started playing American Legion baseball for Post 416. Talk about fun, a bunch of 16, 17 and 18 year olds driving around Southeast Missouri playing baseball against any and all challengers. With all the characters on those teams it's no wonder that our manager, Bob McKinney, lost his hair at an early age. This league was very important to many players because at the time, Farmington High School didn't have a baseball program. American Legion gave many of us a good baseball experience as well as exposure to scouts of colleges and the pros.

One of the scouts to notice me was Hal Loughary from Mineral Area College. Coach Loughary offered me a scholarship to play at MAC, which I gladly accepted. My two years at MAC were very instrumental in my progression as a ball player. The conference was very competitive and it showed me that I could compete at a higher level. Our teams had a lot of local players who were not only talented but also a great bunch of guys to be around.

For my final two years of college, I attended the University of Arkansas. My success as a junior was not as good as I expected, but I was still drafted by the Cleveland Indians in the fifth round. Everything started to fall in place during my senior year. As a designated hitter, I earned All-America honors as the college designated hitter of the year, while posting a 9-2 record as a pitcher. I signed with the New York Yankees in

June 1978 and reported to the AA Eastern League in West Haven, CT .

Fortunately, I didn't have to spend much time in the minor leagues. I got called up to pitch for the Yankees in June 1980. What an experience! Our team was loaded with so many future Hall of Famers that even I wanted to collect their autographs! We went to the playoffs against Kansas City, but the Royals beat us in that best of five series. The following spring training, I got traded to the San Diego Padres.

The most enjoyable years of my career were with San Diego. It was very rewarding to be an important part of an organization that in a four-year span went from losing almost 100 games to winning the National League pennant and making it to the World Series. In 1984 we won the National League West and then defeated the Cubs in the NL playoffs. I started game four of the playoffs when we were down two games to one. That game is most memorable as the Steve Garvey game in which he hit a home run late in the game to tie the playoffs. We won the fifth game and then got to square off against Detroit in the World Series, but they proved to be too much to handle and beat us in five games. I started game three of that series but it wasn't one of my stellar performances and we lost the game 5-2. Playing in my first World Series was quite an experience. I never knew how much adrenaline your body could produce until then. Fortunately, Detroit wasn't very far from Farmington, so my family and some close friends were able to join us for the Series. San Diego was also very important to me for personal reasons. I met my wife while she was working for a local television station. We now have three great children who have shown lots of athletic ability as well.

During the winter of 1984, I was traded to Chicago White Sox where I spent a half-season before being traded to the Boston Red Sox. In 1986, our Red Sox team won the American League East and then in the playoffs made a remarkable comeback against the California Angels, so I was headed to the World Series for a second time. Unfortunately, the final outcome would be the same, as we lost to the New York Mets in seven games. I've never been so close to winning as we were in the sixth game when New York scored three runs in the bottom of the ninth to tie the Series. We then lost game seven and it was a long flight back to Boston. My last year in the Majors was 1986, but I played a little longer in the Miners before retiring in 1988.

Baseball has given me many great treasures, but none of the opportunities for me would have been possible without the support of Betty, my mom, and the rest of my family, including my sister, Janis Chatman, and my nephew, Joe Chatman. Also, if not for the personal sacrifices of men like Jim Boyer, Bob McKinney, Bob Bone and Wayne Province, to name only a few, I and many of Farmington's youths would have never had an opportunity to learn this great game!

Farmington was a great town in which to grow up. Everyone was your neighbor and the area had such great enthusiasm and support for its youth.

I say with pride that I grew up in your wonderful community.

Life Sketch Of St. Francois County Pioneer: Thomas Smith McMullin

Born in Henderson County, KY on January 18, 1825, Thomas Smith McMullin lived in St. Francois County, MO until his untimely death in Farmington September 16, 1880, at age 55. He was a Tennessee native of English and Irish parentage. As a young boy on the Kentucky frontier, Thomas and his brother sawed lumber by hand to rebuild the family homestead, still standing nearly one century later. Following an accident as a teenager where he had a gun explode, resulting in the loss of three fingers of his right hand, Thomas took up the photographer's trade using the daguerreotype system. At age 19 he traveled to California, crossing the river at Ste. Genevieve and hooking up with a wagon train of immigrants at Jefferson City, MO. He left the wagon train at Salt Lake City due to illness, he joined with another group of immigrants in driving a herd of cattle west. While in California he earned a living as a hunter, selling the meat to the mining camps.

Once while hunting near Mari Posa, CA, he came upon a bear which charged him, and Thomas was compelled to escape by jumping off a high bluff. On his landing he sprained his ankle. In another close call, Indians attacked his camp without warning, though he later related that he managed to kill them in his escape.

In 1852 Thomas returned to Kentucky, where in 1854 he married Harriet Sorrels. Two children were born to this union. Later in the 1850s he returned to Missouri, and settled in Farmington, MO where he followed the trade of the gunsmith. Harriet died in 1861 and Thomas remarried in February 1862, this time to Ruth Elizabeth Fraser of neighboring Ste. Genevieve County. He and Ruth had seven children.

While in Farmington, he took an active interest in local government and was appointed marshall of Farmington. A short while later he was elected as sheriff of St. Francois County and served from 1861-1864, this being in the unsettled time of the Civil War. He later was engaged in the nursery business on his farm near Farmington and was elected sheriff again in 1877, serving until his death in 1880. The year 1880 was certainly a trying time for him. He had been involved in solving the brutal murder the previous October and arrested Charles Hardin for the murder of Robert Ferguson. Hardin was sentenced to hang, and on January 23, 1880, Sheriff McMullin carried out this unpleasant task. On September 13, 1880, he was involved in an altercation with one Henry Horn in an alley next to the Trapps Saloon in Farmington. Witnesses related that Sheriff McMullin advanced on Horn and shot Horn in the hand. Horn then returned fire, striking Sheriff McMullin with two well-placed shots in the stomach and chest. It was believed that there had been a long standing grudge between the two. Thomas died three days later on September 16, 1880. Mr. Horn survived the shooting and claimed self-defense at his trial.

Ruth McMullin remained in Farmington following the death of her husband and raised their family, later moving to Charleston, MO.

where she lived with a daughter. She passed away at the age of 65 and is buried next to Thomas McMullin in the Masonic Cemetery in Farmington. She was survived by three daughters and one son.

Sarah Barton Murphy

Sarah Barton Murphy is considered the Founder of Farmington. She was born on May 8, 1748, to Joshua and Sarah Dubart Barton. Her family were all God fearing people. She grew up in a deeply religious family and also believed that Jesus was her Savior and that God is Almighty.

Joshua Barton met and married his wife while in Pennsylvania. Sarah was born in Maryland. Joshua's parents were originally from Ireland and settled in Massachusetts, later moving to Pennsylvania. They had two sons before moving to Maryland where Sarah was born and later, Elizabeth was born. The pioneer family moved to North Carolina, and it was here that Sarah's mother died. Her Grandmother Jane helped with the household chores. Five-year old Sarah helped whenever possible, including the care of Elizabeth, just turning three. Assuming they had a cow, she may have milked it herself. Life on the frontier was hard and Sarah learned at an early age the "art of survival." Her father eventually remarried to a Susannah Dodd and several more children were born. Sarah was a member of a blended family.

Sarah learned to read and write. It is assumed that she was home-schooled as there were no schools on the frontier. Her grandfather, who was educated, believed that education was important. There were no schools where they lived in this country so he home-schooled his children. Likewise, Joshua home-schooled his children.

While living in North Carolina, other pioneer families settled near the Bartons. Two of those families were those of Daniel Boone and Rev. William Murphy Sr. These three families remained lifelong friends. The Bartons moved to Virginia and then to Eastern Tennessee. The Boone and Murphy families followed. Daniel Boone moved on to Kentucky. When Rev. William Murphy arrived in Eastern Tennessee, he was a widower with five children. He began courting Sarah Barton and they were eventually married sometime before July 21, 1767. Upon saying, "I do", she immediately became a stepmother to his five children, the oldest being just two years younger than she. Sarah was 19 and Rev. William was 37 when they married. In 1769, they had the first of their six children. Again, Sarah was living in a blended family.

The Reverend William Murphy was a Baptist minister. One of his brothers was also a Baptist minister. They were well-known and popular preachers. Later, his oldest son, John, became a Baptist minister. Also, Sarah's brother, Isaac, became a Baptist minister. (Some research material states that Sarah's father was a Baptist minister while other material makes no mention of this.)

In 1774 a terrible tragedy occurred in the Barton family. Her father, an older brother and her younger half-brother, Joab, who was only seven years old, were on their way to the mill when they were attacked by a party of raiding Shawnee Indians. They killed and scalped her father and older brother and kidnapped Joab, which the family thought was a fate worse than death.

Later, Sarah's brother, Isaac, married Keziah, Rev. William Murphy's daughter from his first marriage. Hence, Keziah was not only Sarah's step-daughter, she was her sister-in-law, and her brother became her step-son-in-law. Rev. William and Isaac were brothers-in-law and now Isaac became his son-in-law, etc.

Reverend William Murphy heard that Spain was giving Spanish Land Grants to those colonists who would settle in the Louisiana Territory west of the Mississippi River. The grant consisted of 640 acres. Coming with him to this area in 1798 were his three sons and a friend, Silas George. Spanish land grants were claimed by these five people. They traveled to New Orleans to secure their claims. Upon contributing to the Spanish King's war fund, all were granted their legal land grants with papers. On their return trip to Eastern Tennessee, Silas George and Reverend Murphy became ill. Silas George died. Reverend Murphy died at his son's, just a day's journey from home.

In 1800 Joseph, William, David and Richard Murphy came to this area by wagon. All brought their families except Richard, who was not married.

Arriving in June of 1802 was Sarah Barton Murphy. Traveling with her were her sons, Isaac and Jesse; William Evans, her 9-year-old grandson who she was raising; an 18 year old hired hand, a Negro woman and a Negro boy. They traveled by keelboat down the Holston River, the Tennessee River, the Ohio River and then the Mississippi River. Surely, God was with them on this dangerous journey! Sarah Barton Murphy was terribly afraid of Indians and they would be traveling through Indian territories, some being friendly while others were not. They traveled only during the night and hid their keelboat by day along the riverbank. None of these people were experienced "river navigators." It had to have been God's will that Sarah Barton Murphy entered the Louisiana Territory and settled in what was to become known as Murphy Settlement and later Farmington.

In 1803 she started a school in her home, teaching reading, writing and arithmetic to all students who attended this free school. She also taught the girls how to cook, clean, and sew; and the boys how to do simple household repairs, plant crops and ride horses.

That same year, she held secret prayer meetings in her home. The people of Murphy Settlement were starved to worship God in their faith. One of the conditions of the Spanish land grants was that the receiver of said grant must sign a pledge saying they would worship in the Catholic faith. Reverend William Murphy, being a Baptist minister, signed that pledge! If he had not, there would be no Farmington, MO, today. He knew that Spain was at war with England and did not have the extra necessary militia to send to the area to make sure the pioneers were worshipping in the Catholic faith, so he did not hesitate in signing the pledge.

In 1803 the United States purchased the Louisiana Territory from France who had obtained said territory from Spain in 1800. News

Marker for the first Sunday School, founded by Sarah Barton Murphy.

did not always travel swiftly or directly and Murphy Settlement did not hear the good news till 1804. Upon learning this, the people in Murphy Settlement rushed to Sarah Barton Murphy's and honored her by letting her say the first public Protestant prayer west of the Mississippi River. She donated one acre of land upon which to build a log church. All denominations worshipped there. She declared that she would give the church to the first minister who came here and would take charge of the church. That person happened to be a Reverend James Oglesby, a Methodest circuit rider. Through this single incident, this is how Sarah Barton Murphy and her descendants became Methodists. A church was built on West Columbia Street. It was named the Murphy-Long Methodist Church. It is also known as the Southern Methodist Church. Today, it is the Free Will Baptist Church.

In 1805, Sarah Barton Murphy thought the young people were not observing the Sabbath as God intended. She saw them going fishing, berrying, nutting, hunting and swimming. She saw the need for a Sunday School so she organized and taught what is believed to be the first Sunday School west of the Mississippi River. There is a stone marker in the northeast corner of the Masonic Cemetery which simply states: "On this spot the first Sunday School west of the Mississippi River was organized and taught by Sarah Barton Murphy in the year 1805, in the log meeting house which was the first Protestant Church west of the Mississippi River. Erected by her great-grandson, Hugh Long."

In 1808 Dubart Murphy, Sarah's son, and his family came to Murphy Settlement. One of his daughters later married Philip Graham Long who had come here from Kentucky. It was he and his wife, Isabella Murphy Long, who built the Long House in Long Park which was donated to the city of Farmington in 1921.

About 1812, Daniel Boone came to Murphy Settlement, bringing with him a young man and a 10-year-old girl. This young man turned out to be her younger brother, Joab, who had been kidnapped by the Shawnee Indians, and his daughter. He had married an Indian maiden. These Indians had migrated to the Meramac Springs area where Daniel Boone had been exploring and met them. He recognized Joab as he looked too much like the Bartons and knew of the kidnapping.

Sarah Barton Murphy became ill in March of 1817 and died. She was 69 years of age. She is buried on their original land grant which is part of the Masonic Cemetery today. Sarah Barton Murphy's influence must have been great if the legends that surround her name are to be believed. Another aspect of her influence is in justice. The rapid shifts in government and the remoteness of the area made formal justice hard to administer. Mrs. Murphy had a reputation as a compassionate and fair arbiter and persons would sometimes come from more than a hundred miles for settlement of their grievances. Through Sarah Barton Murphy's devout Christian influence she established a religious atmosphere that survives in this town to the present time.

Devotion to her persists to this day around Farmington where her descendants proudly claim their lineage.

Gilbert "Gus" Owen Nations

Judge Nations was born in Perry County, MO, August 18, 1866, and grew to manhood on a farm in Ste. Genevieve County. He married Sallie McFarland at the age of 20 and to this union seven children were born.

Judge Nations practiced law and was probate judge of St. Francois County from 1903-1911. He became the only Farmingtonian to ever receive the American Party's nomination for President of the United States in 1924. That was the year Calvin Coolidge was elected to succeed himself.

Judge Nations held five academic degrees at the time of his death. For many years he taught at the American University, Washington, D.C.

In addition to being superintendent of the Farmington Public Schools around the turn of the century, Judge Nations was a noted speaker and appeared on public platforms with William Jennings Bryan and other prominent citizens.

At the time of his death five of the seven children were still living: Karl McFarland Nations, Paul Douglas Nations, Myrtle Frances Ellis, Florence Emily Pyatt, and Zora Caroline Ritter.

On February 13, 1950, Judge Nations passed away at his residence in Silver Springs, MD. He was buried on February 15, 1950, at Parkview Cemetery in Farmington, MO.

Dan Peek

As a ninth generation descendant of Sarah Barton Murphy and an eighth generation descendant of William Murphy, founder of Farmington, I have a special place in my heart for this, my adopted "Hometown." Both William and my own father served in our Nation's military. William, in the Revolution and my father, Milton, in the Military Occupation of Japan.

In fact my lineage to the Murphys comes on my maternal side. My mother, Geraldine, regaled her children with tales of her ancestors and instilled a deep respect and love for those roots. Because of Dad's military postings we grew up literally around the world and until I "discovered" Farmington and my heritage here, I always felt a sense of something missing.

I attended 20 different schools growing up

in Japan, Pakistan, England and the U.S. I never actually set foot in Farmington until I was 14 years old. My older brother Tom and I played in a rock-band at Long Hall in the mid-60s, during the time I was living with my grandparents on a farm near Doe Run. I then fell in love with Farmington and the beautiful countryside of this part of Missouri.

Two years later my parents established a home in Farmington, but again we were on the move, with a three-year stay in London, England. I had started playing guitar and singing at age 12 while living in Pakistan. While in London, I formed the pop-group America with two high school pals from my London alma mater. Within a year of forming the band we had a worldwide hit record, *A Horse With No Name.*

My career in America kept me globetrotting and for many years able only to visit Farmington. I also brought members of the band here who fell in love with Farmington and the surrounding area.

America was tremendously successful and kept us all very busy for a number of years as we toured globally and played the music from our hit records. It was a very exciting life and gave us the opportunity to travel, work and live in various locales around the world.

However, when the opportunity presented itself, I moved here with my wife, Catherine. We relish our time here and make the most of the outdoor activities possible in this lovely country setting. Though we have moved from Farmington in times past, we always come back to our "Hometown U.S.A."

Barney Pelty

Barney Pelty, who collapsed on the street on last Thursday evening and has been in a critical condition since, passed away about 7 o'clock on Wednesday morning at the State Hospital where he had been removed earlier in the week. Mr. Pelty's death was attributed to a cerebral hemorrhage. On Monday and Tuesday, it was believed his condition had shown some improvement though he was reported as being very weak from the loss of blood. However, on Wednesday morning his condition suddenly grew worse and the end came. He was 58 years, 8 months and 14 days of age.

Barney Pelty was one of our city's best known citizens. Marty became interested in football, and for 10 years, from about 1900 to 1910, he was an outstanding pitcher in the Major Leagues. His baseball career first started with a season in Memphis, and from there he went to Cedar Rapids, IA. He soon demonstrated his powers as a hurler and was sent to Cleveland in the Major League, where he remained for a part of one season, when his contract was bought by the St. Louis Browns. He remained with the St. Louis Browns for about 9 years, playing all the rest of his time, except the last season he was in baseball with that team. He was with the Washington Senators his last year in professional ball. Following his retirement from baseball, he became interested in politics and took an active part in the work of the Republican Party. He was appointed by Governor Hyde to a place in the State Pure Food and Drug Administration Department and remained in this department

Barney Pelty

through the Hyde, Kaker and Caulfield administration.

He was born in Farmington on September 10, 1880, the son of the late Samuel and Helena Pelty. He was one of six children. In 1903 he was married to Eva Warning and to this union, one son, Lawrence, who with the wife survives. He is also survived by two sisters, Miss Gertie Pelty and Mrs. Pauline Detrick, both of Farmington, and a grandson.

Funeral services will be held this afternoon, Friday, at 3:30 p.m. at the Cozean Funeral Home.

Kyle D. Richardson

Kyle Richardson was born in Farmington on March 2, 1973. He is the son of Jack and Susan Richardson. He attended school K-12 at Farmington, graduating in 1991. While in high school he participated in the student council and was a member of the football, the basketball and the track teams.

As an all-around excellent athlete, Kyle compiled numerous awards and honors, some of those being All-Conference for football, basketball and track and All-District for the same three sports. In 1991 he was a member of the KREI Dream Team for both football and basketball, Most Valuable Athlete his senior year and Most Valuable Player for basketball.

Kyle played several different positions on the football team: defensive back, receiver, kicker and punter. During his senior year, the Farmington Varsity Football team finished the season third in the state.

Besides playing the above mentioned sports, Kyle also was a member of the Farmington Swim Team, baseball team, involved in his church, and a member of the Boy Scouts, earning the Eagle Scout Award as a young man.

After high school Kyle attended Arkansas State University at Jonesboro, AR. He was a "walk-on" punter and received a full four-year football scholarship as a result of his skill. He was the holder for the kick-off team as well as the punter. Kyle graduated with a BS degree in Fine Arts, majoring in Graphic Design.

The sports awards didn't stop with high school. In college they continued to accumulate, beginning with four football letters, AT&T Long

Distance Award for a 75 yard punt, Big West All-Conference Honorable Mention, as punter his junior year, Big West All-Conference First Team and his senior year Member of the football Academic Team

Kyle finished his Arkansas career with the most punts in Arkansas State University history and was the third all-time punter.

In 1996 Kyle began his professional career playing for Rhein Fire of the World Football League (WFL of Europe) in Germany as a punter and a holder. He finished the season second in the league in average punts and first in league in net average.

Kyle D. Richardson

In 1997 he played three games for the Miami Dolphins and two games for the Seattle Seahawks.

In 1998 he signed with the Baltimore Ravens, playing the entire season with the Ravens as their punter and holder.

Kyle has two brothers, Clark, his wife Sandi and daughter Brooke, and Alex and his wife Jean.

C.E. "Pal" Wood

C.E. "Pal" Wood was born on a farm near Doe Run, MO on March 25, 1879, the son of Franklin and Rebecca Ann Wood. He was one of three children from this union, a sister having died in infancy and one brother, Carson E. Wood. Pal Woods had two step-sisters, Mrs. Eya Radle and Mrs. Florence Jones and two step-brothers, Clarence Morris and Emmett Morris. His father died when he was quite young and his mother married B.I. Morris and with her two sons moved to Farmington where "Pal" continued to make his home throughout his entire life.

He played on the first Carleton College football team along with his brother, Carson. Pal was a painter by trade and sometimes he was unable to get off on Friday afternoon when Mr. Wesley Pratt was rushing his men to finish a job.

Every evening, Saturday afternoons and Sundays you could find Pal in McKinney's ice cream parlor (later at Laakman's) waiting to "kid" or to be "kidded" and during the winter months generally sipping a hot chocolate.

His hobby was collecting old pictures of Farmington, specializing in football teams.

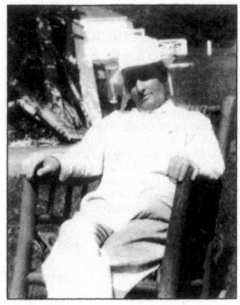
C. E. "Pal" Wood

When Fred Asbury (brother to Herbert) a St. Louis printer, heard of this, he furnished him with a large scrap book in which Pal pasted the pictures and donated it to the Farmington Public Library. It was titled "Farmingtonia." Pal was also a pioneer in sportsmanship and clean living. He had no patience with an athlete who smoked or did not observe strict training habits.

Pal was a lovable character and will never be forgotten by those who knew him well. Pal died on March 23, 1947, and is buried in Pendleton Cemetery at Doe Run, Missouri.

MILITARY HISTORY

Grand Army of the Republic Veterans in 1906.

WW I men in front of the courthouse.

REVOLUTIONARY WAR SOLDIERS

Revolutionary War soldiers who settled in the St. Francois County area were James Cunningham of the Virginia Militia; James Caldwell of the Virginia Militia; William Murphy Jr. of the Virginia Militia, buried in the Murphy Cemetery on Old Fredericktown Road; Joseph Murphy Sr. of the Virginia Militia who is buried in the Masonic Cemetery in Farmington; William Nicholson of the Pennsylvania Continentals; Thomas Arman of the Virginia Continentals, and William Alexander, who is buried in the Alexander Family Cemetery, behind Parkland Hospital.

Information taken from Houck's History of Missouri.

Captain James Caldwell

On September 6, 1836, Captain James Caldwell, a patriot and soldier of the Revolutionary War died in Farmington, MO and was buried on the home place. This became the Judge William Carter place and after Judge Carter's death the Carter property was laid off in town property of lots, streets and alleys. The grave of Captain Caldwell was left in the alley running east and west back of the Carter House.

Last Monday Dr. J.P. Sebastian of Williamsville, Wayne County, MO came to Farmington to superintend the disinterment of Captain Caldwell's body and have the remains as might be found after 80 years reintered in some cemetery. The doctor in this was animated by a sentiment interwoven with the Caldwell and Sebastian families and was assisted in this work to preserve the memory and mark the resting place of the Old Solider and a Pioneer of St. Francois County by the Sarah Barton Murphy Chapter of Daughters of American Revolution. This disinterment took place Tuesday morning. All that was found of the body, were the skull, the thigh and shin bones. These were carefully stored in a box in charge of Milton Spaugh and will, at a date not yet decided upon, be given a final resting place in Parkview Cemetery with the appropriate ceremonies under the auspices of DAR local chapter.

Captain James Caldwell was a native of Virginia and after the Revolutionary War, in which he served with distinction, he moved to Crab Orchard, KY and thence in 1810 to Missouri to the Cook Settlement. In that settlement, in 1813, a baby boy was born and an hour afterward the spirit of the mother passed into silence.

Captain Caldwell and his wife took the motherless babe to their hearts and reared him to manhood. The babe was Edwin C. Sebastian, who became a prominent and successful citizen of the county and a leader in the Christian Church at Libertyville. He reared a large family, only three of whom are now living, Dr. J.P. Sebastian of Williamsville, MO; Hon. W.P. Sebastian of Austin, Texas; and the youngest, Ella, Mrs. J.W. Williams of Springfield, MO.

Captain Caldwell was the speaker of First Assembly of Missouri which convened at St. Charles in 1820. In 1831 or 1832, he moved to Farmington and engaged in merchandising and

Joseph Murphy Sr., born Mar. 12, 1759, died Nov. 2, 1833.

Thomas O'Bannon, born Oct. 20, 1832, died Oct. 12, 1913

bought a tract of land south of Farmington. He died September 6, 1836.

CIVIL WAR IN THE FARMINGTON AREA

Historians and students of the Civil War in Missouri, 1861-1865, would probably agree that these were some of the most devastating and trying times in Missouri history. St. Francois County and the Farmington area shared in this turmoil. A large number of the early settlers in our area had roots in states that had succeeded from the Union: Virginia, North and South Carolina, Tennessee and others. Many of these settlers brought their slave families with them. The 1860 slave census of St. Francois County shows approximately 204 owners of 875 slaves. Most of these were small family units. Many of the slave-owning families were loyal Union people and stayed that way throughout the conflict. In fact, the majority of Missourians were determined to remain neutral. As events unfolded in early 1861, neutrality became impossible as more and more people were forced to take sides.

The Federal Government, under the new President Lincoln and the Republican Party, realized that keeping Missouri a loyal state was critical in many ways. Control of the Mississippi River and the area west of the river was vital. While most of rural southeast Missouri favored succession, there was strong Union support in the more populated areas, such as St. Louis with its large immigrant population.

Attempts were made to compromise the situation. In a convention held in February 1861, the delegates voted not to secede at that time. Mr. Milton P. Cayce of Farmington was a delegate at this convention. Mr. Cayce was a native of Virginia and a slave owner.

In April 1861, with the firing on Fort Sumpter in South Carolina, open warfare began and Missouri was forced to take sides. President Lincoln's request for Missouri troops was denied by Governor Claybourne Jackson, who was ready to take Missouri into the Confederacy. The state government under Jackson had formed a Pro-

Confederate militia, the Missouri State Guard.

After Governor Jackson's removal from office, the Unionists placed Hamilton Gamble as Provisional Governor and formed their own militia, the Union Home Guard. Now Missouri had two governors and two militias, one favoring each side in the conflict.

The Union had moved in Federal troops to establish law and order and all of Missouri was placed under martial law. Citizens rights were denied. Property could be seized, elected officials removed from office, and loyalty oaths were required of teachers, ministers and people wishing to hold public office. Military provost marshals were put into power to enforce the laws. In St. Francois County the elected sheriff and collector, T.S. McMullin, refused to have anything to do with war-related matters but was encouraged to stay on as collector.

Our area was important to the Union for several reasons: the iron and lead mines, and nearness to the St. Louis and Iron Mountain Railroad, which was vital for the movement of these products and the troops which were needed for its protection.

Fort Davidson at Pilot Knob was the southern end of the railroad. Troops from the fort were active in the Farmington area throughout the war. In April 1861 southern sympathizers demonstrated at Farmington, where they raised the Confederate Flag, made speeches, and paraded. One observer believed that the people of Farmington wanted immediate succession. Other meetings were held in county communities supporting the southern cause. It was a time when everyone was trying to join somebody's army.

On July 4, 1861, it was reported that a force of Union Home Guards were attacked at the courthouse in Farmington and driven out. They soon reclaimed the town.

During the War several other skirmishes were held in and around the courthouse. In mid-October 1861 Confederate General M. Jeff Thompson, from his camp in St. Francois County, issued a proclamation calling for residents to join his cause. He promised to assist them in throwing out the invaders. All these activities caused dissension between friends, families and neighbors. It was reported that many who favored succession just moved away to more favorable areas to carry on their lives. Those who remained were subjected to harassment and threats. Those who were loyal to the Union were also targeted by groups of guerilla fighters and bushwhackers who favored the Confederacy.

By the end of 1861 the region had become one of Union support. Confederate forces were making raids into the area and disrupting the mining operations as well as raiding the railroad by burning bridges and tearing up tracks.

There is little activity reported in the official records of the Union during 1862. It is certain that guerilla and bushwhacker activity in and around Farmington was carried out by both sides. The only major skirmish in 1863 was a raid on one of the railroad bridges over Big River by Confederate General J.O. Shelby.

In November of 1863 the official record tells of a raid on Farmington made by the bushwhacker Sam Hilderbrand and a group of about 20 men. Union officials sent orders for this group to be pursued and "if found to kill the rascals."

Sam Hilderbrand was from St. Francois County. Both he and his family had been badly mistreated by units of the State militia. During the war years he made numerous raids in the area, avenging the misdeeds that had been done to him and his family. Sam survived the war and was later killed in southern Illinois. Several books have been written that tells Sam's story.

There were several other Confederate bushwhacker units that raided in the Farmington area. These groups not only killed their supposed enemies but took livestock, food and other property from the civilian population, making life miserable for many families. This practice was also carried out by Union people, as well as militia units.

The year 1864 saw much of the same activities going on in our county. The Union controlled through the use of martial law. The required loyalty oaths kept Union sympathizers in control of county government. This also extended to the school teachers and ministers. More of southeast Missouri was counted in the Union camp as the war continued. The Union now had control of the Mississippi River, and the Trans-Mississippi branch of the Confederacy was cut off from the help and supplies of the eastern Confederacy. Grant, now in control in the eastern war zone, was pressing hard on Lee's Confederate Army. Grant had moved many of the Federal troops from the western theatre, leaving control here to the local militia units.

The Confederacy thought this would be their chance to take Missouri back from the Union. A grand plan was devised to raid the State and put the elected Governor Jackson and his people back in power then capture the large Union arsenal at St. Louis. The result of this plan was the largest skirmish to take place in Farmington during the war.

General Sterling Price, ex-governor of Missouri and a popular figure with the Missouri Confederate population, was placed in charge of the raid. He thought these supporters would rise up and join him when he arrived in their midst. His unit commanders were also well-known in Missouri: Generals Shelby, Marmaduke and Fagan. On July 28, 1864, Union General Rosecrans,

commander in Missouri, issued General Order 134, telling citizens of the area that this raid was in progress and called for units of Voluntary Missouri Infantry to be organized. The 47th regiment Missouri Volunteers was to be organized at Pilot Knob and counties in the area were to supply companies of 100 men. St. Francois County was designated as Company F. These 100 men were to be enlisted for six months. The county court authorized the sum of $5,000 to be used in forming this company. Each of the men were to receive $50 dollars, $25 at the time of enlistment and $25 when mustered out of service. The company was lead by Captain Wm. P. Adair and contained many men from Farmington and the surrounding area. These soldiers didn't have long to wait before seeing action.

On September 24, 1864, while on duty in Farmington, a patrol of about 25 men under the command of Lt. Christian Helber were attacked by advance units of Confederate General Shelby's command. They fought well but were faced with a large force and had to retreat to Pilot Knob. On September 26, 1864, General Price's Confederate Army attacked Fort Davidson. After a gallant fight under heavy odds the Union troops was forced to evacuate, retreating northward to Leesburg, MO. It is said that the men of the 47th fought both in the fort and on the forced retreat.

The Confederates suffered a terrible defeat at Pilot Knob in loss of men, equipment and time. The planned raid into Missouri was abandoned; following defeats in central and western Missouri, the Confederates were forced to retreat back into Arkansas. Except for incidents of bushwhacker activity, this ended Confederate military actions in our area. By all reports civilians in the county were left in a destitute condition by war's end. Some interesting old courthouse records, diaries and stories passed down through the years are all that remain of the Civil War days in the Farmington area.

General James Robinson McCormick

General James Robinson McCormick, a resident of Arcadia Valley, fought at the Battle of Pilot Knob and was reportedly wounded and had his horse shot out from under him during the battle. After the retreat of the Union forces, McCormick remained in the area for a short time to care for the wounded on both sides. Once the Confederates learned he had fought in the battle, staying behind would have meant imprisonment, so McCormick fled toward Perry County and Cape Girardeau. After the war, he returned to Arcadia to resume his medical practice and to open a drug store.

General McCormick was married first to Burchette Caroline Nance and second to Susan Elizabeth Garner in 1866. Two children were born of the second marriage, one died in infancy and the second was James Edward McCormick.

In 1866 he was elected to the Missouri State Senate. In 1867, he resigned this position to fill the unexpired term of Thomas E. Noel in the United States Congress. He was elected to three additional terms before his retirement from politics.

In late 1873 or early 1874, General

McCormick moved to Farmington and built a home. The home, located at 324 W. Columbia Street, has recently been declared a historic site. General McCormick established a drug store and pharmaceutical business. Although he was a prominent physician and surgeon, he no longer practiced medicine.

General McCormick was a Ruling Elder of the Farmington Presbyterian Church. He was a member of the Masonic fraternity and was a 32 degree Mason. On March 15, 1871, he was one of the founders and charter members of the Midian Royal Arch Chapter No. 71 of the AF&AM, which was the first chapter south of St. Louis.

After suffering a stroke which caused a feeble condition and paralysis, he could still be seen taking short walks and riding in his surrey. On May 19, 1897, Brigadier General James R. McCormick died. He is buried in the Masonic Cemetery in Farmington in the McCormick family plot.

(Based on *St. Francois County Notable - General James Robinson McCormick*, by Gene Murdock; St. Francois County Historical Society January 1999 Newsletter.)

Platt Pearsall
Corporal, Company C
30th Ohio Volunteer Infantry
"The Forlorn Hope"
Congressional Medal of Honor

Platt Pearsall was a young man of 21 years from Meigs County, OH, when he joined the 30th Ohio Volunteer Infantry. The regiment was formed in August 1861 and was assigned to the Army of the Potomac in August 1862. In January 1863 the Regiment joined General U.S. Grant's Army near Vicksburg, TN. It was thus that Platt and the 30th Ohio found themselves in front of the Vicksburg defenses on May 2.

By this time Grant had encircled the city on three sides with a battle line over 10 miles long and on the fourth side was the Mississippi River on which Admiral Porter's warships rode. Grant decided that a frontal attack, if successful, would avoid a long and costly siege. The point of attack was in front of the 15th Corps and the regimental commanders explained the attack to their men and called for volunteers. One hundred and fifty men were asked as a "Forlorn Hope" to lead the attack against the ramparts. Part of their job would be to bridge a ditch and place the scaling ladders on the sides of the ramparts to be used by the general assault brigades. These men would be the targets of heavy enemy fire and it was expected that only a few would survive. Over 400 men volunteered, the first 150 unmarried men were chosen, and Platt Pearsall was one of them.

The "Forlorn Hope" started out toward the ramparts at a full run and within the first 80 yards half of them were down. When the survivors reached the ditch, it was impossible to build the bridge since so many had been lost, along with the material required for construction. They were now trapped below the ramparts and under weathering fire from the defenders directly above them. They fought back. Private Howell G. Trogden planted the flag of the storming party on the parapet of the fort and fired at any confederate who reached out to take it. The Union brigades advanced to the support of the stormers but fell back under heavy fire. Only 30 men from the Eleventh Missouri with two officers reached the ditch, planted their flag and fought along side what was left of the "Forlorn Hope." The bottom of the ditch was strewn with mangled bodies.

The overall attack faltered and the Union brigades began to withdraw all along the line. The men in the ditch were unable to retreat or advance and not only held their position but weakened the fire from the rebel guns by shooting down the gunners. All through the day the unequal fight went on and only after nightfall did the little group of survivors crawl out of the ditch and with their bullet-riddled flags made their way back to their own lines. Of the storming party, 85 percent were killed or wounded. It would be almost two more months before Vicksburg fell on July 4, 1863. It is said the citizens of Vicksburg did not celebrate July 4 with the rest of the nation until 1933.

Corporal Pearsall returned to Ohio after the war, married, and worked in the lumber business. His war-time travels had taken him through the St. Francois County, MO area and he knew he wanted to return since the amount of timber he had seen in and around the local would be an excellent source of material for the lumber trade. He returned to Missouri with his wife Martha, purchased 160 acres of timber and went into the charcoal business. They had two sons.

Platt Pearsall was awarded the nation's highest honor on August 14, 1894. The citation reads, "For Gallantry in the charge of the Volunteer Storming party, May 22, 1863". Platt died in 1931 at the age of 90 and is buried in the Pendleton Unity Baptist Church Cemetery in St. Francois County. His great-grandsons and their families still live on the family farm today.

Sources:

1. Boyer, W.F. *Deeds of Valor*, Long Meadow Press, 1903, pp. 190-197.

2. Civil War Medal of Honor Recipients - http://www2.army.mil/cmh-pg/mohciv2.htm

3. 30th Ohio Infantry - http://www/infinet.com/~1stevens/a/civil.htm/

World War I

After war was declared on Germany by US President Woodrow Wilson in 1917, young men from Farmington and the surrounding area were quick to do their part in seeing the world was made safe for Democracy.

During the Great War, the "war to end all wars" over 1,300 men from St. Francois County served their country.

While many voluntarily entered the service, others were drafted under the new Selective Service Law.

This item was from the *Farmington News* Feb. 15, 1918.

The local Exemption Board had been following the policy of placing all men married since May 18 in Class One and permitting them to appeal to the District Board at Poplar Bluff. The board received a letter regarding newly married men that read in part:

"At a conference Col. McCord expressed himself very strongly in regard to Boards adhering to the rule laid down directing us to consider all such marriages where proof has not been consummated for the purpose of evading Selective Service Law. The marriages are to be disregarded only in those cases where the proof failed to show that the marriage was not for the purpose of evading military service.

"Col. McCord stressed that practically all of the marriageable men of the U. S. were now registered for military service and that it was not the policy or the desire of the government to discourage marriage and that the only intention was to stop marriage for the purpose of evading military service."

Those men whose appeals had been submitted were reclassified as class two or class four.

The citizens of the county rallied to the patriotic cause of supporting the war effort and the Bank of Farmington proudly announced they had been appointed by the U.S. Government "as an agent to sell and distribute Thrift Stamps and War Savings Stamps without any recompense whatever" for its services. Thrift stamps could be purchased for 25 cents apiece and war savings stamps were $4.12 to $4.32 each. Interest was four percent compounded quarterly.

The St. Francois County Chapter of the Red Cross was formed with J.C. Morris serving as chairman. Other officers were Mrs. Henry Giessing, vice chair, J.P. Cayce, treasurer, H. Edward Kaschmann, secretary and Emma Lang was membership chairman. Members of the board were J.C. Morris, M.P. Cayce, and C.B. Denman. The executive committee consisted of M.P. Cayce, J.C. Akers, W.L. Johns, E.J. McKinney, Barney Pelty, W.R. Lang, C.B. Denman, J.W. McCarthy, Ed Helber, Genevieve Logan, Charles Schuettler, and the Misses Emma Lang and Anna Menge. Henry Rinke was chairman of the Christmas Roll Call.

Lt. Walter Bennick of Flat River was in charge of a company of returned soldiers that toured principal towns and put on programs that consisted of military drills, four minutes of speeches and four minutes of songs. To keep the support of the war strong, similar groups staged programs like this all over the country and became known as the "Four Minute Men."

Everyday life went on and The Young Men's Club entertained with a Valentine Dance in the club room; an entertainment and pie supper were held at the Knob Lick School; and such movies as Mary Pickford in *Hulda from Holland* and Fatty Arbuckle in a two-reel comedy *Reckless Romeo* were shown at the Monarch Theater.

Several boot-legging joints were permanently enjoined by the circuit court for allegedly selling or permitting the sale and use of liquor on their premises in defiance of the Local Option Law then in effect in St. Francois County.

The St. Francois County Railroad Company continued in service with M.P. Cayce as President and F.H. Dearing, secretary.

Wage increases were posted by the Federal, St. Joseph and Doe Run Lead Companies ranging from 25-75 cents a day. Shovelers and underground workers granted an increase of 15 cents per day, due to the shortage of underground workers.

During the war a great miner's riot broke out in Flat River over the hiring of immigrant

WW I Stanley Overall, Sr. (left) with a fellow serviceman.

workers at the mines to replace local men, who were expected to be called up for service. Rampaging miners eventually rounded up all of these workers and their families, marched them to the paymaster to collect their wages and then on to the train depot where they were given one-way tickets out of the area.

And then, there were those who served:

According to a record carefully compiled by the Missouri State Historical Society and published in the *Farmington News* on June 27, 1919, St. Francois County had a total casualty list in the great World War of 106 men, all serving in the Army and Marines. Of this number 33 made the supreme sacrifice of which 11 from the Army and three Marines were killed in action; seven Army men died of disease, eight died in camp and two from accidents of other causes. Eighteen Army men and seven Marines were severely wounded, 25 Army men slightly wounded and 17 Army men and one Marine were wounded but the extent undetermined according to available records. Not a single St. Francois County man was taken prisoner.

These casualties were higher than many had believed but were remarkably low when consideration was given to the number of men in the service and the number and kind of battles in which they participated.

The article went on to say that "specific mention of personal achievement has been purposely omitted in these columns since personal achievement was more or less secondary to the big task of winning the war and because the unquestioned ultimate of personal achievements surely belongs to those men who so gallantly made the supreme sacrifice. By best count 1,312 men from St. Francois County served their country during this Great World War."

The first St. Francois County man to lose his life in action in the World War was Norman Jackson of East Bonne Terre, who was killed in action in France on April 15, 1918; but the first man to lose his life in his country's service was Andrew Au Buchon of Bonne Terre, who was killed in an accidental manner in December

1917. The first Farmington man killed in action was Walter H. LePere, son of Jacob and Sally LePere. He was killed in France in October of 1918. His two brothers, Jack and Oscar LePere, were still serving in France. All three of the LePere boys were members of the Marine Corps.

These excerpts came from an article by the editor in the *Farmington News* in 1918.

Jacob LePere tells us he is in receipt of a letter from his son, Jack, written from France on November 10, 1918, the day before Armistice was signed, stating that both he and his brother, Oscar, were well.

He knew nothing of his brother Walter's death as the latter was in a different regiment and they had not seen one another since they enlisted in the service. It will probably be some time yet before Oscar and Jack will learn the news of their older brother's death.

"N.A. Kinkead of Rt. 1 told the *News* he had just received a letter from his son, Gladden, written from a hospital in France on November 10, the day before Armistice was signed, stating he had about recovered from the wound he received when a machine bullet passed entirely through one leg, and he expected to be back with his regiment in a few days. He also said Fred Kerlagon was attached to the hospital where he was then located.

"Following is a list of men from St. Francois County who made the supreme sacrifice in behalf of their Country and in the cause of Liberty and, who have been most fittingly called the Country's Immortals:

Edward C. Aderman, Everett Angel, Harold M. Antoine, Andrew Aubuchon, Clanie C. Belknap, William P. Black, Hervey L. Blaylock, Carl J. Boyer, John L. Bradley, George M. Buchholtz, Charles C. Conover, David F. Cooksey, Erwin L. Dann, Charles F. Davis, Earl Ferguson, Frank H. Fleming, Coleman P. Frazier, William Gallagher, Harry J. Griffin, Norman R. Jackson, Walter J. Jones, Richard F. Kirkpatrick, Walter H. LePere, George A. Mund, William E. Parker, Gus Scott, Robert J. Ste. Gemme, Jackson Stewart, Henry Thomas, Clarence J. Thomure, Frank Tucker, Jesse M. Van Sickle, Lawrence T. Vaughn, Evan P. Wells, Floyd S. Young, Ralph A. Abernathy, Firmin E. Clay, Nathaniel J. Cowley, Charles C. Franz, Harry L. Gruner, Claud R. Haile, William A. Kendall, John Knight, Elmer C. Lewis, Elmer A. Polk, Ivan R. Robinson, Hardy M. Rogers, Theodore R. Steinmetz.

Today, the names of those heroes are immortalized along with the names of their fallen comrades from succeeding wars on the St. Francois County War Memorial located at the courthouse in Farmington.

Robert E. Brooks
Commendation Ribbon With Metal Pendant

Sergeant Robert E. Brooks (Service No. RA17264305), Artillery, United States Army, distinguished himself while a prisoner of war in North Korea from December 1950 to August 1953. Sergeant Brooks completely refused to accept the Communist program presented by his captors and sabotaged their teachings by inspiring others to resist. He was a leader among the anti-Communist groups of prisoners of war and remained steadfast to his democratic principles even when imprisoned. Sergeant Brooks' courage and inspiring devotion to duty are in the highest tradition of military service.

(Of all the Army personnel taken prisoner in Korea, 35 men received the Army Commendation Ribbon with Metal Pendant.)

Fred Lesh on D-Day
June 12, 1944

"During the first few days following the landing I witnessed many acts of heroism and plain old-fashioned kindness, which made me feel proud to be an American".

"For me it was a day that ran the gamut of human emotions. This was a memorable day not only because of what I accomplished but mainly of what did and did not happen to me. What did happen is explainable, but the did nots still baffle my mind".

Taken from a letter by Fred Lesh on his experiences and memories of D-Day.

Darrell Samuel Cole
Congressional Medal of Honor

The Congressional Medal of Honor has been presented posthumously to Sergeant Darrell S. Cole, USMCR, Esther, MO, for action during the assault on Iwo Jima on February 19, 1945. The citation reads as follows:

For conspicuous gallantry and intrepidity at the risk of his life above and beyond the call of duty while serving as leader of a Machine Gun Section of Company B, 1st Battalion, 23rd Marines, 4th Marine Division, in action against enemy Japanese forces during the assault on Iwo Jima in the Volcano Islands, February 19, 1945. Assailed by a tremendous volume of small-arms, mortar and artillery fire as he advanced with one squad of his section in the initial assault wave, Sergeant Cole boldly led his men up the sloping beach toward Airfield No. 1 despite the blanketing curtain of flying shrapnel and, personally destroying with hand grenades two hostile emplacements which menaced the progress of his unit, continued to move forward until a merciless barrage of fire emanating from three Japanese pillboxes halted the advance. Instantly placing his one remaining machine gun in action, he delivered a shattering fusillade and succeeded in silencing the nearest and most threatening emplacement before his weapon jammed and the enemy, reopening fire with knee mortars and grenades, pinned down his unit for the second time. Shrewdly gauging the tactical situation and evolving a daring plan of counterattack, Sergeant Cole, armed solely with a pistol and one grenade, coolly advanced alone to the hostile pillboxes. Hurling his one grenade at the enemy in sudden, swift attack, he quickly withdrew, returned to his own lines for additional grenades and again advanced, attacked and withdrew. With enemy guns still active, he ran the gauntlet of slashing fire a third time to complete the total destruction of the Japanese strong point and the annihilation of the defending garrison in this final assault. Although instantly killed by an enemy grenade as he returned to his squad, Sergeant Cole had eliminated a formidable Japanese position, thereby enabling his company to storm the remaining fortifications, continue the advance, and seize the objective. By his dauntless initiative, unfaltering courage, and indomitable determination during a critical period of action, Sergeant Cole served as an inspiration to his comrades, and his stouthearted leadership in the face of almost certain death sustained and enhanced the highest tradition of the U.S. Naval Service. He gallantly gave his life for his country.

Darrell Cole was born July 20, 1920, and was married to Margaret Willott in San Diego, CA. He was killed on February 19, 1945, at Iwo Jima and is buried at Parkview Cemetery in Farmington, MO. Darrell's parents were Samuel Randall Cole and Mary Magdalena Williams. His grandparents were William James Cole and Francis M. Vandiver.

Leaving for WW I at DeLassus depot in 1918.

Leaving for WW I on March 4, 1918 at the Doe Run depot.

129

War Memorial

Dedicated in the memory of those from St. Francois County who gave their lives in conflict overseas during times of war.

World War I

Aderman, Edward C.
Antoine, Harold
Belknap, Clanie C.
Black, William C.
Blaylock, Henry L.
Boyer, Carl J.
Bradley, John L.
Conover, Charles
Cooksey, David F.
Cowley, Nathaniel J.
Dann, Ervin C.
Davis, Charles F.
Eaton, Charley M.
Fleming, Frank B.
Franz, Charley C.
Frazier, Coleman P.
Gallagher, William
Griffin, Harry J.
Hale, Claude R.
Humphrey, Jake
Jackson, Norman
Jones, Walter J.
Kendall, William A.
Kirkpatrick, Richard F.
LePere, Walter
Munds, Arnold G.
Parker, William F.
Polk, Elamer A.
Ritter, Jesse
Robinson, James A.
Roggers, William J.
Scott, Gus
Steinmetz, Theodore R.
St. Gemme, Robert J.
Stuart, Jackson
Thomas, Henry
Thomure, Clarence J.
Tucker, Frank
Vaughn, Lawrence T.
Wells, Even S.
Wells, Even P.
Young, Floyd S.

World War II

Asher, John E.
Bader, Troy R.
Barker, Harold J.
Bayless, Joseph W.
Black, Earl W.
Boatright, George J.
Bone, Alpha J.
Bradley, Rolla C.
Callaway, William E.
Cash, Cecil J.

Clark, Audery L.
Clay, Harold D. Jr.
Cole, Darrell S.
Cooper, Buford E.
Counts, Harold
Counts, Winiferd U.
Cox, Emanuel E.
Crepps, Paul E.
Crump, Alva L.
Denman, Charles W.
Dewey, John W.
Douglas, Harold W.
Eddington, John F.
Fenton, Louis
Frago, Kenneth
Fortner, Harold
Gardner, Harvey T.
Gibson, Harold E.
Gibson, Harold G.
Gilliam, Warren H.
Gremmels, Ralph
Grider, James S.
Griwach, John Jr.
Hamman, Thomas E.
Hardesty, F. Marvin
Hawkins, Lindley E.
Henry, Harold G.
Herman, Elmer J.
Highley, Carlton B.
Hollinger, Harry L.
House, Louis E.
Hughes, Laverne G.
Huitt, Kenneth
Janis, Robert L.
Johnson Forrest W.
Johnson, Charles E.
Johnson, Gerald E.
Jones, Henry A.
Kellison, Cecil E.
Kellums, Kenneth
Kendall, Leon J.
Kenton, Lewis J.
Koen, Willard R. Jr.
Kohut, Joseph M.
Kirchner, Ellis E.
Kistner, Charles L. Jr.
Kulasaza, Anthony
Lace, George A.
Long, Milton R.
Long, Robert W.
Lunsford, James A.
Luther, Francis E.
Mahurin, Omer L.
Mathews, Andrew J.
McCalister, William F. Jr.
Meyer, Paul B.
Miller, Leman B.

Milne, Britton J.
Missey, Hubert J.
Moore, Charles
Moser, Edwin P.
McGeorge, Carl
Myers, Jerry W.
Morris, Tommy
Nations, Hildon H.
Nelms, Charles E.
Orr, Smiley A.
Perry, Harry
Pettus, Winford L.
Phillips, William C.
Pinkston, Robert E.
Portell, Charles A.
Pryor, Morris E.
Pogue, Roy D.
Pulliam, Robert O. Jr.
Radle, Clarence H.
Rawlins, Eli B.
Rigdon, Norman L.
Rickman, Gilbert
Rolens, William E.
Rippee, Burl H.
Roome, Charles G.
Roome, Wilburn M.
Russell, Edgar E.
Shaner, Leonard P.
Sherman, Harold H.
Shoemake, Eldon T.
Shumake, Lytle
Sitton, Ruben W.
Skaggs, James W.
Stegall, Joseph
Stausser, Clifford
Steele, Howard
Stewart, Bengie
Stewart, Thomas
Stoll, Milton
Stroup, Ray E.
Sutton, Carl
Thomure, Harold C.
Thomure, Jasper E.
Thurman, Afton J.
Thurman, Glendal M.
Tongay, Darrell
Tucker, Ralph
Turner, Howard J.
Tyndyk, Mike
Van Doren, Louis
Vaughn, Adolph
Van Lear, J.H.
Weible, James H.
Watson, Willard E.
Woodcock, Marion
Westover, Martin W.
Whaley, Leonard L.

Williford, Harry E.
Walker, Donald
Walker, Tom
Young, James E.

Korean

Brown, Alvin L.
Clinton, Robert
Cole, John
DeGrant, Gilbert L.
Edgar, William T.
Fingers, Donald E.
Gibson, Howard J.
Hanaver, Alan M.
Hurst, Charles M.
Kohut, John L.
Laird, Rob R.
Long, Junior E.
Marler, Glenwood E.
Overall, Forest L.
Pettus, Firman E. Jr.
Rose, Edward R.
Sliter, Alford
Thornton, Donald
Vallo, Eugene S.
Welker, Eugene P.
Wilfong, Leeman D.

Vietnam

Carter, Jery R.
Cortor, Francis Jr.
Cleve, Reginald
Ellis, Earl
Freeman, David
Graves, Gary
Hardie, Anuthony
Isgrig, Dennis
Johnson, Roger
Meador, Billy J.
Pipkin, Thomas D.
Reese, Delbert
Rhodes, Donald L.
Silvey, Harold
Seabourne, Benny
Suggs, John F.
Trammell, Roger
Vandiver, Harry M.
Werley, Robert W.

Gulf War

Hurley, Patrick

WORLD WAR II

DEDICATED IN MEMORY OF THOSE FROM ST. FRANCOIS COUNTY
WHO GAVE THEIR LIVES IN DEFENSE
OF OUR GREAT NATION DURING TIMES OF WAR

ASHER, JOHN E.	JOHNSON, FORREST W	RICKMAN, GILBERT
BADER, TROY R	JOHNSON, CHARLES E.	ROLENS, WILLIAM R.
BARKER, HAROLD J.	JOHNSON, GERALD L.	RIPPEE, BUEL H.
BASLESS, JOSEPH W	JONES, HENRY A	ROONE, CHARLES G.
BLACK, EARL W.	KELLISON, CECIL L.	ROOME, WILBURN M
BOATRIGHT, GEORGE J.	KELLUMS, KENNETH	RUSSELL, EDGAR E.
BONE, ALPHA J.	KENDALL, LEON J.	SHANER, LEONARD P.
BRADLEY, ROLLA C.	KENTON, LEWIS J.	SHERMAN, HAROLD M
CALLAWAY, WILLIAM L.	KOER, WILLARD R. Jr.	SHOEMAKE, ELDON T.
CASH, CECIL J.	KOBUT, JOSEPH W.	SHUMAKE, LYTLE
CLARK, AUDREY L.	KIPCHNEE, ELLIS J.	SUTTON, RUBEN W
CLAY, HAROLD D. Jr.	KISTNER, CHARLES S. Jr.	SKAGGS, JAMES W.
COLE, DARRELL E.	KULASZA, ANTHONY	SEEGALL, JOSEPH
COOPER, BUFORD E.	LACY, GEORGE A.	STRAESSER, CLIFFORD
COUNTS, HAROLD	LONG, MILTON P.	STEWART, RENGIE
COUNTS, WINFRED O.	LONG, ROBERT W	STEWART, THOMAS
COX, EMANUEL E.	LUNSFORD, JAMES A.	STOLL, MILTON
CREPPS, PAUL E.	LUTHER, FRANCIS E.	STROUP, RAY E.
CRUME, ALVA L.	MAHURIN, OMER L.	SUTTON, CARL
DENMAN, CHARLES W	MATTHEWS, ANDREW J.	THOMURE, HAROLD C.
DEWEY, JOHN W.	McCALISTER, WILLIAM N. Jr.	THOMURE, JASPER E.
DOUGLAS, HAROLD W.	MEYER, PAUL B	THURMAN, AFTON J.
EDDINGTON, JOHN E.	MILLER, LEEMAN B.	THURMAN, GLENDAL W.
FENTON, LOUIS	MILNE, BRITTON J.	TONGAE, DARRELL
DRAGO, KENNETH	MESSEY, HUBERT J.	TUCKER, RALPH
FORTNER, HAROLD	MOORE, CHARLES	TURNER, HOWARD J.
GARDNER, HARVEY T.	MOSER, EDWIN P.	TYNDYK, MIKE
GIBSON, HAROLD L.	McGEORGE, CARL	VAN DOREN, LOUIS
GIBSON, HAROLD G.	MYERS, JERRY W.	VAUGHN, ADOLPH
McKILLIAM, WARREN M.	MORRIS, TOMMY	VAN LEAR, S. H.
GRIMSLEY, RALPH	NATIONS, HELDON H.	WEIBLE, JAMES H.
GRIDER, JAMES S	NEEMS, CHARLES E.	WATSON, WILLARD T.
GRIWACH, JOHN R.	ORR, SMILEY A.	WOODCOCK, MARION
HAMMAC, THOMAS E.	PERRY, HARRY	WESTOVER, MARTIN W.
HARDESTY, F. MARVIN	PETTUS, WINFORD L.	WHALEY, LEONARD E.
HOPKINS, LINDLEY E	PHILLIPS, WILLIAM L.	WILLFORD, HARRY E.
HENRY, HAROLD G.	PINKSTON, ROBERT E.	WALKER, DONALD
HERMAN, ELMER L.	PORTELL, CHARLES A.	WALKER, TOM
HIGHLEY, CARLTON B.	FRYOR, MORRIS E.	YOUNG, JAMES T.
HOLLINGER, HARRY L.	POGUE, ROY D.	
HOUSE, LOUIS E.	PULLIAM, ROBERT O. Jr.	
HUGHES, LAVERNE G.	RAILE, CLARENCE H.	
HUFF, KENNETH	RAWLINS, LEE R.	
ROBERT L.	RIGDON, NORMAN J.	

City of Farmington bomber flying in combat during WW II.

City of Farmington bomber and crew. Cecil Hulsey, fourth from left.

The USS Farmington

WW II Bomber named City of Farmington.

Dedication ceremony of war memorial.

MISCELLANEOUS

The Hanging Day

by Leroy Sigman

Less than a year after Farmington officially became a city, Charles H. Hardin disappointed a large crowd waiting for his hanging by giving a religious speech rather that a confession.

It was a cold, bitter day on January 23, 1880, when the courthouse lawn, the trees and even the roof of the courthouse itself filled with area residents. Between 4,000 and 5,000 people came to the city's courthouse square from distant locations to watch. At 1 p.m. Hardin was hanged in full public view.

Hardin was found guilty of killing Robert Ferguson in a camp along Indian Creek. As the story goes, Hardin stopped at Ferguson's camp on Indian Creek near the village of Haggai, located three miles southeast of Iron Mountain. He soon discovered Ferguson had $350 on him.

During the evening, Hardin decided to rob Ferguson and Ferguson's son who was also at the camp. Hardin approached the fire, picked up a stick and started to stir the fire.

Ferguson was seated near the fire when Hardin, stick in hand, began hitting Ferguson in the head several times. Hardin threw Ferguson's body into the creek, where he was later discovered by his children. He fled with the child to Columbus, KY, taking the money, along with the wagon and team of horses. He was captured in Columbus, KY and returned to stand trial in Farmington.

The account of the hanging says the scaffold was built by Messrs. Lang and his brother, who were wagon masters at the time. The necktie was adjusted by Sheriff Thomas McMullen after Hardin was allowed to say his last words. He had been brought from the county jail in a wagon accompanied by his attorney, Jasper N. Burks.

According to those who witnessed the gruesome event, Hardin slowly climbed the steps in to the gallows shortly after 1 p.m. He was dressed in a brownish plaid business suit, spotless shirt and a cravat. Hardin knelt to pray and then addressed the gathering crowd.

"My sentence is a hard one, but it is just," he began. "I have nothing to say against the judge, or the jury, or against Mr. Carter. He is a perfect gentleman, but I do think some of the witnesses didn't do me justice. I forgive them all. The people here treated me very kindly, a great deal better than I had any reason to expect." Hardin's speech continued. Instead of the expected confession, however, he gave a lengthy religious oration.

As he was led to the trap-door, he said, "Farewell vain world, this is the way Jesus supports a man in my condition."

There were five physicians on hand to pronounce Hardin dead. His death by strangulation rather that a broken neck caused the *St. Louis Globe-Democrat* to report it as a cruelly managed event.

Although Hardin's hanging was the only legal execution in the county, there were other illegal ones conducted, many reported to have taken place during the Civil War.

Reprinted with permission from *The Daily Journal,* April 4, 1987

Last legal hanging 1880.

It Happened Here

•Perhaps the most tragic event in Farmington's history occurred on April 2, 1979, when a fire at Straughn's Wayside Inn, a retirement and boarding home just outside the city limits, killed 25 residents. This was the deadliest fire in Missouri since 1957, when 72 residents died in a fire at a Warrenton nursing home.

•Farmington entered the modern age in October 1891 when the city's new power station began generating enough electricity to run 20 street lights. Many townspeople expressed a desire to hook up to the new system as quickly as possible. Elmwood Seminary announced it would convert entirely to electric lights. Up to now, most homes and businesses used coal oil lamps for illumination. The availability of electricity would also permit the manufacture of ice and other products in Farmington.

•The movie theater has played a prominent place in Farmington history since the turn of the century. The first films were shown here in Tom Brohm's "Old Picture Store" in 1903. It featured "moving pictures and illustrated songs." The city's first modern-day movie theater was the Monarch, which opened its doors in 1913 at a location that is now the parking lot of Ozarks Federal Savings and Loan Association. The building was made of wood with a metal exterior and could accommodate 500 patrons. In January 1927, the structure and all of its contents were destroyed by fire. Shortly after work was begun on a new brick structure, renamed the Ritz, which opened to rave reviews by 1700 ticket holders on April 9, 1928. The new building was designed to present both movies and vaudeville acts. With seating for 1,000, it was one of the largest theaters in this part of the state. The Ritz featured an orchestra pit, dressing rooms under the stage, and a loft over the stage from which scenery could be lowered, and a balcony. In 1930 the first sound films were shown with the newly-installed Vitaphone sound-on-disc system. This equipment was soon replaced with the more practical sound-on-film system. In 1954 the Cinemascope wide screen system was added.

•The Ritz was an important gathering place, where its huge 65-foot-wide stage featured such varied offerings as variety shows, club meetings, church services, square dances, and even occasional monsters to thrill audiences at horror shows. During World War II, two big stars, Gene Tierney and Anthony Quinn, stood on the stage to help sell war bonds. In the golden era of movies, the Ritz was the flagship of a chain of area cinemas known as the Lead Belt Amusement Co. Theaters during the 1930s and the Edwards and Plumlee Theaters after 1947. (See related article in chapter.) The coming of television and competition from other sources of entertainment in the post-war period caused a major decline in movie attendance. The fatal blow for the Ritz came on May 27, 1964, when a fire in the adjoining P.N. Hirsch store (later the Dollar Store) severely damaged the theater. The last film shown at the Ritz was *Fancy Pants,* starring Bob Hope. Today, movie goers attend the Maple Valley Four, which features four screens and 300 seats. Although the Ritz is gone, it is not forgotten.

•On January 23, 1880, Farmington was the scene of the only legal hanging in the county. Despite the bitter cold, more than 4,000 people turned out to watch Charles H. Hardin drop to his doom. But Hardin died of strangulation rather than a broken neck in what the *St. Louis Globe-Democrat* called a cruelly bungled event. The deceased had been found guilty of killing Robert Ferguson after robbing him of $350. Another noted hanging occurred in 1843 when an angry mob broke into the county jail and lynched James Layton.

•A deadly shootout at a large public picnic

in Doe Run was featured as the lead article on the front page of the August 19, 1900, edition of the *St. Louis Post Dispatch* in what was described as the "Dooley-Harris" family feud in which five men and a woman were shot, two of them fatally.

•Farmington got a grand dose of baseball in April 1946 when the old St. Louis Browns used Wilson-Rozier Park as a training site for 125 baseball players from their many minor league ball clubs. Just before and after World War II, Wilson-Rozier Park was also the home of its own professional baseball team, the St. Louis Blues. Another sports note: Robert F. Karsch, who taught political science at Westminister College in Fulton, wrote the music that same year for the now famous Mizzou Tigers' "fight song." Karsch was the son of Mr. and Mrs. Fred Karsch of Farmington.

•In 1947 John M. and Cecil W. Roberts, founders of the *Farmington Press*, dissolved their partnership. Cecil got the newspaper while John took over Roberts Office Supply. Later in August, Cecil sold the *Press* to Art Freeman and Wally Stewart, two employees of the newspaper. Soon after, Cecil opened KREI, a 1000-watt radio station in Farmington. KREI-FM went on the air in 1949.

•One of the early "stars" on KREI was Johnny Rion, who hosted a morning show at the station. Rion later went to St. Louis, where he broadcast a popular country western show on KSTL. During his long career, he wrote many of the songs he sang on his shows. Today Johnny Rion is best remembered for his rendition of the ballad *Iron Mountain Baby*, which was written by J.T. Barton, a United Baptist preacher who lived near Iron County. The song tells the story of a baby boy who was thrown from a speeding train at the Big River bridge near Irondale in 1902. The baby, stuffed in a suitcase, was soon discovered by a farmer, Bill Helms, who was attracted by the infant's cries. Helms raised the boy as his own. The story of this modern-day Moses quickly attracted the attention of the nation when it was printed in newspapers around the country. After ending his radio career, Johnny Rion became a popular evangelist, but his signature song was always *Iron Mountain Baby*.

•One of the most exciting events in Farmington occurred at 7 p.m. on February 6, 1932, when 7 of the 32 prisoners at the county jail escaped by dynamiting a large hole in the building. However, their freedom was short lived: one was killed, another was shot and wounded, and the others were recaptured. The incident sparked interest in building a better jail, but nothing came of it at the time. However, in 1996 St. Francois County finally built a new jail on the site of the old dairy barn of State Hospital No. 4.

•Much speculation surrounds the whereabouts of Farmington's fort, constructed in the early 1800s by city founder William Murphy to protect residents from native Americans. The fort was dismantled after Indians were removed from this part of the state in 1824 and its logs were used to build homes in the area. Some of the nails used to build the fort, made by a local blacksmith, were stored and later placed on display at the St. Louis World's Fair in 1904. The location of those nails and the exact site of the fort remain a mystery. Local lore suggests that the fort stood in the south section of Farmington, somewhere near Harrison Street, which was the location of Farmington's original southern boundary.

•In 1963 a Farmingtonian, SP-4 Donald Halton, drove one of the cars in the funeral procession of assassinated President John F. Kennedy. His was the second car from the front. Known to his friends as "Shorty," he attended Farmington High School and is the son of Mr. and Mrs. Frank Halton of Rt. 2.

LAYTON'S LYNCHING AT FARMINGTON, 1843

On June 17, 1843, the first, and so far as I have been able to learn the only, lynching that St. Francois County ever indulged in occurred in Farmington. The events that led an outraged public to take the execution of the law into their own hands on this occasion may be briefly stated as follows:

On the night of January 10, 1841, James Layton, a desolate worthless character, living in Perry County, came home drunk and drove his wife and little son out into the winter night and storm. Mrs. Layton, who was Layton's second wife, was at the time about to become a mother; and in her helpless condition, she and her little stepson attempted to make their way through the darkness to a neighbor's. But she was pursued by the drunk-maddened demon that overtook her and the child as they were crouching over and trying to warm themselves by the embers where some laborers had been burning that day. Seizing one of the green sticks that had been burned to a sharp point, at the first blow he struck down his helpless and unresisting victim and continued to beat her till life was extinct. Then, with brutality from which an ordinary savage would have turned from in horror, he thrust the pointed club through her body and thus laterally pinned to the earth his wife and unborn child.

Layton at once fled, leaving his little boy who had been a witness of the whole horrible affair alone with his dead stepmother. The child made his way to a neighbor's house and related the tragic story. The next morning the neighbors flocked to the scene of the tragedy and were horrified by what they saw. Though at that time the telegraph was unknown and the newspapers few and far between, the news spread quickly over Perry and all the adjoining counties. It was, never-the-less, nearly a year before Layton was arrested. He was found in hiding in Wayne County and brought back to Perry where he was put on trial charged with murder in the first degree. His own son, the little 9-year-old boy, who fled with his step-mother on the fatal night, was the only witness that was put on the stand. But so clear and convincing was his story that no cross-questioning of the lawyers could confuse or shake it; and upon the conclusion of the trial, the jury was scarcely 10 minutes in bringing a unanimous verdict of guilty. The interest in the case, instead of dying out, had increased; and now that sentence has been passed on which the whole country breathed easier in the belief that justice at last was about to be meted out to the wife murderer.

But on an appeal, which Layton's lawyer took to the Supreme Court, the judgment of the trial court was set aside and the case remanded for a new trial. Then followed another tedious delay, during which the case was brought on a change of venue to St. Francois County. At the May term of court 1843 the case came up for trial the second time; and as before, Layton's little son was the only witness called. On his testimony the father was again convicted and sentenced to death on the following June 17. Owing to the peculiarly atrocious features of the murder and the long delay that had already followed its perpetration, the deepest interest was felt in the approaching execution by 10 o'clock on the morning of the 17th fully 3,000 people, many of whom had come 10 to 30 miles, were assembled in and about the public square in the then little village of Farmington. All were eager to witness the execution.

The jail in which the prisoner was confined was a two-story log structure, the first story being built with triple walls. Access to the "dungeon," as it was usually called, could only be had by a flight of stairs on the outside to the second story, from which the entrance was by a trapdoor near the middle of the floor. Through this the jailer descended by means of a movable ladder, which was drawn up after being used and the heavy trapdoor shut down and securely locked. Around this dingy little building the people crowded, each morbidly eager to see the culprit when he would be brought to his death. At a few minutes after 11 o'clock the sheriff with considerable effort crowded his way through the dense mass of humanity to the foot of the stairway that led to the jail. As he ascended the stairs, it was observed that he held a paper in his hand and it was taken for granted that this was the death warrant and that as soon as it was read to the prisoner he would be brought out and the execution would at once take place. On reaching the top of the stairs, however, hc paused, turned toward the crowd and waved the paper above his head to attract attention. Amid almost breathless silence, he announced to the crowd that the paper he held in his hand and which he had, but a few minutes before received from the governor, contained an order for a stay of execution for 30 days.

The effect of this announcement was keen disappointment and was quickly succeeded by a feeling of deep indignation as the honest farmers recalled the mutilated form of that young wife and her unborn babe. That appeal to their manhood was too strong to be suppressed, and what at first was only a murmur of dissatisfaction in a few minutes swelled into a roar of indignation that would be satisfied with nothing short of life. No one knows how or by what process the determination was reached, but in a few minutes it was universally understood that the jail was to be forced and the prisoner hanged without further delay.

A few of the more conservative citizens pleaded with the mob to allow the law to take its course, and in deference to this suggestion a vote was ordered and all in favor of hanging were requested to take one side of the square, while those opposed were to take the other. It was found that an overwhelming majority was in favor of hanging.

In another minute a rush was made for the jail, and with heavy iron bars and sledgehammers the door was soon beaten down. The trapdoor to the "dungeon" was next pried up and half a dozen of the lynchers descended. After they tied the prisoner's hands behind him and placed a rope around his neck, they carried the trembling wretch back up the ladder to the second floor and out on the platform at the head of the stairs. An open buggy, from which the horse had been unhitched, was backed up to the foot of the stairs, and in this the victim of the mob's vengeance was placed and willing hands took hold of the shafts and rapidly drew the vehicle under the rude gallows tree improvised for the occasion. At this juncture the culprit was given an opportunity to speak, but on his declining to avail himself of it, the rope was thrown over the beam and secured and the buggy was quickly drawn from under. The body swung back and forth for several minutes and then was still. The brutal murder of Mary Layton was avenged. The crowd quickly dispersed, the body cut down and buried.

TRAIL OF TEARS NATIONAL HISTORIC TRAIL

In 1830 Congress endorsed the Indian Removal Act that forced the remaining Indians west of the Mississippi. The Indian tribes that were relocated included Cherokee, Chickasaw, Creek and Seminole.

In May 1838 the Cherokee were rounded up by federal troops and placed in camps. Although the troops were told to treat the Indians humanly, this was not the case as families were separated, some forced out at gunpoint with nothing but the clothes on their backs.

Before General Winfield Scott ordered the forced removal of the Cherokee on May 23, 1838, several groups of Cherokee had already started voluntarily for Oklahoma. Late in 1837, a group lead by B.B. Cannon left Tennessee and set out on what in now called the Northern Route which passed through Missouri. Eleven detachments of Cherokee used the Northern Route to travel to Oklahoma. They landed near what is now Trail of Tears State Park and at Smith's Ferry at Bainbridge, several miles south. This crossing was made in December 1838 and January and February of 1839.

From Cape Girardeau they traveled through Jackson on to Fredericktown, then north to Farmington. Many of the detachments, which were to follow, came through Farmington as stated in a diary by Rev. Daniel S. Buttrick. His February 21, 1839, entry states: "This morning we passed through Farmington, a pleasant village."

Due to the horrible weather conditions and lacking proper clothing and supplies the Cherokee endured sickness, cold, hunger and, of course, the sometimes hostile reception from the townspeople. Sometimes the local merchants took advantage of this traveling group as B.B. Cannon recorded in his journal on November 21, 1837.

"A considerable number drank last night, obtained liquor at Farmington yesterday; had to get out of bed about midnight to quell disor-der; a refusal by several to march this morning."

The route continued southwest from Farmington through DeLassus and Doe Run and then on west toward Springfield and into Oklahoma.

The removal and forced march of the Cherokee from the southeastern United States to Indian Territory has come to be known as the Trail of Tears. In 1987 Congress acknowledged the significance of the Trail by establishing the Trail of Tears National Historic Trail, which commemorates the forced removal of the five civilized Indian tribes from the east. The National Park Service administers the trail in cooperation with federal, state, and local agencies, the Cherokee Nation and the Eastern Band of Cherokee Indians, interested groups and private landowners.

Dick Ockermorre and wife.

Thrashing wheat around 1902.

Thrashing machine, early 1900s.

Thrashing machines, 1889.

FAMILY HISTORIES

At right: Mildred and Mabel Casteel
Below: Schramm wedding day, 1920.

ALCORN - "Life itself won't give you joy, unless you really will it, life just gives you time and space, it's up to you to fill it" (unknown). This is Dan Alcorn's philosophy.

Dan, born Aug. 20, 1936, Leadwood, MO, moved to Farmington in 1958 with a new baby and pregnant wife, Barbara Edwina Harrington, born Feb. 18, 1935. He had just served a tour in Germany with the army and was anxious to begin his married life as a civilian. His wife

Dan R. Alcorn, 1998 Mineral Area College

had been in Germany with him and his son Dennis Keith, born 1957, Frankfort, Germany. Thirteen months later, his daughter, Patricia Joan, was born at the Bonne Terre Hospital in 1959.

After settling in Farmington, Dan immediately started to Flat River Junior College. Besides carrying a full load of classes, he worked full time at the Farmington State Hospital #4. Then after graduating from Washington University, he continued working at the hospital. He established the first juvenile educational program and was the first teacher in the history of the hospital. He also established the first juvenile ward and formed the first Boy Scout troop consisting only of young patients.

In 1961 Dan left the state hospital to pursue a career with the Missouri Department of Elementary and Secondary Education, Division Vocational Rehabilitation in Cape Girardeau. Five years later, he returned to Farmington as a supervisor for vocational rehabilitation with the task of setting up a rehabilitation unit at State Hospital #4. During the next 20 years this unit discharged hundreds of hospitalized patients into training programs and employment opportunities. During its height, it had a staff of 75 employees of which 30 were professional positions. Dan successfully established and supervised this unit on the hospital grounds until the state hospital became Farmington Correctional Center. In 1986 Dan moved the unit off the grounds to the community where vocational rehabilitation continued to serve St. Francois and surrounding counties.

Dan has always been active in the community. Farmington has been the town where he has lived, worked and raised his two children. He is a member of the Baptist Church, past-president of the Farmington Lions Club and a member of the board in various civic organizations.

During his vocational career, Dan received numerous recognitions. When he was appointed supervisor for vocational rehabilitation, he was the youngest supervisor in the Department of Education. He received one of only two commissioner awards within a seven-state area for his work in vocational rehabilitation. He has served on several committees, chairing many of them. Also, he is past state president of the Missouri Rehabilitation Association. Dan has made several trips to Washington, DC in regard to the Americans with Disabilities Act. Presently, he has more seniority with the Department of Elementary and Secondary Education than any other employee.

Dan credits his accomplishments to his many friends and co-workers who have provided him with the substance for his accomplishments. However, no one influenced him to the extent that his father, Harold Henry Alcorn Sr.. Throughout his life his father's example in integrity, work ethic and morals shaped and focused Dan's career. *Submitted by Dennis K. Alcorn.*

ALLEN - Archiles Vernon Allen was born April 13, 1838 in Gallatin County, IL and moved to rural Farmington, in Ste. Genevieve County around 1843. He lived with the Jobe Mayberry family. He served three years in the Civil War and married Sarah Jane Boyd Aug. 2, 1867. He died in January 1882 and was survived by his wife and 11 children. Most of these families remained in Farmington and Ste. Genevieve County.

Sidney Counts Allen, the ninth child, married Nora Hampton. In 1939 he purchased a farm on Route 3, Farmington, and lived there until 1956. He resided in Farmington until his death in 1958. He was a member and deacon of the Pleasant Hill Baptist Church. They had one son, Marvin.

Kenny, Reba, Clara, Beverly, Gene Allen

Marvin Henry Allen attended the Avon schools and married Clara Jane Gregory. They both worked at the State Hospital and later moved to St. Louis where he was a truck driver for the Kroger Company. Around 1940 Marvin purchased a farm next to his father on Route 3. In 1942 he moved his family to the farm and went to work for the St. Joe Lead Company #9 as a safety man. He loved baseball and played every Sunday with some of the area fellows until his death in 1958. He was a member of the Pleasant Hill Baptist Church and Libertyville Masonic Lodge. His wife, Clara, age 92, resides with a daughter in Farmington. They had four children.

Marvin Eugene Allen married Jean Zimmer. He is a graduate of Ste. Genevieve High School and worked for the Farmington US Postal Service for 30 years. After retirement he worked real estate part-time and loves fishing. He is a member of the Lutheran Church. He and Jean have three children, and all are Farmington High graduates.

Rebecca Allen married Barry Kiesel and Tom Crawford. She had two children, Adrienne and Jacob Kiesel. Becky is assistant director of Grants and Planning for USOC and resides in Colorado.

Jane Allen resides in California and works as regional sales manager of Guidant, Inc. She travels all over the world.

Randall Allen lives in Farmington and owns and operates Hard Rack Restaurant and Billiards in Bonne Terre, MO.

Beverly Allen married Don McGuire. She is a graduate of Ste. Genevieve High and Missouri Beauty Academy of Farmington. She left Farmington in 1963. Bev and her husband, Don, a Southern Baptist minister, have served in several churches over the past 35 years. They are now retired and reside in Farmington. They have three children.

Richard McGuire married Debbie Reed and lives in Steelville, MO. He is a mechanic and has two children, Waylon and Angela, and two grandchildren, Katie and Trenton.

Bruce McGuire married Kelly Brigham and lives in Clarksville, MO. He is an attorney in Louisiana, MO. They have three daughters: Emily, Rachel and Jessica.

Jennifer McGuire married Andrew May and lives in St. Louis. She works as an information specialist for the State of Missouri and has a son, Malachi.

Reba Allen married Robert Mell. A graduate of Missouri Beauty Academy, Farmington, she owned and operated a beauty salon for several years. She has been secretary for Cooper Oil the last 28 years. She is a member of the Lutheran Church. She and Bobby have four sons and all are graduates of Farmington High, members of the Lutheran Church and reside in the Farmington area.

Michael Mell married Sharon Stacey. He is in masonry construction and they have three children: Shaun, Stacey and Jeri, and two grandchildren, Justin and Rachella.

Terry Mell married Sandy Jones. He owns and operates Mell Masonry Company. They have two children, Luke and Abby.

Gregory Mell married Caron Hull. Greg works for Mell Masonry and they have a son, Andy.

Dennis Mell married Ellen Roosman. They own and operate Custom Technologies in Farmington. They have one son, Jonathan.

Kenneth Duane Allen married Sheila Creswell. He is a graduate of Farmington High and served in the US Air Force. He is a member of the Methodist Church, President of the Farmington High School Alumni Association, and employed by the city of Farmington as recreation manager for the Civic Center. They have a daughter, Laura Jane. *Submitted by Beverly J. McGuire*

ALLEN - John William Allen, born in 1903, of Greenville, MO and Nancy Ruth Rawlings, born 1913, of Sullivan, MO were married Sept. 2, 1931. They had three children: Deloris Jean, born 1932; Donald Paul, born 1934; and William Lynn, born 1948.

John and Ruth Allen moved to Farmington in May 1943 with their two children, Deloris (10) and Donald (9). They moved to Farmington to establish an Assembly of God Church. They had been pastoring an established church in Salem, MO when they felt God leading them to move to Farmington. They rented a house on the northern edge of Farmington and set up a tent on the lots that are now 104 South Washington Street to hold services.

Rev. John William Allen and Nancy Ruth Allen

On Aug. 15, 1943, while still holding services in the tent, a Sunday School was organized with eight members present, four of them being the Allen family. On Aug. 23, 1943 the Southern Missouri District of the Assemblies of God purchased (for $600) a corner lot at First and Franklin Streets where Dr. John Jackson's dental office is now. The basement was dug mostly by hand by Rev. Allen. Occasionally people passing by would stop to help, and whenever he could Tom Gibson, who owned a team of mules, would help. On Dec. 5, 1943 the first services were held in the basement with 18 members present in Sunday School. The church continued to grow and the main auditorium was built and dedicated on Sept. 14, 1947. Two additions were built to the church, one in 1954 and another in 1961. On Oct. 1, 1943, the Allens purchased the remainder of the lot (204 West Harrison Street) and built their home which later became the parsonage. The Allens pastored the church for more than 25 years and retired in 1969.

Rev. Allen was a highly respected individual and minister. He had a reputation of leading people to Christ. Mrs. Allen was a faithful and dedicated pastor's wife. A lot of her days were filled with cooking for visiting ministers and their families. Both Rev. and Mrs. Allen were always available when members of their family, church or community needed them. Rev. Allen died in 1984. Mrs. Allen is still a resident of Farmington.

ALLEN - Donald Paul Allen was born in March 1934, Elmont, MO, son of John William and Nancy Ruth Allen. He moved to Farmington in May 1943 with his parents. He graduated from Farmington High School in 1952 and worked for Klein Grocery and for Wetterau Foods. He married Lillie Carolyn Gibson, born 1935, on Sept. 25, 1953. Carolyn was a graduate of Farmington High School in 1952 and the daughter of Casper Edward Gibson, born 1909, and Ethel Myra (Wann) Gibson, born 1910. Donald "Bud" and Carolyn have two children, Greg Edward, born 1961, and Donna Beth, born 1966. The family moved to Scott City, MO in September 1962 when Wetterau Foods moved. They lived in Scott City, MO, until December 1969 when Donald became disabled because of blindness. The family returned to Farmington at that time.

Greg and Donna both graduated from Farmington High School, Mineral Area College and Southeast Missouri State University. Greg married Jane Marie Boesch, daughter of Don and Finian Boesch, in 1985. Jane is also a graduate of Farmington High School, Mineral Area College and Southeast Missouri State University. They have two children, Bryant Christopher, born 1988, and Bryana Marie, born 1992. Greg is president of First State Bancshares.

Donna married William Russell Drye, son of Dan and Sherry Drye, in 1990. William is also a graduate of Farmington High School. They have two children, Kayla Bryanne, born 1993, and Donald Patrick, born 1996. Donna teaches second grade at Washington-Franklin Elementary School and William is manager of the Farmington Dairy Queen. They are expecting their third child in April 1999.

Donald died Jan. 14, 1996. Carolyn is an assistant secretary at Ozarks Federal Savings and Loan Association.

ASHER - I, Donald Glen Asher, was born June 12, 1934, son of Lewis Glen Asher and Maude Catherine (Eugas) Asher, in Yount, MO. My father's paternal grandparents were Rebecca Asher and maternal grandparents were Joseph Chaboude and wife Jennie (Turpin) Chaboude. Joseph came to America from Bourdeaux, France when he was 2 years old. Alice Gertrude was one of their nine children.

My mother's paternal grandparents were William Eugas and Dora (Heitman) Hahn Eugas. Henry Elijah was the youngest of their seven children. My mother's maternal grandparents were Henry Franklin "Cap" Johnson and Barbara Amelia (Yamnitz) Johnson. Mary was the third of 11 children. Henry Elijah and Mary's children were: Hazel Myrtle, Maude Catherine and Lester William Eugas.

My father's father, Sylvester Asher, married Alice Gertrude (Chaboude) on Oct. 19, 1899 and their children were James Henry, born Sept. 14, 1901, died Sept. 29, 1901; Ada Irene Roberts, born Aug. 29, 1902, died April 10, 1990; Nora Lucille, born Nov. 22, 1904, died Feb. 27, 1905; Lewis Glen, born May 24, 1906, died Jan. 1, 1977;

Naomi Gertrude, born April 7, 1908, died July 2, 1923; Daisy Christine, born July 8, 1912, died July 21, 1913; Milton Sylvester, born May 23, 1914, died Feb. I, 1992; George Martin, born May 22, 1916, died Aug. 8, 1990; Harry Ross, born Aug. 8, 1910, died June 7, 1993; Harriet Annette, born Dec. 11, 1921.

Maude, Lewis, Donald, Jean and Larry - late 60s or early 70s

My father, Lewis Glen Asher, married Maude Catherine Eugas on Sept. 25, 1929. Their children are Anita Imogene, born Jan. 2, 1931; Donald Glen, born June 12, 1934; and Larry Martin, born Dec. 23, 1950. My sister, Jean, married Dennis Eugene Herbst Jan. 15, 1949. Their children are Dennis Eugene, David Lewis, Catherine Irene and James Herman. My brother, Larry, has two children, Christina Marie and Carrie Nicole.

I married Janice Waldrop of Randolph, MS on Aug. 11, 1957. We have one child, Tracie Janice, born Jan. 5, 1965. Tracie married James Stanton Aug. 5, 1989 and they have two children, Grady Asher Stanton, born April 3, 1992, and Clara Marley Stanton.

My sister, Jean, and her husband, Gene, have grandchildren, Kassidy Rene and Kaylan, from their eldest son and his wife, Kristin Rene (Voertman). Second son, David Lewis, and wife, Laurie (Hill), have children: David Michael, Lindsey Ann and Samuel Martin. Catherine Irene and husband, Leeman Schwent, have children Myranda Lea, Nicholas Eugene Starkey and Valeria Schwent. Jamie and wife, Mary (Spraul), have children Dennis Eugene and Benjamin Thomas.

My brother Larry's grandchildren are from his daughter, Christina, and her husband, Jimmy Church; Johnnathan Ray, Ciarra and Sabrina Ann.

My family moved to Farmington when I was 2 years old. In approximately 1941, my father started working for the Presbyterian Orphanage, later to be called Presbyterian Children's Home and now called Presbyterian Children's Services. The Home's first farm was on the west side of town, just south of Maple Street and about where N. Alexander Street is located. In the summer of 1942, the Home bought the Kosksy farm at the end of Pine Street. They later bought the Giessing farm adjoining on the east side of the Kosksy farm.

They had laying chickens, hogs and at the start, a few dairy cows, also a garden where Dad raised a lot of their vegetables. They later went to an all registered Guernsey herd and at one time were milking over 30 head of cows. In the early 50s they started raising broiler chickens on the Giessing farm. Once the boys in the Home reached approximately 12 years of age, they moved out on the farm where two cottages had been built. Later there was a cottage built featuring a kitchen and dining hall. The boys helped with the farm chores such as milking cows, putting up hay, gardening and fence building. Not only was my father the farm manager, but he and my mom were house-parents in one of the cottages. When the third cottage was completed, my mom also cooked for a while. Maude and Lewis

were affectionately referred to as "Mom and Dad," and often after the boys left the Home they would come back for visits with Mom and Dad.

I attended Farmington Public schools and graduated from high school in 1953. I was in the Navy for four years. I met my future wife while going to radar school in Millington, TN. In 1957 we were married and moved to Ironton, MO where Jan taught home economics at the high school. I worked for the telephone company. In June 1962 I was hired by the Federal Aviation Agency and we moved to Olathe, KS where we lived until my retirement Sept. 1, 1989. In December 1990 we returned to Farmington to live. *Submitted by Don Asher.*

ASLINGER - Thelma Virginia Pogue, born Aug. 16, 1926, was the sixth child of Felix and Laura Pogue. Thelma's family moved to Farmington in 1936 and owned and operated a neighborhood grocery store near the corner of West Liberty and Alexander Streets. Thelma graduated from Farmington High School in 1944 and met and married Arthur L. Aslinger, known to everyone as "Jack."

Thelma Aslinger

Jack served in the US Navy, and after he and Thelma were married and he was discharged from the Navy, they opened "Jack's Drive-in Restaurant" located on Ste. Genevieve Ave. This was a very popular hangout for teens and adults. The Aslingers had four children: Linda, Kathy, Geoff and Jacque.

Jack, Thelma and their family moved to the Fenton area where Jack worked for and retired from the Chrysler Corporation. Jack passed away in 1983 and Thelma now resides near her brother, Eugene Pogue, and her sister, Goldie Koen, in Farmington. Thelma is a member of the First Baptist Church of Farmington and enjoys her 13 grandchildren and five great-grandchildren. *Submitted by Thelma V. Aslinger.*

AUCHTER - The history of the Auchter family in Farmington began in 1946 when newly married Fred and Dorotha moved from Wichita, KS. In the spring of that year Fred, Claude Lovitt and Harry Peterson formed the Farmington Aviation Corporation and in May, Farmington's first airport opened for business. The airport quickly became a thriving enterprise and Fred and Dortha settled into life in Farmington, building their home adjacent to the airport in 1947.

Two daughters soon followed, Barbara in 1947 and Norma in 1950. Fred became active in local organizations and was a founding member of the Elk's Club. Dorothy, Dot to many of her friends, was active in, and an officer of, Beta Sigma Phi Sorority and later in the local garden club. Fred remained an owner and the operations manager of the airport until his accidental death in 1956. That year Dorotha was also involved in a serious accident. Despite entreaties from her family to return to Kansas, she chose to remain in Farmington. She operated a private accounting business until her death in 1973.

Barbara and Norma graduated from Farmington High School. Barbara attended Temple University in Philadelphia, and later graduate school in St. Louis. She currently lives in Pennsylvania with her husband, Frank Anders, and has been a business owner since 1950. Norma is a graduate of Culver-Stockton College in Canton, MO. She and Michael Thurman of Farmington have been married for 25 years and are parents of three children: Christopher, Katie and Timmy. They reside in Webster Groves, MO.

Fred was born in Philadelphia, PA in 1916. He attended aeronautical school in Philadelphia and earned an aircraft engine mechanic license. In 1940 he made his way to Wichita to work for Beach Aviation as an aircraft inspector. In his spare time he took flying lessons and met his future wife, Dorotha. In December of 1941, he moved to the Farmington area to be an instructor at the National Defense Training School in Flat River. Impressed with his surroundings he wrote to Dorotha: "The country is marvelous, trees, trees, trees, millions of them. Woods and hills and streams that are full of game." While in Flat River he met many local aviation pioneers, including his future partners. The school closed in 1943 and Fred returned to Wichita, Dorotha and Boeing Company where he joined the test crews flying B-29's. When B-29 production ended, he returned to Farmington.

Dorotha was born in Oklahoma in 1920 and moved to Wichita in 1922. She attended the University of Wichita on a scholarship, graduating cum laude with a degree in business administration in 1942. While in school she worked part-time at Kansas Gas and Electric Co., and upon graduation became secretary to the company president. She visited the Farmington area in 1942 and met first-hand the country and company which had so impressed Fred.

Throughout their short lives, Fred and Dorotha never avoided challenge. They came to Farmington with a spirit of adventure and determination to succeed. *Submitted by Barbara Auchter and Norma Auchter Thurman*

BAILEY - Rev. James M. Bailey was born June 11, 1865, Woodford County, KY, was a graduate of Transylvania University, Lexington, KY and ordained as a minister in the Christian Church, June 10, 1890. He married Annie Dearson of Richmond, KY. Seven children were born to the union. (Two children died during the teen years.)

Allie Mae, John, Edna, Virginia, Anna D., Georgia, Rev. Bailey, Annie Bailey (somewhere between 1910-15)

James M. Bailey moved to Farmington in 1911 where he served as pastor of the Farmington Christian Church for 27 years, performing over 1,000 marriage ceremonies and 2,000 burial services. Rev. Bailey was interested in sports, attending Farmington home football games. Being an avid St. Louis Cardinals and Browns fan, he listened to the games on an Atwater Kent radio which was one of the first radios to use 110v AC. (The radio is still kept within the family.)

Rev. Bailey's son, John W., played football for the first Farmington team and then played college football. John W. received an MD degree and practiced medicine in Wheelwright, KY for 30 years. Two of Rev. Bailey's daughters, Alley Mae and Virginia, were nurses at St. Luke's Hospital in St. Louis. Another daughter Edna, my

mother, married Emmett D. Swink. We lived on a rice plantation in Humphry, AR before my father purchased a 500-acre farm in Farmington. A fourth daughter, Georgia, married Walter Thurman and lived in Detroit. Following Walter's death, Georgia returned to Farmington and taught at W.L. Johns Elementary School for many years.

Rev. Bailey lived in the parsonage until 1927 when he built a home on W. College. As his grandson, I helped with the planting and care of two trees in his front yard. These trees are now 20 to 30 feet tall and add to the beauty of College Street. Following the death of his wife in January 1929, Rev. Bailey moved in with us, the Emmett Swink family. His brother, Lee, also lived with us. Lee's job was to haul shelled corn to four farms owned by Judge Swink. Since the cattle had to be fed daily, Lee would leave with his team of mules at 3:00 a.m. each day, rain or shine. His route was through the middle of Farmington on to old Route 67 to Libertyville. He returned home before dark.

On a cold night in February 1934, the Swink's lost their home to fire. Thanks to the barking of the family dog, our family was awakened and escaped from the fire still wearing our nightshirts. We were barefoot in about six inches of snow. Our family had lost all our belongings. While watching the fire, a man loaned his top coat to Grandfather Bailey. Later when at Grandpa Swink's home and standing by the fireplace, Grandfather Bailey pulled a quart of whiskey from the man's top coat which had been loaned to him. For several years we teased him about hiding the bottle.

Two weeks before his death in 1938, Rev. Bailey retired as pastor of the Farmington Christian Church. He had also served part time at the Libertyville, Festus, Bismarck, Bonne Terre and Flat River churches. Rev. Bailey's funeral was performed by 10 ministers. All the businesses in Farmington were closed in honor of the late Rev. James M. Bailey. *Respectively submitted by John E. Swink, grandson.*

BAKER - Henry E. Baker, born July 1824, lived in Bollinger County, MO where most of his children were born. He died Feb. 22, 1912 in Knob Lick, MO. He was married to Mary Marella Schell, born Feb. 13, 1828. She died in Knob Lick, MO, March 10, 1928, age 100. They were parents of eight children.

1) Martha Adeline was born in 1853 and married first Mitchell Raby. They had a son, Mitchell Andrew, born Dec. 20, 1874, who married Mary Jane Skaggs. Their children were Della who married George Burch, Rose married John Mecey, a daughter who died in infancy, Edgar, Cecil, Noah, Evelyn and Olen. Mitchell died Jan. 21, 1950 and is buried in Doe Run Memorial Cemetery. Martha married second to Mr. Woods and third to William Eaves.

2) Solomon Columbus was born in 1855 and married first to Anna Isabella Key and had infant (unnamed), Julius Walter, Andrew, Delo and Luther. Solomon married second to Rachel Levina Eaves and they had Ethel (who married Fred Brewen), Eddie and Charles. Solomon remarried to Sarah James.

3) Cynthia Melcanie was born June 25, 1856 and died Feb. 12, 1961, age 106, and was buried in the Pendleton Cemetery in Doe Run, MO. She was married in 1877 to Barton Crawford, son of James M. and Isabella Cartee Crawford. They were parents of seven children: Mary Jane, born in 1878, married John Murray; Sarah Ellen married William Pritchett; George, born 1885, married Carrie Weiss; Gertrude, born 1889, married Frank Chapman and had seven children; James R., born 1892, married Mary Clark; Samuel married Louise Kremminger in 1917 and had Robert

who married Alta May Williams; Elijah, born 1896, married Genevieve Smith.

4) Malinda Catherine Harriet, born 1861, married first to Noah Baker and had Tony. She married second to Steward Snowdell.

5) Sarah Emaline, born March 2, 1862, married Wesley Bess and had five children: Henry, Pearl, Stella, Annie and Mary. Sarah died Aug. 31 1946 and is buried in Knob Lick.

6) Renee Arlene Ellen, born Dec. 14, 1874, died Feb. 13, 1924, is buried in Knights of Pythias Cemetery in Farmington. She married Thomas Heck and they had Emmett, Herman, Everett and Jesse. Jesse, born Feb. 24, 1908, Ste. Genevieve County, died March 19, 1989, was married to Helen Rickus and had a daughter, Joan Ellen. Jesse owned the grocery store on Columbia and later where the Press Paper is located. Herman, born Oct. 14, 1900, died Dec. 30, 1972, married Alpha Mitchell. He is buried at Hillview Memorial Gardens Cemetery.

7 & 8) Elizabeth and Henry (no information on either).

BAKER - John Baker was born Nov. 10, 1819 in North Carolina and is listed in the 1850 Perry County, TN census. They lived in Kentucky where the youngest son was born in 1856. They moved to St. Francois County, MO where they lived on property owned by the Mine LaMotte Company, south of Knob Lick, MO. They moved to Syenite where he died in 1874. He married Jamima (last name unknown) who was born Oct. 10, 1817 in North Carolina and died Aug. 7, 1888. John died in  *Mary Emily Politte Baker, Hattie, Lorenzo Baker and Minnie (ca. 1892)* 1874 and they are both buried in Knob Lick but have no markers and the site is unknown. They were the parents of six children.

1) Pinkney A., born March 10, 1840, in Coke County, TN, and died June 16, 1888 in Shelby County, TN. He married Sarah Jane Short June 16, 1867 in St. Francois County, MO. She was born in St. Francois County in 1848 and died in May 1895 in Kerrville, Shelby County, TN. They were the parents of seven children: 1) Ruth E. (no dates) who married a man named Sanders, 2) Wesley (no dates), 3) James was born May 5, 1873, 4) Hattie was born Jan. 12, 1875, 5) Franklin P. was born Sept. 6, 1878, 6) Samuel E. was born Oct. 6, 1882, 7) Thomas E.was born Aug. 10, 1885. Pinkney served under Missouri State Guard General M. Jeff Thompson from Aug. 4, 1861 to Jan. 4, 1862. Post war records show that he took an oath of loyalty in June 1862. Pinkney was 24 years old when he enlisted in Co. F at Ironton, MO on Sept. 25, 1864. He was later paroled near Union, MO and on Oct. 2, 1864, and rejoined his company. November saw him in DeSoto and on Dec. 1, 1864 the company was back in Farmington with orders to leave for Nashville, TN. Arriving on Dec. 23, 1864, Baker and the remaining soldiers in Co. F completed their enlistment in TN. They were mustered out at Benton Barracks on March 29, 1865. He moved to Kerrville, Shelby County, TN in March 1878.

2) Mary E. was born Aug. 16, 1844, married John Miller and had two known children, Frank, born 1861, died 1945 in Madison County, MO, and George W., born 1865.

3) Susannah, born Sept. 1, 1846, married John Singleton.

4) George William, born March 4, 1848, married Sarah Elizabeth Ferguson. They had three children: Noah A., born 1876; Nora, and Barney who married in 1918 to Jennie McGinnis, daughter of William and Eliza Jane White McGinnis. She was born in 1892 in Madison County, MO. Barney and Jennie were the parents of two children: Howard, born in 1919, married Imogene and had five children. George W., born in 1922, married Venita Harnettaux in 1947 and had two children, Larry and Janice.

5) Lorenzo Dow, born April 9, 1840 in Tennessee, died Sept. 13, 1939, was married to Mary Emily Politte in 1888. She was the daughter of Joseph and Nancy Politte and was born Jan. 1, 1872 and died Oct. 3, 1898. They had six children: Minnie, born 1889, married John Chapman. They were the parents of seven children: Golda, Olen, Paul Jesse, Laura, Bessie and Charles. Paul was killed in WWII on the Rhine River between Belgium and Germany in 1945. Hattie, born 1890, married Charles Clemons and they were parents of six children: Ethel, Lloyd, Emma, Carl, Bertha and Irene. Hattie and Charlie, with the youngest three children, died in an accident when their car was hit by a train in Colorado in 1931. They are buried together in one grave in the Knob Lick Cemetery. Lorenzo and Mary Emily are also buried in the same cemetery. The old community church, now torn down. The oldest children then went to live with relatives. Ida Viola, born 1892, married Eugene Williams and had nine children: May, Hazel, Lawrence, Beulah, Chester, Helen, Melvin, Carl and Laverne. Ernest, born 1893, married Emma Hurst and had four children: Irene, Arthur, Earl and Norma Ruth. Dewey, born 1898, married Virgie Marler and had two children, Lorena and Julia.

6) John W. was born in 1856 and died in 1915. His family is unknown but lived at Annapolis, MO. John and Jamima are buried in Knob Lick, probably behind the Baptist Church, but the stones are missing. The family were granite workers and farmers. *Submitted by Chester Williams.*

BANNISTER - Gene Bryan Bannister Jr. and Michelle Anne Logan were married May 19, 1998 in a private ceremony at the family home in Farmington. Michelle Anne Logan is the daughter of Vernon Logan originally of Wright City, MO and Berniece Brown of the Perryville area. Gene Bannister Jr. is one of seven children of Gene B. Bannister Sr. of Farmington and Patrechia JoAnn Beck of Desloge. Jeffrey L. Bannister and family live in Bismarck. Margaret Abney and family live in Farmington. Donald J. Hamm Jr. and family live in Daytona Beach, FL, as does Harold L. Hamm. Rebecca Wolfe and family live in Plato, MO.

Gene Bryan, Michelle, Kayla, Jacob (December 1998)

Diane Clinton and family live in Farmington. Pamela Williford and family also live in Farmington. Elizabeth Abney is of Desloge. Gene Sr. is the son of Richard William Bannister Sr. of Bonne Terre and Ruby Lee Zolman of Farmington. Richard's parents were Edward Lee Bannister of Bonne Terre and Eliza Josephine Skaggs of Washington County. Edward was the son of George Washington Bannister who served with the Union Forces during the Civil War. Ruby Lee Zolman was the daughter of John Phillip Zolman, respected area justice of the peace who performed thousands of marriage ceremonies in St. Francois County, and Mary Leota Level, daughter of William Julian Level and Emma Shannon. J.P. Zolman was the son of Joel Zolman who was the son of Phillip Zolman who was, incidentally, married to the granddaughter of city founder, Rev. William Murphy.

Members of the family have served in every major conflict in the history of the United States. Most recently Gene Jr. served in the 34th Signal Division during the Persian Gulf War where he earned the Army Commendation Medal. Lynn Bannister Jr., a cousin living in Little Rock, AR, served during the Vietnam Conflict. His father, the late Lynn Z. Bannister Sr., served aboard the USS *San Juan* during the WWII. Michelle's father, Vernon, served in the Korean Conflict. Michelle's maternal grandfather, Bert Donald Brown of Farmington, served in the United States Navy. Gene Sr.'s step-grandfather, the late Harry Mitchell, served during WWI. Patrechia Bannister's brother, John Henry Beck of Louisville, KY, was a colonel during the Vietnam and Korean Wars. George Washington Bannister served during the Civil War for the Union Cause; and on Patrechia Bannister's side of the family, Maj. Sam Hildebrand served the Confederate Cause. Pat's mother, Edith Mae Hampton, was married to Alphonso Beck. Edith Mae was the daughter of John N. Hampton and Ida Mae LaRose. The Murphy side of the family served during the Revolutionary War, the Indian wars and other battles.

Gene Jr. and Michelle Bannister have two children, Kayla Dawn and Jacob Lynn. Gene is currently attending Mineral Area College with an expected graduation date of December 1999 with an associate's degree in English literature with education option and plans on attending Southeast Missouri University in 2000. Michelle is currently a housewife who will be returning to college in 2000.

BARTON - Donald and Jane Barton moved to Farmington in June 1963 as Don was to begin work at Farmington State Hospital #4 as a psychiatric social worker. They met at Central Methodist College where Jane graduated with an education degree. Don graduated from Missouri University, Columbia, with a master's degree in social work. He worked for the state for two years to fulfill a work study scholarship obligation. Jane taught first grade that year in the Farmington School District at the Washington School. Their daughter, Laura, was born in Columbia, MO and was 6 months old when they moved to Farmington. Their son, Craig, was born in 1965.

Donald and Jane Barton

Through the years Don moved into different positions in the State Hospital and in 1990 became superintendent of what is now called Southeast Missouri Mental Health Center. At one time early in his career Don was the only certified social worker in St. Francois County, and he was honored in the 80s as the Southeast Missouri Social Worker of the year. Jane went back to teaching in the Farmington schools after the children were in school and taught 23 more years, being elected president of the Farmington Teachers Association, Teacher of the Year, and retired in 1995.

Both their children graduated from Farmington High School. Laura is living in Ballwin, MO and is married to Michael Ruest. She received an AB degree from the University of Missouri, Columbia, in English and creative writing and did further study at the University of Iowa in sociology and writing. Craig lives in Burbank, CA and received an AB degree from the University of Missouri, St. Louis, in communications, and in June 1999 he received a master's of divinity degree from Fuller University, Pasadena, CA to become a Presbyterian minister.

Jane and Don both grew up in St. Louis and considered it to be home until they moved to Farmington and found all the family roots they both had in St. Francois County. Don's paternal grandfather, Samuel Barton, was the son of Tally M. Barton and Catherine Mills. The Bartons gave the land for the Barton School on Highway D.

Samuel went to St. Louis to become a motorman on the street car lines and married Mary Jane Beer; they had four children. Melvin, Don's father, married Isabelle Mothershead and they had three children: Virginia, Donald and Diana, and seven grandchildren. Don's maternal grandfather was Addison Mothershead from DeSoto, MO, who was a conductor for Missouri Pacific Railroad for over 55 years. Addison married Mabel Beck from DeSoto whose father was John R. Beck, born in England, and her mother was Mary A. Cape. The Mothersheads had three children: Dr. Robert Mothershead, a dentist in St. Louis and Farmington State Hospital for 30 years. He and Hazel Haug had three children: Julie, Jerry and Robert, all graduates of Farmington High School. Dr. John Mothershead, M.D., practiced in St. Joseph, MO. Isabelle married Melvin Barton, son of Samuel, and raised their children in St. Louis, MO. Melvin was a fireman and then engineer on the Missouri Pacific Railroad for 33 years. Isabelle's family lived in Bismarck for a time, and she played piano for the silent movies at the Bismarck Theatre. Don's sister, Virginia, and her husband, William Mounts, have retired from St. Louis to Farmington.

Jane's maternal grandmother and grandfather were from Doe Run, MO. Rebecca Cartee married Jack Smith who was the farm manager for the Murphy family in Bonne Terre. They had 11 children, one being Millie Jane Smith who married Stephen Douglas Hill from Bonne Terre. Stephen Hill was the underground foreman at the Bonne Terre Mine in the early 1900s, and was crippled in a slide about 1916. He was one of the first patients at the Bonne Terre Hospital. They moved to Knoxville, TN with their six children and then moved to St. Louis after Mr. Hill died. Helen was the youngest and married Henry J. Amrhein from St. Louis. They had one child, Jane. Jane's father was the son of German residents of St. Louis, Margaret Brummel and Francis Amherin.

Jane and Don only planned on living in Farmington two years and have now been here 36. They found it was a great place for raising children and making lifelong friends. *Submitted by Jane Barton.*

BECK - Herbert William Beck moved to Farmington from St. Louis along with his two sisters, Ruth and Grace, in 1949 when the three of them became residents of the Presbyterian Children's Home. Within the year Herb's two sisters were adopted by Mr. and Mrs. Oscar Groh of St. Louis. The children did not see each other again until 1959.

Herb lived at the Children's Home through graduation from Farmington High School. After four years in the Army he returned to Farmington and commuted to St. Louis to work at McDonald Aircraft. In 1964 he married Janet Cole of Farmington (see Oral and Verna Clubb Cole Family History). Janet had just graduated from Southeast Missouri University and began teaching English and business education at the high school in Bonne Terre, MO. Herb left his job at McDonald Aircraft and attended Flat River Junior College to study art. After Herb completed two years at FRJC, Herb and Janet moved to Linn, MO in 1966. Janet taught business at Linn High School and Herb finished his degree in art education at Lincoln University and then taught art at Linn High School for one year. Herb and Janet moved to Concordia, MO in 1969 so they could complete graduate degrees at Central Missouri State University. Janet taught at Concordia High School and Herb had a teaching assistantship at the University. After completing graduate degrees, Herb and Janet returned to Farmington in 1970 to take positions as teachers in the North County School District.

Herb left teaching in 1978 and formed a construction partnership, Cardinal Home Builders of Farmington. He is now owner of Oak Ridge Enterprises, the principal venture being the sales of the Hardy Outside Woodburning Furnace. Janet retired from North County School District after teaching for 32 years. She now teaches graduate courses and professional development workshops for teachers and does the office work for Oak Ridge Enterprises.

Herb and Janet have two children, Erin, born 1971, and Shanna, born 1976. Both girls graduated from Farmington High School. Erin graduated from Washington University and completed teacher certification through Webster University. She is a science teacher at Central High School in Park Hills, MO. Shanna is a graduate of the University of Missouri in Columbia with a degree in fisheries and wildlife. She works for the Missouri Department of Conservation.

Herb and Janet live outside of Farmington in a home that Herb built in 1975. Herb was reunited with his two sisters in 1959. Grace is married and living in St. Louis; and Ruth and her husband, Tom Christmann, moved to Farmington in 1995 and are neighbors of Herb and Janet. *Submitted by Janet Beck.*

BELL - Clifton R. Bell, Ph.D., was born in Fredericktown, MO on May 22, 1910. His parents were Henry Bell, born in 1877 and died in 1965, and Nancy Stanfield, born in 1884 and died in 1965.

Henry was from Alton, MO and his ancestors migrated from Tennessee. He was of Scots/Irish descent.

Clifton moved to Flat River, MO when he was two years old, with his parents and sisters, Beatrice and Helen. There he graduated from high school and junior college in 1929. He was an elementary and high school teacher at Marquand, MO

from 1931-1937. That was the beginning of a long and amazing career, not only in the education field, but in other fields as well.

He received his BS in education from Southeast Missouri State University in 1935, majoring in history and English. He received his MA in sec-ondary school administration at the University of Missouri in 1940. He was superintendent of schools at Centerville, MO from 1937-1942. He became superintendent of schools at Farmington, MO from 1946-1958. He completed graduate work at the Universities of Colorado and Minnesota during 1949-1950. He received his doctorate degree in education from Washington University in 1957, majoring in education administration. He was a professor at Truman University from 1964-1976.

On Jan. 17, 1931 he married Alma Lorance, whom he had met while teaching school at Marquand, MO. Alma was born in Marquand, MO June 6, 1913, daughter of Newt Lorance and Virginia Sitzes.

During WWII, Clifton was special representative, US Civil Service Commission in 1942 at the St. Louis Regional Office. He served in the US Navy from 1942-1946, attending Cornell University at Ithaca and Harvard University. He was stationed at Key West, FL and sent to Panama. Clifton stayed in the Reserves for over 20 years and retired as Commander, USNR. He has a multitude of stories about his duties while in the Navy.

Clifton and Alma had one daughter, Judith V. Bell, born Jan. 28, 1947 in Farmington. Judy graduated from Galesburg High School, received her degree from the University of Kansas, and her MS degree from the University of California. She now lives in Aspen, CO and travels extensively with her career as program director for Rocky Mountain College of Aspen, CO.

Alma attended college at Flat River and Cape Girardeau, receiving her BS degree from Washington University and doing graduate work at Western University. She taught school at Centerville, Bismarck, Farmington, and Galesburg, IL, where she was the assistant principal of the Weston School.

Under Dr. Bell's guidance the Farmington School District Board of Education and staff members implemented some of the following changes and improvements: Triple AAA status; established first PTA; established the first Vocational Department; established the first technical school in the county; established a National Honor Society; organized the first high school band; saw to the construction of a new elementary and high school buildings and began the first counselor program.

Dr. Bell and his family left Farmington in 1958 and moved to Galesburg, IL where he was superintendent from 1958-1964. He left there to become professor of education at Northeast Missouri State University, now Truman University in 1964. Alma stayed in Galesburg and continued to teach while Judy attended school. Dr. Bell commuted between Kirksville and Galesburg on weekends. They both retired in 1976 and returned to Farmington where they now reside on Kinley Drive.

Prior to his retirement Dr. Bell was involved in numerous organizations such as: secretary in the North Central Association; a member of the Governor's Commission for Handicapped Children; a member of the Resolutions and Programs Committee, Illinois Association; past president of Missouri Association of School Administrators, chairman of Missouri Association of Professors of Education Administration.

Since Clifton and Alma retired he has continued to stay busy by serving as a trustee for the County Health District, member of State Legislative Committee AARP, member of the Farmington Public Library Advisory Board, Chairman of the Financial Campaign of Methodist Church, Chamber of Commerce board member, District Coordinator National Retired Teachers, adjunct professor at Washington University, chairman of Facili-ties Library and Special Merit Award, past president of Kiwanis, and receiver of a Lifetime Achievement Award from Chamber of Commerce in 1994.

He and Alma both were active supporters in the building projects for the Farmington Public Library and the Civic Center. *Submitted by Dr. Clifton R. Bell.*

BEST - Ellis John Best, born 1904, died 1947, married Nellie Carol Murphy, born 1909, died 1993, on Aug. 23, 1930 at the Lutheran parsonage in Perryville, MO.

Nellie was a direct descendent of William Murphy Sr., Sarah Barton Murphy and David Murphy. David Murphy, son of William Sr., donated 52 acres of land on which the community of Farmington was established.

Born Oct. 7, 1909 in Ste. Genevieve County, Nellie was the daughter of Robert F. Murphy, born 1877, died 1969, and Lydia Ann McGee, born 1878, died 1963. There were four other children born to the Murphys: Ethel Irene, born 1906; Helen Roberta, born 1908, died 1997; Lehman Frederick, born 1913, died 1996; and Anna Marie, born 1920.

Nellie attended Farmington schools and was a 1925 graduate of Farmington High School. She was a graduate of Flat River Junior College and attended Kirksville Teachers College (now

Adult woman, Nellie C. Murphy Best; adult man, Ellis J. Best; left child, Robert E. "Bob" Best; middle child, Agnes Ann Best Mattli; right child, Edward J. "Eddie" Best

Truman State University). She graduated from Southeast Missouri State University in Cape Girardeau with a degree in education. After college, Nellie taught in area schools. Assignments included teaching all eight grades in rural one-room schoolhouses. Upon marrying Ellis, Nellie put her teaching career on hold.

The Best family traces its roots to Germany. Ellis was the son of Henry C. Best, born 1857, died 1922, and Lydia Agnes Morgan, born 1869 and died in 1918. He was born Jan. 21, 1904 near Farmington. He had three brothers: Cletus, his elder brother who died in infancy; Edwin and Clarence; and a half-sister, Sophia.

Ellis was baptized and confirmed at St. Paul's Lutheran Church in Farmington. He attended St. Paul's Lutheran School and was a graduate of Farmington High School. After taking courses in herdsmanship from the University of Missouri, Ellis began a career in dairy herd management. Ellis helped introduce a number of innovations to dairy farming in St. Francois County. He also helped establish a thriving 4-H program and was recognized for his involvement.

After their marriage in 1930, Ellis and Nellie moved to Jefferson City where Ellis managed dairy herds for the State Prison System after receiving an appointment from the governor. While living in Jefferson City, their first two children were born, Robert Ellis, born July 25, 1931, died Nov. 21, 1993, and Agnes Ann, born Nov. 14, 1932. Ellis later managed dairy operations for the state and also for private companies in Bonne Terre, St. Albans (near St. Louis), Concordia and Farmington. While living in Bonne Terre, their third child, Edward John, was born on Aug. 27, 1935. He died Aug. 5, 1998. Upon returning to

Farmington in 1940, Ellis managed the dairy herd at the State Hospital #4.

Ellis and Nellie enjoyed living and raising their family in Farmington. The children attended St. Paul's Lutheran School and the family worshipped at St. Paul's Lutheran Church. Ellis started his 4-H activities and became quite involved along with his three children. Nellie was also very supportive of the program. While living in Farmington Ellis became ill, and after a long sickness, he passed away at the Lutheran Hospital in St. Louis on Sept. 23, 1947, age 43. Nellie returned to teaching after Ellis' death. She taught in area public schools, including Doe Run, and finished her career as an elementary teacher in the Fox (Arnold) School System in 1975. Nellie led a very active retirement. She traveled throughout the United States visiting family and friends. Even with her busy schedule, she found time for her beloved hobby of quilting and her passion of genealogy. She was an active member and officer in the Sarah Barton Murphy chapter of the Daughters of the American Revolution and the Daughters of the American Colonists. She was also an active member and officer in the Society of Descendants of Washington's Army at Valley Forge, having traced her lineage on her mother's side to John Frost, who served as a bodyguard for General George Washington. As a descendant of Edward Diggs, a pilgrim and colonial governor of Virginia in the 1600s, Nellie was granted membership in the National Society of the Sons and Daughters of the Pilgrims. Her intensive genealogical research was rewarded with her membership in the Dames of the Magna Carta. Nellie traced her ancestry back through 30 generations to establish kinship with five of the 25 English barons who forced King John to sign the Magna Carta, considered to be the cornerstone of British constitutional law and containing the origins of the US Bill of Rights, in the year 1215.

Nellie was an active member of the St. Paul Lutheran Church Ladies Aid, the Missouri Historical Society and the Missouri Retired Teachers Association. She had also been a long time member and former president of the St. Francois County Historical Society. Her activities never kept her from family, regularly visiting and receiving visits from her sisters, children, grandchildren and great-grandchildren. She was always a part of Christmas and other holiday family gatherings, birthdays and baptisms. She always made time for her friends, both well and ill. Faithfully, she visited invalid friends until her own health failed. After a short illness, she passed away June 16, 1993, at her daughter's home in Poplar Bluff. She was 83.

BIESER - To the best of our present knowledge our ancestors were part of the Holy Roman Empire that was ruled by the Germans and Romans for some 300 years. It was through the Holy Roman Empire that our ancestors have handed down Christian names of Anton, John, Richard, Jacob, etc. Otto I was married to a Byzantine queen and Otto III was married to a Byzantine princess. After the crusades the families moved into Flanders, on to Belgium and to Alsace-Lorraine. The Biesers settled in such German towns as Frankfurt, Mainz, Oberhilbersheim, Offenburg, Darmstadt and

Henry and Elizabeth Bieser Weiler, Nov. 4, 1919

Mannheim. In the mid-1800s several Biesers entered the United States with scores of other German immigrants.

In 1852 Anton and Caroline Bieser arrived in Ste. Genevieve from Germany. Anton was born Jan. 1, 1822, in Oberhilbershiem, Germany. On Dec. 22, 1854, they bought a farm in Ste. Genevieve County on the historic Plank Road. Caroline, his wife, died in childbirth and is buried in the Zell Parish Cemetery. They had three children. Anton then married Maria Anna Stutz on April 23, 1857. They had 11 children, of which three died at infancy. Anton died May 30, 1879, and is buried in the Weingarten Cemetery. Maria Anna died Jan. 17, 1920 and is buried in the Old Calvary Cemetery in Farmington, MO.

In the late 1890s, Frank and Henry Bieser, the youngest sons of Anton, along with their mother, Maria Anna, purchased land three miles east of Farmington on Hwy. 32 near Wolf Creek. They were known as Bieser Brothers and were enterprising farmers. In 1916 they built a two-story brick home where both of them and their families lived. Henry was known throughout the neighborhood for his ability to work with the big draft horses. When the neighbors had a sick horse or one needing shoes, they called Henry. Henry and Frank continued to farm until Frank died in 1943.

Frank Bieser, born May 27, 1873, married Sally Katherine Weiler, born Aug. 1, 1875. They had two daughters, Alvina (Mrs. Charles Horn), born March 7, 1900, and Matilda "Tillie" (Mrs. Ellis V. Moore), born June 17, 1905.

Henry Edward Bieser, born Oct. 14, 1875, married Nov. 4, 1919, at Weingarten Catholic Church to Elizabeth Theresa Weiler, born June 17, 1888. They had a son Francis Edward, born Nov. 10, 1920, and a daughter, Dorothy Marie (Mrs. Edwin Mount), born Jan. 28, 1926. Henry Bieser died Jan. 30, 1953 and his wife Elizabeth died March 1, 1977. They are both buried in the Old Calvary Cemetery in Farmington.

On June 2, 1945 their son, Francis, married Eva Bernice Lukachick, born Sept. 16, 1921. Francis continued the farming tradition of the Biesers. He and his brother-in-law, Mike Lukachick, established a dairy farm near Farmington. Later, Francis's son, John, continued the dairy operation. Francis and Eva Bieser both died in 1995. Francis died June 30 and Eva November 7. Both are buried in the New Calvary Cemetery in Farmington. Their four children and 10 grandchildren all survive.

Family of Helen Marie, born Sept. 27, 1946, and John Thurman, born Jan. 11, 1941, includes Eva Marie, born May 13, 1968, married Randy Michael Keup, born Oct. 23, 1964, and Catherine Sue, born Jan. 16, 1970, who married Brett James Kirner, born Aug. 21, 1969.

Family of Carol Sue, born June 21, 1950, and Gary Darrell Inman, born Sept. 20, 1948, includes the following children: Thomas Gary, born Sept. 12, 1972; Matthew Francis, born Sept. 24, 1974; and Timothy Laverl, born Sept. 14, 1976.

Family of James Edward, born July 17, 1954, and Mary Kay (Rulo) Bieser, born Aug. 25, 1956, includes Jared Michael, born Nov. 29, 1985; Sarah Jessica, born Oct. 23, 1988; and Kyle Edward, born July 26, 1990.

Family of John David, born Nov. 6, 1955, and Shirley Joan (Seabaugh) Bieser, born Sept. 8, 1955, includes Mark David, born May 23, 1983, and Amanda Frances, born Aug. 8, 1986.

On May 8, 1948, Henry and Elizabeth's daughter, Dorothy Marie Bieser, married Edwin W. Mount, born June 5, 1919. Their three children and five grandchildren include:

William Henry, born March 3, 1951, married Deborah Kay (Boyer) Mount, born Oct. 9, 1953, and has two children, Bryan Matthew, born Aug.

3, 1978, and Andrew Paul, born Jan. 22, 1981.

Mary Ellen, born June 11, 1954, married Steven Coble, born July 31, 1952, and has child, Kyle David, born Nov. 27, 1980.

John Robert, born Oct. 26, 1959, married Tamara Sue (Briley) Mount, born Oct. 19, 1961, and has two children, Jennelle Denise, born May 23, 1987, and Kara Nicole, born Sept. 13, 1991.

The Biesers were all members of St. Joseph's Catholic Church in Farmington. Henry was on the church building committee when it was erected in 1912. For many years Henry and his brother Frank supplied wood to heat St. Joseph's rectory. Henry and his son, Francis, were both active members of the Knights of Columbus. Francis was a 4th degree Knight holding such titles as grand knight, district deputy and financial secretary with Council 1088. Francis served on the St. Joseph Parish Council. He was also president of the Farmers Mutual Insurance of St. Francois County and first president of the Wolf Creek Fire Protection District until his death in *1995. Submitted by John D. Bieser.*

BLAINE - Tessa Ella McClanahan and Warren Blaine were married in Venice, IL in 1926. Tessa Ella was the daughter of James Valentine McClanahan and Tessa Ella Highley of the Sprott area in Ste. Genevieve County. Tessa Ella Blaine returned to Farmington in 1938 with her three children: Robert Warren "Bob," Charlotte Lavern and Theodore Valentine "Ted." She was joined by her husband a short time later. The family resided at 401 N. Franklin Street in Farmington where in 1940, Edward Homer "Eddie" was born. In 1942 the family moved to 422 N. Washington St., where they resided until the early 1960s.

Bob joined the US Navy in 1944 and served in the Pacific Theater of Operations during the closing period of WWII. Bob married Mille Lindaman and they had four children. Following is a list of their children with the area they are now located and their occupations.

Robert Steven, a businessman living in Smithfield, VA; Roger Scott, law enforcement, living in Conway, AR; Riochelle S., paralegal, Houston, TX; and Renee Susanne, physical therapist, living in Alice, TX. Bob is now retired from civil service and living in Port Arthur, TX.

Lavern married Hugh Carter Burris and moved to the St. Louis area in 1946. They had six children: Hugh Carter living in St. Louis area; Bruce Wayne of Doe Run area, transportation; Janice Theo of Fort Oglethorpe, GA, transportation; Tessa Kathleen "Kathy" Summerville, GA, small business owner; David Lee, Park Hills, MO; Lisa Jo Ann of Kingston, GA, retail sales. Lavern and Hugh are now both deceased. They were living in Summerville, GA at the time of death.

Ted joined the US Army in 1955 and is now retired and living in Desloge, MO with his wife, Virginia. Ted married Janis Gayle Short in 1959; they are now divorced. Their four children are Jeffery Lynn of Kansas City, Kansas area, associate engineer of Grain Valley; Dawn Re'nee of the Farmington area, x-ray technician; Brian Kelly of Farmington area, transportation; Michelle Dianne of Kansas City, Missouri, University of Missouri at Kansas City Theater Department.

Eddie attended the University of Missouri on a football scholarship and received a bachelor's degree in zoology in 1962 and a Ph.D. in physiology in 1970. He played professional football for the 1962 world champion Green Bay Packers and later for the Philadelphia Eagles. He married Susan Cring of Brentwood, MO in 1963; they were divorced in 1992. They have two children, Jennifer, an accountant, living in Ballwin and Marquis Edward, a journalist, living in Eugene, OR.

BLAIR - Farmington, MO became home for Bill and Joanne "Jody" Blair in October 1970. Bill became the second administrator of Farmington Community Hospital which had opened in the spring of 1969. The family included daughters, Teresa Ann, age 10, and Lori Lee, age 7, and a third daughter Patricia Jo joined the family in December 1971.

Both Bill and Jody are from Hutchinson KS. Bill was born in Hutchinson and Jody in nearby Newton, KS. They graduated from Hutchinson High School, attended Hutchinson Junior College and Bill selected Kansas State University, graduating with a BS in business administration. Jody graduated from University of Kansas with a BS in nursing. They

Bill and Jody Blair

were married in Hutchinson in 1957 after Bill completed four years in the Navy. He was an officer on a LST ship, making several trips to Japan and Alaska.

Bill was employed by Union Carbide in 1957. During the next 10 years with this company, promotions required moves to Dallas, TX; Indianapolis, IN; Charlotte, NC where Teresa and Lori were born; Asheboro, NC and Philadelphia, PA. In 1967 Bill decided upon a profession change, entering Duke University graduate school in Durham, NC and graduating in 1969 with a master of hospital administration. Two years were spent in Jacksonville, IL. Bill was assistant administrator at Passavant Hospital and Jody worked for the Morgan County Health Department as a public health nurse.

During Bill's 27 years at Farmington Community Health Center, later renamed Parkland Health Center, the hospital experienced three periods of major growth. Bill was active in the American Hospital Association and the Missouri Hospital Association, becoming board chairman in 1980. Local civic responsibilities included the Farmington Chamber of Commerce Board, member of the R-VII School Board and Memorial United Methodist Church Administrative Board.

Jody was employed for 16 years by Mineral Area College in Park Hills, MO as an instructor in the Allied Health Department in the Associate Degree Nursing Program. The last three years of her employment she served as chairperson of the department. While she was a member of the faculty, she attended Southern Illinois University at Edwardsville and acquired a master of nursing in 1987. She is a member of the Honor Society of Nursing, Sigma Theta Tau. Civic responsibilities included the American Cancer Society Board, American Red Cross, United Way Board, Girl Scout leader and troop organizer.

The three daughters graduated from Farmington High School. After Teri graduated in 1978, she attended Central Methodist College. Teri lives with her family in St. Louis and is a reimbursement specialist for the Unity Health System. Lori graduated in 1981 and continued her education at Southwest Missouri State University. Lori lives in Bolivar, MO and teaches fourth grade in Morrisville, MO. Patti graduated in 1990, attended University of Missouri at Kansas City and is completing a Family Practice Residency Program in South Bend, IN.

Farmington, MO has been a good community to raise three daughters and is a good place to retire. Jody retired from Mineral Area College in 1996; Bill retired from Parkland Health Center

in 1997; and they continue to enjoy family, friends, and the Farmington community. *Submitted by Jody Blair.*

BOSWELL/HELBER - The Boswell Helber family's association with Farmington began in 1852 when Christian and Catherine Helber arrived from Lewisburg, OH. The Christian Helber family of five children: Jacob, Laura, Emma, John Wesley and Edward, made their home on East Liberty Street. Christian Helber became the first postmaster of Farmington in 1863. He also served as a lieutenant in the Union Army and fought in the Battle of Pilot Knob (Fort Davidson) and was killed in action Feb. 26, 1865, in Tennessee.

On Dec. 5, 1874, their daughter, Emma Helber, married Dr. Robert French Boswell from Tennessee, who was the first resident dentist in Farmington. He died in 1870, leaving a young widow with two small sons, Jesse V. and Robert L. Boswell. Emma taught in the Farmington public schools from 1880-90, and for many

Oldest, Emma Helber Boswell; Robert Leslie Boswell; Hilda Boswell McHenry; youngest, Robert Eugene McHenry

years taught children in Sunday school in both the Methodist and Presbyterian Churches. In 1890 she and her brother, Edward Helber, began a business of hardware and metal work. The Boswell-Helber Tin Shop was on East Liberty Street next to the Helber home.

Emma's brother, Jake Helber, married Emma Carleton. He was another successful businessman who had a furniture and hardware store. Their daughter, Mae Helber, married Edd Holler. Their historical home still stands on Ste. Genevieve Street in Farmington. Jesse V. Boswell, born 1876, died 1972, was Emma Boswell's oldest son and a nationally recognized dentist in Springfield, MO for 50 years. Jesse Boswell married Anite Campbell from Nashville. Their daughter, Mary Kathryn, married James McClosky and they retired to Springfield. Their son, James McClosky, is living in Virginia.

Robert Leslie Boswell, born 1878, died 1945, was Emma Boswell's youngest son and became a successful businessman in Farmington. He assumed leadership of the Boswell-Helber Tin Shop after Edward Helber's death in 1927. Boswell Hardware remained a family enterprise operated by Mr. Boswell. He married Alma Krekel of rural Farmington in 1906. Their children were Hilda Mae, Robert Krekel and Harry Eugene Boswell. In 1928, after Alma's death, Robert L. Boswell married Lena Revoir. For almost a half century Rob Boswell was one of Farmington's most progressive civic-minded citizens. Mr. Robert L. Boswell served four years as city alderman representing the First Ward, a charter member of the Rotary Club, a member of the city's municipal band and a past Noble Grand of the IOOF. He was also a lifelong, faithful and active member of the Carleton Memorial Church. He died in 1945.

Robert Krekel Boswell, born 1912, died 1967, son of Robert Leslie Boswell was an active business leader in Farmington. In 1945 the Helber-Boswell family home on Liberty Street was demolished; and under the ownership of Robert K. Boswell, the Boswell Hardware Store was enlarged featuring plumbing, household and farm appliances and furniture. Robert K. Boswell was president of the Farmington Chamber of Com-

merce in 1964. At the time of his death in 1967, he was serving on the board of directors of the Farmington Development Corporation, the Farmington Community Hospital and the St. Francois County Country Club. He was a charter member of the Farmington Kiwanis Club, past Exalted Ruler of the Farmington Elks Lodge and an active member of the Presbyterian Church. He married Elizabeth Owen from Lexington, KY. She passed away in 1977. Their son Robert O. Boswell was manager of the Boswell Hardware Store from 1967 until his death in 1969, and the family store was sold in 1977.

Harry Eugene Boswell, born 1914, died 1983, youngest son of Robert L. Boswell, married Jewell Woodard of Farmington. They had various business and real estate holdings, as well as farms in Farmington. Harry Boswell was a member of the Farmington Lodge #132 AF&AM and the Scottish Rite Valley of St. Louis, MO. The Boswells were active members of the Presbyterian Church. They retired to New Symra Beach and Daytona, FL and continued in the real estate business. Jewell Boswell is presently living in New Symra, FL. Their daughter, Harriet Jane Clair, is living in Highlands, NC.

Hilda Mae Boswell McHenry, born 1907, the surviving child of Robert L. Boswell, married Pope R. McHenry of rural Farmington. They lived in Flat River, MO for 67 years. Hilda Mae was active in the Taylor Avenue United Methodist Church, Eastern Star, Girl Scouts, DAR Regent and gave private piano lessons for 50 years. Pope McHenry was assistant postmaster in Flat River and raised cattle on his farms in St. Francois and Ste. Genevieve counties. Their children are Robert Eugene McHenry of Adrian, MI; Milton Randolph McHenry of Santa Ana, CA; and Martha McHenry Cassity of Litchfield, IL. Hilda Boswell McHenry (91 years of age) is living in Litchfield, IL. *Submitted by Martha McHenry Cassity.*

BOYD - The Boyd Family can be traced back to County Ulster in Northern Ireland and to Kilmarnock in Southwestern Scotland where the family castle was donated to the city of Kilmarnock in 1975. Members of the family came to the United States in 1764, landing and settling in Virginia. Some lived out their lives there, but others migrated west to Kentucky and Tennessee and then to Louisiana, Texas and Missouri. Of those entering Missouri in 1819, a group went to the Independence area, perhaps to join a wagon train further west, but the branch that came to this area settled in the Saline Township of Ste. Genevieve County in an area that became known as "New Tennessee."

Two brothers, John, born 1814, and William Boyd, who moved to the area now known as Avon, MO, married Martha and Sarah Counts, sisters, who had moved here from Tennessee. John and Martha had five sons and seven daughters, one of whom was Joel Elijah, born 1846, died 1898, who married Harriet Sebastian. Joel and Harriet had five children: Henry, who fell into a scalding barrel and died at age 6; Eddie died of "the fever"

at age 19; Mary married Everett Barron; Nathaniel married Dora Allgire; and John William married Ellen Haney.

John and Ellen had six children: the first, a daughter, died at birth; Marion, married Mae Richy; Elijah Jerry, born in 1910, died in 1997, married Hazel Kennon, born in 1911; Alelies, married Velvie Williams; Thomas William married Dorothy Head; and Harriet, married Clark Kinkead.

Elijah Jerry, known by most as "E.J.," and Hazel had four children: Mary Lou, born 1930, married James T. Eames; J. Lee, born 1940, married Jessie Mae Harvell; and Dennis Gerald "Jerry," born 1942, died 1997, married Paula Herberlle; and Lois Jane, born 1950.

J. Lee and Jessie had five children: Tommy Lee, Faith Ann, Teresa Ellen, Dennis Lee, and Elijah Joel Lee Boyd. The J. Lee Boyd family moved to Farmington in 1972 from the family farms at Clearwater, MO (J.C. Nations store and Post Office), near Pine Log Church (built by Joel Boyd and family), which is a few miles beyond Coffman on State Route WW.

Coffman (which was founded by Thomas Boyd) was once a thriving town. It had two sawmills, a railroad-tie yard, stores, taverns, lumberyard, bank, undertaker, post office, and a roundtable on the Houck Railroad which ran from Farmington to Perryville through Minnith and St. Marys.

J. Lee became a police officer in Farmington Oct. 13, 1975; Jessie retired in 1999, after 27 years with SEMO-MHC (Farmington State Hospital No. 4); Faith is married to Jimmie Gann Jr. and has two daughters, Jessica Kaye and Jennifer Faye; Teresa is married to Daniel Govereau and has two children, Joseph Daniel and Emma Grace; Dennis is married to Susanne Pratte and has one son, Bradlee Taylor "Tater" Boyd (whose duty it will be to keep this story going!)

BRAUN - In the summer of 1975 the Braun family moved from Des Peres, MO to a 110-acre farm on the St. Francois River three miles west of Farmington.

David was tired of a suburban lifestyle and fighting rush-hour traffic. Linda wanted to go back to work and had a position in social services at the state hospital. Rachel, age 6, started kindergarten that fall while Marc, age 2, stayed home to "help" his dad rebuild the old farmhouse.

After a few horses, a few cows, a few goats and five years as a gentleman farmer, David and his family moved to Farmington. Rachel and Marc attended St. Paul's Lutheran School where Linda taught third grade. David was working as director of Family and Community

Chelsea, David, Alyse and Carla

Services for the Presbyterian Children's Home while building a private practice in marriage and family counseling. Ironically, strains in his own marriage led to a separation and divorce in early 1981.

Both parents remained closely involved with both children, sharing parenting responsibilities while living just three blocks apart. Each then remarried, David marrying Carla Ragsdell, a native of Farmington, and Linda marrying John Mullins of Ste. Genevieve.

During the next two years, John and Linda lived out of state, while Rachel and Marc stayed

with their dad and Carla, finishing high school in Farmington. Both then attended the University of Missouri on Bright Flight scholarships. During their high school years, Rachel and Marc enjoyed some "extracurricular" excitement in addition to cheerleading and

Stevie and Marc

football. During the homecoming parade on Oct. 17, 1986, a little sister was born, Chelsea Terese "Chels," and then another sister, Alyse Elizabeth "Ali" arrived three years later on Nov. 30, 1989, just in time for a Friday night football game.

David and Carla were thrilled with these new "additions" to the old white house on Columbia Street, bought in 1988, as it was soon filled with family and friends and older furniture (some actually antiques). This home was also Carla's studio where she did freelance art work for businesses, prior to buying and developing her own business, Minuteman Press, a printing business downtown.

David's career was changing, too, as he began doing more training and consulting with area businesses. In early 1994 he and his partner, Marlene Brockmiller, started Workforce, a full-service employment firm that later opened several offices in southeast Missouri.

Rachel married Blake Fagan from Joplin, MO in July 1992. She worked as a physical therapist for several years in Chicago and Nashville while Blake finished medical school at Vanderbilt University. In 1998 the Fagans moved with their daughter, Rebecca, born June 30, 1997, to Asheville, NC to complete a three-year residency in

Blake and Rachel

family practice. Marc's BS in chemical engineering led him to begin a career with Dow Chemical where he has worked in Texas and at their Pevely, MO facility. Marc lives with his best friend, "Stevie," a beautiful honey-blond mixed breed lab, who is encouraging him to go on with his education and get an MBA.

Chelsea writes music, plays piano and loves singing and dancing, especially ballet. She enjoys sketching and is a regular at the Roller Zone. Some of her natural leadership she probably came by honestly. She seems unusually comfortable with almost any audience, whether she is juggling, acting in community theater, or performing in the Nutcracker Ballet.

Alyse has inherited some of her mom's strengths. She is quite artistic, loves designing things, is in the Pages class, and is very organized. Holidays are her favorite times, but she enjoys cooking and playing with dolls year round. Real babies, however, especially her niece Rebecca, are her favorites.

Rebecca

Carla and David have been actively involved in the growth of Farmington, working closely with the Chamber of Commerce and the business community as well as the schools, neighborhood associations and other community organizations.

When Carla graduated as the valedictorian of her Farmington High School class, she could not have foreseen owning her own business and raising her own family here. Nor could David have envisioned the changes in his life and the growth and opportunities for his family and children that Farmington has presented in these years leading up to the Bi-Centennial Celebration. *Submitted by David Braun.*

BREWER/SULLIVAN - The Brewer/Sullivan family has resided in St. Francois County since the mid-1800s. James Edwin Brewer was born in Annapolis, MO on Sept. 20, 1882. Four years later on May 22, 1886, Anna Josephine Bangert was born in Bonne Terre, MO. They were united in marriage in 1905. Edwin was a conductor on the MR&BT Railroad, so he and Anna moved to Doe Run, MO. Since many of the passenger trains began their run to St. Louis from the Doe Run or

Madeline Brewer Sullivan left, Josephine Bangert Brewer right.

Rock Springs railroad stations, many of the railroad's personnel lived in Doe Run. The Brewers moved into the home that had been owned by F.P. Graves, owner of the Doe Run Lead Company. Mr. Graves had sold his home when the mines closed. The house had 18 rooms, plus three rooms that had been used as servants' quarters. The electricity that had been generated by the mines were no longer available, so the huge house had to depend once again on oil lamps for lighting. To Edwin and Anna's marriage two children were born, Madelyn Irene Brewer Oct. 8, 1910 and James Edwin Brewer Feb. 23, 1910.

In 1916 the Brewers moved to "A" Street in Farmington. Edwin was elected county collector of St. Francois County in 1918 and re-elected in 1922. In 1926 when Edwin completed his terms as county collector, he purchased the St. Francois Hotel on the Courthouse square. The hotel was the only hotel at that time between St. Louis and Cape Girardeau that had hot running water in each room. In the hotel there was a large formal dining room which was often used for social events and receptions. In addition, a restaurant and a coffee shop were located just off the lobby on the front side of the hotel. Many travelers and salesmen stayed in the hotel as they traveled eastern Missouri. In those days, it was common for cattle and mules to be herded through downtown Farmington to DeLassus to be loaded and transported on the railroad. The Swink family was one of the large farm families who made these drives.

Mr. Brewer continued to operate the hotel until the economic downward spiral of the Depression made it no longer profitable. At that time, the Brewer family moved to the corner of "A" and Maple streets. In addition to owning the St. Francois Hotel, Ed Brewer was a partner in several other businesses in Farmington: the Willis-Knight car agency, a furniture store, and a service station in downtown Farmington.

After graduating from high school Madelyn and James Edwin rode the streetcar from Farmington to Flat River Junior College. It was there that Madelyn met a football player from DeSoto, Albert Charles Sullivan. They were married March 23, 1926. In 1935 they moved to St. Louis. Albert worked for the federal government and Madelyn taught elementary school. They had two children: Albert Charles Sullivan Jr. Sept. 19, 1940 and John Edwin Sullivan Oct. 8, 1946.

While working at the State Hospital, young Edwin Brewer met a nurse named Clyo Clark. She was from Illinois and they were married in 1931. On Sept. 11, 1933, a daughter, Mary Jane Brewer, was born to Edwin and Clyo.

In 1932 the senior Ed Brewer moved the family from "A" street to the family farm on the St. Francois River on Highway W. He built a home on the site where Clarence Wade's home now stands. In 1935 Ed Brewer passed away. Three years later at the age of 28, young Edwin Brewer was killed in a tragic accident. Edwin left behind his young daughter, Mary Jane, and his wife Clyo. Clyo continued to work at the State Hospital until her retirement. She passed away Nov. 12, 1967. Anna Josephine Brewer, Madelyn and Edwin's mother, continued to live on the family farm until her death Jan. 6, 1956.

On Jan. 8, 1960, Albert Charles Sullivan Jr. married Patricia Diane West from Steele, MO. They met during their college years at the University of Missouri in Columbia. To this marriage one daughter, Sally Diane Sullivan, was born Dec. 17, 1961. Albert Sr. and Madelyn retired in 1968, built a new home on the family farm, and moved back to St. Francois County. Albert Jr. and Patricia were divorced in 1969. Madelyn died Aug. 27, 1977 and Albert Sr. died March 3, 1989.

Sally Diane Sullivan and Gregory Lee Shinn were married Oct. 24, 1987. On July 30, 1991, a daughter, Madelyn Fuller Shinn, was born to this marriage. In 1993 Albert Jr. married Nancy G. Rohrer and moved to her home on the corner of Center and Maple streets.

John Sullivan currently resides in Indianapolis, IN while Albert, Nancy, Mary Jane, Sally, Greg and Madelyn live in Farmington. Albert Sullivan retired in 1998 after 35 years as an administrator at Mineral Area College, and he continues to raise horses on the family farms. Nancy Sullivan is an elementary school teacher at Washington-Franklin Elementary. Greg Shinn is a certified public accountant, and he works for the city of Farmington as the director of finance. Sally Sullivan Shinn is an educator in the Farmington School District, and Madelyn Fuller Shinn is a student in the Farmington School District. *Submitted by Sally Sullivan-Shinn.*

BREWSTER - In the second decade of the 1900s, Zeno and Frances Brewster moved their family to a farm on Sprott Road (Hwy EE) in rural Farmington. The family grew to include Clifford, Paul, Grace and Edgar.

Clifford worked as a young man for Russell Straughn on his farm. At age 18, he took a job at a service station owned by Harvey Roberts located on North Washington just south of the laundry. Within a few months, Roberts acquired a station at the intersection of Potosi and Liberty where Cliff continued employment. In the early 1930s this station sold out to Standard Oil. They tore the old building down to build a new one. During this time Cliff drove an oil truck for Leo Johnson, the Standard Oil dealer. When the new station was built, he went back to the station.

Meanwhile, he had been keeping company with Mary Haynes. Mary, daughter of John and Mary Haynes, lived on the Old St Louis Road (D Hwy). Mary's family included Blanche, Dan, George, Helen, Kossuth, Lucy and Bill. Due to the economics of the nation, they weren't married until 1935. They had one daughter, Frances.

Clifford Brewster and Edgar Brewster in front of Brewster's Service Station in about 1940

A Mr. Ball, Cities Service Oil, built a station at 32 E Liberty where Cecil Hulsey is now located. Jim Newman was the manager and he asked Cliff to work with him since Cliff had experience in the oil business. In 1936 Jim sold the business to Cliff. The accompanying picture is of Cliff on the left with brother, Edgar "Buck," when the business was in this location.

In 1945 Cliff and John Schafer bought the deserted Tetley Klein Lumber Company building on the corner of Liberty and Henry and built a station that opened in the fall of 1946. The highway to by-pass Farmington (Karsch Blvd.) was being built, but Cliff knew his customers were local and knew he could make a go of it. He and John built to the east and put in a restaurant and warehouse (Vess Cola). A little later the two buildings were joined and became the Bunny Bread outlet and warehouse. They now house law offices and a retail establishment. At various times, brothers, Paul and Edgar, and brother-in-law, Howard Cole, worked with him in his business.

In the early 1960s Cliff and John sold the service station to a group of local businessmen. The other two buildings eventually were sold. Cliff continued to run the Rustic Rock Service Station until he sold it to Tommy Hayes. Cliff continued to work until Tommy knew the business and the customers. In 1968 Cliff retired to his farm on D Hwy to spend his remaining years with Mary and his black Angus cattle.

After being closed for a while, the service station was acquired by Wilburn Hayes and he currently operates his business there.

BROCKMILLER - Paul Brockmiller and Marlene Mullaney met at the University of Florida in late 1983. Marlene was working toward a BS in public relations while Paul was almost finished with a BS in building construction. He had graduated from Farmington High School in 1980 and was determined to follow in his father's footsteps and someday return to help him run the construction business back in Farmington.

Paul graduated from the University of Florida in 1984 and moved to St. Petersburg, FL to accept a project manager position with Federal Construction Company. He and Marlene kept up a "long distance" relationship with both of them traveling every weekend to spend time together, until Marlene graduated in June 1986. They married in October 1986 at St. John's Catholic Church in St. Petersburg. Marlene's father, Bill Mullaney from Atlanta, and sister, De Lyons from Jacksonville, FL, were in attendance. Marlene's mother, Betsy, had passed away in January of that year. Although the decision to continue with the wedding plans as scheduled was difficult, she had known and loved Paul and everyone involved felt it was what she would have wanted.

Unfortunately, in December 1987, Paul's father, Don Brockmiller, passed away in his early 50s. Paul immediately moved to Missouri to take over Brockmiller Construction Company and

Marlene followed several months later. They lived in Oakville, MO for five years. Paul commuted one hour to Farmington each day while Marlene commuted one hour to Westport Plaza to her job as a branch manager for Kelly Assisted Living.

Paul's family has a deep-rooted history in Farmington. Paul's grandfather, Walter Brockmiller, started Brockmiller Construction, Inc. in 1926 (then known as Walter Brockmiller, Inc.) When Walter died, his son, Don, took over the company. Don was married to Barbara "Bobbi" Steinke in 1961. They had two children, Paul, born 1962, and Deborah, born 1964. Don and Bobbi divorced in 1970 and Bobbi married Dr. Alvan Karraker. Dr. Karraker is recently retired from Medical Arts Clinic. They have been married for 27 years. Don married Marlys Pietz in 1975. Marlys is a kindergarten teacher at Truman Kindergarten Center in Farmington.

When Paul took over the company, he had one office employee, no computers and a small building. Today, he has 10 staff employees, a fully automated office and more field personnel than ever. Brockmiller Construction has been instrumental in the progress of the city, including such structures as the Farmington Community Civic Center, the Maple Valley Shopping Center, several schools and churches and the Farmington Police Station.

In March 1992 their first daughter, Lauren Elizabeth, was born at St. Luke's Hospital in St. Louis. Fueled mostly by the desire to raise their daughter in a smaller area closer to family, Marlene and Paul decided to move to Farmington. They moved into the first (and Paul says the last) home built by Brockmiller Construction. In January 1995 their second daughter, Taylor Mullaney, was born at Jefferson Memorial Hospital in Crystal City; in June of 1997, their third (and final!) daughter, Morgan Georgia, was born at Parkland Health Center in Farmington. All three girls have middle names that have a family meaning. Lauren Elizabeth was named for Marlene's mother, Betsy. Taylor Mullaney has Marlene's maiden name and Morgan Georgia was named for Paul's maternal grandmother, Georgia Steinke.

After being a stay-at-home mom for six months, Marlene started Workforce, Inc. with partner, David Braun, in June 1994. With offices in Farmington, Perryville, Ste. Genevieve and Cape Girardeau, Workforce continues to grow and serve all of southeast Missouri.

Paul and Marlene have both been active in civic and community activities since moving to Farmington. Paul is on the First State Community Bank Board of Directors, the Parkland Hospital Foundation Board and the Civic Center Advisory Panel. Marlene has worked closely with the Farmington Chamber of Commerce, serving as president in 1999, and she has also been involved with the Federated Women's Club and the Industrial Development Authority. They have also co-owned The Pasta House Company with Mike and Nancy Silvey since 1996. Mike and Paul were childhood friends and the two couples formed "Pasta Partners."

The Brockmiller family has been honored to become part of a community where they have developed lasting friendships, successful business partnerships and that offers a special place to raise their daughters. *Submitted by Marlene Brockmiller.*

BROOKS - Mr. and Mrs. Robert E. Brooks Sr. moved to Farmington in May 1962. They are the parents of four children: Constance Marie, Robert E. Jr., Cynthia Sue and stepson, Martin. Robert Sr. was born in Ellington, MO, and wife, Deloris, was born in Manning, IA. Robert served in the US Army from 1950-1953.

Veterans Day Parade, Robert Brooks, Gib Cresswell, Bill Cleve, Sam Saylor, Ott McKinney, Elmer Chaplan

He was a prisoner of war in Korea from 1951-1953 and received the Commendation Medal for service beyond the call of duty. He worked for Wichman Motors for 25 years and for Wohlschaeger Motors until retiring in 1983. He formed a ritual team from members of the Farmington VFW Post #5896 which performed graveside and memorial services for deceased veterans. This ritual team still holds Memorial Day ceremonies at many local cemeteries and the county courthouse. For several years, he was responsible for the parade on Veterans Day. He was responsible for setting up the Korean War Memorial at Mineral Area College with the help of Harold Pratte. He was a dedicated veteran to God and his country.

Robert Sr. and Robert Jr. are both past Worshipful Masters of the Farmington Masonic Lodge #132. Connie (1972) and Cindy (1983) are past Honor Queens of Bethel #34, Farmington. Deloris Brooks served as guardian of Bethel #34. She also served as president of the Women's Auxilliary VFW Post #5896 in 1982-1993. She retired from Wal-Mart in 1983, after working several years as a department manager in the jewelry department.

Grant, Nicole, Gabrielle, Ashley and Courtney - Easter 1997

All of their children graduated from Farmington High School. Connie graduated from Mineral Area College and is married to Jim Lintz. They currently reside in High Ridge, MO and have two daughters, Nicole and Ashley. Robert Jr. graduated from Vatterott College and is married to Becky Thomason. They currently reside in Farmington and have a daughter and son, Courtney and Grant, who are twins. Cindy graduated from Mineral Area College and is married to John Rupp. They currently reside in Potosi and have one daughter, Gabrielle. Martin graduated from Mineral Area College and currently resides in Farmington.

BURCHAM - Tom R. Burcham Jr. and his wife, Mary Ann, along with their 1-year-old daughter, Teresa Marie, moved to Farmington in February 1963. Tom joined the Medical Arts Clinic as a family practice physician. One month after arriving in Farmington, a second daughter, Mary Ellen, was born. In 1965 a son, Paul Riordan, was born. He

died the following day. A fourth child, Tom R. Burcham III, was born in 1967.

Tom R. Burcham Jr. was born and grew up in Doniphan, MO. He attended grade and high school in Doniphan where his father was a high school mathamatics teacher and coach as well as a merchant. Tom went on to graduate from Central Methodist College in Fayette, MO then graduated from St. Louis University Medical School in 1958.

Mary Ann grew up in St. Louis, attended grade and high schools there and graduated from St. John's Hospital School of Nursing in 1959. Tom and Mary Ann met while at St. John's. Mary Ann's parents immigrated to the US from southern Ireland in the 1920s.

Tom R. Burcham Jr. Family (1984) Top: Tom R. Burcham Jr., Tom Burcham III, Mary Ellen Argana. Bottom: Mary Ann and Teresa Kehr

Tom and Mary Ann were married in St. Louis in 1959. Tom spent several years at St. Louis City Hospital participating in an internship and residency program. Mary Ann worked as an RN at the same hospital. They then moved to Doniphan, MO, where Tom practiced for several years before moving to Farmington.

Tom and Mary Ann's children attended St. Joseph's Grade School and Farmington High School. Teresa went on to St. Louis University to obtain bachelor's and master's degrees in nursing. Mary Ellen graduated from the University of Colorado with a degree in pharmacy. Tom III received an undergraduate degree from Tulane University in Louisiana and his law degree from Catholic University in Washington, D.C.

Teresa is married to Donald R. Kehr and lives in Cave Creek, AZ. Mary Ellen is married to Charles Anthony Argana. They live outside Farmington with their four children: Charles Thomas, Tom Christopher, Will Burcham and Mary Teresa. Charlie is a practicing pharmacist. Tom lives in Farmington with his wife Leslie and their two sons, Tom R. IV and John Christopher. Tom is a partner in the law firm of Roberts, Roberts and Burcham.

Dr. Burcham practiced family medicine at the Medical Arts Clinic for 14 years. He then went to St. Francis Hospital in Cape Girardeau where he practiced emergency medicine until he retired in 1998. Despite Tom's working out of town over this period the family has continued to make Farmington their home for the past 36 years.

BUSH - Farmington, MO is celebrating its 200th birthday this year. My family has lived in Farmington since its begining starting with Rev. William Murphy and Sarah Barton Murphy. My mother's father, Hugh Kent Bush, was born in Farmington. A niece, Patricia Cangelosi, resides in Ironton, MO, which is about 18 miles southwest of Farmington. Even today, our family has ties to this city.

The Farmington Library has most of what has been published about our ancestors, Rev. William Murphy, Sarah Barton Murphy and Philip Graham Long. Therefore, would like to tell a little about our grandfather, Hugh Kent Bush, son of John F. Bush and Catherine E. Long. Hugh was born in Farmington, MO Oct. 6, 1865. His was the fourth generation to have lived in Farmington and the third generation to have been born there. He became deaf at the age of 17 months from a

overdose of quinine. Hugh attended the Ohio School for the Deaf, the Missouri School for the Deaf and Dumb (Kendall) and Galaudet College in Washington, DC. While at Galaudet, he was a member of the football team which beat Navy (16-0). He also set a running record that held for years.

A note of interest, did you know that the "Huddle"

Hugh Kent Bush

was started by the hearing impaired, so that the play could be made known to teammates and the opposition would not see what was being signed. Today all football teams use the "Huddle" for the same reason. He was one of the founders of the Dixie Association of the Deaf of Virginia. He spent his last years there, but continued his caring of the hearing impaired throughout the South and Southwest.

Hugh's parents were John F. Bush and Catherine E. Long. Catherine was the daughter of Philip Graham Long and Isabelle Murphy Long; Isabelle was the daughter of Dubart Murphy and Sarah Bacon.

The Long family was one of the first to bring commerce to Farmington when they started the first tanning business in Farmington, The Long Bisby Tannery. Long Memorial Hall is dedicated to them. Our family also built the first grist mill in Farmington.

My family has lived in the Farmington, MO area over three generations. Sarah Barton Murphy, my great-grandmother (seven generations back) has been recorded as having the first Bible class west of the Mississippi. John F. Bush was a state senator from Farmington. Two other ancestors were in the Revolutionary War, Joshua Barton and Michael Bacon.

Isaac Barton, a cutler, and his son, Joshua, were friends of Daniel Boone and helped blaze the Wilderness Trail from Tennessee to Kentucky. They also helped build Fort Boonesbrough and died defending it.

Isabella Murphy Long, my great aunt, was the first white girl born in Murphy Settlement (now known as Farmington). Her father, Dubart Murphy, was the son of William Murphy, a minister who came to settle on the land with his family. At his death, his wife, Sarah Barton Murphy, decided she would continue his ambition, and with their children and a couple of helpers, she came to what is now Farmington and began to carry out their dreams. The rest is history.

Although my grandparents, Hugh Kent Bush and Martha May Lantz Bush had only two daughters, Elizabeth Julia "Alta" Bush Coleman Eanes, three boys and my mother, Isabella Jenny Bush Carter, eight children; the family has grown by their 20 grandchildren and more than 25 great-grandchildren.

Farmington, MO can be proud of producing such a family of ministers, lawyers, senators, doctors, tanners and teachers.

Several years ago we visited Farmington seeking information on the families "roots" and there is still that southern hospitality present in all we met. (The Library, City Hall and the Chamber of Commerce.)

CARROW - Francis Carrow was born in Farmington in a small brick house at 314 E. Spring Street. His wife, Beulah, was born in Esther, MO. They were married in Farmington April 7, 1951 at St. Joseph Catholic Church. The parents of

Francis Carrow were Orval "Sixty" Carrow and Genevieve Antoine Carrow. Orval Carrow's nickname of "Sixty" was derived by his occupation as an automobile mechanic and he could take a Model "A" Ford and adjust it to where it would go 60 miles an hour.

Bobby Joe, Francis, Lester, Charles and their father, Orval Carrow

Francis had three brothers: Charles, the oldest, referred to as "61;" Lester, referred to as "62;" Francis as "63;" and Bobby Joe as "64." These nicknames stuck with the four boys several years while they were growing up. The Carrow boys all went to St. Joseph parochial school and then to Farmington High School. Francis graduated from Farmington High in the Class of 1946, then went to Flat River Jr. College and graduated from there. Francis enlisted in the US Air Force in November 1951. After basic training he was assigned to Headquarters Air Defense Command in Colorado Springs, CO, where he was in statistical services for the Air Force and served all four years there. He attended night school at Colorado College while in service. He was discharged in 1955 and came back to Missouri University in Columbia, MO where he graduated from business school in 1956. He, his wife and small son came back to Farmington and established an insurance agency. In 1968 he went to work as executive secretary for St. Francois County Savings & Loan Association. He retired as president of the association in 1994.

Orval and Genevieve Carrow

Francis and Beulah have two sons, Stephen F. Carrow, born April 14, 1955, and Gerard W. Carrow, born March 23, 1961. Stephen's wife is Nancy and they have two sons, Thomas is 13 and Samuel is 10. They live in St. Louis, MO. Jerry and wife, Sherry, have a girl, Melissa, age 5, and Christopher, age 14, step-son of Jerry. They live in Houston, TX.

Beulah's father and mother were Edward Huber and Ruth (Carver) Huber. Beulah has five sisters, all living in Farmington except one. Also, two brothers, both deceased. Mr. Huber worked for St. Joe Lead Company for over 40 years. Yes, Farmington has truly been our home and will continue to be.

CAYCE - Milton Pleasant Cayce, pioneer and entrepreneur, was the patriarch of the Cayce family in Farmington. He was born in Charlotte County, VA in 1804 and married Susan Ellis in January 1830. That same year Milton, his bride, father, siblings and a number of slaves emigrated to St. Charles, MO.

In 1832 Milton moved his family to Farmington where he acquired and made his home on property described as the Milton P. Cayce addition to Farmington. Milton's father, Pleasant, followed him to Farmington in 1834. Pleasant was born in Chesterfield County, VA and died in Farmington. Upon his arrival in Farmington, Milton immediately affilated with the Presbyterian Church which he

Milton Pleasant Cayce, 1804-1888, came to St. Charles from Charlotte County, VA in 1830. Came to Farmington in 1832 with wife Susan Ellis.

served as an elder for 55 years and was one of its most liberal contributers. He engaged in the mercantile with John D. Peers and continued in merchandising for 53 years while pursuing numerous other activities. A lifelong Democrat, he was elected county treasurer in 1836 and held the office for 20 years, sheriff for two years and postmaster for several years. He was a member of the constitutional convention of 1861.

In 1847 Milton founded on his homesite a private school for children. In 1886, in cooperation with the Potosi Presbytery, Milton, his son, Ellis, and others erected a brick building for Elmwood Seminary for young women. In 1914, with the advent of public education, Elmwood closed and the building was then used as a Presbyterian Orphanage. It is now the site of the Farmington Children's Home.

In 1853 Milton and S.A. Douthit erected the first grist mill. In 1855 he purchased Douthit's interest, enlarged the mill and continued its operation until destroyed by fire in 1875. He was also interested in a blacksmith shop, a tanning yard and farming. He built the first ice house in the county and was said to have purchased the first piano.

Milton and Susan had two children: Ellis Plummer Cayce was manager of the Iron Mountain Company store and succeeded his father as county treasurer. Nettleton D. Cayce spent several years in the gold fields of California during the 1860s. He probably went to California to avoid serving on either side in the Civil War. Susan Ellis Cayce died of pneumonia after riding horseback from Potosi to Farmington in 1843.

Ellis and his wife had three children: Elsie married Robert Forsythe, an artist and nurseryman. Adele married James Carson Morris, a clothing merchant with Morris Brothers store. Later, he was for a time mayor of Farmington. Julian Paul Cayce married Katherine Peers Forster in 1903. Julian Paul was a long time, highly respected attorney who was associated with Robert Manley in later years. He operated a savings and loan, was a trustee of Westminister College in Fulton, MO. Paul was a devout member of the Presbyterian Church which he served as elder and clerk of the session.

In March 1850, Milton received a letter from a William Morton urging him to visit Charlotte County, VA to meet some of the available young ladies. Part of the letter is excerpted below: "I was glad to find that you had not entirely forgotten our fine Virginia girls, especially the Marble Hill beauties. Come over and let us have a good talk over the points. I was at Marble last week, and, of course, your name is always brought up, as I am known to be your warm advocate. The girls looked very sweet and interesting, but as I remarked to my friend on leaving the house that Jinny was decidedly the choice of the flock. She is a lovely woman, and if you stop one moment to count the distance when you think of such a woman and the prospect of uniting in the happy bond of matrimony, I shall scratch you from my books. I think you love her, if not, I know you would if you knew her as well as I do. We have talked about you frequently. She says you are slow in coming and if you don't get here before autumn she will go down the Ohio River on her way south or west looking for a home she knows not where, and would be glad to meet you halfway if you can't get to old Virginia. Now my friend come to Virginia, come quickly, and I think you can get one of the old dominion's loveliest daughters. What can I say to induce you?"

Milton and Virginia Catherine Dupuy "Jinny" were married Nov. 6, 1850.

Milton's son, Ellis, married Emma Dupuy of the Marble Hill family in 1862. The Dupuys had an illustrious history in France dating back at least to the 12th century, participating in the crusades. Raymond Dupuy was one of the founders of the Knights of Malta. In later years the Dupuy family was identified with the Huguenot reformed religion of France. The family fled persecution of the Huguenots and in 1700 arrived in Virginia settling on lands granted to Huguenot refugees.

Milton and Virginia had six children: Alice, unmarried; Elizabeth married Martin Linn Clardy who was elected to congress and later vice president and general counsel of the Missouri Pacific Railroad; Anna married Kossuth W. Weber, attorney and organizer and later president of the Bank of Farmington; J. Harry emigrated to Colorado and died in Denver in 1891; William D., a pharmacist, proprietor of the City Drug Store and died unmarried in 1901; Milton Pleasant Jr., better known as M.P., carried on the traditions of the Cayce family. He was one of the organizers of the Bank of Farmington and served as cashier for many years. M.P. was credited with considerable influence in bringing the State Mental Hospital to Farmington. He died after a long and productive life in 1962 at the age of 96.

The Cayces were a large and influential family in the first 160 years of Farmington's history. There are no longer any members of the family left in Farmington as all are either deceased or have moved on. According to family tradition the Cayces were originally from France.

CHALK - Oscar Chalk was born in 1883 on the family farm in Illinois, just across from Paducah, KY. He married Metta Belle Wood and two children were born, Carson and Velma, now Mrs. Leo Dugal. Metta died when Velma was 3 years old. Oscar later married Pearl Hull, and they had one daughter, Virginia.

Oscar worked 52 years for Missouri Pacific Railroad. He was the station agent in DeLassus for many years before transferring to DeSoto. They moved back to Farmington after he retired. Both died in 1971. Carson played football for Farmington and right after high school learned to fly. Carson operated his own airport in Adel, GA, where he did crop dusting. When WWII started, the government converted his airport into a training station for pilots and put Carson in charge of training fighter pilots for the Army Air Corps.

One of Oscar's brothers was Burns Chalk, who operated a small repair shop in Illinois. A barnstorming pilot came through and had a serious engine problem. Burns repaired his airplane in return for flying lessons. Burns started flying in 1911. He enlisted in the Marine Corps during WWI and became a fighter pilot. After the war, Burns started the first international airline service in Miami flying passengers from Miami to Cuba and other islands in the Caribbean. His planes were all seaplanes, taking off and landing in the ocean.

Many famous people preferred to fly with Burns, namely: Errol Flynn, Lana Turner, Ava Gardner, Arthur Godfrey, Ernest Hemingway, Al Capone, Howard Hughes, Stuart Symington, Adam Clayton Powell and heavyweight boxing champion, Gene Tunney. The Wright Brothers became very good friends of Burns. When Burns retired at age 83, he was the oldest airline pilot in the world still carrying a valid commercial license, number 708. When Dictator Gerardo Machado was overthrown in 1933, he called Burns to rescue him. They took off in a hail of gunfire as the Army was trying to kill him, but they safely escaped from Cuba.

The Chalk family history has been traced back to 1066 when William the Conqueror invaded England at the Battle of Hastings. One of the signers of the Magna Carta was a Chalk ancestor named Richard de Clare. Many of the Chalk men were sea captains, bringing treasures back to England from India, Australia, and the West Indies. One Chalk was living at Jamestown, VA in the early 1600s, but didn't like frontier life and returned to England, later becoming the mayor of London. The Chalk family owned a large farm where they raised the finest celery. Today, the farm is in the area called Wimbledon, where the tennis matches are played.

About 1802, James William Chalk and his brother, Edward, left London and came to Newburgh, NY. James married a widow who owned a 120-acre farm on Manhattan Island. She died in 1804 leaving James the 120-acre farm. James moved to Paducah, KY, and while there, suffered a fire which destroyed all of his possessions including the legal papers showing he was the rightful owner of the 120-acre farm. James never returned to New York. The records do not show any sale of the farm, and it is believed it is now part of the 840-acre Central Park.

There are many notable Chalk ancestors mentioned in the family history. The grandmother of Oscar Chalk was Mary Jane Burns, a second cousin of Robert Burns, the Scottish poet. One of his most famous writings is *Auld Lang Syne*, the traditional song of New Year's Eve. Robert Burns wrote more than 200 songs.

Another famous family in the Chalk line is the Blackburn family. Two of their daughters married nephews of George Washington and lived at Mount Vernon. Both are buried just 20 feet from George and Martha Washington's tomb at Mount Vernon.

CHAMBERLAIN - Nathan Chamberlain and wife, Mary Minnix Chamberlain, came to Missouri from Tennessee about 1852 with five children. They lived in Missouri for about six years and had three more children, then went to Arkansas for two or three years (another two children) and returned to Missouri about 1863. They settled at Irondale near the Washington-St. Francois County line and had two more children while living there bringing the total to 12 children over 22 years. Nathan and their oldest son, John, enlisted in the union cause of the Civil War at Irondale. They were both listed as farmers. Nathan was released due to his age although he may have served in the Missouri militia.

John married a Civil War widow, Barsheba Rice Wigger, who had two children, and they were listed on the census of St. Francois County in 1870 with her children and their daughter. A son, William, would be born in October of that year. Barsheba died in October 1872 at Irondale. John married again to Elizabeth Whaley in 1873 and they were living in Barton County, MO in 1880 with his children and their five. Records from the Split Rock (Brightstone) School and land records show John and his brother, Alex, and their families moved to the area southwest of Knob Lick in 1881 and purchased property there. This was near the quarry which was operated by the Missouri Granite Co. They may have all worked in the quarry business. John was shown as a driller in 1885 and, in fact, had an eye put out as the result of a drill bit breaking off and hitting him in the eye. Some of the Chamberlains worked in the timber as railroad ties were in demand at that time. The 1901 St. Francois County map shows the railroad line extended to the Missouri Granite Co.

Another brother, James Thomas "Tom," also lived in the area. Their father, Nathan, moved to the area in 1881 and was listed as a taxpayer there through 1884 when he moved to the Buck Mountain area near Doe Run.

Nathan's second daughter married Americus McLeod of Reynolds County in 1867. She had twin sons, Mason and Henry. It is not known if her husband died but she and her sons were living in the household of her father, according to the Washington County census of 1870. Although she remarried later to a Snowdell and then in 1883 to Samuel Brim in St. Francois County, the McLeod grandsons continued to live with Nathan and his family. They were all shown in the church book of the Pleasant Hill Christian Church which was located near Doe Run. Most of the McLeod families living in the area today are descendants of Henry.

Other sons of Nathan, Bailey and Robert, lived in the Bismarck and Doe Run area. Bailey later lived in Washington County, although some of his sons lived near Doe Run. Granville lived in the area now known as Terre DuLac. His son, John, lived near Bonne Terre, and Earl near Farmington. Most of Alex' family lived in the Knob Lick *and* Doe Run area and many descendants still do.

John's great-grandson now owns some of the same land John once owned in southwest St. Francois County even though it changed owners many times through the years. The land is still farmed. Most of John's children lived in the area their entire lifetime. His son, James, though he never married, donated land for the Brightstone School to be moved to the top of the hill and Brightstone Presbyterian Church.

Nathan died in Reynolds County in 1894 and it is believed he is buried in the Doe Run area, as his widow lived there after his death. *Submitted by Ruth Hahn*

CHATMAN - Earliest recorded information on the Chatman family history dates back to Yorkshire, England in 1206 A.D. The oldest recorded family Bible dates back to Yorkshire, England in 1613 A.D. There is in existence today a family Bible over 365 years old that was located in Pueblo, CO in 1973. Earlier recorded information of the Chatman family shows arrival from Yorkshire to America in 1734.

The family traveled from Pennsylvania into Virginia, crossing the Potomac River at Harper's Ferry. Eventually, they traveled over the Cumberland Gap to Tennessee and finally to the Lead Belt of Missouri.

Originally our name was spelled "Ceapman" or "Cypeman," indicating our forefathers were merchants. Much speculation has arisen to whether the spelling should be Chapman or Chatman. Records from England show the name to be spelled Chapman; however, early land transfer records from the 1800s indicated the spelling to be Chatman.

Records show John Monroe Chatman, third child of William H. and Elizabeth Bullock Chatman, born Sept. 20, 1870, married Martha Lucinda Scaggs, born March 6, 1879. John's first wife, Mary Jackson, died shortly after the birth of their son, John Edward. Children born to John and Martha: Elmer, born Aug. 25, 1897, died Aug. 21, 1961, married Mahala Burch; Ernie, born Aug. 10, 1899, died Nov. 21, 1901; Mary, born Nov. 4, 1901, died Oct. 2, 1992, married Adam Wilkerson; Mattie, born April 13, 1904, died May 27, 1923; Oscar, born May 7, 1906, died Jan. 23, 1963, married Edyth Hibbits; Ida, born Sept. 30, 1908, died Jan. 5, 1918; Nolis "Chat," born March 31, 1912, died April 25, 1983, married Ruth House; Lonis, born July 7, 1914, died April 17, 1963, married Opalene Kollmeyer; Otto, born Jan. 3, 1918, died Jan. 2, 1999, married Wanda Carver; Mildred, born March 17, 1921, married Alvin Reed; Lola "Jackie," born Sept. 2, 1923, died July 1, 1997, married Wilfred Boevingloh.

John and Martha resided on a farm located on AA Highway southwest of Farmington. John built the house from locally mined granite. John died March 10, 1931. Martha and the younger children continued to live on the farm until approximately 1934. Martha died March 18, 1958. She resided in Farmington at the time of her death.

The Chatman family relied heavily on their faith in God, and church was a very important aspect of their lives. At one time the Chatman family attended Washita Church, often walking the distance from their home to the church. Many of the children attended Washita School. The three younger children also attended school in Farmington. Humor (often dry and subtle) was, and still is, evident as a Chatman family characteristic. Those who knew the family will surely remember this as, almost, a trademark of the family. The history above has been provided by descendants of Nolis who married Ruth House on Feb. 14, 1934. Ten children were born to Nolis and Ruth: John Albert, Gary Gale, Sharon Elizabeth (Mrs. Winfred Strange), David Noel, Nola Ruth (Mrs. Bradley Covell), Ange-La (Mrs. Frank Sutherland), Jessie Mae (Mrs. Michel Williams), Jeffrey Lyle (deceased twin of Timothy), Timothy Kyle, Martha Jane (deceased shortly after birth).

The Chatmans lived for a time in the old Frankclay house in Frankclay, MO until the closing of the mines led them to Colorado. They resided there until Nolis' retirement, at which time they returned to Farmington. Throughout his life, Nolis was active in his church, served as a Boy Scout leader in St. Francois County, served on the Frankclay School Board and the St. Francois County School Board. Ruth was active in church, social organizations, and was a writer of stories and poetry. She was also a talented painter. Ruth was a daughter of Albert and Lula House and a descendent of Adam House, who settled House Springs and was massacred by the Osage Indians.

Many of John and Martha's descendants are residents of the Farmington area today. You will find them involved in local businesses, churches, schools, and civic organizations. Other descendants can be found in several different states and foreign countries. Even though we are scattered, the bond of the Chatman family remains strong. We are proud of our heritage, be it Chapman or Chatman.

CHILTON - Vivian and Viola Greb LePere Chilton were married on Sept. 3, 1934 and resided in Farmington.

Vivian was born the son of Earnest and Lillian Lewis Chilton of Annapolis on Feb. 28, 1906. He had four sisters, Myrtle, Eunice, Velma and Wanda, and six brothers, Elva, Marvin, Oren, Harold, James Elmer and Garvin.

Viola was born to Emma Clara Kerckhoff Greb and William Robert Greb of St. Louis County on June 22, 1910. Viola's mother, Clara Greb, died at her birth and Viola was raised from infancy as the foster daughter of her aunt and uncle, Jacob and Sally Greb LePere of Manchester, MO. Viola, "Babe," had two brothers, Robert and Erwin Greb and six foster brothers and sisters: Matilda, Emma, Walter, Oscar, Jack and Ethel LePere.

Viola and Vivian Chilton and daughter Janet, September 1940

The LePeres moved to Farmington in 1915 to be near Carleton College. Emma LePere Phelan had graduated from Carleton College in 1913 and made many friends while in Farmington. Oscar, Jack and Ethel also planned to attend upon their graduations from high school. Before their graduation, Jack and Oscar, along with their brother Walter, all joined the Marines and served in France during WWI. Walter was killed in action there, and later both the Farmington and Manchester American Legion Posts were named in his honor. Jack and Oscar returned to Farmington and graduated with the high school class of 1920.

Babe's tenacious nature developed at an early age as her mother reported in a letter she wrote both Oscar and Jack while they were in service. The letter read in part, "...the rabbits are eating the lettuce in my garden as quickly as it comes up. I want to put out something to get rid of them, but 'baby' thinks it is the Easter Rabbit and just will not give up on the subject. Therefore, we are still plagued with rabbits."

Babe was a person who always enjoyed having a "good visit" with family and friends. She belonged to the Memorial United Methodist Church, Town and Country Homemakers Club, Women's Society of the Methodist Church, Pythian Sisters and was a charter member of 55 Plus Club. She died Nov. 4, 1992 at the age of 82.

Vivian served in the US Army prior to WWII, and was discharged after developing rheumatic fever while stationed in Hawaii. While in service he developed his love for cooking. His biscuits became a family legend and his innovative approach to cooking led to such startling sights as smoke drifting from an old refrigerator, which he used to smoke his hams and turkeys.

After service, Vivian entered his lifelong trade as a carpenter. He worked with McCarthy Brothers Construction in Panama in 1940 and, in later years, became a millwright and worked on such large construction projects as Pea Ridge Mines, Taum Sauk Electric Plant and Hannah Mines at Pilot Knob. He passed away Oct. 15, 1972 at age 66.

Vivian and Viola had one daughter, Janet Vivian Chilton Douglas of Farmington and one grandson, Mark Wayne Douglas of California. Janet is presently editor of *Farmington Press* and active in the Memorial Methodist Church and several organizations including Shepherd Center, Mineral Area Council on the Arts, Kiwanis, Farmington BPW, Downtown Farmington Organization, Chamber of Commerce, and Farmington History Book Committee. *Submitted by Janet Vivian Chilton Douglas.*

CLAY - Eleazer Clay, a pioneer resident of St. Francois County, was born in Virginia Oct. 4, 1779, the eighth child and youngest son of James and Margaret Muse Clay. After James Clay's death in 1790, Margaret and her family moved to Granger County in east Tennessee. On Jan. 22, 1802, Eleazer married Mary Dunville who was the daughter of Robert Dunville, a Methodist minister. Mary was born Dec. 26, 1784 near Camden, SC. Their first child of record was Margaret, born 1803. On Mary's birthday in 1806, she gave birth to twin boys, James and William; and Nancy was born in 1809. These four are listed as born in Tennessee. On Oct. 12, 1811, Waide H. was born in Kentucky; this may have occurred on their trip to the Missouri Territory, for records show they arrived in Missouri about this time. Eleazer and Mary settled land located on Doe Run Creek, about one mile southeast of present town of Doe Run. We believe Eleazer brought with him from Tennessee a family of slaves he had inherited from his father's estate. The 1830 census shows he owned eight slaves, of which only two were adults. There was much to be done clearing land and building a homestead. The family seemed to progress very well. By the year 1820 four more children were born: Eleanor in 1814, Eleazer Green in 1816, Robert D. in 1817 and Morgan S. in 1820.

When St. Francois County was established in 1821, Governor McNair appointed Eleazer one of two justices of the peace for Pendleton Township, an office he held for several years. He was also on the venue of the first jury selected in the county. From 1823 to 1826 three more daughters were born: Mahalia, Mary Ann and Angeline. By the early 1830s the older children began to marry and establish their own homes, some moved to other areas; however, sons, Waide H. and Eleazer Green, aquired land adjoining their parents. By the mid-1850s Eleazer and his two sons owned about 750-acres of adjoining land. During these years as happens to all families, the family burying ground has claimed several family members. Waide's wife, Menica; Eleazer's daughter, Mahalia, and possibly others. Also, son William had died in Madison County. Then on April 16, 1852 Mother Mary Clay was called away.

The known marriages of Eleazer and Mary's children are as follows. Margaret to George Carder, James W. to Polly Ann Spradling, William S. to Sarah Murphy, Waide H. to Menica Musick and second to Mary E. Sutherland, Robert D. to Luvica Hunt, Eleazer G. to Susan Chilton or Shelton, Angeline to Alvin Rucker, Nancy to Perry Moore and Mary Ann to William Bumbaugh.

As far as we know, daughter, Margaret Carder, and some of her children and grandchildren were the only family members left in the neighborhood. The census of 1860 lists Eleazer, 80 years of age, as the lone member of the household, with a real estate value of $8,000 and personal property value of $9,800; this figure would include his slaves. The clouds of Civil War were gathering and surely affected the closing years of Eleazer's life. On Feb. 18, 1863, he was found dead in his home. Doctors said he had suffered a stroke. The inscription on his gravestone has these words, "I have finished my work, I have kept the faith."

CLAY - Jack and Ann first met in January 1946 and were married March 13, 1946. Jack had lived in the Lead Belt area all his life, and had been discharged from the Army in November 1945 after 39 months of service in WWII. Ann had lived in Flat River since about 1943. She was born March 6, 1926, near Quaker in Washington County, MO. Her parents, O.W. and Sally (Tedder) Martin, had been lifelong residents of Washington County, living near Quaker, then Belgrade and

Potosi. Mr. Martin was a carpenter by trade and had moved to Flat River to be closer to his job helping build the Prisoner of War Camp near Weingarten, MO. Ann has three sisters: Helen Blair, Virginia Dix and Rosemary Crocker, and one brother, Glenwood Martin.

Jack's parents were Paul J. and Beulah Iahn Clay. He was born Jan. 2, 1924, and has one brother, Bob Clay; one sister, Shirley Slover; and another sister, Polly Ann,

Jack and Ann Clay

died in infancy. Jack and Ann moved to Farmington in 1947, where the family operated a feed and produce store under the name of Paul J. Clay and Sons on Jackson Street. Their first home in Farmington was on North Street and in about 1950, they moved to a residence on Trimfoot Street. Then in 1956 they moved to their present home at 506 North A. Street. Their first child, Linda, born Dec. 31, 1946,, married Lawrence K. Schlichter and they live on a farm north of Farmington. Linda and Larry have three children: William, April and Wesley; also twin granddaughters, Rachael and Jacqueline Schlichter. Their second child, a son, Joseph M. Clay, born Sept. 27, 1949, lives in Florida. Joseph was twice married: first to Beverly White and they have a son, Scott J. Clay. Joe later married Marianne DeMarco; they have no children. Joe works as a salesman for a company selling supplies to golf courses.

Jack went to work for W.R. Sheets DVM in September 1949 at the office on Harrison St. in Farmington. In 1951 Dr. Sheets built a new clinic on Karsch Blvd. in Farmington. Jack worked at this clinic for about 39 years until retirement in 1988. Since then he has worked parttime with J.O. Swink, Jr. at the Farmington Livestock Market.

Before marriage Ann worked in St. Louis, also at the Shoe Factory in Flat River and Foulon's Drug Store. After marriage she, beside being a housewife and mother, became an excellent seamstress. After her children were grown she worked at the high school cafeteria and as a receptionist for the Medical Arts Clinic. Jack and Ann became interested in collectables, which they still enjoy as a hobby. Ann also crafted many different items, such as dolls, bears, quilts and other items. The couple has always been interested in gardening and their yard and garden contain many flowers, herbs, and vegetables are plentiful in season. They also belong to the St. Francois County Historical Society, helping on projects to preserve old county records and other items of interest. They are members of the Memorial United Methodist Church, which they joined soon after moving to Farmington.

Jack is also a life member of VFW Post 5896. Their family has always been the source of much enjoyment and love, to see the children, grandchildren, and now great-grandchildren grow up, makes the sacrifices and worry all worth while. The children showed their thanks by hosting a celebration on their parents 50th wedding aniversary in April 1996. *Submitted by Jack Clay.*

CLAY - Paul J. Clay and Beulah H. Iahn were married March 18, 1921. Paul, a son of Robert L. and Mattie (Hardin) Clay, was born Feb. 8, 1899. Beulah, daughter of William H. and Katherine (Gould) Iahn, was born Feb. 23, 1903. Paul spent his childhood years in the area around Frankclay, MO, along with his brothers: Roy L., Charles R.,

Virgil E. and a sister, Pearl E. His father, Robert, worked at several jobs including miner, store clerk and farmer. Also living nearby were other Clay families, including the grandparents, Robert J. Clay and wife, Nerceniae; also, Mattie's parents, Louis M. and Mary Laura Hardin. Beulah was born and raised in the Desloge and Leadwood, MO area along with her sister, Bernice. Another sister and brother, Melba and Freddie, died in infancy. Her father, Wm. H. Iahn, was killed May 3, 1911, in Frankclay, MO. Katherine Iahn kept her young family together by furnishing room and board to miners. Kate, as she was called, was a very strong willed person. She later married George Cain and they spent the remainder of their lives in Leadwood. Beulah went to school in Leadwood, after which she went to St. Louis and worked for Western Union.

Paul J. and Beulah H. Clay

The Robert L. Clay family moved to Farmington from Frankclay in about 1911, hauling their possessions in a farm wagon. Robert had obtained employment in the Farmington Post Office. Paul finished his schooling in the Farmington Public Schools and attended the Ozark Business College in Farmington. He often talked of his days growing up in Farmington and the many friends he had at work and play. He was employed for awhile on the farm and nursery of the Butterfield family. After attending the Ozark Business College, he went to work in the office of the Federal Lead Co. in Flat River, MO. His transportation to this job was by taking the electric trolley to Flat River. In 1918, Paul received his notice for the draft in WWI. He said he sold his clothes and other possessions and was waiting to leave when the Armistice was signed in November and the call was cancelled.

After this, his work consisted of selling for various businesses, mainly in automobiles and Delco Electric. When Paul and Beulah married in 1921, they lived in the Crawley Bottom area of Flat River. Later, they bought property in Leadington near the new Highway 61, and this is where the family was to live for several years. Their first child, Billy Bob, was born on April 15, 1922, and on Jan. 2, 1924, Jack was born. It wasn't until Feb. 26, 1929, that a daughter, Polly Ann, arrived, but on May 6, 1931, she passed away; the victim of scarlet fever. Another daughter, Shirley, was born July 4, 1932. Their children all attended the Esther, MO, School.

During the depression years, Paul worked at various jobs. Then in 1934, he was elected County Clerk of St. Francois County. He served in this position for 12 years, leaving office in January 1947. The family had moved to a farm east of Esther in the mid-1930s, which is now the location of Mineral Area College. They moved to Farmington in the late 1940s, where they operated a feed and produce store. After this he became a realtor and remained in this business until retirement.

Their children's marriages are as follows: Bob married Maxine Mueller and has two daughters, Connie Barnes and Cathy Davis, and two grandchildren, Shawn Barnes and Kimberly Duncan. Jack married Ann Martin and has two children; Linda Schlichter and Joseph Clay; four grandchildren: William Schlichter, April Schlichter, Wesley Schlichter and Scott Clay; and twin great-granddaughters, Racheal and Jacqueline Schlichter. Shirley married Dual Slover and has four children: Ray Slover, Paul Clay Slover, Polly Ann Klasek and Max Slover; and six grandchildren: Bryan and Erick Slover, Laura and Paula Klasek, Rick and Chuck Hess.

Paul and Beulah were married 69 years in March 1990, and Beulah passed away in November 1990, at age 87. Paul died in June 1993, at the age of 94, with burial in Parkview Cemetery in Farmington. They were lifelong members of the Methodist, Free Will Baptist and United Baptist Churches. They enjoyed their family, many friends, and were wonderful parents.

CLEVE - A bicentennial history of Farmington will be written by those who have chosen to settle here recently, and by those who have local family backgrounds which span several generations. Albert Louis Cleve and his family can look back to many ancestors who contributed to the 200-year history of Farmington. Through both of his parents, John F. and Bernice Worley Cleve, Albert can trace his roots to four pioneer families.

His great-grandfather, Louis Henry Cleve Sr., came to this country from Klein-Rhuden, Germany in 1845, first settling in Cape County and later coming to St. Francois County. Louis' father, Johann Heinrich Cleve, born Oct. 6, 1802, and Louis' mother, Auguste Luise Friderike, born 1802, also came to Missouri. "Grandpa Cleve," as Louis Cleve was called, was a carpenter by trade. He first settled on the farm known as the present Elwood Wigger farm which joins the Karl Cleve farm on Busiek Road. He built the house which still stands on the Wigger farm today. When he was not farming or doing other carpenter work, he also built coffins. Living in this area during the Civil War was trying, according to stories that have been passed along. Bushwackers were a real threat to settlers with good horses and other animals during that time. To elude the bushwackers, he would hide his horses in the willows along the creek and hide his family in the cornshocks. When he died, it was reported that the funeral procession was the largest ever seen in the county. In the procession from the home in Farmington to the little country church, two miles south of town, were about 100 carriages containing members of the family, neighbors and his friends.

Original old family about 1910 Front Row: Emma Brockmiller, Mary Halter, Louis Cleve Sr., Louise Cleve, Louise Gaebe, Elizabeth Cleve. Back Row: Edward Cleve, George Cleve, William Cleve, Charles Cleve, John Cleve, Louis Cleve Jr.

Albert's paternal great-grandmother, Louisa Rickus Cleve, came to Farmington in 1846 from Darmstadt, Germany with her parents, John, born 1799, and Mimone "Minnie" Rickus. Louis H. Cleve Sr. and his wife, Louisa, had 10 children, nine of whom married and several of whom raised families in St. Francois County. These were: Charles married Emma Miller; Mary married Andrew F. Halter; Louise married Carl Gaebe; Elizabeth married Theodore Kiepe; Emma married John Brockmiller; John married Ellen Bowling; Louis Cleve Jr. married Mary Hillebrecht; George Cleve married Thresia Miller; Edward Cleve married Selma Kneise; William never married.

Louis Cleve Jr. children about 1940 Minnie Cleve, Elizabeth Mell, Walter Cleve, Adalia Hoehn, John Cleve, Alma Zieba

Albert L. Cleve's father's maternal grandfather, Ernest Hillebrecht, born Jan. 13, 1818, came from Germany and settled in Iron Mountain about 1860. On April 3, 1862, he married Johanna Christina Pumpel, who was born in 1832, in Germany. She died about 1882, while Ernest lived until Nov. 21, 1900. Their children and spouses: Minnie married Conrad Meyer, Mary married Louis H. Cleve Jr. and Louise married Charles Frederick Rickus. Johanna Christina Hillebrecht had two children by a previous marriage. They were Anna Hoffmeister (married Ernest Wichman) and Fredericka Hoffmeister (married August W. Wichman). Louis Cleve Jr. and his wife, Mary, had six children: Minnie never married, Elizabeth married William Mell, Walter married Bertha Hoehn, Adelia married Carl Hoehn, John married Bernice Worley and Alma married Frank Zieba.

Apple butter time, a family tradition for Cleve family about 1975. Back row from left: Fred Smith, Alma Zieba, John Cleve, Fred Smith. Front row from left: Andrew Smith, Charles Smith, Bernice Cleve with Jennifer Cleve, Marjorie Smith, Karen Cleve, Elizabeth Mell, Steve Worley, Erma Worley. The smaller of the two kettles, from the Hillebrecht family, has been passed down from generation to generation and used at this yearly family tradition.

Albert L. Cleve's maternal great-grandfather, Andrew Worley, came to Reynolds County from Hickman County, TN and fought as a Union soldier in the Civil War. Andrew's son, Albert Worley, came to St. Francois County from Reynolds County to work in the lead mines in Flat River. Albert's maternal great-grandfather, George W. Reynolds, came to St. Francois County from Cumberland County, KY in the 1840s. He purchased property in the northwestern part of the county where he and his family lived until 1858 when he sold the property and moved to Jefferson County.

In 1883, one of George W. Reynold's sons,

William F. Reynolds, married Sophia Shipton Bowen, and one of their children, Mae Reynolds, married Albert Worley. William F. Reynolds worked for Valles Mines for 39 years, being responsible for the furnace at the smelter. William F. Reynolds and his family lived in a mining company house, which still exists, until he and his family came to Flat River in 1904. Albert Worley and Mae Reynolds had eight children: Thelma married Lester Price, Gladys died in infancy, Bernice married John Cleve, Theron married Erma Horton, Henry died in infancy, Helen married Noah Shirrell, Dorothy married Mack Brann and Norma married William Johnson. Albert L. Cleve's parents and many of his grandparents were engaged in agriculture, although his mother's father, grandfather and great-grandfather had been employed in mining at some point in their lives.

Cleve family about 1980. Back Row: Albert Cleve, Wayne Johnson, Fred Smith, Charles Smith . Middle Row: Karen Cleve, Dorothy Johnson, Andrew Smith, Marjorie Smith, Fred Smith. Seated: John Cleve holding Kathryn Cleve, Bernice Cleve holding Jennifer Clev.

Albert L. Cleve and his two sisters, Marjorie and Dorothy, attended public school in Libertyville near the family farm which their parents bought in 1939. His two daughters, Jennifer (Cleve) Blum and Katherine, have added to their father's Farmington background. Their mother, Karen Botkin Cleve, is a daughter of Robert and Wilma Botkin, one of the earlier owners of Botkin Lumber Company which has been part of Farmington's history since 1951. Soon after graduating from Farmington High School in 1966, Albert attended Lincoln University in Jefferson City and Mineral Area College. Karen also attended Mineral Area College.

Albert and Karen have been active in their lumber company and in the operation of their Percheron draft horse farm, Blue Ribbon Farms. Albert's lumber business has expanded to new facilities in Taylorville, IL and Cape Girardeau. Jennifer graduated from William Jewell College in Liberty, MO in 1997, and Katherine began her junior year there in 1998.

In addition to lumber and draft horse enterprises, Albert L. Cleve continues to be involved in the cattle business and operates the family farm near Libertyville. His mother, Bernice Worley Cleve, still resides in the house which is the scene of extended family gatherings whenever his two sisters, Marjorie (Mrs. Fred) Cleve Smith of Fenton, MO and Dorothy (Mrs. Wayne) Cleve Johnson of Nacogdoches, TX, travel to the area. Researching and compiling family history remains an enjoyable pasttime for the family. Up until just a few years ago, the descendants of Louis Henry Cleve Sr. had an annual family reunion on the Copenhagen Cemetery grounds, where he and Louise are remembered, as they rest in peace. *Submitted by Dr. Wayne and Dorothy (Cleve) Johnson*

COLE - Gene was born June 28, 1917 in DeLassus, MO to Lorris Dell and Lucinda (Hunt)

Cole. He had one brother, Lorris. Gene graduated from Farmington High School, Flat River Junior College, and completed one year at Missouri University, leaving there to take a position at the Farmington Post Office in 1936. Gene married Joyce Swink, who passed away in 1987. Gene spent 33 months in the Army during WWII serving in the European Theatre of Operations. In January 1989 he married Maxine Overall Beckett.

Maxine was born in Farmington, Nov. 1, 1926, to Stanley and Frances Ethlyn "Ethel" (Barton) Overall. She was one of seven children and had a wonderful childhood among this large family. Her father

Gene and Maxine Cole, Oct. 20, 1992

worked hard to provide for his family and her mother tried to make ends meet during the depression years. Maxine graduated from Farmington High School in 1944 and went to work as an operator for Southeast Missouri Telephone Company. After the war, she married Medford Del "Muff" Bequette. They had two children, Nancy Del and David Lynn. Nancy married Michael E. Wamble of Esther in 1975 and they are the parents of Rebecca, Elizabeth and Katherine. David married Jeanine Chapman of Columbia in 1986 and they are the parents of Mitchell and Caroline.

Maxine's husband retired from St. Joe Minerals in 1983 and passed away of cancer in 1986. She had just retired from the Farmington School District R-7 after 23-1/2 years. She then filed and was elected as City Treasurer for a two-year term. In 1989 she married Gene.

Maxine and Gene are both active in their churches and civic clubs. She is a member of First Baptist and he is a Presbyterian and serves as treasurer. Gene has been a Mason for 48 years, a 46-year member of Odd Fellows, a member of the American Legion and VFW.

Maxine is a member of Beta Sigma Phi, Monday Club, PEO Chapter HJ, a member of the Parks Board, and served on the Planning and Zoning Board for 15 years. Maxine's grandparents on the Barton side were farmers in the Three Rivers Community and came to this area from southeast Missouri. The Overall family originated in Tennessee. John A. Overall was a carpenter and helped build buildings at the State Hospital #4. John was married to Nettie Kinzer.

Gene's lineage comes from the Murphy family who founded Farmington. His great-grandfather was Franklin Murphy, great-grandson of Sarah Barton Murphy. Gene's father operated a grocery store in DeLassus. The Hunt's side were farmers. His grandfather, Giles Hunt, was a Civil War veteran as was his grandfather, Zachriah Cole, who was also sheriff of St. Francois in 1880. *Submitted by Eugene M. and Maxine B. Cole*

COLE - Oral Cole, born 1917, grew up in St. Francois County, attended school in Desloge and worked on his father's farm. Oral began working for St. Joe Lead Company but was drafted into the Army when WWII began. He served in the Pacific and was awarded a Purple Heart. He and Verna Clubb were married in 1941. Their three children are Janet, born 1942, married to Herb Beck (see Herb and Janet Beck family history); Rita, born 1947, married John Stam (see John and Rita Cole Stam family history); and Michael, born 1952, married to Kathy Houlihan Cole.

After the end of WWII, Oral and Verna lived

in Flat River and then Irondale for a few years, finally settling in Farmington to raise their family. Oral continued to work for the lead mines until retirement. Over the years, Verna worked for Trimfoot Shoe Company, Wabash Mfg. Co. and Presbyterian Manor. Oral and Verna still make their home on Fourth Street in Farmington.

The earliest known member of Oral's family is John Cole, born 1669. John married Johanna Garrett ca 1690 in Maryland. John and his children owned several large parcels of land where Baltimore, MD is today. Members of the Cole family that remained in Maryland for a generation or two are Thomas, born 1690s, and Thomas Jr., born in 1718. Being pioneers, several members of the Cole family traveled to claim land in Kentucky, but returned to Maryland and died in Maryland. Thomas Jr. willed his land in Kentucky to his son, Salathiel, born prior to 1747, and grandson, Micajah, born in 1768. The family migrated to Kentucky in the late 1790s (Thomas Jr.'s son, Salatheil and Salathiel's son Micajah). They moved west again to Washington County, MO in the early 1800s. Micajah's son, Thomas H., was born in 1795 and moved to St. Francois County ca. 1820. Thomas H.'s son, Leonard, was born in 1824 and farmed in St. Francois County. Leonard's son, William James Cole, was born in 1845 and married Frances Vandiver in 1865. William and Frances had nine children born between 1866 and 1887: Richmond, Idella, Leonard, James Earl, Job, Sevilla, Samuel, Zeno, Anne. The birth and death dates of the tenth child, Winnett, are unknown.

Oral's grandfather, Richmond, born 1866, married Josephine Lindsay. Richmond was an engineer with the lead company. He and Josephine had nine children: Roy Lee, Jhonce Herbert, Consula, Essie, Mildred, Ollie, Ogan, Evelyn and Myrna. Richmond, Josephine and some of their children are buried in the Doe Run Cemetery on Hildebrecht Road just outside of Doe Run, MO. Oral's father, Roy, was born in 1893. He married Ethel Jones from Elvins in 1914. They lived in several locations in St. Francois County before moving to Farmington in the early 1940s. After living in town for many years, they bought a farm on Old Fredericktown Road, but after a few years they sold the farm and moved back to Farmington. Roy was a mining captain for the lead company. He and Ethel had four children: Ogan is deceased, Oral, Harold Lee, deceased; and Norma, Mrs. Gerald Kerr of Union, MO. Roy and Ethel are both buried in Parkview Cemetery in Farmington, MO.

Verna's great-great-great-grandfather, John Devenport Sr., born 1784 in Virginia, and his wife, Delilah Abernathy, born 1783, migrated to Missouri in 1820 as part of a wagon train made up of 70 families. They settled in Bollinger County, MO. John and Delilah had eight children. John died in 1851 and Delilah died in 1860. They are buried in Old Union Methodist Cemetery in Marble Hill, MO. Delilah's ancestors can be traced back to Robert Abernathy, born 1635, in Jamestown, VA.

Verna's great-great-grandfather, Joab Q. Devenport, born 1820, was the seventh child of John and Delilah. Joab, a successful farmer, died about 1848, leaving his wife, Jane Wilkinson Devenport, with four young children. James Wooster Devenport, born 1846, their fourth child, was Verna's great-great-grandfather. He married Julie Camren and they had six children. Julia died at age 30 and James later married Julia Miinch or Muench. He and his second wife had 11 children. James' daughter by his first wife, Emma Dora Devenport, born 1878, married Henry Juan Moyers. Henry and Emma Devenport Moyers, Verna's grandparents, had 15 children. Verna's mother, Clara May Moyers, born 1897, married

Henry Ira Evrette Clubb, born 1894. Both are buried at Marcus Cemetery, Fredericktown, MO. Verna's parents had 10 children; all but one are still living. *Submitted by: Janet Cole Beck*

COLE - Watson Cole, born 1802, died 1876, was a brick-layer when he met Louisiana Murphy, born 1806, died 1874, daughter of David Murphy and Rachel (Jones) Murphy. They were married Dec. 1, 1823, at the Murphy home in Farmington. They lived in Farmington for several years before deciding to leave. They had decided that the town was becoming too wicked to raise children in such an environment.

They received a grant for 1500 acres on Cub Creek in Washington County, which is 12 miles west of Belgrade, MO. Men were sent to clear the land, build the fences and sheds to house the domestic animals and fowls. A temporary log house was built with a picket fence around it to protect the house. The move to Cub Creek took two days. Several wagons were used to take the family's belongings, tools, furniture and supplies. The large animals were driven. These were cattle, sheep, horses and hogs. Upon arrival all animals were sheltered except the hogs that were put in the narrow yard surrounding the house. All were in bed when the wolves began to howl with their blood curdling cries and a commotion started among the hogs. Watson jumped up from bed and grabbed a firebrand from the fireplace and ran to see what was happening. He was met by an old sow being chased by a big black bear. He threw the firebrand at the bear who fled in terror. The sow escaped but Watson was knocked down. He returned to bed. There would be many such nights as the Cole family lived there until 1917.

Homestead - Watson Cole and Louisiana Murphy's home on Cub Creek built in the 1850s has many of its original features. Wire fence nearly 100 years old. Civil War was real to them there. Now owned by Mrs. Valle Barr

People were coming into the community. A Baptist Church and a Methodist Church were built plus a school was added to the community. One cold winter night, Watson and a Mr. Huitt decided to visit the Baptist Church. There were very few members present. The Baptist minister called on his members to pray. Each "begged to be excused." The minister said, "Brother Watson, you pray." Brother Watson felt slighted and said in a loud voice, "Pray yourself if you want anyone to pray." William Huitt could hardly wait to tell Louisiana.

Watson was a hard worker and learned to farm (or starve) and to be a great hunter but his large orchards were his pride and joy. Louisiana was an excellent homemaker and very good at weaving, knitting and baking. She also taught her children at home until the school was finished. Farmington didn't prove to be too wicked for the second generation. They came to Farmington for advanced schooling. They went to universities including Missouri University, Northwestern University, which seemed to be the favorite, and Harvard receiving master and doctorate degrees.

They scattered all across the United States and Asia as teachers, missionaries and ministers. One person spent years teaching Indian children on a reservation.

Descendants of the Watson Coles (as a whole) are successful. They have the same ideals as their forefathers. They are interested in religion, education, community improvements, environmental issues, charities and their families. They are my cousins. I admire them as they rise to meet the challenges of an approaching future. *Submitted by Margaret Cole Barr, great-great-granddaughter of David Murphy; Mrs. Herman Barr, Desloge, MO; assisted by Anna Sue Turner, GGGG-granddaughter of David Murphy, daughter of Joe and Sue (Rowe) Turner, Desoge, MO*

COLSON - David Lee Colson and his wife, Norma Lee (Aslinger) Colson, moved to Farmington in 1960. Dave and Norma were both reared in Desloge, MO, graduating from Desloge High School. Dave joined the Navy for one year (the only one year enlistments this country has ever had) in 1948. When his enlistment was up, he returned to Desloge. In October of 1948, Dave and Norma were married.

Dave is the son of the late Emerson and Faustine (Meadows) Colson, and Norma is the daughter of Irene (Aldrich) Aslinger and the late Arthur L. Aslinger of Desloge, MO. Both parents worked for St. Joseph Lead Company. Dave and Norma both graduated from the University of Missouri in 1952. Dave received a BS in statistics, and Norma received a BS in elementary education. They moved to St. Louis, MO where Dave attended St. Louis University Law School and Norma taught in the Farragut School close to Old Sportsman Park. After law school they moved to Flat River, MO where Dave opened his law office and Norma taught in Elvins, MO. Dave was assistant prosecuting attorney for St. Francois County in 1966 and prosecuting attorney in 1956. Dave and Norma have five children and 10 grandchildren: Craig and his daughters, Anne and Rachel; Lee Ann and husband, Frank Gentile, and their sons, Dominic and Lang; Susan and husband, Dan Freund, and their sons: Matthew, Alex and Luke; Beth and her husband, Greg Wade, and children: Marcus, Andrea and Alison; and daughter Jill and husband, Stewart Mackay.

Norma received her master's degree from Southeast Missouri State University and taught special education in the Farmington School System. In 1993, after 32 years of teaching, she retired and is now owner of Mercantile Antiques in Farmington. Dave continues to practice law with his daughter, Jill, Thomas L. Ray and Gary W. Wagner.

COLYER - Marv, McClire II, the youngest of eight children to Jesse Andrew and Jenny Mae Murphy. Jesse's family immigrated from Scotland to Monroe County, TN, mid-1800s. As was typical of the day, William Colyer married a young Cherokee maiden, Alice. In 1905, traveling in a Conestoga wagon, the family of seven children migrated west to the fertile farm land of the Mississippi bottom lands of southern Illinois, Pulaski-Alexander County. Jenny's Irish family, the Buckles and Murphys, also settled in Pulaski-Alexander County.

Pat, New Bern, NC, the third of four children of Robert P. O'Neal, of Santa Monica, CA and Nancy Monroe of Quincy, IL. Robert's family migrated to the West, Nevada and California, as physician and ranchers during the Gold Rush and Silver Lode era. Nancy's dad worked with her grandfather, Edward N. Monroe, developer and manufacturer of Monroe Chemical Co. producing Putnam Dyes in Unionville, MO, beginning in

1870, later, Quincy, IL. Pat's father, a thermodynamics engineer, served in the US Marine Corps Aviation for 34 years. The family maintained a permanent residence in New Bern, NC, near the Cherry Point Marine Air Station, while Robert was often aircraft carrier based, on deployment to Japan, the Philippines, Korea and Vietnam.

Kimberly and Jeff Coleman

Marv and Pat met at a professional seminar. He was a student at St. Joseph's School of Nursing, Alton, IL and she at Duke University's Watts School of Nursing, Durham, NC. Marv's a graduate of Southwest School of Anesthesia, Springfield, MO. A captain in the US Army during the Vietnam War, San Francisco and Okinawa, Japan, 1965-1969. Via HAM short wave radio contact with a friend, he learned of two new hospitals opening in the Spring of 1969. First accepting the Ste. Genevieve position, and later moving to Farmington.

Marv, Kimberly, Pat and Andy

Two weeks after the relocation in November, Kimberly was born. Together with her brother, John Andrew, almost 3 years old, the family was completed. Family interests vary from music, sailing, flying, running and walking, gardening, classical and social dancing, swimming, basketball, canoeing, family history and traveling.

Marv's professional activities include serving on the Missouri Association of Nurse Anesthetists board of directors; member, president and chairman of State Governmental Affairs Committee; founder of the Southeast Missouri Continuing Education Seminars; and federal political director. They co-chaired the St. Francois County Fund Raising Campaign for John Hancock, Secretary of State candidate.

Pat's activities have included membership in the Federated Women's Club; member and president, Twenty-Five Gardeners Club; flower show arranging winner; floral displays at Citizens Center and Farmington Community Hospital; Japanese Ikebana floral arranger; 1976 bi-centennial parade co-chair and chairman of local efforts; Governor Kit Bond's campaign to "Save the George Caleb Bingham Art Works for Missouri;" display and sales, at Ozarks Federal Savings & Loan; Mineral Area College Arts Council Annual Fund Raising Committee 1988-1997; decorating co-chairman 1996 and chairman 1997; ambassador volunteer at Farmington Community Hospital, now Parkland Health Center, president 1996-1997; project chairman of the 50th anniversary celebration of the founding of Medical Arts Clinic and unveiling of the Medical History Wall, Oct. 18, 1998.

The Colyers have owned 10-4 Aircraft Sales; were Amway ruby direct distributors; senior vice-president of A.L. Williams Financial Services; and an extension of their hobby, they own "Go Travel." Travel Agency.

John Andrew "Andy," is well known for his love of piano music. He has played solo and has accompanied classmates from Washington-Franklin School through high school, 1985; vocal music, 1980-1985; Mr. Don Veith's Acapella Choir, Choraliers, All State Choir, 1985; Cub and Boy Scout Troup 471; Life Award, S-F and Philmont Scout Ranches; Bugler for Annual Memorial Day Celebration honoring Veterans, 1980-1987, under the direction of Bob Brooks, North Korean Prisoner of War Camp, 1952-1955; Farmington swim team, 1972-1981; basketball, 1979-1985; track, 1979-1990; 1500 and 3000 meter distances; first Show-Me State Olympics Gold Medalist 1500 and 3000 meters; 1985 National Honor Society.

Colleges: Mineral Area College, Music Scholarship; recipient of the Music Department Student of the Year, 1987; student government; Phi Theta Kappa Honor Society; Junior Piano Recital; Honor Graduate, Rhodes, Memphis, TN, AB 1990; Gold Medaled in the 3000 Meter Steeplechase, Division III, Southern Athletic College Conference; Senior Piano Recital; Logan College of Chiropractic, Chesterfield, MO; founder and president, Student Sports Council; Student, ACA President; Pi Kappa Chi professional fraternity' 1993 Alumnae Award Honor Graduate; Student Doctor of the Year, 1993; certified strength and conditioning specialist, founder and director of Parkland Pain and Rehab, Farmington; professional piano musician; owner of Eclipse Studios.

Kimberly's activities: Farmington swim team, 1972-1975; Flute, 1982-1988; first chair, piano 1966-1988; choir, 1882-1988; Acapella and Choraliers, 1996-1998; Brownie and Girl Scouting; artistry color-coordination consultant, 1982-1984; student of Ballet Arts Studio, Kimberly Gavin Jeude Director, Bonne Terre, 1979-1988; spring recitals, summer informal performances in the park and bi-annual Christmas performances of the Nutcracker Suite in various roles, Sugar Plum Fairy 1993 & 1997. Choreographed own ballet for participation in 25th Annual Sweetheart Talent Competition, music from St. Elmo's Fire, crowned Sweetheart Queen, 1997. National Honor Society and Honor Graduate, 1998.

Colleges: Rhodes, Memphis, TN, AB, political science, 1992; athletic trainer; Kappa Delta Sorority; St. Louis University accelerated bachelors in nursing degree, 1994; Sigma Theta Tau Honor Society; University of Missouri St. Louis; advanced practice program, Women's Health Specialty, 1998. Married Jeffrey Coleman, CRNA, June 5, 1997, graduate Potosi High School, 1982, band, tennis team, University of Missouri, Columbia, 1996, Sigma Chi Fraternity, St. Mary's University, School of Anesthesia, Winona, MN. They reside in Clayton, MO.

CONRAD - John Ireanus Conrad was born at Alliance, MO on May 20, 1867. He was the third son of Peter Rudolph and Anna Elizabeth (Nugent) Conrad, the grandson of David Rudolph and Mary (Bollinger) Conrad.

John married Josephine (Barks) Conrad, Jan. 9, 1887. To this union 14 children were born, two dying in infancy.

John and Josephine lived on a farm joining his father's farm on Big White Water Creek near Alliance, MO. They built a four-room log cabin where 11 of their children were born, or possibly one or two older ones were born at their grandfather's farm.

In 1906 John sold his farm to his younger brother, Arthur O. Conrad and wife Ida (Murray)

Conrad. John and Josephine bought a farm on Village Creek about three miles north of Fredericktown, MO and moved there in March 1906. Their three youngest sons were born on this farm near Fredericktown.

The John and Josephine Conrad family (1911) Front Row: John I, James, Theodore, Anna, Stanley and Josephine. Back row: Peter, Cora, Daniel, Herman, Chauncey, John and Edwin.

John was a farmer, but always wanted to be a railroad engineer. He had only eight years of formal education, but was an avid reader and furthered his learning on his own. He subscribed to a goodly number of a magazines and newspapers, and his self-education gave him the equivalent of a college degree of his time. John became an elder of the Presbyterian Church of Fredericktown and remained in that position the rest of his life. He was active in politics and other public affairs, serving as a judge at elections, on the Village Creek School Board, and backed the teachers in any way he could. He was a surveyor and surveyed numerous parcels of land in Madison County. He was a member of the Odd Fellow and Modern Woodmen lodges in Fredericktown.

We, the children of John and Josephine, have much to be thankful for. Their lives were a good example for us, both in religious pursuit and education. Not all of us attended college, but most finished high school. We always attended the circus when it was in town, went to St. Louis Zoo on education trips, attended lectures, music or acting programs, increasing our educational experiences. We had a radio in the home after WWII and always had a phonograph and piano. We all loved to sing. My father probably never saw a television.

The above information was taken from a letter written April 14, 1986 by their last living child, Anna Marie Conrad (Dilingham) Coffman. Anna Marie passed away in August 1987.

CONRAD/KORBER/MOORE/NORMAN/ DARROUGH - This the family history of Stanley Winslow Conrad and Wilma Marie Korber. Stanley, son of John and Josephine Conrad, was born on a farm near Village Creek, at Fredericktown, MO. Later he moved with his family to Farmington where he met and married Wilma Marie Korber, daughter of Alvin Edward Korber Sr. and Adeline Barbara (Bieser) Korber. To this union was born two daughters, Martha Marie and Josephine Adeline.

Stanley and Wilma spent the first few years of their marriage in Farmington, then moved to a farm near Libertyville, which still remains our home place. In addition to running the farm, Stanley worked as a cream buyer on Harrison Street in Farmington where he purchased cream from farmers and sold it to Sugar Creek or Beatrice Creamery. He also had a cream buying business in Fredericktown at the back of Sonderman's Store.

Stanley had suffered from polio at an early age, and there was not much the doctors could do for victims of this terrible disease. As a result

of this affliction, one of his legs was about three inches shorter than the other. Wilma helped out at the creamery station until she finally went to work at Trimfoot Shoe Company where she remained until her retirement.

Following the death of Stanley, Wilma married Paul Lee Ervin from Knob Lick, MO, and they continued to live on the farm. Paul had served in the Battle of Normandy and other engagements in Northern France where he was wounded and received the Silver Star and a Purple Heart.

Martha married, then divorced, having two children, Donna Marie and Ray Lynn Moore. Both children graduated from Farmington High. Donna married Murray "Bud" Norman and has two children, Nicholas Murray and Jennifer Marie. Bud works for the City of Farmington as Director of Parks and Recreation. Donna is a homemaker and good mother.

Stanley and Wilma with daughters, Martha and Jody

Ray Lynn married, divorced and has two children, Ryan Lynn and Ashley Marie. Ray served in the US Army in Korea and Germany, then served in the Missouri National Guard. Ashley was born in Germany, Ryan in Colorado Springs, CO. Ray is now married to Esther Rowe and has two step-daughters, Laryssa and Kaycelyn.

Martha has been married for the last several years to Bobby Ray Darrough, son of Marguritte and Irving Darrough of Parrish, AL. Martha attended Libertyville Grade School and Farmington High School. She worked at Biltwell and Thorngate as a machine operator then as a supervisor and retired after 26-1/2 years.

She met Bob when he was working at building the Community Hospital, as a drywall and taping foreman, for a company out of Memphis, TN. He later worked at the same profession for construction companies in St. Louis. Both are now retired and enjoying life at a slower pace. Martha is a member of the Eastern Star #430, Bob a member of St. Francois Lodge #234 at Libertyville, a 32nd Scottish Rite Mason, Three Rivers Shrine Club at Poplar Bluff, and American Legion #0416 and IOOF #48 of Farmington.

CONRAD/TINNIN/RATCLIFF - Josephine Adeline "Jody" Conrad born in Farmington, MO to Stanley Winslow Conrad, son of John I. Conrad and Josephine Barks Conrad of Farmington and Wilma Marie (Korber) Conrad, daughter of Alvin E. Korber Sr. and Adeline Barbara (Bieser) Korber of Farmington, MO. Josephine went to Libertyville Grade School and Farmington High School. She married Marvin P. Tinnin, son of Thomas P. and Agnes Tinnin of Fredericktown, MO. Five children were born to this marriage, Sherry Jo, Thomas Winslow, Cynthia Ann, Terry Lynn and Gregory Lynn. They divorced and she later married Charles David Ratcliff, son of George and Opal Ratcliff of Farmington. To this marriage two children were born, Tracey Wayne and Christopher Scot. Josephine was a homemaker most of

her time. She worked for Missouri Home Care for six years helping the elderly. Then went back to homemaking and babysitting her grandchildren. She is a member of Ladies Auxiliary Ozark Hills Eagle 3350 of Deslode, MO, Ladies Auxiliary VFW 5896 of Farmington, MO and Farmington Order Eastern Star #430. She lives in Farmington.

Children: Sherry married Claude Andy Huitt Jr., son of Claude Andy Sr. and Marry Huitt. They have two children, Christopher Andrew and Collin Joseph, and live in Farmington. Andy works for Western Press in Leadington, MO and Sherry works for Eric Scott Leather at Ste. Genevieve, MO. Thomas married Pam Doss, daughter of Gene and Lela Doss of Farmington, and they had one daughter, Carmen Nicole, who lives in Bossier City, LA. He divorced and then married Faith Miller, daughter of James and Brenda Miller of East Prairie, MO and has two sons, Dalton Blaine and Cody Alex, and lives in East Prairie, MO. Thomas is an over-the-road truck driver for Riechmann Transport in Granite City, IL. Thomas also is in the Missouri National Guard, Co. A, 1140th Engineer Bn. in Farmington, MO. Faith works for Jakel Inc. of East Prairie, MO.

Cynthia, Terry and Gregory were adopted at an early age. Cynthia married a Howard of Piedmont, MO and they have one child, Amanda. Cynthia is now married to Jerry Stout and they live in Piedmont, MO. Nothing is known about the where abouts of Terry and Gregory. Hope someday to find them.

Tracey married Tina Horn of Deslode, MO, daughter of Wilburn and Ileane Horn. They have three children: Matthew, Michael and Rachael. They all live in St. Charles, MO. Tracey is the manager of St. Peters Wal-Mart. Tina is a good mother and homemaker. Christopher married Denise Heberlie O'Neal, daughter of Stanley and Joyce Herberlie of Farmington. To this marriage one son was born, Ethan. Christopher has two step-children, Justin and Colleen O'Neal, and all live in Farmington. Christopher is an athletic trainer at Farmington Sport and Rehabilitation Center and is a 2nd lieutenant in Missouri National Guard, Co. A, 1140th Engineer Bn. of Sikeston, MO. Denise is a fifth grade teacher at St. Joseph Catholic School in Farmington.

Josephine's husband Charles, was an over-the-road truck driver for different trucking companies. He retired early from Overnite Transportation Company in St. Louis, MO due to cancer which took his life in April 1998. He received many safe driving awards and a lot of long mile awards. He loved hunting, fishing, gardening and helping others however he could.

COOK - Jessie Louise Eaton, daughter of Roy W. and Mildred Hughes Eaton, granddaughter of Aaron and Lucy Wells Eaton, and Arthur and Ida May Ford Hughes, was born in St. Francois County, March 3, 1945. She started school in a one room schoolhouse at Cedar Falls, attended three years at a three room school in Washington County, and completed her high school at Farmington, graduating with the Class of 1962. Her first job was in the office of Trimfoot Shoe Company, where she remains working at this time.

Her marriage to Mike Statler ended in divorce, with no children involved. In June 1969, she married James Leon Cook, son of Raymond and Pearl Merritt Cook, grandson of Sam and Belle Goodfellow Cook, and Frank and Elma Robbs Merritt. Jim was born Feb. 14, 1945 in St. Francois County. He also started school at Cedar Falls School, finishing high school in Deslode. His first marriage to Shirley Coram ended in divorce, and they have a son, Mark Allen Cook.

Jim spent a short time in the Army Reserves,

but his main employment has been installing overhead doors and operators. He is self-employed.

Jim and Jessie have one daughter, Jaime Gayle Cook, who is finishing her college in Springfield, MO, after attending two years at Mineral Area College in Park Hills. Mark is married to Debbie Bova of St. Louis. They have a son, Joshua James, born April 1998. They make their home at Troy, MO. *Submitted by Jesse Eaton Cook.*

CORBEN - June Arnold Corben and wife, Mardsena Frances, settled in Farmington in March 1995. For years they had driven from Rolla to visit their daughter, Lynn, her husband, Dale Crites, and their children living here.

June and Frances met in Missouri and were married March 17, 1942 in Muskogee, OK. As June served prior to, and throughout WWII in the US Navy, the couple moved to San Diego where June was stationed. When his unit was transferred to the European Theater of Operations, Frances returned to Oklahoma.

At war's end, June rejoined his family in Oklahoma. June was transferred to the Active Naval Reserve in which he served until retirement. The Corbens continued to make their home in Oklahoma. Their two daughters, Marsdena Kay "Dena" Walker and June Lynn Crites, were born in Muskogee.

In 1955 the family moved to June's native state

June and Frances Corben, 1982.

of Missouri and have called Neosho, Rolla, and Farmington home. Dena and Lynn grew to maturity in Rolla where they met and married their spouses.

June and Frances have six grandchildren, nine great-grandchildren and one step-great-grandchild, all living in Missouri.

June retired from federal civil service in December 1977. After rearing their girls, Frances also worked as a federal employee, resigning when June did.

In early retirement they traveled extensively and soon adopted an RV lifestyle. Their trips often followed ancestral pathways as they became interested in genealogical research. After many years, when they decided it was wise to replant roots, they chose Missouri to be near their progeny and June's siblings in Missouri and Illinois.

June and Frances both have ancestral roots deep in Missouri soil. June was born in Lewis County, MO, one of ten children, nine of whom lived until recent years, six are still living. His father, Seth Arnold Corben, and mother, Selna Maude Walker, were born in Clark County, MO in 1882, where they married in 1900.

Seth Corben descends from Corbin (spelled with an i), family who immigrated to Virginia from England in 1650. Corbin descendants settled in Bourbon County, KY, later some trekked westward. Seth's father, James Jasper Corbin, was born in Missouri in 1858 when his parents settled in Clark County in the early 1850s. Here James married Lucy Elizabeth Dow from Ohio in 1879. Seth was their second son.

June's mother, Selna Maude Walker, was a direct descendent of Benjamin Walker who served with the Third Pennsylvania Regiment in the Revolutionary War. Selena's father, Hugh Scott Walker, was Benjamin's great-grandson. Hugh was born in 1852 in Illinois. Soon thereafter, his parents moved to Clark County, MO. He married

Sarah Elizabeth Ketchum, born in 1857 in Illinois, Clark County, in 1881.

France Corben and an older sister, Lindsay, were born on a cotton plantation south of Little Rock, AR. Their parents, Oliver McKay and Esther Galloway Lippeatt, Arkansas natives, were married in Russellville, AR in May 1917. Sadly, Frances' father, Oliver McKay, died young. After numerous moves, Frances' mother, Esther McKay, with her two little girls, Lindsay and Frances, moved to Fort Gibson, OK to be near Esther's maternal grandmother.

Oliver McKay's father, Dr. Thomas McKay, born in Ireland, immigrated as a young man. Dr. McKay died when Oliver was a boy, and with Oliver's own death at an early age, little is known of the McKay lineage.

Oliver's mother, Hattie Oliver McKay, was born in Howard County, MO in 1880. Hattie's father, Jonathon Butler Oliver, was born in Tennessee in 1843 and came to Missouri as a boy. In 1862, at age 18, he enlisted in the 11th Missouri Infantry, a Confederate Unit. Following the Civil War he married Sarah Madora Green in Howard County, MO in 1867. Hattie, through her mother, Sarah Green, descends from two ancestors who fought in the American Revolution. They are Stephen Green, who was a member of Lee's Legion, Continental Forces of Virginia, and Claibourn Johnson, who served in the Virginia Militia. Descendants of Stephen Green came to Missouri in 1821, settling in Howard County. Claibourn Johnson brought his family to Howard County, MO about 1830.

Frances' mother, Esther Gallows Lippeatt, was the daughter of John William "Jack" Lippeatt whose family immigrated from England when Jack was 11 years old in 1884. His family were miners. Jack married Bentita Marsdena Gallows in Sebastian County, AR in 1897. Marsdena's mother was a native of England and her father an immigrant from Canada.

The Corbens are members of the First Christian Church of Rolla, MO. June is a 50-year Mason, a past master of that order, and is a current member of Farmington Lodge No. 132. Also, he is a 50-year member of the Scottish Rite and the Bedouin Shrine. He and Frances are 50-year members of the Order of the Eastern Star and are Past Patron and Past Matron, respectively, of that order. *Submitted by June and Frances Corben*

COUNTS - Neoma Counts and her five children: Darlene, Ernest, Olga, Eddie and Jerry, moved to Farmington in August 1957. Before this they had lived at various places in Reynolds County and briefly at Doe Run. Carter Counts, the husband and father, had been engaged in sawmilling. Following a divorce they moved to Farmington.

The children all went through high school in Farmington. Darlene was a freshman when they moved there and Jerry, the youngest, was in the third grade. Neoma went to work as an attendant at the State Hospital in October 1957 and worked there 17 years. They lived on

R-L Bottom Row: Jerry, Olga, Eddie. Top: Neoma, Ernest, Darlene

Doubet Road just behind the State Hospital.

They did not have any transportation and the only way to get into town was to walk through the State Hospital grounds. The children soon found a lot of interesting things to do at the hospital. They visited the canteen and bought snacks. They enjoyed the beautiful gold fish pond in front of the Administration Building. They took a blanket and attended the outside movies each week that the hospital had for the patients to watch all summer. Then in the winter they went inside and enjoyed the movies with the patients. They attended the dances and other entertainment for the patients. They got to swim in the swimming pool at certain times.

Some people were afraid of the mental patients and would not think of doing the things that the Counts children did. All the children except Jerry worked at the state hospital for a while after they graduated from high school. Darlene worked as a secretary in the accounting department. Ernest worked in custodial work. Olga worked as an aide and nurse and Eddie worked as an aide on the wards. Eddie did many hours of volunteer work in the community relations office with Charlie Mink. He even won a trip to New Orleans one year as the "Volunteer of the Year."

Ernest, Eddie and Jerry all delivered the *Daily Journal* on bicycles. They had routes in Farmington and DeLassus. They all had paper routes at the same time. Jerry was only nine years old when he started. That was a busy time at the Counts house when they brought the three big bundles of papers. Everyone helped get them rolled and got the boys started on their route. They delivered them rain or snow, on bicycles. Jerry won "Carrier of the Year" one year. Darlene and Olga did baby sitting and house cleaning for a lot of people.

Darlene married Bob Lerche from Fredericktown and they are still living on a farm in the Silver Mines area. They have a girl and a boy. Shirley lives in the Los Angeles area and does art work. Keith married Kim Tripp and they have a son, Clay. Keith and Kim live in Fredericktown and have an insurance business. Ernest married Pat Rowe from Hammond, IN and they still live in Hammond. Ernest and Pat have three children. Stacy is attending college and Rachel is a senior in high school. Little Ernie is in the second grade.

Olga (Gayle) married Paul Byington and they have three girls. Karen married Terry Kelch and they live in Arnold. They have Courtney and Christian. Cheri married David Goldsmith and they have Danielle and Devin. They live in Farmington. Carmen married Peter Venezia, they live in the St. Louis area and have one little girl, Isabel. Olga later married Jim Bledsoe and they live in Arnold. Olga (Gayle) is a registered nurse at St. Anthony hospital in St. Louis.

Eddie lives in Philadelphia and works as a computer programmer for a company called Center for Professional Education.

Jerry married Beverly Stanton and they have two children, Michael and Heather, who are both students at Missouri University in Columbia. Jerry is a pharmacist and owns and operates his own drug store in Marshfield, MO. In 1996 Jerry had a heart and kidney transplant at the same time from the same donor. He is in good health and works six days a week now. *Submitted by Neoma Counts*

COUNTS - Jeff Counts, a young man of 23, was working with a threshing crew near Hazel Run. When the crew came to the Kennedy farm, Jeff saw a lovely young girl with blue eyes and dark hair swinging on a gate. Jeff said to a fellow workman, "I'm going to marry that girl!" Two years later, he and Sallie Kennedy were married.

Jefferson Douglas Counts was born in 1873 to Jefferson Nicholas Counts and Mary Douglas

Jefferson Douglas Counts

Farmer, on a farm just out of Farmington. Gus, an older brother, was the first rural route mail carrier from Farmington. He rode a horse and carried the mail in a saddlebag. He was also a frequent winner in fiddling contests and a collector of folk songs. He had 100 verses to *A Froggy Went A'Courtin*.

Sallie Kennedy was born in 1880 to William A. Kennedy and Leanora Glascock in Paducah, KY. The family moved to Hazel Run when Sallie was 3 years old. Later they lived in Farmington. Sallie attended Carleton College before her marriage. William Kennedy served in the Civil War. He was the last Civil War veteran in Farmington.

Sallie and Jeff had seven children: one boy, Jeff Jr.,

Sallie Kennedy Counts

and six girls: Lucille, Jessalyn, Minnie Alva, Maghenrye, Marie, and Yalette. The family was living on the Counts farm when Jeff was elected to the office of county judge in the mid-20s. Before his term started, he was stricken with tuberculosis and confined to bed. The family moved to town because Governor Sam Baker ruled that if Jeff met with the other judges a certain number of hours a month, he could keep his position, so the court met in Jeff's bedroom. Later, Jeff was able to join the other judges in being the first court to occupy the new courthouse.

In 1929 Jeff, Sallie and the three youngest children joined Lucille in Pasadena, CA, where the mild climate would be better for Jeff's health. M.W. Rickus (Bus) drove them across country in an open Buick touring car. They traveled on Route 66, which was not paved except through towns. One motel advertised "Electric Lights." It cost $2.50 a night! The trip took 10 days. They were happy that there was Missouri air in all four tires when they arrived in California! Marie and Bus did not stay long in Pasadena. On June 2, 1930, they were married and went back to Farmington.

The seven children led productive lives. There were four teachers: Lucille and Yalette in California, Jessalyn in the Lutheran School in Farmington and Minnie Alva in several country schools in St Francis County. (She later worked in social welfare.) Maghenrye held several positions in the St. Louis area. Jeff Jr. was a tile contractor in Southern California. Marie worked 27 years in "The Factory." After she retired, she volunteered almost 2,000 hours in the hospital. Three of the girls were married to local men: Jessalyn to Earl Meyer, Minnie Alva to Jerry Rickus and Marie to M.W. Rickus. Jeff and Sallie continued to live in Pasadena with Lucille. Jeff died in 1937, Sallie in 1967.

Farmington has always been a special place to the Counts family. Lucille, who traveled extensively, always said there was no place more beautiful than the Missouri Ozarks. When Yalette visits Marie and her family every year, she says she has lived in California 70 years, but coming to Farmington is coming home. *Submitted by Yalette Counts Gore*

COUNTS/HARTER - Cora Bell Counts, born March 17, 1874, lived in Farmington and attended Baptist College before teaching school for three years in country schools. During her teaching career, she met Frank Thomas Harter, born Jan. 18, 1874, and married him Nov. 2, 1897. They lived in Ste. Genevieve County and became the parents of John Counts Harter, Orval Francis Harter, Viola Harter Wade, Burl Thomas Harter, Emmett Simon Harter and Joseph Lyde Harter. Frank and Cora Harter were farmers on Route 3, Farmington until 1946 when they retired and moved to Farmington.

Their eldest son, John, known as J.C., married Harriett Gregory, daughter of Thomas

Cora Counts Harter

J. and Myrtle Dell Blanton Gregory, on Oct. 2, 1919 in Farmington. J.C. and Harriett lived in Farmington for a few years before moving to St. Louis County where J.C. worked as a mechanic for Kroger Company. After a few years, they moved with their three boys to Ste. Genevieve County to a farm near Coffman.

During the next 12 years, they had six other children. They were the parents of Thomas J. Harter, William S. Harter, Robert D. Harter, James R. Harter, Cora Dell Harter Johnson, Betty Harter Miller, Doris Harter Gannon, John G. Harter and Joseph David Harter. The Harters were staunch supporters of education with Mr. Harter serving on Board of Education of rural school districts in Ste. Genevieve County.

J.C. and Harriett moved to Farmington in 1955, where they owned and operated a launderette. They later became employees of State Hospital #4 and Mr. Harter became self-employed with aluminum window and awning sales and service. Their children, with the exception of Cora Dell, who is married to Sherman Johnson and lives in the area today, moved to various parts of the country, but gathered back at the Harter home for many enjoyable family reunions and celebrations.

J.C. and Harriett were active members of First Baptist Church, Order of Eastern Star and ECMO Shrine Club in Farmington. They had the good fortune to celebrate their 50th, 60th, 65th and 70th wedding anniversaries with their loving children, grandchildren and great-grandchildren in attendance. The last six years of their lives were spent at Presbyterian Manor in Farmington. Their close union ended in 1990 when Mr. Harter died in May and Mrs. Harter died in November after 70+ years of marriage. *Submitted by Cora Dell Johnson*

COZEAN - Rolla was born Nov. 16, 1881, at Cornwall, MO and died July 5, 1961. His parents were Elias and Martha (Stephens) Cozean. Both were born in Madison County. Elias was of French heritage and Martha, Irish. They resided on a farm in Cornwall and had nine children. Elias died at the age of 54, resulting from injuries incurred when thrown from his horse. Martha tilled the fields to eke out a living. She could pick up a snake by its tail and snap off its head. The girls did the housekeeping. The older boys left home when they were young and sent monies from their wages to help support the family. Martha was fun loving, sharp witted, and had many friends.

Rolla's grandparents were George and Eliza (White) Cozean. George might have been born in Kentucky or Arkansas. Eliza was born in Arkansas. They married in 1838 in St. Francois County and had four children. Eliza's parents were Elias and Elillies (Barron) White.

Rolla and Elva (Rinke) Cozean were married June 15, 1910 at Flat River where he worked in the mines.

Elva was born May 3, 1885 at De Soto and expired April 9, 1967. Elva's parents were Henry and Catherine Rutledge Rinke. Henry was born in Soest, Germany to Lutheran parents. He came to America in 1873, being 13 years old, avoiding conscription into the Prussian military. Having little formal education, he worked at various jobs while in the Jefferson County area. In 1901 he opened Rinke Undertaking and Tin Company in Flat River. He enabled three sons-in-law to become undertakers. These were Rolla Cozean, Alvin Hood and Raymond Caldwell. Henry was the first mayor of Flat River.

Elva's mother, Catherine, (Rutledge) Rinke was born near Rush Tower, Jefferson County. She was one of seven children born to John and Drucella (Henry) Rutledge at the family farm.

Rolla and Elva purchased the Farmington Undertaking and Furniture Company from Henry Rinke in 1915. Later the business moved to North Washington Street and was re-named Cozean Funeral Home, with the family residing upstairs. There were four children: Hugo (Zelda Martin), Caroline (Clifford) Detring, Bud Harriet Miller) and Jack (Frances Munzer).

When Rolla was appointed postmaster, Elva and son, Hugo, formed a partnership. Later, the business was moved to the present location on Columbia Street. Hugo soon became sole owner with Elva continuing to work in the office.

Elva was a good cook and homemaker, known for her home made bread and angel food cakes. She was a devout Baptist and loved pretty hats.

Rolla, lastly, was a probation officer. He served as city alderman and was a staunch Democrat. He enjoyed pinochle and the kitchen would be blue with cigar smoke and reek with a terrible odor when friends would join him for a game. He enjoyed fishing and liked sports. He had a perpetual whistle and always carried chewing gum to give to those he met. He was affectionately referred to as "Pop" Cozean by many who knew him. He was a member of the Odd Fellows and Masonic Lodges. He was particular about his appearance and one could often detect a faint scent of "Old Spice" after shave. *Submitted by Caroline Cozean Detring and John M. Cozean*

COZEAN - "Ah, what an actress," is the way the Cape Girardeau High School yearbook, *The Girardot*, described Zelda Martin in its 1932 edition. Following her marriage to Charles Hugo Cozean May 19, 1935, Zelda put her acting abilities to good use over the years in a variety of community activities in the Farmington area before her death on Nov. 28, 1984.

A seventh generation descendant of the Rev. William Murphy and Sarah (Barton) Murphy who founded Farmington, Zelda was born Dec. 31, 1913, at Quaker, MO, the oldest of seven children of Harlan Edward and Josephine (Jarvis) Martin. Her brothers and sisters were Edsel, Cullen, Lowell, Meredith "Jack," Geneva Martin Klein and Charlotte Martin Rocket.

Hugo Cozean was born March 21, 1911, at Flat River, MO, the son of Rolla and Elva Cozean. Elva was one of six children of Henry Rinke and Elizabeth Rutledge. Henry was a pioneer embalmer, funeral director and community leader in the Lead Belt dating back to 1901. In his obituary printed April 26, 1929, *The Lead Belt News* noted that "perhaps no man in Flat River was better known than was Henry Rinke." He was elected the first mayor of Flat River following its first incorporation. Rolla Cozean was born in Madison County,

Charles Cozean Jr., age 3

one of nine children of Elias Milburn and Martha Ellen (Stephens) Cozean. Soon after his completion of embalming school, Rolla and Elva moved to Farmington where they purchased the former Lang Undertaking Co. from Henry Rinke in 1915. Hugo, who was often called "Zip" because of his running skills on the Farmington High School football team, began working at the funeral home in the mid-1930s.

The Cozeans were involved in many community activities. Zelda was frequently asked to give programs at a wide variety of civic functions. Hugo was County Public Administrator for a number of years and also served on the Farmington Public School Board for a record 30 years and on the Mineral Area College Board of Trustees for 10 years up to the time of his death in December 1982.

Zelda Cozean in 1932

They are the parents of six natural children: Charles H. Cozean, MD, of Cape Girardeau, married to the former Carole Eberhart; Jon D. Cozean, Ph.D., Farmington; Robin Cozean, Neosho, MO; Mary (Mrs. James) Alexander, Ph.D., Panama City, FL; Nancy Jean (Mrs. Donald) Jacob, Poughkeepsie, NY, and Josephine Elva (Mrs. Harry) Styron, Branson, MO. There are eight grandchildren: Laura (Mrs. Bart) DeBrock, Vincennes, IN;

Charles Hugo Cozean Sr.

Charles H. Cozean III, McLean, VA; and John Eberhart Cozean, Columbia, MO; Kevin Alexander, Irving, CA; Josephine Lauren Jacob, Poughkeepsie, NY and Cole Jarvis Styron, Richard Henry Styron and Thomas Cozean Styron of Branson, MO. Great-grandchildren are Erica and William DeBrock of Vinennes, IN.

Nine chosen children of Zelda and Hugo are Betty Yeager, Patricia Patterson, Judith Butler and Edward Mackley, all of Farmington; Mary Christy, Poplar Bluff; Linda Foreman, Quincy, IL; Elaine Moore, Colorado Springs, CO and Richard and Kenneth Mackley of Columbia, MO.

CRITES - Dale Wayne Crites was born in Poplar Bluff, MO Jan. 8, 1947. His parents are Dale Edward and Mildred Fern (Brotherton) Crites. They lived in Dexter, MO until 1957 when his father, who was a Missouri State Patrolman, was transferred to Rolla and put in charge of the Patrol Training Academy. His grandparents were Ira McPherson and Anna Columbia (Shirley) Crites of Patton and Charles Edward and Nellie Estelle (Tinnin) Brotherton of Fredericktown. Ira's parents were Davault and Martha Ann Delilah (Rader) Crites. Anna's parents were William

Sgt. Dale W. and Lynn Crites

Andrew Jackson and Hettie Adaline (Lawson) Shirley; Charles's parents were John Lewis and Susan Jane (Fronabarger) Brotherton; Nellie's parents were Andrew King and Frances Ellen (Baker) Tinnin. Most of Dale's ancestors lived in and around Madison, Bollinger and Cape Girardeau Counties.

June Lynn (Corben) Crites was born in Muskogee, OK, Aug. 27, 1948. Her parents are June Arnold and Marsdena Frances (McKay) Corben. They lived in Ft. Gibson, OK until 1954 when the family moved to Neosha, MO. From there they moved to Rolla, MO in the summer of 1958.

Dale and Lynn are the typical high school sweethearts. They both had mutual friends and knew of each other but didn't begin dating one another until 1964. Dale graduated from Rolla High School in 1965 and Lynn in 1966.

On Oct. 28, 1967 Dale and Lynn were married. On Feb. 4, 1968 Dale entered the Missouri State Highway Patrol Academy at Rolla, graduating in

Jason W. Crites and his buddy, Kozmo

May 1968. On graduation day the new troopers learned to which troop they would be assigned and Dale found out he was going to Troop C. Dale and Lynn drove to Troop C that same day and learned from Capt. Barton they were coming to Flat River and the Leadbelt. Dale was thrilled. Being a small town boy and having grandparents in Fredericktown and Patton he was familiar with the area and knew he would love working in St. Francois and Washington Counties. On the ride back to Rolla, Lynn asked Dale "Where in the world is the Leadbelt and what in the world is a slime pond?"

In June 1968, Dale and Lynn moved to the Leadbelt and rented a house in Desloge. While living there their first son, Jeffery Scott, was born Feb. 22, 1969. In October 1970 they bought their first home at 408 S. "A" Street and moved to Farmington. This was the first time a state trooper had been allowed to make permanent residence in Farmington. On Feb. 27, 1975 their second son, Jason Wayne, was born.

Dale was promoted to corporal in 1980 and transferred to St. Louis County where he worked for one year. In 1981, the Troop C satellite station at Flat River was completed and the position of investigative officer was added to the personnel at the satellite. Dale requested a transfer to the satellite station and applied for the investigative officer position. Dale received the transfer and became a criminal investigator for the highway patrol assigned to the Intelligence and Investigation Division.

In February 1982, Dale and a fellow trooper left to attend the Canadian Police College in Ottawa, Canada. There he received training to become a certified polygraphist. Dale and his fellow classmate were the first two troopers sent from Missouri to receive training outside of the United States and the third and fourth police officers from the United States to receive training in the Polygraph Examiners Training Course. While in Canada, Dale was promoted to the rank of sergeant. He graduated from polygraph school and returned to Missouri in June 1982 to continue his investigative and polygraph career.

While Dale was working and attending numerous investigative schools, Lynn was raising Jeff and Jason and taking her turn at being room mother and Boy Scout den mother. In January 1984, Lynn began volunteer work at the Farmington Public Library. In February 1984, she began working there part-time. In 1985, she was promoted to assistant librarian and in the spring of 1988 she took over the job of library director, the job she continues to hold today. One accomplishment of which she's particularly proud is the expansion to the library in 1992. This literally doubled the size of the existing library, allowing for a larger children's area, meeting rooms and a separate genealogy room.

Dale and Lynn's older son, Jeff, graduated from Farmington High School in 1987 and attended Mineral College. On Nov. 14, 1992, he married Margie Christina "Crissy" Taylor.

Their younger son, Jason, graduated from Farmington High School in 1993. While in high school, Jason was a member of the tennis team his sophomore, junior and senior years, Oui-Si Club his junior and senior years, on the basketball team his freshman, sophomore and junior years, and spent several summers lifeguarding at the city pool. He attended one year at Mineral Area College before attending college at Southeast Missouri State where he is now pursuing a career in wildlife management.

On Aug. 31, 1998, Dale retired from the Missouri State Highway Patrol after working 31 years. He is currently an investigator for the State Judicial Commission on Retirement, Removal and Discipline. He will continue to do this as long as it doesn't become a full-time job or interfere with his grandkids, golf, fishing or restoration of his '51 Chevy truck.

Dale is a current member and past master of the Farmington Masonic Lodge #132, Farmington Elks Lodge, Sword of Bunker Hill, Scottish Rite and a member of the Missouri Polygraph Association. Lynn is the current president of the Farmington Kiwanis Club, vice-president of the United Way of Farmington, a member of the Missouri Public Library Directors and chairman of the Bicentennial History Book Committee.

Lynn continues to work at the library, but may hang it up if Dale seems to be having too much fun in his retirement. In the summer she loves to work in her flower garden and golf with Dale and wants to devote more time to the family genealogy. *Submitted by Lynn Crites.*

CRITES - Jeffrey Scott Crites is the son of Dale and Lynn Crites of Farmington. He was born Feb. 22, 1969, at Madison County Memorial Hospital in Fredericktown. In October 1970, his family moved from Desloge to 408 S. "A" St. in Farmington. He graduated from Farmington High School in 1987. While in school he played on the

football team all through middle school and into and through his junior year in high school. Upon graduation he attended Mineral Area College and worked for Wal-Mart.

In April 1991, he joined the Farmington Police Department, working as a radio dispatcher. In July 1992, he was commissioned as a police officer and worked the road as a uniformed patrolman. In January 1995, he was transferred from patrol duty to the Detective Division. In December 1998, Jeff was promoted to the rank of corporal and made head of the Detective Division.

Taylor, Jeff, Crissy and Corben Crites, 1999

On Nov. 14, 1992, he married Margie Christina "Crissy" Taylor, daughter of Darrell Wayne and Margie Ellen (Jones) Taylor of Irondale, MO. Crissy was born Aug. 4, 1970, at Farmington Community Hospital, Parkland Health Center. Her grandparents were Jessie Albert and Mary Emma (Pratt) Taylor of Irondale, MO and Joel Lester and Margie Alberta (Hampton) Jones of Doe Run, MO. Crissy attended West County High School and graduated in 1988. While in high school she played on both the basketball and volleyball teams, was a member of the concert band, choir, and National Honor Society. After graduation she attended Mineral Area College. Crissy worked as an office manager at Helzberg Jewelry in South County Center and as a receptionist for the Mineral Area Program in Mineral Area Regional Medical Center.

On Oct. 8, 1995, their first son, Taylor Wayne, was born and on Aug. 15, 1998, their second son, Corben Jackson, was welcomed into the family. Crissy is now self-employed, taking care of children in her home so she can enjoy watching her own children grow as well.

Jeff is a member of the Farmington Masonic Lodge #132 and the Farmington Elks Lodge. Jeff, Crissy, Taylor and Corben are members of the First Baptist Church of Farmington. *Submitted by Jeff and Crissy Crites*

CROUCH - Our family traces its Farmington roots back to 1845. Our daughter, Jennifer, is the fifth generation of our Farmington family. Please refer to the Crouch-Manley family biography for further information on John's side of the family.

John, Kathryn and Jennifer Crouch

John is the son of the late Dr. F.R. Crouch and Mary Manley Crouch. He came from a family of four children. John is a CPA and in 1975 founded an accounting firm that now employs 15 people. He works within a few blocks of where his father, grandfather and great-grandfather worked. John received a BS from the University of Missouri and a master's degree from the Uni-

versity of Illinois. He served in the Army for two years from 1970-1972 during the Vietnam era. John was born in Farmington in 1947.

Dr. F. R. and Mary Crouch

Kathryn is the daughter of Edward Frystak and Virginia Skorupa Frystak. Kathryn was born and raised in the Chicago area. She has a BA from Saint Xavier College and a master's degree in library science from the University of Illinois. She is a professional librarian but has devoted her full-time to the home in the last 12 years. Her father and mother were both also raised in the Chicago area. Her father was an accountant and worked for various companies in the Chicago area in comptroller and chief financial officer positions. Her mother took care of the home and raised Kathryn and her younger brother, Eric. Edward Frystak and Virginia Skorupa Frystak were both born in 1925. John and Kathryn met at the University of Illinois and were married in 1973.

John and Kathryn were blessed with the birth of their daughter, Jennifer, in 1987. Jennifer is a student at Saint Joseph Catholic School.

Kathryn's grandmother on her mother's side was named Victoria Misiaszek Skorupa. She immigrated to the United States from Tarnow, Poland at the age of 23 in 1921. Her ocean voyage lasted three weeks. Her first sight of America was the Statue of Liberty followed by Ellis Island.

Kathryn's grandfather, Walter Skorupa, immigrated to the United States from Tarnow, Poland at the age of 15 in 1913. Walter was one of the first owners of a Model T Ford in Chicago. As a young man he traveled over the western United States working on the crews that built the giant railroads for our country. His best friends during this period were an American Indian and a Chinese man. They did not understand each other's languages so they communicated by gestures. He became a car and truck mechanic. Kathryn's grandparents married in 1923, and settled in Chicago where they resided for the rest of their lives.

Kathryn's grandmother on her father's side was named Pauline Piecuch Frystak. She immigrated from Poland in 1915 and settled in Chicago. She worked as an ironer in a hotel. Her grandfather, Louis Frystak, immigrated from Poland in about 1900. He settled in Indiana. He worked as a cook on the Sante Fe Railroad. They married and lived in Chicago for the rest of their lives.

MANLEY/CROUCH - The Manley family history in Farmington covers four generations. Henri Manley was born in 1845 in Ste. Genevieve. At 17, he enlisted in the Union Army. After the Civil War ended he worked on wagons carrying ore between Iron Mountain and Ste. Genevieve. He settled in Farmington opening a shop, making and repairing shoes. He married Sophia Louise Kinneman. Her grandparents were German immigrants to the St. Louis area; her parents moved to a farm near Knob Lick. Six children were born to Henri and Sophia. The second son, named Henry William, stayed in Farmington after finishing high school, worked at Klein Grocer Company, and became principal owner of the store. Henry was prominent in civic affairs, influential in establishing the first street lighting, and carried a leadership role in his church. At the time of his death he was called the #1 citizen of Farmington.

Family of Henry W. and Madia K. Manley in 1927. Front Row: Bessie, Alice with Madia, Henry, Helen. Back Row: Robert, Jack, Betty, Mary, James

Henry W. and Madia Katherine McKamey were married in 1908. Education was very important to them. They were proud to see all eight of their children with college degrees, unusual at that time. Madia was the daughter of Susan Bragg and Robert McKamey, farmer and landowner in northeastern Arkansas. His ancestors were among early Scotch and Irish immigrants to the American colonies. Robert served the Union Army during the Civil War. Susan's family were Confederates, so they combined the Blue and the Gray. She was second cousin to General Braxton Bragg, and also traced her ancestry to Betsy Ross, maker of our country's first flag.

From the third generation of Henry and Madia's family, two have remained citizens of Farmington. Robert Bragg Manley received the JD degree from University of Michigan, then served in the Navy during WWII as an officer on a destroyer. After the war, he became a prominent attorney in this area until his retirement in 1997. He is married to Reba Geogianna Rickus, a former schoolteacher. Her parents, George and Birdie Griffin Rickus, moved to Farmington from a farm in southeast Missouri.

Virginia Mary Manley met and later married Francis Richard Crouch, from New York State, when he came to Missouri for college and medical school. His parents, Harry Ensign and Mary Pierce Crouch (she is a relative of President Franklin Pierce), had lived on land settled by their ancestors, early immigrants from England and Wales. When his training was completed, Dr. Crouch chose Farmington for his medical practice and joined Dr. George Lancaster Watkins in 1938. During WWII he left to serve with the 21st General Hospital in Africa and Europe. After his return in 1945, he and Dr. Watkins established the Medical Arts Clinic, which grew into a large group of physicians serving patients from a wide territory.

In addition to his busy practice he was a leader in community, church and Boy Scout affairs. He died in 1977. Mary has also been a responsible citizen also with leadership roles in PTA, schools, Red Cross and church. The Crouch-Manley family had two sons and two daughters. One son, John, chose to stay in his hometown. He will add the story of the 4th generation of Manley. *Submitted by Mary M. Crouch*

CROW - Edward Crow, born 1720-1790, is the first known ancestor to be listed in Crow genealogy records. He was of Irish descent and born in Frederick County, MD. His wife, Pricilla Farmer, was born in 1724 in Maryland. They were par-

ents of 12 children. Son, Joshua, born 1760, died 1830, and wife, Mary Wayman, born ?, died 1827, started the move of the Crow migration westward. They settled in western Kentucky and were parents of eight children.

Their son, Henry W. Crow, born 1803, died 1876, was born in Kentucky and was the first Crow resident of St. Francois County. His wife, Virginia T. Moore, born 1810, died 1882, was born in Kentucky. Before settling in St. Francois County, they made several moves. They, with son Henry and daughter Ellen, moved first to Bloomington, IL where Lucy was born. From there, they settled in Osceola, MO where Spotswood, Marianna, Wayman and William were born. John C., born 1849, died 1928, and Robert were born in St. Francois County.

When Henry first arrived in Farmington, his brother, Wayman Crow, of St. Louis, and Henry were in the merchandising business. Henry soon bought land in Cook Settlement/Libertyville from Zeno Blanks in 1847. He farmed and spent the rest of his life on what has become to be known as the Crow Farm. Zeno Blanks had built a small brick home on the farm. The bricks were made and baked on the farm by brick makers named Samuels of Cook Settlement. Henry had a large addition added to the home by the same brick makers. At this time in 1998, the home is one of the oldest in the area. It has withstood two destructive tornadoes, 1917 and 1969. Henry and Virginia's son, John Cobb Crow, continued the operation of the farm after their death. John bought cattle in the surrounding area and shipped them by rail from Knob Lick to St. Louis market.

John C. Crow married Anne Green Sebastain. They were the parents of one son, Harold W. Crow. Harold was a graduate of Cape Girardeau Normal College in 1908 and taught school in St. Francois County.

Harold married Lydia Ann Detring. At this time, John and Anne moved from the Crow Farm to West College Street in Farmington and John opened a harness and saddle shop on what is now Columbia Street. Harold and Lydia became the operators of the Crow Farm. They were the parents of one son, Wayman Detring Crow, born Nov. 20, 1916. Harold established a herd of Polled Hereford cattle and sold breeding stock. He passed away in 1939. Son Wayman and Lydia continued farming through 1943.

Wayman married Barbara E. "Betty" Conrad. He continued farming and cattle business until his death in 1981. The farm has been managed by his wife since his death. They were the parents of John Wayman Crow and Mary Janet Crow.

John graduated from Rolla in 1966 and has been a designing engineer for Caterpillar Company for 25 years. He married Nancy Aubuchon. They are the parents of Jerry W., Sharon and Terry W. Crow.

Jerry W. Crow married Joy (Harris) Crow. Children: Rebecca and John Matthew Crow. Sharon Crow married Brian Reeves. Children: Corrine and Evan Benjamin Reeves. Terry W. Crow married Trisha Quigley. Mary Janet Crow graduated from St. Louis University with a degree in medical records and allied health services. She married Richard D. Sidelnik and they live in Austin, TX. Mary is assistant to the bureau chief of the State Health Department of Texas.

The following Crow family members are buried in the Libertyville Christian Cemetery: Henry W. and wife, Ellen Crow; Lucy Crow Hill and husband, John Hill; John C. Crow and wife, Anne; Harold W. Crow and wife, Lydia; and Wayman D. Crow. *Submitted by Barbara E. Crow Griffin*

CRUNCELTON - John Paca and Elizabeth Smith Paca had two sons. One son, William Paca, born

1740, died 1799, was a US statesman; signer of the Declaration of Independence; born in Hartford County, MD; governor of Maryland, 1782-86; and district judge, 1789-99.

William and Caroline Cruncelton celebrated their 50th wedding anniversary in front of their home at 929 North Washington, Farmington, MO. At that time their property was not in the city limits or when George and Iva Williams purchased the property in the '50s. Grandpa had chickens, one mule and one cow. He took milk to the George Beck family. Uncle Ora used the mule to make sorghum molasses and sold for extra income. In later years, Grandpa became blind.

Another son, Aquilla Paca, had a daughter named Priscilla who married Richard Boothby Dallam. They had a daughter, Frances Ann Dallam, born March 6, 1806, in Hartford County, MD. The Dallams moved to Kentucky in 1806. Frances Ann Dallam married William Christopher Ashburn who was born Oct. 7, 1833, in Hickman County, KY, and died in St. Francois County, MO on April 23, 1899. George Henry had married Julia Mostiller and they had a daughter, Caroline Pearl Ashburn, born April 20, 1863, died March 25, 1953. Caroline Pearl Ashburn married in March 1880 to William Mortomore Cruncelton, born March 6, 1856, died Oct. 12, 1936. From this union, William and Caroline's children were as follows:

1) George Ora, born April 16, 1881, died Dec. 27, 1969, never married.

2) Anna Bell, born Sept. 1, 1883, died July 10, 1945, married James Frederick Holmes, born Feb. 19, 1876, died July 21, 1970. Their family includes:

Raymond Russell, born July 25, 1905, died March 28, 1993, married Dec. 15, 1926 to Reva Kerlagon, born Oct. 9, 1903, died Nov. 18, 1987. Their son Norman Francis, born Nov. 17, 1928, married Helen Cunningham, born Aug. 24, 1929. Their children: Mark, born Feb. 23, 1960, and Daneen, born July 10, 1964.

Mary Caroline, born Feb. 28, 1907, married Aug. 10, 1923, to Wilburn A. Cunningham. Their children are Homer Lee, born April 20, 1925, died Jan. 11, 1933, Ronald Ray, born April 1, 1933, and Jean Marilyn, born Dec. 3, 1938.

Bernice, born Oct. 21, 1908, died Sept. 24, 1983. Married Nov. 2, 1925 to Ernest David Kerlagon, born May 16, 1907, died Nov. 29, 1980. Children: Harold Eugene, born Jan. 31, 1927, and Charles Edward, born Jan. 8, 1944.

Audra Lucille, born Aug. 27, 1912, died May 21, 1957, married December 1931, to Orville B. Pratt, born Nov. 19, 1905. Children: Annabel and Dale Lee.

Marvin Lee, born May 22, 1919, died Oct. 7, 1939, married July 1939, to Gladys Bollinger. Son, Marvin Lee Jr., born April 11, 1940.

Stepsister, Hazel, married Claude Mitchell. Children: Mardoni, Mable, Happy, Claude, Clark and Mark.

3) Julia, born April 17, 1885, died March 28, 1971, married Frank Cole and their child was James Lee.

4) Charles Lee, born June 7, 1889, died June

14, 1918, married June 26, 1912 to Elsie Glover, born March 27, 1894, died May 25, 1972. Children:

Arthur, born May 26, 1913, died Aug. 1, 1971, married Sophie and had no children.

Caroline, born May 27, 1915, married April 18, 1936 to James Henneberry, born ?, died Sept. 1, 1993. Children Mary Jane, born Oct. 12, 1940, died Aug. 25, 1988, and Judith Ann, born Jan. 13, 1951.

5) Rose Ione, born April 22, 1891, died Feb. 13, 1973, married Nov. 1, 1908 to Fred Joseph Landolt, born Sept. 3, 1887, died Oct. 28, 1942.

Son Lee, born Feb. 15, 1910, died March 4, 1976, married Aug. 4, 1928 to Mary Wunning, born Sept. 25, 1910, died April 9, 1990. Children: Anna Lee, born Aug. 9, 1931, Charles Ray, born Feb. 14, 1934, died Sept. 23, 1986 and Shirley, born Nov. 1, 1937.

Harold, born Sept. 10, 1911, died March 10, 1972, married Jan. 22, 1931 to Loretta Horn, born June 19, 1913, died April 9, 1988. Their children: Gene, born Dec. 21, 1931, died April 3, 1994, and Janet, born Aug. 4, 1943.

Lena Mae, born May 14, 1914, died July 17, 1997, married Jan. 23, 1932 to Rae Thurman, born May 13, 1912, died June 29, 1986. Their children: Juanita, born July 10, 1932; Donald, born Oct. 17, 1933; Barbara, born March 28, 1942.

Iva Louise, born Nov. 29, 1918, died Jan. 24, 1992, married Oct. 12, 1935 to George Williams, born July 21, 1912, died June 30, 1954. Their children: Georgia, born July 1, 1936, and Darlene, born Feb. 19, 1939.

Ruby, born Oct. 5, 1921, married Sept. 18, 1938 to Earl Faircloth, born Aug. 19, 1917. Their children: James, born Oct. 24, 1941, died March 31, 1988; Darrell, born May 10, 1945; Nancy, born June 24, 1952.

Reva, born Oct. 5, 1921, married Feb. 9, 1944 to Perry Morris, born July 10, 1919. Their daughter Patsy was born May 17, 1944.

Fred Joseph Jr., born Feb. 20, 1926, married Oct. 7, 1944 to Helen Hager, born May 11, 1926. Their children: Joyce, born Nov. 7, 1945, Carol, born Jan. 27, 1948, Jerry, born Jan. 3, 1949, and Fred Joseph II, born Nov. 26, 1956.

6) Clara Louise, born July 29, 1893, died Sept. 14, 1979, married Clinton Cunningham. Their children:

Melvin, born March 2, 1915, died July 11, 1995, married Aug. 20, 1937 to Darline Killarley died Jan. 23, 1994. Their children: Carol died August 1992 and Doug.

Marvin, born April 2, 1917, married July 31, 1937 to Glena Songer. Their children: William Bruce, born April 24, 1941, Robert, born Nov. 27, 1942 and Benita Lou, born Feb. 11, 1946.

Ila, born Feb. 29, 1920, married George Bixler. Their children: Barbara, George, Thomas and Ila. Ila divorced George and married Donald Soltman.

James William, born 1925, died at 6 months in 1926. Clara was divorced and married Allan Morrison in 1941.

7) Jennie May, born March 12, 1898, died Sept. 30, 1980 married Walter Barron. Walter had a son, William, and a daughter, Elizabeth, by a previous marriage.

8) Thomas Earl, born Jan. 24, 1900, died Nov. 28, 1982, married Feb. 21, 1921 to Bethel David, born Aug. 23, 1901, died Feb. 13, 1978. Their children:

Marie, born June 15, 1921, died Aug. 13, 1973, married Aug. 26, 1943 to James Edward Burnette, born Nov. 12, 1917, died May 1, 1993. No children.

Virginia, born May 28, 1924, married June 24, 1944 to Cecil Putman, born Sept. 9, 1923, died Sept. 21, 1990. Their children: Karen, born

April 2, 1945, and Keith, born Oct. 22, 1951.

9) Lena Agusta, born Aug. 17, 1904, died June 23, 1990, married Williard Cunningham and had no children. They divorced and Lena later married Eurial Gohn.

The family has remained close and the first cousins remaining are Mary Cunningham, Caroline Henneberry, Ruby Faircloth, Reva Morris, Marvin Cunningham, Ila Soltman and Virginia Putman. As of April 1998, the property no longer belongs to the family. We cherish our memories and continue to share them with each other. We praise God for blessing our family in good times and bad. One keepsake I have of great-grandpa Cruncelton is his mustasche cup still in perfect condition. *Written by Darlene McWilliams, daughter of Iva Louise Williams, grand-daughter of Ione Landolt and great-granddaughter of Caroline Cruncelton*

CUNNINGHAM - Revolutionary War Patriot James Cunningham (Rev. War file No. SI6746 certificate No. 2.345MO) was born in January 1756 in Augusta County, VA. He died in April 1844 in St. Francois County, MO and was buried on his homestead near Farmington. His wife, Elizabeth, died before the 1840 census was taken.

The Revolutionary War record for James, summarized below, is found in his pension papers and in the research done by his descendant, Camilla Bricker Cox. She provided the first proof to be accepted by NSDAR that James served in the Revolutionary War.

In August of 1775, James Cunningham volunteered for service in a militia unit commanded by Capt. William Russell and Lt. Bowen. In May 1776, James was called into service to guard the frontier with a militia company and took part in the Battle of Long Island Flats. Sometime later, James joined a detachment of militia to protect the frontier against the Cherokee Indians. In the fall of 1780, James was employed as a waggoner to haul lead from the Chissel Mine in Virginia, to General Greene's army, then stationed in North Carolina. In 1833, James applied for a pension as a veteran of the Revolutionary War. It was granted and he received $40 a month until his death.

Shown in the picture taken in the early 1900s are Mrs. Harriet Cunningham McDaniel and daughter Minnie (Mrs. Reuban Appleberry). Their house still stands on the corner of Liberty Street across from the Presbyterian Home.

Sometime before 1802, James, with his wife and family, arrived in what was later the state of Missouri. In that year he received permission from Pierre De Luziere, Commandant from New Bourbon, District of Ste. Genevieve, to settle on a grant of 1500 arpens (a French arpen is 7/8 of an acre) in what is now St. Francois County, MO. Later, the Board of Land Commissioners, through survey No. 829 by Nathaniel Cook, gave James Cunningham clear American title to the land lying in Murphy's Settlement. In 1827 according to records in Deed Book "A," James and Elizabeth

deeded parcels of this land to each of their sons as "parents affections for a son." Copied from "James and Elizabeth Cunningham" forward by Elizabeth Covington Hoagland.

After the settlement, James Jr. remained on his portion of the land. He was married to Jane Harris and they had a large family, one of whom was Reece B. Cunningham. James Jr. later married Mahala Berry Thomas and they also had children. He died in 1873 and was buried on the estate. Reece B. Cunningham grew to young manhood at the old home and walked the three miles into Farmington to attend school. In 1853, he married Nancy Monroe Williams. He became a blacksmith by trade. After 12 years of "smithing" he returned to his first love, farming. He continued to till the soil until old age. (From the notes of Genevieve Bartch). He then built a home on Liberty Street in Farmington near his daughter, Harriet (Mrs. David McDaniel). Shown in the picture taken in the early 1900s, are Mrs. Harriet Cunningham McDaniel and daughter Minnie (Mrs. Reuban Appleberry). Their house still stands on the corner of Liberty Street across from the Presbyterian Home.

Many descendants of James Cunningham Sr. can still be found living in and around Farmington. A book containing their history and genealogy has been presented to the Farmington Library. *Submitted by Dorothy Bess*

DANE - Thomas D. Dane and Nancy K. Dane settled in Farmington in April 1975, shortly after their marriage in Belle Plaine, IA. Nancy was born in Belle Plaine, IA, Jan. 7, 1950, to Albert F. Lyman and Ruth Nebendahl Lyman. She was the second of four children. Brothers and sister are David, William and Peggy. Nancy graduated from Belle Plaine High School in 1968 and received her BS in elementary education from Iowa State University in 1972.

In November of 1972, she moved to Farmington to work as a house parent at the Presbyterian Home for Children and eventually worked with Tom's mother there. Tom was born Thomas Dorzinski, Jan. 28, 1954, the fifth child of Joseph Dorzinski and Jacquelyn "Jackie" Klotz Dorzinski. Sisters and brothers are Joseph "Skip," Linda Kowalski, Daniel, Frances "Frank," and Philomena "Mimi." The family name was later changed to Dane. Though born in Miami, Tom was raised in Milwaukee, WI, and graduated from Franklin High School in 1972. He worked as a mechanic following graduation.

After a six month stay in Milwaukee following their marriage, Tom and Nancy made the move to Farmington. Nancy taught at St. Joseph Catholic School and Tom worked at Plaza Tire (then located at the corner of Potosi and Karsch). Nancy quit teaching with the arrival of son Damion Thomas, Sept. 26, 1976. Jason Charles was born May 22, 1978. As the boys were growing, the family was active with the Cub Scouts and Boy Scout Troop 471. Both boys achieved the rank of Eagle Scout. Damion graduated from Farmington High School in 1994, Mineral Area College in 1996 and was in his junior year at Southeast Missouri State University when he died of cancer Feb. 17, 1997. Jason graduated from Farmington High School in 1996 and is attending Mineral Area College.

The family presently lives outside of Farmington. Tom is employed at Ozark Steel Fabricators and still works with the Boy Scouts. Nancy is employed by Bodine & Boyd, Inc., teaches Sunday school at Memorial Methodist Church, and is active with the Order of the Eastern Star.

DANIELEY/ANDRIANO - Donald Philip Danieley, son of Charles Everett Danieley and Myrtle Sarah Boyd, was born on the family farm in Ste. Genevieve County. This farm stayed in the Danieley family until 1987. Don's brothers and sisters are Charles, Benton, Dean and Alice (Danieley) Rudloff.

Maxine and Don Danieley

The Danieley family is of Scotch/Irish heritage and can be traced back to James Danieley of Alamance and Guilford Counties in North Carolina. The Bethel Church in Alamance County, NC is near the Danieley Cemetery in which several ancestors are buried. Don's great-grandfather, James, married Mary (last name unknown). His grandfather, John T. Danieley, married Margaret C. Alexander.

In 1949 Don graduated from Ste. Genevieve High School and was farming with his father on the family farm near Coffman, MO in Ste. Genevieve County. Don also worked as a farm operator on a farm owned by a St. Louis man.

Back L to R: Diane, David, Steve, Marcia. Front L to R: Don and Maxine Danieley.

On Sept. 19, 1952, Don married Maxine Elizabeth Andriano in Farmington. Don owned the American Family Insurance office in Farmington and retired after 42 years in that business. During his insurance career, Don won the American Family Insurance "All-Star Award;" the top honor given by American Family Insurance Group. Since retirement, Don has enjoyed raising cattle on their farm south of Farmington.

Don and Maxine have four children: Donald Stephen and Glenna who live in Oklahoma with their two daughters, Stephanie and Leslie; Phil and Marcia Ann Pease and son, Robby, live in Farmington; Barrett P. and Diane Marie Upchurch live in Chesterfield, MO with their daughters: Katherine, Natalie and Jennna; David Michael and Laura Hill Danieley and daughter, Haleigh, live in Farmington. David and Marcia have continued the family business, each having their own insurance agency in Farmington.

Maxine was born in Neosho, MO, daughter of Felix F. Andriano and Mary Julia Deagle. Mary Julia Deagle was born in Boston, MA of French heritage. Maxine's parents owned Andriano's Department Store in Fredericktown and, upon their retirement, moved to Casa Grande, AR. Mary's passion is painting porcelain china.

Maxine was named after her grandfather, Maximillion Joseph Andriano, and grandmother, Elizabeth. Maximillion was born in Germany of Italian descent. His lineage can be traced back to the Laga De Como area of Italy, with their coat-

of-arms established in 1690, and family history to 1625, with some as early as the 1400s.

Maxine's grandfather, Maximillion, was a very interesting man. He was vice-president of First National Bank of St. Joseph, MO. One fine day just outside the bank he had an encounter with a young man who said to him, "you're a pretty young fellow to be carrying so much money, aren't you?" He replied, "I always mind my own business and will thank you to do the same," not realizing this young man was actually "casing" the bank. The next day he learned that the notorious bank robber, Jesse James, had been killed. He went to view the body and was surprised to see it was the same young man who had stopped him the day before. Maximillion said Jesse laughed at his remark when he told Jesse to mind his own business, and Jesse had the most satanic smile he had ever seen on a man before. This information was taken from a St. Joseph newspaper story written by well-known author Ernie Pyle. Maxine has a copy of this article and many others written about him, as well as poetry he wrote.

Jesse James wasn't the only well-known individual with whom Maximillion came into contact. Maximillion was a soldier during the Indian uprising and was stationed in the Dakota Territory. He served as quartermaster under the command of General George Custer and witnessed events that led to the massacre of Custer's army at Little Big Horn in 1876.

The Andriano's left Italy during the invasion and fled to Germany. Albert Andriano came to America, landing in New Orleans and moving up to the Mississippi River. He spent two years in St. Louis then later moved to St. Joseph. Albert invented the first soda water in April 1853 and first flavored fountain soda. From this he started Andriano Bottling Co. of St. Joseph. The company was sold to Hund & Edgar Co., who later sold it to Coca Cola Co. Albert wrote many of his experiences in a housebook (diary), he kept entitled *Journey to America.* Maxine has a copy of this diary.

Maxine is a distant cousin of Bettina Brentano. In the book entitled *Bettina A Potrait* by Arthur Helps and Elizabeth Jane Howard, Bettina Brentano is described as talented, musical, exciting, a romantic, and very beautiful, with long, dark hair. In fact Napoleon was to have inquired, "Who is this young person?" Bettina led a very exciting life, moving in the same circles as Goethe, Beethoven, Schumann and Brahms. Letters to her from Beethoven were auctioned by Sotheby's of New York Auction House. Schumann dedicated *Gesaenge der Fruche* to her, while Brahms dedicated his first volume of *Songs to Bettina.* Bettina Brentano married Achim Von Armin. Maxine has a copy of this book, which she values highly. *Submitted by Maxine Danieley.*

DEFREECE - Vergil and Sylvia Defreece came to Esther (now Park Hills), MO, in 1955. He became pastor of the Esther Baptist Church, where he served for 22 years. Both were born and reared in Arkansas, Sylvia at Huff and Vergil at Newark. Vergil was born in a labor camp where his father worked on a temporary job helping to build the railroad from Newport, AR, to Springfield, MO. Vergil is the son of Walter and Bertha (Sturch) Defreece. Bertha died when Vergil was very young, and his father married Irene (Wade) Defreece. Vergil, his brothers: Orvil, Malcolm and McGrady, and his sister, Mabel, helped their parents farm.

Sylvia is the daughter of Robert and Ethel (Smith) Ingram McKee. She helped her mother raise her sisters: Emily, Elsie, Mattie and Mary Etta, as well as her brothers, John and Edgar Lee. Vergil received his bachelor of arts degree from

Ouachita University in Arkadelphia, AR in 1946. Sylvia attended Ouachita and later Harding College, Searcy, AR. She served as a public school teacher for many years. Vergil has been in the ministry now (1998) for 66 years.

Vergil and Sylvia Defreece

Vergil spent the first 23 years of his ministry in Arkansas. He was pastor of Central Baptist Church, Bald Knob, AR before he left to come to the Esther Baptist Church. After retiring from Esther Baptist Church, Vergil served a number of churches as an interim pastor. These include First Baptist of Farmington, Bonne Terre, Bismarck, Ste. Genevieve, Knob Lick, Three Rivers, Chestnut Ridge and Doe Run. He now serves First Baptist Church of Doe Run and has served there for more than 18 years.

Vergil and Sylvia Defreece had three children: 1) son, Dale, who graduated from Ouachita University, attended the University of Missouri at Rolla, and is now retired from McDonnell Douglass Corporation; 2) son, Dean, who was killed in an auto accident while in the US Air Force in Germany; 3) a daughter, Jeanie, a teacher and organist who graduated from MAC, SEMO and MU. Jeanie is married to Dr. Darrell Griffin, now with Medical Arts Clinic in Farmington. The Defreeces have eight grandchildren and six great-grandchildren.

DENMAN - Charles M. Denman was born Jan. 23, 1892, in Bollinger County, MO, the son of William Denman and Melissa Kathryn Hawn. William Denman was the son of the Reverend Jabez and Sarah Denman and brother of Walter M., Harris E., Clinton H. and Cyrus B. Denman.

Charles attended Carleton College for a short period prior to his marriage to Flora B. Ward, daughter of William and Mary Biffle Ward, Dec. 17, 1913. Charles and Flora Denman moved to the

Charles M. Denman

Farmington area in 1926; first operating a farm between DeLassus and Doe Run and then later purchasing a 12 acre farm on Wallace Road. He worked at St. Joseph Lead Company and the State Mental Hospital at Farmington while operating his farm as well as leasing land to raise cattle.

To this union was born: Leonard M., Mary Kathryn, Lewis M., Ruby H. (Mrs. Fred Bruce), Charles W. Ward, Anna Mae (Mrs. Emmett Wampler), Eugene D. and Barbara Berneice (Mrs. Kenneth Panchot). Leonard was killed as the result of an auto-truck accident in Indiana in 1937; Charles W. Ward was killed during the D-Day invasion on the beaches of Normandy in WWII, June 5, 1944; and Kathryn (Mrs. James W. Hawn) died in 1967.

Charles died at the Bonne Terre Hospital Thursday, Dec. 24, 1953, at the age of 61. His wife, Flora B., passed away at the Madison Memorial Hospital on Saturday, March 25, 1967.

DENMAN - Cyrus B. Denman, the son of the late Rev. J.H. and Sarah King Denman was born in Bollinger County, MO. He attended a one room school, and spent three years at Carleton College at Farmington. Leaving college in June 1901,

C.B. Denman

he worked in the mines at Flat River, serving then as a reporter for the *Farmington News* for two years.

On June 3, 1903, he married Anna Martin, daughter of Dr. J.J. Martin. In 1904, he was elected county collector and served two terms. In 1910, he purchased the W.F. Miller farm at Copenhagen, southeast of Farmington, later adding the Beck farm and part of the Jerry Hopkins farm. He also operated the 8,000 acres Eleven Points Ranch in Oregon County for about 15 years.

Most of his farming was in livestock production and marketing. A breeder of Hereford cattle, he assisted in organizing a cooperative sales service for the breeders of this county. He helped organize the County Farm Bureau, got the first county agent and represented this county at a meeting where the Missouri Farm Bureau Federation was organized. This was the first state Farm Bureau and that movement led to the American Farm Bureau Federation. He served as Director of Organization of the State Federation.

In 1922, he became the president of the Producers' Live Stock Commission Association at the National Stock Yards, which later joined with some 20 other locals in the National Live Stock Producers' Association, the largest cooperative marketing association in the United States. Mr. Denman also served the National as president until drafted by President Hoover to be the live stock member of the Federal Farm Board in 1929. Following this service he was again president of National Stock Producers until 1937 when he became agricultural counsel to the Nation Food Chains in Washington, D.C., until his retirement in 1949.

Cyrus was a director of both the Farmers and First State Banks, the National Farm Loan Association and for many years treasurer of the Farmers Mutual Insurance Company. He helped organize and served as vice chairman of the Missouri 4-H Foundation of Columbia, and as a director of the Poultry and Egg National Board. For 20 years, he was on the board of directors of the National Live Stock and Meat Association.

Mr. Denman was a lifelong member of the Methodist Church. During his residence in Washington, D.C., he was the chairman of the Finance Committee of Foundry Methodist Church. Cy and Anna gave a Lincoln Memorial window in memory of their preacher fathers, Jabez H. Denman and Dr. J.J. Martin, each having known Lincoln personally. Abraham Lincoln was a life member of the Missionary Society and his membership certificate, along with his likeness, is reproduced in this window.

When the local Carleton and Murphy Long Churches merged in 1950, Mr. Denman was made chairman of the board of trustees, a member of the Building Committee and taught a young adult Sunday School class. In 1953, he directed a campaign for an endowment to supplement pensions

paid retired members of the St. Louis Conference of the Methodist Church.

In 1958, during graduating exercises, Central College conferred the honorary degree of doctor of law on him. He died in 1958, and his wife, Anna, died five days later. He was survived by one daughter, Mary (Mrs. Elgin) Hartshorn; a son-in-law; two grandsons, Elgin D. and John, of St. Louis; one granddaughter, Marianna (Mrs. Robert) McGuire, of Kansas City; and five great-grandchildren; also a brother, Clinton H. Denman, of Sikeston, and other relatives.

DENMAN - Eugene D. Denman is the fourth son of Charles M. and Flora B. Ward Denman, born March 15, 1928 in Farmington. Gene served in the US Army Signal Corps for a period of two years, 1946-1948. In 1952, he married Lorene (Norma) J. Hodge of Leadwood, daughter of Joseph S. and Lula Banks Hodge, who died in 1984. Gene and Norma adopted two children; Stephen

D. of Albuquerque, NM in 1959 and Laura K. (Mrs. Robert Coon) of Houston, TX in 1960. He has two grandchildren, David and Katie, both living in Albuquerque.

Gene is a graduate of the Farmington High School (1945) and received his higher

Eugene Dale Denman

education at Washington University (BSc in electrical engineering, 1951), Vanderbilt University (MSc in physics, 1955) and the University of Virginia (DSc in electrical engineering, 1963). Prior to receiving his doctorate, he was employed by Alcoa Aluminum, the Magnavox Co., Sperry Gyroscope Co. and Midwest Research Institute. After receiving the doctorate, Gene joined the faculty at Vanderbilt as an associate professor of electrical engineering and assistant professor of medicine. He moved to the University of Houston in 1969, as a professor of electrical and systems engineering, where he remained until his retirement in 1988. Gene has served as a consultant to the NASA Space Center in Huntsville, AL, through the Boeing Company, to NASA Space Center in Houston, TX, through the Lockheed Company. He was also a consultant to several other firms during his career.

He has been involved in the writing of several technical books; as an author of one, co-author of another, and co-editor of two others. In addition, he has compiled two books on genealogy; his father's (Denman) and mother's (Ward) families. During his professional career, Gene was listed in *American Men of Science*, *Who's Who in the Southwest* and *Who's Who in America*. The honorary engineering societies, Tau Beta Pi and Eta Kappa Nu, elected Gene to membership while at Vanderbilt for his professional work. He is a life senior member of the Institute of Electrical and Electronics Engineering. He has continued his professional involvement with several groups including having served as a committee member of the National Council of Examiners for Engineering and Surveying for seven years.

Gene is a member of the Farmington Kiwanis Club, serving as president and lieutenant governor of the MOARK District in past years, and Memorial United Methodist Church of Farmington. He has resided at 7449 Hillsboro Rd., Bonne Terre, MO since 1990.

DENMAN - Harry E. Denman was born in Bollinger County, MO, on March 23, 1875, son of

the late Rev. Jabez H. and Sarah King Denman. After attending country school in Bollinger County, he came to Farmington and graduated from Carleton College. His newspaper career started early in life and his first venture was at Fredericktown, where with the late George Gale, he helped publish the *Democrat News*. Staying at Fredericktown only a short time, he went to Licking, MO and bought the *Licking News* which he owned and published for two years. Upon selling the

Harris Edward Denman

Licking News he returned to Farmington in 1900, and with his brother, Clint H. Denman, who then had graduated from Carleton College, purchased from the late T.P. Pigg, *The Farmington News*, of which he had since been co-owner and publisher.

On Oct. 23, 1898, he was married to Lou Freeman, of Licking, MO. They were the parents of seven children, two of whom, Mrs. Grace White and Harry King, with their mother, preceded him in death. The surviving children were Wilma (Mrs. C.E. Carleton), Ted R., Mack F., of Farmington; Bess Newcomb of University City and Smith Denman of Oklahoma City, OK; 12 grandchildren and five great-grandchildren. He was survived by two brothers, Clint H., of Sikeston, and C.B. Denman, of Farmington. One sister, Mrs. Ella Ellinghouse, and two brothers, Will and Walter, preceded him in death. His death occurred exactly 31 years, to the day, after the death of his father. Harry, as he was known, died in 1951 at the age of 76. His wife, Lou, died in 1950.

Through all of his mature, life he was devoted to his chosen profession as a newspaper publisher. However, he found time to take a leading part in the religious, civic and fraternal life of his community. He was honored by his fellow newspaper publishers by being elected president of the Missouri Press Association in 1928, and twice served as president of the Southeast Missouri Press Association. He served the City of Farmington two terms as a member of City Council. He was named as census supervisor of the old 13th Congressional District in 1930, and had served in three sessions of the legislature, being a member of the 66th General Assembly. He was first elected to serve out the unexpired term of the late John W. Gaebe. In connection with his work as a member of the State Legislature, he had devoted much of his time and effort in trying to improve conditions in the State Eleemosynary Institutions, for both the patients and the employees and, was a member of the important Appropriations Committee of the Legislature during his office term.

He had served Farmington as a president of the Chamber of Commerce, was a member of several fraternal organizations and had been a life-time member of the Methodist Church. He had for many years been a member of the official board of the church, had served both as superintendent of the Sunday School and member of the Men's Bible Class. In the few years before his death, he had been giving much time and efforts to the Church Building Fund of Memorial Methodist Church, looking forward to the erection of new church property.

Two of Harry Denman's sons continued with him in the newspaper business. Mack and Ted joined their father in the mid 1920s. Mack served as editor and Ted as press supervisor for many years. Mack was also active in the Chamber of

Commerce and Republican politics, succeeding his father in the Missouri legislature for an unexpired term. He was a delegate to two Republican National Conventions. Mack's son, Harry, joined the *Farmington News* as a third generation in 1957 and retained the newspaper in the Denman family until 1972.

Ted had one son, Rex. Mack, married to MayOra Sloan, had six children: Bettie Lou, Robert, Mack F. Jr., Harry, Wilma June and Sheri Sue. Gerald Boring, OD, is a son of Bettie Lou and Bill Boring. He is the only direct Mack Denman family member still living in Farmington.

DENMAN - Jabez Harris Denman was one of a family of 11 children, the fourth son of Smith Denman and Elizabeth Dixon who came to Illinois in 1820. Of this family there were only three living in 1912; Jabez H. of Farmington, Smith of Kirksville, MO and Mrs. Mary Benson, wife of C.H. Benson of Chicago, IL. Jabez H. was a direct descendant of John Denman who came to Salem, MA from England in 1635.

J.H. Denman was born in McLean County, IL in 1830. He was educated in the common schools of Illinois and at Wesleyan College, now Wesleyan University of Bloomington, IL. When about 20, he entered the ministry of the Methodist Episcopal Church. Before and during the Civil War, he preached in northern Illinois where in August of 1855 he was married to Miss Jane Odell of Rock Island, who died prior

Sarah Ann King Denman, wife of Jabez H. Denman

to 1866. To this union four children were born of whom only one reached the age of maturity. In 1866 Reverend Denman moved to southeast Missouri. One of his first pastoral duties was to assist in the organization of the First Methodist Episcopal Church (Carleton Memorial Church) of Farmington, MO, which merged with the Murphy-Long Methodist Church to form the Memorial United Methodist Church in 1950.

From Farmington, he went to Bollinger County as a circuit rider of the Methodist Church, where on Aug. 16, 1867, he married Miss Sarah Ann King, daughter of the late George W. and Sarah Ward King. George W. King was lieutenant colonel of the 42nd Missouri Infantry and saw much action in the Civil War. George W. King was the 20th pastor

Jabez H. Denman

of the Methodist Episcopal Church of Farmington as well as being in charge of one of the circuits of the St. Louis conference of the church and president of Carleton College. His father, Suggars King, was a soldier in the Revolutionary War, as was Jabez's grandfathers, Mathias Denman and John Dixon.

To Rev. Denman's second marriage five children were born. They were William "Will" H. and Walter Mathias, farmers of Bollinger County; Harris "Harry" Edward and Clinton Harvey; and Cyrus "Cy" Benson of Farmington; all connected with the Farmington News. Rev. J.H. Denman died in 1920 followed by his wife, Sarah, in 1927.

DETJEN - Change was in the air in 1975 for Bill Detjen and family. The 39-year-old red-headed carpenter, who was born and raised in the Webster Groves area of St. Louis County, moved his wife, Mitzie (Marcia Spencer) and four children: Vickie, Tom, Billy and Lori, to 214 Patterson Street and began the transition from city life to country life and adopted Farmington as their home.

Bill commuted to St. Louis for about a year. Then in February 1976 became carpenter superintendent for Don Brockmiller where he continued until his retirement in August 1998. Bill was known for his

Vickie, Tom, Mitzie, Lori, Bill, Billy (June 1976)

pleasant disposition and excellent work throughout the area. After about three years of remodeling the Patterson Street house, the family moved to the Holiday Park area for 13 years.

Mitzie, a licensed practical nurse, began working for Medical Arts Clinic in December 1975, first being an office nurse for Dr. Dierker for about 10 years, then returning to the clinic as Nurse On Duty in 1988 after working a short time for the State Prison and in a private cardiologist's office.

Billy and Lori loved riding their bikes to downtown where they went to the Ben Franklin Store, the pet store or the swimming pool in the summer. Billy caught hundreds of snakes in Harlan Park, bringing them all home. Vickie was a sophomore, an excellent student, being in National Honor Society and the wrestling manager. She graduated in 1977 and then went to Mineral Area College. She then transferred to St. Louis where she got her associate degree and licensed medical technologist certification, working first at Farmington Community Hospital, then at St. Anthony's Hospital where she has been employed for 17 years. In 1981 she married Steve Huckstep and resides in the Fenton area with their two children, Jessica and Robert.

Tom was a freshman when moving to Farmington. He started playing football and wrestling. He was Athlete of the Year and was voted All District Football player and State Wrestler. Tom graduated in 1979 then started a career in the Army until his retirement in 1997. He is now with Procter and Gamble and has a farm out of Patton, MO. Tom was married to Laura Layton for 13 years and they divorced in 1997. They have one daughter, Danielle.

Billy bore many hardships as he was born with congenital birth defects and multiple learning disabilities. Farmington School was unprepared for such as Billy and many many concerns arose with his education. He graduated in 1987 and lives at Cedar Brooks apartments. Billy is known by all for his helpful ways and happy smiles. He spends hours working on his pick-up truck and going fishing. He attends the Church of God.

Lori started 1st Grade at Washington School and loved the two block walk. In high school, she was talented and vivacious. She worked on the school paper, ran for Sweetheart Queen and Miss Farmington. She was in Rifles for three years. She graduated in 1987, then received her science degree from SEMO and teaches science at the Middle School in Steeleville, MO where she has a farm and lives with her son, Austin Bequette. Lori remarried in 1997 to Dan Gilmore who is also a teacher.

In 1992 Bill and Mitzie moved from Ever-

glades Street to the real country on five acres off of Hildebrecht Road where they enjoy the serenity of quiet starry nights, rustling leaves and the sound of coyotes in the distance. You can find them digging in the yard in the spring or in a canoe on the rivers in the summer. The winters are spent on the hill reading or just enjoying the country. They belong to the Farmington Christian Church and feel blessed by the path they chose that led them to Farmington.

DETRING - Clifford was born March 25, 1923, at Libertyville in the house which sibling William and Minnie (Miller) reside. Formerly known as the Harris place, slave quarters on this farm have been razed.

Clifford's parents were Albert and Frieda (Schaefer) Detring. Sister, Nadine (Duane) Thomas, resides near Farmington. Another sibling, Albert Jr., is deceased. Their parents' farm was near the city limits, part of the Sarah Barton Murphy tract. Albert was an appraiser for Production Credit. He and Freda enjoyed many friends and

Clifford E. Caroline Detring

were well thought of in the community. They were members of St. Paul Lutheran Church.

Paternal grandparents, William and Margaret (Strohlman), were born in Germany and parented 13 children, there being three sets of twins. William farmed in the Libertyville area.

Maternal grandparents, George and Mary (Johncke) Schaefer, were born in Germany, parenting seven children and farming at rural Farmington. Clifford graduated from Farmington High School, was drafted into the Army in 1943. He served in WWII in a regimental combat team in the Philippines and Japan, as sergeant and stevedore foreman. Gasoline was loaded and shipped to Korea, pending the next war. After discharge, he returned home to farm with his ailing father.

Clifford married Caroline Cozean, Oct. 3, 1953. She was born on Oct. 20, 1921. Her parents were Rolla and Elva (Rinke) Cozean. Siblings were Hugo, Rolla "Bud" and John "Jack" Cozean. (Refer to Rolla Cozean Family)

Clifford and Caroline purchased 200 acres of land from J.C. Cayce in 1967. The property joined Clifford's home place and is also part of the Sarah Barton Murphy tract. He farmed both properties. They have two children, David and Debra (Organ), who live in Farmington, as does daughter, Susan Leonard. In 1959 the Detrings sold acreage to the city of Farmington for construction of the airport.

Due to Clifford's health, Caroline returned to work at Division of Family Services in 1964. Clifford gradually recovered and resumed farming. Caroline retired in 1983 and Clifford is semi-retired. Clifford likes to tinker with old tractors and is a bee keeper. He has a dry wit. Caroline likes antiques, flowers, cross-word puzzles, reading books, as well as attending church and social functions. They both enjoy short vacation trips, friends, grandsons, Jason and Tyler, and watching baseball games. They are active in the Lutheran Church. They are interested in Farm Bureau activities and Clifford is on the Board of St. Francois County Farmers Mutual Fire Insurance Co. He participates in environmental waste planning and is a member of the VFW and the American Legion. *Submitted by Caroline Cozean Detring.*

DETRING - Henry Charles Detring was the 12th of 13 children born to William and Margaret Strahlman Detring. He was born near Libertyville, St. Francis County, MO in 1899, to German immigrant parents.

William Detring was born in 1855, at Rahden, Germany, the son of Conrad and Engel Meier Detering. His paternal grandparents were Jacob Spreen Detering and Anne Marie Stormer of Kleindorf, Germany.

Henry Charles Detring

The maternal grandparents were Frantz Heinrich Meyer and Anne Schoeteler of Varl Luebbeke, Germany. Conrad died in 1859 in Espelkamp, Germany.

William Detring's sister, Dorothea, and a Clara Detring left Germany in June 1867 on the ship *Weser*. Five years later, William, age 17 years, and his mother, Engel, age 57 years, set sail for St. Louis on the same ship. They settled in Addieville, Washington County, IL.

Margaret Strahlman was born in 1860 at Abbehausen, near Oldenburg, Germany. She was the daughter of Diedrich and Margaret Cornelius Strahlmann. Her maternal grandparents were Reinhart and Margaret Haase Cornelius. After Diedrich died in Germany, a marriage was arranged between the widow, Margaret, and Conrad Kiepe of Farmington, MO by her brother-in-law, Henry Gaebe. Margaret and her two young children, Margaret and Diedrick, arrived in New York in 1870. The daughter, Margaret, married William Detring in 1879 in Washington County, IL. Shortly thereafter, they moved to St. Francois County, MO.

William Detring died in 1919, while son Henry was working near New Salem, North Dakota on the Will Detring farm there. Margaret died in 1931 and both were buried at the Copenhagen Cemetery.

In 1923, Henry Detring married Ethel Rosalee LePere and eventually bought the Detring farm south of Libertyville. Henry was a cattle farmer specializing in polled Hereford bulls. Breeders from a wide area purchased bulls from him. Sheep, hogs, horses, and chickens were raised in the early years. Corn and hay were raised to feed the livestock on the 200 acre farm. Besides raising quality cattle, Henry was known for his hard work and dedication to farming.

The two story, federal style home was built using bricks which were made on the property by slaves. At one time, there was a slave graveyard marked by fieldstones and several slave houses near the barnyard. Rainwater was collected in a cistern. Butter, milk and cream were kept cool in a nearby springhouse. After refrigeration, watermelons were still cooled there.

In 1972, they sold the farm and lived their remaining years in Farmington. In town, they still had a large garden. Rhubarb from the garden was used in Ethel's rhubarb custard pie. Henry took pride in growing large cantaloupes. Henry and Ethel Detring had four children: Walter, Dorothy, Kathryn and Stanley, all raised in the Methodist faith. Walter married Geraldine Shannon and lives in Farmington. Dorothy lives in Aurora, CO and "Kitty," married to Dr. Bedford Knipschild, lives in Marshall, MO. Stanley married Gail Stigall and they live in Morganfield, KY. Henry died in 1977 and Ethel in 1985, both are buried in Hillview Cemetery. Their seven living grandchildren live in Tennessee, Kentucky, Alabama and Missouri. *Submitted by Dawn Dement Detring*

DETRING - Walter Charles Detring married Geraldine Shannon on May 25, 1948, and recently celebrated their 50th wedding anniversary.

Walter Charles Detring was the first child born to Henry Charles and Ethel LePere Detring. He was born at 609 W. Liberty Street in Farmington at the home of Jacob and Salome Greb LePere, his maternal grandparents. Walter was named for his mother's brother, Walter LePere, who had been killed in

Walter and Jeri Detring

France during WWI. His middle name, Charles, was the same as his father's. Walter was raised on a farm south of Libertyville, MO.

Geraldine Shannon was born at Flat River (now Park Hills) the fifth of six children born to Lewis Cole and Anna Belle Meredith Shannon. Jeri's mother died when she was 2 years old. Her baby sister, Betty June, was raised by her paternal grandparents, Lewis Cole and Cynthia Manorah Sigman Shannon. The Shannon family immigrated from North Carolina to Robertson County, TN in the early 1800s. They came to St. Francois County, MO prior to the Civil War. The Sigman family immigrated from Alexander County, NC to Madison County, MO in the mid-1800s.

Anna Belle Meredith was the daughter of Alonzo and Orrie May Williamson Merideth. They came to Madison County, MO shortly after 1900 from Marion and Jefferson County, IL. Alonzo and Orrie are buried at Crossroads Cemetery in Madison County. Anna taught school before she married in 1922. Anna Belle Meredith had six children within 10 years time which was thought to contribute to her untimely death from pneumonia. After her death, Lewis married Elizabeth "Bessie" Eaves and they had two sons.

Walter and Jeri had two sons, Kenneth Charles and Gerald Wayne Detring. When their sons became teenagers, Walter and Jeri attended college at Southeast Missouri University during the summers. They took every class together and graduated in 1971 with teaching degrees. Wayne and Kenneth worked on the family farm and especially helped while their parents were attending college.

Walter taught school for 13 years with seven years at Belleview, MO. He also worked in later years as a substitute mail carrier. He enjoyed taking cross-country motorcycle trips on his Gold Wing cycle. Walter and Jeri moved from the farm in Libertyville to Farmington in 1985 after his mother died.

Jeri taught first at St. Joseph Catholic School. After graduating from SEMO in 1971, Jeri was hired by the Farmington Public School System to teach 3rd grade. She taught there for 19 years. Jeri and her husband, Walter, are members of the Libertyville United Methodist Church.

Their oldest son, Kenneth Charles, married the former Dawn Dement and they reside in Jackson, MO. Their daughters are Amanda Rose, Meredith Dawn and Sarah Elizabeth Detring. Ken graduated from SEMO in 1974 and the Illinois College of Optometry in 1980. He owns Eye Care Center of Jackson. Wayne Detring married the former Barbara Crane of Nashville, TN. They live in Goodlettsville, TN and have one son, Derek. Wayne graduated from SEMO in 1976 and from Vanderbilt School of Law in 1979. His law practice is in Hendersonville, TN. *Submitted by Dawn Dement Detring*

DETRING - William Detring came to America from Germany soon after the death of his father, Conrad. He was a small boy when he came with his mother, Engel Meier Detring, and his sister, Dorothea. They settled in Addieville, IL, in 1867.

William met his wife-to-be, Margaret Strahlman, through the Gaebe family. Margaret's mother, when she arrived in America, married Conrad Kiepe, who had children, and one of his daughters, Louisa, married a Gaebe from the Addieville area.

William and Margaret were married May 17, 1879, in Addieville. He was 24 and Margaret 19. Their first daughter, Emma, was born March 1, 1880, in Addieville. Soon after, they moved to near Libertyville, on a farm owned by N.C. Sebastain. After living on the A.K. Harris farm, William purchased the T.C. Highley Williams farm just south of Libertyville, where he lived until his death.

William and Margaret Detring

William and Margaret were the parents of 13 children, including three sets of twins. A son and daughter, Dora, died in infancy. It is said William was St. Francois County's leading farmer. He and his eight boys and three girls worked hard on the 300 acre farm. He raised his family in the German Methodist Church. He is remembered by his goatee, shown in every picture. William died in Farmington Aug. 27, 1919, at 63 years of age. Margaret passed away at the home of her daughter, Lydia Crow, on Dec. 8, 1931, at the age of 72.

Their children:

1) Emma Detring Gaebe, born March 1, 1880, died Sept. 13, 1962, and had one child, Esther.

2) Lydia Detring, born Nov. 20, 1883, died Nov. 30, 1969. She married Harold Crow and had one son, Wayman.

3) William Detring Jr., born Nov. 20, 1883, died July 30, 1959. He married Carrie Klusmann and had three children: Edna, Lois and Bernice.

4) Franklin Detring, born June 29, 1886, died Nov. 14, 1971. He married Maggie Lewis and had two children, Frank and Marguerite.

5) Conrad Detring, born June 29, 1886, died Nov. 15, 1961. He married Grace Graham and had two children, Edgar and Van.

6) Louis Detring, born March 9, 1889, died Jan. 23, 1973. He married Ruth Gay, no children.

7) Albert Detring, born March 26, 1891, died Oct. 8, 1948. He married Freida Schaeffer and had three children: William, Clifford and Nadine.

8) Antonia Detring, born April 5, 1893, died Nov. 1, 1975. She married R.C. Graham and had five children: William, Chester, Eugene, Max and Mable.

9) Elmer Detring, born April 28, 1897, died Aug. 17, 1953. He married Clara Anthony and had two children, Norman and Ralph.

10) Dora Detring, born April 28, 1897, died April 28, 1898.

11) Henry Detring, born Sept. 4, 1899, died June 11, 1977. He married Ethel LePere and had four children: Walter, Dorothy, Kathryn and Stanley.

12) George Detring, born May 19, 1902, died

March 18, 1998. He married Elizabeth Klein and had six children: Patty, Barbara, Charlotte, Jean, Ray and Paul. *Submitted by Edgar Detring*

DETRING - William Detring was born in St. Francois County, MO near Farmington on December 25, 1920. He was the son of the late Albert and Frieda (Schaeffer) Detring.

William's father, Albert, was born in 1891 and served with the 89th Division as a Military Police of the US Army in WWI. He served in France, Germany and Belgium. He and wife, Frieda, had three sons and one daughter. William's father and grandfather were farmers.

His grandfather, William Detring Sr., came from Hahlen, Germany in 1867, age 12, with his mother and sister, Dora. They settled first in Addieville, IL. Later they moved to St. Francois County, MO near Farmington in the late 1870s, where he became a very successful farmer.

He and his dear wife, Margaret Strahlman Detring, also of rural Farmington, were married in 1879 and raised eight sons and three daughters. His wife came from Oldenburg, Germany at the age of 10 with her mother and younger brother. Mr. Strahlman had died in Germany.

William (third generation) and wife, Minnie Miller, were married in February 1945. They are the parents of three children: Joann, born in 1947, married Hugh Boyle; Linda Detring, born 1948; and Richard Detring, born 1955, married Karen

Back Row: Joann (Detring) Boyle, Richard Detring, Linda Detring. Front Row: Minnie (Miller) Detring, William Detring

Burns. Six grandchildren have joined the family: Cynthia, Karen and Hugh John Boyle; Brad, Jill and Jenna Detring.

William followed in his father and grandfather's footsteps. He lives and farms on the same farm his father and grandfather farmed since 1901. William A. moved to the farm in 1942, his wife joined him in 1945, and they have spent all their married life there. This farm had several slaves in its early years and there were five known slave cabins on the farm.

Their son, Richard, is the fourth generation and grandson, Brad, is the fifth Detring generation to work the land on this farm. Minnie's father, William Daniel Miller, was born near Farmington in 1873. He was the son of Daniel C. and Minnie (Eggert) Miller, born in Hasselteich, Germany.

Great-grandfather Daniel Miller was born in Otzendorf, Germany in 1797 and his wife, Annie, was also born in Germany. They came to the United States about 1834, settling first in Ste. Genevieve, MO until 1838, then moved to Farmington and purchased a farm in what became known as Copenhagen Community. Great-grandfather was a tailor by trade. His tailor shop was located at Henry and Columbia Streets in Farmington. They were the first German family to settle in St. Francois County.

Minnie's Grandfather Miller fought in the Civil War. He was a member of the Union Army. Being left alone on the farm created a hardship on his wife and small children. Minnie's father married Clara Kleinschmidt, of near DeSoto, MO in 1917 and they were the parents of two children, Lawrence, born 1918 and died at 18 months of age, and Minnie, born 1922. Her father was a farmer and loved the land. Our grandparents left

us a beautiful heritage, all living their Christian faith. *Submitted by Minnie (Miller) Detring*

DOBBINS - In November 1938, my mother became very ill; my father could not work and handle seven children. The youngest three were taken care of by family members, the four older were brought to the Presbyterian Home for Children in Farmington, from Kansas City, MO.

I, Ruth Elvira (Weeks) Dobbins, was 11; my sister, Norma, was 10; my brother, Leonard, was 8; and my sister, Weymuth, was 6. We lived in the "Plantation House." Norma and I were on the 3rd floor; Leonard and Weymuth were on the 2nd floor. We were not allowed to see them because Leonard was a boy and Weymuth was a baby. Everyone had chores to do. I cleaned the parlor, ironed twice a week, helped the little girls with baths twice weekly, and with washing their hair on Saturday nights.

When Mrs. Stinson was the superintendent, we had oatmeal everyday for breakfast. When Mr. Fischer was there, we had cornflakes everyday instead. No matter what, we could have all the bread, milk and syrup we wanted.

Although I was only here a short time, (I went home in May 1935, my siblings returning home in August 1939), my stay there had such a profound impact on my life that I returned 60 years later, May 1999, to see the site and find if the facts went with my memories. *Submitted by Ruth E. Dobbins*

DOUGHTY - The Doughty family first came to Farmington from Ohio in the early 1830s. James Doughty was born 1779 in New Jersey and his wife, Margaret Maring, traveled with their son, Mahlon Maring Doughty, born 1804 in New Jersey, his wife Harriet Jackson, and Mahlon's first born daughter, Sophronia. The Doughtys purchased a small farm on Fredericktown Road from the Murphy family. Their descendants still own a portion of this property today.

Mahlon and Harriet added nine more children after settling here: Daniel, born 1835; James, 1836; Sarah Margaret, 1838; Alfred Mahlon, 1840; David Jackson, 1842; Prudence Hathaway, 1844; Milton Cayce, 1847; Marcus Lodge, 1849; and Ira Jackson, 1851. At least three of these brothers fought in the Civil War. Daniel served in the Union infantry and died of wounds and exposure during the retreat from the Battle of Pilot Knob. David Jackson Doughty served in the Union Navy, survived the war and became one of the area's finest cabinet makers. He also helped to found the Farmington chapter of the Grand Army of the Republic.

Alfred Mahlon Doughty fought on the side of the Confederacy. After the war he married and spent many years living in Arkansas; not being welcome to come home since the rest of the family had been Union loyalists.

Marcus Lodge Doughty, being too young to serve during the war, became active in community affairs in Farmington. He was instrumental in the formation of the city's first public water works in 1902, the reorganization of the local telephone system and the building of the Carleton Memorial Methodist Church. He served three terms as Farmington's postmaster, before moving to Chicago in 1912 where he achieved business success with a commercial laundry.

One of the younger brothers, Milton Cayce Doughty took over the operation of the family farm upon the death of his father in 1873. In 1877 he married Sarah Jane Wood. The couple had two boys and three girls. Only one of the girls lived to adulthood.

The youngest of these children, Walter Wood Doughty, born 1888, married Minnie Melinda

Burch and became the fourth Doughty and third generation to operate the Doughty farm. Walter modernized the family dairy business. The resulting Locust Ridge Dairy served the milk and butter needs for many of the local restaurants, grocers, and families for many years.

Walter and Minnie's children were Nellie May, born 1912; James Melbourne, born 1914; Glenda Ruth, born 1917; Glenwood Hubert, born 1920; Alfred Wesley, born 1924; and Donald Eugene, born 1929.

Melbourne farmed for many years before taking a job with Missouri Natural Gas until his retirement. Glenwood spent a number of years in Alaska as a construction contractor before returning to Farmington to raise cattle. Part of his farm was in the original Doughty acreage. Glenda also lived in Alaska for many years where she owned a beauty shop, and along with her husband, Ervin Miller, ran a camper sales agency. She now lives on part of the family farm with her daughter, Carole, and son-in-law, Ron Sumpter. Alfred became a veterinarian and has lived for most of his life in Illinois. Donald spent almost 25 years as a Missouri Highway Patrolman in the St. Francois County area. His wife, Donna Baughn, is retired from a position as director of the Learning Center at Mineral Area College. They also live on part of the original farm.

Don's eldest son, Ed, lives in Farmington with his wife, Rhonda Jarvis, and daughters, Brandi and Kaitlin, where he has operated a business for several years. His second son, Glen, lives with his wife, Sheila Jarvis, in England. His daughter, Kelly, lives in Sedalia, MO with her husband, Bruce Gabriel, and daughter, Deanna. *Submitted by Ed Doughty*

DUGAL - The grandfather of Edward Frank Dugal came from Canada to Iron Mountain, MI then to Iron Mountain, MO where he worked in the mines. His ancestors originally came from Scotland. Edward Frank Dugal's grandfather was drafted into the Union Army during the Civil War. His wife had previously died, leaving him with a son who was 13 years old when his father was drafted. The boy had no one to live with, so he went with his

Edward Frank and Nannie Elizabeth Wood

father and stayed with him throughout the war. Both the father and son were in the battle of Fort Davidson at Pilot Knob in 1864. Gen. Hewing was the commanding officer of Fort Davidson.

When this boy, Edward Lewis Dugal, grew up, he met and married a lady who had immigrated from Germany and she gave birth to Edward Frank Dugal.

Edward Frank Dugal met and married Nannie Wood. Nannie's father and mother were members of a wagon train from Kentucky on their way to Texas in 1880. While passing through St. Francois County, they camped overnight near Haggai, a thriving village at that time. The next morning some of the children were playing and found the body of a man named Ferguson. The entire party was detained because the authorities suspected a member of the wagon train killed Ferguson. A man named Hardin was soon arrested, confessed to the killing and was hanged in Farmington. The temporary detention of the wagon train made them many friends who sympathized with them for the predicament in which they had innocently and accidentally been placed.

So much did they appreciate their new-found friends, that the entire party abandoned their plans to go to Texas and stayed in St. Francois County.

Edward and Nannie Dugal raised five children: Leo, Robert, Berniece, John and Earl. At this writing, only Leo is still living. All four of their sons served in the military during WWII. Berniece's husband, Frank McCreary, also served and fought in the Battle of the Bulge. This battle was the beginning of the end for Hitler, as 110,000 Germans were captured, and they suffered almost 100,000 other casualties. *Submitted by Ronald V. Dugal, grandson.*

DUGAL - Leo Dugal was raised in Doe Run and Velma Chalk was raised in DeLassus. Both attended Farmington High School, graduated in 1929 and were married Jan. 30, 1930. Leo's mother and Velma's mother were both named Wood, but were not related.

Seven children were born to Leo and Velma, four daughters and three sons. Bill, Ronald, Connie, Carole and Richard were born before Leo left for the Army in March 1944. Velma was expecting their sixth child when Leo was drafted. Sandra was born in November 1944 and Janice in 1947.

Leo was trained as a surgical technician and served in India and Burma. Leo was assigned to the 95th Field Hospital in Burma, where fierce fighting was taking place against the Japanese. Leo was later assigned to the 30th Station Hospital just before being discharged in 1946.

When Leo was drafted, he and Velma had milk cows and operated a small dairy operation in Farmington. Back during the depression, everybody worked to make ends meet. Leo was working at Klein's Grocery Store across the street from the post office. Each day before he went to work and again after he got home, Leo would milk the cows. Velma would sanitize the milk bottles and bottle the milk. Then, the whole family would pile in the old Model A Ford and deliver the milk to various customers around Farmington. This continued up until Leo was drafted. Before he left for the Army, the cows had to be sold.

After being discharged, Leo returned to the grocery business (Klein Grocer Co.) where he had worked since 1931. Leo worked 65 years in the store. He bought into the business in 1954 and eventually owned four stores in Farmington, Flat River, Bonne Terre and Poplar Bluff. Velma worked with him in the store for many years, and their daughter, Janice, and her husband, Dave Spane, now own the store in Farmington.

Leo and Velma made sure all of their children attended Sunday School and worship services every week at the First Baptist Church, where Leo had more than 50 years of perfect attendance, except for the years in the Army.

Leo and Velma's oldest son, Bill, passed away in 1994. Ronald and his wife, Shirley, live in the area. Connie and her husband, Norman Caringer, live in Poplar Bluff. Carole and her husband, Ron Short, own and operate Dicus Drug Store in Farmington. Richard and his wife, Dorothy, own and operate a motel in Branson. Sandra and her husband, Kenny Stoll, live in north Little Rock, where Kenny is the assistant US Attorney.

Leo and Velma's family now number more than a 100 members counting children, grandchildren, great-grandchildren, sons-in-law and daughters-in-law.

Leo and Velma celebrated their 68th wedding anniversary this year. Leo said his most exciting memory of his Army experience was the day his ship sailed into New York and the Statue of Liberty was welcoming them home. He knew then he was almost home. *Submitted by Leo B. Dugal*

DUNCAN - Marilyn Gayle Eaton, daughter of Roy and Mildred Hughes Eaton, granddaughter of Aaron and Lucy Wells Eaton and Arthur and Ida May Ford Hughes, was born in St. Francois County on March 8, 1940. She started school at a one room school in Cedar Falls, east of Desloge. She went two years at Bell Fountain, a three-room school in Washington County and graduated from grammar school at Potosi. She finished high school in Farmington, then went to St. Louis to find work. She started in an office job in the warehouse of Lammert's Furniture Store.

In July 1958, she married Tom J. Griffin and started her married life with him at Fort Benning, GA. Following his discharge from the Army, they returned to St. Louis. Their son, Jeffrey Linn Griffin, was born July 15, 1959, at Mineral Area Osteopathic Hospital. This marriage ended in divorce.

She later married Larry Duncan of Flat River, MO and they lived in the St. Louis area for several years. Their only child was Dawn Lynette Duncan, born at Mineral Area Osteopathic Hospital.

When Dawn was 10 years old, they left this area and went to Denver, CO. Jeffrey finished school in Denver, then entered the Navy and trained in San Diego, CA. He also served in the state of Washington, Vallejo, CA and in Hawaii. He chose to serve in the submarine service. While in Washington he married Margaret and are the parents of two sons, Zachary and Travis. Later, he was sent to the East Coast, serving in South Carolina and Norfolk, VA. He was on duty at Norfolk in June 1966 when he was struck down in a crosswalk and fatally injured. He is buried in a military cemetery in South Carolina.

Dawn went to Grand Island, NE to go to college. There she met and married Darryl Krecklow and their children are Katie and Jake.

Marilyn and Larry were divorced in Denver and she later spent some time working in California, but returned to Denver and started working at Four Winds Trading Company in Boulder, CO. In December 1995, she was diagnosed with lung cancer and started radiation therapy. She continued to work as long as she was physically able to do so. In April 1996, she came back to Farmington where she had family to take care of her. She passed away June 17, 1996, at Mineral Area Hospital, just 11 days after her son, Jeff, lost his life. She is buried at Bismarck Masonic Cemetery.

EATON - David Allan Eaton, son of Roy W. and Mildred Hughes Eaton, grandson of Aaron and Lucy Wells Eaton and Arthur and Ida May Ford Hughes, was born Sept. 14, 1953, at Mineral Area Osteopathic Hospital in Farmington, MO.

He attended school in Farmington, MO and while in high school and a short time afterward, he worked at Davco Auto Supply. He then enlisted in the Navy, choosing to serve on Nuclear Powered Submarines. His boot training was at Orlando, FL, followed by training at Vallejo, CA and Idaho Falls, ID. He has since served at Charleston, SC, one three year hitch in Guam, in Connecticut and at Norfolk, VA, where he now serves.

While in Idaho he met and married Carol Jessica Bahr, who was raised in Hawaii. They have two children, Kristen Marie and David Allan II. Carol passed away in December 1989, suffering from an inoperable brain tumor. She is buried at the Masonic Cemetery in Bismarck, MO.

Four and one half years later, he married Ellen Tolson of Norfolk, VA. She has one daughter, Holly, from a previous marriage. Holly is married to Kirk Anderson. Kirk is serving with the US Navy in Groton, CT. They have one son, Kyle Patrick, born in April 1998.

Kristen is attending her third year at Virginia Wesleyan College in Norfolk, VA. David II is starting an internship in computer drawing at a technical school in Virginia Beach, VA and is employed by the city of Virginia Beach.

EATON - Dennis Wayne Eaton, son of Roy W. and Mildred Hughes Eaton, grandson of Aaron and Lucy Wells Eaton and Arthur and Ida May Ford Hughes, was born at Mineral Area Osteopathic Hospital on Aug. 17, 1952, the same year the hospital was established.

He attended school at Farmington, including training in auto mechanics at the trade school in Bonne Terre, MO. He has his father's natural ability for auto maintenance, and while yet in high school worked at the trade. He is is still with auto maintenance, as an assistant service writer for Feld Toyoto dealership in south St. Louis.

He married Carolyn Fink, daughter of Paul and Ila Mae Oder Fink. They have one daughter, Amy Christine Eaton, who is starting this year as a teacher's aide for the Farmington School System. This marriage ended in divorce. A short marriage to Peggy (last name unknown) resulted in a son, Daniel Joseph Eaton, of whom we know little. He is presently married to Linda Hart Bailey who had two children from previous marriages, Scott Vaughn and Charmin Bailey. Linda is employed by Trimfoot Shoe Co.

EATON - Frankie Leroy Eaton, son of Roy and Mildred Hughes Eaton, grandson of Aaron and Lucy Wells Eaton and Arthur and Ida Ford Hughes, was born Aug. 9, 1941, in St. Louis County. He spent most of his younger years in St. Francois County, with a short three years spent in Washington County. He started school in a one room school, at Cedar Falls. He went three years in Washington County to a three room school, finishing his schooling in Farmington. He enlisted in the Army, spent two years in Germany and was discharged from Fort Riley, KS. He worked a few years at Davco Auto Parts in Farmington, before buying a dump truck and has been hauling on his own until the present time.

He married Katie Lynn Sturgess, daughter of Wm. Archie and Eva Winch Sturgess, granddaughter of John Wesley and Maggie Oden Winch and Edward and Katie Lynn Allen Sturgess. She was a professional hairdresser, having her own shop in Farmington for several years. More recently she has been working as a realtor for Coldwell Banker Hulsey Real Estate of Farmington. They were blessed with three children: Frank Jr., Krista Lynn, and Eeron Michelle. Frank Jr. is a member of the US Army, stationed at Fort Benning, GA. He is a ranger and a member of the Special Forces. He is married to Judith Kristine Ray who has two daughters, Robin and Marissa Ray, by a first marriage. They make their home in Alabama. Krista was called home to be with her Maker, when she was almost 17. She was the victim of an auto accident. Eeron is married to Oliver Siebert, of St. Genevieve, and they have two children, 4-year-old Oliver Jr. and 4-month-old Olivia. They make their home in Farmington.

EATON - Robert Linn Eaton, son of Roy W. and Mildred Hughes Eaton, grandson of Aaron and Lucy Wells Eaton, and Arthur and Ida May Ford Hughes, was born May 6, 1943, in St. Francois County. He started school in a one room schoolhouse at Cedar Falls, attended three years at a three room school in Washington County, but finished his schooling in Farmington. He enlisted in the US Navy, took his boot training at Great Lakes, IL, spent time in Puerto Rico; Key West, FL; Millington, TN and Norfolk, VA.

Following his boot training, he married Janet Lea Moore, daughter of Alonzo and Charlotte Bingham Moore, granddaughter of George and Maryetta Bingham Moore, and Charles and Irene Bingham. They were blessed with two children, Teresa Ann and Robert Linn Jr. Teresa finished high school in Virginia Beach, VA; came to Farmington when her dad retired from the Navy and has worked since in the office of Trimfoot Shoe Company in Farmington. She married Scott Clauser of Farmington and has two lovely teenagers, Amber and Megan Clauser. Scott is affiliated with the St. Francois Glass Company in Farmington, where they make their home. Robert Jr. finished high school in Farmington, enlisted in the Navy and spent 12 years, mostly at Norfolk, VA, before deciding to leave the Navy for civilian life. He married Maryetta Murphy, also of Farmington, and they have two children, Dustin and Amelia Beth. They reside near Farmington.

EAVES - Albert Eaves was the 4th son of William Bartlett Eaves who came from Henry County, TN in 1849 to Dent County, MO. He was born in 1840, in Henry County. William Bartlett and wife, Carolina Wofford Eaves, came to Dent Country, MO with their first six children. They had six more children after they came to Missouri.

Elisha, born in 1834, was in Co. F with Albert throughout the Civil War and was ordained a minister in 1867.

Albert married Susanna W., Aug. 28, 1858, in St. Francois County, MO. She was born in August 1845, to Daniel and Sarah Jones W in Possum Hollow near Knob Lick. They were the parents of nine children. Albert enlisted in Co. F, Aug. 23, 1864, in Ironton, MO and was in the Battle of Pilot Knob, then went to Ten-

Susanna Williams Eaves

nessee. He was captured by the enemy in September of 1864, but was shortly released. In March 1865, he was discharged and returned to Doe Run, where his wife and children were living. He died in May 1883, in Iron County, MO. Albert is buried in the Possum Hollow Cemetery off Possum Hollow Road. Susanna is buried in the Knob Lick Cemetery. Albert was a farmer. Following are their children:

1) John Wesley, born 1860, in Syenite, and married Lillie White, Aug. 10, 1884. She was born in December 1868 to John J. Their children were Hattie, born 1885, Syenite, MO and married Thomas Bell; William F., born 1895, Syenite, MO; Bertha, born 1888, married a Mr. Boyer and had three children: Marie, Jessie, and Katherine; Albert B., born 1890; Ida P., born 1894, married Fred May and had Elmer, Helen, Arthur and Doris May; Edgar, born in 1896; Bessie, born in 1898; John W., born Feb 1, 1892, died July 10, 1893. John Wesley is buried in Knob Lick.

2) Daniel, born l862, died l869, is buried at Possum Hollow Cemetery.

3) Albert, born 1866 in Salem, died 1939 in Flat River, MO. He married Lou Wallace and they owned a store in Flat River. They are buried in the Knob Lick Cemetery.

4) Edward Franklin, born 1872 in Salem, MO, died l940 in Knob Lick. He married first, Ida Jackson; second, Clara Newcomer Jennings, and had one daughter Elsie Pauline who was born in l896. She married James Benton and had children, Clara May and Jesta Lee.

5) Ida Cora, born 1871 and died 1936 in Yount, MO. She married Oliver French, the son of Alexander and Mary Jane Shaw French of Perry County, MO. He was born in 1867 and died in 1938, Floyd, born in 1896 Perry County, MO died in 1963. He is buried in the Whitewater Cemetery in Yount, MO. Floyd had a furniture manufacturing business in Desloge and later moved to Farmington where Hester gave music lessons to students. He married Hester Lawrence who was born in 1900 and died in 1979. They had twins, Aletha and Alvada, Eldon, Norvin, Melvin, Floyd, Dorothy, Iris and Daisy. Daisy married John Hodges and has a son, Alex, and daughter, Soroya. They live in Farmington, MO. Arthur married Ellen Heaps and had Kenneth, Clovis, Wanda, Curtis, Ruby, Leona, Herbert, and Judy. Myrtle married Edgar Parsons and had a daughter, Nadine. Bertha married Marcus Kennon and had Eugene, Alvin, Nevada, Roger and Levada. Elva married George Shaw. Harley married Ella Pittman and had Wilma and Leroy.

6) Laura May, born 1878 in Doe Run, died 1898 and married William French in 1894. He was the brother of Oliver. They had two daughters, Ethel born 1895 and Hazel born 1897. He married Zora Henderson in 1901, and they had eight children: Jesse, Beulah, Roy, George, Lena, Chancel, Wilburn and Vernon. Laura is buried at Silver Lake, Perry County, MO on their home place. Ethel married John Hughes and had George, Cecil and Opal. Hazel married John Surina and had John, William, Florence, Ethel, Jessie, Melba and Wilma Fay. Wilma, born 1929, married Leslie Highley in 1946. Their children are Leslie and John Paul.

7) Thomas J. born 1880, no info.

8) Rhoda, no info.

9) Maude born 1883, married Edward Laturno in 1892. They had Charlie, Walter, Cecil, Clifford, Gilbert, Lena Fay and Floyd. They were listed in 1910 census in St. Francois County in Liberty Township, Knob Lick, MO. Edward, age 29, married 10 years, born in Illinois; Maude, age 27, six children, four living, born in Missouri; Charlie, age 8; Walter, age 7; Cecil, age 4; Clifford, age 11 months. There are a lot of the Eaves family who moved to the Farmington area and are well known. Most who carry that name are descendants of William Bartlett Eaves and Carolina Wofford Eaves. *Submitted by Daisey Hodges*

EAVES - Solomon Eaves was born in 1807 in Davidson County, TN. His parentage is unknown. He married Sarah Williams Jan. 6, 1826, in Davidson County. She was the daughter of Lodowich and Susanna Williams. Their first two children were born in Tennessee. They moved to St. Francois County, MO around 1833, and are listed in the 1840 census in Pendleton Township, with wife and four children. They were the parents of the following six children:

1) Susan, born 1828, Tennessee, married Lewis Casto Sept. 19, 1850 in St. Francois County and had five children: Sarah E., born 1852; Julia Ann, born 1857, married August Tollman in 1876; Lucy, born 1862; Newton, born 1866; and William, born 1871. The Tollmans lived in Iron County.

2) Thomas, born 1830 in Tennessee, married Talitha Murray in 1853, and had eight children: Solomon married Barsheba Chamberlain and had Rachel and Charles, William married Martha Baker, Sarah married James Horne and had Maggie, Alexander, James R., Mary T., Alice, Eva and Anna. James Anderson, born 1866, married Lilian Watson in 1901 and had Mayme who married Charles Stewart, Nellie married first to Elmer Ketler and second, Leroy Field, John Thomas, born 1907, married Mary Benko and had Marvin Thomas who married Ruth Anna Parker

and Bonnie June who married Harold McGee, Bessie married Cole Shannon, James married Mayme Resinger, Irah married Thomas Hocker, Marvin, born in 1916, died in a motorcycle accident in 1938, Arthur married Dorine Slaser, Burl married Catherine, Rachel married Columbus Baker in 1889 and died in childbirth. Her daughter, Ethel, was raised by William and Martha, Joseph married Clara Groves in 1900. Their children: Bula, Earl, Russell and Buford. Catherine married William Wells in 1894. He was the son of Eli Wells and Rachel Mayo Wells and was born in Knob Lick. They had eight children: Thomas, Mary, Bertha, Henry, Emmett, Addia May who married Orville Hamm.

3) Martha, born 1834, in Missouri, and married Jacob Murray 1853. He was the son of William and Mary Murray.

4) Meekie, born 1837, in Missouri, married George Bayless in 1858. George Calaway J. was born Dec. 30, 1838, was one of the soldiers in Co. F from the state of Tennessee. He was the son of Joseph and Polly Bayless. He enlisted Aug. 27, 1864, in Farmington and was in all the actions in Missouri and later in Tennessee. He contracted pneumonia and died in the hospital in Pulaski, March 19, 1865, and is buried at Stones River. Their children were Joseph and Martha. Meekie remarried April 14, 1871, to James Thomas Arnold but divorced in 1891. Joseph, born 1860, married Laura McDowell in 1881. She was the daughter of William and Sarah Jacobs McDowell, was born in 1856 in Knob Lick, and they are buried there. They had five children: Clara Beatrice, married George Wallace, George William married Edith, Charles, Cyrus B. married Maggie Milne, McDowell married Leona Chastain. Martha, second child of George and Meekie, married Harvey Hibbits. She was born 1862 and died 1918. Harvey, born 1859 and died 1915. He was the son of William and Martha Ann Jacobs Hibbits. They had four children: Thomas, Aubrey, Allen, born 1899, and married Mary Frances Williams, born 1907, daughter of Elias Jefferson and Harriet Ann Barnes. Their children were Bernice, Harvey, Herbert, Woodrow, Robert, Paul, Thomas, Pauline, Ina and Mary. Ina, a twin to Allen, was born in 1899. Harvey married Iva and had James, Milo and Edith. Meekie and Thomas Arnold had three children: John, Mary Eliza and Louisa Alice.

5) Sarah, born 1841, married John Arnold in 1858. He was born in 1836, in Henry County, TN, the son of John and Jean Arnold. John was a farmer 6'2" tall. He enlisted in Co. F Aug 24, 1864, in Farmington and saw action in Missouri and Tennessee. They had 12 children: Sarah, Martha, Frances, George, Thomas, Lucinda, Leander, Rocky, Emma, Maggie and John. In the 1870 census, John was a railroad watchman. Later, he worked in the rock quarry where he died from an explosion Sept. 1, 1885. John is buried in the Possum Hollow Cemetery.

6) Mary A., born 1844, died 1899, Fredericktown, MO, married first to Timothy Landrum and second in 1869 to John Killilee, born 1839, Indiana, died 1886 in Fredericktown, MO. They had seven children: William, Frank, Alonzo, Mary, Charles, Leo and John W.

Solomon was a farmer and it is unknown when Solomon and Sarah died or where they are buried, but they lived in the Knob Lick and Pendleton Township area. *Submitted by Mrs John Thomas Eaves*

ECKHOFF - Eileen Marie Eckhoff (nee Knittig) is the fourth child of Frank J. and Rosemary J. Knittig, born June 18, 1958 in St. Louis, MO. The fun-filled early years of her life were spent at Rt. 2, High Ridge, MO, where she went to kindergarten. Because of the Highway 21 expansion project, the family was forced to move in 1967. Eileen began first grade at St. Joseph's Catholic School in Farmington, MO. This is where she remained until 8th grade graduation. In 1976, after graduation from Farmington High School, she attended Mineral Area College for two years.

With an associates degree in secretarial science, she began work at the Missouri State Probation and Parole Office in 1978. Three years later she had the opportunity to begin work at Missouri Division of Family Services where she continues to work today. Since July 1995, Eileen has enjoyed most of all, being a Mary Kay Consultant. With a light and bubbly personality, she is just right for this career.

Eckhoff's Christmas (1993)

Mark D. Dalton, son of Willard and Bertha Dalton, and Eileen moved into their home on Middle Street in Farmington after their marriage on May 19, 1979. Then just four years later, after their divorce, she moved to Desloge, MO to begin a new life.

On July 21, 1984, at the Centenary Methodist Church of Bonne Terre, Eileen and Gary Eckhoff, son of Buryle (deceased) and Erma Jean Eckhoff of Potosi, were united in marriage. With his two sons, Duane born Dec. 23 1976, in St. Louis, and Christopher born April 22, 1979, in St. Louis, the couple bought a home at 307 S. Main Street in Desloge. And to this family, two more sons were born, Kyle born Sept. 7, 1985, in Farmington and Dylan born Sept. 11, 1993, in St. Louis. Having outgrown their present home, the family moved to a spacious four bedroom home in Terre Du Lac in April 1996. Gary keeps busy at his privately owned auto body repair shop, while Eileen enjoys making new friends with her Mary Kay Cosmetics. Their youngest sons along with their two grandsons, Wyatt born Dec. 15, 1995, and Austin born Dec. 8, 1996, (parents are Duane and Jody Eckhoff) enjoy playing in the spacious yard of this quiet neighborhood.

EFFAN - Originally from Missouri, William Effan moved to Farmington in 1996, with his wife, Patricia, and her mother, Goldwyn Hughes Smith, whose uncle was the "famous" Howard Hughes. Formerly Will lived in San Diego, CA, where he served on active duty in the US Navy and where he met and married Patti. After his retirement from the Navy, they relocated to Yuma, AZ, where Will received his associate of arts in chemistry. While in Yuma, Will worked part-time at the Shilo Inn and Patti was the dining room manager at the Yuma Golf and Country Club. In preparation for their move, Patti left her job in Yuma, ending a 32 year career in the food service industry. After Will's graduation they settled in Farmington where most of his family lives.

Will works for his brother, Terry Effan, who is the St. Francois County Surveyor, but shortly expects to start working for the US Postal Service. During

William, Patricia, Goldwyn (Scotties: Winnie, Kerry and Bear)

his naval career Will specialized in non-destructive testing, and was for 10 years, stationed on submarine tenders. Other duty assignments included general ship maintenance, planning, estimating and technical librarian. Through his career, Will served on five ships and made nine Western Pacific deployments. Patti, a native of Mobile, AL, is a homemaker. She is

James and Sarah Sebastian

also primary care-giver for her mother, an Alzheimer's/Parkinson's patient. Spare moments are spent crafting and tending their three Scotties and one abandoned Black Lab pup. They raise Scottish Terriers and hope to expand their kennel, "A Passel of Scotties in Farmington, MO." In the works is an on-line shopping page featuring an all Scottie selection of products for Scotties and their owners.

Will is a Sebastian on the maternal side of his family, through his mother, Marilyn, whose parents were James and Sarah Sebastian of Libertyville, MO. The Sebastians have been in this area since the early 1800s. His great-great-great grandfather, George W. Sebastian was one of the founders of Libertyville, MO. Since before the founding of Libertyville, the Sebastians have been active in county politics and law enforcement, including three circuit court judges, one doctor of medicine, one state legislator, and one sheriff, known from documents dating back to 1839. Descendants now living in St. Francois County include James and Sarah's children and grandchildren, George and Fern Sebastian and their children: Linda, Judy, George T. and Ben Lee; David and Cora Sebastian and their children, Edward and Diane; Helen Holt and her children: Joseph, Timothy and Nancy; Marilyn and Harvey's children include Terry and Ruth Effan and their son Steve, Alan and Jo Ann Effan, Will and Patti, and Harleen Miller and her daughter Mary Jo.

With a rich military history, the Sebastians and Effans have served their country in nearly every war since the Civil War. James M. Sebastian served during the Civil War, as did 13 of his cousins. Earl Sebastian, former St. Francois County Treasurer, served in the US Navy during WWI. The Effan family's service includes Will's fraternal grandfather, August Effan, who served in the United States Army during the Spanish American War, his father, Harvey W. Effan, served in the US Army Air Corps during WWII, his brother, Alan Effan, served in the US Army, completing two tours in Vietnam, and Will's service in the US Navy in the Persian Gulf War at Jebel Ali in the United Arab Emirates.

EFFREIN - Edward B. Effrein became a resident of Farmington when his parents, Benjamin and Anna Karl Effrein, moved here from Ste. Genevieve, MO when Benjamin Effrein became employed as a wagon maker by Lang Brothers Co.

Benjamin and Anna Karl Effrein were the parents of seven children; Hilda Moran, Augusta Seitz, Leona Hoffman, Emma Munger, Johanna Swink, Edward Benjamin and Thomas Bernard Effrein.

Edward Benjamin Effrein was born May 3, 1895, in Ste. Genevieve and was married to Juanita McAtee Effrein in 1921. Juanita was born Sept. 16, 1901, in Jackson, Mo, the daughter of Stephen and Lily Ross McAtee. Four children were born to

Edward and Juanita Effrein: Edward Jr. of Chicago, IL; Donald of Farmington; George of Quincy, IL; and Janet, who died at age 18 of pneumonia while attending college in Lafayette, LA.

Edward Effrein became a successful and respected business person in Farmington and was the owner and operator of Effrein Shoe Store for over 50 years until his retirement in 1970. Effrein Shoe Store was first located in the 100 block of E. Columbia Street in the building that originally housed the Theodore Lockridge Harness Shop. In its early years it was known as The Quality Shoe Store. Later the business moved across the street next to Kirkland's 5 cent and 10 cent store in, what was then, the Odd Fellows Building. This is the same site where Ozarks Federal Savings and Loan is located today, of

Mrs. Edward B. Effrein; son, Donald; daughter, Janet; son, Edward J. (1936)

which Edward's son, Donald, is president and chairman of the board.

Edward Effrein was an Army veteran of WWI, member of the Norman L. Rigdon VFW Post and Commander of the LePere-McCallister American Legion Post 416 in Farmington. He was also a member of the St. Jospeh's Catholic Church. A forward looking man, Edward took part in many community organizations and activities and simultaneously served as president of the Farmington Rotary Club and the Farmington Chamber of Commerce. During his tenure as president of the chamber, he and a

Edward Effrein, the father; daughter, Janet; sons, Edward and Don (George was not born at the time)

group of progressive businessmen were instrumental in securing a commitment from Trimfoot Shoe Company to locate in Farmington. Trimfoot opened its factory and headquarters in 1941 and remains here to the present day.

Edward Effrein Jr. is semi-retired from his insurance business in Chicago, IL. He is married to Mary Lou and has five children: Susan, Mark, John, Danny and Michael.

George Effrein is married to Mary and has three children: David, Craig and Janet. He is retired from a retail business in Quincy, IL.

Donald Effrein and his late wife, Dolores Bell Effrein, made their home in Farmington, MO. He has one son, Steve Effrein of Farmington, one daughter Stephanie (Mrs. Douglas) Helfrich of St. Peters, and three grandchildren. Besides his position with Ozarks Federal Savings and Loan, Donald Effrein is active in numerous professional organizations and carries on his father's tradition of being supportive of community organizations and activities that further the progress and growth of Farmington.

EMILY - Melvin Dan Emily, born in Richwoods, MO in 1886, was descended from grandparents who came from France. He served in France during WWI. In Bonne Terre, MO he met Mary Lucille Snowden of Fort Worth, TX, who was visiting relatives, and they married. Lucille was born in 1897.

As a young man, Dan was an accomplished musician, and a local newspaper at that time stated that he was much in demand at social gatherings. He played his violin at the movie theater at Flat River (now Park Hills) and his niece, Florence Mostiller, played the piano for him.

After their marriage, Dan and Lucille lived in Nevada, MO for a time, and then at Marshall, MO where he worked at the State Hospital and where their only child, Patricia, was born in 1927. They also lived in St. Louis a short time before settling in Farmington in 1928. Dan was a machinist at St. Joseph Lead Co. from the time he moved to Farmington until his retirement. They lived on a farm across from the old County Infirmary on what is now Weber

Dan and Lucille Emily

Road. Later they moved to Boyce Street in Farmington, where they lived when Patricia met and married Elmer Burns of Esther, MO, in 1946.

Lucille and Patricia were active in the Murphy Long Methodist Church South, where Lucille taught a girls Sunday School Class for several years. She was also active in the Oak Grove Home Economics Club. Dan died in Farmington in 1953. Lucille then made her home with Patricia and Elmer.

In 1955 they moved to Cincinnati, OH, where Elmer was employed as a machinist for General Electric. Lucille died of leukemia in 1970 in Cincinnati and was buried beside Dan in Parkview Cemetery near Farmington.

Patricia and Elmer have four children and six grandchildren. Their children are Richard (and Bonnie), Janet (and Mark) Gilbert, Nancy Lynn Burns, and Tom (and Kim) Burns. *Submitted by Patricia Emily Burns.*

FAIRCLOTH - Carol Currington Faircloth is a native of Farmington and with the exception of 1-1/2 years in St. Louis, has resided here all of her life. She is the mother of two children, Brent Alan, 29, and Amy Lynne, 24. Carol is the daughter of Kathryn Meyer Currington and the late Lindell T. Currington of Farmington.

L-R: Carol, Brent and Amy Faircloth

Lindell grew up in Flat River. He was born in 1914, the son of the late Wallace T. and Hattie Lee Fitzwater Currington. In his early years he, along with L.C. Mayes, ran a gas station and taxi business. It was there at his business on Ste. Genevieve Avenue (now a barber shop) where he met his bride, Kathryn Meyer.

Kathryn is the daughter of the late Adam and Katie Kollmeyer Meyer and was born in 1918. Her family's farm was located on the east end of Ste. Genevieve Ave. which is now the East Gate Trailor Park and Farm Bureau. Lindell (nicknamed Slim) and Kathryn were married at St. Paul Lutheran

Church in July 1939. They were the parents of three children: Gary Lee, born 1940; Dennis Ray, born 1945; and Carol Jean, born 1946. All three children are graduates of Farmington High School. Gary married the former Joyce Black of Farmington in 1963 and has two daughters, Shawn Aveningto of Rescue, CA, and Traci Schrampf of St. Louis. Shawn and her husband, John, have three children: Jimmy (9) and twin daughters, Ashley and Nicole (7-1/2) Gary and Joyce reside in Fenton where he is employed with Unigraphics Solutions, Inc. as regional business manager.

Denny is married to the former Janet Woodruf of Dexter, MO and they reside in San Diego, CA.

Carol married Darrell Faircloth of Bonne Terre in 1969 and they divorced in 1981.

Lindell worked underground in the St. Joe Lead Mines #17 in Flat River until June 1963, when he died at the early age of 48. Kathryn worked as cashier at P.N. Hirsch in Farmington for 27 years, retiring in May 1983. She still resides in Farmington.

After graduating from high school in 1964, Carol attended one semester of Flat River Junior College. In February 1965, she began working at United Bank of Farmington (now Mercantile) in the bookkeeping and proof departments. She resigned in July 1968 and moved to St. Louis where she was employed as a secretary for one year at Washington University School of Medicine. Carol and Darrell were married in St Louis and moved back to Farmington after the birth of their son, Brent Alan. Carol returned to United Bank until January 1974. In December 1975, she began working at her current employment, Ozarks Federal Savings and Loan Association. She began as the receptionist and has held various duties, including purchasing, public relations, marketing, advertising, new accounts and drive-up teller. Carol has been active in the Farmington community for several years, having been president of the Beta Sigma Phi sorority, Downtown Farmington Organization, United Way and the Farmington Business and Professional Women's Organization. She currently holds the title on the BPW state board as Public Relations Chair. Carol and her family are members of St. Paul Lutheran Church. Both of Carol's children are graduates of Farmington High School. Brent currently resides in Doe Run and is employed with Southeast Missouri Mental Health Center. Amy married Scott Lix of Farmington in October 1998 and they reside in Farmington. Amy is employed as a pharmacy tech at CMS and is a full-time student at CMC on the campus of Mineral Area College in Park Hills. She will receive her BS in business at the end of 1999. Scott is employed as plant supervisor, Mosler Co. (formerly LeFebure in Farmington) and attends Southeast Missouri State University in Cape Girardeau, majoring in industrial business.

Carol returned to Mineral Area College, attending night classes. She received her associate's degree in 1991.

FITZ - The first Fitz family to move to Farmington was headed by Charles Samuel Fitz, who was affectionately known as "Sam." Sam Fitz was the son of Thomas Purrington Fitz and was born Sept. 10, 1887 at DesArc, MO. During WWI he served in the Navy as a radio operator.

He was employed as a railroad tie inspector subsequent to the war. He married Lucy S. Horton from Poplar Bluff, MO on May 5, 1920.

In 1935 Sam Fitz purchased the Chevrolet Auto dealership in Farmington from John M. Morris. He later acquired the Buick automobile franchise in 1938. He died Feb. 16, 1960, having been

a car dealer for 25 years.

C.S. Fitz was an active member of the American Legion and served as commander of the LePere-McCalister Post in Farmington. He was a member of the Farmington Presbyterian Church and a deacon and ruling elder

Charles Samuel Fitz

for many years. His wife, Lucy Fitz, served as church organist and was active in the Red Cross blood bank program.

C.S. and Lucy Fitz had two sons, Thomas Patterson and Milton Sherwood. The youngest sibling was a daughter, Alice Louise, born Sept. 17, 1930. She married Alex Phillips from Rivermines. They lived in Columbia, MO until she died July 31, 1980.

Thomas Fitz attended the University of Missouri and graduated with a BS degree in business administration in 1943. That same year he was commissioned and assigned to the 86th Inf. Div. as an artillery officer during WWII. The division was sent to the European Theater of Operations and to the Philippines.

Tom returned to Farmington in 1947, where he established the Tom Fitz Sales Company, an appliance and farm equipment dealership, which he sold in 1953. Tom became general manager of Fitz Chevrolet-Buick, Inc.

Tom was a member and served as president of the Farmington Chamber of Commerce, the Kiwanis Club and the Farmington Board of Education.

In 1948 he married Lois Ann "Tanny" Rutledge from Crystal City. She served on the faculty of the Farmington Public Schools for 16 years. To this union two children were born, Sarah "Sally" H. Fitz on Sept. 2, 1952, and John Rutledge Fitz on June 7, 1956.

Sally attended the University of Missouri, graduating in 1975 with a degree in journalism. She also attended the Institute of European Studies in Vienna, Austria. She was employed as a TV anchor for WTVS in Miami, FL, where she worked for 12 years. She was chosen parade marshal in 1991 for the Farmington Country Days activities. Sally now lives in Chicago, IL with her husband, Michael Morrison, and son, MacArthur Morrison.

John Rutledge Fitz graduated from Farmington High School in 1974. He attended Duke University and the St. Louis University School of Medicine. He became a resident in ophthalmology at the University of Missouri.

In 1986 Dr. Fitz returned to Farmington where he established his practice in ophthalmology, known as Precision Eye Care. In 1999 he also was instrumental in establishing the Surgery Center of Farmington.

In 1983 he married Elizabeth Rohan from St. Louis. They had three children: Martin, Harrison and Hillary.

Milton S. Fitz was born July 11, 1925 and died Aug. 24, 1987. He joined an ASTP unit prior to his graduation from Farmington High School. He attended Westminster College at Fulton where he joined Delta Tau Delta social fraternity. Two years later he transferred to the University of Missouri, taking courses in economics and business administration.

He served in WWII as a member of a chemical mortar battalion from 1943 until 1946. He later joined the Army Reserves and was promoted to first lieutenant.

Milton was employed by Fitz Chevrolet-Buick as business manager. He was a member of the Scottish Rite, Rotary and VFW in Farmington.

He married Barbara Elizabeth Hulsey on Dec. 19, 1954. She was employed as a teacher for 29 years with most of her career being a librarian at the Farmington Middle School. They had two children, Cynthia, born Aug. 20, 1959 and James, born Sept. 15, 1966. Cynthia attended the University of Southwest Missouri, graduating in 1985. She is employed by Huffy Bicycle Company as Human Resources manager.

Cyndi married Les Lamb, an industrial engineer with Chrysler Corporation. Her children are Travis LaBruyere and Suzanne Lamb. The family resides in Farmington.

James Fitz attended Mineral Area College and graduated with a degree in engineering from the University of Missour-Rolla in 1993. He lives in Hibbing, MN where he is employed as an electrical engineer with Internet. On Sept. 24, 1999 he married Karen Forsteum from Minnesota. Submitted by Thomas P. Fitz.

FLANERY - Isaac Flanery, born in Illinois in 1820, came to Farmington around 1840, where he bought 39 acres of land from the "Deluziere Tract" in St. Francois County. On Nov. 6, 1848, he married Nancy Tabor, born Aug. 27, 1825, of Anderson County, TN, and they had three children: John, William and Emma. He made his living In the lead mining business and fought in the Civil War as a Union soldier at Pilot Knob. He died at age 58 in 1878, and Nancy died at age 88. Both are buried in the Pendleton Cemetery in Doe Run, MO.

John, born 1852, in Huzzah, MO, married Esther Ann Wood of Ohio. Esther Ann, at the age of 13, along with her family had to wait for the Mississippi to freeze over before crossing. After marriage, John and Esther Ann purchased 54 acres of land from the "Deluziere Tract," donating land for the Flanery School which existed for many years. Esther Ann wove her own rugs. She would hang them on a line, beating them with a rug beater to clean. She would return them after scrubbing the floor and covering it with newspapers to keep out the cold. John was an ordained Baptist minister who rode the circuit of several churches and also farmed to support nine children: Nancy, Martha, Charles, Lizzie, Otto, Jess, Fred and two who died young. Early on, his was one of only three telephones in the area. Sons, Otto and Jess, served in WWI. Esther Ann died in 1928, John died in 1944 (age 92) and both are buried in Doe Run Cemetery.

Radford, Darrell, Elton, Bernice, Rowena, wife of Charles, Opal, T. Lee

Charles Flanery was born in 1882, in the old farmhouse. He and his first wife, Nellie Scaggs of Leadwood, had three children. Within two years, Elva (age 4), Ted (age 1-1/2) and wife, Nellie, died. A daughter, Trixie Lee, survived and became a nurse. Her son, Barnard Baker, has two daughters.

Charles then married Opal Westover of Bonne Terre in 1910. Opal had been a talented

milliner. They had five children: Radford, Rowena, Darrell, Bernice and Elton. The family lived in Doe Run on a small farm then moved to a house in Farmington where the Taylor Funeral home is now located. They then moved to St. Louis for nine years, returning to Farmington. Charlie was a carpenter who built many homes in Farmington. All of the children but Radford graduated from Farmington High School. While living on Jackson Street, they watched the high school burn. The students were transferred to Carleton College to complete the year. This family was musically talented. The three boys played and sang in bands that performed for school programs and local entertainment spots.

Radford married Marguerite Williams of Farmington and settled in Tulsa, OK with four children. He died in 1991 at the age of 80. Rowena, born in 1913, married Louie Crouch and had four children: Howard, Wayne, Ann and Paul. She worked as a beauty shop operator. Louie died in 1972. Rowena married Clarence Hill. She died in 1991 and Clarence died in 1996.

John D. and Esther Ann Flanery about 1872

Darrell, born in 1915, had two children and lives in California. He worked for the zoning commission. Elton, born in 1918 had four children. He is a WWII veteran. He ran his own contracting business and is now retired and living in Maryland.

Bernice, born in 1917, married in 1936, then divorced and married Guy Roux who had one son with two children, Mike and Linda. Guy died in 1980 and is buried in Hillview Gardens. Bernice then married Louis Cochran of Farmington. He had one son, Dennis. Lou died in 1994 and is buried in Zolman Cemetery, Farmington. Bernice worked as a medical records technician. Bernice is the only Flanery living in Farmington at the present time. There are many relatives in surrounding states and counties. *Submitted by Bernice Flanery Cochran*

FLIEG - Indeed the Flieg family is a pioneer family! It is believed that Josef Flieg came to America in the mid-1840s. Working as a (Schreiner) cabinet maker in St. Louis before settling in Zell, MO, Ste. Genevieve, CO. He came from Weilheim, Germany in the area of Burg Hohenzollern, South Germany. He was about 17 years old. He bought 38 acres, the original home place, where he built the first home. Later it was used as a chicken house and still used in that capacity on Henry Flieg's departure in 1941. Later a larger home was constructed of logs, straw, and mortar, boxed inside and out and added to, section by section as needed as family increased.

Ancestral line starts with Joseph marrying Rosa Hoog. They were married March 1, 1859, at Zell, MO. To this union 14 children were born as follows: Catherine, Henry, Anastasia, Juliana, Charles, Francis "Frank," Theresa, Elizabeth, Peter, Ludwig, Tony, Tom, Andrew and George.

Son, Andrew, was 9 years old when Grandpa died on Feb. 2, 1892. Rosa continued living at home place until her death; when it was pur-

chased by son, Andrew. The children walked three miles to Zell through pastures, barn lots and wheat fields to school.

Henry Joseph Flieg, son of Andrew Flieg, at about 5 years old remembers Grandmother Rosie. He remembers her falling at home and couldn't

Josef Flieg, Germany, Henry Flieg, Ste. Genevieve

get up until someone came home to help, and he remembers her body in state at home and the lines of wagons going through fields from home to St. Joseph Church and cemetery in Zell for burial on Dec. 19, 1922.

Back Row: Herbert and Henry Flieg. Front Row: Alois, Rosemary Kreitler, Lorene Gegg, Richard, Francis and Sr. Mary Vera Flieg

Andrew bought the home place and raised his family there. Later he moved to a trailer and he expired in Ste. Genevieve Hospital on July 23, 1972, at age 89. Andrew and Philomena Grass Flieg were married April 7, 1913, and had eight children: Juliana (Sr. Mary Vera), Herbert, Henry, Alois, Lorene Gegg, Richard, Francis and Rosemary Kreitler. All living except Herbert who expired in 1997.

Son, Francis, bought old home place and added new sections to house for expansion. Francis's son, Steve, demolished the older home and built a new home on the original 38 acres, where he resides with his wife, Carol, and two children, Jennifer and Kevin. He continues with farming and gardening as his occupation.

Andrew and Philomena's children are all retired, doing farming and stock raising, and live on acreage in Zell and Weingarten area. On the weekend of Aug. 10, 1997, The Flieg family was chosen as Pioneer Family of the Year for Ste. Genevieve's Annual Jour de Fete. Indeed an honor!

Andrew and Philomena Flieg

Local descendants of Anton Flieg and Mechtildis Beck of early 1700 from Weilheim, Germany, joined several committees and compiled our ancestral genealogy. Trips to Germany and with communications, we located a fifth generation cousin, Josef, living in same locale in Weilheim, Germany, where Grandfather Joseph originally came. Josef visited with all family relations during Jour de Fete and when accepting award for traveling the farthest says, "He has more relatives in United States than in Germany consisting of father, brother and two nieces." Josef is entering family tree in computer, also keeping in touch with US family regularly. A family re-united again after being separated for many years. *Submitted by Evelyn Flieg*

FORSYTHE - Joseph Leo Forsythe was born May 14, 1902, in Elvins, St. Francois County, MO, and died June 6, 1966, in Fredericktown, MO. He was the son of Zacharia Jesse and Mary Downs Forsythe. Zacharia Jessie Forsythe was born in Cornwall, Madison County, MO, Aug. 14, 1872, and was the son of James Patrick and Sarah Snow Forsythe, who came from Lincoln County, TN. Jesse died in a underground mine accident Aug. 3, 1922, in the National Lead Mines at Flat River. He is buried in the Woodlawn Cemetery in Leadington, MO. He was married to Mary Downs in 1898, the daughter of Henry and Emma Frizzell Downs, born 1877, died 1970 in Illinois. They were the parents of five children: Joseph; Thelma, born in 1905, married Harry Long; Vera, born in 1907, married Charles Walker; Juanita, born in 1910, married George Greenwell; and Harold Morgan, born 1912, married three times. They all lived in Illinois and St. Louis, except Joseph Leo and family.

L-R: Theodore (middle), Dwayne, Warren, Leo and Cordelia c. 1942.

Joseph Leo Forsythe married Cordelia Ellen Weiss on March 29, 1923, in Doe Run, MO. She was the daughter of Peter and Cora Honeycutt Weiss. Cordelia was born May 18, 1908, in Doe Run, MO and died July 5, 1992, in Farmington, MO. Peter was the son of Heinrich and Mary Mueller Weiss who came from Germany to Doe Run, MO. Cora Ellen Honeycutt was born in 1876, in Wayne County, MO. They were en route to St. Francois County from Arkansas. She was the daughter of Charles and Cordelia Murray Honeycutt. Leo and Cordelia lived in Flat River. They moved to Hurryville, then bought a farm on D Highway in Ste. Genevieve County. Joseph Leo was a farmer and worked in the St. Joe Lead Mines for 39 years. When he retired, they moved to Farmington and lived there until he died in 1966. He and Cordelia are buried in the Hillview Cemetery in Farmington, MO. They had four children.

1) Theodore Morgan Forsythe was born Jan. 22, 1926, in Flat River and married Laverne Williams, born Jan. 22, 1931, in 1948. She was the daughter of Eugene and Ida Baker Williams and was born in Doe Run, MO. They had four children: (1) Danny, born and died Aug. 30, 1949. (2) Steven, born Dec. 3, 1950, married Gale Centrone in Virginia, where he was stationed while serving in the US Navy. They are the parents of Daniel, born 1983; Katherine, born 1987; and Stephanie, born 1989. After retiring from the US Navy, Steven went to work for United Airlines in maintenance in San Francisco and after eight years transferred in October 1998, to Indianapolis, IN. His wife and children are living in Farmington where the children are in school but plan to move to Indianapolis at a later time. (3) Karen Leigh Forsythe, born April 29, 1957, married Terry Pyeatt in 1977 but divorced. They lived in Grand Junction, CO where their daughter, Tera Danielle, was born Jan. 17, 1978. Kirk was born May 7, 1981, in Greeley, CO. Karen and Tera now live in Missouri. (4) Linda Carol Forsythe, born Jan. 1, 1959, was the first baby born in St. Francois County in the new year. She mar-

ried Allen Manning but they divorced. She has a son, Nathaniel Joseph, born March 19, 1990, in Greeley, CO. She is married to Dennis Smith and they live in Valmeyer, IL.

2. Warren Forsythe, born Feb. 11, 1928, in Flat River, died July 20, 1992, in St. Peters, MO, married Betty Koen in 1951 and they had Pattie Marie, born 1952, who wed Dennis Smith. They have two children, Jacob and Sarah. Terry Forsythe was born in 1955, and married Melissa. They have two children, Justin and Christian. Warren was retired from the Navy.

3. Dwayne Forsythe was born April 30, 1932, in Flat River and married Betty Lou Johnson. They have three children: Dianne is married to John Anderson and has two sons, Mark and Eric; Vickie married Larry Mitchell; Cathy married George Cadman and they divorced. She has a son Jayson. Dwayne is retired from NASA. He and his family live in Texas.

4. James Forsythe, born May 2, 1945, married Linda Clark and had three children: Cheri who was born in 1968, and married first Shawn Snell, they divorced. She has a daughter, Kristara Ann, whose father is Walter Long. Misty, born Oct. 24, 1970, died Oct. 26, 1970, and is buried in the Weiss Cemetery in Doe Run, MO; Scott was born in 1972, in California. James married second to Stephanie Johnson. *Submitted by Karen Forsythe*

FOX - James Andrew "Andy" and Sophia Irene (Harris) Fox began married life in Washington County. Shortly after WWII, Sophia sought employment at State Hospital #4 in Farmington. Soon, Andy, too, obtained employment at the hospital and they moved their family to Farmington. After a short while they purchased a home in DeLassus where they lived until retirement. Their family included John, Florence, Elsie, Linda and Pamela.

Following retirement they moved back to Irondale where they felt they would find perfect retirement. They loved friends, family and the familiarity of Irondale, but soon found they missed the friends, church and business affiliations of Farmington. In 1973, they returned to Farmington, moving to a home on Clover Lane just outside the city limits of Farmington. Andy and Sophie are now deceased but two of their children, John and Pam, remain Farmington residents.

Sophia and Andy Fox, 40th wedding anniversary

FOX - John P. Fox moved to Farmington with his family as a young boy. In 1955, he enlisted in the US Air Force and moved to Texas. In 1956, he returned to Farmington to marry Frances E. Brewster. They soon had their family, Mary Anne and John P. Jr. The family traveled to bases around Texas, Arizona, Nevada and Tripoli, Libya.

In 1968, the family moved to Kennett, MO where John became the Air Force recruiter. In 1970, the family returned to Farmington where John was Air Force recruiter until his retirement in 1975. Following retirement, John took a job with the Farmington Police Department but left after a few months to become owner/operator of dump trucks and operator of a small family cattle farm.

Meanwhile, Frances had worked in several positions in Farmington and finally went to work at the Farmington Post Office. After a number of years, she transferred to a supervisory position at the Bonne Terre Post Office. She retired in 1992.

John and Frances are long standing and

active members of the Independent Order of Odd Fellows (IOOF), John as an Odd Fellow and Frances as a Rebekah. Both belong to the other units of the order. John is past department commander, Department Council of Missouri; general commanding (retired), Patriarchs Militant of the World; past grand master, Grand Lodge of Missouri; and past grand patriarch, Grand Encampment of Missouri. He is a member of the Ancient and Mystic Order of Samaritans (AMOS). He is a Master Mason and presently going through the chairs of George Washington Lodge #9. Frances is past president, Rebekah Assembly of Missouri and past president, Ladies Association Patriarch Militant of Missouri.

General John Fox and Lady Frances Fox

Several years ago John served on Farmington's City Council for six years, five of these he was mayor Pro-Tem. They continue to live in Farmington with John serving on the Board of Adjustment and Frances serving on the Planning and Zoning Commission.

FRANCIS - Fred Edward Francis was born April 2, 1935, to Clarence Edward and Esther (Jordan) Francis, in Madison County, MO. He was the oldest of five children (two died in infancy). His brother, Harvie and Mimi Francis, live at Holden, MO, and sister, Shirley (Jackie) and Craig Wright, live at Alburnett, IA. Fred graduated from Fredericktown High School in 1953, worked in St. Louis for awhile and served in the US Army from 1955-1957. On July 20, 1957, he married Carol Faye Monie at Second Baptist Church, Fredericktown, MO. Carol was born on Aug. 13, 1939, to Marion and Lillie (Cobb) Monie. She was the youngest of three children. Sister, Viola Myers, lives near DeSoto, MO, and brother, Lewis, and Pauline Monie, live at Farmington. Carol graduated from Fredericktown High School in 1956.

Fred and Carol Francis

Fred and Carol moved to Farmington in 1959. He worked at Trimfoot Co. from 1957-85. In 1985, Fred purchased Farmington Small Engines, a local business at 125 North Washington, selling and servicing chain saws and lawn/garden equipment. Fred relocated the business to 207 East Liberty where it remained until the business closed in 1996 after his death. Fred died on July 5, 1995, of a brain aneurysm.

Carol began working for Farmington School District in 1970, serving as a teacher aide and secretary at Farmington High School. She transferred to the school administrative offices in 1986 and continues to serve as secretary to the superintendent and to the Board of Education. Fred and Carol are the parents of two sons, Mark Edward, born in 1960, and Rodney Lynn, born in 1962.

Mark lives in Price, UT and is self-employed in a business called Startech (computer/telephony integration). He also manages the airport at Price and enjoys flying. Mark has a daughter, Megan, and stepdaughter, Laura. Rodney has three children: Kendra, Keith and Kerick, who live in Iowa. Rodney lives in Virginia Beach, VA with his wife, Sandy, and two stepdaughters, Celeste and Amanda. He has been in the nuclear submarine service of the US Navy since 1985.

Fred's parents were born and raised in Madison County, but moved to Viburnum, MO in the late 1950s when the lead mining operations moved to that area. Clarence Francis, born April 11, 1912, was killed in a mining accident in 1972. Esther, born Sept. 1, 1918, married Ralph Pirtle (deceased 1990) in 1980 and she lives at Farmington.

Carol's parents were married in Bollinger County, MO. In the early years of their marriage they lived on a farm near Marquand, MO and Marion operated a sawmill along with his brother, Arthur Monie. They moved to Fredericktown in 1949 and Marion turned to carpentry for his occupation. He and his son, Lewis, helped build many houses at Fredericktown and Farmington. Lillie devoted her life to her family, church and writing poetry. Her children plan to self-publish a book, *Surrounded by Love,* for friends and family so that her poetry can be shared with future generations. Marion was born in 1892 and died in 1978. Lillie was born in 1901 and lives in a nursing home. *Submitted by Carol Francis*

GENTGES - Bernard Thomas Gentges was favorably impressed with Farmington when he arrived on the streetcar along Columbia Street in 1914. A son of John J. Gentges, a Belgian emigrant who settled in Quincy, IL before the Civil War, Bernard came to take over the "Jet White" commercial laundry which he renamed "The Farmington Laundry" (now Midstates Laundry).

Mr. Gentges was a widower with two daughters, Mary and Cecelia. In 1916, he married Elsie Buckman Miles, daughter of an old Kentucky family who had settled in northeast Missouri. She was a widow with two children, Tom and Velma. A son, Charles Robinson, was born in 1918, and daughter, Anna Johanna "Nancy" in 1922. Cecelia, Charles and Nancy are still living.

Mary became Mrs. Bert Bragg and moved to Pennsylvania. Tom, Velma and Cecelia graduated from SE Missouri State Teachers' College at Cape Girardeau. Velma married Ford Thurston and lived in Wisconsin; Tom and his wife, Sarah Tucker, of Farmington, moved to St. Louis where Sarah still resides.

"At Farmington, Mayor B.T. Gentges and his wife and children: Cecelia, Charles and Nancy, at home." From a 1935 St. Louis newspaper photo supplement section.

Cecelia taught school, then returned home to help in the laundry business, remaining through the war until her dad retired at age 77 in 1953.

The Gentges family lived in the tall house at 418 N. Washington from 1920 to 1964. Mrs. Gentges was known for her tailoring skills, her flowers, and her many club memberships where she was in demand to give book reviews.

Mr. Gentges was mayor of Farmington for five years during the 1930s. During the Depression, Mr. Gentges managed to keep on almost all his employees, despite great personal loss.

The family was active in St. Joseph's parish, where they comprised all four vocal parts of the choir as well as the organist.

Of the two younger children, Nancy went to Mount Mary in Milwaukee to become a dietitian, took a job in Portland, OR and married Gerald Janson in 1947. Their five children and families live in the northwest; since Gerald's death in 1998, Nancy continues to reside in Vancouver, WA.

Charles was drafted in 1941 and served in the US Infantry, Red Bull Division, in Ireland, England, North Africa and Italy, being wounded three times. After a four-year wartime correspondence, he and Florence Schwartz of Farmington married in October 1945. Daughter, Mary Elizabeth, was born in 1947. Charles and Florence went into retailing in 1951 and spent almost 30 years in the variety store business in central Missouri and Colorado, retiring in 1982. They and daughter, Mary, now reside in St. Marys, KS.

After her dad's retirement, Cecelia returned to education, teaching at Farmington Middle School for 19 years. She cared for her stepmother and father who died in 1963 and 1964, respectively.

Cecelia was active in the Business and Professional Women, the Monday Club, the Historical Society and was well-known in St. Joseph's parish where she had been organist for 35 years and a charter member of the Legion of Mary. The last Gentges in Farmington, Cecelia (now 92) moved in 1997 to Our Lady of Mercy Country Home, Liberty, MO.

GIERSE - Frank Henry Gierse came to this country from Herschberg, Germany about 1880. He married Mathilda Best, daughter of Karl and Maria Best, of rural Farmington. They moved to Farmington and purchased the building and property at 106 West Columbia. Frank started the Frank Gierse Merchant Tailor business in 1882. At that time the business took up part of the building and the rest was used for their living quarters.

Frank and Mathilda had two children, Charles Theodore and Frederick John. Frank was Catholic and raised Charles in the Catholic faith. Mathilda, whose father helped found St. Paul's Lutheran Church of Farmington, raised Fred in the Lutheran Church. All of Fred's

Martin and Ailene Gierse

descendants have remained active in the Lutheran Church.

Frank died in 1900, at the age of 49. Mathilda took over the business until her sons could manage it. Charles stayed and ran the business while Fred went to Cut Make and Trim School in Chicago in 1908. Charles married Louise Schwaner of Fredericktown, Fred married Bird May Keller of Farmington. In 1913, Charles sold his interest to Fred and moved to Poplar Bluff, to open a shop. In 1912, Fred added dry cleaning to his business.

Fred and Bird had five children: Martin K., Virginia, Winifred "Winnie," Charles F. and Margaret L. All the children were born in the home at 713 West Liberty. Fred had purchased this land and built his home there. The Gierse family still owns seven acres behind the original home

In the 1920s, Fred took his family to Phoenix, AZ hoping the climate would cure his sinus problems. He kept the shop in Farmington open by having John Miller run it in his absence. Fred did some tailoring while in Phoenix and Martin has fond memories of going to grade school there.

Fred's mother, Mathilda, became ill. Then a fire in the cleaning plant caused Fred and family to return home. Mathilda recovered. Fred then took his oldest son, Martin, along with a family friend, to Mercedes, TX. There, he purchased land and built a home. Bird brought the rest of

Gierse Family Home c. 1944, 713 Liberty St., Martin Keller Gierse, Ruth Ailene Edwards Gierse, Viginia Lucille Gierse Giddens, mother - Bird May Keller Gierse, father - Frederick Gierse, Charles Frederick Gierse, Margaret Louise Gierse, Winnifred May Gierse Nelson, Raymond Leyden Nelson.

their children and her mother, Sophie Keller, to Texas. The climate didn't help Fred, so the Gierses returned to Farmington. They kept the Texas property for several years.

Martin went to West Palm Beach, FL, where he spent several winters learning newer methods of dry cleaning. Due to his father's ill health, Martin took over running the business in the 30s.

In 1938, Martin married Ailene Edwards. He served in Europe during WWII and while Martin was in the service, Fred Gierse helped John Miller keep the business going. Martin returned to Farmington in 1946.

Virginia married Paul Giddens, moved to California and raised a family. Winnie married Raymond Nelson from Bonne Terre. They had one son, Ray Lynn. Winnie, Ray Lynn and his wife, Kathie (Kauffman) and daughters, Anna and Katie, reside in Farmington. Charles married Melbe McDaniel and they moved to Florissant and raised two sons, Charles Jr. and James. Margaret married Leon Seitz and they moved to Phoenix, AZ.

Martin and Ailene had two children, Keller Edward and Robert Martin. When Fred Gierse passed away in 1950, Martin became sole owner and kept the business going with the help of Ailene until they sold the business in 1986. The Gierses had owned the business 104 years and they still own the building.

Martin and Ailene remain in Farmington. Their son, Robert, his wife, Nancy Wiley, and their children, Rebekah Erin and Alex Wiley, also live there. Their son, Keller, lives in St. Louis and his son, Christopher, lives in Scottsdale, AZ.

GIESSING - After coming to America, he changed his name to Charles. Giessing was born Dec. 12, 1823, in Waldeck, Germany, also a vicinity of Niederinghausen, Germany. He immigrated to America in 1847. His parents were Carl Friedrich Giessing, born 1789, died 1846, and Marie Friedrich Schaabe, born 1789, died 1833, from Adorf, Germany.

Carl Adam Friedrich Giessing

Charles Giessing married Mary Hoehn, in Missouri, on April 15, 1851. Charles and Mary Hoehn Giessing had seven sons and two daughters. One daughter, Mary, died in infancy. Elizabeth never married. The sons were John, Charles, Peter, Henry, Frederick, Dan and William.

Charles immigrated from Germany and settled in Iron Mountain, MO. Through years of efficient service he held many prominent positions with the Iron Mountain Mining Co. Charles became head foreman of the Foundry Department. In this capacity he became one of their highest salaried workmen, earning $1,800 per year.

Children of Charles Giessing and Mary Hoehn Giessing in 1880. Top: Dan, Peter, Henry, Fred and Will. Bottom: John, Elizabeth and Charles Jr.

In 1860 he and his brother-in-law, Peter Hoehn, purchased a flour mill in Valley Forge, located a few miles east of Farmington, MO on the old Plank Road, leading from Iron Mountain to Ste. Genevieve, MO. The flour mill was situated on Wolf Creek. The power in the mill, to grind the wheat into flour, was obtained by a water wheel.

Giessing Family Reunion at the home of Mr. and Mrs. D. F. Giessing at 317 North Jefferson Street in Farmington, Nov. 26, 1908. Back L to R: Miss Bettie Giessing, D. F. Giessing, Charles Giessing, John Giessing, Peter Giessing, Henry Giessing, Charles H. Giessing, Jr. Middle L to R: Mrs. Charles Giessing, Mrs. Charles H. Giessing, Mrs. Peter Giessing, Mrs. John Giessing, Norma Giessing (Mrs. George Herbst), Mrs. Henry Giessing, Melvin (Pete) Giessing, Mrs. D. F. Giessing, Mildred Giessing (Mrs. Arthur Soergel). Bottom L to R: Miss Maymie Giessing, Mrs. Emma Patton, Miss Elizabeth Giessing, Theodore Giessing, Marian Giessing (Mrs. Wesley Holler), Mrs. H. Edward Koschmann, Cecelia Giessing (Mrs. Herbert Schramm) and Mrs. Minnie Kowert.

In 1867, Charles and Mary moved to Valley Forge. In 1897, the mill was moved to Farmington, MO. Charles died Feb. 18, 1880, and Mary Hoehn died in April 1893. They are buried in the Odd Fellows Cemetery on Ste. Genevieve Ave. in Farmington. This information was obtained from Mildred Giessing Soergel and from a letter written to me from Maime Giessing in 1969. *Submitted by Louise Holler Craddock, great-granddaughter of Charles Giessing and Mary Hoehn Giessing.*

GIESSING - Charles Henry Giessing, known as Charlie to his friends, was born Dec. 20, 1878, in Valley Forge, St. Francios County, MO. He was the oldest son of John Henry Giessing Sr. and Johannetta "Nettie" Reuter. Charlie was young when his family moved to Farmington in 1880. He attended grade school at the Lutheran School in Farmington, Farmington High School, and Walter College in St. Louis.

On April 9, 1901, Charlie married Lydia Vollath, the daughter of George and Doretta Vollath. Charlie built a home at 511 Forster St. for his family and the couple lived there all their married life. He also built a house next door for his widowed mother-in-law, Dorothea Vollath. Charlie and Lydia reared four children: Theodore, born 1903; Cecelia (Mrs. Herbert Schramm), born 1906; Mignon (Mrs. Carl Webb), born 1913; and Walter Karl, born 1919.

Charles Henry Giessing, 1878-1962

Charlie worked as an assistant cashier at the Bank of Farmington from 1901-1916. In 1916, he went into business with his father, John Giessing Sr., and his brother, John, in the Farmington Milling Co. on East Columbia Street. He was closely associated with Farmington civic and business affairs. In 1917, he filled out a term of mayor of Farmington and was re-elected for the 1918-1919 term. He served intermittently as an alderman of Farmington for 40 years. He was associated with the Farmington Home Building and Loan Association for 25 years and served as the association president for 15 of those years. Charlie also served as manager of the St. Francios Railroad for 21 years. In 1948, Charlie semi-retired from the milling business but remained active in civic and church affairs. Charlie and Lydia Giessing were active members of St. Paul's Lutheran Church all their lives and Charlie served in a number of offices in the church.

Charlie and his wife, Lydia, were privileged to celebrate not only their Golden Anniversary but also their 60th wedding anniversary. On Sept. 5, 1962, Charlie died suddenly of a heart attack. Lydia remained in the family home until her death on Feb. 8, 1965. Charles Giessing was a man advanced in business enterprises and was always interested in new technology. He loved to try new inventions. He possessed fine leadership qualities which he used to benefit his church and the community of Farmington.

GIESSING - Daniel Frederick Giessing was born May 1, 1868, at Valley Forge, MO, the son of Charles Giessing and Marie Hoehn. He was baptized into the Lutheran faith at Pilot Knob and was confirmed at St. Paul's Lutheran Church in Farmington. He attended St. Paul's Lutheran School and later attended Carleton College in Farmington. When he was 20 years old, he went to the International Business School in St. Louis where he received a degree in accounting.

His career started as the manager of Valley Forge General Merchandizing Company at Wolf Creek. He was also the postmaster. In 1897, the Giessing Milling Company at Valley Forge was dismantled and moved to North Washington St. in Farmington. At this time, Daniel and two of his brothers, Peter and Henry, took over the operations of this flour mill.

On Dec. 12, 1905, he married Pauline Keiser of Mount Olive, IL. Their union was blessed with three children: Mildred (Mrs. A.F. Soergel), Alberta (Mrs. E.D. Eifert) and Vernon (Mrs. Helen Bode).

Daniel was active in local business and civic activities for more than a half century. He was on the board of directors of the Bank of Farmington, United Bank, Ozark Federal and was president of Farm Equitable Building and Loan Association. He was included in a group that underwrote and managed the St. Francois County Railroad Co. and was one of 16 local citizens who took over supervision of the Carleton College property. He was a member of the courthouse commission that supervised the construction of the present courthouse. He also was a member of the building committee which built the first St. Paul's Lutheran school building.

Back L-R: John, Charles, Peter, Henry, Fred, William and Daniel. Front L-R: Joanetta, Louisa, Tillie, Annie, Rachel and Pauline.

Daniel's great-grandson and family, William B. Giessing II, now reside in the old family homestead built in 1905 at 317 North Jefferson. Daniel died June 12, 1954, and his wife, Pauline, followed him in death May 9, 1967. Both are buried in the Lutheran Cemetery near Farmington. *This information was obtained from Mildred Giessing Soergel*

Daniel and wife, Pauline (Keiser) Giessing

GIESSING - In 1882, John and Charles II moved to Farmington and purchased the Farmington Milling Co. from Rodeheaver and Boyce. The other boys continued to operate the mill in Valley Forge until 1897, when the mill was dismantled and moved to N. Washington St. in Farmington and rebuilt. This mill was operated by Peter, Henry and Daniel. Frederick was in East St. Louis, IL with Schaub Hardware Co., and William was in Desloge, MO in general merchandising.

Giessing Milling Co.

Giessing Milling Co. continued to be a thriving business. During WWI the mill ran 24 hours a day. Flour was shipped by the carloads to the US Government to supply the Army with this staple. In 1925, Peter and his family moved to California, and Henry and Dan continued to run the business. In 1935, Daniel's son, Vernon, and Henry's son, Melvin, entered the business. Later in 1948, the mill was sold to MFA who operated it until 1978, when the entire plant was razed. Washington Square currently occupies this land, but the memories of what once stood there can never be erased. *History is from Mildred Giessing Soergel Submitted by Louise Holler Craddock*

GIESSING - John Henry Giessing Sr. was one of seven sons of Carl Adam Friedrich Giessing, who immigrated from Germany to St. Franclos County, MO in 1845. His mother was Mary Hoehn, who immigrated from Prussia in 1850. John was born

John Henry Giessing Sr., 1852-1930

Jan. 13, 1852, in Iron Mountain, MO, where his father worked in the iron mines. Due to near blindness from working in the foundry, John's father purchased the Valley Forge Flour Mill on the Old Plank Road leading from Iron Mountain to Ste. Genevieve. In 1867, the family moved to Valley Forge just east of Farmington. The name of the mill was changed to the Giessing and Sons Flour Mill. From an early age, John worked in the flour mill at Valley Forge and became bookkeeper and general manager. After the death of their father, John and his younger brother, Charles, moved to Farmington and in 1882, purchased the Farmington Roller Mills on E. Columbia St. for $7,000. The mill became known as the Farmington Milling Co. The principal brands of flour they sold were Fancy Patent, Snow Drop, Blue Ribbon and Red Ribbon. They shipped flour as far away as New Orleans. On Jan. 12, 1878, John married Johannette "Nettie" Reuter, the daughter of Frederick Reuter, in Valley Forge. Nettie had arrived in America a few years earlier with only a few dollars in her pocket and was a domestic worker for the Giessings. John and Nettie built their home on Ste. Genevieve St. They raised four sons and three daughters: Charles, born 1878; Frederick, born 1880; John, born 1882; Peter, born 1887; Elizabeth, born 1887; Minnie (Mrs. Henry Kowert), born 1889; and Anna Peter 1884, (Mrs. Edward Koschmann), born 1891.

In 1906, needing a convenient means to transport goods to and from his mill, John entered into an agreement with the St. Francios Railroad, Schramm's Ice and Coal Storage Co. and Lang and Brother's Manufacturing and Mercantile Co. to construct a railroad spur from DeLassus into Farmington. During WWI, the mill ran 24 hours a day to ship staples to the Army. John remained active in the milling business until 1921, when he turned the management of the mill over to his sons, Charles and John.

A devoted Lutheran, John donated the land on which St. Paul's Lutheran Church was erected. He and his wife remained active in the church all their lives. John passed away on March 13, 1930, at his home in Farmington. His wife, Nettie, died on Dec. 1, 1936. Both are buried in the St. Paul's Lutheran Cemetery.

GIESSING - Peter Giessing was born Feb. 1, 1858, in Iron Mountain, MO. Peter attended the public schools of Iron Mountain and Farmington. His school days ended before he was 20 years old, and for several years prior to that time he had been employed, more or less, in his father's mill. His parents were Charles and Mary Hoehn

Giessing. After quitting school, he went to work regularly in the mill and for eight or 10 years was the engineer of the establishment. In 1882, two years after his father's death, he became one of the principal owners of the Giessing Milling Co., his associates being his two brothers.

Peter Giessing and Louise Knoche Giessing

In 1882, he remodeled the plant at Valley Forge, changing the process of manufacturing to what is known as the roller system. Until 1893, this plant was operated under the name of Giessing & Sons. The death of his mother, Mary Hoehn Giessing, brought about a readjustment of affairs, and the Giessing Milling Company was organized with Peter, Henry and Daniel F. Giessing as partners. In 1897, the mill at Valley Forge was dismantled and the same year the brothers erected a large flour manufacturing plant at Farmington. He was a successful manufacturer and a good citizen in all that the term implies.

Peter Giessing was a resident of Farmington for over 30 years during which he was prominent in all civic matters. He was one of the promoters and the first president of the local electric railroad and was active in bringing that enterprise to a successful completion. He was a director in the Bank of Farmington, a leading member of the Lutheran Church and at the front in all matters of interest to the community, giving generously of his time and means to all public enterprises. He was treasurer of the State Hospital No. 4 during the administration of Governor Hadley. Peter took an active part in the conduct of political campaigns as a member of the Republican State Central Committee. He was an active member of the Lutheran Church.

On April 6, 1897, he married Louisa Knoche of Onarga, IL. The Giessing family and the Knoche family both resided at Iron Mountain, MO upon immigrating from Germany. Louisa was born in Iron Mountain. In 1861, her father moved to Onarga, IL. Peter and Louise Giessing had one child named Marian Anna Giessing born in Farmington, MO. In 1925, Peter sold his interest in the Milling Co. to his brothers, Henry and Daniel F. Giessing. The next year he and his wife, Louise, moved to Los Angeles, CA to reside near their daughter, Marian Giessing Holler. Peter died on April 14, 1941. Louise Giessing died April 8, 1952. Their resting place is at Forest Lawn Cemetery, Glendale, CA. *Submitted by: Louise Holler Craddock, granddaughter of Peter and Louise Giessing*

Marian Anna Giessing Holler, daughter of Peter and Louise Giessing, born April 1, 1898, in Farmington, MO. She married Wesley C. Holler, Feb. 20, 1923, at the Peter Giessing home in Farmington, MO. She died May 27, 1986

GIESSING - There are not many people who live all their life in the same town they were born in. Vernon Giessing did, and he never really ever left home. He was a true Farmingtonian!

Vernon Keiser Giessing was born July 19, 1913, in his parents' home at 317 North Jefferson. He was the third child, and only son, of Daniel and Pauline Giessing. He was preceded by two older sisters, Mildred "Midge" Soergel, and Alberta "Bert" Eifert. Vernon was a popular young man. He attended St. Paul Lutheran School and Church, and later graduated from Farmington High School in 1931. While in high school, he played basketball, tennis, and took part in numerous civic and social groups. He attended Valparaiso University, where he met his future bride, Helen Bode, of Echo, MN. Vernon graduated with a bachelor's degree in business administration in 1935. The next year he and Helen were married. They took up residence next door to the Giessing family home at 313 North Jefferson, and have lived there ever since. Vernon and Helen had three children, Daniel, William and Rosemary.

After graduating from Valparaiso, Vernon worked in the Giessing Flour Mill, owned by his father, Daniel, and his uncle, Henry Giessing. Vernon kept the books and made local sales calls. During this time, he was also on the board of directors for United Bank. When the Giessing mill closed, in 1948, Vernon moved across town and joined his cousin, Walter Carl, in operating the Farmington Milling Company. Vernon's true love was banking, and in 1953, at the invitation of Wendell Dearing, he became the vice-president of United Bank. In 1954, he became president of the United Bank. While president of United Bank, the bank became an affiliate of Mercantile Bank Corporation and in March 1973, Vernon was president of Mercantile Bank of Farmington. He remained in that position until he retired in 1978. Vernon continued to serve on the board of directors until 1983. Aside from the banking business, Vernon was also very involved in other church and civic organizations. He was president of the Farmington Chamber of Commerce, a member of the Farmington Kiwanis Club and he was on the board of trustees for the Farmington Community Hospital. He was a stalwart supporter of St. Paul Lutheran Church, serving 17 years as Sunday School superintendent, 11 years as president of the congregation, and over 40 years as a member of the church choir.

Vernon Giessing passed away Oct. 5, 1998. His loving wife, Helen, his sister Midge, and his children, Daniel and (Janet) Ward, Bill and (Polly), and (Jay) and Rosemary Ward survive him. He was the proud grandfather of Vernon Keiser Giessing of Mark Giessing, Bill Giessing II, Kristen Bowers, Jeff Giessing, Angela Bortel, Chris Giessing, Kelly Suhl and Brian Ward. In addition, his life was blessed with 11 great-grandchildren: Carolyn Abrams, Michelle Bower, Kevin Giessing, Joshua Bortel, Zachary Bower, Jessica Giessing, Allison Bortel, Emily Bower, Grant Giessing, Zachary Giessing, and Rebekah Bower. *Submitted by Helen Giessing*

GIESSING - Walter Karl Giessing, 1919-1984, was mayor of Farmington for three terms, elected first in 1965, as was his father Charles Henry Giessing, mayor of Farmington for two terms, first elected in 1917, and also served in 1934, after the death of Mayor Tetley.

Walter Karl Giessing was born in Farmington, MO July 31, 1919, at 511 Forster Street. He was a life long member of St. Paul's Lutheran Church, a charter member of the Farmington Lion's Club, a policeman and member of the Farmington volunteer fire department from 1943 to 1975. He served in the Merchant Marines and the US Navy during WWII and was a member of American Legion Post #416.

Leora and Walter Karl Giessing

He was a 4th generation to work in the flour milling business. In later years, he owned and operated the Farmington Printing Company, 1971-1983, which published the *County Advertiser* and the *Farmington News* newspapers.

Walter went to work for his father at the Farmington Milling Co. Married in 1939 to Leora Bernice Blanton, daughter of James Carter and Mary Evelyn Wallen Blanton of Bismarck, MO. Walter and Leora are the parents of two sons, Don Karl and Charles Richard. Don Karl married Martha Kay Ruble and has one son, Eric Karl. Charles Richard married Doris Elaine Miller and has one son and one daughter, Bradley Kyle and Cara Danille. Eric Karl married Donna Michelle Russ and has one son and one daughter, Kodi Michael and Karli Nicole.

Walter Karl was the son of Charles Henry and Lydia Vollath Giessing; had one brother, Theodore J. and three sisters: Cecilia (Mrs. Herbert Schramm), Mignon (Mrs. Carl Webb) and Rosalie who passed away in infancy.

Walter's father, Charles Henry Giessing, was the son of John and Johanetta Reuter Giessing who served 15 years as cashier at the Old Bank of Farmington. A servant of the community having served as mayor and member of the city council at various times for 40 years. He succeeded his father in part ownership of the Farmington Milling Co. until Charles Henry's death in 1962.

Walter's grandfather, John Giessing, was the son of Carl Charles Adams Freidrick and Mary Hoehn Giessing. John married in 1878 to Johanetta Reuter and they are parents of four

sons: Charles Henry, Frederick William, John Ernest, Peter Daniel and three daughters: Elizabeth, Wilhamina and Annie. John and his brother, Charles, bought a mill in Farmington from Boyce and Rodehaver in 1882. They called it the "Steam Flouring Mill," which had been partly destroyed by fire. The mill was re-built as Giessing and Brothers and later named as Farmington Milling Company about 1903.

Carl Charles Adam Freidrick Giessing, son of Carl Freidrick and Marie Schaabe Giessing, married Mary Hoehn and came to America from Germany. He found work in Iron Mountain, MO, moved to Valley Forge, MO and bought the mill of Mr. Pickles. The children of Carl and Mary are John, Charles, Peter, Fred, Henry, Daniel and William. Two daughters, Mary (died young) and Elizabeth.

Carl Freidercke Giessing married Marie Rosine Becker. His parents are Johanna Jacob and Catharina Henkeler Giessing. Their parents, Johann Friedrick and Anna Elizabeth Engelhard Giessing. Their parents, Johannes and Anna Catharina Happe Giessing, 1681-1740. *Submitted by W.K. Giessing*

GIESSING - William "Bill" Bode Giessing II is the great-grandson of Daniel and Pauline Giessing and the grandson of Helen and the late Vernon Giessing. He is the son of Helen and Vernon's second son, Bill, and Polly Giessing. He spent many a summer vacation playing at 313 N. Jefferson, home of Helen and Vernon. Bill grew up in Houston, TX and St. Louis, MO. He graduated from Parkway South in Manchester, MO in 1981, and from Texas A&M University in 1985. He spent seven and a half years as an officer in the Army Corps of Engineers, during which time he met and married his wife Cathy (Carter) and became a father to Carolyn (Abrams).

After his military career, he was an area manager for Pizza Hut Corp. in Des Moines, IA. While in Des Moines, Bill and Cathy adopted their son, Zachary Giessing. After the arrival of Zachary, the family decided that a change in lifestyle was in order. The desire for more family time, a slower pace, and a smaller community lead the family to

Bill, Carolyn, Zachary and Cathy

think about Farmington. As luck would have it, Bill's great aunt, Mildred (Giessing) Soergel, was looking to sell the family home, built by Daniel Giessing in 1905, at 317 N. Jefferson. After signing on with his old childhood friend, Paul Brockmiller, as a project manager at Brockmiller Construction, Bill and family made the move to Farmington, and into 317 N. Jefferson in July of 1995.

The newest members of the Farmington Giessings followed in the family's footsteps. They are members of St. Paul Lutheran Church, where Bill is on the board of education for the school, works on the annual school auction, and coaches the A-girl's volleyball team. He represents Brockmiller Construction on the

Farmington Chamber of Commerce. He has served on committees for the Rails to Trails bike

path, and he organized the William Bode Giessing II Farmington Community Band for the bicentennial celebration, playing in the percussion section during performances. The family has had the luxury of living right next door to Bill's grandparents, Helen and Vernon.

All of the reasons for moving to Farmington have been justified for this Giessing family, they have found good friends, small town values, and a safe environment to raise their children. They have no intentions of leaving Farmington anytime soon, and hopefully their children will be in the next generation of Farmington history. *Submitted by Cathy Giessing*

GILLIAM - The family includes Jason, Dana, Colin, and Garrett.

Jason Wayne Gilliam was born July 6, 1973, at the Osteopathic Hospital in Farmington. He is the son of Donald and Marilyn Gilliam of rural Farmington. Jason was raised in Esther, MO and graduated from Central High School in 1991. He served as a volunteer with the Esther Fire Department from 1990 to 1992. Jason was on active duty in the United States Ma-

rine Corps from 1992 to 1996. During this time, he was stationed at Camp Pendleton, CA. When he returned to Missouri, he served as a volunteer with the Leadington Fire Department for two years. He moved to Farmington in 1996, after accepting a position as radio dispatcher for the Police Department. Since moving to Farmington, Jason has also worked for the Fire Department as a part-time and full-time firefighter and is currently a building inspector with the city. Jason graduated from Jefferson College in Hillsboro, MO in 1999, with an AAS in fire science technology.

Dana Ann Springs was born at St. John's Mercy Medical Center in Creve Couer, MO March 5, 1970. She was raised in Festus, MO where she attended Our Lady Catholic School. Her family moved to Farmington in 1984, when her father transferred with the Highway Patrol. She is the daughter of Dale and Verna Springs of Farmington. Dana graduated from Farmington High School in 1988. Dana has been employed in the past with Mineral Area Regional Medical Center and as a licensed cosmetologist. She is currently serving as a radio dispatcher with the Farmington Police Department. Dana attended Mineral Area College in Park Hills.

Dana and Jason are members of Memorial United Methodist Church in Farmington where the family has attended since 1998. They were married at the church Nov. 7, 1998. They have two sons, Colin and Garrett Martin. Colin Phillip born Aug. 5, 1990, at Mineral Area Regional Medical Center and Garrett Andrew was born Feb. 11, 1992, at Mineral Area Regional Medical Center. Colin and Garrett attend school in Farmington.

GRAHAM - Mr. and Mrs. Kenneth W. Graham and young children, Sarah Renee, born 1971, and Michael William, born 1976, returned to the Farmington area following Ken's college years at the University of Missouri in Columbia, MO, where he received his BS, MA and specialist degrees. He taught one year in Rolla, MO. Ken is the son of William and Mildred Graham of Farmington, MO. Michael was 1 week old when they returned to their home town of Farmington.

Kenneth began a teaching career with

Farmington School System as the agriculture instructor in 1976. The youngest son, Brian Matthew, was born in 1978. Ken's wife, Sheri, is the daughter of Vernon G. and Helen L. Montgomery of Farmington, MO. She received her AA degree from Mineral Area College in Park Hills, MO and BS degree from National Louis University in St. Louis, MO.

She began her career as director of Human Resources with Parkland Health Center in 1980. The Graham children graduated from Farmington High School and attended Mineral Area College. Sarah, who received her BS degree from the University of Missouri in Columbia, now resides in Jefferson City, MO and teaches landscape design and turf management at Linn State Technical College in Linn, MO. She is engaged to Mr. Steve Denkler, who resides at Lake of the Ozarks.

Michael who will graduate from the University of Missouri, Columbia, MO in May 1999, will be an agriculture instructor. Michael is engaged to be married to Miss Kendra Kollmeyer, who will also graduate from the University of Missouri at Columbia in May 1999.

Kendra is the daughter of Kenny and Sharon Kollmeyer, Farmington, MO. Brian Matthew resides in Springfield, MO, where he continues to study music at Southwest Missouri State University. A member of the Blue Knights Drum and Bugle Corps for two years, Brian received distinguished honors for his solo performances on 'quads' in national competition. The Grahams have been active members of the Libertyville Methodist Church, where Ken serves as lay leader and Sheri as assistant Sunday School Superintendent. Ken is a member of the St. Francois County Fair Board, a member of the Farm Bureau Board of Directors, a past member of the MFA Board of Directors, a member of The Missouri State Teachers Association, and past president of the Missouri Vocation Association and the Missouri Vocation Agriculture Teachers Association. Sheri is a member of the Southeast Missouri Human Resource Professional Association, the National Healthcare Quality Assurance Association, a supporter of Farmington School's A+ Committee and School to Work Programs, a member of the board of directors for the Farmington Training Institute and is a certified human resource professional. She is a past Cub Scout den mother and Girl Scout leader.

GREGORY - Thomas Jacob and Myrtle Dell Blanton Gregory, were married April 2, 1899. They lived in Jefferson County, IL, and came to Missouri in 1914. They traveled with seven children, the youngest 2 months old, by covered wagon and crossed the Mississippi River by ferryboat at Ste. Genevieve, MO. They traveled Hwy 32 to Miller's Switch, crossed through the Pinery (now Hawn State Park) and came out on county road AA, where they arrived at their new home in Missouri.

Thomas Jacob, known as Papa Tom, had traded his farm in Illinois for the Missouri farm. His wife, Myrtle, known as Mama Myrt, told that the weeks of travel was one of the happiest times of her life. Two more children were born after they moved to Missouri. They were members of the Pleasant Hill Baptist Church. The children all attended the Oak Grove School, located on the land next to the farm.

Papa Tom had a sawmill. He owned a threshing machine and traveled throughout the area, threshing for the neighbors. Mamma Myrt was very interested in education. She taught all her children songs and poems that they could still quote to their children during their lifetimes. The families gathered every weekend at Papa Tom and Mama Myrt's. There was always a big meal served. The men ate first, then the ladies. The

Thomas Jacob and Myrtle Dell Blanton Gregory 1949 Golden Wedding Anniversary. Thomas Jackson (1918-1996), Henry Earl (1903-1972), John William (1913-1998), Esta Vay (1907-1987), Clara Jane (1906-), Harriett Ethel (1904-1990), Gertie Leota (1912-1988), Elsie May (1909-1993). Missing is Charles Edward (1916-1940).

children came in and ate all that was left. The girls loved to laugh and share memories. In 1954, Papa and Mama moved into Farmington and lived until their deaths. Charley died early in life, and Jack lived in East St. Louis until his death. The girls: Harriet (Mrs. J.C. Harter), Elsie (Mrs. Hillard Gray), Gertie (Mrs. Harold Rickard) Hellon, Esta (Mrs. Claud Gray Hughes), all lived in Farmington until their deaths. Clara (Mrs. Marvin H. Allen), age 92, resides with a daughter in Farmington.

GREIF - The Greif family came to this community somewhere around 1914.

Martin Greif married Anna Earl Sanders May 13, 1887. They had five children: Lorena, Fadalias, Rollie, Katy and Irvin. Martin Greif was an active miller for 62 years and retired at the age of 82. He worked for the Giessing Milling Companies in Farmington for 30 years, operating both the upper and lower mills at Farmington.

Irvin "Greasy" Greif was the only child to stay in the community. He married Catherine Lewis in 1935. They had twin sons, William and Robert. Irvin Greif started and operated the local Phillips "66" service station for 25 years. The service station is still located on Main Street today.

In 1947, Irvin Greif and Carl Moranville built and operated the Clover Club located between Farmington and Flat River. In the early 1950s, Irvin became the sole owner and ran the Clover Club until 1956, at which time he converted the Clover Club into Suburban Furniture. Suburban Furniture burned to the ground Dec. 9, 1960, but was back in operation by February 1961. Irvin and Catherine, better known as Katy and Greasy, were joined by their twin sons, Bill and Bob, in 1967. They operated the furniture store until 1982 at which time it was sold.

Robert Greif married Norma Welker of Perryville and they had seven children: Cynthia, Deborah, Martha, Jennifer, Margaret, Robert Jr. and Sarah. William Greif married Margaret Boyer of Flat River and they had three sons: Michael, Mark and Matthew. Martin Greif died at age 87; Irvin Greif died May 7, 1977, age 62; Catherine Greif died Jan. 23, 1980, age 62; Robert Greif died Nov. 5, 1987, age 52.

William Greif retired May 1982. On Feb. 1, 1986, he was ordained as a permanent deacon in the Catholic Church and was assigned to the parish of St. Joseph in Farmington by Archbishop John Mays. He presently continues his work in the church. William's sons are keeping the Greif name alive: Michael has a son, Braden Tate Greif, and Mark has a son, Miles Thomas Greif. *Submitted by William Grief*

GRIFFIN - Darrell, the son of George and Arleen (Gillespie) Griffin, grew up on a family farm in ru-

ral Ste. Genevieve, MO. Darrel, his brother, David, and sister, June, helped their parents work the farm in an area originally settled by Tennessean George Harvey Griffin after the Civil War.

Darrell, Jeanie, Matt, John, David, Josh, Julie Griffin

Jeanie, the daughter of Vergil and Sylvia (Ingram) Defreece, moved to Flat River, MO, from Arkansas in 1955, when her father accepted the pastorate of the Esther Baptist Church. Her brothers, Dale and Dean, were in the Air Force at that time.

Darrell and Jeanie graduated from Esther High School, Flat River Junior College, and Southeast Missouri State University. Darrell went to medical school at the University of Missouri in Columbia, graduating in 1970. Jeanie completed her M.Ed. degree in 1969. They were married June 7, 1969, and spent the summer working in a mission hospital in Bangkla, Thailand. After medical school and an internship at St. John's Mercy Hospital in St. Louis, MO, Darrell served in the US Air Force at Columbus AFB, MS. He, Jeanie, and their newborn son, Matthew Patrick, born 1973, returned to Columbia for Darrell to complete a pediatric residency. John David was born into the family in 1975. In 1976, the Griffin family moved to Farmington for Darrell to begin a pediatric practice with Medical Arts Clinic. David Defreece Griffin was born in 1977 in Farmington.

In 1979, the Griffin family moved briefly to Auburn, AL, then on to Dayton, OH for Darrell to complete a residency training in dermatology. Joshua Daniel was born into the family in 1980. The Griffins moved back to Farmington, MO in 1982 and Darrell opened his practice in dermatology. Julie Elizabeth was born in 1985, completing the family of seven.

During the years, Jeanie has served in numerous churches, playing the organ and piano, as well as working with Kid's Praise (choir and drama for children), and Youth Choir (drama, choir and dinner theatre). She has also taught school in several Missouri schools (Arnold, Ladue, Columbia, and Mineral Area College).

Both Darrell and Jeanie enjoy spending time with youth at church, at home, and on mission trips. They also spend as much time as possible with their own family: Matt in Boston, MA; John in Columbia, MO; David in Wheaton, IL; and Josh soon to begin college. It becomes more of a challenge each year to get the family of seven together in one place at one time.

GRIFFIN/SMITH/TUCKER - Karen G. Griffin and James C. Tucker met as seniors in high school in 1960 and were married in the Farmington Christian Church Jan. 25, 1964. Karen, born in St. Louis to J.V. and Elizabeth "Betty" Griffin, lived in Festus until 3-years-old. Then the family moved south of Farmington to farm land originally owned by William J. Griffin, J.V.'s father. Jim, oldest of three children, was born in St. Charles to George R. and Elsie M. "Peppers" Tucker. He attended Flat River schools and Flat River Junior College. He has worked at Boeing Aircraft in St. Louis for 36 years.

L-R: David and Jane Maloney, Karen holding Conrad, James, Stacy and Kyle Tucker

After graduating from Lutheran Hospital School of Nursing, Karen worked for a physician until Nov. 30, 1966, when Jane Carol was born and the family moved to Flat River. Karen worked at Bonne Terre Hospital before becoming school nurse in the Central District, then later transferred to the Farmington district where she retired after 26 years. A second child, Kyle Gentry Tucker, was born July 1, 1969, in Farmington. Jim, Karen, Jane and Kyle moved to Farmington in 1974 and built a home on J.V. Griffin's farm.

Jane married David Maloney Dec. 29, 1990. They are the parents of Conrad James. Jane is a physical therapist and David is a CPA. Kyle married Stacy Lyon on Sept. 9, 1995. Both are engineers and live in Michigan.

Karen's paternal great-great-grandfather, Lott Griffin, of Irish descent, moved from North Carolina to Pennsylvania in 1785 and then to Mississippi County, MO. Great-grandfather, Andrew J. Griffin, came from New Madrid County, MO to the Unity Community in 1812 and married Lavina Maze. Grandfather, William J. Griffin, was born there Jan. 25, 1863. In 1889, he married Annie Moore. They farmed briefly in New Madrid County where J.V., Karen's father, was born Aug. 26, 1907. J.V.

Smith Family. Front Row: Elizabeth. Second Row: George, Amanda (mother) and Noel

was one of eight children: Clara, Myrtie Lee, Curran, Willa Marie, Moore, J.B., J.V. and Nona. J.V.'s family moved back to the Farmington area in 1910, buying the Doss farm near the Independence School. Three of J.V.'s sisters married three Kollmeyer brothers. These siblings remained close and farmed land along old Highway 67 towards Libertyville. At present all of the six farms but one are still home for their children or grandchildren. J.V. lived all of his life on this farm except for 10 years when he and his wife Elizabeth "Betty" (Smith) Griffin lived and worked in Festus, MO. They returned to the farm in 1945. J.V. and his daughter, Karen, attended first through eighth grades at the same one-room school house, Independence, later known as the Busiek School. Karen was also in the first public kindergarten class in Farmington in 1947. J.V. drove a Busiek school bus for 21 years and also landscaped many new homes in this area. Betty graduated with Missouri Beauty Academy's first class in 1936 and worked as an operator for 30 years, owning Cinderella Beauty Salon on Columbia Street. She also worked at Kirkland's Dime Store, Trimfoot Shoe Factory and the former State Hospital.

Karen's great-great-grandfather, William F. Moore Sr., immigrated from Ireland to Virginia in

1821, coming to New Madrid County in a covered wagon, marrying Nancy Younger. Great-Grandfather, William F. Moore Jr., married Martha Eblin and grandmother, Annie "Moore" Griffin, oldest of their six children, was born in Libertyville, Nov. 18, 1870.

Griffin Family. Front Row: William and Annie. Second row: Myrtie, J.B., Willa, Moore, Clara and J.V.

Karen's maternal great-grandfather, Thomas William Santee, was of French descent and married Harriet Elizabeth Hibbits. Grandmother Amanda Jane was born July 6, 1875. She had two brothers and married Pleasant Gentry "P.G." Smith, born July 22, 1881, oldest of four children. His parents, George "Wash" Smith and Annie (Whatley) Smith, farmed near the Pleasant Hill Baptist Church in Ste. Genevieve County. P.G. Smith farmed, was a store owner and a popular auctioneer in this area. P.G. and Amanda Smith had three children born in the Unity Community on what is now Best Road. Elizabeth "Betty," Karen's mother, was born March 4, 1911 and had two older brothers, Noel Carleton and George Eldon. *Submitted by Karen Griffin Tucker.*

GRIFFIN - Lott Griffin came to St. Francois County, MO from Tennessee and was listed in the 1840 census in Liberty Township with wife and six children. His wife's name was Meeke, but her parents are not known. She was born in 1794 in North Carolina. Lott died before the 1850 census and his wife was listed as head of house. She was age 64, born in North Carolina. Her son, John W., 34, born in Tennessee and daughter, Meeke C., age 18, born in Missouri. A daughter, Elizabeth Tucker, age 22, born in Missouri, a widow, and her daughter, Martha J. Tucker, age 1, all in same home. They were the parents of seven children:

1) Josephus P., born in Tennessee and died in 1846.

2) Andrew J., born in 1811 in Tennessee, married Lavinia. They were listed in the 1870 census with eight children: Meeke, age 24; Lott, age 22; Sarah J., age 21; Joseph, age 19; Mary, age 14; Martha, age 12; William, age 7; Andrew, age 3; and Meeka C., sister, age 49.

3) John Wesley, born March 15, 1812, died April 16, 1899, in Missouri. He married Artemisia Williams, daughter of Daniel and Sarah Jones Williams. She was born April 1837, in St. Francois County, MO. John and Artemisia, who were married Jan. 18, 1855, lived in Pendleton Township, Doe Run, MO. They had one son, John Wesley Griffin, born in July 1865, Doe Run, MO and died May 1, 1939, Venice, IL. He married Martha Jesse Snodgrass Oct. 30, 1895. She was born Feb. 20, 1876, in Lesterville, MO and died April 30, 1954, in Venice, IL. They had five children: Bessie, born in Doe Run, MO (no dates available). Frederick Wesley, born Aug. 11, 1899 in Doe Run, MO and died Feb. 5, 1965, in Granite City, IL. He married Minnie Luettia Wheeler April 28, 1923, who was born June 4, 1903 in Madisonville, KY. They had 10 children: Frederick Ted, Lucy Ellen, Melvin Leon, William Wesley Frank Norman, Bonnie Ruth, Jesse Lee, Raymond Roy, Joyce

Luettia, Dale Wayne. Frederick Ted was born May 21, 1923, in Venice, IL and married Delores Ziegler and had eight children: John, Fred, Katherine, Doris, Julia Ann, Melvin, Theresa Lynn and Joe. Theresa was born Sept. 15, 1952, in Granite City, IL and married Teddy Ray Crawford April 24, 1971, in Graniteville, MO. He was born Aug. 31, 1952, and they had two children, Christopher Scott and Shawn Eliott. Theresa now lives in Ironton, MO.

4) Lucinda, born 1816, in Tennessee, married Pleasant Mays May 2, 1844.

5) Rhoda married William M. Sweeney May 27, 1847, and was in the 1870 census living with Elizabeth Mason age 50.

6) Elizabeth, born 1828, married John Tucker May 4, 1848. She must have married a second time since she is in the 1870 census as Elizabeth Mason, age 45, with children: Edward, age 15; Meeka, age 14; Mary E., age 9, with Rhoda Sweeney, age 45.

7. Meeka C. born 1821.

It is believed that Lott and Meeke are buried in the Knob Lick area but where is unknown. John Wesley and Artemisia lived in Knob Lick and were listed in 1860 census in the Liberty Township. In the 1870 census, Artemisia was living with her son in Liberty Township and was a widow. In 1900, she was living in Doe Run with her son, John W., age 34, and wife, Martha J., age 24, and their son, Fred, age 9 months. Artemisia, age 63, died in 1911.

The will of Lott Griffin, dated Sept. 1, 1841, "left personal property to following children, to wit, Josephus P. Griffin, John W. Griffin, Andrew J. Griffin, Rhoda D. Griffin, Lucinda S. Griffin, Elizabeth H. Griffin and daughter, Meekee C. Griffin. Remaining property and the farm upon which I now reside to my wife Meekee Griffin, for the support of my daughter, Meeke, during her natural life." Exr. Not named. No witnesses. St. Francois County. Samuel P. Harris and John Cobb witness that the said Lott Griffin signed and acknowledged the will in their presence. Recorded Nov. 22, 1843. (W&B:99-100) L/T granted Meeke Griffin on Dec. 3, 1842. Sec. Joseph P. Grifffin and John W. Griffin. (W&B: 103) *Submitted by Theresa Crawford*

HAGER - Robert and Georgia moved to Farmington in 1990. Both were born in St. Francois County and raised their family, two sons and a daughter, here. They have lived here all their lives except four years when they resided in St. Louis while Robert was employed by Laister Kauffman and McDonnell Air Craft Companies. After returning to St. Francois County Robert operated a dairy farm for 33 years. He also was an agent and has served on the board of Farmers Mutual Fire Ins. Co. for approximately 30 years.

Georgia was employed in St. Francois County Recorder of Deeds office as a deputy recorder for eight years and then retired from Mineral Area Hospital as dietitian and food service supervisor after 13 years. In 1979, they sold their farm and moved to Desloge where they lived for 11 years before moving to Farmington.

Hager Family, 1958-1959

Robert's grandfather, John Hager, was born in Germany in 1863, immigrated to the United States February 1885, where he lived in Farmington and Bonne Terre. Robert's father, George F. Hager, was born in St. Francois County in 1890. He was married to Bessie Shy and they lived in New Madrid, MO before moving back to St. Francois County in 1913, where he operated a farm and later a dairy farm, raising a family of six sons and three daughters.

Robert and Georgia's oldest son, Bob Hager, taught in Farmington public schools for 16 years. Also Robert's brother, Floyd, taught in Farmington High School for 22 years and served as mayor of Farmington for seven years.

HALL - James is the son of Claude and Ernie (Wood) Hall of Poplar Bluff, MO and was the sixth of eight children. After Jim graduated from the Poplar Bluff High School he enlisted in the United States Navy. On May 17, 1964, while serving in the Navy in Long Beach, CA, Jim married Teresa Carr, daughter of E.E. Bus Carr, one of the first sports announcers in the Boothill, and Mildred (Clark) Carr of Poplar Bluff, MO.

Brian, Jim, Terry and James Hall

Jim and Terry moved to Farmington in September 1968 when Jim was offered a job with the Missouri Natural Gas Company, a position he held for 31 years. Terry worked for the Farmington Public School System and is now employed as the reference librarian at the City Library. Jim and Terry have been blessed with two wonderful sons of whom they are very proud. Jim Jr., who now lives in Poplar Bluff and works for the Hastings Book, Music and Video Company, and Brian, who lives in Cape Girardeau and is employed as computer technician specialist with the Cape Girardeau School System.

HAMPTON - Eric "Ric" Lee Hampton son of Thomas and Patty (Pogue) Hampton was born Sept. 30, 1968, in Oklahoma City, OK. Ric and his family moved to Farmington, MO in November 1969, where Ric graduated from high school in 1986. Ric attended Mineral Area College on a music scholarship. He then attended SEMO in Cape Girardeau, graduating in 1991 with a degree in physical education and health.

Eric, Jordan and Abigail Hampton

Ric married Kimberly Rae Crews in 1989 and they were blessed with two children, Jordan Lee,

born February 1991, and Abigail Sue, born April 1994. Ric and Kim divorced in 1995 with Ric getting custody of the children.

Ric is presently employed with the Jennings School District in St. Louis County, teaching health and PE. He was previously employed at Farmington School District, Midwest Learning Center and Centerville Missouri School District. He is presently working towards a master's degree in counseling at University of Missouri at St. Louis (UMSL).

Ric enjoys golf, sand volleyball, his family and many friends.

HAMPTON - Thomas Hampton, son of Lawrence Ray Hampton, an Assembly of God minister of North Little Rock, AR, moved to Fredericktown, MO with his family in 1952. Tom was a freshman in high school at the time. In 1953, Tom met Patty Jean Pogue of Farmington, daughter of Eugene and Larna Pogue. After Tom graduated from Fredericktown High School and Patty graduated from Farmington High School, Tom joined the US Air Force and he and Pat were married Sept. 30, 1956 and moved to Marietta, GA where he was stationed for four years. While in Marietta, their daughter, Jeanna Lea was born May 20, 1959.

Thomas and Patty Hampton

After Tom's discharge in 1960 they moved to the St. Louis area where Tom went to work for International Shoe Company. In 1963, Tom went to work for Phillips Petroleum Company and shortly after was transferred to Kansas City, MO for five months and then on to Bartlesville, OK, where they lived for six years. In October 1968, they were thrilled with the arrival (by choice) of a baby boy whom they named Eric Lee. Eric was born Sept. 30, 1968, the 12th wedding anniversary of his new parents.

In November 1969, the Hampton's moved back to Farmington, MO and Tom attended Molar Barber College in St. Louis and Patty went to work for Mineral Area Osteopathic Hospital. In June 1970, after completing barber college, Tom went to work at the OK Barber Shop on Columbia Street with his father-in-law, Eugene Pogue. In 1974, Tom went to work for Millers Mutual Insurance Company and worked there until 1980, when he went into business for himself and is still active in the insurance business. Tom has been an active supporter of the National Association of Life Underwriters having served as president, Life Underwriter training chairman and professional development chairman for the local association, Scenic Rivers Life Underwriters Association.

In 1983, when their son, Eric, began playing high school basketball Tom organized three teams of high school players taking them to St. Louis to play in an Amateur Athletic Union (AAU) tournament. The following year Tom began running AAU basketball tournaments in Farmington, and in 1995 organized the Mineral Area Flyers Sports Club, Inc., a youth basketball program that involves over 700 youth, ages 5 through 19 and over 100 adult volun-

teers from St. Francois and surrounding counties. Tom is very active in the Lions Club, having held several offices in the Farmington Lions Club and served on the District and State Athletic Committee for several years. Tom was a founding member of the St. Francis River Pow-Wow and continues to serve as their treasurer and as a deacon at First Baptist Church of Farmington. Friday mornings finds him delivering meals for the Nutrition Center "Meals on Wheels" program.

Patty was treasurer for First Baptist Church from 1983-96 and in January 1998 retired from Mineral Area Regional Medical Center where she was insurance supervisor. Patty has also done volunteer work with the tax aide program and the CLAIM program.

Tom and Pat are very active in their church and enjoy their two children and five grandchildren who visit them often.

HARRINGTON - Byron Harrington was born in Esther, MO to the late E.J. and Carolina (Morris) Harrington, on July 6, 1912. Byron was very knowledgeable in the field of agriculture as his father was a prominent farmer and businessman in this area. On Dec. 20, 1936 he married Hazel Oleatha Thurman, daughter of Lawrence and Clara (Williams) Thurman, long-time residents of St. Francois County. Hazel's grandfather, Jeff Williams, and Byron's father, E.J. Harrington, both served on the first jury trial in the St. Francois County Courthouse. Byron helped, with a team of mules, to dig the basements of the St. Francois County Courthouse and the post office in 1926.

Byron and Hazel's 50th anniversary Dec. 20, 1986. Back Row: Dwight Harrington, Diana Sitzes, Delores Gross, Sandy Sales, Linda Treaster, Randy Harrington. Front Row: Hazel and Byron Harrington.

Byron and Hazel lived for the first few years of their marriage at the Harrington Homestead on old Highway 61. In 1940 they moved to the original Alexander farm and leased it from Mr. William Day and were able to purchase it in 1944. This property included 180 acres of land and a house which was built in 1902. Byron was a hard worker, was successful and was able to purchase 105 acres from J.B. Reinhardt, whose property adjoined his land. However, Byron was not as successful fighting the needs of a growing community and state. The present day high school and football field and BJC Parkland Health Center are located on part of the original farm land. In the early 1960s the route of Highway 67 cut directly through the property, leaving 130 acres on either side. The present Maple Valley Drive resulted in the farm land being split again. The Harrington cows have adapted to the changes and can reach the pasture in the front of the high school by going under the bridge and can go under the culvert of Highway 67 and Maple Valley Drive to get between the fields.

This farm was a family farm in which all the children learned good work ethics early. The children helped with all the chores needed such as milking and feeding the cows, tending to the chickens and gathering the eggs, driving the tractor and farm equipment, plus the housework, which included cooking and canning. Hay time meant putting up square hay bales which was always quality family time! Byron loved to teach the children and grandchildren, always encouraged independence and being conservative, and "living within your means." The farm was originally a dairy farm, with the milk being transported to Schramm Dairy and later to the Perryville Cheese Factory. Hundreds of baby chickens were purchased in the spring to provide fresh eggs and fresh fried chicken. Hogs were raised and butchered on the farm. There were always fresh vegetables and fruits raised in the well-cultivated gardens. Assorted fruit trees, grapes and strawberries provided wonderful fruit pies, jellies and preserves. It was a family affair to clean and prepare food for freezing and canning.

Hazel was a wonderful cook and prepared a large meal for all who could come to eat at noon. Hazel was a special mother and loving grandmother who loved to baby-sit, rock and sing to the little ones. Byron and Hazel were blessed with their love and were given 63 years together. Hazel passed away at home on June 3, 1997, after a lengthy illness. Her family was her main caregiver the last 10 years of her life, thereby, returning the nurturing and love she had given to her family and allowing her death with dignity.

There were six children born to this union: Dwight (June) Harrington, born Feb. 3, 1943; Diana (Mrs. Verdell) Sitzes, born Jan. 1, 1945; Delores Gross, born Dec. 27, 1949; Sandra (Mrs. Alan) Sales, born Sept. 4, 1952; Linda (Mrs. Tom) Treaster, born Nov. 7, 1953; and Randall Harrington, born Aug. 9, 1955. There are nine grandchildren: Edward (Beth) Harrington, Byron Ray (Jennifer) Harrington, Dawn (Mrs. Larry) Kekec, David Ross (Sarah) Buerck, Brent Gross, Dustin Sales, Randall Sitzes, Matthew Treaster, and Jared Treaster. There are three great-grandchildren: Jamie and Whitney Harrington and Kourtney Kekec.

This close-knit family is unusual since the children and grandchildren live in this area and most visit daily and still help on the farm. The family loves to gather at the dinner table daily to eat the delicious food raised mainly on the farm and welcome all who can attend. The television series, *The Walton's*, describes the Byron Harrington family.

HARRINGTON - *Our Ship Came in But, We Missed It!* Back in the late 1800s the Edgar Harrington Family received a telegram from England stating that the Harrington family must come to England to claim their rights to the Harrington Ship Lines. Back in those days, $2000 was a large sum that the Harrington's could not muster. Therefore, the Harrington's running ships went to the Parliament.

Edgar Harrington and Reva Williams were united in marriage and to their union three sons were born: Edward, the first son, died in infancy; Edgar Lynn, the second son, presently lives in Farmington with his wife, Dorothy. He has one son, Eddie, who also resides in Farmington. Ray, the third son, deceased in 1994, married Shirley Smith from Flat River, MO and moved to Farmington in 1963. Ray and Shirley have two children, Janet Lea (Harrington) Stricklin (Mrs. Richard Stricklin) and Keven Ray Harrington and Lynn (McDowell) Harrington, all who reside in this area. Shirley's mother and father, Clifford and Corrine (Mueller) Smith, lived in St. Francois County all their lives. Shirley has one brother, Don, and one sister, Janet Marie (Smith) Seabaugh.

Shirley has four grandchildren: two grand-

daughters, Tiffany and Kayla, born to Richard and Janet (Harrington) Stricklin; and Mitchell and Mason, born to Keven and Lynn (McDowell) Harrington.

The Harrington family prided themselves on honesty and hard work. Ray and Shirley's mothers both worked at the State Hospital for 35 years. Both their fathers worked at State Hospital No. 4 in construction, and Shirley's father was a bus driver for Esther School for over 20 years.

Ray and Shirley were known in this community as an entrepreneurial couple, starting several businesses here in Farmington. Some of their business ventures were: Harrington's Bakery Outlet located on Karsch Blvd. in the late 1970s, Harrington's Bakery and Lunch Bar, located in Park Hills in the late 1960s, Harrington Dixie Cream Donuts in Farmington in 1982, Harrington & Son Construction Co. in the early 1970s, Delta Outdoor Advertising, started in 1978 and was then sold in 1992.

Ray also worked for the Missouri State Highway Dept., office manager at Hartrup Real Estate, and had just started Proline Graphics shortly before his demise.

Shirley had employment over the years with Trimfoot Shoe Co., Missouri State Hospital, Harrington Real Estate, Farmington Clinic, and Wetterau (now known as Super-Valu) in Desloge. Ray and Shirley both obtained their real estate brokers license. Both of their children were involved in the family businesses and graduated from the Farmington School System. Janet is a pharmacy technician at Medicate Clinic Pharmacy and Keven is the owner of Signs Etc., here in Farmington.

Ray was a member of Farmington Elks, Odd Fellows, the Missouri Real Estate, and the Esther Nazarene Church. Shirley belonged to Esther Nazarene Church, a member of Farmington School Board (1980-83), Missouri Real Estate, and the Rebekah Lodge. She served on many boards in this community.

Even though their ship did come and they missed it, they led very productive and satisfied lives right here in Farmington, MO.

HARRINGTON - One of the oddities in Edward Joshua Harrington's family history is the spelling of Harrington. In 1910, two Edward J. Herringtons were shipping cattle through the DeLassus stock pens at the same time and on the same train. To avoid a mix-up at the St. Louis stock yards, E.J. Herrington of rural Farmington said: "That is easy done and that won't bother me because, bill my shipment as Edward J. Harrington."

Edward Joshua Herrington (E.J.) was born at Pevely, MO, Jefferson County on Oct. 29, 1864. He was the eldest of three sons born to Samuel T. and Elizabeth Jenneatta (Hagen) Herrington. In 1871, the family lived in Irondale, MO where Samuel served as constable of Concord Township in Washington County. The first tragedy in E.J.'s life occurred on Oct. 3, 1871 when Samuel, responding to a disturbance at the local tavern, was stabbed in the stomach. He died the next morning.

E.J.'s mother, Jeanetta, along with her three sons, ages 6, 3 and 2, went to live with her sister, Mrs. John Tullock (Flucum, Jefferson County). Five years later, the second tragedy happened in 12-year-old E.J.'s life. His mother died. E.J., James Walter and Samuel were "bound out" to Mitchell McCormick of Plattin Station (Jefferson County) to work on the McCormick farms.

Tragedy struck again in E.J.'s early marriages: Jerushia May (Pinkie) McCormick married in 1889 and their only daughter died. His second wife, Julia Caroline Frazier, married 1893, and their first two daughters died. Their third daugh-

ter, Eva Lena, born Sept. 24, 1894, lived and married Antone "Tony" Columbus Hager of Bonne Terre.

On Dec. 27, 1899, E.J. of Hazel Run and Caroline Ann Morris, born Aug. 4, 1873, eldest daughter of James and Mary (Mostiller) Morris of Hazel Run, MO, were married at Farmington. Eight sons and a daughter were born to them: Irvin Lee, James Edward, Mary Jeannetta, Byron Ross and Willis Samuel. Four sons died in infancy.

Ed. J. Harrington cutting his prize winning corn.

On Feb. 27, 1905, E.J. and Caroline Ann purchased a 96 acre farm located on the old Potosi Road midway between Farmington and Flat River. The road divided the farm. On one side of the road, E.J. built a comfortable nine-room, two-story house with a large, wrap-around porch. Directly across the road, he built a huge cattle and horse barn; hung on the front of the barn was a big sign that read, "E.J. Harrington & Sons."

The convenient location of the farm was a "perfect fit" for E.J. and Caroline's personality. Their sons and daughter reminisce about the many friends that visited and ate lunch with the family. Also, Caroline's immediate family, along with her aunts and uncles, were a close family that had family "get-togethers" and reunions.

E.J. was a successful farmer. He had fields of oats, wheat, corn and sweet clover. The farm equipment was horse or mule drawn: a team of mules pulled the plows, a horse-drawn mower cut the hay, and mules or horses pulled the wagons and dump rakes. Since E.J. and Caroline had a large family, they had a vegetable garden, a five-acre fruit orchard, and of course, grapes. E.J. Harrington was known for his grape wine, which he shared, but never sold.

E.J. and Joe Hague co-owned The Hague Butcher Company (1898-1914), operating three butcher shops in Elvins, Flat River and Desloge. E.J. as the chief buyer, purchased cattle, hogs, turkeys, chickens, guineas, sheep and goats for their slaughter houses. His buying trips meant going by horseback, being gone four or five days, and traveling as far as 40 miles from Desloge.

E.J. took an active roll in civic affairs. In 1913, he was elected to the board of directors for the Bank of Flat River and the Bank of Desloge. He also served on the board of directors for one of the Farmington banks, the Bank of St. Francois County. With a strong interest in education, he was elected to the three-person school board for the Oak Hill School. Having had a life-long interest and involvement in agriculture, E.J. served on the first St. Francois County Fair Board as chairman of the cattle and horse department, as well as ringmaster at the horse races. In 1927, the St. Francois County Courthouse was completed and ready for its first court session. E.J., along with many of his personal friends, served on the first jury.

The final tragedy of E.J.'s life happened on March 1, 1924. Caroline died following complications from a gallstone operation at the Bonne Terre Hospital. She was 50 years old. Their 13-year-old daughter, Jeannetta, assumed her mother's household duties, but E.J. always hired a woman to help his daughter with the work. Twelve years later on Nov. 23, 1936, E.J. died at his farm from cancer.

E.J. and Caroline's gracious hospitality, as well as their many community involvements, made them a popular and well-known couple throughout the county. They were known as good neighbors, true friends and outstanding citizens of St. Francois County.

HARRINGTON - Long-time resident of Farmington, Irvin Lee Harrington was a descendent of Edward Jasuah and Caroline Ann Morris Harrington. Irvin, the second oldest son, was born in Desloge, MO, April 30, 1902.

His parents moved to a farm between Flat River and Farmington in 1905. Irvin farmed with his father, buying and selling cattle, raising chickens and hogs, fixing fences and gardening. The farm equipment was horse drawn, plows were pulled by mules.

He attended a one room school house at Oak Hill. He met Mary Emeline Wiles (known as Emma) at a church revival. They were married in St. Louis, MO, June 23, 1923. He worked at the National Laundry in St. Louis. Later moved to Farmington on a farm on the Hillsboro Road. He worked as a mechanic at Antones Garage in Flat River. Later worked for the County as a road grader operator, then went to work for St. Joe Lead Co. #17 till his retirement.

Mr. and Mrs. Harrington had five children: Doris Lee Urick of Euphrada, WA; Maurice Irvin Harrington of Farmington, MO; Walter Harrington of Irondale, MO; Eva Lou Propst of Farmington, MO; and Larry Harrington of Akin, SC. They also raised a grandson, Gene Harrington.

Irvin and Emma Harrington

Emma passed away in June of 1978. Irvin stayed on the farm for four years until his health began to fail (diabetes). He then went to the Presbyterian Home. He passed away Nov. 16, 1984, at the age of 82.

HARRINGTON - Good citizens make good communities. James Edward Harrington was that type of citizen that contributed to Farmington. Father, farmer, miner and friend, he was born to Edward Joshua and Caroline Ann (Morris) Harrington on Aug. 24, 1905, at Desloge, MO. Except for a short period of time, he lived his entire life in the Farmington area.

On July 4, 1925, he married Beulah Jane Clay of Webster Groves, born Aug. 21, 1905, daughter of John Edwin and Nellie (McKeighan) Clay at Ironton, MO. To this union five daughters were born: Ellen Caroline (Mrs. Horace Eugene O'Dell) Pevely, MO; Clara Jeannetta (Mrs. Lawrence Francis Hale) St. Louis; Barbara Edwina (Mrs. Dan Richard Alcorn) Farmington; Eva Jane (Mrs. Ronald Eugene Simms)

James Edward Harrington, Taken at David Allen's Wedding October 1989.

Farmington; and Beulah Ann (Mrs. David William McCreery) Arnold. Tragically, on July 22, 1973, Beulah (his wife) died suddenly at their home. James died 17 years later on Nov. 3, 1990.

Early in James and Beulah's marriage, the couple lived in Webster Groves, close to her family. James worked for the Pevely Dairy. However, it seemed that their young daughter, Ellen, was frail, and the doctor advised the family to raise her in the fresh country air. So he moved his wife and two children to an isolated farm owned by his father on Plattin Creek in Jefferson County. This proved to be a difficult time in the family's life. After a none-too-brief stay on the rural farm, he moved his wife and now three daughters to the Farmington area.

This was a challenging period for James and Beulah. Coming from a farming family, James continued to do what he knew best, farming. But now with a family of five girls, he needed to supplement his farm earnings, so this is when he started working for the St. Joe Lead Company at the Flat River mine, mainly as a crusher operator. Even though he spent 17 years in the mines, his true love and lifelong occupation was that of a farmer. He owned two different farms that were close proximity to the northwest city limits of Farmington.

Everyone liked and respected James. He possessed a touch of class with his friendly, outgoing personality. Because he was social and interested in his fellow man, he was an unofficial authority on local genealogy. However, since he lived in the Farmington area the majority of his life, James knew most of the families.

Later in life his favorite recollections were in regard to the days when he first worked for his future father-in-law, Mr. Edwin John Clay, on a large farm. Or possibly the high point of his career was during the first few years of his marriage when he and Beulah lived in St. Louis where he was employed by the Pevely Dairy Co. Not only did they develop lasting friendships, but it gave Beulah a time to renew her childhood friendships.

James Edward Harrington, without a doubt, was a solid citizen. To him, family and friends were important. Although he never held a public office, he never failed to vote in any election. Needless to say, James Edward Harrington is the type of citizen upon which Farmington was built.

HARRINGTON - I GOT IT FROM MY DAD! Keven's father and mother, Ray and Shirley (Smith) Harrington, were married in 1963 in St. Francois County. He and his sister, Janet Lea, became part of the Harrington legacy. Both of his parents were hard working entrepreneurs who enjoyed new adventures and new businesses. As a result, he became an entrepreneur with Farmington values and dreams of growth. While attending Farmington High School, Keven worked at McDonald's and for his dad at Delta Outdoor Advertising before starting his own business. He

Keven, Lynn, Mitchell, Mason Harrington

then opened his business, Signs Etc. in 1992 on 918 Weber Road in Farmington. This site was a former restaurant, service station in the 1950s.

Signs Etc. offers custom made banners, vinyl lettering for cars, storefronts and many other forms of advertising and signs, as well as screen printing on all types of products. Included in the

business are many types of advertising specialties. Keven is presently planning on expanding and adding a new business called WFO International that sells through catalog sales throughout the US and will also sell products internationally.

Keven and Lynn McDowell had met as children in the Esther Nazarene Church. It wasn't until they were teenagers that they "discovered" each other and later married in 1990.

Lynn is the daughter of Dan and Janet McDowell who are also life-long St. Francois County residents. Lynn has a sister, Carrie, and a brother, Tim McDowell. Lynn works at the Farmington Police Department as the secretary to the chief of police.

Both Keven and Lynn continue to be active members of the Esther Nazarene Church. Keven is also a member in good standing of Elks Lodge 1765 of Farmington.

Keven and Lynn (McDowell) Harrington were blessed with two sons, Mitchell Ray and Mason Daniel, who will "with little doubt," grow up to have the Farmington spirit of "Tradition and Progress."

If you would ask Keven where he got the idea to be a business owner, he would say, "I got it from my dad!"

HARRINGTON - Walter Preston Harrington was born June 30, 1899, at Jay Dee, just east of Bonne Terre, MO, to James Walter Harrington and Elba Rebecca Buchanan. On June 10, 1923, he married Irene Miller. Irene was born Oct. 9, 1901, to Alfred Miller and Alice Caroline Chandler. To this union five children were born: Norma Jean, Helen Mae, James Robert, Mary Louise and William Preston.

Back: Mary Louise, Helen Mae, Norma Jean and William Preston. Front: Walter Preston and Irene Harrington. Preston Harrington Family 1943

Preston attended school in Desloge, MO through the eighth grade. As a young man he tried his fortune in the lumber camps and copper mines of Nebraska and Wyoming. He also traveled to Texas and worked in the oil fields there. He returned home and went to St. Louis to find work. He was hired at Munger Laundry as a driver. There he met Irene Miller who would become his wife. Upon leaving the laundry he opened a tire retreading business on Easton Avenue in St. Louis. He left there in 1927 and moved with his family back to the Farmington area.

He farmed on rented farms until November 1933 and moved his family to San Antonio, TX. His health failed and the family returned to the Farmington area where he again engaged in farming. He sold *Globe Democrat* newspaper subscriptions to rural areas until he died on Aug. 3, 1945. From 1937-1944 he ran a service station in Farmington and also owned a used furniture and antique store in town.

Upon his death, Irene went to work at Wulfers Furniture, and finally at a restaurant in Farmington. She was educated in the Farmington schools and graduated from high school with the class of 1920. She also attended the Ozark Business College in 1920. She moved to St. Louis and worked at Nugent's "Grand Leader" Department Store. She married Harry Slater Feb. 2, 1921. The marriage ended in divorce. While at Nugent's, Irene and another girlfriend felt very honored to be invited to lunch with Charley Chaplin, the famous actor. The invitation was accepted and she found him to be very pleasant and friendly. She passed away Sept. 18, 1958.

Both Preston's and Irene's ancestry goes back to the arrival of the earliest colonists. These pioneer names are found in the settling of this area, our state and country. Preston's lineage contains the names of Herrington (Harrington), Drennan, Helderbrand (Hildebrand), Hagan, Ricard, Hubardeau, Patterson, Poe, McNair, Totten, Buchanan, Bryant, and Beavins. His families came from Ireland, Scotland and France. Bartholomew Herrington, William Drennan, Adam Poe and John Totten all served in the Revolutionary War in the Pennsylvania Line. John Helderbrand served with Illinois in the Virginia Regiments under George Rogers Clark. Joseph Hagan served with the Maryland Patriots. We are sure there are others of these lines who served but at this time we have not proven them. These people came to these far shores in search of land, freedom and a better way of life. In 1799, the King of Spain offered land west of the Mississippi River to anyone who had served against England during the Revolution. To receive this land you were required to pledge allegiance to Spain and vow that you were Catholic since Spain was a Catholic nation. They were attracted here because of the rich fertile lands and mining industry.

Irene's lineage contains the name of Chandler, Edwards, Harrod, Burks, Thomas, Grant, Lunsford, Miller and Zimmer. Abiel Chandler and Elisha Lunsford both served in the American Revolution. These men were on her mother's side of the family. The Millers came from Germany and settled in the Farmington area about 1828. He was a farmer and tailor. The Zimmers came later and settled near Doe Run. They were farmers. *Submitted by Norma J. Fuchs, Sept. 6, 1998*

HARRINGTON - In remembrance of Willis Samuel Harrington.

Byron Harrington, Jeanetta Stevenson and Willis Harrington

Willis was the youngest son of Edward J. and Caroline Ann (Morris) Harrington. His mother died at the age of 52, when he was 7 years old. He was raised by his father, brothers and sisters, especially Jeanetta. He attended Oak Hill School, a one-room rural school, Flat River Junior and Senior High School and the Flat River Junior College. He later graduated from the University of Missouri with a BS degree in secondary education with a major in social studies and a minor in biology. He taught for 14 years.

In 1959 he became a licensed real estate broker until 1992. He lived in Farmington, MO all of his life until he passed away Jan. 25, 1993.

HASTINGS - The Hastings (Haston) family of Farmington arrived in St. Francois County in the mid-1850s when Daniel Marion Haston and his brother, David Crockett Haston, arrived there to be close to an uncle, David McComsky Haston, after the deaths of their parents, Thomas and Margaret Haston, of Butler County, MO and formerly of Van Buren and White Counties, TN.

Harold and Virginia Hastings

Daniel M. Haston married Minerva Jane Tabor, daughter of John and Margaret Tabor, of Doe Run, MO on Oct. 22, 1857. Daniel died from complications of measles and pneumonia in the Civil War on Jan. 9, 1865, at Louisville, KY, where he is buried at Cave Hill Cemetery. Daniel enlisted in Co. B, 68th Regt. of the Missouri Militia of St. Francois County on March 4, 1864. Their children were: Francis Marion, born Oct. 20, 1858, died March 29, 1911, and Louis Princeton, born June 29, 1860. The family name was changed from Haston to Hastings during the 1860s, and has remained with the Hastings spelling since that time.

Francis Marion married Clara W. Ledbetter, born Feb. 22, 1859, died March 26, 1932, daughter of Reuben P. and Nancy (Weems) Ledbetter, and were the parents of seven children: Clara Ethel, born 1883, died 1883; Cora Antoinnette, born June 24, 1885, died July 20, 1901; Francis K., born Nov. 26, 1887, died Jan. 3, 1946; Francis Phillip, born Nov. 14, 1889, died June 13, 1906; Grace Ledbetter, born 1892, died Dec. 18, 1971; August DeWitt, born Aug. 1, 1895, died Nov. 11, 1940; and George Lee, born Dec. 27, 1899.

Francis K. "Koss" Hastings married Estella M. Currington, born Feb. 5, 1887, died May 24, 1974 on Nov. 2, 1912. They were the parents of seven children: Gladys Marie, born Feb. 2, 1913, died July 30, 1992; Lelia Arlene, born Feb. 25, 1915, died Nov. 28, 1985, Harold K., born Sept. 7, 1916; Doris Estella, born Oct. 16, 1918, died April 4, 1920; Helen Geraldine, born Dec. 15, 1920, died Dec. 19, 1990; Mabel Maxine, born Jan. 16, 1922, died Sept. 20, 1970; Cletus Clifford, born Dec. 8, 1924, died Feb. 24, 1982.

Harold K. Hastings, son of F.K. and Estella (Currington) Hastings was born in Flat River, MO, the third of seven children. Virginia Lee Schafer, second daughter of John F. and Daisy J. (Robertson) Schafer was born in Farmington, MO Dec. 20, 1916 and died Dec. 25, 1996 in St. Louis, MO, and is buried at Parkview Cemetery, north of Farmington. Harold Hastings and Virginia Schafer were married in Farmington, MO on Oct. 6, 1940. Harold and Virginia Hastings were the parents of four sons: Harold G., born April 3, 1943, married Phyllis Pemberton); Larry L., born Dec. 10, 1946, married Deborah Johnson); John R., born June 3, 1948; and James D., born June 18, 1951.

Harold K. Hastings currently resides in Farmington in the house he has lived in since 1941. He worked for St. Joe Lead Co. for more than 35 years. He was affiliated with the *Lead Belt News* in Flat River, MO for more than 40 years; was a St. Francois County deputy sheriff for more than 10 years; owned and operated Whistle Vess Bottling Co. in Farmington during the early 1960s; and has made and sold Plastic Seal Auto Polish since 1954, which he does to this day. Virginia Hastings was a devoted housewife and mother during the 56 years of their marriage. They were members of the United Memorial Methodist Church of Farmington.

Harold G. and Phyllis currently reside in Farmington where Harold has a business and Phyllis teaches school. They are the parents of two sons: Scott of Farmington (Scott and wife, Regina, own a photography studio in Farmington and are the parents of Tristan, the first great-grandson of Harold and Virginia [Schafer] Hastings) and Sean of Aux Vasse, MO. Larry L. and Debbie reside in Coffman, MO. Larry is head of maintenance at Presbyterian Homelife in Farmington. They have three sons: Brian and Mark Garner, and Larry L. Hastings Jr., all of Farmington. John R. resides in Farmington and works for Mississippi Lime in Ste. Genevieve, MO. He has three children: Matt, Jason and Katie. James D. lives in St. Louis where he owns his own business. *Written by James D. Hastings, St. Louis, MO and submitted by Harold K. Hastings, Farmington, MO.*

HENDERSON/MURPHY - James Henderson Jr. was the fourth great-grandfather of Esther M. Carroll. He was born in Tennessee in 1791 and was the son of Hannah Sollars and James Henderson Sr. James Sr. died in 1793 and Hannah remarried to James Tallant in 1799. In the early 1800s, the Henderson/Tallant family left Greene County, TN and came to southeast Missouri and were among the early settlers of what would later become the town of Farmington in St. Francois County. At that time it was still part of Ste. Genevieve County since St. Francois County was not formed until 1821.

The Carroll Clan with Santa - Christmas 1994. Santa, Gene and Esther Carroll and their three "kids" - Brandy (left), Sandy (center) and Candy (right). Esther is a descendant of James Henderson, an early settler in Farmington.

In 1817, James Henderson signed a petition for construction of a road beginning at the James Bryan plantation on Flat River and intersecting with the road from Mine A Breton (now known as Potosi) in Washington County to Jackson in Cape Girardeau County. In October 1818, James was paid $2 by the county of Ste. Genevieve for killing a wolf. In 1819, James signed a petition to construct a road leading from the county road to St. Mary's Landing. In May 1820, James Henderson appraised a stray horse which had been taken up by Isaac Cunningham. In 1857, James Henderson purchased a four-horse wagon from Milton P. Cayce for $45.

James Henderson married circa 1819 and he and his wife, Hopy, eventually had six children: Jane, who was first married to William S. Brim and later to a Mr. Graham; Mary Ann, who was first married to her cousin, John Henderson Jr. and then later to Robert M. Markham (Mary Ann and John Henderson Jr. were the third great-grandparents of Esther M. Carroll); Samuel S., who went to Oregon; Corbin A., who was first married to Elizabeth Mitchel and then to Emma Martin; Nancy Telithy, who was married to James M. Mitchel; and Eleanor, who married Henderson "Henry" Strickland.

The Henderson family was related to the prominent Murphy family. Rachel Henderson was the wife of William Murphy, Jr. According to the book, "*Rev. William Murphy and His Descendants*," Rachel Henderson was born in the famous Shenandoah Valley of Virginia in 1764. William and Rachel were married in Greene County, TN in 1782. They came from the vicinity of Knoxville to St. Francois County, MO, 1798-1802, and settled south of what would later become Farmington.

William and Rachel had a large family. One of their sons, David Henderson Murphy, born 1802, was the first child born in the "Murphy Settlement." In adulthood David H. Murphy was the guardian of George W., James M., Elizabeth and Almeda Henderson who were the children of Mary Ann and John Henderson Jr. and the grandchildren of James Henderson Jr. and John Henderson Sr. In 1821 William Murphy's brother, David, donated 52 acres of land upon which Farmington, the county seat of St. Francois County, was established.

Joseph Murphy, brother to William and David, acquired survey #340 in 1799. This survey was 550 arpents, or 478.88 acres. The northwest part of present day Farmington takes up much of this claim from west of Highway 67 to and including part of Maple Valley Shopping Center, to way north and east of Mineral Area Regional Medical Center. In 1814 James Tallant purchased 91 arpents of land from Joseph Murphy. In 1824, James Tallant gave this property to his stepson, James Henderson, in return for Henderson taking care of Tallant and his horse in his old age. Since there was no mention of James Henderson's mother, Hannah, in this document, she was probably already deceased. For whatever reason, the arrangement between James Henderson and James Tallant apparently did not work out, for a year later Henderson agrees to purchase the property from Tallant over a three-year period, and Tallant left and went to Alabama.

In 1830, James Henderson was residing between Joseph Murphy and Charles B. Cunningham. In this same year, James Henderson sold his property to Cunningham. James Henderson then moved to Pendleton Township where he resided for about 30 years. This property was on the west end of what is now Raby Rd. James Henderson died circa 1863-1870. Many of his descendants still reside in and around St. Francois County. *Researched and written by Esther M. Ziock Carroll*

HENNRICH - Jeanna Lea (Hampton) Hennrich was born May 1959 in Marietta, GA to Thomas Lee and Patty Jean (Pogue) Hampton. After living in Farmington, as a baby for about 10 months, moved to Fenton, MO, Kansas City, MO and Bartlesville, OK before her move back to Farmington in November 1969 at the age of 10.

Seth, Kate, Jeanna and Levi Hennrich

Jeanna graduated from Farmington High School in 1977 and in March 1978 married Stephen Paul Hennrich. Three children were born

of this union: Seth Augustus, born Nov. 11, 1982, Levi Thomas, born Aug. 27, 1984, and Kathleen "Kate" Gale, born May 23, 1987.

Jeanna attended Mineral Area College and graduated from SEMO, Cape Girardeau, MO in 1993 with a degree in elementary education and early childhood education. She is presently employed as the kindergarten teacher at St. Paul Lutheran School in Farmington, a position she has held since graduation. She is currently working towards a master's degree in education through Southwest Baptist University.

Jeanna and her children are very active in their church, First Baptist of Farmington, and reside on the family farm on Bray Road which they purchased several years ago from her grandparents, Eugene and Larna (Hicks) Pogue.

HENSON - In June 1973, Charles "Chuck" and Ardith "Ardie" Henson moved to Farmington so Chuck could begin what would become a lifetime career as a teacher, coach and administrator in the Farmington School District. Chuck began in August 1973, as varsity basketball coach and social studies teacher at Farmington High School. He would later become head volleyball coach also. He would continue to coach basketball until 1979 and coach volleyball until 1993. In 1976, he was one of a limited number of coaches to win two regionals in one season: the 1976 basketball team was defeated by Charleston; however, the volleyball team went on to finish third in the state. His lifetime record as a volleyball coach was 348 - 104 - 7. He continues to serve as athletic director and assistant principal at Farmington High School.

L-R: Chuck Henson Family, Ardie, Shawnna, Keenan, Shannon, Chuck, December 1998.

Chuck and Ardie met at Mineral Area College while students. They married in 1967 and moved to St. Louis where Chuck continued his basketball career at University of Missouri at St. Louis. While at MAC, the Cardinals were rated third in the nation; and at UMSL, Chuck also was fortunate to be a part of a winning team as the Rivermen advanced to the NAIA National Tournament his junior year. Chuck's first teaching job was at Windsor High School in Imperial.

Chuck is originally from Piedmont, MO. His parents were Leroy "Pete" and Esther Kathleen (Williams) Henson. Both the Henson and Williams families were from the Wayne County farming communities. Chuck's parents moved briefly to California with his maternal grandparents and Chuck was born in Woodlake, CA in Sequoia National Park Hospital. His grandparents were Charles Clay and Mable (Noble) Williams and Roy Lee and Gertie (Babb) Henson.

Ardie was born in Bonne Terre, MO to David Arthur and Vera Imogene (Bradley) Province. The Provinces were part of the farming community of Hazel Glen and Irondale, MO. The Bradleys were lead miners in the Leadwood Community. Ardie's grandparents were David Seabourne and Myrtle Priscilla (French) Province and Fred and Matilda Ann (Pitts) Bradley. Ardie lived from 1948 to 1960

in Fredericktown where her father was the conservation agent for Madison County. Her mother, Imogene, retired from SEMO Treatment Center and continues to work part time at Parkland Regional.

Chuck and Ardie's children are Shawna Kay (Mrs. John) Robinson, Shannon Keith, and Keenan Lee. Shawnna graduated from SEMO University and was director for BKTV in the early years. She and John are the parents of John Charles, born 1993 and Chloe Elizabeth, born 1997. The Henson's eldest son, Shannon, is a graduate of SEMO and is a biology teacher and coach in the Fredericktown School District. He is engaged to Rebecca Domazlicky of Cape Girardeau. She is a chemistry teacher in the Farmington School District. Their youngest child, Keenan Lee, is attending Maryville University where he is majoring in mass communications and playing basketball.

Chuck and Ardie have been active in community organizations including Lions Club, Flora Garden Club and Beta Sigma Phi. They have been most active in their church, First Baptist. Chuck is a deacon and has served as Sunday School director for many years. Ardie has served as Baptist Women president, GA teacher, Sunday School teacher, Vacation Bible School and is the drama director for the annual Easter play "Joy Comes in the Morning."

Chuck and Ardie enjoy sporting events, gardening and spending time with their family. They were honored to be selected as Mr. and Mrs. Country Days in 1986 and are proud to be part of the Farmington Community.

HERBST - The two-story house at 513 North "A" Street in Farmington was bought by my dad, Will Herbst, in 1912 for $2,750 and was animated by the Herbst Family from 1912-68. During those 56 years, it was a hub of activity.

Dad bought the property to entice his parents to "move to town." The idea delighted Grandma, now she was at leisure to garden, cultivate her flowers and was convenient for her aged father. Grandpa's ingenious talent with wood promptly altered the landscape, his "court yard" between the smoke house and the horse barn had a "windbreak" fence on the north, enhanced by picturesque fencing and gates on the south. The big leaning maple tree seemed pleased.

Emmett Herbst in Antarctica 1976 - South Pole Pointing to Sign: Farmington, MO 8300 miles

My dad and mom were married in 1917, and by 1920 they had a family; then grandpa and grandma bought a home on North Franklin Street, adjoining their daughter and son-in-law, John and Anna Bohs.

Now the new occupants of 513 North "A" Street were Will and Mary Herbst plus young Leonard, Marvin, about 20 chickens, a buggy horse named Prince and Mom's promising strawberry patch.

Many apple butter cookings, hog butcherings, vegetable cannings, celebrations and sorrows happened at 513 North "A" Street;

Grandpa and Grandma were very sincere people, making a life good for all the family.

My brother, Emmett, was born in 1925, enhancing the aura. But we were so saddened when Grandma (Caroline Herbst) died in 1926. Dad, Mom and Grandpa (William Herbst) kept our hopes intact. My sister, Edith, was born in 1928 and Evelyn in 1933. Thus, there were five young Herbst's bouncing out to meet the world of the 1930s.

The Depression made life difficult, yet stimulating. We youngsters were required to work, still we had time to investigate everything that might attract a youngster's interest; the papaws with their many turtle dove nests that grew in a fence row where Karsch Blvd., now rages. We admired the ever present rabbits and the plethora of birds living in the big trees of the neighborhood.

There were 12 boys in the neighborhood inciting ball games, fishing and camping expeditions. We enjoyed school but soon it was time to get jobs. I was lucky at Schramms Ice Plant at Festus, engines compressors, etc., I was elated. Marvin followed the next year. Marvin came upon an airplane magazine and to our surprise, he was in the Naval Air School shortly.

On Dec. 10, 1941, 700 young men along with Marvin "got their wings." Marvin was in the Pacific through all the war. By V-J Day Marvin was one of seven survivors. Emmett was drafted after high school, served in the Philippines, survived but shaken. Emmett diligently pursued the study of geology; with a rewarding career, taking him to many parts of the world.

The atmosphere from that home inspired us to many interests.

Included is picture of Emmett pointing the way to Farmington, MO from the South Pole in 1976. *Submitted by Leonard Herbst*

HERBST/SHANNON - Benedict Heinrich Herbst, son of August and Mary Herbst, was born Aug. 22, 1884, in the Cartee Community, southwest of Farmington. August Frederick Herbst's parents, Henry Carl Herbst and Wilhelmina (Hildebrecht) Herbst, immigrated about 1850 from Brunswick (Duchy of Braunschweig), Germany. August was their first child born in America. Marie Elizabeth "Mary" Heck was born at Iron Mountain, MO, on March 2, 1859, daughter of Benedict and Elizabeth (Rinderly) Heck. The Hecks were from Baden, Germany. Shortly after their marriage Nov. 14, 1882, August and Mary moved to Cartee Road. They are buried in the family cemetery there. Descendants still own the farm. August died May 10, 1897, leaving his widow and seven children: Ben, Sue, Lena, Emma, Herman, Denis and August. Ben, age 13, became the man of the family.

Mary Elizabeth Shannon

Mary Elizabeth "Lizzie" Shannon was born March 11, 1887, to William Shelly and Lucinda (Resinger) Shannon. William's parents, Rev. John Crabtree and Caroline (Shelly) Shannon, came from Robertson County, TN about 1849. Lizzie attended the Valley Forge School east of Farmington. In 1910, the widowed Lucinda lived next door to Mary Herbst. Lizzie worked as a maid and telephone operator. Ben farmed and worked for the railroad. They courted seven years and were married March 2, 1912.

They rented the Kirstein farm in the Cartee Community for about 30 years. Ben did not want to be a landowner. He bought his first threshing machine, which was powered by a steam engine, in 1914, and threshed grain for farmers all over the county until the late 1940s. Ben and his sons liked to hunt. One cold winter, 32 dressed rabbits hung in their smokehouse for days without thawing. Ben read the *Globe Democrat*, a Republican paper, faithfully. There were two kinds of people in his world: good guys and Democrats. Lizzie played piano and taught Sunday School at the Cartee Community Church. They moved to California in 1952, and Ben worked in their son's farm equipment manufacturing and repair shop. They returned to Missouri in 1954 to live in Madison County near daughter Mildred's family. Lizzie died Oct. 26, 1970. Ben followed June 12, 1973.

Five children survived to adulthood. Benjamin "Bus" T. Herbst married Eva May Larby of Farmington. Their son, David Herbst, carries on Herbst Manufacturing, Inc. in Esparto, CA.

Mildred Herbst married Edgar Chamberlain. Ben Elvis Chamberlain lives in his parents' farm in Madison County. His sisters are Mary Porter and Ruth (Mrs. Wayne) Hahn.

Mamie Herbst married Ondis Pritchett. They purchased a farm on Highway H in 1939 and raised four daughters there: Joyce Glasgow, Bonnie (Mrs. Freeman) Pearsall, Betty Pritchett and Judy Pritchett.

Raymond "Jack" Herbst moved to Sacramento, CA and married Marian Peter. They were the parents of Charlene (Mrs. John) Moorhead and Eric Herbst.

Hazel Herbst married Richard Gerlach of Knob Lick. The US Navy took them to Portugal, Turkey, Korea and finally Arlington, VA. They are the parents of Gerald Gerlach and Sandra (Mrs. John) Wilkinson.

HERBST/PRITCHETT - Ondis Pritchett married a woman with money. Mamie Herbst was employed by the Rice-Stix shirt factory in Farmington when they married Aug. 10, 1938, and she brought with her a life savings of $355. Ondis was employed by St. Joe Lead Co., earning $5 per day. In March 1939, they bought 65 acres of land for $1,000. With it came a team of mules, one milk cow, 65 chickens, several pieces of farm equipment, corn in the crib, fodder in the loft and the old family dog. The farm was home for 60 years and main source of income, albeit a grudging one, after a one runaway ore car ended Ondis' mining days in 1942. Ondis called his farm "Barely Do Ridge." On it he raised chickens, cows and four daughters.

Ondis Pritchett

Community meant a great deal to the Pritchetts. Mamie was born and raised in Cartee, the daughter of Ben and Lizzie Herbst. Ondis lived in Elvins and Bismarck before moving to Cartee at age 13 when his mother, Rosa Moore Pritchett, married William Robinson. The Cartee Community during the early days of their marriage was still a farm community. Neighbors worked together, played together and prayed together. Farmers traded work. One fall day Ondis was laid up following surgery, when to his surprise, teams and wagons began to pull up. The neighbors had come to harvest his crops for him. One night a month the ladies sat in a member's kitchen for the Loyal Workers Extension Club meeting, and the men sat in the living room talking farming and politics.

The hub of the community was the one-room Cartee School. The site was donated by James W. and Christiana (Turpin) Moore to the congregation of the Church of Christ of St. Francois County in 1906 for the use of the Cartee congregation. The church transferred the property in 1913 to the school district. G.W. Bess, G.W. Barnes and Lena Williamson (formerly Lena Tetley) were trustees of the congregation. Trustees of School District No. 47 were August Klob, William Crepps and Walter Cartee Weimer. Cartee School records go back to 1869. At one time 89 children were on the rolls.

The first school building was a log cabin which sat across the road from the later site. A second school building was later moved and used as a corn crib. The third building was built in 1912. The school building was also used for nondenominational Sunday School classes. Mamie served many years as Sunday School treasurer. Both Mamie and Ondis served regularly on the school board until the district was consolidated with the Busiek School District about 1960. One hot summer day, the Cartee School burned to the ground. Thirty-seven neighbors attended a basket dinner on Aug. 26, 1961 and decided to build a Cartee Community Center on the site. All expenses were paid by donation. Ondis, Herman Herbst and John Mund became the first trustees.

HIBBITS - Ebenezer H. Hibbits was a native of Iredell County, NC and was probably of Irish extraction. He was reared in Iredell County, following agricultural pursuits, but became a teacher after coming to Missouri. He married Margaret Green in North Carolina and moved to Hardin County, TN where they lived three years before coming to Madison County, MO, then to St. Francois County, MO. He died May 29, 1865 and Margaret died in 1877. They were the parents of nine children:

1) John Green, born 1828, married Sarah Poole and had three children. Luther who married first Lucy Vandergriff and second Mary Stephens. They had seven children. John married Olive Bone and had Wayne, Virginia and Betty (married a Kollmeyer), Ellen, Ruth, Everett, George W. (a minister), Mary and Margaret (married Grover Hardesty), Emma (married Ed Sikes), William Lee (married Ada).

2) William M., born 1837, married Martha Jacobs and had seven children. They were John R., Robert, born 1858 and married Sarah Elizabeth Williams, the daughter of Arthur and Charlotta Williams. Robert and Sarah were the parents of seven children: Nellie, John, Grace, Mary, Noah, Blanche and Bryan. Harvey, born 1859, died 1915, is buried in Knob Lick. He married Martha Bayless, the daughter of George and Meekie (Eaves) Bayless. They were the parents of John, Thomas, Aubrey, Allen who married Mary Francis Williams, daughter of Jeffrey and Harriet (Barnes) Williams. They were the parents of 10 children. Ina, James, Milo, Edith who married Oscar Chapman, Elizabeth, Mary, James and Nancy.

3. Nancy Caroline married first Thomas Holsted in 1855 and second, Cincinnatus Poole in 1864.

4. Sarah Eliza, born March 5, 1837, died Jan. 29, 1923 in Doe Run, MO, married Loderick Williams, Nov. 18, 1858, in St. Francois County, MO. He was the son of David and Ziba (Hailey) Williams who came from Davidson County, TN. They were the parents of John, Frank, Mary, Narcissa, Drullah, Johanna, Margaret and Alice. Loderick was born Sept. 21, 1835, in Nashville, TN and died Jan. 20, 1907. He is buried in the Doe Run

Cemetery. He was a highly esteemed citizen and worked as a pattern maker and inspector of machinery of the Doe Run Lead Co. where he had been employed ever since it was organized. He was highly skilled as a master mechanic, a man to be trusted, of upright character, and possessed a gentleness of manner and consideration for others that made everybody his friend.

5. Harriett, born 1842, married Thomas Santee in 1867. They had a son named George.

6. Margaret. no information.

7. Malvina. no information.

8. James, born 1846, died 1922, married Mary Scott.

9. Lewis Bernard, born 1848, married Elizabeth Wheitt. They had three children.

HILL - John Watson Hill was born in 1808 in Kentucky. On March 17, 1847, in St. Francois County, he married Emeline Mallory Poston. Emeline was born in Missouri Feb. 3, 1819. Her mother, Nancy, was the widow of Henry Poston. Emma had a half brother, Dr. Henry Poston.

John purchased what was known as the Jeptha Bradley farm in November 1846, originally owned by William Murphy Sr. The land was situated in Murphy's Settlement on the waters of the St. Francois River. In April 1849, he bought the 110-acre Henderson Murphy farm.

Nellie May Hill Robinson, daughter of John Warren Hill and Sarah Elizabeth Ragsdale.

It is said John had a crew who built many of the old buildings in Farmington, including the second jail. He also had teams of wagons and oxen that went to Kansas, Texas and Mexico with lumber and supplies.

Born to John and Emma were:

Mary Jane, born 1848; unlisted in census reports after the age of 12, and not included in any of her father's court records; Nancy Emma "Nannie," born 1850, married James Donnell and had one son, Charley.

Anna Eliza "Annie," born 1852, married Walter Combs and had one son. They lived in Kentucky, Kansas, and Washington, D.C. John Warren (Warren), born 1852, twin of Annie. Overton "Ovie," born 1854, never married, see below. Jenny May (year unknown), married Dr. William F. Emerson and had four children. They owned Dred Scott of the famous Dred Scott case. It is said John also owned land at Austin, TX, and Jenny's family moved there.

John Warren married Sarah Elizabeth Ragsdale "Lizzie," Dec. 5, 1872. Lizzie was the daughter of Thomas Ragsdale and Nancy (Brown) Townshend, who lived near Cook's Settlement. He worked in the St. Joe Lead Mines. One daughter, Nellie May, was born to them Dec. 22, 1873. Eventually Warren and Lizzy sold their properties in St. Francois County and moved to a farm in Washington County. Family history tells us John Warren died circa 1885 at the age of 26 of TB and was buried with the folks in Farmington.

Ovie never married. He was studying at Louisville, KY to be a physician when he got sick and returned home. He had a will made April 8, 1875, which stated all his possessions were to be left to his dearly beloved brother, John Warren Hill, his sister-in-law, Elizabeth, and their children. Most of the items listed had just been purchased at his mother's estate sale in October 1874. Ovie died

April 25, 1875 at about 20 years of age. The final settlement for Ovie was published in *The New Era.*

Records show that Dr. George Williams sat with John Watson several days before he died on Dec. 7, 1855 when he was about 46 years old. His coffin was bought for $10. Family history tells us John was buried where the old Farmington airport was.

John died without a will, and in those days women were not allowed to handle legal matters, so Emma selected her friend, Elisha Arnold, to be her attorney and agent. His appraisement list of Jan. 8, 1856 included deeds, shares of St. Genevieve, Iron Mountain and Pilot Knob Plank Road Stock, slaves Henry, a negro man, James "Jim," 16; John, 13; Sanford, 7; Katherine, 38, with 5-month old child, Betsey, 12; Fanny, 8; Louvinna, 6; Rose, 23, and her child, Sally. Also included was one family Bible, numerous books, clocks, a looking glass, furniture, pistol, one old Mexican saddle silver, pleasure carriage, grain and livestock totalling $8,435.37.

On Jan. 25, 1856, Emma's attorney petitioned the court for permission to retain in her possession, for the use and benefit of herself and family, certain livestock, furniture, tools, wagon and pleasure carriage. Proceeds from public sales, held February 1856 and March 1857, were used to settle the estate debts. A case was filed March 30, 1857 against Emeline for selling livestock, a slave named Henry valued at $1,000, leasing eight other slaves, the Bradley place, the Meadow farm and a house and lot in Farmington and not reporting it to the court.

Emma paid taxes on eight pieces of ground in 1867. As curator of the minor heirs of John W. Hill, she asked the court on Sept. 2, 1867, for permission to sell the Bradley and Murphy farms, for the purpose of educating properly said minor heirs of John W. Hill. Family history says Emeline was known to be a society person and went to St. Louis for a short time to do just this.

On May 14, 1871, the court divided the land, owned by John W. Hill, between his heirs. This included 257 acres northwest of what is now Westmeyer Road, 31 acres, one-half mile east of Farmington, bound on the north by the Gravel Roads, now known as St. Genevieve Ave., Lot 57 fronting 95 links on Columbia St. and 3.5 chains on Jackson St., where the US Post Office now stands, and 25 acres known as the Hill's Addition to Farmington, situated between Long, Donnell St. (Main), Henry St., and Forster and four lots lying on the west side of Henry. Two of the streets were named Warren and Overton.

Emeline died Sept. 17, 1873, and was buried beside her son, Ovie, in the Masonic Cemetery in Farmington.

HINKLE - William Gale Hinkle, son of Herbert and Essa (Lashley) Hinkle of Bruno, and Rachel Lee Smith, daughter of Lee Edward and Lucy (Green) Smith of Farmington, married March 5, 1955.

Born to them were three children: Mark William, born at Medical Arts Clinic, Farmington, Nov. 15, 1955; David Alexander was born in Bonne Terre, Aug. 10, 1960; and Lucinda Jo was born in Fredericktown Jan. 13, 1962.

The family moved to Michigan in the early 1970s. It was there Mark met and later married Sarah Ann Jackson on Aug. 17, 1974. Due to complications, Mark and Sarah lost three children at birth. They were Tracy Lynn, Christine Renee and Duane Allen, but Sept. 2, 1978, God blessed them with a son, Patrick James, and then again on Feb. 3, 1980, with Nathaniel Robert.

For just a few short years, they knew their loving grandmother, Rachel, but then on Dec. 9, 1982, they lost her to cancer.

Due to a shutdown of the Ford Tractor Plant in Romeo, MI, Mark was transferred to the St. Louis Assembly Plant and the family moved to DeSoto, MO, in 1986.

Although it meant a farther drive to work, the family agreed to move to Farmington in 1991 due to the outstanding school system. Both Patrick and Nathaniel had been active in the school band since middle school. Both won many awards and were tuba section leaders in their junior and senior years.

In front: Mark, Sarah and Nathaniel. In back: Patrick

Patrick graduated from Farmington High School in 1997 and promptly entered the United States Navy.

Nathaniel has played in the Community Band since it was organized in 1997 and is in the Class of 1999 at Farmington High School. He is planning to continue his studies and enter the field of architectural engineering.

Mark's brother, David, moved to Missouri in 1980. He went to college and received his degree and now teaches at Clearwater High School in Piedmont, MO.

Their sister, Lucinda, moved to Missouri in 1980 also. She married Richard Lee Ross on April 19, 1982 and they lived in Piedmont. He passed away from a heart attack on Dec. 24, 1995. She has two sons, Benjamin and Richard Dale, and now lives in Farmington.

Although the family genealogy compiled goes back to Sarah (Barton) Murphy, our family has many special people. One of them was our mom and grandma, Rachel Lee (Smith) Hinkle. We would like to dedicate this short history to her.

HOEHN - Imogene (Hoehn) Cook celebrated her 70th birthday on July 15, 1998. More than 50 of those years, she has lived in Farmington, MO. She was born in Doe Run, MO to Benjamin and Johanna Hoehn and is the only living child of this union. On June 17, 1943, she was united in marriage with Charles Edward Cook of Mayfield, MO. Three boys: Wayne, Gary and Jeff were happily raised by this couple. Imogene worked in the Farmington school system in the cafeteria for many years before her retirement in 1998. Charlie was a veteran of WWII and worked for the Pilot Knob Pellet Company. Together, Charlie and Imogene enjoyed visiting family and attending auctions. Charlie died May 22, 1982, at their home in Farmington.

Wedding picture of Imogene Cook's parents, Benjamin and Johanna (Lorenz) Hoehn, Sept. 7, 1912

When Imogene was a girl, she was raised in the Pendleton Township and attended the Hildebrecht School. She enjoyed childhood with six older brothers and sisters: Tom, Effie, Dick, Ethel and Charles. Her father, Benjamin Franklin Hoehn, was born in Doe Run in 1891 and worked as a farmer all of his life. As a child, Imogene can remember watching the wheat threshing that took place at their farm, first with the steam engine and then with a tractor. Frank, as he was called, was united in marriage Sept. 7, 1912, to Johanna Magdalena Lorenz. She was born in 1895, also in Doe Run, to Charles and Elizabeth (Saling) Lorenz. Both of Johanna's grandparents, Saling and Lorenz, traveled from Germany and settled in the Iron Mountain, MO area. Frank died in 1961 and Johanna in 1972.

Frank's father was John Adam Hoehn. He was born in Illinois in 1863 and on June 16, 1887, married Margaret Weitzel at Iron Mountain. She was born 1869 in Pilot Knob, MO to Benjamin and Mary (Blattner) Weitzel. Margaret and John were blessed with eight children: Henry, born 1888; Benjamin, born 1891; Edward, born 1893; Albert, born 1895; George, born 1899; Paul, born 1902; Mary, born 1905; and Rozie Ann, born 1907. John passed away in 1939 and 12 years later Margaret joined him in eternity at the age of 80.

John's parents were both born in Germany. Wighand and Maria (Reutzel) Hoehn came to America and were married in 1856. They settled in the Iron Mountain, MO area and had five children. Other than John Adam, the couple had Jacob, who never married; Mary "Molly" who married Allen S. Brown; Henry who was married to Mattie Arnold and then Emma Beiser and Catherine who was united in marriage with Joe Hanks. Joe was born in Lawrence County, IL in 1837 and, after moving to Missouri, enlisted in the 28th Illinois Inf. in 1861 and served during the remainder of the Civil War.

Wighand Hoehn died in 1889 and is buried in Iron Mountain Cemetery. Maria remarried Mathias Heddesheimer and they are both buried in Doe Run Memorial Cemetery.

Imogene (Hoehn) Cook is very proud of her heritage and loves to tell the colorful stories of her past to her sons, nieces and nephews, and we all enjoy hearing them. *Submitted by Susan Baird*

HUANG - George and Amy Huang moved to Farmington, MO, from Los Angeles, CA, in the 1980s to start a business, Royal China Restaurant.

Royal China Restaurant began in June 1987, and at that time it was the only Chinese restaurant in Farmington. Royal China, actually known as the Golden China Restaurant, had opened in September 1986. About seven months later, ownership changed hands and was renamed Royal China.

George was originally from Taiwan, Republic of China. He has been an American citizen since 1980. He was formerly a chef at the Hilton Chinese Restaurant of Los Angeles in 1980. Amy was employed in Los Angeles until the couple married and chose to start a business.

The same couple now resides in Farmington and oversees the business daily. They have two daughters, Jenny and Jamie, who both were born in Farmington, MO.

Since Farmington as a whole has grown dramatically, it has directly affected Royal China Restaurant. As a result of increase in business, an additional dining area was built to the existing building six years ago. Since then, Farmington has gained many other businesses, including two other Chinese restaurants.

HUCKSTEP - Dr. Huckstep, wife Mary (Pilant) Huckstep and children, David Robert and Carol Sue, arrived in Farmington June 1955.

Robert A. Huckstep, MD, joined the Medical Arts Clinic June 1955. He was the son of Frank Arnold Huckstep, born June 22, 1889 in Linn, MO, died July 2, 1938 and Elizabeth Ann (Penning) Huckstep, born in St. Aubert, Dec. 27, 1897, died March 30, 1959. Robert obtained his pre-med at

Washington University, St. Louis, MO, and his MD from Washington University Medical School. He interned and had residences at St. Luke's Hospital, Missouri Pacific Hospital and Jefferson Barracks VA Hospital in St. Louis. He served in the US Army Pacific theater in WWII and was a lieutenant commander in USPHS during the Korean War.

Dr. Robert A. Huckstep and Mrs. Mary Huckstep

In Farmington, he served on the Farmington school board and the Mineral Area College board of trustees. He also worked at the Southeast Missouri Mental Health Center.

He was a member of AMA, Internal Medicine Society, Mineral Area Medical Society and Farmington Kiwanis Club.

He, along with Leroy Mitchem and Kelso Ballantyne (architects), built Camelot Nursing Center. Leroy Mitchem is Dr. Huckstep's cousin. The Huckstep Cardiac Rehab Center, located in Parkland Medical Center, was named in his honor.

In 1958 a second son, Stephen Charles Huckstep, was born at Bonne Terre Hospital.

Dr. Huckstep passed away Nov. 28, 1992.

Mrs. Huckstep, daughter of the late Charles William Pilant, born in Knoxville, TN and Laura Marjorie (Harkins) Pilant, born in St. Louis, MO, attended Harris Teachers College at Teresa and Park in St. Louis. She did substitute teaching in the Farmington school system and as of 1998 was the choir director of the Farmington Christian Church (Disciples of Christ) for 43 years.

She is a former member of the Nancy Weber Garden Club, Mineral Area Medical Auxiliary, Federated Club and past president and present member of Chapter H.J., P.E.O. She is also an alumna member of the Alpha Lambda chapter of Sigma, Sigma Sigma.

Son, David, married Diane Inez Ellis of Farmington; and Carol Sue married Steven Louis Jones of Farmington and they have one daughter, Erica Blythe Jones. David and Carol Sue live in Farmington.

Stephen Charles married Vickie L. Detjen of Farmington. They have a daughter, Jessica Lane Huckstep, and a son, Robert Spencer Huckstep. They live in Fenton, MO.

Dr. Huckstep's Ancestry: the Huckstep ancestors came to America from County Kent in England and originally settled in Richmond, VA. The Penning side came from Stadenhousen, Germany and settled in Missouri Osage County. *Submitted by Mary Huckstep*

HUFF - In 1900 Merrifield W. Huff purchased the house at 403 Doss Street (corner of C St.) and moved his family there. Merrifield's father, William Davis Huff, was a collier and had moved to Missouri to work in the iron industry. The company eventually changed from charcoal to mineral coal, and William bought a farm in Washington County where he and his wife lived out the rest of their lives. Merrifield had gone to law school at Washington University and had practiced in St. Louis, where he also had met his wife, the former Charlotte Martling. He moved to Farmington be-

cause he thought it would be better for his health. The house, which became known as "The House of Surprises," remained in the Huff family until 1983.

The family consisted, besides Merrifield and Charlotte, of six girls and three boys: Louise, Merrifield, Ruth, Margaret, Lottie, Dorothy, Emily, William and Ells. The oldest was 16 and the youngest just a year old when they moved to Farmington. They experienced many of the tribulations that were common in those times. The children suffered typhoid fever; and Margaret died of diphtheria in 1901 at the age of 13. Merrifield died in 1906 of an apoplectic stroke. One of his sons, who suffered from diabetes, has expressed the opinion that his father may have also been a victim of that disease and that it may have contributed to his death.

The family was active in the community, especially in the Farmington Presbyterian Church. The children attended the elementary schools. At least two of the girls, Lottie and Dorothy, attended the academy that occupied what is now the oldest building of the Children's Home. The younger Merrifield attended a college that existed in the town for a time. The other two boys and four of the girls (Louise, Lottie, Dorothy and Emily) attended Drury College in Springfield, MO. Ruth attended Southeast Missouri State Teachers' College in Cape Girardeau. Louise taught in the Farmington schools for a time.

As time passed, the children grew up. The boys all married and one of them, Merrifield Martling Huff, remained in the area (Flat River and Bonne Terre) and remained active in the church. Three of the girls: Ruth, Dorothy and Emily, all married; Dorothy and her family, and Louise and Lottie (who never married), lived in St. Louis for many years, as did Emily; Louise, Lottie and Emily (before her marriage) taught in the St. Louis schools.

Charlotte Huff died in 1923; by that time all the children had homes of their own. But all of the children had a great attachment to the "House of Surprises" and brought their children there as often as possible. In particular, Dorothy with her children and her unmarried sisters, Louise and Lottie, spent every summer there. Often other cousins would be there for shorter times. The property consisted of nearly an acre; and even with nearly half of it devoted to a garden, there was plenty of room for such things as a croquet court, as well as several maple trees that were grand for climbing.

In the early 1950s, Louise and Lottie retired from the St. Louis school system and returned to Farmington to live in the "House of Surprises." After Dorothy's husband died in 1955, she joined them. Emily had moved back to Farmington after her husband retired. Eventually, Emily (by then widowed) and Louise moved into Farmington Manor. Both died there in 1980. Dorothy and Lottie remained in the family home. By 1983, however, they found themselves unable to maintain it by themselves, and sold it and also moved to Farmington Manor. Lottie died in 1985, and Dorothy in 1989.

There are no longer Huffs in Farmington. But Merrifield Huff's grandchildren and several of his great-grandchildren, remember it fondly.

HUGHES/EATON - Just past the middle 1800s, Harvey Drury Hughes along with his wife, Sarah M. (Hayes) Hughes, brought their family from Indiana to Missouri and settled near Steelville, MO. Their children were John, Martin, Arthur, Azro, Jim, Wayne, George, Mary Hughes Hampton, Tremella Hughes Hayes and Amanda Hughes Usher.

Around the same time, James P. Ford, born

Nov. 5, 1851, in Tennessee, son of Thomas and Elizabeth (Stephenson) Ford, met Laura D. Richardson, born in Kentucky, March 26, 1864, daughter of Harrison Richard. How they met is not clear, but they were married in Arkansas, May 5, 1878. They, too, settled in the Steelville area. Their children were John, Ida May, Mattie and Bessie.

Left to Right: Reva Eaton Young, Roy Eaton, Aaron Eaton, Vernie Eaton, Lucy Wells Eaton, Raymond Eaton, Lucy Eaton McClintock, Verba Eaton Hughie.

The Hughes and Ford family were united when Arthur Hughes chose for his bride, Ida May Ford. They were married at Cooks Station, MO, Sept. 22, 1896. Their children were Verline Hughes Propst, Laura Hughes West, Everette, Paul, Marion, Jim, Tremella Hughes Poston, Orville, Dorothy Hughes Womack, Mildred Hughes Eaton and Clifford. They moved around quite frequently in their early marriage, wherever he could find work, some timber cutting, some lead mining, but farming was his first choice, so they settled in St. Francois County and worked the farm.

Orville Hughes, Paul Hughes, Mildred Hughes Eaton, Clifford Hughes, Laura Hughes West, Marion Arthur Hughes, James Hughes, Ida May Ford Hughes, Verline Hughes Propst, Everette Hughes, Tremella Hughes Poston, Marion Hughes, Dorothy Hughes Womack

From Sullivan County, IN, Aaron Jesse Eaton, son of Matthew and Sarah (Hayes) Eaton, settled in St. Francois County. Their children were Matthew, Aaron, Porter, Abraham, Bill, Marvin, John, Gallant, Nancy (Eaton) Forshee, Martha (Eaton) Shepherd and Cynthia Eaton.

Living in St. Francois County near Desloge was the Nesbit Wells family, consisting of Claude, Lucy, Lillie, Fred, Aubry, Nellie (Wells) Winch, and Ollie.

Aaron Eaton chose Lucy Viola Wells for his bride. Their family was Vernie, Reva (Eaton) Young, Verba (Eaton) Hughie, Roy, Lucy (Eaton) McClintock and Raymond.

On May 6, 1939, Roy W. Eaton and Mildred Hughes were married in Knob Lick, MO, at the home of the Rev. Charles Meyers and settled in Farmington. Their children were Marilyn (Eaton) Duncan, Frank, Robert, Jessie (Eaton) Cook, Dennis and David. Roy worked at various jobs, but he was an excellent maintenance man and finished

his working days in maintenance for the Presbyterian Home for Children. He passed away Feb. 28, 1981, and is buried at the Masonic Cemetery in Bismarck, MO. Mildred retired from Trimfoot Shoe Company in 1981, and has worked the past several years at the Farmington Public Library.

Marilyn married twice: first to Tom Griffin of St. Louis, MO, and they had one son, Jeffrey. Later she married Larry Duncan from Flat River and they had one daughter, Dawn. Marilyn passed away June 17, 1996, 11 days after Jeffrey was struck by a car and killed at the Norfolk Naval Base in Norfolk, VA. He is buried in South Carolina and Marilyn in Bismarck, MO.

Frank is married to the former Katie Sturgess of Avon, MO. They had three children: Frank Jr., Krista and Eeron. Frank Jr. is in the Special Forces, stationed at Ft. Benning, GA and a member of the Rangers. Krista was killed in an auto accident, May 18, 1987, and is buried at the K. P. Cemetery in Farmington. Eeron is married to Ollie Siebert of St. Genevieve and now lives in Farmington.

Robert is married to Janet Moore and has two children, Teresa and Robert Jr. Teresa is married to Scott Clauser of Farmington, and Robert is married to Maryetta Murphy and lives in the Farmington area.

Jessie is married to James Cook of Desloge, MO and has one daughter, Jaime, and a stepson, Mark, who lives in Troy, MO. Jaime is presently attending college in Springfield, MO.

Dennis married Carolyn Fink of Farmington and has one daughter, Amy. Following a divorce he married Linda Bailey. Linda has a son, Scott, and a daughter, Charmin.

David married Carol Bahr and had two children, Kristen and David II. Carol passed away in December 1989. Later he married Ellen Tolson, who has one daughter, Holly. David and Ellen live in Virginia Beach, VA, where he is stationed as a member of the USN.

HUNT- HAWN - Florence Hunt Hawn is the great-great-great-granddaughter of Farmington's founding family, Sarah (Barton) Murphy and Rev. William Murphy. Florence Hunt was born Jan. 23, 1905, and is the daughter of Ella (Highley) Hunt and Phillip G. "P.G." Hunt. Her grandmother was Sarah Long Hunt. Her great-grandmother was Isabella (Murphy) Long. Her great-grandfather was Dubart Murphy who was the son of Sarah (Barton) Murphy and Rev. William Murphy.

Florence Hunt married Alexander "Alex" A. Hawn on Oct. 3, 1932. Alex Hawn died Oct. 7, 1975. He was a marketer for Sinclair Oil Co. His mother and father were Etta (Moore) Hawn and E.K. Hawn.

Florence Hawn championed the cause of saving the Long House in Long Park from demolition. In 1921, her aunt, Jane (Long) Bisby, willed the Long House to the city of Farmington. In the spring of 1951, the city decreed to raze the house because of its age and uselessness. James Morris was mayor at this time. His wife told Florence about the city's decision and decided to save Long House. Both were members of the Monday Club. They took their concerns to the members of the Monday Club. As a result, the Monday Club protested the destruction and in the spring of 1952 offered to lease the house from the city for a short period to enable the group to determine how it could be saved as a place of historic interest. A

council was formed utilizing various clubs and civic organizations in town. Work was completed in late summer 1954. To defray part of the expense, the Monday Club sponsored a Community Stunt Night on July 31, 1954, which netted $300 and the first Farmington Homecoming to celebrate 150 years of existence. Old Settlement Days were held next. Monies raised rescued the Long House from destruction and it is now one of the few landmarks of the old Farmington.

Florence Hawn's uncle, W.H. Hunt, donated the four clocks on the current courthouse. Her aunt, Jane (Long) Bisby, built Long Memorial Hall in memory of her brother, Dubart Long.

Florence Hawn is an active member and elder of the Presbyterian Church. She is also active in and belongs to The Monday Club, P.E.O. and the Daughters of the American Revolution. She loves Farmington and is civic-minded. She has witnessed the growth of Farmington from a small town to the thriving community that it has become today. *Submitted by Elma Jennings*

KEITH HUNT - Keith Hunt is the sixth generation of his family to live in the Farmington area. His great-great-great-grandfather, Henry Hunt, came to Farmington in the 1820s. Henry was born in North Carolina, Dec. 6, 1777. He married Nancy Jackson and moved to the Shelbyville, KY area in the early 1800s. Ten children were born to this marriage: Martha, John Giles, Mary, Elizabeth, Nettie (Pernette), Lewicey, Jane, Lucinda, William and Henry. Henry made his living from farming. He and Nancy are buried in the family cemetery at 846 Potosi St.

John Giles, the second child of Henry and Nancy, was Keith's great-great-grandfather. He was born Oct. 17, 1815, while the family lived in Kentucky. After the family moved to Farmington, John married Lucinda Alexander June 2, 1839. Lucinda's parents were William and Elizabeth (Fish) Alexander of Farmington. Her father had fought in the American Revolutionary War. There were nine children born to this marriage: Martha, Henry P., William B., Elisa Jane, Nancy Lucinda, Giles, John, Shelby Wilson and Pinckney Luther. John, like his father, made his living by farming. This farm was located off Beal Road just west of Farmington. It is also the resting place for John and Lucinda.

Pinckney Luther, the ninth child of John and Lucinda, was Keith's great-grandfather. He was born May 26, 1859, on the Hunt farm on Beal Road. He married Cora V. Wood, Nov. 24, 1892. Cora's parents were Nelson and Mary Jane (McKnight) Wood. Nelson Wood fought in the Civil War with the 36th Ohio and join the Missouri Militia when the family moved here from Meigs County, OH. Mary Jane's parents were Samuel and Elizabeth McKnight who were from Dumfrieshire, Scotland. Cora and Pinckney had nine children: Blondy, Bessie Lois, Eunice, Verna, Mary, Luther, Theodore (Dick), Helen and Pinckney Bradberry. Pinckney carried on the family tradition of being a farmer on the Hunt farm. Pinckney and Cora moved off the farm in the late 1920s to a house in DeLassus on the corner of Chestnut and Second. The final resting place for Pinckney and Cora is the K. P. Cemetery off Highway H in Farmington.

Blondy Hunt, the first child of Pinckney and

Cora, was Keith's grandfather. He was born Jan. 25, 1894, on the Hunt farm. He married Beulah Hill, Oct. 16, 1919. Beulah's parents were Jason Allen and Jetrude Ann (Manning) Hill. Jason Hill was a judge in this area. Blondy served in Co. C, 110 Engineers during WWI. Blondy and Beulah had two children, Shelby B. and Blondy R. Jr. The family tradition of being farmers was changed by Blondy as he became a brick mason to make his living. Blondy and Beulah made their home just three houses up Second Street in DeLassus from his parents. The final resting place for Blondy and Beulah is also the K. P. Cemetery.

Blondy "Bob" Hunt Jr., the second child of Blondy and Beulah, is Keith's father. He was born Jan. 6, 1930, in his parents home. He married Karene "Kay" Lemons, Nov. 24, 1951. Karene's parents were Thomas and Charlotte (Bates) Lemons of Poplar Bluff, MO. Blondy served in the AAF in 1948 and the USAF in 1950. There were four children born to this marriage: Keith, Glenda, Edward and Tammy. Bob is a retired brick mason and Kay is a retired recreational therapist. Bob and Kay have lived most of their married years in DeLassus. They moved into his grandfather's old house in 1961, where they presently reside.

Keith Hunt, the eldest of Bob and Kay's children, was born Nov. 26, 1952, in Bonne Terre, MO. Keith married Pam Fox in July 14, 1973. Pam's parents were James A. and Sophia (Harris) Fox. Keith and Pam grew up together as next door neighbors in DeLassus. Keith and Pam moved to Columbia, MO shortly after they were married. On April 4, 1977, a daughter (Jennifer) was born to Keith and Pam. Keith moved his family back to Farmington in October 1977. Two more children were born to this marriage, Sarah, born Dec. 11, 1979, and Kara, born Oct. 31, 1983). Keith has worked 25 years for the postal service. During this time he has held many different job positions. Keith is currently postmaster at Doe Run, MO.

HUTCHINGS - Records from his family Bible show that Richard Hutchings Jr., born April 22, 1811, in Robertson County, TN, and Mahala Holland, born Feb. 20, 1812, were married April 12, 1832. Rev. Jackson performed the ceremony, witnessed by Aaron Burr and Sedelia Gregory. Richard Jr. was the son of Richard Sr. and Dicey Baker Hutchings who are buried in the Redfearn Cemetery in Logan County, KY.

Firman - age 7 years. Irene, age 5, born Jan. 21, 1908, Glenwood, age 20 months.

Leaving Robertson County and traveling by wagon train with other families, Richard and Mahala with their children, Dicey, Mary Margaret, John Baker, Frances Marion, Virginia and William Richard and eight slaves arrived and settled in Marion Township, St. Francois County, MO, in 1848 on land acquired by a Spanish land grant. Here Richard and Mahala built their home. Another son, George W. was born in 1851.

Richard Jr. and Mahala, known as Hallie, were active members in the Methodist Church, South. Some years later rumors were heard that property was wanted in the area on which to build a tavern. Knowing that according to restrictions at that time a tavern had to be some distance from a church, George W. donated the road frontage of his property to be used for the building of Marvin Chapel Church, located on K Highway,

Bonne Terre, MO. George W. and his wife, Cynthia Ann (Wiggins) Hutchings had built their house a short distance behind the church which was now accessible only by going through the churchyard. The house is long gone and the little road going to it is all grown over.

Gene and Elzie Smith Hutchings

The children, as well as several grandchildren of Richard and Hallie, attended the Lambert, Mosteller and Patterson schools. With the exception of Frances Marion, who left and settled in Pinckneyville, IL, their children all married and settled in St. Francois County.

Richard Jr. and Hallie both died in 1886 and were buried in the family cemetery on their farm. Their heirs, upon their parents' death, sold the farm to Mr. Berry Snyder, who later sold it to Mr. Emanuel Peterson. Mr. Peterson's son, Ed, and his wife are the present owners.

Numerous descendants of Richard and Hallie and their children still reside in St. Francois County. Rosetta (Hutchings) Lawson of Bonne Terre remembers the slave cabins that were built on the property as well as being told her great-grandfather, Richard, had informed his slaves of their freedom, yet offered them homes there if they wanted to stay. Some of them are believed

Helen Fahnestock Earley, age 5

to have settled near Granite City, IL, and some are buried in the old Hutchings Cemetery.

Today, among other descendants living in the Farmington area are Helen Earley and Larry Hutchings. Larry, a successful local builder, is the great-grandson of William Richard Hutchings and the son of Shirley and the late Aubrey Hutchings. Aubrey retired from the Farmington VII School District. Larry and his wife, Joni, have a daughter, Lori, and a son, Mark. Mark is presently playing in the Minor League with the San Francisco Giants in Bakersfield, CA. Helen is the great-granddaughter of George W. Her parents were Cloid and Irene (Hutchings) Fahnestock. Irene was the daughter of Gene and Elzie (Smith) Hutchings.

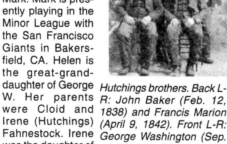
Hutchings brothers. Back L-R: John Baker (Feb. 12, 1838) and Francis Marion (April 9, 1842). Front L-R: George Washington (Sep. 10, 1851) and William Richard (June 1, 1847).

Helen was a teacher in the Mehlville school district and upon retirement moved to Farmington. She has a son, Kip Lewis. Family reunions have been held annually since 1989. At that first reunion over 150 members of the Hutchings Family attended, several coming from other states and countries; a far cry from one little family in a wagon seeking and finding their destiny on a hillside in Missouri.

JANIS - The Janis family originated in France, immigrating to Quebec and then to Kaskaskia, IL, in the 1700s. They helped George Rogers Clark capture Fort Kaskaskia from the British during the Revolution. From there they moved to Ste. Genevieve and other communities, eventually coming to Farmington.

In 1912 David Eli Janis, born 1870 in Ste. Genevieve, was married to Bertha Warren, born 1885. Warren Street is named for her family. Their nine children were born around Festus, MO. They were Alvin, Jesse, Eli, Ruby Edna, Marguerite, Norvel, Robert and Ruth. In 1925 David Eli, the remaining family, moved to DeLassus. They later moved to a farm in the Chestnut Ridge area.

In 1934 Jesse, born 1915, was married to Mary Helen McClanahan of Esther. Their two children were born in St. Louis. They were Virginia, born 1936, and Larry, born 1937. After a year in California, Jesse's family returned to the Farmington area in 1943. In 1946 Jesse became an ordained Southern Missouri Baptist minister. Rev. Janis pastored several churches near Farmington, including Stono, Pine Log, Washita, Little Vine, Silver Springs, Roselle and Coffman, which he began as a new church. After retirement he continued church work as president of the Carondelet Baptist Church School Board and deacon for the Kingshighway and Lindenwood Baptist churches in St. Louis. Mary was active in all the churches, singing in the choirs and leading various groups as needed. They moved back to Farmington in 1991, where they resided until their deaths in 1996.

The Janis's daughter, Virginia, is married to Teddy W. Chapman. Teddy and his brother, Drexel, operated Chapman's Plumbing for over 23 years. Teddy later worked for the city of Farmington Water and Sewer Department until his retirement. Virginia retired after 35 years of teaching; 31 of which were in the Farmington R-7 School District. She taught at the Doe Run, W.L. Johns, Truman and Lincoln buildings and Cartee and Ironton Elementary schools. They have resided in Farmington for 39 years.

The Chapman's have three daughters: Tina, born in 1960, is an LPN at Parkland Hospital. She is married to Shane Verges and has two daughters, both born in Farmington, Megan in 1986, and Caitlyn in 1988. Shane has two children, Matthew and Cara. The Verges family resides in Farmington. Rebecca, born 1962, resides in St. Louis. She is employed in the accounting department of Enterprise Leasing. Rachel, born 1964, resides in Wood River, IL. She is a medical biller in St. Louis, is married to Michael Galbraith, and has one daughter, Samantha, born 1991 in Farmington.

The Janis's son, Larry, is married to Patsy Rucker. They have one daughter, Susan, born 1970 in St. Louis. Larry is retired from teaching at Tower Grove Baptist School in St. Louis and seven years in Alaska. Patsy worked in day care for many years and Susan also teaches at the same school. They reside in St. Louis.

JASTER - Donald E. Hawk moved his wife, the former Evelyn Jaster, and his children, Charles and Sally, to a six-acre farm about two miles from Elvins. Three more children were born to this union: Kathe, Cynthia and Bonita. After six years in the Marine Corps, he wanted to farm. Evelyn L. Jaster was born June 2, 1925, in Bonne Terre, MO, to Frederick A. and Leona Marie (Mouser) Jaster. Three other children were born to this union of marriage: Loretta, Thomas and Donald.

In 1937 a raging fire destroyed their home resulting in the death of mother, Leona, and son, Thomas. Loretta, Donald and Evelyn went to live with their Grandmother Mouser and family until they married. Loretta married Lyman Hoehn, Evelyn married Donald E. Hawk and Donald wed Flo Pierce. Donald E. Hawk perished in a mining accident. Loretta and Lyman expired from natural causes.

Fred A. Jaster expired in 1935, from occupational hazards: typhoid fever and pneumonia. After this sad event, Leona did laundry and house work to raise the remaining children.

Frederick W. and Emma (Renz) Jaster

Fred A. Jaster's grandparents were Augustus and Anna Elizabeth (Glienecke) Jaster. Both, being born in Germany and coming from different areas, immigrated to the United States in 1852. Anna Elizabeth came from Weimar, Germany. Acquaintances began on the boat and in 1853 they were married in New Orleans, LA, port of entry. After living in Ste. Genevieve, Iron Mountain and Bismarck, they finally settled in Bonne Terre in 1880.

During the Civil War Augustus enlisted in Ste. Genevieve, MO, mustering in Sept. 5, 1864, and discharged March 29, 1865. They had three children: Frederick W. Jaster (married Emma Renz), Caroline Sophie (wed Charles Selzer) and Louis E. (never married). Augustus Jaster passed away May 24, 1881 and Anna Elizabeth lived until Feb. 15, 1917.

Frederick W. and Emma (Renz) Jaster, affectionately known as Grandpa and Grandma Jaster, had four boys: Frederick A., August William, Edward L. and Carl Herbert. Herbert and August never married. Edward married Agnes Mouser and Fred A. married Leona Marie Mouser. Brothers and sisters marrying equals double cousins of Ed and Agnes's two children and Fred and Leona's four children: Leroy and Eddie, and Loretta, Evelyn, Thomas and Donald. Of the above mentioned, Evelyn and Donald survive and live in the Farmington area. Evelyn (Jaster) Hawk remarried Aug. 10, 1991, to Henry J. Flieg from Ste. Genevieve, MO. Mr. Flieg had four children from a previous marriage. Their names are Mrs. Ellie Gegg, Art, Norbert and Mark Flieg.

Jaster and Mouser family descendants still live in the area. Most of the men-folks made their living in the lead mining industry. Anna Elizabeth lived the latter part of her life with her daughter, Mrs. Caroline Selzer.

JENNINGS - Benjamin Harrison Jennings was my great-grandfather and was born in 1888. He was the son of Z.B. Jennings and Settie (Bequette) Jennings. He was born on a farm in what is now a part of Esther, MO. He attended grade school in Esther, but quit after the eighth grade so he could find a job. He first traveled to Joplin, MO where he worked in the lead mines for a couple of years.

B.H. Jennings

After returning to Esther he went to work at his father's saloon that was located there. He tended bar and did chores on the family's farm.

When the prohibition laws were enacted, his father had to close the saloon. So he went to work for the Federal Lead Company. He worked above as a ground laborer, but later he was promoted to hoisting engineer. His job was to let the men and the ore up and down the mine shaft.

While he was working the hoisting machine for the Federal Lead Company, he established a coal business. In the evenings after he got off work at the Lead Company, he would go and deliver coal with a wagon and horses to the different homes in Flat River. Sometimes he would be out delivering coal past midnight in the freezing cold in the dead of winter. He thoroughly enjoyed all of his work because he got to talk and visit with a lot of different people. He sometimes had to get up in the morning before work and deliver coal again. He worked hard at both jobs all winter and then spring finally came.

One warm and sunny spring morning he got up early to deliver some coal before work. This started out as any typical busy day with a lot of coal to deliver and then go to work at the mines. He grabbed his lunch box and headed straight for work after his deliveries and made it there ten minutes early. So he began getting the hoisting machine ready for the morning crew of miners to go down. After all of the miners were down in the mine, he sat down to have his usual morning cup of coffee. His boss, who was a tall, slim man, poured himself some coffee and sat down. He sat there silently for a minute and then said, "B.H., you are going to have to make up your mind. You either work for us and give up your coal business or quit. You can't do both. I'll give you a couple of days to decide." B.H. stood up and said, "I have just made up my mind." B.H. walked over and picked up his lunch box and said, "You can worry about getting the men and the ore out of the mine because I quit!" By the time the boss found somebody that knew how to run the hoister it was quitting time and the miners were about 20 minutes late getting out of the mine.

During this time, about 1910, he was united in marriage to Reva Heitman. They had two children, Virginia Mae in 1911 and Harry F., in 1912. His wife and children were his pride and joy. I'm sure he gave them his desires for the better things in life.

From 1917 to 1928 he bought and sold one small business after another, see-sawing back and forth from Arkansas to Flat River. These businesses included such things as a restaurant, a grocery store and a general merchandise store. In 1928 he established the B.H. Jennings Lumber and General Merchandise Store in Flat River. He also went into the building business where he built and sold homes. In 1929 the depression years started, but with his uncanny ability he was able to hold his business together. He continued to build houses and let people work in return for groceries and rent. This made him loved by many people.

In 1932 he established another lumber yard in Farmington which is still being operated by the Jennings family. B.H. had always thought there should be another bank in Farmington. At the age of 65 he walked up and down the streets of Farmington calling on his many friends and selling them stock for the new bank. With this and his assets, he organized in 1954 what is now the First State Bank of Farmington. (It would later be renamed the First State Community Bank of Farmington.) He did this not only for his own benefit but for the benefit of the people of Farmington.

B.H.'s favorite charity was the Presbyterian Children's Home. Every year he would slaughter a big beef and donate it to the Home. He saw to it that each child received a Christmas present every year. He also donated a farm to them which is located on Castor River near Marquand, MO. The Home was named Camp Jennings in his honor. The kids at the home still enjoy the camp each summer.

B.H. was a very mild and kind man. He was very polite and easy going until someone stepped on his toes. He was not afraid of any man. When he was a young man on a train from Elvins to Ste. Genevieve, four guys jumped on him for some reason and he worked all four of them over before the fight was broken up. Even with the few fist fights like this that he had, I feel there was no man that had anymore friends and loved people more than my great-grandfather, B.H. Jennings.

This article was written by Jeffrey E. Jennings for a class assignment while a senior in high school in 1977-78.

JENNINGS - The story of my family is not one of heroes. There are no celebrities in my ancestry. These are real, hard-working people. A simple family tree diagram can never show the love, the struggles, and the tragedy that my kin experienced. My family includes the biological members that try to better their relatives and themselves.

On my mother's side of the family, the history is rather tough to find. In the past, the families have had financial troubles. Ergo, family lineage was not kept track of very well. Nonetheless, the stories that are available on this side are still very intriguing.

My father's side of the family has many fascinating stories and legends. The earliest stories and legends come from way back in the early 1700s. Joist Hite, a native German, travels to America in 1710 on his own boat, The Swift. He brings 16 families to Kingston, NY, goes to Germantown, PA, and later travels to the Shenandoah Valley in Virginia in 1731. He is the first white settler there, and his granddaughter, Sara Jane Froman, was born Nov. 15, 1732. She is claimed to be the first white child born there. Joist, who is the justice of the first court of Orange County, becomes wealthy and is killed by Native Americans. They also kidnap his son and daughter. They make the daughter a squaw, but she escapes, marries and lives for only two more years.

William Pinckney Overall, Joist Hite's great-great-grandson, comes to Missouri in quite a unique way. He is on his way to California for the Gold Rush in 1846, but his wife contracts smallpox on the way, and he has to stop at Cook's Settlement in Missouri. Their firstborn child dies there, and later goes to DeLassus. He buys 58 acres of land for $700, and he later buys up to 80 acres. He builds a log cabin that holds well, but he later builds a two-story, six-room house. William makes his own bricks for the house, and it still stands today.

During the war, armies have to live off of the land and, at times, raid homes and farms for food. Sometimes, if the troops' horses are in bad shape, they take the farmer's horses, leaving the farmer no hope of raising his crop. If they do not take the horses, they take whatever they can get their hands on. William lives in Missouri at this time, and armies from the Union and the Confederacy can each be found there. Since the armies are bitter to those not in their ranks, and William has not joined either side yet, he digs a ditch to hide in case an army raids the house. Somehow he gets word that an army, family history does not distinguish which one, is on its way, and he hides in the ditch under some leaves until they leave. Since this is in the morning, the soldiers demand Elizabeth make breakfast for them. When she does this, one of the soldiers pesters her, but the lead officer demands him to stop because she is doing what she is told. When the enlisted man persists, the officer knocks him on the floor with the butt of his rifle. This calms everything down, and then the troops eat breakfast and leave.

Back in the early to mid-1800s, there lives a man named Baron Von Niegglehoff in Sharlo, Austria. He has a son who is kidnapped and taken to a ship to be held for ransom. The ship's captain, Capt. Johnson, catches the kidnappers. Since there is little communication or transportation, the kidnappers and the boy must stay on the ship bound for the New World. Capt. Johnson adopts the boy. The boy, who later takes the name Johnson, is killed in the Civil War in the Battle of Pilot Knob in southeast Missouri.

Also, there is a relationship involving the Ledbetters, a family that is still prominent today in Farmington, MO. Rueben Phillips Ledbetter succeeds in farming while living in Tennessee. He is elected to the state legislature in 1867, but it is not known how long he serves.

Another interesting tale is one involving Sarah Lucas. She is one-half Choctaw Indian. Most of her tale is family legend and hearsay. It is believed that a wealthy Lucas family in St. Louis hires Native Americans to be their housekeepers. One of the men starts taking a shine to one of the Native American women and that is how Sarah is born. She dies of tuberculosis at the age of 33. There is to this day a Lucas and Hunt Road in St. Louis that many of my relatives believe can be traced to Sarah Lucas' family. It is also believed that they owned the land where the St. Louis County Courthouse, Busch Stadium, and Union Station are currently located. However, they are never duly compensated. On an interesting side note, Sarah's sister, Louvina Nolan, marries five times. Her last husband kills her, and then himself.

More recently, there lives a man by the name of J.B. Laws. Those are not initials. That is his real name. J.B. was a diehard St. Louis Cardinals baseball fan, and he played a square dance fiddle that is believed to date back to the 1600s. Since his name is just those letters, when he went to hotels, they would not let him have a room if he does not fill out his whole name. After bickering with the clerks about this, he finally relents by writing his name as "Jay Bee Laws."

At about this time, Benjamin Harrison Jennings, or B.H., is starting his successful business. It starts when he is working at St. Joe's Lead Company. This part of southeast Missouri is known as the Lead Belt because that is an abundant resource and almost everyone works in this field. B.H., who also sells coal during evenings and weekends, tries to find ways in which he does not have to work in the lead business. One day his boss at St. Joe's tells him that he can either work at St. Joe's or start his own business. Just like that, B.H. leaves and founds Jennings Lumber Company. Since there are only two lumber companies in the area at this time, the business is nearly a monopoly. The Jennings Lumber Company stays a family business for four generations.

Debbie Denison, Markus and Doris' fifth and final child, meets Jay Jennings when they are still in the church nursery. Since Debbie is a year and a half older than Jay, she remembers him as a youngster, but he does not recall her. Jay and Jeff, his younger brother by two years, are in the nursery together and they are typical wild boys. Debbie thinks those two are just terrible.

In high school, they meet again when they are dating each others' best friends. Many nights they talk on the phone about their respective boyfriend and girlfriend. As it happens, Jay breaks up with his girlfriend, and Debbie wants to do the same, but then she could not go to the prom with anyone on such short notice. Jay jumps on this opportunity by saying that he will go with her, and then they start dating.

Soon afterwards, the two got married. Debbie has just graduated from Farmington High School, but Jay is still a senior there. Since he is the student body president, many teachers feel that it is a bad example for him to be married while in high school, and there is some talk of "impeaching" him, but this never happens. Strangely, if Jay is absent during his senior year, Debbie has to call the office and sign the notes to excuse him instead of his parents. Debbie gives birth to Amy that year, and I am born six years after her.

Now, the torch is being passed to me. Only time will tell if I will play an integral role in this family or if I just keep the spirit going. Personally, I hope to continue in achieving by hard work and determination like others in our family have. No matter what, the contributions paid by family and possibly myself can never be shown by a simple family tree diagram.

More Than Just A Diagram was written by Jason Jennings as a class assignment in January 1998. Jason lives with his parents in Cary, NC. He is the grandson of Sonny and Elma Jennings and Marcus and Doris Denison of Farmington.

JENNINGS - Elma Overall and Sonny Jennings met one another in the sixth grade. Elma had gone to the North Ward (Annie Lloyd) School and Sonny had gone to the South Ward (W.L. Johns) School for their first five years of elementary education. They became "girlfriend and boyfriend." This friendship evolved into a marriage 14 years later and they were married Dec. 26, 1955. They have three children, all boys: Jay Barton, born May 3, 1958; Jeffrey Edward, born May 8, 1960; and Ben Harrison, born July 22, 1970. Jay married Debbie Denison and they are the parents of

Elma and Sonny Jennings

two children, Amy and Jason. Jeff is married to Kim Hickman and has one son, Adam. Ben married, divorced, and is the father of one daughter, Riley.

Elma and Sonny graduated from the University of Missouri at Columbia. She earned a BS in education and Sonny a BS in forest products marketing in 1957. Elma taught speech therapy in the public schools until 1981. Sonny managed the Jennings Lumber Company until it closed in 1983. Together, they opened a business called Country Jenny and sold it in 1993. Elma was the first woman elected to the Farmington School Board of Education and the first woman president of said board. She was also the first woman president of the Farmington Chamber of Commerce. She is currently treasurer of said organization and has been since 1991. Elma was honored by being asked to portray Sarah Barton Murphy, foundress of Farmington, for its bicentennial year, 1998.

Sonny's paternal heritage goes back 10 generations to Jean Baptiste Becquette who came to this country from Cambrai, France. It was Jean Baptiste Becquette's grandson, also named Jean Baptiste, who built the Bequette-Ribeau House in Ste. Genevieve. Lucetta Bequette married Bradford Jennings Dec. 24, 1880. One of their sons was Benjamin Harrison who married Reva Heitman. B.H. Jennings started a sawmill in Belleview while employed at St. Joe Lead Company. Later, he started and built a lumber yard in Flat River, and in 1931, built a lumber yard in Farmington. He

also organized and started the First State Community Bank of Farmington in 1954. They had two children, one being Harry Francis Jennings, who was Sonny's father.

Sonny's paternal grandmother's heritage goes back to 1751 when Johannas Hahn came to this country from Germany. Johannas Hahn brought his family to America on the ship *Janet*, arriving Oct. 7, 1751. Johannas was a weaver. Sonny is the eighth generation in this country. They lived in North Carolina, and the succeeding generations moved to what would later be named Bollinger County and Yount, MO. Christian Hahn was Johannas' son. A story was written down years ago about his "language." He owned an old breachy sow, and coming back from the morning church service with a preacher on either arm, he saw a sow in his garden. He yelled, "Sal, look at the Cot Damt old sow in the garden." Christian's language was taken up by the preachers with Joe Neece, one of his best friends. Joe told them "By fire, you'd better get the bug out of your eye before looking for a gnat in Chris's eye!" The matter was dropped and Chris continued his Bi Cots and Cot Tams, whenever he was riled, but was loved by everyone.

Sonny's maternal heritage originates in Wales when John Laws came to America in 1745. The Laws settled in North Carolina. The descendants later moved to Virginia, Kentucky, Tennessee, Illinois and then to Missouri. Sonny is the seventh generation in this country. The Laws were among the early pioneers to settle in the Farmington area, mainly the Chestnut Ridge and Valley Forge areas. Sonny can remember his grandfather, J.B. Laws Sr., telling the story that his father had leased land in Illinois to farm. There were two extremely hard winters and when they went to Illinois, they drove their wagon and team of horses across the Mississippi River which was frozen solid with ice.

Sonny's maternal grandmother's heritage can be traced to Lott Griffin in North Carolina. The Griffins eventually migrated to this area. Lott Griffin's grandson, also named Lott, married Ann Elizabeth Hopkins who was the daughter of Lewis Hopkins. Lewis Hopkins bought some of the original Spanish land grant of William Murphy who came here in 1800. One of their daughters was Alice Mae Griffin who married J.B. Laws Sr. Sonny is the sixth generation in this country.

Harry Laws "Sonny" Jennings is the son of Clarabelle Laws (Jennings) Dicus and Harry Francis Jennings. He has one sister, Alice Mae Settle, and one half-sister, Jennifer (Jennings) Brincat. His maternal grandparents were J.B. Laws Sr. and Alice Mae Griffin Laws. His paternal grandparents were Benjamin Harrison Jennings and Reva (Heitman) Jennings.

Elma's paternal heritage can be traced to Joist Hite who owned his own ship, the *Swift,* and brought 100 families to New York in 1710 from Germany. In 1716 they moved to Pennsylvania and are reported to be the first white settlers in the Shenandoah Valley. He obtained grants for 140,000 acres and settled over to Tennessee, to West Virginia, to Eastern Tennessee and then to Missouri. William Pinckney Overall was probably the last pioneer of the Overall clan of our ancestry. William Pinckney Overall, a farmer, came to St. Francois County in 1854, by covered wagon. He and his wife were on their way to California to strike it rich by looking for gold. Elizabeth (White) Overall, his wife, was pregnant with their first child. She contracted smallpox and the baby was stillborn in St. Francois County. They decided to stay and bought 80 acres in DeLassus. He built a log cabin in the center of the tract and later made his own brick and built a brick house which still stands today in 1998. He was also a surveyor.

A story about Great-Grandfather Overall has

been passed down. Missouri was one of the states that was the victim of renegades, gangs and the Yankee and Confederate Armies raiding where they could take advantage of anyplace they could find booty. When they heard one of armies was coming or had word that they were on their way, Great-grandfather Overall went down to a particular ditch which ran through the woods and covered himself with leaves until they left his farm. An army came through one morning and demanded breakfast. Great-Grandmother Overall proceeded to cook breakfast when one of the men began to pester her and the officer-in-charge told him to let her alone as she was doing what they asked of her and they were hungry. The soldier persisted in abusing her and the officer in charge hit him in the head with the butt of his rifle and knocked him out on the floor. This put an end to the rowdy behavior of the soldier and after eating breakfast, they went along their way.

His son, John Asbury Overall, received one-fifth of the farm when he married Nettie Kinzer. He built a two-story house himself as he was a carpenter. This house was still standing and inhabited until August of 1994 when it was bought and burned down for construction of the new Huffy plant. Overall Road in the Industrial Park is named for the Overalls. John Overall was also the head carpenter of State Hospital Number 4. One of his sons, Stanley Overall Sr., was Elma's father. He always claimed to be a "jack of all trades and master of none." He worked at Trimfoot Shoe Company until his retirement. Prior to that, he had worked at the National Lead Mines and worked with his brothers who were stone masons, brick layers and painters. He also worked for the WPA and helped build the public swimming pool and Wilson-Rozier grandstand.

The Overalls are of English ancestry, representatives of the name being prominent in England for several centuries. The American branch of the family is directly descended from Bishop Overall, who was the author of the convocation books mentioned by Macaulay in the history of England. He was also one of the 60 men chosen by King James to translate the Bible and he and Bishop Cosen compiled the Book of Common Prayer of the established church.

Grandfather John Asbury Overall married Nettie Kinzer. Kinzer Street in Farmington is named after this family. The Kinzers are descended from immigrants from Holland who settled in Dutch Pennsylvania. Our branch eventually settled in Middle Tennessee. They were a very religious people, intelligent, industrious and frugal. They were mostly prosperous, well-to-do farmers with an occasional one going into politics.

Elma's maternal heritage on the Polston line can only be traced to when they lived in Alabama and a short time in Tennessee. They eventually moved to Ste. Genevieve County in the area of Three Rivers. The Barton heritage is more obscure. Elma's Great-Grandfather Talley Machus Barton married Sarah Lucas who was one-half Choctaw. They came to Three Rivers from Mississippi County, MO. They had two children and Sarah Lucas passed away and he married his son's-in-law sister, Mary Catherine Mills. They had 11 children. Grandfather Franklin Barton was very popular and well-liked and respected. He was superintendent of the Three Rivers Baptist Church Sunday School, treasurer, trustee, deacon and taught the Adult Bible Class. He had served as school director of his district for 15 years. His obituary states that he was a man who took interest in his church and welfare of his community.

Elma's parents were Stanley M. Overall Sr. and Frances Ethelyn Barton. Her siblings are Stanley Overall Jr., Norma Jacob, Lorene Kollmeyer, Maxine Cole, Doris Hawkins and Mar-

garet Norton. Her paternal grandparents were John and Nettie Kinzer Overall. Her maternal grandparents were Franklin and LuLu Polston Barton.

Also see Lorene and Vernon Kollmeyer's history.

JOHNSON - Noel, wife Esther, daughters Anna and Margaret, and son Larry, moved to the Farmington area in April 1950. They had purchased the Elmer Jarnigan Farm on Colony Church Road. Formerly they had lived in East Bonne Terre where Noel was employed by the Bonne Terre Farming and Cattle Co., a subsidiary of the St. Joe Lead Co.

Noel and Esther grew up in Crawford County on farms along the Huzzah Creek east of Steelville. Noel, born January 1911, and Esther, born January 1912, were married in July 1933, at the Baptist parsonage, Bonne Terre, MO, by Rev. Ragsdale. Daughter, Anna, was born in October 1934 on the Slowensky homestead where her mother was born.

Noel Johnson Family Christmas 1997

When Noel was employed by the Bonne Terre Farming and Cattle Co. in August 1935, he moved his small family to St. Francois County. They lived in a three-room upstairs apartment with no running water or bath and wood fuel for heating and cooking. Wood and water were carried upstairs and waste water and ashes carried back down. Noel recalls that rent was $4.50 per month, wood was 50 cents a load and wages were $37.50 per month. When a house became available on the farm, they were privileged to move into it rent free. During this time, daughter Margaret was born in October 1936, and son, Larry, in March 1940.

Left to right: Noel, wife Esther, daughters Anna, Margaret, son Larry Johnson, in front of their home on Colony Church Road around 1950.

Noel worked on the dairy farms, and in conjunction with Purity Dairy in Bonne Terre, Grade A milk was processed and distributed in the Lead Belt for nine cents per quart. When St. Joe Lead Co. decided they no longer wanted the responsibility of their subsidiary, the farms, dairy and company-owned grocery stores were sold. After 14 years on the dairy farms, in December 1949, Noel was transferred to another Bonne Terre Farming and Cattle Co. enterprise, the National Warehouse and Supply Department, located at Flat River, MO. Here a source of essential supplies

for lead mining was maintained. Noel retired December 1975, after a tenure of some 40 years with the Bonne Terre Farming and Cattle Co.

During those busy years of rearing a family, Esther worked at the shoe factory in Bonne Terre and at State Hospital No. 4 in Farmington. Youngest daughter, Nancy Sue, was born July 1956.

Their children were educated in St. Francois County schools: East Bonne Terre Elementary, Bonne Terre Schools, Valley Forge School, Farmington Schools, Flat River Junior College and Mineral Area College.

Daughter, Anna, graduated from Bonne Terre High School, Flat River Junior College and Missouri University. She and husband, Glenn Branson, retired teachers, taught at Desloge, North County and Central Schools. They live on Colony Church Road. Their daughter, Glenda, husband, Steve Pulley, and daughters, Amanda and Lauren, live in Farmington. Their son, Alan, and wife, Dana, live in Cape Girardeau.

Daughter, Margaret, graduated from Farmington High School, Flat River Junior College and Oklahoma Baptist University. Margaret and husband, Clifford Heil, live in Cobden, IL. Margaret is a retired kindergarten teacher, and Clifford is pastor of the Congregational Church. Their daughter, Marva, husband, Dennis Watson, and children, Daniel. Maribeth, Melissa and Rachel, live in Gainesville, FL. Their daughter, Malina, husband, Kevin Bonifield, and daughters, Jessica and Jennifer, live in Carterville, IL. Their son, Tom, wife, Nancy, and son, Taylor, live in Springfield, IL.

Son, Larry, graduated from Farmington High School, Flat River Junior College, Southeast Missouri State University, Southern Seminary and New Orleans Theological Seminary. Larry was an educator with North County Schools, director of education at Farmington Baptist Church, and is now president of the Baptist Home, Ironton, MO. His wife, Jane, a former teacher at North County Schools, is also associated with the Baptist Home. They live on Valley Forge Road. Their son, Todd, wife, Kimberly, and daughters, Audrey and Savanna, live in Tallahassee, FL.

Daughter, Nancy, graduated from Farmington High School, Mineral Area College and Southeast Missouri State University. She teaches math at Farmington High School. Nancy, husband, David Stroud, and children, Susan and Matt, live on Colony Church Road.

The Johnson family has been active in the Baptist Church. Noel pastored Blackwell Baptist Mission, Washita Baptist Church and First Baptist Church of New Offenburg. Son, Larry, and son-in-law, Clifford, have pastored churches in Oklahoma, Kentucky, Missouri and Illinois.

Noel and Esther still live on the farm on Colony Church Road. They consider Farmington their home and feel a great indebtedness toward St. Francois County and Farmington for the quality of life they have enjoyed through the years. *Submitted by Noel C. Johnson*

JONES - Calvin A. Jones was born in 1831 in North Carolina and was the son of William Henry and Lydia Jones. He married Sarah M. Mitchell, who was born March 1836 in Indiana and was the daughter of Henry and Martha Mitchell. Henry owned land in Pendleton Township in Doe Run, MO. He gave land to his daughter and her husband, who donated some of their land to build the Pendleton Baptist Church and land for the cemetery. Calvin and Sarah were married April 14, 1857. They were the parents of six children: 1) William Henry, born 1861, first married Jessie and had a son named Edward, born 1880. He married second to Maggie Campbell in 1884. She was born December 1857 and they had seven children: Fred John was born Feb. 7, 1884, and died Aug. 2, 1952, in an accident in the mines. He married Mable Viola Karsch in 1908 and had one daughter who died in infancy. Hattie L., born 1886, married a man named Swyers. Myrtle, born 1888, died 1972, married Christopher Hulsey in 1908 and had Oliver and Esther. Maud, born 1889, married James L. Hulsey in 1908. They had Lydle, Vollie and Orville. William, born 1896, died 1981, married Hester Edwards, born 1897, died 1957. They were the parents of Aline, born 1919, died 1972; Charles Frederick, born 1918, married Helen Ragsdale and they were the parents of Sue Ann, Charles Fred and Richard Linn; Annie Katheryn, born 1920, died 1993, married Howard Holdman and had son, William Jeffrey, and stepson, Gregory; Kenneth Eugene, born 1921, died 1974, married Bessie Miller and had a daughter, Nancy; Barbara Ellen married Charles Kirkpatrick and had a daughter, Janice Lynn; Emma Jean, died in infancy; Mary Lou married J.L. Weiss; and David Robert, died in infancy. Zerilda was born in 1898. Ethel was married first to Barney Wilborn and second to John Senack. The children of the first marriage were Edward, Bernice and Darrell. She married second a man named Randel.

2) John F., born 1861, married Sarah Lawson, Sept. 1, 1886.

3) Martha A., born 1867, married a Mr. Bennett.

4) Mary E., born 1867, married James E. Vartee, Dec. 28, 1886. She died in 1924.

5) James Marion was born August 1873, died 1936, and is buried in the Pendleton Cemetery. He married Millary Cartee, born Feb. 1, 1878, died Jan. 16, 1953, and buried in Pendleton Cemetery, on June 21, 1894. She was the daughter of James E. and Nancy (Pritchett) Cartee. They were the parents of 11 children: Emma, Anna, Ellen, Ethel, Frank, Gilbert, Pearl, Bertha, Jetta, Jesse and Homer.

6) Joseph A. "Joel," born 1879, married Ella Louise Putman and were the parents of nine children: William Henry, John, Lester, Clarence, Woodrow, Tony, Joyce, Earl and Virgil.

Calvin and his family lived in Pendleton Township and are probably buried in the Pendleton Cemetery but the stones were destroyed when it was cleaned off; and although the cemetery is full of graves, they are mostly unmarked. Some of Calvin's grandchildren and other relatives are buried there and have stones. His father, William Henry, was born in 1792 in Fairfax Haven, Wales. They lived in North Carolina, then came west, first to Ste. Genevieve County, MO, then to St. Francois County. There were several of the Jones' who came to St. Francois County that were related to William Henry.

JONES - I am Sharron Kay Jones. My maiden name was Brewer. As of today, Sept. 23, 1998, I am 29 years old. I am originally from Farmington, MO and was born in Madison Memorial Hospital on Oct. 13, 1968, in Fredericktown, MO, because there was no community hospital in Farmington yet. As a child, I attended the First Baptist Church of Farmington. As for school, I attended the Washington-Franklin Elementary School in Farmington and went on to attend the Farmington Middle School, which was located on Franklin Street in Farmington (now located on Fleming Street). I went to the Farmington High School until I was 16, dropped out, and went to Mineral Area College (MAC) where I worked toward my General Education Diploma, which I received Sept. 13, 1990. I attended the St. Charles County Police Training Center when they came to the campus at MAC. I graduated with 120 hours in police training on June 18, 1992. I am now enrolled at MAC as a sophomore studying for a degree in elemen-

tary education. I am married and have three step-children: Carrie Sue Jones, born July 26, 1978; Shane Ray Jones, born Nov. 8, 1986; Andrew Wayne Jones, born Jan. 1, 1988. I have a wonderful life.

Larry and Sharon Jones

I am married to Larry William Jones, son of George Raymond Jones and Virginia May (O'Farrell) Jones. Larry and I married Sept. 9, 1995 at 1331 Columbia St. where his brother-in-law and sister resided at the time. Reverend Robert Webb officiated the services. Our wedding was decorated in teal, including the cake. George helped us pay for our cake; Larry's brother, Raymond, provided chairs for the wedding, helped finish the last minute details in the yard, and stood by his brother's side as "Best Man." Michelle, Larry's sister, decorated the yard with deep red-colored mums for the wedding and took pictures. Crystal Shields was my bridesmaid; her daughter, Ashley Withrow, was our flower girl; and my two stepsons were the ring bearers. My brother, Al, took my arm, walked me to my groom, and gave me away (what a wonderful feeling to have my big brother by my side).

My father is Virrell Eugene Brewer, son of William Jefferson Brewer and Edna (Lee) Brewer. He is one of 12 children. My mother is Melba Berniece (Bayless) Brewer, daughter of Noah Robert Bayless and Bessie (Weddle) Bayless. She is one of eight children. My mother and father were married on Jan. 13, 1968. Nine months later they received a joyous challenge—ME. My father and mother both had come from previous marriages. My mother had previously been married to Jay Carl Cook, also from Farmington, with whom she had six children before myself: Velma Fay (Cook) Bell, James Albert Cook, Janet Sue (Cook) Wolk, Darrell Wayne Cook, Steven Ray Cook, and Cynthia Lou (Cook) Wofford.

My hobbies are writing poetry, listening to country music and crafts. Larry's hobbies are playing guitar, carving crafts (wood) and junking.

Illnesses: heart disease, high blood pressure (father's side), sugar diabetes, high blood pressure, schizophrenia, cancer, emphysema (mother's side).

JONES - The Joneses were originally from Wales. In very early documents this name appeared as Johonnies. Not until about 1140 did it appear as Jones. My personal records of my family began April 10, 1855, when Jeremiah John Jones was united in marriage to Fannie Mandeville Westover, both of whom were residents of St. Francois County. They had seven children, the eldest being William Jeremiah Jones who married Maggie Cordelia White, daughter of Carroll White and Mary Jane (Mason) White May 3, 1888.

They began their life together in a two-room house built by William which was "out in the country" in those days. The house is still standing on the same spot at the southwest end of Perrine St. The house was expanded as the family grew to a total of 10 children: Zeno, Jessie, Carroll, Clarence, Mary, Dorothy, Roy, Earl, Mabel, Elsie.

Zeno, the eldest and my father, married Margaret Ellen Crawford, daughter of William Samuel Crawford and Ruth Elizabeth (Short) Crawford on June 1, 1910. My mother's family were farmers and lived in a log cabin in the Doe Run area. My parents met when both were employed at what was known then as State Hospital No. 4. Our family grew to four children: Helen, Harold, Glenda and Leslie "Buck."

My father was employed as a machinist with the National Lead Co. located in what is now Park Hills. He traveled to and from work on the street car which ran very near our house on what is now Janey St. My mother was an early "entrepreneur." She raised and sold chickens and "took in" sewing for extra income. We children grew up in this house and attended and graduated from Farmington High School.

Jones Family Crest

This house was built by William Jeramiah Jones in 1888 and was the family homestead for 100 years.

In 1930 when the Great Depression happened, profound changes occurred in our lives. The National Lead Co. moved to St. Louis and my father had a choice of moving with the company or finding another job. In the face of many nay sayers, he made a decision to go into business for himself. We sold our home, bought machinery, and the Jones Machine Shop was established. When Harold graduated from high school, he joined my father in business. He took time out to serve in the USN during WWII.

Having sold our home, we lived in town for two years and then moved back to the old neighborhood directly across the street from our former home. Our neighbors had a daughter about Helen's age who had tuberculosis. Helen, a very caring person, read to Mary every afternoon. Although she was careful in her visits, she contracted TB herself and died within a year.

Harold married Frances Divine, daughter of Willie M. Divine and Bertha (Matkin) Divine of Bismarck, Oct. 7, 1949. They had one son, Hal Brett.

My mother died Jan. 25, 1962. On May 2, 1963, my father married a long-time friend, Ada Mae Feezor. He died Feb. 9, 1970. Harold kept the machine shop going, moving it to Bismarck in later years. He was still working part-time when he died June 24, 1998, of a heart attack, following the death of Frances the day before. She had had a massive stroke while visiting him in the hospital.

Brett married Patti Crocker, daughter of Bill and Melba Crocker of Bismarck. Patti had a daughter by a previous marriage, Crystal, who Brett adopted. She is now a student at Mineral Area College. Brett and Patti had a son, Colton

Brett, born Nov. 27, 1991. They were later divorced and Brett married Carol Means of Bismarck. Carol is a nurse at Country Meadows Nursing Home and Brett is employed by Farmington Welding and Fabricating.

Jones Machine Shop, established in 1932 by Zeno Jones, located in the Ferd Thompson Farm Implements building at the corner of First Street and South Henry. Pictured are Zeno Jones, on left, and son Harold, who continued the shop after Zeno died in 1970.

In the summer of 1946, Dr. Fred Walker, superintendent of Presbyterian Home For Children went to McCormick Seminary in Chicago to find a student to do summer work at the home. That student was Donald Stanley Tyner who came to Farmington in May. About the same time the Christian Church had purchased a new Hammond organ and I was the organist. One Sunday evening when the Presbyterian Church was not having services, the junior boys at the home wanted to go to the Christian Church to see the new Hammond organ. When my husband would tell this story he said, "The boys saw the organ but I saw the organist." And the rest Is history. We were married August 14, and I went back to seminary with him while he finished his final two semesters. His seminary work had been interrupted when WWII began and he volunteered for service in the US Army. He was ordained to the Christian ministry in Westminster Presbyterian Church, Lincoln, NE, his home church, on March 7, 1948. We served churches in Missouri, Kansas, Iowa and Nebraska. He was still in the active ministry when he died of cancer, Sept. 27, 1985. I returned to Farmington, having been gone 40 years.

My younger brother, Buck, married LaVera Pulliam, daughter of Oscar and Nellie Pulliam of Farmington. They had three daughters: Sharon, Gloria and Pamela. Buck spent 22 years in law enforcement and safety work in St. Francois County and with the Missouri State Highway Patrol. He had just been elected and sworn in as chief of police of Farmington when he died of cancer, May 8, 1977. LaVera was a cashier at the IGA grocery until she retired. She resides at Brookside Manor. Buck's life had also been interrupted when he served in the USN during WWII.

Sharon married Don Williams, son of Roy and Nina Williams. They had two sons, Todd and Troy. Don died Jan. 31, 1971. Sharon married Gary Cleve, June 30, 1972, son of Melvin "Shorty" Cleve and Delores Cleve. They had three sons: Craig and twins, Tad and Chad. Craig died in infancy. Sharon teaches at the 5th and 6th Grade Center in Farmington. Gary is employed by the USDA. Todd married Gina Pirtle of Park Hills. They have two children, Emilee, 10, and Ty, 3. Todd works for the Missouri Natural Gas Co. of Farmington. Gina works in the office of Dr. Daniel Reiter.

Troy married Susan Droege of Bismarck. They have two children, Bailey, 3, and Tanner, 5 weeks. Troy is employed by MFA. Susan works with "Parents as Teachers" for the Farmington School District.

Tad is supervisor for Botkin Lumber Co. in Cape Girardeau and is a student at SEMO State University.

Chad is singing and dancing with the Andy Williams Show in Branson, MO.

Buck and LaVera's second daughter, Gloria, married Rev. Joe Kochis, son of John and Ruth Kochis, originally from Czechoslovakia and they have made their home in Colorado. Gloria and Joe have two children, Leslie and Joe II. Rev. Joe Kochis is assistant minister at the Assembly of God Church in Farmington. Gloria is a nurse practitioner with the St. Francis County Health Dept.

Leslie married Charles Hasty of Bismarck and has two children, Kaitlyn, 8, and Taylor, 5. Leslie directs the Pays Program for the Farmington School District. Charles is athletic director for the Central School District.

Joseph II is foreman at the Flat River Glass Co.

Third daughter, Pamela, married a farmer, Larry Sebastian, son of Harry and Merceliete Sebastian. They have two daughters, Wendy and Brandi. Pamela is secretary to the counselors in the Farmington School District. Wendy is employed at Spokes Restaurant. Brandi is a student at SEMO State University. *Submitted by Glenda Lois Jones Tyner, daughter of Zeno and Margaret Jones, granddaughter of William and Maggie Jones, great-granddaughter of Jeremiah and Fannie Jones*

KARSCH, see page 259.

KILMER - Emmett Lee Kilmer, the ninth of 10 children born to William Henry Kilmer and Ora Bell Greenhaw, was born April 13, 1920, at Madison, IL. In 1938 he entered the USN and advanced to the rank of chief electrician's mate. During WWII, he was captured by the Japanese while serving at the Corrigedor in the Philippine Islands and was a prisoner in Manchuria for 44 months. Emmett remained on active duty until 1958 when he transferred to the Fleet Reserve, retiring in 1969.

After retiring from the Navy, he worked at Granite City Steel in Granite City, IL. He married Minnie Marie Warden in 1968 and lived near Potosi, MO. After the death of Minnie in 1980, Emmett moved to Farmington where he lives at this time.

On July 16, 1983, he married Golda Virginia Irene (Koester) Moon. Shortly after their marriage, they moved to Washington, DC for one year to serve in the Washington Temple of the Church of Jesus Christ of Latter-Day Saints.

Golda, born Aug. 5, 1915, at Koester, MO in northern St. Francois County, is the oldest of five children born to Carl Gustave Adolf Koester and Ida Pearl Henroid. The other children in the family are Clyde, Mable, Geraldine and Bernice. Golda married Homer Perry Moon on July 4, 1941. Homer was born in 1902, near Blackwell, MO to David Austin Moon and Harriett Rosene Richardson. Homer and Golda's son, Stanley Perry Moon, married Eileen Rogers. They have two sons, Charles and Paul. Charles Moon lives in Farmington.

Homer and Golda lived on the family farm on D Highway north of French Village. After Homer's death in 1973, Golda continued to live on the farm until 1976 when she moved to her current home in Farmington.

KING - William Thomas King, son of Ambros and Rachel King was born June 22, 1854, and departed this life Feb. 2, 1934, aged 79 years, 8 months and 9 days. His death came as a shock to his family and neighbors, although he had been in failing health for two years. He was well as usual

and went to the barn to do the morning chores and became suddenly ill and died a few moments later. He spent most of his entire life near Brunot, MO, coming with his parents from North Carolina when he was a small child. With the passing away of this man, Iron County has lost one of its oldest and most respected citizens. He was converted many years ago but, at the time of his death, did not belong to any church. He loved to read and talk of God's word. A few years ago he told his wife he was ready to go and wanted her and his children to be ready to meet him in Heaven.

Pearlie Mae Hickman King and daughter, Oberia King.

W. T. King (1857-1934) and Osborne King, son, killed in 1935.

L-R: Pearlie Mae Hickman King, William Hickman (father) and W. T. King, Jr. (husband).

He was first married to Sarah Jane Babb and to this union were born 11 children, of whom seven are living. The mother died Nov. 30, 1901. He later married Cora Hickman. To this union five children were born, one dying in infancy. He leaves to mourn his death, his widow and eleven children: Ambros of Ruble, MO; Henry, Osborn and Mrs. Cassa Morris of St. Louis; Mrs. Theresa Smith, Holcomb, MO; Norah, Desloge; Mrs. Charity Chilton and Mrs. Rachel Miller of Brunot, MO; Jewel and Mae, at home. There are also 34 grandchildren and a host of relatives and friends.

KINKEAD/ASHBURN - In 1810 Samuel Kinkead, with his young bride, claimed land south of Farmington known as Libertyville, the beginning of the farming tradition in which the Kinkead family still imparts. Samuel's son, Andrew, continued the family homestead, followed by his son, Nicholas A. Kinkead, who married Harriett Marks whose family had settled land east of Farmington. Nicholas and Harriet's son, Gladden Kinkead, married Frances Ashburn, daughter of Paca Vincent and Sara (Doss) Ashburn. The Ashburn family claim was east of Bonne Terre; the Doss' homestead was just northeast of Farmington. All four family homesteads date between 1810 and 1835. The purchase of another farm, north of Farmington at Hillsboro Road and O Highway, took place in 1900, a Centennial Farm in the year 2000.

In the late 1800s the Ashburns brought the very first Hereford cattle into St. Francois County.

1967, Vincent Kinkead with five Hereford bulls recently purchased from Edgecliff Farm, Potosi, MO.

The Kinkeads were, originally, Shorthorn breeders. In addition to raising Herefords, Gladden Kinkead's sons, "Paca" Vincent and (the late) Robert, expanded the family operation to include a large Jersey dairy herd. Still today, Vincent's son, David Kinkead, continues the family tradition of raising Hereford cattle. During its peak, the Kinkeads farmed over 1,000 acres and 500 head of cattle. In addition, the Ashburns and the Kinkeads were founders of the St. Francois County Farmers Mutual Fire Insurance Co.

Patriotism is part of the Kinkead heritage. Samuel Kinkead was a captain in the War of 1812. Gladden Kinkead received the Purple Heart for his efforts in WWI. Robert Kinkead served in the Philippines during WWII, later telling of an eight-day-and-night battle that left him with bullet holes in his shirt. Vincent's son, Nicholas Kinkead, currently a captain in the US Army, served in Bosnia and received the Bronze Star for his service in Operation Desert Storm. David's wife, Bonnie (DeGrant) Kinkead, also served our country in the USAF.

Church worship and community service has been a priority of the family since settling the Farmington area over 200 years ago. Samuel Kinkead donated the ground in Libertyville for the first "house of public worship" in 1843. The United Methodist Church, its growth, its activities and its service to the community, has been a part of all the family. A 1904 membership list of the Methodist Episcopal Church, South (which later merged with other local Methodist churches to become Memorial United Methodist) shows the Ashburn family as members. Vincent Kinkead met his wife, Evelyn (Gault) Wood, (a widow with three children: Maude, Sandra and Willard Wood) at Memorial United Methodist Church and married there in 1960. Evelyn's grandparents (Overall) originated in DeLassus and were also on the 1904 roster of the Methodist Episcopal Church, South.

The heritage of our family is the force that motivates us to continue farming, to serve God, our church and community. Farmington is rich in tradition and continues to grow and prosper. No matter how far outlying Farmington expands, to us Farmington will always be referred to as just "TOWN." *Submitted by Vincent Kinkead*

KIRKLAND - Marcus Kirkland (1888-1964), and Minnie (White) Kirkland (1892-1978), were Farmington business people from 1930-1947. Marcus was born in Downing, MO in Schuyler County to Mr. and Mrs. Charles H. Kirkland. After graduating from Downing High School, Marcus worked for Heinz 57 Varieties Co. but moved to Flat River in 1915 to join his brother, John, in the furniture business.

During WWI, Marcus enlisted in the Army and served two years (one in France) in the Medical Corps. Sergeant Kirkland was discharged in 1919 and returned to Flat River.

Minnie was born in Bruno, MO to Luke and Mary Susan (Albright) White. She attended school in Madison County and Carleton College in Farmington. She began teaching in Elvins, MO. She and Marcus were married June 26, 1919.

In Flat River Marcus belonged to the Masonic Lodge and the Flat River Methodist Church, which was pastored by Rev. William Stewart. He was a charter member of the Coleman-Frazier Post 39, later serving as commander. He was Worshipful Master of the Eastern Star. For six years he was on the board of directors of the Flat River Building and Loan Association and for five years served on the board of directors of the YMCA.

Marcus Kirkland, Minnie Kirkland wedding day, June 26, 1919.

In 1923 the Kirklands purchased the Flat River Variety Store, operating it until 1930 when they purchased the Ben Franklin Store in Farmington.

After moving to Farmington they transferred their church membership to Murphy-Long Methodist Church, which later became Memorial Methodist Church of which Marcus was on the board of trustees.

The untiring efforts of Marcus, along with Dr. L.M. Stanfield, C.C. Gower and Harry Denman, resulted in the birth of the Farmington Rotary Club. It was chartered Feb. 16, 1934 with Marcus serving as president the first two years. He had a perfect attendance record for 27 years.

From 1945-47, Marcus served as 13th District American Legion commander (LaPere McCallister Post 416) while Minnie served as president of the auxiliary during the same period. He served as judge advocate for several years to the National American Legion Trophies Awards and Ceremonies Committee. He had 45 years of continuous membership. He was president of the local chamber of commerce for two years; a member of the board of trustees of the Mineral Area Osteopathic Hospital since 1952, serving for several months as acting administrator; and was a member of the St. Francois County draft board for 17 years.

Minnie was active in her church, American Legion, Eastern Star lodge and many civic organizations. The Kirklands benevolent character continued after their death by leaving their entire estate to The Mineral Area Osteopathic Hospital.

The Kirklands were blessed with many nieces and nephews as both had several sisters and brothers. Mrs. Charles Raglin (Catherine) was one of Minnie's sisters who lived in the Farmington area. Norma Ruth (Raglin) Williamson, who still lives in this area, is Mrs. Kirkland's niece.

KLEIN - Emil Klein's family came from Hannibal, MO. He became a well-known and long-time groceryman. All of this came about as Emil worked for Maul's Grocery in St. Louis. While working in St. Louis, Mr. Maul sent Emil down to Farmington to investigate the possibility of getting apples that he heard were quite plentiful there. This was during the time the first mine shaft was sunk in this area. We cannot say whether he found apples or not, but he did find a new home.

Emil stopped working at Maul's and rented a building from Karsch's Boot and Shoe Factory. This was the beginning of Klein's Grocery in Farmington. Emil and his family lived in the upper story of the store. Edward and his brother helped in the store and his sister, Anna, kept house for the brothers. Later on a new store was built, the same store that Leo Dugal was in until it burned.

Mr. Emil finally sold his part to his brother, Ed. Early on, Emil had brought a family of cousins to Farmington to help in the store, August and Chris Menge. These two brothers

Eddie and Thelma Klein taken in the 1940s.

became and integral part of the Farmington community. August was involved in city affairs and Chris became a well-known farmer. The lady cousins that came kept house for August Menge.

Emil became a school man and was on the school board for several years. Edward was also involved in city government in Farmington.

Marriage And The Greater Family: Emil married Elizabeth Tetley and to this union three children were born: Edward O., Annetta and Gay. Emil's brother, Edward, married Anna Karsch and they had six children. One of the sons was Elliott, who was the father of Dr. Jones Klein, the dentist in Farmington whose office was behind the post office for many years. Dr. Klein was in WWII. Then he practiced several years after the war, but died rather young. Eddie and Thelma both graduated from Farmington High School in 1927. In high school Thelma played the violin in the school orchestra. Eddie bought a saxophone and played in the town band. After high school Eddie went off to St. Louis to Pharmacy School where he graduated in 1930. Thelma remained in Farmington, attending Ozark Business College and graduating in 1928. The next year she taught in the college's Commercial Department. Thelma worked at the United Bank of Farmington for 40-odd years under several different bank presidents.

Eddie worked for his brother-in-law, Yancy White, in City Drugs for a few years. He worked for Laakman Drugs for about seven years before opening his own store at Medical Arts Clinic. This he did after serving in WWII. He was at Medical Arts Pharmacy for many years where he served so many of the Farmington residents their medicine, as well as serving the outlying communities.

Eddie reports that Thelma would not have much to do with him while they were in school. She told him the reason was that his ears were too big and stood out. This did not last very long after graduation, because they fell in love and later became husband and wife in 1933, married by a minister from Bismarck. They went to St. Louis for the honeymoon. Returning to Farmington, Eddie bought a house on South "A" Street Boyce Street and furnished it for his new bride. The attendants for their wedding were Gay T. Klein and Thelma's sister Cornelia.

Thelma passed away December 1998 and I had the privilege of having the funeral message. The theme of the message was "The Two Were One." This truly was God's theme for marriage recorded in the Holy Bible.

"Edward O. Klein and Thelma (Fry) Klein were truly outstanding citizens of the Farmington Community all their life. They were born here and both intend to die here. Thelma in her 90s and Eddie now in his 90s will leave an outstanding legacy of good citizenship through exemplary living and giving of themselves and so many gifts for the good of so many in and around Farmington. They truly represent the spirit of Farmington."

His brother, Gay T. Klein, married Gertrude Black. They had one child, Mary Ann, who now lives in Massachusetts.

Annetta and Yancy White had two children, Nancy who lives in Florida and Charles "Bud" who lives in St. Genevieve, MO.

This report was prepared by Chester L. Self, the billing clerk for the pharmacy's credit business for 25 years. Mr. Eddie gave me the information from his bed at Farmington Presbyterian Manor.

KLINKHARDT - Walter Klinkhardt and his wife, Clara, his daughter, Mary Louise, and his son, Walter Phillip Jr., moved to Farmington, MO, October 1953, from Hayti, MO, an area in the bootheel of Missouri.

Walter was born in Perry County, IL, in the town of Old DuQuoin on April 9, 1920. His parents were Theo and Louise Klinkhardt.

W. Phillip, Walter, Clara, Mary Lou and Jim.

His wife, Clara Litzler, was born in Stoddard County, near Dexter, MO, on March 3, 1919. Her parents were Mike and Mary Litzler.

They were married on July 30, 1940, at St. Ann Catholic Church in Malden, MO. After their marriage they lived in southeast Missouri. Before moving to Farmington, they were farmers in Pemiscot County, except for his years in service during WWII. In July 1953 Walter became an employee of the Protection Division of the Missouri Department of Conservation.

He received his training to become a wildlife conservation agent in Jefferson City, MO, and on Oct. 1, 1953, he was assigned as an agent to St. Francois County. In 1982 after 29 years of employment in this county and throughout the state, he retired from the Department of Conservation.

Walter and Clara have three children. Their daughter, Mary Lou Brady, and their son, Jim Klinkhardt, live here in the Farmington area, and their son, Phillip, lives in Lansdale, PA.

Their daughter, Mary Louise, was born at the Kennett Hospital in Dunklin County, MO, on April 29, 1943. She attended St. Joseph Grade and High School and graduated from St. Joseph High, in Farmington in May 1961. On May 3, 1969, she married Elroy Brady Jr. She is employed at the First State Community Bank. They have two sons, John Gerard and James Christopher. John lives near Imperial, MO. Christopher received his BA from Missouri University at Columbia in December 1992. July 20, 1996, he married Kim Harris. They live in Fort Meyers Beach, FL.

W. Phillip Klinkhardt was born in Mississippi County, AR at the Blytheville Hospital on Feb. 23, 1948. He attended St. Joseph Grade and High School in Farmington and graduated in 1966. In 1970 he received his BA from Westminster College in Fulton, MO. On Aug. 19, 1976, he married Pamela Simmons of Independence, MO. They have five children: Alexandra, who attends Cornell College at Mt. Vernon, IA; Olivia is a senior in high school; Phillip Devlin, Tessa and Grace attend grade schools in Lansdale, PA. Phillip is employed by the ICT Group in Langhorne, PA.

Jim Klinkhardt was born in St. Francois County, MO, at the Bonne Terre Hospital on Jan. 11, 1955. He attended St. Joseph Grade School and graduated from Farmington High School in 1973. He received his associate degree from Mineral Area College. He married Jane Ann Goggins Sept. 4, 1976. They have two sons, James Matthew and Brandon Joseph. Matthew graduated from Farmington High School, Class of 1998. Brandon is a junior at Farmington High School. Jane Ann is a teacher at the North County School District. Jim is the manager of Goggins Drilling Co., which they own and operate.

Walter and Clara Klinkhardt are members of St. Joseph Catholic Church. In past years they worked in 4-H and other community organizations. They are active in the LePere-McCalister American Legion and Auxiliary. Walter is a charter member of the Farmington Auxiliary Police. He has been a Red Cross first-aid instructor and for many years was a Hunter Education instructor.

Their hobby is bowling. They have been on leagues for the last 40 years. Clara was Farmington Women's Bowling Association secretary for 18 years, and Walter is the secretary-treasurer of Farmington Men's Bowling Association since 1961.

They have lived in Farmington for 45 years and it is their home.

KNITTIG - In September 1964, Frank Knittig came to Farmington looking up an old friend, William Laut. Having worked for 18 years at Mississippi Valley Structural Steel Co., the last four years on the night shift, he sought a new job at Ozark Steel Co., owned and operated by Mr. Laut and Norman Carron. Within two weeks Frank and his family moved into a rental home on Trimfoot St. from Rt. 2, High Ridge, MO.

Frank J. Knittig and Rosemary J. Hupfeld were married on July 23, 1949, at Assumption Catholic Church in St. Louis County. With their five children: Sharon J., born Sept. 18, 1950; David G., born March 31, 1953; Cecelia A., born Sept. 17, 1955; Eileen Marie, born June 18, 1958; and Nancy L., born May 24, 1960. They lived for only a few months on Trimfoot St. Finding a larger

Frank and Rosemary Knittig, June 1987

home, they moved to First Street. While living here, Frank Jr. was born at Mineral Area Osteopathic Hospital on April 3, 1966.

Along with his many years experience as a steel inspector, Frank had earned his license to sell real estate in 1960. While working for Strout Real Estate Co., he came across a home on Airline Dr. Since the house was right next to Lee's Shopping Center where Rosemary worked and being so close to St. Joseph's Catholic School where the children went to school, Frank purchased the house from the late E.M. Horton estate in 1969.

In 1972 after labor problems caused the closing of Ozark Steel, Frank went to work for Cecil Hulsey Real Estate Co. The family soon moved onto the Jacob and Minnie Greenfield property, two miles out of town on Highway H. Three years later in 1976, Frank sold this property to Eric and Cecelia Davis and moved back to town on A Street until their new home was built on Highway D. Frank, Rosemary and their three remaining children moved into their new four-bedroom home in 1977. With the family shrinking due to the girls' marriages and David in the service, Michael and Sharon Vargo bought this home. Having still owned the Airline Dr. property, Frank, Rosemary and Frank Jr. decided to no longer rent it out and moved back into this house in 1979.

Today Frank and Rosemary enjoy their retirement in their Airline Dr. home. Frank is a member of the Knights of Columbus. Retired from Flat River Glass after 15 years of service, Rosemary is a charter member of the Desloge Chapter 3350 Eagles Lodge. They both are members of the Mineral Area Elks Club. With their fifth-wheel camper, they enjoy traveling and the visits from their family, numerous grandchildren and great-grandchildren. *Submitted by Sharon Vargo in cooperation with Frank and Rosemary Knittig January 1999.*

KNITTIG - Frank and Rosemary Knittig's youngest son, Frank Joseph Knittig Jr., was born April 3, 1966, at the Mineral Area Osteopathic Hospital in Farmington, MO.

Frank Knittig Jr. and Ashley Williams

As a young boy, Frank enjoyed all the normal boyhood things. One of his favorite pastimes was climbing trees. On one particular occasion while climbing a tree, he fell out. When he hit the ground, the impact knocked him unconscious and gave his parents quite a fright. As a result of the fall, he suffered a concussion and two black eyes. Resembling a raccoon, he spent the next few days in Farmington Community Hospital recovering from the concussion.

Frank Jr. went to St. Joseph Catholic School for his first two years of school. Third grade was at Busiek school and fourth through sixth grade was at public school. The last two years of grade school was again at St. Joseph's Catholic. He graduated from Farmington High School in 1984.

After graduating he spent two years in Phoenix, AZ working as an electrician. In November 1986 he moved to Norfolk, VA where he was in the assistant management program for 7-11 stores. The Farmington-born native returned home in 1987. February 1988 he began work at Flat River Glass Co. where he still works today in the Quality Control Dept.

Among Frank's many enjoyments are the outdoors, fishing, playing pool, gardening, woodworking and working with computers. Frank Jr. and his daughter, Ashley Renea, born Nov. 15, 1991, in Farmington, live in rural Farmington on nine acres on Cartee Road.

KOEN - James Edward Koen was born Oct. 6, 1929, in Farmington, MO, the second son of Willard and Margaret (Barbier) Koen. Jim joined the USAF in 1947 and was stationed in South Carolina and Alaska. He was discharged in 1949 and attended Molar Barber College in 1950. At that time, Jim was recalled into the US Air Force and on July 29, 1950, he married his high school sweetheart, Goldie Viola Pogue. Goldie, born April 6, 1932, was the eighth child of Felix and Laura Pogue. Goldie's father was presiding judge of St. Francois County at that time. Jim and Goldie were stationed in Spokane, WA for two years and after Jim's discharge in 1953, they moved back to Farmington and Jim owned and operated the OK Barber Shop. Around 1962 Jim sold his barber shop to his brother-in-law, Eugene Pogue, and went into auto sales. In 1969 Goldie went to work at Farmington Community Hospital and worked there until her retirement in 1994. Jim presently deals in antiques and fishes in his spare time. Jim and Goldie are the proud parents of three children: Dana (Mrs. David) Richards of Marquette, MI, Laura (Mrs. Mike)

Jim and Goldie Koen

Apple of Marquette, MI and Steve and (Jeanine) Koen of Farmington. Jim and Goldie love to travel to Michigan to visit their children and grandchildren. They have seven grandchildren and two great-grandchildren whom they enjoy greatly and also love their church, the First Baptist Church of Farmington. *Submitted by Goldie Koen*

KOLLMEYER - Lorene "Spanky" Overall and Vernon C. Kollmeyer were born, raised and live in Farmington. They met as seniors in high school in 1942 and married April 13, 1947. They have

four children: Terry, born March 12, 1949; twins, Tim and Kim, born May 16, 1951; Lorri Jane, born March 23. 1960. Terry married Betty Baker and became the step-parent of two children, Connie and Wade. Tim married Linda Christian, parents of Missie, Mica, Kevin; Kim married Ruth Ann

Vernon and Lorene Kollmeyer

Bradley, parents of Carie and Jennifer; Lorri Jane married David Gilliam, parents of Alex.

Lorene was a homemaker, president of the Home Economics Extension Council, later worked in a jewelry store, worked as a telephone operator and presently works in the Farmington R-7 School District.

Vernon's great-grandparents, Henry P. Stienhaus and Catherine Wilhelmina Kohlmier came from Prussia in 1850. In those days the husband took the wife's name (perhaps because she was wealthier) and the spelling Kollmeyer evolved from Kohlmier. They purchased 200 acres in 1854 after becoming citizens. Henry and son, William Kollmeyer, were two of the nine members to organize St. Paul's Lutheran Church in 1874.

Vernon and his father, Frank, farmed 300 acres, milked cows, raised corn, wheat, hay and raised and sold registered Angus cattle for over 50 years. They purchased the first corn combine in the county in 1959. They also were in the feed and fertilizer business and trucked livestock to the stockyards in East St. Louis, IL. Vernon had one brother, Melvin, who died in 1959 of Hodgkin's Disease. He had married Betty Clubb in 1955, had a daughter Vickie, 1957.

Vernon's maternal great-great-grandfather, William Moore, emigrated from Ireland to Virginia in 1821, coming to New Madrid County in a covered wagon. He married Nancy Younger, a sister of the infamous Younger brothers who rode with Jesse James and his gang.

Vernon's great-great-grandfather, Lott Griffin, migrated from North Carolina to Pennsylvania in 1785 and later to Mississippi County, MO. Great-grandfather A.J. Griffin came from New Madrid County, MO to the Unity Community near Farmington in 1812. Grandfather William J. Grif-

fin was born there in 1863. He married Annie Moore. They were farmers and were the parents of eight children; one was Willa Marie who is Vernon's mother. Willa Marie celebrated her 100th birthday July 12, 1998 with five generations being present: Vernon, Tim, Missie and Madelynn Tripp. Three of the Griffin sisters married three of the Kollmeyer brothers; all lived within five miles of one another and all were successful farmers.

Lorene's maternal great-grandparents, the Polstons, came from Tennessee, the Bartons from Mississippi County, MO. All settled at Three Rivers in Ste. Genevieve County. Her great-grandfather donated the grounds for Three Rivers Cemetery. Her great-uncle, John Barton, donated the land for the Barton School north of Farmington. Her grandfather, Frank Barton, was a farmer, well respected in the church and community. He married Lulu Polston.

Lorene's paternal heritage is a descendant of Joist Hite, the first white settler in the Shenandoah Valley about 1700. He had become very wealthy and was later killed by Indians. They also kidnapped his son and daughter and confiscated all property and jewelry. The daughter was made a squaw, later escaped, married and lived only two years. Her grandfather, John Overall, married Nettie Kinzer. Kinzer Street in Farmington is named after this family. John and Nettie lived in DeLassus. He was a carpenter, built his own home and a beautiful fireplace mantel that is in the possession of the family today. He also built a concrete fence surrounding his property. Overall Road is named after this family. They raised 10 children, Stanley Overall Sr. being my father. He married Ethel Barton. He was a painter, concrete finisher, helped build the city pool, Wilson Rozier Grandstand and the rock fence at State Hospital No. 4. Both of her parents retired from Trimfoot Shoe Factory. Lorene's siblings are Stanley Overall Jr., Norma Jacob, Maxine Cole, Doris Hawkins, Margaret Norton and Elma Jennings. *For additional information on Overall and Barton families, see Elma Overall Jennings and Harry Laws "Sonny" Jennings History.*

KOPPEIS - Kopie and Lucille moved to Farmington in 1950 with their two young daughters, Suzanne and Patricia. Kopie had recently returned from six years service in the USN. Serving during all of WWII, he was a chief petty officer. His brother, Francis, was a pilot in the US Air Force, and another brother, Carl, served in the Marines.

Jennie Sonderman Belken and Charles J. Belken Sr.

Kopie's father, Florian, came to this country from Austria as a teenager, having already completed an apprenticeship as a baker. He owned a large bakery in St. Louis; and at the time of retirement he and Kopie's mother, Margaret, owned and operated a bakery in Fredericktown. Lucille is a daughter of the late Charles J. and Jennie Sonderman Belken of Fredericktown. Mr. Belken was a Missouri state senator from St. Francois

County following WWI. He later worked many years for the Missouri State Highway Dept. in Fredericktown. Mrs. Belken was a homemaker, well known for her cooking and baking skills, especially her all angel-food tiered wedding cakes.

Kopie and Lucille Koppeis

Kopie worked 18 years as a Jewel Home Shopping salesman in this area and 20 years selling for Capital Supply of Farmington until his retirement, due to health concerns. Kopie is a member of the VFW and 4th Degree Knights of Columbus and a former Elk. He was the first president of St. Joseph's Parish Council and was involved in all church activities, with Lucille's help. For many years they volunteered weekly at the local nursing homes. Also, at Christmas time Kopie volunteered as Santa Claus at many area churches, schools, hospitals, nursing homes, the Ursuline Academy and wherever he could help. Kopie has one sister in this area, Margaret Barber.

Florian and Margaret Koppeis

Lucille was a homemaker for 14 years before her employment as a clerical supervisor. She worked 30 years for the State of Missouri, 28 years at Farmington State Hospital, now known as Southeast Missouri Mental Health Center. Lucille was a Girl Scout leader for 15 years. She also trained all the altar boys and taught them the Mass in Latin for St. Joseph Church. She has three sisters living in Farmington: Edna Woodward, Maxine Strong and Kathryn Miller. The late Jo Boyd was also her sister.

Kopie and Lucille Koppies

Kopie and Lucille are the parents of nine children, two having died in infancy: Richard (twin of Michael in 1952, and Judy Clare in 1964. The seven surviving children are Suzanne, Patricia, Theresa, Michael, Joseph, Charles and Jennifer. All seven children were married in St. Joseph's Church in Farmington, where both Kopie and Lucille have been active members since moving here. Kopie and Lucille celebrated their golden wedding anniversary in 1997.

Suzanne, a registered nurse, is married to Frank Luechtefeld, M.D., an orthopedic surgeon in St. Louis. Dr. Luechtefeld, comes to BJC Parkland in Bonne Terre on alternating Wednesdays. They have four children: Mark, Michelle,

Dan and Karen. Mark has a law degree from St. Louis University and is an attorney in San Francisco. He is married to Laurel, a physical therapist. Michelle works in communications, having a degree from St. Louis University. Dan is married to Tricia, an executive with a health insurance firm in St. Louis. Dan works as an insurance broker. Both Dan and Tricia have degrees in business from St. Louis University. Their son, Luke, is two. The Luechtefeld's fourth child, Karen, will complete her communications degree from St. Louis University next year.

Patricia "Pat" Burch is the second child of Kopie and Lucille. She and her husband, Michael, live in Farmington. Pat has taught in special education at North County High School for 27 years. She is nationally known from seminars she has presented throughout the country and awards she has received including: Sharing Our Pride Award, Missouri State Proclamation, MO LINC Distinguished Services Award, Distinguished Graduate Award from St. Joseph's School and Best Practice Award from the MO Department of Education. Mike is a vocational rehabilitation counselor and frequently assists Pat in presentations. He plays a vital role in the placement of students in employment as they finish school. Mike has also been singled out to receive the Sharing Our Pride Award and several times has received the Outstanding Counselor's Award from Missouri Department of Vocational Rehabilitation. The Burchs have four children: Christopher, Clarice, Jeremy and Nicholas. Christopher "Chris" has a psychology and criminal justice degree from SEMO University and is employed as a deputy juvenile officer. Clarice has a SEMO University degree in social work and continues working toward her master's. BJC Behavioral Health Services employ her. She is married to Mark Brackett, an employee of Pepsi Cola. The Burch's son, Jeremy, is in construction work locally for Amsden Construction Co. Nicholas is a freshman at Farmington High School.

The Koppeis's third daughter, Teresa, resides in Festus with her husband, John Ponzar. She has taught 26 years in the Fox system, having her master's in education. Theresa is highly respected as an outstanding fourth grade teacher, especially of Missouri history. She presents an all fourth grades musical, semi-annually, in which she helped to compose *Show Me Missouri*. Each year she takes her class to several historic sites, including a tour of the state capitol. The Missouri Senate presented her with a proclamation noting her outstanding work. Theresa's husband will be retiring soon from Chrysler. The Ponzars have two children, John and Katie. John, a SEMO University graduate, is married to Shannon Blume, also a SEMO University graduate. John is a physical education teacher in the Fox school system and continues to work toward his master's. Shannon is the manager of the deli at the Holly Hills Market Place. Katie is a sophomore at Jeffco Community College. Katie will marry in June 1999 to Scott Burkard, a deputy sheriff in Jefferson County.

Michael, twin of Richard, is married to Patricia O'Connor, a BSN at Southeast MO Mental Health Center. Michael works in medical sales. They have three children: Richard, Joey Kathleen and Julie. Kathleen Marie is their granddaughter. Richard is the bakery manager for both of the Market Place grocery stores. He plans to marry Stephanie Williams in May 1999 at St. Joseph's Church. Richard has one daughter, Kathleen Marie. Joey Kathleen graduated with honors from SEMO University. She is pursuing her master's in education while the university employs her as an English instructor. Julie graduated from the ADN program at SEMO University and continues

working toward her BSN while employed at St. Francis Medical Center in Cape Girardeau. Michael has hosted the Belken-Sonderman family reunion for the past two years. He enjoys team penning with his horses.

Joe is married to the former Patty Saylor, daughter of Earl and Carol Saylor of Farmington. Patty is the granddaughter of the late Ernie and Genevieve Jones, who for many years owned the Wishing Well Gift Shop in downtown Farmington. Joe and Patty live in Columbia, IL with their son, Justin. Justin is a freshman at Gibault Catholic High School in Waterloo, IL. He excels in athletics, especially soccer and basketball. Joe is his soccer coach. They have varied business interests: owning supermarkets, shopping centers, and other land developments. Their first store, The Market Place, is located in Columbia, IL. The Market Place of Holly Hills recently opened in St. Louis.

Charles "Chuck" is married to the former Christine Crites, daughter of the late Leo and Mildred Crites of Farmington. Chuck works in heating and air conditioning and owns several rental properties, which he has renovated in the area.

Christine is a clerical supervisor at Southeast Missouri Mental Health Center where she has been employee of the month three times. She is also chairman of the Employee Relations Committee. Charles and Christine have four children: Chuck, Amy, Eric and Brian and one grandson, Austin, son of Chuck Jr. and the former Michelle Boyer.

Chuck is an apprentice electrician in Farmington with Billy Beard Electric Co. Amy is a senior at Farmington High School and an outstanding athlete in track, volleyball and basketball. Eric is in the fourth grade at St. Joseph's School. Brian is five years of age.

Chuck and Chris bought an old three-story brick home, constructed in 1904 for the Kollmeyer family. It was very run down and they completely restored the property into the beautiful home it is today on the corner of South Washington and Park in Farmington, adding a large matching brick garage and an in-ground pool.

Kopie and Lucille's youngest child, Jennifer, resides in Festus with her husband, Kevin Linhorst, and their two sons, Joseph and Thomas. Kevin is manager of the Holly Hills Market Place. Jennifer is a teacher in learning disabilities in the Fox System. She received her bachelor's degree from SEMO University and her master's from Maryville University. Their son, Joseph, attends kindergarten and Tommy is two years old.

The Koppeis-Belken family continues to be active in civic affairs, St. Joseph Church and Farmington Public Schools. They feel blessed to have originated from and to continue to live in a community as great as Farmington.

LACHANCE - Orville Leo LaChance, born Sept. 13, 1906, married Blanche V. Mackley on July 27, 1929. Orville is a descendant of one of the earliest settlers in this part of Missouri.

Orville and Blanche LaChance

Earliest records go back to Nicholas Calliot dit LaChance, a native of France, who came to America's Mississippi Valley before the Revolutionary War. As a settler of Kaskaskia, he rose to positions of prominence and influence before the Revolution, and after Americans drove out the British, LaChance became one of the first magistrates of the new government of Illinois Country.

Father of a large family, LaChance spent the last decade of his life under Spanish rule at Nouvelle Bourbon in Upper Louisiana's Ste. Genevieve District. He was born in 1733 in France, sailed to the port of New Orleans for the French Company of the Indies and headed north to Kaskaskia. He was associated with the rebuilding in stone of Fort de Chartres. Nicholas married Marianne Girard, daughter of Jean Baptiste Girard, in Kaskaskia's Immaculate Conception of Our Lady Church on Nov. 22, 1757.

Nicholas and Marianne became parents of 13 children: Nicholas Calliot, born 1759; Marianne, born 1760, died very young; Jean Baptiste, born 1762; Antoine, born 1764; Gabriel, born 1766; Francois, born 1768; Joseph, born 1771; Michel, born 1772; Marianne, born 1774; Pelagie, born 1775; Charles, born 1777; Benjamin, born 1778; and Louis, born 1783.

Some of this family moved to New Bourbon, a community to be settled by the Royalists from France. Mining in the Mine La Motte area began in the early 1700s and was increasing by the latter part of that century. Several settlers from New Bourbon went to the Mine La Motte area to mine. Thirteen of them were given grants of land totaling 5,200 arpents in an area where the city of Fredericktown is located. Six of the original 13 were Nicholas LaChance's sons. They were Antoine, Joseph, Francois, Michel, Gabriel and Nicholas. Since Nicholas, the father of these children, had been a Knight of the Grand Cross of the Order of St. Michael, this could account for the name of the new village, St. Michaels, later changed to Fredericktown.

Orville's lineage comes through Francois LaChance. In 1798, Francois married Pelagie DeGuire, and they had three sons and one daughter. One son was Francois Belona Edmund, the father of Alexander LaChance, the father of Mary Ruth LaChance, Orville's mother. Mary Ruth married William Benjamin LaChance, the son of Benjamin LaChance and Millie O'Daly Beeves.

William and Mary were married Aug. 22, 1900. To this union were born 11 children. All of these children settled and married in the Washington, St. Francois and Madison Counties. They are Richard, Dona, Harry, Orville, Viola, Lillie, Lawrence, Agnes, Mavis and a set of twins who died at one month. Mary was a life-long resident of St. Francois County, living in and around Knob Lick and the Doe Run area, and died in 1978.

Orville worked approximately 30 years for St. Joe Lead. He worked at Mine La Motte, Federal in Flat River, Bonne Terre, Pimville and Indian Creek. Orville and Blanche lived most of their lives in either Knob Lick or Mine LaMotte. Orville and Blanche had four children: Rosalee, Betty, Gerald and Beverly.

Rosalee, born June 15, 1931, married Donald Huffman. They had two children: Kevin Donald, born Dec. 21, 1959, died Dec. 3, 1976, and Rebecca Lee, born Dec. 21, 1962. Becky is married to Donald Halphin, and they have three children. Donald Huffman passed away in 1967. Rosalee is currently married to Everett Hampton, and they live in Farmington.

Betty, born Oct. 15, 1938, married Jack Skinner in 1958 and has three sons: Terry, born 1960, married Jan VanHerck and has one son; Christopher, born 1965, married Angela Bullock and has two sons; Shannon, born 1971, married Jennifer

Meinz, and has one daughter and one son. Jack and Betty have lived in Farmington for the past 32 years.

Gerald, born Aug. 13, 1942, was united in marriage to Myra Firebaugh. They continue to live just outside Fredericktown. To this union was born two children: Pamela, born 1963, married John Brewen and has three children; Michael, born in 1967, married Tracey Montgomery and has four children.

Beverly, born in 1945, married Gary Miller and has one daughter, Lynette, who married Scott Perkey and has four children. In a second marriage to John Wilson, a son was born, Johnnie Ray. He married Jamie Snelling and has three children. Beverly and families live in Florida.

Orville passed away Feb. 15, 1983. At that time, Blanche moved to Farmington and has lived here ever since.

LANDRUMS - The Stuart Landrums moved to Farmington from Fredericktown in June 1958. We had three children, Michael age 15, Stuart Jr. age 13 and Rebecca "Mimi" age 5. We moved into the house at 515 W. College where Stu set up his office for State Farm Insurance, a company he had recently joined. One year later we bought a house from Joe and Lenore Ruble at the other end of the block to 503 W. College.

In 1961 Stu became president of the Chamber of Commerce and in his acceptance speech he set as his goal for the year a movement to build a hospital. We had wonderful doctors, but no hospital. Stu worked for six years along with many dedicated citizens until finally in 1969, after many set-backs, the doors of Farmington Community Hospital were opened.

Also about 1961 we had a terrible hailstorm and the manager of Coghill Insurance Agency died. Stu went to Mr. Coghill and told him that he would like to manage that agency for him and also have an option to buy it. This he did, changing the name to Landrum-Coghill and later dropped the Coghill name.

In the early 60s the Mineral Area College District was formed and Stu was elected to the first board of directors. The college was at that time in Flat River in an old brick building. Stu was very instrumental in convincing the board to buy a large tract of land and build a new campus. These two efforts, the hospital and college were sources of great pride and joy for Stu. He remained on the hospital board for 25 years.

The only one of our children to return to Farmington was Stuart Jr. "Mit" returned in 1947 to work with Stu in the insurance agency; and when Stu retired, Mit and Mary Beth Baker bought him out. Mit had two sons, Stuart III "Buck" and Michael. In 1988 Mit married Christine Klemp and this marriage brought three lovely girls into our family: Jessica, Briana and Rose.

Michael has one child, Betsy, and he and his wife, Peggy, live in Blooming Grove, NY. Rebecca "Mimi" is married to Haunt Rama and lives in Novato, CA. Stu died in September 1997.

I still live at 503 W. College and count my blessings that I live in this lovely town of Farmington.

LAWRENCE - Henry Lawrence, merchant of Doe Run, was born in Brunswick, Germany, September 3, 1832, and is the son of Henry and Josephine (Jergens) Lawrence. The father was a native of Germany, born in 1805, who immigrated to America in 1844, and died one year later. Mrs. Lawrence died in 1845 at the age of 39. She was the mother of eight children. Henry Lawrence Jr. immigrated to the United States with his parents, and at the end of nine months moved with them from New Orleans to Cape Girardeau in the vi-

cinity of Jackson. After the death of his father he attended school for a short time and then, with the rest of the family, moved to Mine LaMotte where he formed the acquaintance of John Whitmore with whom he went to St. Genevieve. In the spring of 1851, Henry worked as a salesman in a mercantile establishment with Messrs. F.C. Rozier & Co., a business in which he afterward became a partner. He engaged in flour milling at Pun Jaub, now Lawrenceton. He remained in this business, milling and merchandising, for 20 years, when in September 1887, he moved to Doe Run and again engaged in merchandising for the firm known as Jokerst & Lawrence. This firm was composed of F.L. Jokerst and Joseph A. Lawrence. Mr. Lawrence erected for the firm a storehouse 30 x 70 feet. They are now permanently settled in business. He married Caroline Siebert, of Ste. Genevieve, on Nov. 20, 1855, and they have 13 children, all living: Henry, Joseph Augustus, Amelia (wife of Henry Schmidt), Louisa (wife of Henry Douglas), Cora, Julia, George, William, Felix, Alpha, Leo, Rosa and Emma. Mr. Lawrence and family are members of the Catholic Church, and he is a Democrat politically.

LAWS - Charles "Charlie" and Inajean "Gene" (Horton) Laws were raised in the Farmington area. They married in 1946 and had five children: Bonnie, born 1947; Peggy, born 1949; Kirby, born 1953; Kerry, born 1955; and Kelle, born 1962. They have three grandchildren: Angela, born 1975; Kellen, born 1982; and Gabriel, born 1983.

A Christmas Family Trip to Arizona. Back row: Patty, Angela, Kerry, Bonnie, Ricky, Kelle, Kirby, Melissa. Front Row: Kellen, Peggy, Gene, Charlie, Gabe

Charlie was the fourth of nine children born to David and Gertrude Laws. David and Gertrude were both born in the Farmington area in the late 1880s. David's family descended from England and Gertrude's family was from Wales. They were farmers. Gene, the third of five siblings, grew up in Weingarten. She was the daughter of Mack and Opal Horton, who were also born in the Farmington area in the late 1880s. Both descended from England and were farmers.

Charlie grew up on a farm outside Farmington. He graduated from Farmington High School in 1943 and served in the US Navy during WWII. Gene graduated from Ste. Genevieve High School in 1944 and taught school in Womack. After they married, they moved to St. Louis where Charlie went to Rankin Trade School and worked for Concrete Transport Mixer. While living in St. Louis, three children were born. In 1953 the family returned to their roots. Charlie became part owner of Farm Equipment Sales where he worked until he retired in 1987. Charlie and Gene bought the old Laws homestead. They now live on their own homestead called Hap-i-Hil. Their time is spent vacationing in their motorhome.

All their children remain close to the family. Bonnie lives in Affton, MO with her dog, Gatlin. She works for the Ritenour School District in accounting. Peggy married Richard Korane in 1977

and lives in Florissant, MO. She teaches in the Hazelwood School District and Richard is an engineer. Kirby still lives in Farmington. He married Melissa Upchurch in 1976 and they have one son, Kellen, who is a sophomore at Farmington High School. They both work for Biltwell. Kelly married Patty Boyd in 1974 and has two children. Angela is a senior at Oklahoma University and Gabe is a freshman in high school. They live in Oklahoma City, where Kerry works for Loves Oil and Patty teaches. The youngest, Kelle, lives in Ballwin, MO with her dog, Swayze, and works for Allegiance as a medical advisor.

The family has always enjoyed many activities. Many summers were spent at Mine La Motte, boating and water skiing. Vacations were a family affair. Visits were made to Washington, DC, Arizona, Alaska, Florida, Texas and many more.

One of the most memorable events was Charlie and Gene's 50th anniversary. After a gala party with family and friends, the family celebrated with a limousine trip to St. Louis to visit places of their past. Many enjoyable memories were shared that day.

The family has shared many wonderful memories over the years. Even though it is sometimes difficult for the entire family to get together, they remain a close and loving family. *Submitted by Peggy Korane*

LAWS - Before writing about the Laws family, I want to state that most of my family information has come from Mrs. Howard (Lee) Laws of Blue Springs, MO, who has spent years researching the family.

It is impossible to write about the Laws family without including information about the Cunninghams since the two families intermarried through the years.

Penelope Nellie Laws, born in Wilkesboro, NC in 1823, was the daughter of John Laws. She married James Milton Cunningham in Farmington, MO in 1844. James Milton was the son of James Cunningham Jr. to whom Pierre Deluzier had given permission to settle land in Missouri. James Cunningham Jr. came to the area in 1809. Both the Laws and Cunningham families came from the country of Wales.

Wilson R. Laws, born in Wilkesboro, NC in

Joel Johnson Laws and Elizabeth Cunningham Laws - date unknown — 1870s or 1880s

1817, came to Missouri in 1834. He was the son of William R. Laws, a brother of the above-mentioned John Laws. He married Margaret Slate of North Carolina. They settled in Ste. Genevieve County, becoming members of the Colony Batist Church which later became the Chestnut Ridge Baptist Church. The couple had 10 children, the oldest being Joel Johnson Laws.

Joel Johnson Laws is pictured with his wife, Elizabeth Cunningham. She was the daughter of James Milton and Penelope Nellie Cunningham. Their marriage in 1869 is recorded in St. Francois County marriages. After living in the county for two years, they became residents of Ste. Genevieve County having purchased a farm near Chestnut Ridge. They became the parents of 14 children.

Most of the Laws families in the area today have descended from this family. The children were Milton, Ervin, Kenneth, Cora, Minnie, Percy,

Nellie (Harter), J.B., David, Maurice, Reese, Margaret (Ryan), Cleve (Wilsey) and Joel. Cora, Maurice and Reese died when young.

Descendants of this family living in Farmington today are Reva Swink (daughter of Nellie Harter Laws); J.B. Laws Jr. and Clarabelle Dicus and family (descendants of J.B. Laws); Joyce Simms, Nellie Kollmeyer, Charles Laws and families of these three (descendants of David Laws).

Both John Laws and William R. Laws were sons of David Laws, born in Halifax County, VA in 1755. He died in Wilkes County, NC in 1841. He served in the Revolutionary War in the Kingsbury North Carolina Artillery Company. *Submitted by Pauline Laws McKamey, daughter of Joel Laws.*

LEDBETTER - The late Witten H. Ledbetter moved his family to Farmington in January 1973, when he bought the *Farmington Press* from Marie Stewart.

Having spent summers here as a boy with his maiden aunt, Miss Mary Ledbetter, on the large acreage bordering Karsch Boulevard, Wit grew to love Farmington. The 18 acres remaining are part of a large farm considered "in the country" when Wit's grandfather, H.B. Ledbetter, built the existing residence in 1904 for $2,000. It is the home of Matt Ledbetter, Wit's son, who owns and operates The Oasis Nursery nearby.

Witten and Anne Ledbetter

Hartwell Brown Ledbetter came to Farmington from Lebanon, TN, in early 1880 to practice law. He served the county as probate judge, county treasurer, representative and public administrator.

He married Georgiana Williams, daughter of William Browning Williams, who left Connecticut in 1840 to come to Farmington to practice medicine. Williams became enamored with his future wife, Mary Hester Cole, who was sitting on her aunt's porch piecing a quilt when he happened by and complimented her handiwork. She forthwith challenged him to wear it around his shoulders and parade around the square. When he did so, he won her heart.

To the union of Georgiana and H.B. Ledbetter three children were born: Mary, who became a schoolteacher in Cicero, IL but always maintained the home place here after the death of her parents; Reuben, an electrical engineer; and Frank, who became the publisher of three weekly newspapers in southern Illinois. It was his son, Wit, who caught the journalistic fever and graduated from the Missouri University of Journalism in 1948.

Wit owned newspapers in Mounds, IL; LaPlata, Missouri; and Nevada, IA before returning to the place of his roots to publish the *Farmington Press*. He took the weekly to daily in 1974 and the town had its first newspaper boys. Readers became familiar with Ledbetter's weekly column, "Quotes and UnQuotes," which won him two master columnist awards from the *Missouri Press Association*. His photographs of local people and events along with his emphasis on home town news brought praise and loyalty from the community. Ledbetter sold the paper in 1978 and was mayor for 10 months before his sudden death Jan. 30, 1980.

Mary Ledbetter, a lifelong resident of Farmington, died two years later at the age of 93.

She was given a plaque by the Chamber of Commerce many years earlier for rallying the garden club members around the community's Christmas tree at the junction of Potosi and Karsch. That action stilled the axes of the highway department.

Wit's widow, Anne, still resides in Farmington and was selected as the first woman to serve on the city council in 1982.

Besides Matt, the couple have two children, Mrs. Christ Covington, of El Paso, TX and Dr. Michael Ledbetter, Camdenton, MO who is a 1975 graduate of Farmington High School. There are seven grandchildren. *Submitted by Anne Ledbetter, Farmington, MO.*

LEE - Rita F. Lee and children, Michael Christopher Mosby and Desiree Yvette Davis, live in Farmington, MO where Rita was born and raised. Rita was born at Medical Arts Clinic Dec. 12, 1957. Her parents are Howard Cobb Lee and Rosie Bridges Lee, (both deceased). Her father, known as "Cobb," was a chef with his own catering service in Farmington. He was well known for his delicious barbecue, but what Rita remembers most was his homemade lemon meringue pies. To this day and I quote, "I have yet to taste a lemon meringue pie as good as his." While Cobb was doing his catering service and

Rita F. Lee, Michael Christopher Mosby and Desiree Yvette Davis.

working other odd jobs, Rita's mother, Rosie, stayed home and cared for her seven children. While the Lee family did not have much as they were growing up, Rita and her siblings never remember ever really wanting for anything as children. Cobb passed away March 31, 1978 at Parkland Hospital in Farmington, MO of cardiac arrest. Rosie went on to care for and love her children as Cobb had asked of her on his dying day.

Rita has three sisters: Patricia Amonette, Diane Blevins and Mary Lee, all of Farmington; three brothers: Larry Bridges, whose life was ended all too soon by means of a car accident in 1964 at the young age of 22; Melvin Lee, whose life also ended at the young age of 39, passed away from complications from surgery due to testicular cancer in 1997; and Steven Lee, also living in Farmington. Rita's son, Michael, was born March 31, 1983, at Parkland Hospital in Farmington, MO. Michael's father, Maurice Mosby, and Rita were never married.

Rita married at the age of 26 to Rodney Charles Davis Jr. of St. Louis, MO in 1984. Rodney joined the military and he and Rita moved to Barstow, CA where Rodney served his four-year term at Ft. Irwin, CA in the Mojave Desert. Rita and Rodney's daughter, Desiree, was born June 10, 1986, at Ft. Irwin Hospital. Rita worked on base during Rodney's term in the Army.

In 1988 after Rodney served his duty, he and Rita moved to Soledad, CA where Rodney became a corrections officer for the Department of Corrections at Soledad Prison. Rita managed a townhouse complex consisting of 32 units for almost four years. In 1994 Rita departed from her husband and she and her two children returned to her roots in Farmington. Rita worked at Wal-Mart Supercenter part time while also going to Mineral Area College full-time in Park Hills, MO where she received a certificate in dental assisting.

Rita's mother, Rosie Lee, the woman with a heart for children, became very ill with cirrhosis and cancer of the liver. Rosie was placed in the Presbyterian Nursing Home in Farmington where she passed away on May 24, 1995. Rita and Rodney finalized their divorce after 13 years of marriage in 1996.

Rita began working at the Farmington Community Civic Center for the City of Farmington as a part-time front desk clerk for two years, a position she loved. During her second year there her brother, Melvin, was diagnosed with testicular cancer. Rita and her two children moved Melvin in with them so they could give him the love and care he needed. Melvin passed away Aug. 12, 1997, at St. Louis University Hospital in St. Louis, MO. Those who knew Melvin know what a kind and gentle man he was. In spite of being an amputee and having cancer, he still managed to smile and be a sweet, loving man who never ever complained about anything, not even to his dying day (you are greatly missed, dear brother). Rita says that year was the most stressful time of her life but worth every second and she would do it all over again.

In 1998 Rita left the Farmington Community Civic Center to accept a full-time position at Little Tikes Commercial Play Systems as a receptionist/switchboard operator in Farmington, MO.

LEPERE - Jacob LePere was born Aug. 12, 1856, in St. Clair County, IL, the son of Peter and Louisa Frantz LePere. He married Salome Katherine Greb on Aug. 28, 1882, in St. Clair County, IL. They had nine children: Edward P. was born in 1883; Matilda "Tillie," 1884; Albert, 1886; Emma, 1888; Walter Henry, 1891; Oscar Robert, 1893; Jacob "Jack" Henry, 1895; Chester Frank, 1899 and Ethel Rosalee, 1901. Two sons died young. They also raised from infancy Viola "Babe" Greb, a niece.

In 1896 the family moved from Illinois to Manchester, MO and later in 1915 moved to Farmington, St. Francois County, MO. The father, Peter LePere, owned land in St. Francois

Jacob and Sally Greb LePere

County and Jacob would travel by horseback to check on it. Family tradition says each son was given a plot of land when they married. The other reason they moved to Farmington was to seek a quality education at Carlton College for their children. In later years, Jacob and Sally lived at 609 W. Liberty St., Farmington, MO.

Jacob's father, Peter LePere, was born Nov. 24, 1824 in Erlenbach, Germany and emigrated with his parents, Johanna Philipp and Margaretha Sutter LePere in 1835 from Havre, France. The family arrived at the port of New Orleans and then journeyed by boat up the Mississippi River to St. Louis where they traveled overland to St. Clair County, IL. The LePeres were of French descent but had moved to Bavaria in the 1700s fleeing from the Huguenots. Thus, the family spoke German.

Peter married Louisa Frantz on April 24, 1848. Louisa was born Jan. 17, 1829, the daughter of William and Elizabeth Frantz. The Frantz family immigrated to St. Louis in 1847 from France. Peter LePere died Aug. 27, 1900 in St. Louis, MO and Louisa died March 9, 1910 in Clayton, MO. Their daughter, Ethel LePere Detring, remembered Louisa's funeral carriage being drawn by six white horses.

Salome "Sally" Katherine Greb's parents were George Johann Heinrich Greb born Oct. 25, 1835, in St. Louis County, MO and Magdalena Rüffenach born July 17, 1836, in France. George died Nov. 19, 1903, and Magdalena died Jan. 7, 1919. Family tradition recalled by Ethel LePere Detring is that Magdalene and Louisa Frantz met on the voyage to the US as children. George had a distillery on his farm in Des Peres, MO that was noted for the production of high-quality peach brandy. At the time of his death, George was president of the St. Louis County Farmer's Mutual Fire Insurance Co.

World War I broke out and the three LePere sons enlisted. Only Oscar and Jacob "Jack" returned. Walter H. LePere was killed and buried in France. After the war, Oscar and Jack went to osteopathic college to become doctors. Jack lived and practiced medicine in Stockton, MO. Oscar operated the LePere Heart Clinic in Texas. Daughters, Tillie married John "Robin" Doss and Ethel married Henry Charles Detring. Another daughter, Emma, married John M. Phelan.

Emma LePere Phelan died at age 42 on May 5, 1931, leaving her husband and three young daughters. Jacob LePere died Nov. 14, 1930, after getting an infection from having a tooth extracted. Sally died March 29, 1931, of an apparent heart attack at her home. Three deaths in less than six months was difficult for the family. Jacob and Sally were survived by four children and 13 grandchildren. *Submitted by Dawn Dement Detring*

LESH - Fred Lesh was born March 6, 1911, on a hill farm in Reynolds County, MO. He is of a family of eight children, six boys and two girls, and the son of Delbert and Ada Angel Lesh. His father was a pioneer railroad builder and a farmer. He migrated from Pennsylvania and was of German descent. His mother was born in Indiana and was of Irish descent.

It was a three-mile walk each day to a one-room country school where he received his elementary education. A horse was his transportation for a 12-mile round trip to the Ellington High School where he received his diploma in 1930. He took a course in teacher training and, after receiving his diploma, he taught his home rural school for two

years. A contract was given him for $70 per month, but the Great Depression of the 1930s came before his first year of teaching was completed. The end of the year found Fred with several warrants that could not be cashed and $15 in his pocket. He began to look for other work. A part-time job was offered him in Cape Girardeau for $16 a month. His decision was to enter Teachers College at Cape and work at jobs in the morning and evening. These jobs, along with food packages from his mother at Ellington, helped him to get a college education. He was only able to visit his family twice in those four years and he hitchhiked to get home.

When Fred was in high school, he developed a rare muscular disease that immobilized him for more than a year. And even though he missed a year of school, he was determined to get his education. This education came to Fred through hard work, long-suffering and determination. He returned to his freshman year still unable to mount a horse. Another member provided a

set of wooden steps for him to climb and mount his horse. Through all kinds of weather and many times returning home after dark, sometimes walking behind his horse in cold weather to keep warm, he persevered. Nevertheless, the hand of providence was good to him; and at the end of the year his muscular affliction had disappeared. He feels that the therapy of horseback riding was the means of the cure for his ailment.

Even though life at best was difficult and trying during the depression, Fred's love for the Ozark Hills was never dampened. Even though there wasn't much money to be had, honesty, security, love, dedication and understanding were molded into this family's life.

Horses and mules played a great role in his life, even before he was born. His mother, astride her favorite horse while returning from a visit to her family, barely made it home in time for his birth. Two weeks later Fred was riding on a pillow in front of his mother for a return visit. Eighty years later he spends much of his time riding the trails in Missouri's Ozark Hills.

After receiving his degree he was employed in 1938 as a coach and teacher at the Doe Run High School. In 1942 he volunteered for the Armed Forces and after a short period of training at Jefferson Barracks, he was put into the European Theater as a medical infantryman. He was sent to Scotland for training with the 175th Inf. Regt. Medical Detachment. His job would be to follow the foot soldier. The foot soldier would carry arms to kill, but Fred would carry medical supplies to save lives. He landed near Omaha Beach on D-Day and, with the vast American Army, met the enemy with great loss of men. There he fought along side other gallant Americans with the same determination that he had as a boy. He was awarded a Purple Heart, two Bronze Stars and a Silver Star. He was in Germany when it surrendered in late 1945.

After the war he returned to Doe Run as a teacher, coach and principal of the school. He was a well-loved and respected teacher, an inspiration to his students and was faithful to his calling. As any of his volleyball girls would tell you, he was a great coach and led the school in many years of winning, rarely losing a game.

He bought a grocery and hardware store in 1948, and in 1952 he retired from teaching and purchased a farm. He returned to his great love of horses by obtaining his first Tennessee Walking horse. He founded the Tennessee Walking Horse Riding Club, which had 500 members from 12 states and served as president for 20 years. He helped organize the reenactment of the Trail of Tears in 1938. He helped organize and rode in the transcontinental wagon train ride of 1976. He is an accomplished poet and has published two books of poetry, Echoes of Memories, with the proceeds of the first going to the Mineral Area Community College of Flat River and to a hospice for the terminally ill and their families. The second is dedicated to trail riders.

He married Betty Santens in 1970, whose daughter, Beverly, Mrs. John Sherrill, Fred considers his own. Fred is still a very active young man at 88 years; and although he is a widower, he has many interests that keep him busy. He has a great sense of humor and is a caring human being who has done a lot for humanity and his community. He is responsible for much he has not taken credit for. Space does not permit me to tell of all his accomplishments. *Submitted by Beverly Sherrill*

LEWIS - Ben Lewis must have had some kind of premonition in late 1936 when he applied to Shell Oil Co., his employer, to withdraw his employee investment account. The money was invested in

Holland. A short time later Adolph Hitler, the German dictator, was in a position to freeze the Shell employee investments, leaving many retirees without funds.

Ben had worked for Shell in Arkansas City, KS, his home town, and later in Wood River, IL. He had decided to use that money to set up a business and he had chosen the newly formed associate program of the Western Auto

Ben and Eula Lewis Circa 1950

Co. Then he discovered that an established store was for sale in Farmington.

Ben and his wife Eula purchased the store from C.A. Anth and took possession March 15, 1937. They moved from Wood River to Farmington and rented a home on North Franklin St. Their son, Richard, attended Farmington High School as a sophomore and their younger son, Robert, attended third grade at the Annie Lloyd School.

Ben quickly developed a reputation for fair dealing and his business boomed from the very start. The year 1937 was nearing the end of the Great Depression. Unemployed men were finding jobs in other cities but many lacked dependable transportation. When possible, Ben Lewis helped them with credit on tires and batteries and even some small loans.

In WWI Ben had entered the US Army shortly after graduating from high school, only to be quarantined in the infamous influenza epidemic, and sat out the rest of the war in an ROTC barracks at the University of Kansas.

During WWII when truck transportation was sketchy, Ben frequently drove his family car to the company warehouse in St. Louis to pick up scarce merchandise needed by his customers. He also served on the local draft board. Ben and Eula were active in the Methodist church. Besides working as bookkeeper at the family store, she was a musician, playing cello at numerous church and civic events.

Elmer Day, Eula's father, moved to Farmington during WWII to help at the Western Auto Store and to operate a 40-acre farm near Doe Run. Jessie Day, Eula's mother, had died in 1929.

Richard Lewis married Margie Pogue on June 27, 1940. Their children were Richard Dale, Pamela and Teresa. Richard enlisted in the Army Air Corps in WWII and flew 35 missions as a bomber pilot over Europe, serving again in the Korean War and retiring later at the rank of lieutenant colonel.

Richard Dale Lewis returned to Farmington with his wife, Gladys, in 1996 after also retiring as lieutenant colonel from the US Army. He operated a furniture business for two years in the same location formerly occupied by his grandfather.

Robert Lewis married Joyce Loeblein Dec. 1, 1946. Their children were Christina, Gregory and Barbara. Robert enlisted in the US Army in the occupation of Japan and later settled in Farmington. Gregory served in the US Army in Korea in 1973.

LINDSEY/SHANER - James Riley Lindsey came to St. Francois County, MO, Feb. 26, 1884, with his parents, James Sargent Lindsey and Melcina Mills Lindsey. Both parents are buried at Hamilton Cemetery, St. Francois County. James Riley was born in Jackson County, IL Dec. 11, 1865, and died April 17, 1938, on his farm in Bismarck. He was one of 11 children.

James Riley married Ada Della Shaner Nov. 27, 1886, in Missouri. Ada was the daughter of George Washington Shaner and Mary Elizabeth Davis Shaner, both were born and died in St. Francois County. Both of her parents and some siblings are buried in a private cemetery north of Bismarck, MO on Kings Road. Ada was born Nov. 5, 1869, in Missouri and died May 13, 1966. She was one of 10 children.

In 1892, James Riley and Ada acquired a farm north of Bismarck that is located at the corner of BB and Wallen across from the Masonic Cemetery. Of this union there were born three sons and one daughter: George Franklin, born Feb. 26, 1891, died Dec. 29, 1928, married Myrtle Chilton; Melvin William born Aug. 24, 1892, died Sept. 29, 1975, married Lola Mae Baum; Ethel Bertha, born Nov. 24, 1901, died Jan. 26, 1986, married Thomas Elmer

James Riley Lindsey, Ada Della Shaner Lindsey about 1935

Strauser Sr.; Bert Evans, born Aug. 23, 1905, died July 4, 1974, married Marguerite Charlotte Link. Most of this family and some children are at rest in the Masonic Cemetery. *Submitted by James Riley Lindseys grandson, Gilbert Evans Lindsey.*

LOLLAR - In the spring of 1964, Homer Lollar realized a lifelong dream of owning his own business when he bought the Taum Sauk Sausage Co. in Flat River (now Park Hills). Homer, his wife, Betty (McHenry), and their two children, Janis, age 11, and Tim, age 8, moved to Farmington from Glendale, MO June 8, 1964. They purchased the Ray Barwick home on North Jefferson St. Betty's mother and stepfather, Sam and Wilma Moore, were already residents of Farmington.

Homer Lollar Family . Homer, Betty, Janis (age 5), Tim (age 18 months)

Both Homer and Betty grew up in Ironton. After the death of Homer's mother when he was 18 months old, he went to live with his cousin, Martha (Mayes) and her husband, Walter Masterson. Walter was vice president of Egyptian Tie and Timber Co., and Martha was a homemaker as well as a midwife for the area. She kept her suitcase of supplies packed in the closet and was awakened many times during the early morning hours to deliver a newborn. Homer served in the US Navy during WWII and the Korean War.

Betty is the daughter of John and Wilma (Colyott) McHenry who moved to Ironton from Lesterville in 1935. Betty's grandmother, Laura (Rayfield) Colyott, owned the Ironton Cafe for many years and was well known for her home cooking and luscious cream pies.

The Lollars were married in 1948 and lived in Poplar Bluff a total of 8 years. Homer was a supervisor with Cities Service Oil Co., which warranted moves to Normal, IL, Affton, and Glendale, MO before the big move to Farmington.

Homer was a trader at heart and sold the meat store in 1967 to buy the old George Smith Furniture Store located behind Dugal's Store in Farmington. He sold new and used furniture and started dealing in antiques. Once, when he stopped to visit a friend in Ironton, the friend admired Homer's new suede jacket. Homer said "I'll trade it to you for that gateleg table in the corner." The table fit nicely in the Lollar family room.

On June 9, 1969, Homer, age 42, was killed in a hunting accident. The furniture store was sold shortly afterwards and the building torn down to make additional parking for Dugals.

Betty was assistant librarian at the Farmington Public Library from 1970-75. She then began working in the office of the Washington Elementary School and remained with the school system for 17 years.

Janis Lollar Chatman received her degree in elementary education from SEMO. She taught in Bonne Terre for 14 years and is presently teaching in Farmington. Janis resides on the old Bieser Brothers' farm just out of Farmington. Her hobbies include working in and around the 80-year-old farm house, horseback riding and attending sporting events of former students. Friends of her son, John B. Chatman, born 1980- died 1995, still visit the farm at Christmas to make cookies. Jan's eldest son, Joe Chatman, attended SMSU in Springfield. He was a member of the wrestling team for four years. After graduating in 1992 he worked for six seasons in the front office for various minor league baseball teams. In the fall of 1999 Joe will attend Vanderbilt University to earn his MBA.

After graduating from Farmington High School in 1974, Tim Lollar attended Mineral Area College for two years on a baseball scholarship. He completed his education at the University of Arkansas in Fayetteville, also on a baseball scholarship. On June 9, 1978, in the Lollar dining room, Tim signed a contract with the New York Yankees. In 1981 he was traded to the San Diego Padres where as a pitcher he compiled a record of 19-6 in 1982. He spent a total of seven years in the Major Leagues, retiring from baseball in 1988. Tim is currently director of golf at Lakewood Country Club in Lakewood, CO. He and his wife, Robyn (Schaub) Lollar and their three children, Chris, 15; Kara, 13; and Karyn, 8, reside in Golden, CO.

Betty Lollar is retired and resides in their home on North Jefferson St.

LONG - Philip G. Long and Isabella Murphy, daughter of Dubart Murphy and granddaughter of Sarah (Barton) Murphy, were married Jan. 15, 1833. They were the parents of 10 children. They reared their family in what is known locally as the Long House in Long Park on Ste. Genevieve Avenue. This house is the oldest house still standing in Farmington. The house was built in 1833 and consisted of one room downstairs and one room upstairs. As the family grew in number, it was necessary to build additions to the original structure. The first addition was on the south side and the next addition was erected on the north side. With each addition, another stairway was included. When completed, the house consisted of seven rooms, two hallways and three unique stairways. The house always welcomed friends and relatives. It was also known as the House of Circuit Riders and also sheltered soldiers during the Civil War. As the children grew into adulthood, some of them moved to Canada; but they always called Farmington their home and visited there often and stayed at the Long House.

Mr. Long loved trees and planted many. He was a tanner by trade and established a tannery on the grounds near their new house. This tannery was the first industry in Farmington. A marker has been erected on the grounds and reads "Philip G. Long Tannery - 1833." This pyramid-shaped marker was erected by descendants of Mr. and Mrs. Long who were still alive at the time. Each relative present the day of the dedication placed a stone in the marker. One descendent who laid a stone on the marker is still living in Farmington. She is Mrs. Alex Hawn (Florence Hunt, direct descendent of Sarah Barton Murphy and great-granddaughter of Philip and Isabella.) (See Florence Hunt Hawn Biography.)

Long House

Many marriages, funerals and social activities were held in the Long House. One article in a local newspaper states a delightful party attended by 150 guests at the Long House was enjoyed by all. The lawn was decorated with Japanese lanterns.

Dubart and Horace, sons of Isabella and P.G. Long, went to Canada where they met George Bisby. These three men established a wool and hide industry. Jennie Long went to Canada to visit her brothers, Dubart and Horace. She met George Bisby. The two fell in love and were married at the Long House, but they resided in Canada.

In her declining years, Isabella Long went to Canada and lived with her daughter, Jennie, who along with Dubart and Horace, attended her with loving care. She passed away Feb. 14, 1901. The remains were brought to Farmington by her son, Dubart. Funeral services were held at the M.E. Methodist Church on Sunday, February 17 and were attended by many relatives and friends. Mrs. Long was a member of the Methodist Church for over 75 years. The interment was at the Masonic Cemetery. Eleven members of the family are buried in this cemetery.

A daughter, Jennie (Mrs. George H. Bisby), upon her death in 1921, donated the Long House to the city of Farmington along with the property to be used as a park for the citizens of Farmington. Also provided in her will were instructions for a building to be built in memory of her brother, Dubart Long. She also had an identical building erected in West Windfield, NY in memory of her husband, George H. Bisby. The building in Farmington is known as Long Memorial Hall on West Columbia Street. The building houses city government offices of Farmington. Mrs. Bisby is buried by her husband's side in New York State.

The Monday Club has restored the Long House and leases it from the city. It is used for their meetings and socials. It is open for tours during Country Days.

Philip and Isabella Long's grandson, W.H. Hunt, donated the four clocks that can be seen on each side of the court house.

It is believed that the Long family donated the beautiful pipe organ at the Murphy-Long Southern Methodist Church. This church is now the Free Will Baptist Church.

The Long family and its descendants had a great love for Farmington and its people. They contributed much for the beautification and pleasure for the citizens.

LYPE - The Lype family name can be traced to Hans Leipp, who married Ursula Vogelsanger of Switzerland in 1635. Their son, Melchoir, married Margaretha Mueller circa 1666 in Germany. Their grandson, Johannes Leipp (Leib), left Germany and sailed to America in 1727 where he settled in North Carolina and raised seven children. One of these children was Godfried Johannes Lype (Lipe, Leib) who married Barbara Rudisell in 1762. They had seven kids of their own, at least three of whom fought in the Revolutionary War. Four of Barbara Rudisell's brothers, in fact, spent the long cold winter with General Washington at Valley Forge. Two of the Lype brothers, John and Leonard, moved west to an area just south of current Murphysboro, IL in 1819. Other Lypes had already settled in the area as evidenced by the officially recorded death of Peter Lipe, who was killed by Potawatami Indians near Kaskaski in 1793. The Lype brothers brought their families with them, which apparently included a son named Daniel, born 1808.

1994 - The Lype Family

Daniel would marry Charlotte Etherton and have a large family before his death at age 80. One of their children was a son named John, born in 1831. John would marry Delila Walker in 1853 and have four boys of his own when, in the summer of 1862, he enlisted in the Union army at the age of 32 to fight in the Civil War. Less than a year later he fell dead in the trenches of Vicksburg, just a few days before the city fell. He left Delila a widow with four young boys and personal property valued at $227 which included a wash kettle valued at $2.50 and 100 lbs. of bacon valued at $8.00. She was given a widow's pension of $8.00 per month and never remarried. Daniel Lype, one of John and Delila's sons, was only three years old when his father left for the war. Perhaps this lack of a father when growing up contributed to his own failed marriage with Molly Davis. Daniel worked as a hired hand on Molly's father's farm and married her in 1882. Molly's father, Abel Cartwright Davis, had also been a Civil War veteran, 31st IL, and would hold many public service positions; including sheriff, tax collector and judge of Jackson County, IL. Abel's grandfather was Dr. John Logan, a medical doctor in the late 1700s and 1800s. This meant that Abel's cousin was Civil War general and politician, John A. Logan, who would eventually run unsuccessfully for the vice presidency of the United States in 1884. Having a general for a cousin apparently didn't help Abel Davis, since his rank was a lowly infantry private. Daniel and Molly had four children before they divorced, one of whom was Jefferson Cartwright Lype, born in 1890. Molly had remarried by the time Jeff was nine, and he apparently resented his father's absence as he would never discuss his father in later life. Jeff was born a salesman, and he used this skill to become a businessman and eventually a popular Baptist minister in E. St. Louis, IL. If he knew anything about his grandfather's death at Vicksburg, he never told his only son Jefferson Lype Jr. about it. Jeff Jr. attended William Jewel College before becoming a decorated pilot in WWII and marrying Jerrylene Benton of Mississippi in 1952. Jerrylene was the 1952 Miss Mississippi College homecoming queen; she also had a father who was a Baptist minister, Bob Hollis Benton. After moving to Troy, IL both Jeff and Jerrylene taught school for many years and reared two sons, Jefferson Lype III and Bob Hollis Lype. Jeff is a successful insurance agent in E. St. Louis and is married to Mary Kay Bostrum of Troy. They have two sons Daniel and Thomas. Bob married Cathleen Hogan, also from Troy, and they have daughters, Corinne and Christine. Bob Lype moved his family to the Farmington area in 1992 where he is a practicing optometrist.

MAGLI/MACKLEY - Hans Jacob Magli/Mackley migrated to America from Bern Canton, Switzerland, in 1749. Jacob was born in 1714 in Switzerland. He married Anna Andregg. Their son, Johannes Mackley, was born in 1746 in Switzerland. He married Magdeline.

Their son, Solomon Mackley, was born in 1774 in Virginia and married Nancy Kelly. One of their sons, Jesse Parker Mackley, born 1814 in Ohio, married Nancy Reed in 1833 in Jackson County, OH. Nancy died in 1838. They had three daughters: Margaret married Joseph Benham of Bonne Terre, MO; Jane first married Edward Whitt, then Hiram Benham, both of Missouri.

In 1839, in Jackson County, OH, Jesse Mackley married Isabell Faulkner who was born in Virginia or Ohio. Her parents were from Belfast, Ireland and they were weavers.

Jesse and Isabell were parents of 13 children: James Henderson died in infancy in Ohio, Mary Ann married Madison Ramsey, Nancy Ann married Joseph Pinkston, Solomon married Lucinda Pinkston, John Woodrow married Mary Ellen Seal, Isabell married Francis Marion Hughes, Lucinda was single, Sarah Ellen married George Washington Ramsey, Deborah Adeline married Charles B. VanSickle, Mallisa Josephine married Arzel Byington, Jesse Parker Jr. married Jerusha B. Turley and Missouri Caroline first married Andrew Jackson Thurman, then Abraham Haines. One child was stillborn on the trip from Ohio to Missouri. Jesse and Missouri were twins.

Jesse, Andrew, Lewis, Solomon, Henderson and their father, Solomon, came to Missouri from Ohio on flat boats.

Jesse and Isabell were hard-working people. He was a farmer and carpenter. She raised herbs and doctored with them. She rode on horseback to doctor the neighbors and deliver babies. She spun her own wool and linen and made all the family's clothes. They had an orchard. Jesse would take the fruit and vegetables to Iron Mountain by way of the Old Plank Road. It took him five to seven days round trip. He would bring back staples for his family and neighbors.

The Jesse Parker Mackley Cemetery is on the old homestead, on what is now Pinkston Road, about 2.5 miles north of Sprott, MO.

Jesse Parker Mackley Jr. at one time owned the whole 700 block of W. Liberty Street in Farmington. He and his wife Jerusha Belle were the parents of eight children: Maude Coyle, Florence Romigh, Jesse E. Mackley, Agnes Harris, Milton Theodore Mackley, Homer Leon Mackley, Rhoda Ellen Moore and one male born and died Dec. 9, 1908.

Mary E. Mackley Maples of Farmington remembers Uncle Park as being more like a grandfather than a great uncle.

WOODROW/MACKLEY - John Woodrow was a blacksmith, tinsmith and gunsmith. He had a shop in Doe Run, MO in the late 1800s until 1908. When something broke at the lead mines, the boss, Mr. C.P. Graves, would say, "Take it to Uncle John; he can fix it." If they sent it to New York, it would be two weeks to a month getting it back.

John Woodrow and Mary Ellen Seal Mackley were the parents of 11 children. Martha died at age 15, Adeline "Addie" Lubkey died in 1909, William Harvey died in 1914, John Solomon died in infancy. James "Jimmy" died at age 17; Jesse Wilburn and Ellen Laodice, twins, died when they were small; Isabell Roselin Shelly; two small children died from eating green apples or green grapes; and John Patrick Mackley.

The story is that Grandfather John played the fiddle and Grandmother Mary Ellen danced the jig.

John died in November 1921. Mary Ellen fell and broke her hip, but she would not have it set. She lived 14 years in bed but was a jolly, lively person and died at age 93.

John Patrick Mackley was a self-employed truck driver. He and Alva Margaret Aubuchon Mackley were the parents of six children: Mary E. Maples, Melvin died at age 5 of pneumonia, Lindle Mackley, Elwood Mackley, all of Farmington, and stillborn twins.

John was in WWI in Co. C, 350th Inf. He was discharged because as a child while splitting wood, he had amputated several toes from his right foot.

Mary E. Mackley married Edward J. Maple, Aug. 21, 1937, in Flat River, MO. Edward died Oct. 31, 1973, at his home in Farmington.

Mary and Edward parented four children: Ardelia "DeeDee" Maples married Frank "Pete" Shoemake, Oct. 6, 1956. Pete died June 24, 1992. They were the parents of four children: Peter Lynn Shoemake, born April 20, 1957, and died in a car accident July 8, 1972; Ada Christine Rawson of Farmington; Valerie Lea Noland of Fredericktown; and Alan James Shoemake of Barnhart, MO.

William "Bud" Maples first married Jeronda McCarron. His second marriage was to Carol Marler. Carol had two children, Tim Marler and Kevin Marler. Elizabeth Ellen Maples Hinkle, died Nov. 20, 1994. She was married to John Hinkle. They had two children, Sheldon Hinkle and Robin Sebastian. Oscar Earnest Maples married Doris Farmer. They had two children, Ernie Lynn Maples and Penny Robertson. Doris' children are Kenny Farmer, Denny Farmer, Tammy Myers and Susan Farmer.

MACKLEY - Mr. and Mrs. Lindle F. Mackley Sr. moved to Farmington, MO in 1968. Mr. Mackley was born and reared in Flat River, MO, the son of John and Alva (Aubuchon) Mackley. He enlisted in the Army in 1944 and served 26 months with that branch of the Armed Forces. He was discharged from the Army and then enlisted in the Air Force, where he served 22 years, retiring in 1968, as a senior master seargent.

In 1951 he was stationed in Fort Worth, TX, where he met and married Tillie Burt. They have five children: Shirley (Mrs. George) Donaldson who lives in Park Hills, MO, owners and operators of Donaldson Security; Lindle F. Mackley Jr. who lives in Farmington and works at Flat River Glass in Park Hills, MO; Joe Mackley who lives in Farmington and is employed as a bricklayer; Melvin Mackley who lives in Farmington and is self employed; and Tracy Mackley who lives in Park Hills and works at Huffy Bicycles in Farmington as well as owner and operator of Mackley's Air and Electric Service in Park Hills, MO. Lindle Mackley Sr. also has one sister, Mary Maples, and one brother, Elwood Mackley, who both reside in Farmington, MO. Their brother, Melvin Mackley, died in infancy. The Mackley family has lived in the Leadbelt area for many years.

Back Row: Joe ,Lindle Jr., Tracy and Melvin. Front Row: Shirley, Tillie and Lindle Sr.

Jesse Mackley, great-grandfather to Lindle F. Mackley Sr., took produce and fruit to Ironton, MO, by way of the old Plank Road. The trip took from five to seven days and longer if a load of iron ore came by, as he had to clear the road since this took priority. Jesse would also bring other supplies back this way. John Mackley, grandfather to Lindle F. Mackley Sr., built a blacksmith shop in Doe Run, MO, back in the 1800s and operated it until he sold it in 1908. John had a brother named Park who lived on West Liberty Street in Farmington, MO. Jesse also had a brother named Andrew who is a great-grandfather to Eddie Mackley who currently resides in Farmington, MO.

There is a Mackley Family Cemetery at Sprott, MO and also near Little Vine which is near Sprott. John Mackley Sr., the blacksmith, and his son Bill, are buried at Little Vine. John's parents are buried in the family cemetery.

The Lindle F. Mackley Sr. family has lived in several states, as well as in Okinawa, Japan for three years, during their many years serving in the Air Force. They are happy in Farmington, MO and think that it is a nice place to live.

MACKLEY - Melbourne, better known as "Pedike" was a local businessman. He and Sylvia parented nine children: Betty Yeager, Mary Christy, Patti Patterson, Judy Butler, Edward Mackley, Linda Foreman, Elaine Moore and twins George Kenneth and John Richard, several of whom still reside in Farmington. The Magli/Mackley family came to America from Switzerland in 1749. *The Gettysburg Compiler* in 1893 praised John Jacob as being a noble patriot, for not only giving of himself but the use of his teams to the Continental Army. They were in Kreider's wagon brigade. To prevent capture by the British the Liberty Bell and some other church bells in Philadelphia were taken in his wagons to Allentown, PA for safekeeping. The Liberty Bell was placed by his direction in Zion's Reformed Church. Melbourne's great-great-grandparents, Solomon and Nancy Kelly Mackley, came to Ste. Genevieve County, MO in the late 1830s to early 1840s along with great-grandparents, Andrew Jackson and Rebecca Lambert Mackley. They are all buried in the Mackley Cemetery at Sprott. Melbourne's grandparents were Hiram Parker and Martha Elizabeth Hipes Mackley. Hiram and Martha had 11 children who married Griffin, Drury, Doughty, Sebastian, Munch, Smith and Laws. Hiram and Martha are buried in the K of P Cemetery in Farmington. His parents were George Morris and Sadie Griffin Mackley. George was elected Marshal in Farmington in the 1930s and 1940s.

The Rickard family is documented in "The Palatine Families of New York 1710" by Henry Z. Jones Jr. Jacob Rickard I was born in Salisbury Township, Northampton, PA in 1794.

Melbourne F. and Sylvia Rickard Mackley

Shortly after his birth, the family moved south to the Shenandoah Valley in Virginia. In 1800 they moved to Kanawaha County, VA which is now Mason County, WV. Jacob and his brother Michael joined the Army in 1812 to fight the British. Upon their return home their father, Adam Rickard Sr., deeded 153 acres of land to each son. In 1819 Jacob met Nancy Oliver and after a short courtship they were married.

Jacob II was born Sept. 2, 1823. In late winter of 1841 Jacob I and Nancy began their journey to Missouri. They settled in the area of what is now Sprott, MO. Jacob and Nancy apparently were with the group that started the "Little Church of the Vine" which is located in Weingarten, MO. They were the donors of land on which the church stands. Jacob II worked as a blacksmith in Sprott. He was known as "Uncle Jake" to the young people of the Rickard Clan. Jacob II married Sarah Smith in Ste. Genevieve, MO. When he died in 1904, he was buried in the Church of the Little Vine Cemetery. William Marion Rickard, born 1846, married Martha Grayson Oct. 6, 1872, in Farmington. William and Martha had eight children. Sylvia's father was John Franklin Rickard, born March 29, 1874. John married Sarah Thurman and after Sarah's death in 1949, he married Della Johnson Holmes. John died June 20, 1953, and he and Sarah are buried in Parkview Cemetery.

Melbourne Mackley drowned in 1952 and Sylvia died from complications of kidney failure a few years later. The nine surviving children remained together as a result of the insistence of Zelda and Hugo Cozean, who became their foster parents. There are now 20 grandchildren and 10 great-grandchildren. *Submitted by Ed and Sandra Mackley*

MACKLEY - Ed, son of Melbourne and Sylvia Rickard Mackley, and Sandy, daughter of Cleo V. and Verna Mae Johnson Skaggs, have been lifelong residents and raised two daughters, Karri Lee and Sarah Catherine, of Farmington. Edward worked for the city of Farmington Electric Department for 19 years and in 1997 retired from his business as Ice Man, which he had owned and operated since 1969. Sandra is a nurse with the Farmington R-7 School District. Karri, born Sept. 3, 1968, graduated from Farmington High School in 1986 and Mineral Area College at Park Hills in 1988. She took a year's leave from school and performed in Europe on a Department of Defense tour to American military bases.

She returned to the States and graduated from DePauw University at Greencastle, IN in 1991. While performing at The Palace at Six Flags Over Mid-America, she met Edwin Lucas II of Plainfield, IN. They married in 1991 in Farmington and live in Atlanta, GA with son, Jonathan Edward Brock Lucas, who was born April 2, 1997. Sarah, born Nov. 9, 1974, graduated from Farmington High School in 1993 and from Mineral Area College in 1995. In 1994 she married Joseph M. Black, son of H. Dan and Barbara

Tessereau Black, also of Farmington. Sarah and Joseph graduated from Truman University in Kirksville in 1997 and now make their home in Marietta, GA.

Edward remembers a tale from his grandfather George Morris Mackley. George told of an attempted jailbreak. The explosion must have been big. Sometime after, the roof on the High School on College Street began to leak. When the cause was investigated, bars from the jail were found imbedded in the roof.

Ed, Sandy, Sarah, Joseph, Karri, Edwin. Oct. 1, 1997, wedding at Eagle Lake Country Club

Sandra's grandparents had a farm which is now Park Street through Mileva and Ava Courts. Her parents built the house at 28 Park Street in the early 1950s when all of that area was pasture or corn fields. Submitted by Ed and Sandra Mackley

MARLER - Steven Ray and Catherine Ann (Rowe) Marler were married Oct. 14, 1975, in the Salt Lake Temple of the Church of Jesus Christ of Latter-Day Saints. Both natives to the area, Steve, son of Garland J. and Mary Ella (Cunningham) Marler, grew up in Elvins. Cathy, daughter of Phillip Darrell and Mary Jennell Politte Rowe, grew up in Flat River and Esther.

Following their marriage they moved to a small, three-room cottage on 00 Highway, just a few miles south of Farmington, where they lived for the next eight months. In May 1976, they moved to Rolla, Mo, where Steve was employed first as personnel director, then as patient accounts manager for Phelps County Memorial Hospital.

PCMH then underwent a name change to reflect its regional status, becoming Phelps County Regional Medical Center. It was in this facility that the couple's three children were born. Andrew Steven was born Aug. 29, 1976, an event Cathy claims was brought on by her having endured eight hours on hard bleacher seats watching Steve's PCRMC team play softball!

Convinced by legions of male cousins that all of their children would be boys, Cathy and Steve were pleasantly surprised when Mary Katherine arrived Sept. 28, 1978. Their suprise doubled when, on April 30, 1980, Laura Ellen joined the family.

The young Marler family enjoyed their years in Rolla, a time of growth and learning to rely on one another, of dear friendships forged and lasting memories made.

The year 1987 brought great change into the lives of the Marlers. Back home, both Garland Marler and Darrell Rowe were experiencing ill health, and the decision was made to return to

Farmington in order to be near their fathers. Remaining in the health care field, Steve accepted a position with Mineral Area Regional Medical Center as patient accounts manager. Cathy was a homemaker by design and relished her role in the rearing of their children. Having been involved in both Cub Scouts and Brownie Girl Scouts, as well as Community Choir, Theater, and Arts Council in Rolla, she continued her involvement in community, family and personal activities. She also worked at the Farmington Public Library where she hosted and produced a public service radio program for the visually impaired, The Radio Library.

Andrew participated in theater at Farmington High School and became editor-in-chief of the FHS yearbook from 1993-1994. He is a voracious reader, a writer and an accomplished computer programmer.

Mary Katherine "Katie" was involved in athletics, played piano, flute and oboe and excelled in academics, graduating third in her class. Following her brother's footsteps, she was also editor-in-chief of the FHS yearbook. She later attended MU at Columbia with a major in accountancy and law.

Laura Ellen, also athletic, played flute, sang in A capella choir, andwas busy as a cheerleader. Excelling in academics as well, Laura graduated as salutatorian of her high school class. Her university plans are for a Ph.D. in orthopedic surgery.

MARTIN - The Harlan E. Martin family moved to Farmington ca. 1930. H.E. operated the Kroger grocery store located at the corner of Washington and Liberty. After living on Liberty and Washington Streets they bought a permanent residence at 502 C Street where they raised their children: Zelda, Geneva, Edsel, Cullen, Lowell, Charlotte and Meredith "Jack." After their education the children began their own families. Zelda married Hugo Cozean, six children: Geneva married Jones Klein, three daughters: Edsel, Cullen and Lowell served in the military. After the war Edsel married, had a daughter in Kentucky, divorced and married Rhonda Merritt, Elvins, MO, and had one son. Cullen married a Bismarck girl, Nettie Mae, and had four children; Lowell married Genevieve Siebert and had six children; Charlotte married John Rockett from Connecticut and had eight children; Jack married Joyce St. Gemme of Flat River and had three children from a previous marriage and one son with Joyce. Only one child of H.E. Martin survives, Charlotte, who lives in Connecticut near her children. Three grandchildren and one daughter-in-law live in Farmington.

"Pop," Harlan E. was the son of William Jordan Martin and Emily Wilkerson, a descendant of John Martin and Ann Tooley of Albemarle, VA. Four sons of this couple crossed the States and settled in the Washington and Crawford counties area.

"Mema," Josephine, was the daughter of Cornelius Lafayette Jarvis and Louisiana Turner. She descended maternally from Rev. William Turner and Sarah Barton Murphy and descended paternally from the Bryan-Cole families of Virginia who came in several wagon loads to Missouri, driving over the frozen Mississippi River at St. Louis, settling in the Crawford County area.

Joyce Martin was the daughter of Robert Glenwood St. Gemme and Bertie Berniece Welch. Glen was descended from Jean Baptiste St. Gemme dit Beauvais, grandson of Gabriel St. Gemme of France. J.B. with two of his brothers immigrated to Kaskaskia, IL in the 1700s. J.B.'s son later moved to Ste. Genevieve and was among the first settlers. Some marriages in the family included the Prattes, Aubuchons, La

Saudrais and Tesereaus. Glen was the son of Benjamin Harrison St. Gemme and Lucy Olive Mae Womack. Ollie's ancestors were settlers of Avon, MO. Her father, Robert Benton, was the youngest son of William R. Womack, who fought in Indian Wars in Florida, brought his family from Alabama and Tennessee and his third wife, Lucy Womack, daughter of William "Buck" Womack and Sarah McBee, who descended from William Womack, an immigrant, ca. 1620 in North Carolina. Ollie's mother was Almanza Evelina Mayberry, youngest child of Catharine Allen and Job Mayberry, son of Frederick, a Revolutionary soldier, and grandson of Frederick Mayberry of Wurtemburg, Germany. The Mayberrys set up iron forges in Pennsylvania. Bertie Berniece Welch St. Gemme was the granddaughter of John Riley Welch, Civil War, who was the grandson of Robert Welch, born ca. 1680 in Ireland. John R.'s father, Fountain Welch, was one of the original settlers of Dent County, MO.

MCCARVER - Shawn Ragan McCarver, born at Bonne Terre, MO May 12, 1960, moved to Farmington in 1991 when he married Farmington resident, Vicky Lee Clark Danieley, on Nov. 9, 1991. He grew up in Park Hills (formerly Flat River), MO where his maternal grandparents, Omer and Rose Ragan, operated Ragan's Drug Store for over 40 years. He is the youngest of two sons born to Jimmie Lee McCarver and Barbara Janet Ragan McCarver. His brother, Michael J. McCarver, is a registered pharmacist and is director of the pharmacy at Southeast Missouri Mental Health Center in Farmington. Shawn is an attorney with an office in Farmington.

Mr. McCarver graduated 4th in the Park Hills Central R-3 Class of 1978 where he was a member of the National Honor Society and co-editor of the high school newspaper. He was active on student council, in various school clubs and played varsity football, earning his varsity letter in his sophomore year.

He worked as a stocker and clothing sales clerk at Golde's Department Store in Leadington while attending Mineral Area College from 1978 to 1979 where he was a member of the Phi Theta Kappa Honor Society. He transferred to Central Missouri State University at Warrensburg, MO and graduated Summa Cum Laude in 1981 with a BS degree with a major in criminal justice administration and a minor in finance. While at CMSU, he was president of Alpha Phi Sigma, a member of Phi Kappa Phi Honor Society and was selected Outstanding Undergraduate Student in 1981. McCarver was accepted to the School of Law at University of Missouri - Columbia where he began working toward his law degree in the fall of 1981. McCarver became a member of the Missouri Law Review after his first year of law school and went on to publish two scholarly legal articles while in law school. At law school, he was elected secretary of the Student Bar Association. He graduated with his JD (Doctor of Law) degree in 1984. McCarver passed all three parts of the bar examination and was sworn in as a member of the Missouri Bar and began practicing law in Park Hills, MO in 1984.

McCarver has had a wide range of experience as a practicing attorney. In addition to his private practice, which he has maintained from 1984 to present (1984 to 1991 in Park Hills and 1992 to present in Farmington), he has served St. Francois County and surrounding areas as a public defender, special prosecutor, counsel for the 24th judicial circuit and juvenile officer (a position he has held since 1985) and he presently serves as municipal judge for the cities of Park Hills (since 1985) and Desloge (since 1987). He also serves the Missouri Bar as an investigator,

mediator and arbitrator for the Bar's fee dispute resolution program. McCarver is a panel attorney for the Meramec Area Legal Aid Corporation where he has helped indigents with low cost legal services since 1984. McCarver also donates numerous hours each year to provide free *"pro bono" legal* services.

In addition to the foregoing areas of practice, McCarver has been a consistent author and lecturer, having published numerous scholarly articles and books related to law, real estate and firearms, and having taught for the Missouri Bar, the American Bar Association, the Bar Association of Metropolitan St. Louis, the Circuit Courts of St. Louis City and St. Louis County and Kansas City, the Missouri Juvenile Justice Association, the Office of State Courts Administrator and having served on the Missouri Judicial College faculty since 1992. Mr. McCarver has also served on the faculty at the Missouri State Highway Patrol Law Enforcement Academy in Jefferson City where he taught juvenile law to new state highway patrol troopers.

Mr. McCarver is also a Missouri licensed nursing home administrator and frequently represents clients in connection with residential care matters (including both residents and facilities), and has given training seminars for numerous local facilities and their professional and direct care staff.

McCarver practices law in the areas of family law, including divorce, legal separation, custody, support, modifications, adoptions, grandparent custody/visitation and related matters, personal injury, social security disability, workers' compensation, real estate, corporations, limited liability companies, partnerships and other business law, estate planning including wills, trusts, powers of attorney, health care decisions directives and related matters and other general civil cases. McCarver has tried numerous cases in court, having appeared frequently in the associate divisions and the circuit courts of Missouri and having argued numerous cases before the Missouri Court of Appeals. He has also appeared before the Missouri Supreme Court.

McCarver attends church at the First Baptist Church of Farmington, where he transferred his membership from the First Baptist Church of Park Hills. He is a licensed private pilot (single engine) and a certified scuba diver.

ADAMS/MCCORMICK - Irene Nixon, wife of Walter Lee Morris, was descended from Scotch-Irish ancestors who came to America in the early 1700s, prior to the Revolutionary War, seeking religious freedom. John Adams, a Protestant, arrived in 1721 after escaping arrest due to his beliefs. He settled in New Jersey and married Catherine, with whom he had six children. He was an early and ardent supporter of the American cause in the Revolution. When Gen. Cornwallis invaded New Jersey in 1776, he and his family moved to Virginia. On March 15, 1777, one of their daughters, also named Catherine, married Andrew McCormick, from Ulster, Northern Ireland.

During the Revolutionary War, Andrew fought for independence in the North Carolina Brigade. After the war, he and Catherine, devoted Presbyterians, helped found two churches near their home. They had seven children. Their first child, Joseph, born Jan. 17, 1778, inherited a deep religious faith from his parents. (Joseph was named for an uncle, a sea captain, whose ship was used to bring emigrants seeking religious freedom to America from Great Britain and Ireland). Andrew McCormick died in 1797 and *is* buried on his plantation in North Carolina.

In 1801 Joseph McCormick came to Missouri and helped organize the Bellevue Presbyterian

Church, the first Presbyterian Church west of the Mississippi River. By 1808 many members of the McCormick family had settled in Missouri. On Aug. 22, 1809, Joseph married Elizabeth Sloan. They built a home on Big River near Irondale and had two children, Fielding Lewis McCormick, born Aug. 20, 1810, and Dorcas Elvira McCormick, born Feb. 11, 1812.

Hattie McCormick Nixon and A.T. Nixon (ca. 1884)

Elizabeth died Aug. 9, 1812. In 1816 Joseph married a widow, Jane Robinson, whose family had emigrated to America from Ireland due to the potato famine of 1812. They had seven children, most of whom lived in southeast Missouri.

In the early 1830s, Joseph and his son, Fielding, came to Farmington with Rev. Thomas Donnell to assist in organizing a new church. While helping to erect the Old Presbyterian Church, Fielding lived with the Boyce family on the southwest corner of Columbia and A Streets. He later purchased the lot directly west of the Boyce property and built his home there.

Another son, James Robinson McCormick, born Aug. 1, 1824, died May 9, 1897, became a medical doctor. He served through the Civil War as a brigadier general. He married Lucy Sloan. In 1861 he was elected to the Missouri Constitutional Convention and in 1862 to the Missouri Senate. He also served three terms in Congress. He was a ruling elder in the Farmington Presbyterian Church and is buried in the Masonic Cemetery.

John Adams McCormick, born May 16, 1826, died April 19, 1899, attended Caledonia College and went west to California with his brothers during the gold rush. He returned to Missouri and on May 12, 1859, married Mary Jane Sloan, daughter of Thomas J. and Bernice (Harris) Sloan. He served in the Missouri Legislature and was a ruling elder of the Presbyterian churches at Bellevue and Irondale. John and Mary Jane McCormick had eight children. One of his daughters, Harriet Elsie "Hattie" McCormick, married Almarine T. Nixon June 30, 1885, and they lived in Farmington. They had two children: Harriet Irene "Irene," born April 9, 1886, died Oct. 16, 1947, and Foster Raymond, born Nov. 27, 1891, died March 1, 1953. (See Nixon/Hoge family history).

MCCOY - William Riley McCoy was born in 1858 in Chucky, TN. He married Sally Stafford, and they came to Missouri in a covered wagon and settled on a farm outside Bismarck, near brother Isaac McCoy. Sally never returned to Tennessee or saw any of her family again. They had two daughters and five sons, of which John Henry was the youngest. W.R. died in 1929 and Sally died in 1946.

John H. was born April 6, 1904, in Bismark, MO. He graduated from Bismark High School and Molars Barber College in St. Louis, MO. He married Florence Moore May 25, 1926. He barbered in St. Louis for a short time. Then he and Florence moved to Farmington, where he was employed by Pete Schmitt at the Sanitary Barber Shop. Marvin Roberts later became the owner.

John purchased this shop from Marvin, later selling it to Glen Sloan; current owner is Bob Bone. The shop is now called Head Quarters. John barbered for 45 years and retired in 1970. He is a member of the Methodist Church and a 50-year Mason. In April 1999 he reached the ripe old age of 95 and is currently in good health and resides at the Presbyterian Manor, assisted living, in Farmington. He and Florence were married 70 years prior to her death in 1996. They had one daughter, Peggy.

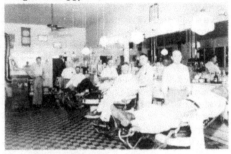

July 11, 1936, Sanitary Barber Shop . 1st chair: Barber John McCoy and patron, Russell Ryan. 2nd chair: Barber Charley Pierce and patron ?. 3rd chair: Barber Tom Roberts. 4th chair: Barber Marvin Roberts. Shoe shiner/porter, Harry Mitchell.

Peggy married Earl F. Wigger and lives in Farmington. She is a graduate of Farmington High School and Mineral Area Junior College. She has one son, Scott, one daughter, Cynthia Wigger Reichert, and two granddaughters. She was employed by the Department of Mental Health and the Department of Corrections until retirement.

MCCREARY - Cota Keith, the son of James Fountain and Anna "Annie" Laura Broadfoot McCreary, was born Oct. 28, 1873, near Hazel Run in St. Francois County, MO. Ada Lee Morris McCreary, the daughter of Donald Morris and Mary Mostiller Morris, was born Jan. 28, 1877, in Ste. Genevieve County, MO. Both the McCreary and Morris families settled in Missouri in the early and mid-1800s respectfully. Cota Keith and Ada Lee were married October 21, Desloge, MO. The marriage license is dated Oct. 19, 1903, AD. The wedding was performed by William J. Selvick, pastor of the MECS of Desloge, MO. The marriage witnesses were S.T. Horn and Eugene C. Mostiller.

Front Row: Marcus "Bill," Ada, Cota and James Franklin "Frank". Back Row: Earl, Marvin, Mary Anna Mae and Raymond "Ray"

Cota Keith was a farmer and Ada Lee was a devoted wife and mother. Both strived to raise a family through sickness and health. Their six children were as follows:

Earl Lehman McCreary, born Aug. 29, 1904, married Roberta Meyer Nov. 10, 1935. Earl died Sept. 25, 1965, in his sleep and is buried at Hillview Memorial Gardens in Farmington, MO.

Marvin Lee McCreary, born Feb. 21, 1906, in St. Francois County, MO, married Mae Garner

on July 4, 1935, at the Methodist Church in Flat River, MO. Marvin died Jan. 26, 1966, in Farmington, MO of a heart attack. He is buried at Parkview Cemetery in Farmington, MO.

Mary Anna Mae McCreary was born July 14, 1909, on the farm at Route #1, Bonne Terre, MO and died of tuberculosis May 6, 1936, at the age of 26, at home on Janey Drive in Farmington, MO. She is buried in Parkview Cemetery near Janey Drive.

Raymond "Ray" Andrew McCreary, born Sept. 29, 1912, in Bonne Terre, MO, was first married to Reba Elizabeth Hunt on April 9, 1936. His second marriage was to Naomi Wickman Ridgeway on Oct. 22, 1976, at First Baptist Church in Farmington, MO. Ray died Oct. 25, 1995, of lung cancer in Farmington, MO. He is buried at Hillview Cemetery in Farmington, MO.

James Franklin "Frank" McCreary, born May 3, 1915, married Berniece Dugal on June 28, 1936, in Farmington, MO. Frank died Sept. 22, 1992, of colon cancer in Louisville, KY at age 77. He is buried in historic Cave Hill Cemetery in Louisville, KY.

Marcus Cody "Bill" McCreary, born Oct. 29, 1919, married Mary Neal Corbitt Sept. 23, 1938, in St. Louis, MO. Bill lives in Florence, AL, where he is owner of Lexington Fabrics Manufacturing Co.

Ada Lee died June 4, 1938, age 61, and is buried in Parkview Cemetery in Farmington, MO. Cota Keith died Jan. 20, 1939, age 65, and is buried in Parkview Cemetery in Farmington, MO. These McCreary parents raised a generation of outstanding community citizens and church leaders.

The following is a newspaper article on Earl McCreary and Leslie Williams 21st birthday celebration, Aug. 29, 1925:

"A large crowd of friends and relatives, consisting of most of the neighbors and some folks from Bonne Terre, Desloge, Gumbo, Esther and Farmington, gathered at the home of Mr. and Mrs. Cota McCreary late Saturday evening, August 29, to help celebrate the 21st birthday anniversary of their oldest son, Earl, and also that of his friend and neighbor, Leslie Williams, their birthdays being on the same day and although no relation they are often taken for brothers; quite a coincident indeed, about the only difference being that Leslie is married, while Earl is yet single. Quite a musical concert was rendered by John Kirk and son, Clarence, Felix Galvin, Harvey Price, Floyd Yount and Clarence McCreary; all taking turns at the violin, guitar, mandolin and harp, which was enjoyed by all. The young folks spent the evening in playing games. Last, but not least, came the refreshments of cake and lemonade, including the large white birthday cake made by Mrs. Leslie Williams and decorated with red candy and 21 white candles, which after being lighted was held aloft by the two men so that all might see the glowing candles. All left at a late hour, declaring that they had had a fine time and wishing Earl and Leslie many more happy birthday anniversaries." *Submitted by Mary McCreary O'Connor, granddaughter.*

MCCREARY - Early in the year 1942, my great-grandfather, James Franklin McCreary, reported for induction to the service on April 8. WWII began on Sept. 1, 1939, when Germany invaded Poland; and at the same time WWII was going on, Hitler's Party was punishing other Germans. It was mid-1942 before the United States of America entered WWII. We entered WWII after the military bases at Pearl Harbor had been bombed. Many historians say the causes of WWII was from business not finished from WWI which was from 1914-1918.

My great-grandfather left Farmington, MO to

serve in the 20th Inf. as a doughboy. A doughboy is an American infantryman. The origin of this term is obscure; but, there are two possibilities offered by the Random House Dictionary of the English Language. Infantrymen wore uniforms that featured "globular buttons" made of brass that resembled globs of pastry dough. Also, dough referred to the white clay used to clean the white uniforms and belts worn by the infantrymen. Doughboys, or infantrymen, were walking soldiers that marched across battlefields.

James Franklin McCreary

My great-grandfather came home on Christmas Day in 1945. Between his induction and his return home was an important period of time. This is when he fought in Germany. It was so important that he kept a diary about walking across the big country of Germany. His diary was so important that it has been saved through the years by our family. I feel very lucky to have had a great-grandfather who fought in WWII and took time to write about this time in his life so that we could learn about family history and world history. English historian Lord McCaulay wrote, "A people that takes no pride in the accomplishments of their remote ancestors will probably produce nothing worthy of recollection by their remote descendants." I am very proud of my great-grandfather, James Franklin McCreary. Written March 1997 by Emma Hutchens (age 11), granddaughter of Bob and Mary Frances (McCreary) O'Connor

FRANKLIN/MCCREARY - James Franklin "Frank" McCreary was born May 3, 1915, the son of Cota Keith and Ada Morris McCreary. He was married to Berniece Dugal, born Oct. 4, 1914, the daughter of Nannie Elizabeth Wood Dugal and the late Edward Frank Dugal on June 28, 1936, in Farmington, MO. The wedding took place at 9 o'clock on Sunday morning in the living room of the Baptist parsonage. The ceremony was performed by Rev. Frank Crockett. Present at the ceremony were Mr. and Mrs. Robert Dugal, Miss Rowena Flanery, Mr. Raymond McCreary and the pastor's family. The bride wore a delphinium blue lace frock with pink accessories and a lace shoulder bouquet of rosebuds with baby breath.

Bernice and Frank McCreary

The bride and groom were graduates of Farmington High School in the classes of 1932 and 1934 respectively. Both Frank and Berniece were active members of First Baptist Church and the local Baptist Association. Frank McCreary was employed by Rozier Store in the clothing department. Before marriage Berniece was a nanny and cook for the Smith family in Farmington, and later she worked at Rice Stix Factory as a seamstress sewing collars on shirts.

When WWII began, Frank was drafted and served in the 20th Inf. Div. He fought in the Battle of the Bulge as a foot soldier. His children remember the story he told about the day he thought he had been shot. Fortunately, it turned out that he had been hit by a burning shingle. While Frank was in WWII, Berniece became a creative baker of cakes in her home. She had her own cottage industry to help feed and clothe her family.

After the war ended Frank knew from his travels that there was a world of experience in other parts of the country, and he wanted his family to have a better life. While unpacking crates of shoes at Roziers, he found a questionnaire saying, "Are you interested in becoming a sales representative for International Shoe Co. of St. Louis, MO? If you are interested in this job, please fill out and mail this form to us." After Frank had mailed the information to International Shoe Co., he told Berniece what he had done. Shortly thereafter, he received a phone call and was interviewed for the job. Frank accepted the offer to become a sales representative, and his first assignment required that he move to Lincoln, NE in 1948. It was a big move for the family that had always lived in the Farmington, MO area. The First Baptist congregation of Lincoln, NE became the family church.

In 1953 Frank was promoted to a better territory, this time requiring that he move his family to Evansville, IN. Eleven years later, Frank was rewarded again with a move to the Louisville, KY territory. With each move new friends were made and new cultures were experienced. Frank had an outgoing personality and Berniece was his multi-talented soul mate whose skills in cooking and entertaining were frequently used.

After arriving in Louisville, while still a sales representative for International Shoe Co., Frank and his good friends, Paul Johnson and Earl Conner, opened three McJohn shoe stores. Selling shoes and Baptist church life were the focal points for the McCreary family of five. The three children born to Frank and Berniece were Mary Frances McCreary O'Connor who married Robert and they live in Louisville, KY; James Franklin McCreary Jr. married Jean Tucker and they live in Brentwood, TN; Marjorie Ann McCreary McCall married Michael and they live in Louisville, KY.

Frank lived an abundant life, always ready to laugh, whistle and sing. Berniece lived a courageous life, always serving her Lord, her family and friends. Frank died Sept. 22, 1992, of colon cancer. Berniece died May 6, 1994, of breast cancer. They are buried in historic Cave Hill Cemetery in Louisville, KY. Wonderful memories of them live on in the minds and hearts of their family and friends. *Submitted by Dr. Robert E. O'Connor Jr., son-in-law*

MCCREARY - James Washington McCreary came to St. Francois County and Farmington area from his birthplace in North Carolina by way of Washington County, MO, where on Feb. 12, 1829, he married Polly Vance, born 1812 in Kentucky and died before 1870. James and Polly's children were John Allen M., Martha A., Samuel K., Rebecca Haseltine, William Milton, Mary J., James Fountain, Philander Thomas and Lucinda S., Susan A. and Alba S.

James Washington lived out his years in Hazel Run, St. Francois County. He is recorded in the home of son, Philander, on 1880 census. The last record we have for James W. is the sale of some property to Philander in August 1883. James' great-great-granddaughter, Mary Frances McCreary O'Connor, has found an incomplete death record at the Boyer Funeral Home, Bonne Terre dated March 27, 1896, for a James McCreary. Payment was made with one load of wood and 140 lbs. of pork.

John Allen M. McCreary and Louisa Hughes McCreary

John Allen M. McCreary, born 1832, died 1920, and Louisa Hughes, born 1836, died 1906, were married in Washington County. He was a master mason. Their children born in Missouri included Naomi Elizabeth, born 1861, died 1935, married Oliver Monroe Darr; Andrew Thomas, born 1863, died 1942, married Ada Louise Dalton; Filander Judson, born 1864, died 1945, married first Mary Fannie Brownwell and second Annie Rice Adams. John A.M. and Louisa moved from St. Francois County to Kaufman County, TX (location now Rockwall County) where their remaining children were born: Elic Spurgeon, born 1868, died 1953, married Myrtle Lee Moore; Walter Warren, born 1871, died 1936, married first to Sarah C. Lancaster Simmons and second, Lemmie L.A. Waldrop Collins; infant daughter; and John Malon, born 1876, died 1948, married first to Lillie Blanche Story and second, Minnie Lee Constable Stubblefield.

Louisa Hughes McCreary died 14 years before John A.M. As a widower, he often visited his children, but considered his home to be with his youngest son, John Malon in Lake Creek, TX. John Malon's daughter, Augusta Glee McCreary, recalled her Grandpa enjoyed walking down into their garden and did not want to be away when it was planted. She remembered his straight back chair with raw hide seat which was on their front porch.

Samuel K. McCreary, born 1836/37, died after 1880, married first to Susan C. Hudspeth. They were in his parents' household for 1860 St. Francois census with their two baby girls, Mary A. (ca. 1859) and Nancy J. (ca. 1860). Samuel married second to Mary Eaton in Washington County where they are on 1880 census. Their children, born 1866 to October 1880, include William A., Louisa, Mildred, Amanda, Ellen, Martin, Maggie, Cyrus and Nettie.

Rebecca Haseltine McCreary, born April 27, 1838, married Andrew P. Tong. Her grandson, Marvin E. Tong Jr., was a resident of Branson, MO in 1970s.

William Milton McCreary, born 1840, died 1903, enlisted in 6th Regiment, Texas Cavalry, 1861, paroled in May 1865. He married first to Isabella Tennessee Heath, Rockwall County, TX. Their children are Charles Milton, born ca. 1867, died ca. 1910, married Nora Vandiver; Philander, born ca. 1869, died before 1894; Ada Bell, born 1873, died 1950, married Jack Hartsough; Willie Ida, born 1874, died 1951, married William Franklin Martin; Mittie Mae, born 1877, married Eugene E. Morris; Howell Stephenson, born 1879, died 1936, married Ola Bostick. Howell was mustered in the Spanish-American War 1898 for two years. William Milton married second to Marietta S. Montgomery, born 1845, died 1919. She received a Widow's Confederate Pension in 1916.

The families of James Fountain and Philander Thomas McCreary are reported elsewhere in this book.

James Washington McCreary's family history as known in 1985 was compiled and published by Grata Jeter Clark in *Connecting Lines* (Volume II of *The Jeter Mosaic*) Submitted by Daphne Gomillion Storey

MCCREARY/BROADFOOT - James Fountain McCreary was born January 1847 to James Washington and Mary Ann "Polly" Vance McCreary in St. Francois, MO. He was the seventh child of nine children. On Oct. 24, 1867, James Fountain McCreary married "Annie" Laura Broadfoot, daughter of James Henderson Broadfoot from Kentucky and Purify Wilson Broadfoot from North Carolina. Anna Laura was born April 9, 1847. James Fountain professed his religious faith at 18 years, uniting with the Presbyterian Church. James Fountain and his father were successful farmers.

Cota, Clarence and Finis McCreary

James and Annie were parents to seven children:

May Duetta was born around 1870 and married Medium Pilliard. Duetta died in St. Louis in May 1944, and is buried in Danby Cemetery near Crystal City, MO.

Cota Keith was born Oct. 28, 1873, near Hazel Run in St. Francois County, MO. Cota married Ada Lee Morris on Oct. 21, 1903, in Desloge, MO. Cota died Jan. 20, 1939, in Farmington, MO and is buried in Parkview Cemetery in Farmington, MO.

Wilton McCreary was born Nov. 25, 1874, and died at the age of 12 years on Nov. 30, 1886.

Lee McCreary was born ca. 1877.

Ewing Tolman McCreary was born Dec. 12, 1880, near Cedar Grove, MO and died Aug. 8, 1885, at the age of 4 years. Wilton and Ewing were buried in Bouyer's Prairie Graveyard, also known as the McCreary Cemetery.

Finis Kenneth McCreary was born Aug. 27, 1882, near Hazel Run, MO. Finis' first marriage was to Ruth Guthrie. On July 19, 1924, he married Settie Thomure Horton. Finis died in his home of a heart ailment Sept. 21, 1945, near Avon, MO.

Clarence McCreary was born around 1885, near Hazel Run, MO. Clarence was married to Lucille. He died in 1944 in Vanport City, WA near Portland, OR. He is buried in Columbian Cemetery.

The family has a document showing that James Fountain McCreary was a captain in Co. H, 97th Regt. of the Missouri Militia. The document is dated Oct. 22, 1867, and signed by the adjutant general officer, Samuel P. Simpson, at the headquarters for the state of Missouri in Jefferson City, MO.

James Fountain McCreary was buried June 19, 1904. Funeral arrangements for one 6-0 No. 26, $25.00; one robe, $3.50; one pair stockings and gloves $.25 with a total of $28.75, were made and paid for by his son, Cota Keith McCreary. Rev. Saffold of Marvin's Chapel near Bonne Terre, MO, conducted the funeral services.

The burial was in Bouyer's Prairie (McCreary Cemetery). This cemetery was located on the old St. Louis Road in St. Francois County near the junction of Hazel Run Road and Highway K. The graveyard no longer exists having been bulldozed clean in 1974. James' obituary stated that "He led a consistent life having prominent traits of character that exemplified a sweet and peaceable disposition always striving to avoid offense and to maintain sociable relations with his fellow human beings. He had a remarkable fortitude during his last illness and said, 'I am ready and willing to go, and I am at peace with all mankind.'"

Annie Laura was part Native American. She is thought to be from the Cherokee Nation. Annie Laura Broadfoot McCreary died of chronic nephritis Oct. 16, 1918, at the age of 71 years and is buried in Parkview Cemetery in Farmington, MO.

In these lives were McCrearys that were law-abiding, family-oriented, patriotic, religious, caring and musical. *Submitted by Cathe O'Connor Hutchens, great-great-granddaughter*

MCCREARY - Philander Thomas McCreary, born 1848, in Missouri and died in 1912, was the son of James Washington, born 1804, North Carolina, and Polly McCreary nee Vance, born 1812, Kentucky. On Nov. 27, 1870, Philander married Lucinda Frances Pyrtle, born 1854 in Tennessee and died in 1914. They had 11 children.

Minnie Belle, born 1871, died 1956, married Charles McClain. Child, Charles "Buster," born 1904, died 1977, married Frieda Molzohn. Children: Winston, Ardith, Patty. Frieda died and he married Marie Nothaker; no children.

McCreary Sisters ca. 1900. Back L-R: Maud, Della, Amo. Front L-R: Minnie, Nellie, Fannie

William Henry, born 1873, died 1939 and, presumably, never married.

Sidney Howard, born 1875, died 1958, married Nell Conn. Children: Hilda, born 1897, died 1993, married Sidney Abbott. Children: Vera and Sidney Jr.; John Conn, born 1898, died 1984, married Edith Martin. Children: Conn Jr., Betty, Howard and Edward. Edith died and John married Mary E. Stimson. No children. Conn Jr., a jockey who won two Kentucky Derbies: "Pensive," 1944 and "Count Turf," 1951; Arnold, born 1901, died 1971, married Theresa Woods. Children: Calvin, Wendell, Betty, Billie Jo; Genevieve, born 1903, married Vernon Evans. Children: Ronnie, Robert and Howard; Leslie, born 1905, died 1983, married Edward Walsh. Children: Edward Jr., Regina, William, Lorraine, Rosemary and Robert; Howard, born 1908, died 1913; Eugene, born 1913, married Thelma Vineyard. Children: Shirley Jean, Judith Ann, Sandra Lee, Nancy Louise; Nelson, born 1916, married Alice Dumbald. Children: Stuart Allen, Stanley Howard, Neal Patrick, Michael Nelson, Dennis Eugene and Timothy Arnold.

Charles Allien, born 1877, died 1901, was a bachelor and died at the age of 24 of complications from typhoid fever.

Alpha Thomas, born 1879, died 1957, married Zollie Bailey. Zollie died and Alpha married Zollie's niece, Essie Bailey. No children.

Eliott Cate "Nellie," born 1883, died 1965, married Lee Gamel. Children: Harvey Lee, born 1903, died 1904; Norvel Francis, born 1905, died 1975, married Martha Rosenkrantz who died. Norvel then married Virginia Knobler. No children; Leona Maude, born 1906, died 1978, married Gus Nothaker who died. Leona then married Riley Hall. No children; Grace Pauline, born 1908, died 1968, married and divorced Franklin Cole. Married Carl Peters. No children; William Albert, born 1911, died 1988, married Louise Tumbas. Children: William Albert Jr., Gerald Lee, Nancy Louise, David Wayne; Robert Glenn, born 1914, died 1961, married Blanche Cohea. Children: Robert Jr., Amy Jean; Dorothy Berniece, born 1916, married and divorced Elmer Kuhlmann. Child: Barbara Joan, married Robert Stamm. No children; Alpha Wayne "Faye," born 1925, married Charles Beintker. Child: Kathy Lee.

Felina Elba "Fannie," born 1886, died 1912, married Lilburn Gipson. Children: Russell, born 1904, and Richard, born 1908.

Della Mae, born 1887, died 1974, married Guy Smith. Children: Richard G., born 1916, died 1984, married Jeanne O'Brien. Children: Richard Jr. and Peggy; Ida Lucille, born 1918, married Joe Ray. Child, Beverley; and Marybelle V., born 1920, married and divorced Keith Main, married Maurice Blumenthal who died, married and divorced Ferd Reich, married George Hayden. No children.

Emma Frances "Amo," born 1890, died 1939, married Jack Fertner and spent her married life in California. No children.

Gertrude Maude, born 1892, died 1935, married Archibald Hall. Children: Hazel Doris "Ruby," born 1916, died 1996, remained single; John, born 1919, died 1986, married and divorced Julie Horton. Child, Beverly, married Veda Griffin. Children: Sherie and Kenneth; Charlotte, born 1920, died 1987, married Elliott Govero. Children: Diana and Melissa; Robert, born 1924, married Evelyn Bowman. Child, Regina; Gilbert, born 1926, married Donna DeRouse. Child, Denise Marie; Gene, born 1930, married and divorced Peggy Boulton. Children: Monte James, Theresa Lynn, Denise Renee and Tina Lee. Married Helen Sproule. No children.

Homa Hoyt, born 1894, died 1966, married Edna Hines. Children: Homa Hoyt Jr., born 1916, died 1975, married Marcella Scharril. Children: Allen, Dennis and Wayne; Robert, born 1918, married Jeanne Gunn. Children: Robert Jr., Rod Patrick and Kathleen.

The McCreary sisters had musical talent (picture ca. 1900), Minnie played the piano, Nellie played guitar and a "mean" hoedown on her fiddle, and Fannie, Amo and Maude were equally talented. When asked what instrument Della played, daughter, Lucille, said, "Why, Momma whistled!"

MCDOWELL - William McDowell came to St. Francois County, MO in the 1840s. He was born April 4, 1822, in North Carolina. He married Sarah Jacobs, the daughter of John W. and Linda Jacobs, born Aug. 3, 1848, in St. Francois County, MO. She was born June 27, 1830, in Kentucky and died Oct. 28, 1893, and is buried in the Knob Lick Cemetery. William died Dec. 14, 1904, and is also buried in Knob Lick. They lived in Knob Lick and had 10 children.

Catherine L. was born in 1850, in Missouri and married Nixon Rogers.

John Samuel was born Jan. 11, 1852, and married Cynthia Isabelle Hill in 1880. They had Floyd, John, Hugh and Pearl. Floyd died in infancy; John Wm. was born Oct. 15, 1882, in Knob Lick and died Nov. 14, 1959, and is buried in Knob Lick. Hugh Blandford was born Oct. 20, 1889, in Knob Lick and died March 20, 1966, and is buried in Knob Lick. Pearl was born Aug. 2, 1892, in Knob Lick and married John McBrien. She died July 28, 1980, and is buried in Knob Lick.

Laura was born Dec. 27, 1856, in Knob Lick and died June 15, 1925. She married Joseph Bayless in 1881, the son of George and Meekie Eaves Bayless. They had Clara, George, Charles, Cyrus and McDowell. Clara was born May 10, 1882, died April 1, 1966, and is buried in Knob Lick. She married George Wallace Dec. 18, 1918, and had three children: Winford, George and Fern Audell. George William, born June 1886, married Edith and they had a son, Joseph, who was born Oct. 10, 1919, and died Nov. 20, 1943, in WWII. Charles B. was born June 1889, Cyrus B. was born March 31, 1891, and died Nov. 12, 1965, and is buried in Knob Lick. He married Maggie Milne June 19, 1919, and they had C.B. Jr. Maggie was the daughter of William and Maggie Skinner Milne and was born Nov. 18, 1890, in Knob Lick, died Feb. 7, 1978, and is buried in Knob Lick. McDowell "Mack" was born Feb. 22, 1894, died Feb. 25, 1968, and is buried in Knob Lick. He married Leona Chastain and they had Jack, who married Theresa Richard; Floyd married Verna Bards; Laura married Leeman Underwood and Norma Jean married Harry Hahl.

Nancy Ann was born Nov. 22, 1858, died July 16, 1924, and is buried in Knob Lick. She married W.F. Martin.

Thomas Jefferson, born March 11, 1860, died Feb. 23, 1930, and is buried in Knob Lick. He married Mary Ann and they adopted a son, Clem.

Ida was born in 1864 and married Daniel F. Eichar in 1884.

Alta E. was born in 1866 and married W.A. Cloud in 1885.

William B. was born Sept. 16, 1871, died Aug. 28, 1932, and married Laura Rudy in 1907. They are buried in Knob Lick.

Sarah E. married a man named Luce. No Info.

Anna B. married a man named Smith. No info.

MCGUIRE - Ancil McGuire, born 1876 in Kentucky, married Addie Shearer in 1900 and had two sons, William Dennis and George Cecil McGuire. The family moved to Farmington in 1915 from Tuscola, IL. He purchased a farm on the Trogden Road and later moved to a farm on the Sand Creek Road and resided there until his death in 1953.

Dennis, Eileen, Donald, Patrick, Michele, George, Robert McGuire family

William Dennis, born in 1901, married Edith Shinn in 1921 and died in 1944. He was employed by the US Post Office, was a member of the Methodist Church and very active in Boy Scouts. He purchased a farm on Valley Forge Road and Hwy. 32. He and Edith had five children: Dennis, Eileen, Donald, Patrick and Michele.

Dennis married Mildred Hargis. He served four years as a pilot for the US Air Force. He worked for the Missouri Highway Dept. as an engineer. He is retired and resides in Farmington. They had two children, Peggy and Penny, and two grandchildren. Dennis and his two daughters are graduates of Farmington High.

Eileen married John Murphy and they lived in St. Louis until retirement and now reside at Terre Du Lac. They have three sons: John, Pat and Danny, and five grandchildren. Eileeen is a Farmington graduate.

Donald married Beverly Allen. He is a Farmington graduate. He served four years in the US Air Force and is a Baptist minister. Prior to his ministry he was employed by Missouri Natural Gas as an accountant. They are retired, reside in Farmington and have three children: Richard, Bruce, Jennifer; six grandchildren; and two great-grandchildren.

Patrick married Linda Kimmel and they live on a farm in Kearney, MO. He served in the US Army and is now retired from the US Treasury Dept. They have three children: Kelly, Tracy, Patrick Jr. and eight grandchildren. He is a Farmington graduate.

Michele married John Northcutt and lives in Farmington. She is employed by the Missouri Department of Mental Health and is the Southeast Missouri Youth Services Coordinator. She has three children: Deborah, Dennis and Bradley Downs, and two grandchildren. Michele and her three children are Farmington graduates.

George Cecil, born in 1905, married Freida Joggerest in September 1928 and had two sons, Robert and George. In the 30s Cecil worked for Geissing Milling Co. and in the 40s for Trimfoot Shoe. Prior to his retirement he worked for Adams Dairy in St. Louis. He resided in Farmington until his death in 1990.

Robert married Marianna Hartshorn and they live in Kansas City, MO. They have two children, David and Susie, and six grandchildren. Bob and Marianna are both Farmington graduates. Bob worked for O'Brien Co. and was head of the industrial design department.

George had three children: Keith, Gary, Mike (deceased) and three granddaughters. George was employed by the US Postal Service as supervisor. He and his wife, Phyllis are retired and live on a farm in the Farmington area. George and his three sons are graduates of Farmington High.

MCHENRY - Because of two sisters remaining so close and one grandfather who thought his sons-in-law should become funeral directors, I eventually became a Farmingtonian.

Elva Octavia (Rinke) Cozean and Elizabeth Georgia (Rinke) Hood were the two sisters so close they somehow managed to spend, along with their families, the holidays together. Because Aunt "Elvy's" family was so much larger, it fell upon her to feed everyone and so the "magic" began. No matter the number of mouths expected or unexpected, there was always enough to go around. Even with everyone sampling, most especially, the turkey as it was being carved. There was enough.

It was my

Norma McHenry

mother, Elizabeth's, part to furnish cookies, candies and especially the cakes - always one sunshine and one angel food. My cousins and I are hoping that one day the original recipe for that sunshine cake will turn up. It used up all the yokes left over from the egg whites used to make the angel food cake.

Such memories that I have of those days long past. Growing up by spending wonderful summer days and nights sleeping on this marvelous screened-in porch and being awakened by the mourning doves, saying "Good Morning."

And so the "magic" has continued into four generations; of course, there have been disagreements along the way. In the second generation I remember a pesky cousin being chased out of the house with a broom. The third generation brought on a tussle over a hobby horse which otherwise had been completely ignored. Fourth generation brought on a trip to California for a first meeting of the children. We worried somewhat about how they would accept each other. They were introduced and hand-in-hand went down the hill to investigate their own interests.

Life took us to other places: Alabama, California, Arizona, etc., but within the fabric of our family there run iron threads and it seems a part of the magic that we return to the rolling hills and the beauty of Missouri and it is home. *Submitted by Norma Hood McHenry*

MCMULLIN - Thomas Smith McMullin was born in Henderson County, KY Jan. 18, 1825, and died in Farmington, MO Sept. 16, 1880. His father was a native of Tennessee, of English and Irish parentage. When yet a young boy, he and his brother, Joe, sawed lumber by hand to remodel the family's three-room house, where they were born. The building was still standing in good condition in 1914.

He suffered an unfortunate accident at a young age when a gun exploded, and he lost three fingers on his right hand. Thomas took up the trade of photography, using the daguerrotype on silver plates, said to be the first pictures in that area. In about the year 1843 he decided to go to California to seek gold, but his parents refused, he being only 18 years old. One year later he got their consent and left for the west, crossing the Mississippi River at St. Genevieve, MO, then overland to Jefferson City, where he joined a company of immigrants. On the journey near Salt Lake City, he became ill and had to be left to recover. After being nursed back to health, he joined another group in driving a herd of cattle to California. There he became a hunter and earned a living, killing deer, antelope and bears, selling the meat to mining camps.

While hunting near Mara Posa, CA, he came upon a bear which charged him; and while escaping, he fell from a bluff and severely sprained his ankle. His hunting experience lasted from about 1848 to 1852. He had a close call once when three Indians he encountered tried to kill him, but he managed to get them instead. After all his western experience he decided to return home to Kentucky, where in 1854 he married Harriet Sorrels and two children were born to this union. He moved to Farmington, MO where he followed the trade of gunsmith. His wife died in 1861 and he married again in February 1862 to Ruth Elizabeth Fraser of Ste. Genevieve County; seven children were born to this union.

Thomas took an active interest in local government, being listed as a voter in local elections as well as being appointed marshall in the town of Farmington. He was elected sheriff of St. Francois County where he served from 1861-1864, this being in the unsettled time of the Civil War. After this he engaged in the nursery business on his farm near Farmington. He was again elected sheriff and served from 1877 until his death (while still in office) in 1880.

The year of 1880 had to be a trying time for Thomas. He had been involved in solving a brutal murder case that occurred in October 1879 and arrested Charles Hardin for the murder of Robert Ferguson. Hardin was sentenced to hang on Jan. 23, 1880. As sheriff, he was in charge of carrying out the sentence of the court.

On Sept. 13, 1880, he was involved in an altercation with one Henry Horn in an alley next to Trapps saloon in Farmington. Witnesses said the sheriff advanced on Horn, fired and hit Horn in the hand. Horn then returned fire, hitting McMullin twice, once in the stomach and another in the chest. Witnesses said there had been a long-standing grudge between the two men. Thomas died three days later on Sept. 16, 1880. Mr. Horn survived the shooting and claimed self defense at his trial.

Mrs. McMullin, after the death of her husband, remained in the Farmington area and reared her family. Later she moved to Charleston, MO to live with a daughter. She passed away at age 65 and was buried next to her husband in the Masonic Cemetery in Farmington. She is survived by three daughters and one son. *Submitted by Jack Clay*

MERRYMAN - Thomas Merryman was born June 25, 1860 in Doe Run, St. Francois County, MO to John W. and Catherine Rogers Merryman. His father, John W., came to Wayne County, TN in 1856 then to Pendleton Township, Doe Run, St. Francois County, MO and learned the blacksmith trade from his father John, who died in Missouri in December 1864. John W. worked at the mines in Iron Mountain about 14 years and bought a farm in Doe Run.

Sarah Williams, wife of Thomas Jefferson Merryman

He discovered lead in the rocks on his land and he sold the property to St. Joe Lead Company for $10,000 in cash and bought another farm. He also owned the land in Farmington where the Parkview Cemetery is located, and several of the family members are buried there. John W. married Catherine Rogers. She was the daughter of William Rogers and they had a son, Thomas Jefferson. John married a second time, when his wife died, to Susan Rennicks, daughter of Lewis and Mary Wilburn Rennicks, who were from Indiana. He and his second wife had eight more children. They were James, Mary Jane, Melissa Frances, Amanda Ida, Martha Ann, Leroy and William. Thomas J. married Sarah Anne Williams, the youngest daughter of Daniel and Sarah Jones Williams who had 13 children. Thomas and Sarah married Oct. 6, 1882, in St. Francois County, MO and were the parents of 10 children.

1. Bertha Merryman, born in 1883, married Pete Warren in 1916 and had one daughter, Elizabeth, who died in 1919.

2. Blanche Merryman, born in 1885, died 1957. She married Martin M. Beck in 1905. He was the son of Henry and Esther Beck and was born in 1869. Sarah and Martin were parents of six children. Anna Beck was born in 1924 and married William Barnhouse in 1947. He was born in 1926. Their children: Bill married Wanda Johnson, Barbara married Vernon Howell, Marilyn married James Martin, Shirley married Darrell Boren and Judith married Edward Pinson. William Barnhouse was the son of Daniel and Amanda Hamilton Barnhouse who lived in Doe Run. Daniel's parents Carico and Emma Woods Barnhouse came from Meigs County, OH. Next child of Sarah and Martin Beck was Jesse who was born in 1907 and married Alma Martin in 1928. They had four children: Paul, Gene, Dorothy and Harold. Henry Beck was born in 1909 and married Oleta Gray in 1935. Their children

were Henry Richard and Charles. Mitchell Beck, born in 1914, married Jean Freeman in 1943 and had one daughter, Carolyn. Rose Beck, born 1919, married Russell King in 1941 and had 10 children: Sherry, born 1942, married Thomas Sales; Rose, born 1944, married Lindell Kennon; Carol, born 1948; Helen, born 1949, married Byron Richardson; Dolores, born 1951, married Jerry Lewellen; Barbara, born 1954, married William Shelton; James, born 1956, married Diedre Umfleet Davis; Catherine, born 1958; John, born 1960; and Patricia, born 1961, married David Easter.

Elsie Beck, born 1927, is the last child of Sarah and Martin. She married Warren Rion and they have one daughter, Donna. Martin and Blanche are buried in the Doe Run Memorial Cemetery but all their children are in the Parkview Cemetery.

3. Rose Merryman, born 1887, died 1966 and married Andrew Burnette in 1909. They had seven children: Harold, Helen, Andrew Paul, Thomas Robert, James Edward, Glen and Earl.

4. Lillie Merryman, born 1889 and died 1969. She married Thomas Rion in 1917 and had six children: Dorothy, Raymond, Thomas, Norma, Paul and James.

5. Mabel Merryman, born 1890 and died in 1975. She married Golf Duncan.

6. Clarence W. Merryman, born Aug. 20, 1892 and died Feb. 2, 1974. He married Josephine Herbst and had one son, William.

7. Myrtle Merryman, born in 1894 and died in 1970. She married John O'Sullivan in 1915 and had three children: Virginia, Marvin and Clyde.

8. William Merryman, born in 1896 and died in 1930.

9. Dewey L. Merryman, born 1898, died 1950, she married George Smith and had a daughter, Lora.

10. Grace Merryman, born 1900 and died 1966. She married Zeno Grifford and they had one daughter, Eula E., who was born in 1921 and married Arthur Freeman in 1943. They had five children: David, born 1946, and died in Vietnam in 1970; Michelle, born 1949; Thomas, born 1952; Mary, born 1955; Margaret, born 1958. Art was active in the Boy Scouts and was a leader for years.

Thomas died Jan. 14, 1933, and Sarah Anne died Dec. 11, 1918, in the influenza epidemic that swept the nation at the end of WWI. Thomas was a farmer and in his later years moved to Farmington and lived there until he died. *Submitted by Rose King*

MEYER - When this bride cut the first piece of wedding cake, little did she know she would be baking a cake every day for the next 35 years. Her husband, and later the children, consumed a total of 12,775 cakes. More on the cake story later.

Sonny and Willa Dean Meyer

Willa Dean Thurman, a Farmington native, was born Oct. 10, 1932, on the Hunt farm, the youngest of seven children born to Lawrence and Clara Williams Thurman. The siblings were Ha-

zel (Harrington), Lee, Earl, Genevieve (Dillard Bauman), Geraldine Zielieke, Lawrence Jr. and Willa Dean. Only Geraldine and Willa Dean are living. Paternal grandparents were Major and Nancy Rickard Thurman from Ste. Genevieve County and maternal grandparents were Jeff and Harriet Ann Barnes Williams of the Sprott area. Arthur Francis "Sonny" Meyer was born in Ste. Genevieve, MO, Sept. 11, 1931, to Francis and Agnes Basler Meyer. Sonny is the youngest of three children: Mary Ann, deceased, and Rosella (Bahr). His paternal grandparents were Frank and Anne Bahr Meyer and his maternal grandparents were Anton and Elizabeth Roth Basler.

Sonny and Willa Dean met at the Casino Roller Rink in 1950. Following a long engagement, they were married at the St. Joseph Catholic Church in Farmington April 14, 1956. All of their married years have been spent in Farmington. Willa Dean worked for the Missouri Department of Revenue as an auditor with her office located in the St. Francois County Courthouse. After 13 years in that position, she stayed home several years with the three children, later returning to work as secretary at the Farmington Presbyterian Church. After 10 years there she became the news editor of the *Farmington Press* where she spent 10 years. Since 1992 she has been the public relations/marketing director for Mineral Area Regional Medical Center. Sonny first worked for St. Joe Lead Co. and in 1958 opened his own business in the rebuilding and sale of automobiles. For 35 years the Meyer family's home has been at #1 Airline Drive and the business is located on their 25-plus acre farm east on Highway 32 in Ste. Genevieve County.

Sonny and Willa Dean are parents of three children: Cynthia Ann, born 1960, married Thomas Butterbaugh and resides in Kentucky; Larry Joseph, born 1962, married Marianne Nackley and resides in St. Louis; Kevin Lee, born 1965, married Robin Mallory and resides in Illinois. Eight grandsons including two sets of twins bless this family tree. They are Austin, Adam, (twins) Sean and Eric Butterbaugh; Ryan and Brandon Meyer; and (twins) Seth and Zachary Meyer. Willa Dean is actively involved in community work and currently serves as chairperson for Farmington Country Days sponsored by the Chamber of Commerce. Sonny shares her interest in community work and both are very involved in the St. Joseph Catholic Church where Willa Dean is a lector and both are Eucharistic Ministers.

The rest of the cake story... Because Willa Dean was raised in an old-fashioned home where the woman's role always was to please the husband and the children, and also because they wouldn't leave the table without dessert, it became a tradition that every day she would bake a chocolate cake with chocolate frosting, half with nuts and half without. Friends of the Meyer children, now grown, comment on those days when they enjoyed chocolate cake at the Meyer home. When Cindy was in college at Murray State, cakes were sent to her and eaten by people that Willa Dean never knew. Cakes were baked and taken on vacation. The truth of the matter is, the family was probably addicted to chocolate and didn't know it! Today, the Meyer kitchen turns out a couple of cakes a week with brownies in between. That tradition may very well have been the secret to a wonderful marriage.

MEYER - Earl Meyer married Jesselyn Counts. They had two children, Virginia Lee and Earl Douglas "Sonny."

They moved to California in the late 1920s to be near Jesselyn's parents, Jeff and Sally Counts. They migrated to California due to Jeff's declining health. He had presided as judge in St.

Francois County. Two years later Earl and Jesselyn moved back to Farmington. Earl worked at Rice Stix Shirt Factory and Jesselyn taught at the Lutheran School for 37 years.

Richard A. Schneider, Richard D. Schneider, Virginia Schneider, Joyce Chalmers, Mary Ross 50th anniversary in 1996

Virginia Lee and Sonny attended the Lutheran School. Miss Della Rickus, Mr. Meyerman and Mrs. Mueller were her teachers. Remembering the first day Virginia attended school was frightening. Then a smiling Virginia Gierse came to meet her, took her hand and kindly walked with her to the classroom. The years that followed were wonderful and cherished, laying the foundation of a strong faith and Christian life.

Richard Schneider, Virginia (Meyer) Schneider, Scott, Joyce, Chalmers, Casey, Adam, Rick and Deby Schneider, James, Jesselynn, Jubal, Mary Ross, Rob, James, Rich

Virginia graduated from Flat River High in 1943. She worked part-time at the Fair Department Store and Revoir Grocery. Employees of the Fair Department waved to the boys leaving for war in the July 4th Parade from the upstairs window of the store. The town and the country had a great feeling of patriotism and pride. Some of our boys came back as men after fighting for our country. Some did not come back but gave their lives for the cause for which they fought.

Sonny Meyer enjoyed sports and singing in the chorus. He enjoyed fishing with his friend, John D. Vincel. He and Duane Thomas, his first cousin, were also good friends and were on a Walther League outing at Chimney Rocks when Sonny fell from a high rock to his death, leaving the town in shock. A sight to behold and cherish was when Miss Daisy Baker brought her school children one morning to the funeral home to say farewell to Sonny.

Off to war

Virginia attended Valparaiso University. After the war she married Richard Schneider. They moved to Rolla where he attended the School of Mines and became an electrical engineer. He worked for Shell Oil in Wood River, was then transferred to California in 1968 and lived in Huntington Beach until retirement in 1982 when they moved to the high desert.

Virginia taught school in Huntington Beach. They had three children. Joyce married Scott Chalmers and has two sons. Adam graduated from West Point and is now an Army Ranger in North Carolina. Casey attends college majoring in accounting.

Mary Lee married Robert Ross and has three sons. Rob recently married Deborah Dowling. He is an ocean engineer. James married Leslie and is employed by an engineering firm in Houston. Richard, the youngest son, attends University of Texas majoring in geology.

Mary is now married to Herb Hildebrand and is a real estate agent for the Woodlands in the Houston area.

Virginia and Richard's youngest son graduated from University of Utah majoring in music. He married Deborah Hall and they have three children: James, Jesselynn and Jubal. They live in Silver Lakes, the same area as their parents. *Submitted by Virginia L. Schneider*

MEYER - Marvin Meyer and his wife, Mildred, were long time residents of Farmington, having built their home at 617 Overton Street in 1937, when their only child, Larry, was 1-year-old. This home was located in the Carleton Addition and was built by the Jennings Lumber Co. for about $3,100.

Mildred "Mickey" was born in 1908 and was the former Mildred Margretta Henderlite, daughter of Alva Clarence and Lucinda Pernice (Bellamy) Henderlite. The Henderlite and Bellamy families were originally from the Sparta, IL area. They settled in Farmington, where Alva worked as a freight hauler and Lucinda did washing and ironing for Farmington residents. Mildred graduated from Farmington High School in 1927 and earned a teaching certificate. She was

Mildred and Marvin Meyer wedding day, April 24, 1929

a homemaker and part-time employee at the H.C. Mell Hardware Store which was located on E. Liberty Street. She died in July 1981.

George (or Marvin) was born in 1902 and was the son of Noah John and Mollie (Griffin) Meyer. His grandparents immigrated from Germany. They were farmers and lived on a 240 acre farm five miles south of Farmington. He attended school through the eighth grade, graduating from Independence School, which was located near the corner of Kollmeyer and Feezor Roads. He was employed by the H.C. Mell Hardware Store and retired after 43 years.

Marvin and Mildred were married on March 24, 1929. They were faithful members of the Methodist Church, loved to fish, play pinochle and socialize with family and friends. He also was a bowler, vegetable gardener, hunter and avid St. Louis Cardinal baseball fan. She was an excellent cook and housekeeper. Summer evenings were spent sitting on their front porch, listening to Cardinal baseball and visiting with friends who strolled the neighborhood sidewalks. He served as an alderman from the Fourth Ward for many years and died in July 1998.

Their only child, Larry, was born March 9, 1936. He attended St. Paul's Lutheran School, Farmington Public Schools, graduating from high school in 1954, spent one year at Flat River Junior College and graduated from the Missouri School of Mines and Metallurgy at Rolla in 1958 with a degree in civil engineering. As a youth, he was active in the Methodist Youth Fellowship, worked at the Howard Tetley Jewelers, the Rozier Store Co., wrote sports stories for the *Farmington Press* and *St. Francois County Journal*, and broadcast Farmington High School football and basketball games on KREI radio. After graduating from college, he began work with the state of Illinois, Division of Highways, at their District 9 office in Carbondale. He retired Dec. 31, 1991.

He married Sharon Lee Bradley, a graduate nurse from St. Luke's Hospital in St. Louis and a resident of Carbondale, in the summer of 1961. They currently reside at 1606 West Lake Road in Murphysboro, IL.

They had three daughters: Lisa Ellen Canivez (Gary), Amy Jo McHose (Jim) and Jennifer Leigh Sykes (Jeff). These lovely daughters have provided them with five grandchildren: Hannah and Sarah Canivez, Cassidy and Cason McHose and Joshua Sykes. *Submitted by Larry Meyer*

MILLER - Berl J. and Juanita Miller moved to Farmington in 1940 when they purchased the well-established Neidert Funeral Home on West Columbia Street. They remained in that business until retiring in 1985, at which time the establishment was sold to David and Ann Taylor.

Left to right : Berl Miller and John Neidert

Berl had started in the funeral business in 1930 and graduated from the Williams Institute of Mortuary Science at Kansas City, KS. Juanita, who was originally from Montana, also became a licensed funeral director after her marriage on June 29, 1935.

Upon moving to Farmington, the Millers immediately became enmeshed in community life. Berl was a member, and later chairman, of the Board of Stewards at the United Memorial Methodist Church and was the first chairman of its Men's Club. He was also a member of the Board of Trustees.

Berl and Juanita Miller

The Neidert Funeral Home had been established by Adam Neidert in 1881 as the A. Neidert

Undertaking Company. Mr. Neidert was one of the earliest licensed embalmers in the state of Missouri. When he first came to Farmington, he was active in and served as president of the Junior Chamber of Commerce and in 1959 was president of the Farmington Chamber of Commerce. He was awarded the chamber's Lifetime Service Award.

In addition, he became the first president of the Kiwanis Club of Farmington upon its organization in 1956 and went on to become his division's lieutenant-governor for the Missouri-Arkansas District. His dedication to the Kiwanis was shown with his 30-year perfect attendance record.

He was Past Worshipful Master of Farmington Lodge No. 132 AF&AM and was the first "Dad" for the Bethel of Job's Daughters. His Masonic affiliations included membership in the Eastern Star, the Scottish Rite and the Shrine. Berl was a past Noble Grand of the Independent Order of Odd Fellows and a charter member of the Elks Lodge No. 1765 in Farmington.

Further service to his community included 15 years on the Farmington Public School Board, three terms as president; coroner for St. Francois County for 16 years and a president of the St. Francois Country Club.

Professional honors included being director of the Southeast Missouri Funeral Directors Association and serving on the State Association Board. He also was honored by being president of the National Guild of Funeral Directors as well as a member of the National Selected Funeral Directors Association.

Mrs. Miller was also an actively involved member of her church, various social organizations and many community endeavors. Throughout their ownership of Miller Funeral Home she worked in the business with her husband.

The Millers had two daughters: Barbara (Mrs. Bennett) Hall of Atlanta, GA, who has two children, Robert and Babette, and five grand-children; Carol (Mrs. Clare "Bud") Jones and her family reside in Dallas, TX. She has two sons, Jeffrey Shumake, who has two children; and William Jay Shumake who has one daughter.

Berl Miller passed away in 1990 and Juanita continues to make her home in Farmington.

MILLER - Daniel C. and Anna Maria Miller migrated to America from Otzendorf, Germany. They had three children born in Germany and seven children born in America. It is uncertain why Daniel and Anna came to America. Daniel and Anna arrived by sailboat to New York, which was a journey of approximately six weeks. From New York they went to Ohio. Upon leaving Ohio, they settled in Ste. Genevieve, MO from 1834 to 1838.

In 1838 Daniel and Anna moved to Farmington, MO. They were the first German settlers in St. Franois County. Their home was located in the 200 block of Columbia Street. Daniel was a tailor by trade in Germany. He continued his trade when he moved to America. His business was located on the corner of Columbia and Henry Streets.

After working in his shop for a few years, Daniel moved his family two miles southeast of Farmington. He homesteaded 200 acres in the Copenhagen Community. Being earnest German Methodists, Daniel deeded two acres of land for a church, parsonage and cemetery in the Copenhagen Community. The cemetery remains as the final resting place of the donors, Daniel and Anna, and their descendants. *Submitted by Jane Miller Robke*

MILLER - Danny Joe Miller and Sandra Taylor Miller graduated from Desloge High School, Danny in 1960 and Sandra in 1964. They were married in the First Presbyterian Church of the Lead Belt in Flat River on Jan. 29, 1966. (January 29 turned out to be the coldest day of that winter.)

Bill and Christine Robbins, Susie and Rodney Miller, Sandra and Danny Miller at Rodney and Susie's wedding Nov. 2, 1997

After living in Jefferson County for several years, Danny and his father, Jesse Miller, started an electrical contracting business, Total Electric Company, in 1972. In 1974 Danny and Sandra decided to move to Farmington. They lived on North Street from August 1974 until August 1997. Their children, Christine and Rodney, graduated from Farmington High School, Christine in 1984 and Rodney in 1986. The decision to move to Farmington was partly based on business but mainly based on the quality of life Farmington offered to families.

They became active members in United Memorial Methodist Church. Christine and Rodney were involved with Farmington Swim Team, the Merchant's Summer Baseball program and many school organizations. Christine was a majorette and played basketball. Rodney was on the wrestling, golf and football teams.

Sandra taught business education classes at MAC from January 1976, until her planned retirement in 2000.

Danny continues operating Total Electric. Rodney graduated from Mineral Area College in 1988, SMSU in 1991, and completed the IBEW Local No. 1 Apprenticeship Program in 1997. He works alongside Danny in the operation of Total Electric. Rodney married Susie Fowler on Nov. 2, 1998. Susie works for the Farmington city government.

Christine graduated from MAC in 1985 and SMU in 1988. She married Bill Robbins March 25, 1989, and they live in Plano, TX, where she is employed by Electronic Data Systems. He works for MCIWorldcom.

In addition to Total Electric, Danny has been involved in several business interests including Kedly, a systems engineering firm, and Pizza Inn restaurants.

Stress relief for Danny is his horses. He has been active in breeding and raising racing stock quarter horses.

Danny's parents, Jesse and Veronica Barton Miller, were raised in the Leadwood area. Danny's great-grandmother was 100 percent Cherokee. When she married his great-grandfather, the family disowned him. That's when the family surname became Miller instead of Mueller.

Sandra's parents were Byron and Rachel Dickson Taylor. Byron Taylor was an M.D. in Flat River for many years and died in 1959. He was from St. Louis. His ancestors included Kit Carson and Robert E. Lee. Rachel was reared in Mississippi. She worked as a RN at Mississippi Lime Company in Ste. Genevieve after Byron's death. In 1977 she married Lothar Fieg.

Sandra has two brothers, Byron and David. Byron married Kay Tripp from Gumbo. They lived in Saudi Arabia for 20 plus years while Byron worked for ARAMCO.

David married Ann Koupal from Flat River. They own and operate Taylor Funeral Service in Farmington. Their two children, Travis and Tracy, are students at Farmington High School.

Danny's sister, Claudia, married Dave Radford from Bonne Terre. They live in Irving, TX. Claudia works for Exxon and Dave is self-employed. Their son, Brian, is a college freshman at College Station, TX.

MILLER - One of Daniel and Anna Miller's sons, William Frederick Miller, married Clara Zimmer in 1869. After they were married, William built a house and barn on 100 acres in the Copenhagen Community. All of William and Clara's 12 children were born in that house. The house is located on what is now called Denman Road. It is still standing but is no longer owned by the Miller family. Family legend passed down through generations was that William traded the farm in 1914 or 1915 for a house in Farmington. The house in town was owned by Sy Denman.

This photo was taken in 1895 of the house built by William Miller in the Copenhagen Community. Family members are from the left: Alfred Miller, Ann (Miller) Nosal, Willie Nosal, Walter Miller, Joe Miller, Elmer Miller, Sam Miller, Clara (Zimmer) Miller, Adam Miller (in wagon), William Miller (on horse) and Kate Miller (on horse)

Yet in January 1896, William wanted more land. He bought 1,000 acres of land eight miles east of Farmington from M.P. Cayce. William and Clara did not live on this land. Instead, two of their sons, Walter and Samuel, lived on the farm. At that time Walter was 14 years old and Sam was only 12 years of age. Many stories have been passed down about this time period in their lives. It is referred to as their bachelor years.

When they first came, they did not have a cook stove. They cooked out in the yard with a dutch oven. They made fresh bread in the dutch oven covered with a lid and set on hot coals and ashes. It was then covered with more hot coals and ashes to bake it. For meat Walter and Sam ate animals they hunted in the woods, mainly rabbit. Their routine was one would cook the meal while the other would walk to Pickle Springs and get two gallons of water. Later they would go to Pickle Springs with a team and wagon to get barrels of water. During this time a log cabin was built, and then another was built a little farther back towards the east. The two cabins were later joined by a dogtrot.

Walter and Sam farmed all of the land they had cleared. In 1901 there was a severe drought. They had feed and corn fodder left over in the barn and corn was in the fields. Shredded corn fodder would go much farther, so they converted the corn in the fields to fodder. They had enough feed to take care of 70 head of cattle over the winter.

In 1904 the two log cabins and dogtrot were enclosed to make a three-room cabin. During that same year, Walter married Annie Roegner. Sam continued to live with them on the farm for 16 years until he married Thelma Hamor in 1920.

Now at the turn of the century, the two children of Walter and Annie Miller, Emilie and William, still live on a piece of that original land bought by William F. Miller. In September 1996 their family farm celebrated its 100th anniversary. The road going back to Emilie and William's home is now named "Miller Lane." Three sons of Sam and Thelma Miller's four children: Charles, A.J. and Earl, made their homes in the Farmington area as well. *Submitted by Jane Miller Robke*

MITCHELL - Jefferson Davis Mitchell, son of John Q. Mitchell and Catherine Day, was born on the family farm near the present town of Leadwood. In 1884 he married Elizabeth Yeargain, daughter of Andrew Patterson Yeargain and Lucinda Westover. This union produced six children: Myra who married J. Ed Swink; Bertha married Taylor Smith; Florence moved to St. Louis and had three sons; Lee was involved in airport management in Tampico, Mexico; Leslie moved to Albuquerque, NM; and Eugene died in Farmington.

Jefferson Davis lived all of his life in St. Francois County, spending the last 23 years in Farmington. He was a machinist in the mining industry and served four years as presiding judge of the County Comissioners Court. At the time of his death he had been superintendent of Farmington City Light, Power and Water Plants for a number of years. J.D. was known to be a public official who could be depended upon to carry on faithfully as he saw his duty.

MONIE - Lewis, Pauline and daughter, Brenda Sue, age 5, moved to Farmington, MO in the spring of 1953 from Fredericktown, MO. They were married in 1946.

Lewis and Pauline Monie

Lewis' parents were Marion Monie, deceased, and Lillie Monie, who is 97. He has two sisters, Viola Myers and Carol Francis. Pauline's parents were the late William and Clara Skaggs. She had two sisters, Jewel, who died in 1982, and a twin sister, Pearline. Two brothers, Everett (deceased in 1988) and Cecil. They were all born in Madison County, MO.

Lewis was working at Gifford Lumber Co. in Farmington, MO as a carpenter when they moved to Farmington, MO. In June 1959 a son, Charles "Chuck," was born into the family. In 1960 they started The Monie Cabinet Shop; in 1969 Lloyd Lamb joined the business and it was renamed Monie and Lamb Custom Cabinets. They were located at 309 East Liberty Street, Farmington, MO. They installed cabinets in Ste. Francois, Madison, Bollinger, Iron, Washington and St. Louis counties. They enjoyed their work and their customers. Pauline helped out in the office.

In 1991 Lewis retired from the cabinet business. He has a shop at their home where he enjoys working with wood. Pauline enjoys working with all kinds of hand work and cooking. They are blessed with a family. Brenda married James "Jim" Caruthers who lives in Vassar, MI and has two sons, Craig and Jason. Jason is married to Kathy Thompson. They all live in Greenville, SC. Charles "Chuck" married Jennifer Crone and they live in Meridian, MS. *Written by Pauline Monie*

MONTGOMERY - Gregory L. Montgomery Sr. was born in Ironton, MO July 6, 1946, son of

Vernon G. and Helen L. (Ellis) Montgomery. The family moved to Farmington in 1949. Gregory attended elementary school at Busiek School and graduated from Farmington High School in 1964. He served in the US Navy from 1965 to 1969 and was stationed on the USS *Forrestal* in which 134 men lost their lives. Gregory was honorably discharged from the Navy in 1969.

He married his high school sweetheart, Brenda Dean Buckley, daughter of Herbert and Clodene (Rhoton) Buckley, also from Farmington, on Nov. 20, 1965. Greg and Brenda became parents of three children: Teresa Sue, Melissa Dawn, and Gregory Lynn Jr.

Gregory Sr. went to work for Southwestern Bell Telephone Co. in 1969, shortly after his honorable discharge from the Navy. He was a member of Libertyville Masonic Lodge where he served as Worshipful Master, 1979-1980. He was also a member of VFW Post 5896 in Farmington, MO.

The Montgomery children were all raised in Farmington and attended school there; however, Teresa Sue graduated from Central High School in 1985 and Gregory Jr. graduated from Central High School in 1991. Melissa graduated from Farmington High School in 1989.

Teresa attended college at Mineral Area College, graduating with an associate of arts degree, then moved to Cape Girardeau, MO where she continued her education at Southeast Missouri State University. In 1990, she graduated with a BS degree in education and began teaching at Farmington High School in the fall. She went on to the University of Missouri in St. Louis in 1993 and graduated in August 1996 with a master's of education in secondary counseling. She is presently employed at Farmington High School as a counselor. Teresa has two children, Kayla Marie, 14 and Ashleigh Nicole, 4.

Melissa attended Mineral Area Regional Medical Center School of Radiology, graduating in 1991. She worked at Perryville Hospital for two years and part-time at Delta Memorial Hospital in Sikeston. She then moved to Chattanooga, TN and attended Nuclear Medicine School in 1993-94. She is currently married to Timothy Postell of Blue Ridge, GA. They have a son, Matthew Gregory, who is 2 years old. Melissa is currently employed at Fannin Regional Hospital in Blue Ridge.

Gregory Jr. is married to Letha Ryals and is currently employed at S.M. and T. Utilities Resources. He and Letha have three daughters: Callie Dawn, 5, Jamie Lynn, 3 and Jessie Sue, 1. They reside in Farmington.

Brenda is employed as a certified nurse's aide at Mineral Area Regional Medical Center. Gregory Sr. passed away May 23, 1998, at Missouri Baptist Hospital following triple by-pass surgery. He was 51 years old.

Brenda, Teresa and the grandchildren attend the Farmington Christian Church, Disciples of Christ.

MONTGOMERY - Mr. and Mrs. Vernon G. Montgomery and young son, Gregory Lynn, moved to Farmington in November 1949 from Ironton, MO. Mr. Montgomery served his country four years during WWII. He married Helen Ellis, who was born and reared in Flat River, MO, on Dec. 16, 1942.

After his discharge from the US Coast Guard in 1945, he worked at The Mountain Echo as a linotype operator. In July 1946 their first child, Gregory Lynn, was born. Mr. Montgomery worked for *The Farmington News*, owned and operated by the Denman family for 30 years. He also worked *at The Farmington Press*, owned by Jess Stewart at the time.

In 1953 and 1956 the Montgomerys became

parents of two daughters, Sheri Sue and Beth Ann. All three of the children went to Busiek School for eight years and on to Farmington High School, and all three graduated from there. Gregory Lynn served in the US Navy during the Vietnam conflict.

Helen and Vernon's 50th wedding anniversary in 1992. L-R: Beth, Vernon, Helen, Sherri and Greg in the middle

He returned to Farmington and made his home there until his death in May 1998. His father, Vernon G., preceded him in death eight months earlier. The Montgomerys loved living in Farmington and were all members of the Libertyville Methodist Church. They were active in their church, the Triple C 4-H Club, PTA members, and both Vernon and Gregory were active members of Libertyville Masonic Lodge, where both served as worshipful master. The Montgomerys have nine grandchildren and six great-grandchildren.

MORANVILLE - Francis George Moranville, grandson of Thomas Moranville and Ella Mae McBride, of Perry County, Anthony Mullersman and Ella Mae Hunold Mullersman, of St. Francois County. Both grandparents were farmers.

Francis, youngest son of George Emmett Moranville and Laura Mullersman Moranville, moved from Ste. Genevieve, MO to Farmington in April 1923. He had two sisters, Pearl and Rita, and two brothers, Paul and Carl.

Francis and Dorothy Moranville, 1991

Mr. Moranville was employed by Esman Blacksmith Shop until 1935 when he opened his own shop on First and Jackson Streets which he operated until his death Feb. 10, 1951. Francis worked in his father's shop as an auto repairman from 1945 until December 1950, when the inhalation of toxic fumes from a welding apparatus caused irreparable optic nerve damage. After some training in 1963 he was employed with the Stand Program for Opportunities for Missouri Blind until he retired in 1980.

On Sept. 30, 1950, Francis married Dorothy Pearl Fowler Turner, widow of Glenn Edward Turner of Bonne Terre, MO. Dorothy, granddaughter of William Davis Fowler and Nancy Pinkston Fowler and John Hunt and Caroline Rickard Hunt. Dorothy was the youngest daughter of Andrew Jackson Fowler and Mary Hunt Fowler.

Dorothy had four sisters: Irene, Bertha, Gertrude and Florence, and two brothers, Willard and Andrew Jr. Mr. Fowler started work for St. Joe Lead Co. in 1891, at age 9, as a water boy. He worked on a number of different jobs with the Lead Co. until he retired in 1948.

The Fowler family lived in the same house in Deslodge from 1920 until May 1957, when the tornado completely destroyed the home. Dorothy retired from Missouri Natural Gas Co. in 1983 after 30 years of service.

MORRIS - John MacCauley "Jack" Morris, of Scottish descent, was born in Louisa, VA Oct. 31, 1838. He fought in the Civil War, including the battles of Appomattox and Chancellorsville, under Gen. "Stonewall" Jackson. He was wounded three times and carried in his shoulder for the rest of his life a bullet received at Gettysburg.

The Morris Family. L-R: Walter Lee Morris, John MacCauley "Jack" Morris, Macy Morris, Molly Perkins, George W. Morris, James C. Morris. Taken about 1897

After the Civil War, he and three Clarkson brothers came to Missouri and started a sawmill in Caledonia. When Eugenia Phillips, born 1851, came from Virginia to visit her mother's relatives, the Clarksons, she met Jack Morris. They were married Dec. 2, 1869. The families established additional sawmills, with adjoining stores, in Annapolis and Des Arc.

Jack and Eugenia Morris had six children: John, died in childhood; George William, born June 10, 1870, died May 10, 1948; James Carson, born Aug. 25, 1875, died July 28, 1957; Munson, died at age 11; Walter Lee, born Feb. 16, 1880, died Nov. 28, 1961; and Macy, born 1884, died 1977. Eugenia died in 1887 when her youngest child, Macy, was three years old. A cousin from Virgina, Molly Perkins, then came to Missouri to help raise the children and remained devoted to Jack, as he was to her, for 30 years until his death.

The Morris Family. Front Row L-R: Frances Irene Morris, Virginia Morris, Eugenia Adele Morris, Howard G. Washburn, James C. Morris. Back Row L-R: Walter Morris, Irene Morris, Mayme Morris, George Morris, Macy Morris Washburn, Molly Perkins, Evelyn Washburn, Jane Washburn - March 16, 1924

Jack Morris retired from the sawmill business in 1900 and moved his family to Farmington, where he and his three surviving sons founded a mercantile store, called Morris Brothers, in a building facing the square at Columbia and North Jefferson. Jack Morris died Dec. 21, 1918, and is buried at Parkview Cemetery. Morris Brothers continued to operate until 1942 and became an institution in Farmington, selling the finest mer-

chandise to citizens from all of St. Francois and adjoining counties, including men and women's clothing, dry goods and furniture.

The three Morris sons all married Farmington residents: George married Mary Isabelle "Mayme" Fitz in 1890. They had four children: Ethel, Virginia, John Munson and Thomas Carson. Grandchildren were John M. Morris Jr. of Rolla and Tom Morris of Kansas City; great-grandchildren include John M. "Jack" Morris III, with the attorney general's office in Jefferson City, and Susan Morris Miller of St. Louis, mother of David and Caroline.

James married Adele Cayce in 1905. He served three terms as mayor of Farmington, April 1947-April 1953. Adele was the organist at the Presbyterian Church for 50 years. They had one daughter, Eugenia, born April 12, 1909. On Dec. 28, 1935, she married Donald McClure, born April 20, 1906 in Farmington, and they resided in Webster Groves. Their daughter, Betty Cayce McClure, was born Sept. 4, 1939. During WWII, while Donald was away in the Army, Eugenia and young Betty lived in Farmington with Eugenia's parents.

Betty married Herbert Salisbury, a Navy officer, on Dec. 28, 1960, and they currently reside near Harrisonburg, VA. Their children are Elizabeth Salisbury Rose of Hammond, LA and Neil Salisbury, of Dallas.

Walter married Irene Nixon in 1910 at the Presbyterian Church. They lived at 321 W. Columbia, the family home of Irene's parents, Harriet and Almarine T. Nixon. Irene was a 1903 graduate of Elmwood Seminary. Walter belonged to the Masonic Lodge. They had one daughter, Frances Irene Morris, born Sept. 6, 1916. She graduated from Farmington High School in 1933, attended Gulf Park College in Gulfport, MS and in 1937 graduated from the University of Missouri, where she joined Kappa Kappa Gamma Sorority. She returned to Gulf Park College to teach math and English. There she met Max H. Koerner, a graduate of M.U.'s School of Journalism. They were married Dec. 11, 1945, at the Presbyterian Church in Farmington and lived in the Kansas City area. On Sept. 23, 1951, they had a daughter, Barbara Irene Koerner (who is called "Irene" after her grandmother). She is a lawyer in Washington, DC. Max died March 16, 1995, and Frances passed away Aug. 27, 1998. They are buried in Parkview Cemetery near Frances' parents.

Macy married Howard G. Washburn, a graduate of the School of Mines at Rolla, and they had two daughters, Jane and Evelyn.

In 1918 they moved to Wallace, ID. Thereafter, their Missouri relatives enjoyed many wonderful visits to Wallace and to the Washburn's summer home on beautiful Coeur d'Alene Lake. Evelyn, a San Francisco resident, died in the early 1970s. Jane married mining engineer, Keith Whiting, and currently resides in Spokane, WA. Their children are Betty Whiting King of Spokane and Richard Whiting of Sevierville, TN.

MOSSMAN - This history begins when George William Mossman was born Dec. 29, 1897, in Bloomfield, MO, the son of Thomas and Cora May (Hester) Mossman. We are told that Cora Hester Mossman was a descendant of the Cherokee Indians. George was one of five children. George came to St. Francois County looking for work as a young man. He met Dorothy Keith Jones and married her Dec. 29, 1923. She was one of the 10 children of William Jeremiah Jones and Maggie Cordelia (White) Jones. George worked at National Lead Company and with the WPA as well as being a painting contractor for many years. He died of cancer in November 1952. Dorothy Jones Mossman was born January 1901 and died

March 1993. Dorothy carried the mail by horse-drawn buggy when she was a young woman. Later in her life she retired from the State Hospital as an aide. George and Dorothy were the parents of seven children.

Back Row Standing (L-R): Floyd Mossman, Audrey Warren, Marilyn Zimmerman, Charles Mossman, Gerald Mossman seated for her 83rd birthday, Dorothy Keith Jones Mossman and Joyce Hoehn

The first-born son was Charles William Mossman, born in September 1924. He married Cynthia Savage and they have three sons: Charles William Jr., Clyde Wesley and Carl Wayne. Charles, Sr. spent some time in World War II. Floyd Milford Mossman was born March 1928 and died March 1994. He was married to Virginia Gramm and they are the parents of two sons, Terri Lynn and Steven Glynn. Floyd died of cancer.

Audrey Marcella Mossman Warren was born Dec. 29, 1929. This was a special day in the lives of George and Dorothy, this being his birthday and their anniversary and the birth of their first daughter. Audrey is married to Ernest Cleo Warren and they have one daughter, Pamela Suzanne. Audrey worked for the Farmington City Light and Water for 32-plus years and saw many changes come and go.

Ernest worked for 43 years at St. Joseph Lead Mines, now named the Doe Run Company. Ernest spent several years in the army during World War II.

The fourth child born was Norma Ruth in October 1931 and died in August 1933. We were told she died of scarlet fever.

Marilyn Norene was born in April 1933. She is married to Charles Edward Zimmerman and they are the parents of three daughters: Karen Gail Munroe, Deborah Kaye O'Shea and Kimberly Diane Leach.

Joyce Nadine was the sixth child, born in August 1935. She married Lee Edward Hoehn and they have two daughters, Robyn Lee Lodholz and Brenda Joyce Raymer. Joyce was associated with the Prudential Insurance Co. for years. Lee Hoehn was a truck driver for a local milk company.

The last Mossman boy, Gerald Wayne, was born in August 1939. He married Rosemary Chandler and they were parents to two boys, Gordon Wayne and Gregory William, and a daughter, Michelle Renee, born in February 1967 and died the same day. Rosie is well known, having worked many years at Medical Arts Clinic. Gerald owns and operates his own big truck, driving many miles a year.

This ends the Mossman history as I know it. Dorothy Mossman kept a record book with names and dates which was a big help as I began to write this, April 15, 1999.

MOUSER - Barbara Weber, daughter of Lawrence and Christine Weber, and Peter Mouser, son of Benjamin Mouser and Mary Grownes Mouser, were residents of Perryville, MO. How their acquaintance began is not known to this writer. In the early census of St. Mary's Township, Peter was listed as a laborer. Barbara was under 18 years, so her father, Lawrence Weber, had to sign papers for the marriage on Nov. 1, 1887.

To this union 14 children were born: Rosie; William, who married Alice Marler and had no children; Ella Leona, Leo Benjamin and Rosie passed away as young children; Florence married Lee Jake Pettus and had no children. Their sixth child, Leona Marie Mouser, married Frederick A. Jaster in 1920 and had four children: Loretta, Evelyn, Thomas and Donald. Agnes married Ed Jaster and had two children, Leroy and Eddie. Lena married Carl Sutterer and had two children, Barbara and Robert. Earl Henry "Dukie," Mabel and Frankie never married. Leon married Dorothy Sumpter and had one child, Janet Counts.

Barbara Weber Mouser

Raging fire destroyed the two-story home of Fred A. Jaster and surviving children: Loretta, Evelyn and Donald, went to live with Peter Mouser family until they married.

This branch of the Mouser family begins when Hans Michael and Agatha Gomminger Mouser came from Ofterdingen, Germany and started the ancestral lineage here in the United States.

In the 1860 census, we find Benjamin Mouser in St. Mary's Township. He and his wife, Mary, had 11 children: Isaac, Sarah, Parlay, Rachael, Henry, Peter, Susan, Amanda Jane, Amelia and Pollyanna.

Leona Marie Mouser Jaster

Peter Mouser was Leona Mouser Jaster's father and grandparent to Fred and Leona Jaster family.

Brothers, Peter and Isaac, migrated to Bonne Terre probably for working opportunities in the lead mines. Writer remembers two of Isaac Mousers sons: Uncle George and William F. Mouser and knew several of their descendants, Ruth Mouser and Virgil Dotson and son, Joe.

Benjamin and Mary lived in the vicinity of Yount where groceries were purchased by the family. Part of the ledger from the store shows the family made purchases.

During the Civil War, Benjamin enlisted in Co. C with Missouri Militia. His son, Isaac, was also enlisted.

Benjamin Mouser is buried in Crossroads Methodist Cemetery, near Yount, MO.

Isaac Mouser family and son, George, are interred in Bonne Terre City Cemetery.

MURDICK - William "Bill" Murdick, Melinda Irene Murdick and their 10-year-old daughter, Nikki Lynn, moved to Farmington in 1957 and settled at 512 West College, where 41 years later they still reside. The land that their home sits on is part of the old David Murphy land grant. Irene is the ggg-granddaughter of Joseph Murphy, the youngest son of Rev. William Murphy and Martha Hodges. After moving to Farmington, Irene said, "I feel as if I have finally come home."

Murdick Family

Bill Murdick is the son of Phillip Sheridan Murdick and Lola Groom Murdick. He was born and reared in Flat River (now Park Hills) and graduated from Flat River High School and Flat River Junior College. He met Irene Hulsey in junior college and after they graduated they were married in 1940. In 1943 Bill was called into service and placed in the Army Postal Unit. He was sent overseas in 1944 and spent 19 months in China, Burma and India, arriving back in the States in May 1946.

Bill and Irene lived in St. Louis for two and a half years. Their daughter, Nikki Lynn, was born in 1947. Bill became very ill in 1948 and spent 13 months in the Veteran's Hospital at Springfield, MO. In July 1950 he accepted a position in the billing department of Missouri Natural Gas Company in Farmington. He later became vice president of operations. When he retired in 1981, he was director of all services and sales for the company.

Growing tired of retirement, Bill got his real estate and brokers license and accepted a position as sales representative with Hulsey Coldwell Banker in 1986, retiring again in 1995.

Bill's father, Phillip Sheridan Murdick, was born and reared in Richwoods, MO, the son of William Joseph Murdick and Sarah Margaret Merseal. Phillip married Lola Ethyl Groom of DeSoto, daughter of George Washington Groom and Mary Jane Hulsey in 1913. Three children were born to them: Floyd in 1914, Virginia in 1916 and Bill in 1918, all born in Flat River, MO. Floyd joined the armed forces in February 1942 and was captured when Corregidor fell in May 1942, spending four and a half years in a Japanese prison camp in Mukden, China. He arrived back home in November 1945 after the war was over. He married Ina Branson of Cuba, MO in June 1947 and one son, Phillip Lee, was born to them in May 1948. Floyd was killed in a car accident the night before Easter near Van Buren, MO in April 1952. Virginia married Monroe Stewart of Flat River, MO. They had two daughters, Sarah Margaret and Marilyn.

William Gano Hulsey and his wife, Nancy Marguerite Blanton, left Washington County, MO in 1887 and followed his father and mother, James Milan and Mary Simmons Hulsey to St. Francois County, settling on a farm near Doe Run. Here Elmer Hulsey, Irene's father, was born. When he was 8-years-old in 1898, his family moved into Doe Run. At 18, he married Melinda Jane Henson, a native of Doe Run, and went to work for St. Joe Lead Company. Three boys were born to them: Luther in 1909, Raymond in 1910 and William Edgar in 1912. Raymond died in 1912. After the mines shut down in 1912, Elmer and Melinda Jane moved to Leadwood in 1913. The two youngest children, Robert Leon and Melinda Irene, were born in 1915 and 1917. In 1920 Elmer was transferred to Elvins where the four children grew up.

Melinda Jane Henson was the daughter of Robert Franklin Henson and Mary Louise Smith. She was the third of 11 children, all of them surviving to adulthood. Mary Louise was the granddaughter of Melinda Murphy, daughter of Joseph Murphy, and one of the first children to be born in the new Murphy's Settlement, later Farmington. Melinda Jane Henson was Melinda Murphy's great-granddaughter.

Nikki Lynn Murdick, daughter of Bill and Irene, graduated from Farmington High School and went on to receive her PHD from the University of Georgia. She married William Richard Craft Jr. of Piedmont, MO in 1967. Two children were born to them, Jason William in 1973 at Columbia, MO and Lynn Christine in 1978 at Farmington. She divorced Richard in 1981. Jason William, now legally William Jason Murdick, married Kelly Maria Sturtevant, June 10, 1996. Christine Lynn is a senior at Fontbonne College, St. Louis, majoring in graphic art. Nikki Lynn is now professor and chair of the Department of Educational Studies at St. Louis University.

All the ancestors of Bill and Irene Murdick came to the American Colonies by the mid-1770s and settled along the eastern seaboard, gradually making their way west as land opened up in their new country. Irene's comment, "Yea, we have a goodly heritage!"

MURPHY - On Dec. 13, 1955, Stanley E. and Conie R., 9th generation to William and Sarah Barton Murphy, were the first children born to E. Lloyd and Norma L. (Cook) Murphy. Fifteen months after the birth of the twins, Cheryl L. was born and Carrie J. Murphy was born in 1960. Later marriages resulted in the birth of Jackie L. Murphy to Lloyd and Shirley Murphy and Brian F. and Teresa A. born to Norma and Frank Pigg.

Dec. 25, 1955 - Front Row L-R: Jean M. Murphy, Diane Coonce, Lydia Murphy, Robert F. Murphy, Norma Murphy, Conie Murphy, Lloyd Murphy, Stan Murphy. 2nd Row: Clarence Pigg, Mattie Murphy, Mary Ann Pigg, Carol Ann Coonce, Clyde Coonce, Lehman Murphy, Anna Marie Coonce, Nellie Best, Helen Pigg, Mary Katie Murphy, Paula Murphy, Jo Ann Murphy

For the first year of the twins' lives, they lived across the field from Lloyd's parents, Lehman F. and Mark K. (Sherlock) Murphy. The twins' grandparents also had a new arrival born six days earlier, their Aunt Paula S. Murphy. The next house down from the brown house lived the twins Great Aunt Jean, Uncle Meredith and second cousins: Danny, Roberta and Pam Keen.

From the beginning, Lloyd and Norma's children were surrounded by family; so, to Conie, Farmington represents family and a wonderful childhood surrounded by people who loved, protected and guided her.

Most weekends, the whole family went to visit either Grandpa and Grandma Murphy or Grandma Lissie (Hurst) Cook. Most of the aunts, uncles and cousins would be there, too, and no one ever got bored. Most of the places the family went were visiting relatives or to the First Baptist Church.

In the early years, the children of Lloyd and Norma remember visiting their Great Grandpa Robert F. and Great Grandma Lydia (Skaggs) Murphy. They would always give their great-grandchildren apples and raisins, and Lydia would thrill the kids by showing them where she had to have her leg amputated from poor circulation. Norma said that Lydia would get a big kick out of it too because the kids would swear in excitement that her stump was growing. The kids' memories of their great-grandpa were that he chewed tobacco and had a can by his chair to spit in. He always had a can of sorghum, butter and bread on the table for a tasty snack.

Front Row L-R: Jeromy D. Leonard, Shawn M. Leonard, Pat Murphy, Debbie and Christopher Murphy, Christina Clubb, Cheryl Perez, Victor Perez, Maryetta Eaton, Jean M. Logan. Second Row: Cindi Reynolds, Timmy Clubb, Dee Medlin, Joshua Medlin, Alice Murphy, Lori Murphy, Mathew Clubb, Polly Murphy, Kara Weems, Amy Eaton, Shannon Zalenski, Laura Murphy, Stan Murphy, Jackie Murphy, Dustin Eaton, Robert Eaton. 3rd Row: Conie Bell, Dennis Weems, Paul Weems, Danny, Jean Kean, Fred Murphy, Mike Murphy, Lloyd Murphy, Angla Pyatt, Clarence Murphy, Sandy Murphy, Stan Murphy, Brian Murphy

Another great-grandparent was Lloyd's Grandma Ida M. (Pinkston) Sherlock who lived outside of Farmington in Sprott until she was in her mid-80s. Ida was a fiercely independent woman. She got her own wood and wouldn't use the electricity in the house because she thought it was wasteful.

Last of all was Norma's grandmother, Nancy (Bequette) Hurst who lived outside Farmington on a farm with her son, Julius Hurst. One of the things Julius raised was popcorn, which he would give to his great nephew and nieces for them to shell and pop. In the early 1900s, Julius worked in Detroit for Ford Motor Co. and saved $1,800 to build a new two-story house on the farm.

Lloyd and Norma's children were taught to put God first, then family, and of course to always do "the right thing." Conie says that this is the most valuable thing her parents gave her and she is grateful for being taught these things, as well as being reared in a community that reinforced these same values.

Conie has lived in Illinois since 1979; but most of the family still lives in Farmington as well as her son, Jeromy D., and her grandson, Shawn Michael Leonard. She visits family as often as possible, but it really isn't often enough to suit her desire to be with family. *Submitted by Conie Ray (Murphy) Bell*

MURPHY - Pat Hardin and her daughter, Cheryl McKelvey, learned years ago that they were direct descendants of Rev. William Murphy and his wife, Sarah Barton Murphy, from Pat's Aunt Jessie (Jessie Murphy Eaves). Aunt Jessie used to talk about her life as a young girl and about growing up at the turn of the century in Bonne Terre, MO on a farm that

Mather Maxwell Murphy

is now a part of Bonne Terre Orchard. Perhaps this is why Cheryl developed such a keen interest in history and the way of life during the 1800s. After listening to stories about long dresses, riding horses, tending gardens and canning foods, a young Cheryl would say, "Boy, Aunt Jessie, I wish I lived back in the 'good ole' days." Aunt Jessie, who passed on in 1984, the last of her immediate family, would chuckle and declare "Honey, these are the good ole days!" Of course Aunt Jessie was referring to the modern conveniences that have made life easier, but she always spoke with such fondness of the simplicity of life back then and the closeness of family, neighbors and friends.

She may not have realized it, but Aunt Jessie also instilled the same pride that she felt in being one of the "Farmington Murphys" into Pat and Cheryl as well. In 1983, Cheryl and her husband, Mark McKelvey, decided to marry at the Farmington Courthouse which stands on property donated by the Murphy family. The Murphy family bond became even stronger when Pat and her husband, Bill Hardin, moved to Farmington in 1992 to property that Pat recently discovered was a part of one of the original Murphy land grants. As Pat and Bill became familiar with the area, they learned of cemeteries where many of the Murphy ancestors were laid to rest. Cheryl lives in Arnold but visits Farmington often and has spent many weekends strolling through these cemeteries comparing names and dates to the "family tree" information that Aunt Jessie passed down to her. A few years ago, Pat and Cheryl discovered that Aunt Jessie's parents, Mather (pictured) and Mary Ann Murphy, were buried in the old Bonne Terre Cemetery directly across Highway 67 from Bonne Terre Orchard. It seems only fitting that this cemetery would overlook the property that was once a part of their farm.

According to Aunt Jessie's documentation, Pat and Cheryl are descendants of the following Murphy line: Rev. William Murphy and Sarah Barton Murphy; David Murphy and Rachel Bacon Murphy; William Murphy and Rhoda George Murphy; Addison Murphy and Mary Ann Megahan Murphy; Mather Maxwell Murphy and Mary Ann Thurman Murphy; Earl Sanderson and Leona Murphy Sanderson (Aunt Jessie's baby sister), William Hardin and Patsy Sanderson Hardin; Mark McKelvey and Cheryl Hardin McKelvey.

Pat and Cheryl are thankful for the precious gift that Aunt Jessie passed down to them, the knowledge of their family's part in Farmington's rich history.

MURPHY - Stan Earl Murphy was born Dec. 13, 1955, the second born twin to Earl Lloyd Murphy and Norma Lee Cook Murphy. Stan and Conie Ray (the first born of the twins) were born at Bonne Terre Hospital. The twin infants were brought home to start life on the Murphy farm, just across the pond from their grandparents, Lehman Fredrick and Mary Kate (Sherlock) Murphy. This was at the junction of Highway D and Murphy Road.

Stan and Vickie Murphy united as one on Sept. 10, 1998

Stan's father, Earl L. Murphy, was an ironworker and helped out part-time at Murphy's Slaughter House on the farm. After a year or two the family moved to Festus to be closer to the bigger jobs.

Two other children were born, Cheryl Lee (now of Richmond, VA) and Carrie Jayne (of Park Hills, MO). After five years in Festus the Murphys wanted to move closer to home and family. They moved to Coffman and settled on the Coffman farm. In 1996 Earl L. bought the Allen farm at Valley Forge on Wolf Creek. The roadbed of the Plank Road from Iron Mountain to Ste. Genevieve is still in use on the Murphy's place. The only remnants of the bridge crossing Wolf Creek are some rusted cables long ago broken and laying on the bank.

In 1972 Stan enlisted in the US Army for five years as a surveyor for special services. During his tour of duty he served in Fort Riley, KS, Korea and Germany. Leaving the service in 1977, Stan was ready to come home.

Early in 1978 Stan started his career with the railroad in St. Louis and commuted daily. The distance and the drive became tedious. In 1979 he bought a house in the suburbs of St. Louis. City life was not to his liking; and after five years, he sold the house and came home.

In 1987 Stan met and married Laura Metcalf. In May 1989 Tyler Earl Murphy was born. In 1990, Stan bought part of the Vandergriff farm 10 miles south of Farmington. The place hadn't been farmed for 50 years, so there was much to do. A house site was chosen, cleared and a road built, a well drilled and a foundation laid. The new road was named Murphy Road South. In 1992 the Murphys moved in. They divorced in 1996 and Stan stayed at the house. In early 1997 he met Vickie Jean Hamman and they were married in September 1998. Today, Stan, Vickie and Tyler still live there. Work is still in progress. A barn is being built and a lake has been started. Plans for a garden have been started and a new fence row has been put in place for future plans to own livestock.

NELSON - Ray Nelson and his wife, Kathie, have lived in Farmington since 1976. Kathie (Katherine Clare Kauffman) is a native of Memphis, TN. Ray attended St. Paul Lutheran School, Farmington High School, and left the area when he attended the University of Missouri. After graduation he served four years in the US Navy where he met his future bride, who was working as a civil servant for the chief of naval technical training at NAS Memphis. Ray is a certified public accountant and partner at Detring & Nelson, P.C. with long-time friend and schoolmate, Terry Detring. Ray and Kathie also have the C Mart convenience stores in Bonne Terre and on Karsch Blvd. in Farmington. They are members of St. Paul Lutheran Church where six generations of the family have attended. Ray's great-great-great-grandfather Karl Frederick Best (also referred to as Charles and Carl in America) was one of the founders of St. Paul Lutheran Church in Farmington.

The couple's two daughters, Anna Christine and Katherine Evelyn "Katie," were born in Memphis, TN. Katie attended St. Paul School and both girls are graduates of FHS. Anna graduated with a degree in psychology from Southeast Missouri University and lives in St. Louis with her son Noah Christian Nelson. Noah was born Oct. 1, 1997. Katie graduated from Bauder School of Design in Texas. She married Mark Wood from Wichita Falls, TX in June 1996 and they reside in Fort Worth.

Ray's father was the late Raymond Leyden Nelson from Bonne Terre, MO. His parents were Rose Young Nelson and R.L. Nelson Sr. Raymond was born in Boone, IA and was the eldest of 11 children. His father worked for the railroad and moved to several locations. Shortly before his marriage to Winnie Gierse, Raymond joined the US Army and served in the European Theater of WWII and also saw action in the Korean Conflict. After returning from WWII they lived in St. Louis and eventually moved back to Farmington. Raymond worked at Boswell Hardware (now Plummer's How To Hardware) and later went to work for Missouri Natural Gas. He was Southeast District manager of Missouri Natural Gas located in Poplar Bluff at the time of his death in 1980 at the young age of 59 years. While still in Farmington, he was active in Boy Scouts for many years and was bestowed the Silver Beaver Award. Raymond was past president of the Farmington Chamber of Commerce and treasurer of St. Paul Lutheran Church.

Ray Lynn Nelson Family, October 1998. Anna, Noah, Winnie, Ray, KatHie, Katie

Winifred May Gierse, Ray's mother, is the daughter of the late Frederick J. Gierse and Bird Mae Keller. (See Gierse Family). Fred Gierse was the son of Frank and Mathilda Gierse who were the original owners of Frank Gierse Merchant Taylor (later Gierse Cleaners) which served Farmington for over 100 years. Mr. Gierse later became the owner of the cleaners and that ownership was passed on to his son Martin Gierse, Winnie's brother. Winnie was a charter member of GFWC Federated Club and has been an active member of Nancy Weber Garden Club and St. Paul Lutheran Church. *Submitted by Kathie Nelson*

NESBIT - Gerald "Jerry" and wife, Jackie, along with sons, Craig and Jack, moved to Farmington in January 1971 from Sullivan, MO, where Jerry had been employed for four years with Kimberlin Oil Co. The Crabdree Oil Co. became available for purchase and the Nesbits decided to take the plunge. The company was renamed Nesbit Oil Co. and remained so until 1974, when Jerry merged with Huber Oil Co. of Perryville. The new name became Inland Energy, Inc. It soon became evident that a new side business of the oil industry had emerged, namely convenience stores. Jerry quickly remodeled his station at Karsch and Washington into the first duel unit in Farmington.

Jerry was born in Herrington, KS to Roy Authur and Ruby Pearl Whitington Johnson. Roy died of pneumonia when Jerry was but 4 months old, leaving Pearl with three small sons. Four years later she married Charles E. Nesbit, a school superintendent, and two girls were born to this union. Charles adopted the three Johnson brothers. Jerry's maternal ancestors, the Whitingtons, originally came from England.

Jerry graduated with a business degree from CMSU, Warrensburg, MO in 1956, joined the US Naval Cadet Program immediately thereafter, and soon was flying multi-engine planes and helicopters. He studied a year at the Naval Post Graduate School in Monterey, CA, and ended his 10-year career as a lieutenant. During his duty station at Lakehurst, NJ he met and married

Jacquelyn Janet McIntosh of Sullivan, MO, daughter of Jack D. and Lily Budrovich McIntosh, on Sept. 23, 1961. Two sons were born of this marriage, Craig Patrick on Jan. 26, 1963, Lakewood, NJ and Jack McIntosh on June 21, 1965, in Oxnard, CA.

Jerry, Jackie and Jack Nesbit. Susan and Craig Nesbit, Aug. 28, 1997

Jackie attended SMSU in Springfield, MO and was a graduate of Miss Hickey's School for Secretaries in St. Louis. She was working at the US Naval Air Station in Lakehurst, NJ, when she met Jerry. Jackie is a descendent of Madam Chouteau, who with her oldest son, Auguste and Pierre Laclede Ligueste, founded the city of St. Louis. Her paternal great-grandfather, Major Eugene Charles Baugher, served as a legislator from both Jasper and Washington counties. Her maternal grandparents, Vincent and Ivanka Soric' Budrovich were born on Hvar and Brac, tiny islands just off the mainland of Yugoslavia. They migrated to the United States where Vincent worked as a cook at the World's Fair in St. Louis in 1904. He subsequently went into the insurance business.

Both Jerry and Jackie have been active in the community since their arrival in 1971. Jerry was a Lieutenant District Governor of Kiwanis, president of the Farmington Library Board, board member of Mercantile Bank, St. Francois County Republican chairman, member of Session of the Presbyterian Church of Farmington, Chamber of Commerce member, president of Board of Directors of the Presbyterian Home for Children, chairman of the Board of Southeast Community Treatment Center, and board member of L.I.F.E. Jackie has also been a member of the Session of the Presbyterian Church, cub scout leader, 4-H leader, president of the Federated Women's Club, volunteer at Presbyterian Manor, choir member, pianist and advisory board of the Presbyterian Home for Children.

In October 1973, the Nesbits purchased the old Clardy home at the junction of Hwys. 67 and W. They did extensive remodeling inside, and it was the scene of many social and political gatherings. In keeping with the rearing of children, it also became home to an assortment of animals. They sold the home in early 1993.

Craig Nesbit received his BA degree from UMC (Mizzou) in speech and communications. There he met his wife, Susan Marie Jimenez, daughter of Dr. Jose and Marie Kodros Jimenez. They married on Oct. 28, 1989, and two children were born to them, Sierra Jimenez Nesbit on June 24, 1996, and Bryce Weston Nesbit on Oct. 23, 1997. Craig is the owner and operator of the T-Rex Convenience Stores and also the Shell Oil jobber for this area. Susan also graduated from UMC with her BS in nursing and her masters of science in nursing in family nurse practitioning. She's currently working with Dr. Edward Dumontier at the Parkland Health Clinic. She and Craig are avid fossil hunters and collectors.

Jack Nesbit received his BFA degree with emphasis on commercial fashion photography

and painting from Columbia College in Columbia, MO. He resides in Los Angeles, CA, and will receive his master's degree in psychology from Pepperdine University in December 1998. He is working as an intern at Hugh's Space and Electronics in Los Angeles.

NIXON/HOGE - In 1682 William Hoge, son of a prominent family of Musselboro, Scotland came to America as a result of religious persecution under the Stuarts. On the ship called *Caledonia*, he met his future wife, Barbara Hume, who had departed her home in Scotland with her parents. Her father, Sir James Hume, was a knight and baron whose family traced its lineage back to Robert Bruce. James, however, differed with the political powers of the day. He was imprisoned and most of his

Irene Nixon Morris and Frances Morris about 1936

considerable property was confiscated. Through the influence of his brother, he was released on condition of his emigrating to America.

William Hoge lived 90 years. He and Barbara were the parents of nine children. From them, over the centuries, came many descendants who were instrumental in the early history of this country, including leaders in church, state and business. William and Barbara first lived in Pennsylvania, but soon settled on the Opequon branch of the Potomac River in Virginia. Among other contributions, William donated land for the first place of worship in the Valley of Virginia. Several descendants became Presbyterian ministers, including the renowned Rev. Moses Hoge, D.D.

William and Barbara's fourth son, James (b. 1706), was the great-grandfather of Eliza Hoge Brawley (b. March 15, 1813, d. Nov. 11, 1873). Eliza married William P. Nixon, who was born Oct. 1, 1815, in Westmoreland County, England, came to Virginia and North Carolina, served in the Civil War, then moved to Missouri. He died Dec. 2, 1887. They were the parents of Farmington resident, Almarine T. Nixon, who was born March 19, 1848, and died Jan. 26, 1924.

On June 30, 1885, Almarine Nixon married Harriett Elsie "Hattie" McCormick. (See McCormick family history). They were the parents of two children: Harriet Irene "Irene" Nixon, born April 9, 1886, and died Oct. 16, 1947, and Foster Raymond Nixon, born Nov. 27, 1891, and died March 1, 1953. Raymond served in the Navy during WWI and lived most of his adult life in Detroit, MI. Irene Nixon graduated from Elmwood Seminary in Farmington in 1903. She married Farmington resident Walter Lee Morris on June 30, 1910. (See Morris family history). They had one daughter, Frances Irene Morris, born Sept. 6, 1916. Irene Nixon Morris died in 1947, and Walter subsequently married Mabel Summers Morris of Farmington. Walter and Irene Morris are buried in Parkview Cemetery.

NORBACK - The Norbacks moved to the Farmington area in September 1994 to grow and promote their custom-made drapery business. Roger Norback and family lived in St. Louis where he utilized his expertise in the garment industry as a director of operations for the Grove Co. (Thermo Jac Sportswear) as well as a plant manager for Modern Jacket in downtown St. Louis.

After much discussion and thought, he opened a sewing factory in Potosi, making medical sewn products, thousands of dozens of sheets and pillow cases, ladies sportswear, postal jackets for the US Postal Service employees, bags and many other products for the consumer and wholesale markets.

After closing the factory, he opened a fabric store that included quilting fabrics, quilting machines and supplies, sewing machine repair, selling sewing machines and many other aspects of the sewing trade.

As an aside, during the floods of 1993, a friend of his had a factory in the flood plane of St. Mary, MO and as the water was moving in the front door of that factory, he was helping move the equipment out the back door to bring it to Potosi, to help give jobs to the people, as well as keep his friends' business from "drowning" in the floods. To continue, adding draperies seemed a natural extension of the sewn products tradition that his father, Howard G. Norback of Springfield, MO, had started more than 45 years earlier. Quickly, the drapery business took on a new aspect and over 75% of the orders were from the St. Francois country area. It was decided to open a store in Farmington, which was accomplished in 1994. The business thrived but personal challenges to family and other unforeseen problems arose and the business was pared back, but never closed.

Meanwhile the children, Tiffany and Tara, graduated from Farmington High School and went on to college in Springfield, MO at Drury College. Tiffany has chosen the direction of veterinary medicine and Tara in the Hammonds School of Architecture. Roger Norback continued on a deliberate process to remain in the drapery business. In October 1998 he became sole owner of Norback Custom Drapery and has since endeavored, with great success, to increase his business in Farmington and surrounding areas.

Roger truly believes that "Norback to the Future" is certainly here in Farmington, MO.

O'BANNON - My paternal great-grandfather was William Isom O'Bannon born in Madison County, Dec. 31, 1818, and died Nov. 28, 1875. My paternal great-grandmother was Martha Washington Hunt born in St.

Francois County on Sept. 1, 1818, and died April 6, 1906. They were married Nov. 24, 1842. My grandfather, John Frank O'Bannon, was born on their homestead April 8, 1848, and died May 11, 1910. My grandmother, Martha Washington Sloss, was born in Madison County on Nov. 2, 1850, and died Jan. 12, 1928. They were married April 22, 1869. They lived *John Frank O'Bannon Sr., Martha Washington O'Bannon nee Sloss, John Frank O'Bannon Jr. (age 6) and Parkhurst Bainbridge O'Bannon (age 2)*

all their lives on 110 acres purchased from William Isom O'Bannon at the time of their marriage. My father, Parkhurst Bainbridge O'Bannon, was born May 8, 1892, and died April 16, 1955. My mother was Clara Lucille Thomas. She was born in Portland, OR May 26, 1905, and moved to St. Francois County in the winter of 1911 and 1912; the family came to Missouri on the train and were snowbound in Denver, CO. My parents were married Nov. 17, 1923. My sister, Martha, was born April 9, 1926, and I was born July 4, 1927. After Grandmother O'Bannon's death, my parents moved back to my father's homeplace and are both interred on the farm. My sister and I still remain

here after my mother's death Jan. 27, 1987.

William Isom O'Bannon homesteaded a section of land in St. Francois County in 1840 and purchased more. After the Civil War he had to sell off land to provide a living for his family, and they lived on cornbread and wild meat until they could make a crop. The northern

Earliest existing photo of J. F. and M.W.O'b? taken after Feb. 23, 1884 (Mary's birth) before March 24, 1886 (Flora's birth). Maggie (Standing), Pattye (J. F.'s lap). Mary (M.W.'s lap), Tressie

army took him to Ironton to stand trial for harboring slaves and giving aid to Sam Hildebrand. Grandmother saddled a horse and went with him. They let him go and they went to Illinois and stayed until after the war was over.

OVERALL - Helen Mae Morrow was born Aug. 2, 1895, in Hebron, IN. On this day the world was blessed with just looking at the little life born, not knowing all she would accomplish in hers.

Nettie Overall, Helen Overall, Lucille LaComb holding Sue LaComb, Leslie Overall, 1945

Helen graduated from Valparaiso University in Indiana in 1916. She and a classmate answered an ad in the paper to go west to teach. In September 1916 they headed on a long journey to Rapid City, first by train, to Chicago; then by stagecoach into South Dakota. On this trip Helen saw the Mississippi River and a rattlesnake for the first time. Creighton was the town with seven students she was to teach; but when she arrived, the school building would not be built for two weeks. Her experiences at this time were new and unforgettable; as she taught, she learned more herself.

In 1917 Helen would go to Chicago to work; as this would be a turning point in her life when meeting Leslie Kinzer Overall. Leslie was in the Navy during WWI and was stationed nearby. He was from DeLassus, MO. The two dated and wrote to each other during the next three years. Aug. 26, 1920, would be another turning point, but this was for all women as they were given the right to vote. Helen voted that year, as all women would, for the president of the US for the first time Nov. 2, 1920. On Nov. 11, 1920, Leslie went to Hebron to make Helen his bride. That day they boarded a train to DeLassus where they made their home next door to his childhood home.

Leslie was a bricklayer by trade and Helen often went with him on jobs. It was while they were on a job in Kansas they had their first daughter, Virginia, born Sept. 3, 1921. Helen stayed at home more often now. On June 10, 1924, their second daughter, Lucille, was born.

Leslie's bricklaying work can still be seen in Farmington today. Leslie was in charge of some projects of Civil Works Administration, such as

the State Hospital fence and the dairy barn, which is the new jail now. He also did brick work on the Memorial Methodist Church, Baptist Church, Children Home, and some houses in Farmington. Leslie passed away Oct. 2, 1970, but his life's work stands strong long after.

Helen kept her hands busy doing one craft or another, especially her crochet. She also was busy in the community, in the clubs she joined and her service in her church. She belonged to the Town and Country Club, Eastern Star since 1917, and Lady's Church Circle. She would donate her crafts she made to the benefit of others in the community. When Helen glanced back through her life, she may have thought she gave up teaching in 1920. Looking at her life, she was teaching all who knew her every day until her passing Aug. 11, 1998. She was a lady with class even then. Helen especially was a teacher to her two daughters, eight grandchildren, 18 great-grandchildren and 17 great-great-grandchildren.

PEACE/FORSHEE - My great-grandfather was John Fletcher Forshee who moved to Missouri from Tennessee sometime after 1851. We know that many of his descendants lived in Farmington part of their lives. These include George Campbell, Mr. and Mrs. J.C. Forshee, and Miss Addie Mae Forshee; as did I in the mid-1970s.

John F. Forshee settled in Washington County, MO with his parents. Around 1870 he married Josephine Polk in Farmington and to this marriage six children were born: Carl Richard, born 1873, died 1951, married Betty Ann

Charles C. Peace and Laura Ellen Forshee Peace

Hill; Laura Ellen, my grandmother, born 1875, died 1912, married Charles C. Peace; Luther Allen, born 1879, died 1932, married Bridgett O'Sullivan; Thomas Lee, born 1882, died 1956, married Allie May Evens; Arthur Milton, born 1887, died 1898, buried in Hopewell Cemetery in Washington County; Ellis Marion, born 1889, died 1956, married Fleta Conroy.

John F. Forshee lived much of his life in St. Francois County before moving to Iowa to live with his eldest son, Carl Richard. John Fletcher Forshee also had two other children by his second wife following the death of Josephine who died in 1890. Their names were Raymond, born 1899, and Walter, born 1901. John Fletcher Forshee died May 20, 1929, in Bonne Terre and is buried in Hopewell Cemetery in Washington County.

My grandmother married Charles Christopher Peace in Flat River where my grandfather was working in the lead mines. By 1905 they had moved to my great-grandfather's farm in Flatwoods in Iron County, MO. Charles Peace was the grandson of Andrew Peace, a circuit rider for the M.E. Church-South in this area. Charles' father, John M. Peace, was a captain in the Confederate Army during the Civil War. Charles' mother, Obedience, was the daughter of Cadmus Lashley. My grandmother died of pneumonia and complications in childbirth of her seventh child, Grace, in January 1912. Baby Grace died soon after. Their six other children were orphaned in August 1913 when Charles Peace was killed when the steam boiler running a saw mill exploded. The children were sent to be reared by the maternal family. The oldest, Gerard Lance, stayed in Iron County area by himself as far as we can determine. Their second child, Harry Ralph Peace, had already died by this time. The girls, Gladys Josephine and Mary Emmaline, along with their younger brother, Willard Fletcher, were sent to live with Grandma's brother, Thomas Lee Forshee, in Festus, MO. My father, Frederick Lee, was sent to live with Carl Richard Forshee, another of Grandma's brothers. My father lived with them until 1926 when he moved to Gary, IN and worked for US Steel for 34 years. On July 4, 1934, he married Edna May Johnson in Granite City, IL. I was born in Gary, IN July 28, 1949. My father passed away in Fredericktown, MO in 1964, and my mother died in Bonne Terre in 1973.

I am married to Russell G. Griffitts and have four children: Lisa, born 1970; Jamie, born 1980, died 1981; David, born 1982; and Vanessa, born 1985. I am very interested in communicating with others that are relatives and their descendants and in just doing genealogy on the Southeast Missouri area. *Submitted by Gloria "Jean" Pearce-Griffitts*

PEEK - Lt. Col. Milton L. Peek retired from the US Air Force in December 1971 and returned to Farmington with his wife, Gerri and six children: Tom, Dan, Debby, Becky, David and Angela. They settled into the home, which they had previously bought in 1966, and named it "Fair Ground on Kinzer." The name derives from its location on the site of the old Farmington fair ground and race track.

Tombstone of William Murphy with DAR Marker located in Murphy Cemetery, Old Fredericktown Road

Although Milton is a native of Alabama and has lived all over the world, he had no problem choosing Farmington as a permanent home. He felt that Farmington was a wonderful town with wonderful people. Gerri was delighted because now she and the children could be near her mother and step-father, Alma and Archie Parks, after years of separation due to military life. Farmington was also very important to her because she was descended from the Murphys who had settled here on Spanish land grants.

Gerri's lineage goes back through two of Rev. William Murphy's sons, William Jr., who fought in the Revolutionary War and is buried in the Murphy Cemetery on old Fredericktown Road, and Rev. William and Sarah Barton's son, David, who donated the land where the Farmington Courthouse stands. William Jr.'s son, John C., married David's daughter, Tobitha. Tobitha Murphy is buried in Calvary Cemetery on Henry Street. Her father, David, and his mother, Sarah Barton Murphy, are buried in the connecting Masonic Cemetery.

John and Tobitha's daughter, Louisa, married Joel Zolman. They are buried on land deeded by Joel Zolman for the Zolman Family Cemetery on Turley Mill Road.

Joel and Louisa's daughter, Margaret, married Alexander Moore. The Moores were Gerri's great-grandparents. Alice Murphy Sturgess, on pages 28 and 29 of her book, *History of Rev. William Murphy and His Descendants 1798-1918*, describes their 50th wedding anniversary celebration on May 12, 1917, at their home, which still

stands on Moore Street. Margaret and Alexander are buried in the Zolman Family Cemetery.

Margaret and Alexander Moore's daughter, Mary Ann "Mollie," married Henry Andrew Mills. For many years they lived in the Moore house. Mollie and Henry Mills, Gerri's grandparents, are also buried in the Zolman Cemetery.

Mollie and Henry Mill's daughter, Alma Lavada, who was Gerri's mother, married James Oscar Ratley. He died and was buried in Los Angeles, CA. Alma was remarried in 1964 to Archie Parks, a Farmingtonian. They are buried in the Zolman Family Cemetery. Milton and Gerri also plan to be buried there. Such an unbroken line of ancestors being born and buried here definitely makes Farmington a special place for the Peek family.

The children have their own reasons for loving Farmington. All attended school here. Tom, Becky, David and Angela graduated from Farmington High School. Dan and Debby's education at Farmington High was cut short by the family's move to London, England, where they graduated from London Central High.

All of the children are now married. Tom married Sheilah Radbourne while the family lived in England. They now reside in Oxfordshire, England near their son, Matthew, and his wife, Victoria Bloomfield. Dan met his wife, Catherine Maberry, in England and later married her while he was a musician with the rock group "America." Debby married Paul AuBuchon, a Farmingtonian, and they have two daughters, Molly and Jane. Becky met and married Dr. Richard Page in St. Louis. They have two daughters, Susannah and Elisabeth. David, who is now a lieutenant in the US Air Force, married Sarah Lund from St. Louis. Angela married a Farmington High School classmate, Robert E. Propes II, and they have two children, Robert E. III and Megan. All of the children still think of Farmington as home. *Submitted by Alma "Gerri" Peek*

PELTY - Samuel and Helena (Haas) Pelty both came from Prussia and lived in St. Louis until they settled in Farmington in the 1870s. Little is known about their early family life, other than they had six children: Bessie, Martha, Pauline, Gustaf, Gertrude (Gertie, as she was known) and Barney. After the early death of Martha, Gertie raised her sister's children, and consequently never married. Gertie, Gustaf and Barney had book stores in

Larry Paul Pelty, Jr., great-grandson of Barney Pelty

Flat River and Farmington. Gertie had the local St. Louis paper distribution business until her death in 1949, at which time her nephew, Herbert Marty, took over the business.

Barney married his childhood sweetheart, Eva Warsing, in 1903. Barney was well known in Farmington and all over the country as a pitcher for the St. Louis Browns baseball club from 1903-12. Barney and Eva had a son, Lawrence Albert Pelty, born July 17, 1906, who later became a well known Farmington High School athlete in the early 1920s. After high school, Lawrence "Bus" attended the University of Missouri Engineering School in Columbia. He married the former Lavina Marie Hampton of Elvins, the daughter of Edward Wade and Daisy Pearl Hampton, in 1929 and went to work for the Missouri Highway Department as a construction engineer. A son, Larry Paul Pelty,

was born June 17, 1931, in Farmington. Lawrence was later employed by the city as an engineer and was responsible for many local construction projects, including the first swimming pool. Their son, Larry, attended the old North Ward and South Ward Elementary Schools and later the W.L. Johns Elementary School.

After war was declared in 1941, Lawrence accepted a position with the US Corps of Engineers and was transferred to Meridian, MS where he was involved in the construction of military air fields in Mississippi and Louisiana. After the war he rejoined private industry and located his family in Maplewood, LA, and later in Houston, TX. His son, Larry, finished high school in Houston, and then attended Rice Institute and the University of Houston where he received his bachelor's and master's degrees. After graduation Larry went to work for Hughes Tool Co. in their Engineering Research Laboratory. In 1954 Larry went into the armed forces and was assigned to a Signal Construction Battalion in Karlsruhe, Germany. Larry was discharged in 1956 and returned to his work with Hughes Tool Co.

In 1960 Larry married Myrtle Lee Eberhardt and was divorced in 1962. He later married Delia Marie Rouse in 1968. Larry and Delia had a son, Larry Paul Pelty Jr., born June 29, 1974.

Larry Sr. was involved in many aspects of the oil drilling tool industry and was awarded a US Patent for a special material used in the manufacture of rock bits. After over 40 years of service he retired in 1994. Larry Jr. attended elementary, middle and high schools in Houston. Upon graduation he was awarded a scholarship to attend the University of Houston. Larry Jr. studied engineering, computer science and psychology at the university. He is presently employed as a manager with a national computer software organization. *Submitted by Larry Paul Pelty*

PETERSON - The first Peterson to settle in the Lead Belt was Victor "Pete" Peterson, son of Mangus and Anna Bryteson Peterson. Pete immigrated to America from Sweden in the early 1900s and married Dora Parmer Peterson. They made their home in Bonne Terre where he worked for St. Joseph Lead Company. Two sons were born, Harry H. Peterson and Carl Franklin Peterson. Anna died on July 1, 1935 and Victor died June 24, 1958 at age 84.

Katelyn, Debbie, Chip, Parks, Harry

Harry H. Peterson made his home in Flat River and married Ethel Burcham Peterson. Three children were born to this union: Harry Lynn, Howard G. "Crockey" and Evangeline Peterson Taylor.

In the early 1920s Harry H. Peterson was the first to bring a beverage called Pepsi Cola, being produced in the Carolinas, to Missouri and the Lead Belt area. Pepsi Cola Bottling Company of Flat River grew and flourished, and locally became synonymous with the name of Peterson.

Harry H. was also a pioneer in air transportation for the area. In 1946 he, along with Fred Auchter and Claud Lovitt, built the first modern airfield in the county, Farmington Airmotive, Inc. The airfield operated as a private corporation until it was disbanded in the mid-1950s. Harry H. died on Feb. 13, 1986.

Both Harry Lynn and Crockey married and made their homes in the county and continued to work in the Pepsi Cola Company. Crockey married Mary Kathryn McLane Peterson and settled in Desloge where their three children, Beth, Chip and A.J. were raised.

Chip Peterson graduated from North County in 1977 and from University of Colorado in Boulder in 1981 with a BS in business administration.

On April 7, 1984 he and Debbie Brown Peterson, daughter of Ron and Sue Brown of Farmington were married. They are the parents of three children: Katelyn, Harry and Parks.

Debbie graduated from Farmington High School in 1977 and, later, from Missouri Baptist School of Nursing with a Nursing degree.

In 1989, after being away for nearly 12 years while working for Pepsi-Cola, the Petersons decided to return to Farmington to raise their family.

Chip took over management of the Flat River Building Center, a business his parents had established, and Debbie worked as a nurse at Farmington Community Hospital.

In 1989 Chip and Joe Burgess also began working on the development of Maple Valley Shopping Center in Farmington, established at the intersection of Highways 67 and 32. Today Maple Valley is a regional shopping center that attracts national franchise businesses as well as local entrepreneurs.

Both Chip and Debbie Peterson are staunch Farmington supporters, heavily involved in the work of their church, Memorial United Methodist, their community, and youth activities.

Chip is an active member and past-president of the Farmington Chamber of Commerce and Dean of Counselors for the American Legion Boys State; has served on the Presbyterian Children's Home Board, the Parkland's Tourism Board, First State Community Bank Board, vice-president of the Farmington Industrial Development Authority and, at present, is a member of the Board of Trustees of Mineral Area College.

For Debbie Peterson the role of parent has first priority, followed by her business activities of overseeing the Farmington Care Center, In-sight Partners (Steak 'N Shake), Maple Valley Car Wash and Kate's. She is an active member of Memorial Methodist Church, a leader for Women of Faith, member of the Federated Woman's Club, Nan Weber Garden Club, and Meals on Wheels.

The Peterson family was named Mr. and Mrs. Country Days in 1997, and served as hosts for Farmington's annual Country Days celebration.

Chip Peterson sums up the philosophy of his close-knit family. "Possessions and job titles go away with time; but family, well, they're always there for you, and I want to be there for them."

PINKLEY - Ancel Eugene Pinkley, wife Lillie Belle and sons, Paul and Jesse, moved to the Farmington area from Bellview, MO in November 1948. Their daughter, Juanita, was married and lived in Bloomsdale, MO.

The Pinkley family began with Michael Pinkley. Michael served in the 7th Maryland Regiment from 1777-1780. He moved to North Carolina, then to Barren County, KY. He and his wife, Elizabeth, had a son, William P. Pinkley. He was born in Kentucky June 9, 1804, and married Mary "Polly" Huckaby in December 1824. William purchased, by land patents, 320 acres during the years 1854-1858. The land was in Madison County, MO when purchased; but when Iron County was established and the county lines were

changed, the land was in Iron County located in the Glover-Hogan area.

William was a farmer and also bought and sold land. He and his wife, Mary, were charter members of Big Creek United Baptist Church, Roselle, MO. William was murdered by bushwackers

Ancel Eugene Pinkley in WWI uniform

who were attempting to rob him. His second wife, Louisa, buried him in an unmarked grave. The exact location is not known, but it is probably on the land now (1995) owned by Asarco. William's son, Jesse A. Pinkley, was born July 25, 1829. He married Susannah Weeks in Tennessee. He served in the Civil War. Jesse died July 19, 1904, and is buried in the Taum Sauk Cemetery near Lesterville, MO.

Jesse and Susanna's son, George Washington Pinkley, was born Aug. 19, 1863, and married Martha Jane Sherrill. Their son, Ancel Eugene Pinkley, was born June 15, 1892. Ancel served in WWI. He married Lillie Belle Conway and had three children: Juanita Pinkley Camden (deceased), Paul Eugene Pinkley and Jesse Allen Pinkley of Farmington. Paul married Doris Jean Mahurin and had three children: Rodger Paul Pinkley (deceased), Paula Jean Pinkley (Mrs. Larry) Gremminger of Desloge, MO and Carolyn June Pinkley (Mrs. Richard) Resinger of Farmington. Jesse married Wilma Faye Archambo and had four children: Charlotte Marie Pinkley (Mrs. Jay) Stewart of Fenton, MO; Randy Alan Pinkley (wife, Beverly Hastings) of Kansas City, MO, Sandra Laverne Pinkley (Mrs. Michael) Gamblin; and Jay Lynn Pinkley (wife, Deborah Foot), both of Farmington.

PLUMMER - Home to Jim (James S.) and Delores Plummer is a late 1800s two-story white house and adjoining 28 acres on the outskirts of Farmington. Although now completely modernized, the original beautiful stairway and matching carved woodwork remain features of this country home. Former owners of the property were Joe Kollmeyer, W.A. Brookshire and John Gegg. Mr. Kollmeyer and Mr. Gegg were dairy farmers, Mr. Brookshire a lawyer.

Jim and Delores Plummer Residence

About 300 yards from this farmhouse is a large, white, well-maintained Dutch-style dairy barn. The barn was built in 1952 by master barn builder, Charles Gerlach of Knob Lick. The original barn on the farm was demolished in a tornado earlier that year. Nearby is Highway H, once a farm-to-market gravel road but now a paved highway used by hundreds of cars, trucks and buses each day. The Plummers are often told by these motorists just how much they enjoy seeing the activities of the farm as they drive into or out

of Farmington. Cattle grazing in the fields, baby calves arriving in the spring and hay making in progress are a delight to the eye to those rushing by. No longer considered a rural area, the farm is now surrounded by homes along Highway H and to the north of Korber Road.

James Plummer family

Jim, the son of Evelyn (Martin) Plummer and Lester Plummer of Knob Lick, and Delores, daughter of Pearl (Bess) Brewen and William J. Brewen of Fredericktown, purchased the farm from John Gegg in 1966 and have reared their three children there. All three recall horseback riding, driving tractors, and playing in the gigantic barn loft. They are Kimberly Plummer Krull, a free lance writer of Kirkwood, MO; Melinda Plummer Marquart, a teacher who lives in Ellisville, MO; and Scott Plummer who now owns and operates the family business, Plummer's Hardware store in downtown Farmington. Two sons-in-law, Chris Krull and Keith Marquart and one daughter-in-law, Tina Plummer, along with six grandchildren: Christopher and Ryan Krull, Matthew and Kellyn Marquart and Dylan and Jackson Plummer, complete the family.

After more than 20 years in the retail hardware and furniture business, Jim and Delores now focus on farm life and travel. Jim also serves on several farm-related boards. Most of the cattle herd is kept on another farm a short distance away on Old Fredericktown Road. Once owned by Delores' aunt and uncle, Stella and Charles Rost, this 185-acre farm includes a large Pennsylvania Bank-style barn built in the 1850s. Both the first floor and the huge loft can be entered at ground level. Hand-hewed sleepers 52-feet long support the main floor and wooden pegs instead of nails were used throughout the barn. According to reports, a crew of 90 men, some mainly supplying muscle power, constructed this massive barn. The barn loft alone can accommodate six hay wagons. Mr. Lewis Hopkins owned the property at that time. In 1941 the farm was sold by the Hopkins family to Mr. and Mrs. Rost, who operated a dairy farm. The Plummers purchased the farm in 1978. At one time this land was granted to the William Murphy family before the Louisiana Purchase. The Murphy family were the founders of Farmington. On the farm property and alongside what is now called Old Fredericktown Road is a small fenced-in burial plot where some members of the Murphy family are buried.

POGUE - Brian Keith Pogue was born April 16, 1967, in Rolla, MO, and was the second of three children born to Jerry and Mary (Schramm) Pogue. Brian's father worked as a civil engineer for Continental Oil Company and Brian lived in Missouri (3 times), Oklahoma (2 times), Minnesota, Louisiana (2 times) and Arkansas.

He graduated from Lake Hamilton High School in Hot Springs, AR in May 1985 and Garland County Community College in Hot Springs in May 1989 and from University of Arkansas in Little Rock in May 1992, with a degree in criminal justice. Brian married Michelle Lynn Flowers, born

Sept. 25, 1961, to Sylvester Flowers and Margaret (Flowers) Leonard. Brian and Michelle were married in Farmington Oct. 8, 1994. Michelle graduated from Poplar Bluff High School and then Southeast Missouri State University with a master's degree in psychological counseling. They both work for the Missouri Department of Corrections and live in Farmington. They were blessed with a son, Spencer Callahan Pogue,

Brian, Michelle and Spencer Pogue

born April 23, 1998. They enjoy their family, friends, church and traveling. Brian, being a Pogue, enjoys fishing and hunting.

POGUE - Eugene Clayborn Pogue, born Oct. 31, 1916, was the first of eight children born to Felix Pogue and Laura (Sikes) Pogue. Eugene grew up farming and working timber in Madison and St. Francois Counties. He went to C.C.C. Camp in Troy, MO, December 1932 for six months.

Eugene and Larna Pogue, Pogue's Store, 1947

On Dec. 24, 1936, Eugene married Larna Lillian Hicks, born April 16, 1916, the daughter of William "Bert" Hicks and Stella (Isabel) Hicks. They opened a grocery store and gas station in 1937 on the north side of Farmington on old Highway 67 (presently Weber Road). Larna also worked at the hat factory in Elvins. Patty Jean Pogue was born Oct. 20, 1937. They sold their business in 1941 to Larna's parents, "Bert" and Stella Hicks. They moved to Flat River where Eugene worked in the shoe factory. Jerry Gale Pogue was born Feb. 16, 1943. Eugene joined the Merchant Marines in 1944.

Eugene and Larna Pogue

Late 1945 they built Pogue's Grocery at 910 West Liberty Street, a two-story building with a residence above the store and full basement. Most customers put their groceries on a bill and paid for them on payday. Some phoned their orders in and had their groceries delivered. After nine years they sold the business to Eugene's parents, Felix and Laura Pogue in 1945. They moved to an 81-

acre farm located 1.5 miles west of Farmington on Bray Road. They farmed and Eugene also worked at St. Joe Mines. Larna worked various times for Felix Pogue's Grocery, Melvin William's Grocery and Woody Hibbit's Grocery.

Eugene graduated from Molar Barber College in 1960 and worked with his brother-in-law, Jim Koen, who owned the OK Barber Shop in Farmington. Eugene purchased the OK Barber Shop. His son, Jerry, and son-in-law, Tom Hampton, worked as barbers with Eugene. There are about 20 barbers in the family. Larna worked in the Farmington Middle School Cafeteria. Mid-1960s Eugene and Larna tore down their barn and installed nine rental mobile homes and operated Pogue's Rentals. Eugene retired from barbering in 1978 and Larna retired from the Farmington School District in 1980.

They moved to Hot Springs, AR in May 1980 on Lake Hamilton where they managed an RV and mobile home park for their son, Jerry. They met lots of new friends and Eugene fished most everyday. They moved back to Farmington in 1990 and enjoy good health and many friends and relatives. Eugene spent a great deal of his life hunting, fishing and gardening as most Pogues do! He's been a Mason for nearly 50 years. Larna is an excellent cook, which is a well-known fact by many! They have been members at First Baptist Church of Farmington since 1945.

They have two children, five grandchildren and 10 great-grandchildren. Their daughter, Patty, married Tom Hampton and has a daughter and son, Jeanna Hennrich and Eric, and five grandchildren: Seth, Levi and Kate Hennrich and Jordan and Abigail Hampton. Their son, Jerry married Mary Schramm and has three children: Bradley, Brian and Stephanie; and five grandchildren. Bradley's children are Ivy, Taylor, Whitney and Evan and Brian has a son, Spencer.

POGUE - Jerry Gale Pogue was born Feb. 16, 1943, in Flat River to Eugene Clayborn Pogue and Larna Lillian (Hicks) Pogue. Jerry's parents owned Pogue's Grocery at 910 West Liberty Street in Farmington from 1945 until 1954 when the family moved to a farm 1.5 miles west of town on Bray Road where they farmed for a living. After high school Jerry went to Molar Barber College and barbered to pay his

Jerry and Mary Pogue

way through college. He graduated from Flat River Junior College in January 1964.

Dec. 30, 1963, Jerry married Mary Doretta Schramm, born Aug. 18, 1943, the daughter of Herbert Henry Schramm and Cecelia Elizabeth (Giessing) Schramm. Jerry and Mary both grew up and attended school in Farmington, MO. They went to kindergarten together and were high school sweethearts. They moved to Rolla in January 1964. Jerry graduated from Missouri School of Mines in January 1968 with a BS degree in civil engineering. Mary graduated from Lutheran School of Nursing in 1965 and is a registered nurse. Jerry worked for Continental Oil Company from 1968 to 1980 as a construction project manager and they lived in Oklahoma (twice), Minnesota, and Louisiana (twice), doing major construction projects. They moved to Farmington in 1970 and Jerry was the city engineer, building inspector, and planning and zoning commissioner for a little over a year before accepting an offer from

Continental Oil Company to return to his previous job.

In 1980 they made a big career change and moved to Hot Springs, AR where they purchased a RV and mobile home park on Lake Hamilton. Jerry's parents moved from Farmington, MO to Hot Springs and managed the RV and mobile home park. Jerry also opened Best Mobile Homes, a manufactured home sales center. He served for a number of years on the Arkansas Mobile Home Association board of directors and was appointed by the governor of Arkansas to serve on the Arkansas Mobile Home Commission.

They live on Lake Hamilton and enjoy lake living and fishing. Both businesses were sold in 1990. Mary works at National Park Medical Center as emergency room charge nurse. She has worked in emergency nursing most all of her nursing career. Mary enjoys needlework and crafts. They enjoy trips on their Goldwing motorcycle. Jerry loves music and plays several instruments, including guitar and trumpet. He plays trumpet in the Hot Springs Community Band and is on the board of directors. They are active in the First Baptist Church of Hot Springs where Jerry is deacon.

Jerry and Mary have three children: Bradley Dale, Brian Keith and Stephanie Dawn; and five grandchildren: Bradley and Gwen (Dees) Pogue and their children, Ivy, Taylor, Whitney and Evan, live in Sulphur, LA; Brian and Michelle (Flowers) Pogue and their son, Spencer, live in Farmington; and Stephanie (Pogue) Graves and her husband, Victor, live in Hot Springs, AR.

Jerry has extensive genealogy information on his family lines and associated family lines that include Pogue, Sikes, Hicks, Isabel, Wilson, Hibbits, Bennett, Brown, Wagganer, Tesreau, Howell, Johnson, Johnston, Hopkins, Jordan, Kirk, Matthews, McNail, Williams, Wright and Ross. On Mary's side he has Schramm, Giessing, Oberbeck, Reuter and Vollath. Please send your related family information or request for information to Jerry Pogue, 110 Silverwood Point, Hot Springs, AR. *Submitted by Jerry J. Pogue.*

POGUE - Joseph Pogue and Elizabeth Marthy (Duncan) Pogue had five sons. Lewis Zachariah Pogue was their first, born March 19, 1810, in Tennessee. Lewis Zachariah Pogue married Fatence "Fatima" Ross about 1830 in Tennessee.

Felix and Laura Pogue and their seven children. 50th Wedding Anniversary.

She was part Cherokee Indian and a near relative to John Ross who led the Cherokees on the "Trail of Tears." John Lewis Pogue was born in February 1836, the third son of Lewis and "Fatima." Lewis Zachariah Pogue married Louisa Flowers Feb. 11, 1848, and moved his family to Reynolds County, MO Dec. 8, 1856.

John Lewis Pogue married Jemima Delana (Wilson) Pogue Jan. 17, 1859. In 1873 they moved to Mine LaMotte. They had 13 children. Annual family reunions for descendants of John Lewis Pogue are held at Fredericktown City Park the second Saturday in May.

William Addison Pogue was born Dec. 11, 1860, to John and Jemima Pogue. He married Lillie Johnston March 5, 1885, and had 11 children. They lived on a farm at Rock Creek on old Highway 67 (now Highway OO). William was a very ardent hunter and fisherman and spent most of his life working in the woods. Their fourth child, Felix Jasper Pogue, was born April 18, 1895, in Madison County.

Felix Pogue, 1954

On April 18, 1915, Felix Jasper Pogue married Laura Mae Sikes, born Nov. 2, 1899, to Edward Sikes and Emma (Hibbits) Sikes. Felix and Laura had eight children: Eugene, Roy, Verna Mae, Rosabel, Margie, Thelma, Nina and Goldie. They lived on a farm (the old Lashley place) on Rhodes Mountain near Silver Mines from 1927-1936. After being severely injured in a mine accident, they moved to Farmington and bought a house and grocery store at the corner of West Liberty and Alexander Streets. Just before WWII Laura managed a restaurant across from Rice Stix Factory. She later owned a dress shop. Their son, Roy, who was in the US Army, was killed in action in Germany Feb. 27, 1945. They eventually had both sons and all six sons-in-law in the military.

Late 1945 their son, Eugene, and his wife, Larna, built a new Pogue's Grocery at 910 West Liberty; and Felix and Laura sold out and moved to 913 West Liberty Street on an 18-acre farm.

Felix was elected presiding judge of the St. Francois County Court and served from 1950-54. In 1954 Felix and Laura purchased Pogue's Grocery from Eugene and Larna Pogue and operated it for a couple of years, then sold it to Melvin Williams and retired. Felix died Sept. 9, 1969, and Laura died Aug. 15, 1979. Of the seven living children, all but one has celebrated their 50th wedding anniversary. There has not been a divorce in the entire group of eight brothers and sisters, which speaks highly of their Christian upbringing, blessings of a long and productive life is prevalent: Felix lived 74 years, Laura lived 79 years, and their seven children currently range from 66 years to 82 years.

Felix was quite a hunter, fisherman and gardener as you would expect of a Pogue! They were always proud of their family, friends and church (First Baptist Church).

POWELL - It has been said that if you have lost something and it comes back to you, it is yours forever. This is true for Frank Powell and Opal Berniece Umfleet.

Opal Berniece Umfleet was born July 19, 1919, in Esther, MO. As a young woman, she decided to serve her country. She served in WWII and was a member of the Women's Army Corps (WAC). Francis Herman Powell was born Oct. 4, 1915, in Stanton, MO. He served in the Army during WWII and he drove a tank in the 409th Infantry. Sev-

Frank and Opal Berniece Powell, 25th anniversary, 1973.

eral years after the war was over, Frank and Berniece met again, dated and married Nov. 8, 1948. Frank worked at Local No. 1 with Sach's Electric Company. He was a loyal member of the Masonic Lodge of Doe Run, MO. Berniece stayed at home to raise their children.

Frank and Berniece had two sons and two daughters. They also lost two sons during infancy. They were very proud of Robert Lynn, Frankie Mae, Nancy Berniece and Billy Gene. The family lived in Doe Run, MO, and could be found riding their Missouri Fox Trotter horses. Frank enjoyed working with the horses and finding a good buy at an auction sale. On occasion he would play poker with Billy and his friends in the shed so Berniece wouldn't find out. Frank's pride and joy were the horses and his granddaughters. He would take them to visit friends and family a few times each week. Frank passed away on June 14, 1978, due to heart disease and pneumonia. Berniece then moved to town. She worked at Biltwell Slack Factory and later at Cozean's Funeral Home.

When she was not working, she could be found spending time with her grandchildren. She had 12 grandchildren to spoil. She loved to go out to eat and she made daily trips to Hunt's Dairy Bar for ice cream. She also liked to sew. She would make quilts and baby doll clothes for the unwanted dolls she bought at yard sales. Berniece became ill with cancer in February 1993 and the doctors found more cancer in September. She fought as long as she could and passed away on Feb. 9, 1994.

Frank and Opal Berniece Powell were hard workers, friends to everyone and devoted residents of the Farmington community. *Written by Sandy Shelley and submitted by Nancy Powell Harris.*

POWELL - Lewis Hopkins Powell and Nettie Emma Meyer were married May 28, 1908, in Farmington, MO. Lewis was born Oct. 2, 1877, and Nettie was born Nov. 13, 1877. Both grew up on farms near Farmington. Lewis and Nettie spent their entire married life farming the Powell family farm. It was first homesteaded by Lewis's grandfather, David Powell, who moved his family to Farmington from Pennsylvania. His family came by train as far as Ironton, MO. They walked on to DeLassus where they camped the first night. The next morning they began their walk on to a spot where Wolf Creek and Sand Creek met, becoming one of the first settlers in this area, homesteading 124.6 acres. They chose this spot for the clear fresh water, and they thought the bottoms here were the richest in the area. The land went to the next generation, Basil Powell, Lewis's father, who farmed and cared for the land.

Lewis Powell, Nettie Powell, Lola Powell, Minnie Powell, Martin Powell, Helen Powell, Robert Harry Powell, in front of a house in Farmington, 1940

Nettie's ancestors came from Germany by boat in 1845 and brought a big German copper kettle. Still today Lewis and Nettie's children, grandchildren and great-grandchildren make apple butter in this very kettle every October. Nettie was noted for her wonderful German cooking. Family and friends remember the homemade light bread and German coffee cake. Her cooking was done on a wood stove in a summer kitchen that was separated from the rest of the house. Nettie and Lewis's children remember cold winter mornings running from the rest of the house where their bedrooms were across the front porch to that old summer kitchen for those wonderful German breakfasts.

Lewis was named after Lewis Hopkins, his maternal grandfather, who was born in Pennsylvania in 1815. Lewis Hopkins eventually came to St. Francois County and settled on the Murphy Settlement in 1858. Lewis Hopkins Powell attended the Valley Forge School in his early years. Later he attended Carleton College and was quite a noted pitcher for the Farmington baseball team.

Lewis Powell belonged to the Methodist "Old Rock Church," also called the Northern Church, while Nettie was confirmed at the age of 13 in the Farmington Lutheran Church. Her father, John Conrad Meyer, was one of the first charter signers. In 1940 Nettie also joined the Carleton Methodist Church with Lewis. In 1904 Lewis attended the World's Fair in St. Louis. He gave his children accounts that the Ferris wheel was the tallest in the world. In 1917 Lewis purchased his first car, a Model T Ford, purchased from Carlysle Rozier, called St. Francois County Motors, costing $350.

John Doughty once wrote an account noting that Lewis was his favorite cousin and that Lewis had once managed to save his life when he found himself in deep Wolf Creek water and could not swim. He also described Lewis as a man held in high esteem and a plain man, "As plain as an old shoe." Dr. C.C.C. Shuttler described Lewis Powell as a humble man in his eulogy in 1965.

His children have many fond memories of those "good old days." There was very little money but a very rich life on that farm in the Valley Forge Community. There were swimming holes in the hot summer, berries to pick and sell for money so they could attend the Fourth of July Picnic at Clardy's Grove, maple trees to tap for syrup, tall trees to climb, watermelons to eat from the watermelon patch. They made homemade soap, butchered all their own meat, canned all the family's vegetables from their garden. There was an old log tobacco barn on the farm; tobacco had been grown there in previous generations. They played many games for hours in that old log tobacco barn. Christmas reminiscing brings to mind one memorable Christmas. The tree was decorated and lit with candles. The tree caught fire. The youngest son, Robert Harry, bravely rushed the burning tree out the front door saving their home from tragedy.

Six children were born at home to Nettie and Lewis Powell. Martin Lewis Powell was born June 12, 1909 and delivered by Dr. George Lynn Watkins Sr.; Herbert Alvin was born 1911 but lived only 3 weeks; Lola Elizabeth was born Oct. 30, 1913; Minnie Agnes was born Feb. 10, 1916; Helen Bernice was born Feb. 1, 1918; and Robert Harry was born May 1, 1920. The last five children were delivered by "Old" Dr. Robinson as he was affectionately known. Nettie and Lewis's influence lives on in our community today with several children, grandchildren and great-grandchildren still residing in this community. *Submitted by granddaughter, Shirley Ingebritsen*

POWELL - Martin Lewis Powell was born June 12, 1909, and died March 19, 1980. He was born in St. Francois County on a farm in the Valley Forge community near Wolf Creek. The farm was one of the first farms homesteaded in the area by his great-grandfather, David Anthony Powell, born 1807, died 1845. David Powell came to Missouri from Pennsylvania by railroad. At that time, Valley Forge was one of the largest communities in the area. The community had a flour mill located alongside Wolf Creek.

Gale Martin Powell, Iva (Patterson) Powell, Connie Jean Powell, Martin Lewis Powell, Fern Joy Powell

Martin Powell's grandparents were Basil Anton, born 1833, died 1901, and Mary Agnes (Hopkins) Powell, born 1854, died 1927. They lived on a working farm and had five children: Belle (Wilson), Jennie (Parker), Kate, Clark and Lewis. Lewis Hopkins Powell was born in 1877 and died 1965. He married Nettie Emma Meyer, born 1887, died 1944, on May 28, 1908. Nettie was the daughter of John Conrad, born 1855, died 1940, and Minnie (Hildebrecht) Meyer, born 1863, died 1905. They moved to the farm with his mother after his father passed away. The couple had six children: Martin Lewis, born 1909, died 1980; Herbert Alvin, died in infancy; Lola Elizabeth Ragsdale, born 1913; Minnie Agnes Cowley, born 1916; Helen Bernice Larby, born 1918; and Robert Harry, born 1920. After Mary Agnes's death, Lewis and Nettie continued to live on the farm and raise their children. The children all attended the Valley Forge School and eventually married and settled in the Farmington area.

Martin married Iva Patterson, born 1915, on Nov. 2, 1935. Iva was the daughter of McAnally Andrews, born 1868, died 1957, and Alice (Covington) Patterson, born l872, died 1950. The Patterson family lived on a farm near Bonne Terre, MO. Iva was the 14th of 15 Patterson children. After renting several places in and around Farmington, Martin and Iva purchased their home located on South Washington Street in Farmington where they raised their children. The couple had three children: Connie Jean, born 1939; Gale Martin, born 1941; and Fern Joy, born 1943.

Martin worked at several jobs, including the Giessing Milling Company, before being hired at St. Joe Lead Company in 1942 where he remained until his retirement in 1972. Iva, a skilled seamstress, was hired by the Rice Stix Factory, later known as the Puritan Factory and now known as the Biltwell Factory. Martin and Iva became members of the Methodist Church and attended services at the Rock Church where Iva joined the church choir. The children were baptized and became members of the Methodist Church. All three of their children attended the Farmington Public Schools and graduated from Farmington High School.

Connie married Robert Mackley Smith, son of Robert L. and Glenna (Woodward) Smith of rural Farmington, on Sept. 19, 1959. They relocated to the St. Louis area and had three sons: Robert Wayne, born 1960; Stanley Martin, born 1963; and Alan Christopher, born 1967.

Gale married Grace Glatt, daughter of Oreal and Irma (Kohler) Glatt of Arnold, on Feb. 4, 1967. They live in Arnold, MO and have three children:

Peggy Grace (Mrs. John) Rabun, born 1968; Rodney Gale, born 1970; and Chad Morgan, born 1977. They have one granddaughter, Maura Alyssa Rabun, born Nov. 12, 1997.

Fern married Paul Eugene Smallen, son of Dewey and Pauline (Walker) Smallen of Desloge, on Sept. 7, 1963. They live in Farmington and have two children, Christina Lynn (Mrs. Thomas) Schrautemeier, born 1965, and Eric Eugene, born 1969. They have one grandson, Andrew Thomas Schrautemeier, born Sept. 5, 1998.

POWERS - Corey Powers was born in Torrence, CA in 1956 and spent most of his young life moving with his family to cities across the country as his father was in the computer industry and was frequently transferred with his job. Corey is the second oldest in a family of four children: Pam, Corey, Leslie and Don. When he was a young adult, Corey completed classes at a junior

Emma Christine Powers

college in Kansas City, MO and then set off to gain a lot of life experience by traveling on his own and learning a number of trades including drilling oil wells, laying asphalt, driving an ice cream truck, setting up trade shows for a silk flower and Christmas decoration company, managing a number of people in manufacturing and much more before settling in Independence, MO with his family.

Corey worked with his parents (Buddy and Sylvia Powers) at their tennis club in Blue Springs, MO. Courtside Tennis Center was definitely the center of the Powers' family

Corey, Julie and Ian Powers - January 1998

life, with Corey, his parents and his younger brother, Don, spending most waking moments maintaining courts, giving tennis lessons, conducting tournaments, etc. After many years of tennis, Corey decided to move into the computer industry and keep tennis as a hobby, which he has done for many years.

Julie Ross was born in Fredericktown, MO in 1967 to Douglas and Pamela Ross of Farmington, MO. She is the second oldest in a family of five children: Kevin, Julie, Brad, Scott and Jenifer (See the Doug and Pam Ross family history for more information). Julie attended St. Paul Lutheran School from kindergarten through eighth grade and graduated from Farmington Senior High in 1985. She received her bachelor of arts degree from the University of Missouri in Columbia in 1989 and worked as a public relations intern at Venture Stores, Inc. in O'Fallon, MO. After her internship she moved to Kansas City where she worked for the Home Builders Association of Greater Kansas City. Julie moved to Melbourne, Australia in July 1991 where she worked for a public relations company. She visited many exciting places on the continent, including scuba diving on the Great Barrier Reef. She returned to the United States in September 1992.

Corey and Julie met in March 1993 while

working together at APS Technologies in Kansas City, MO. Corey worked in purchasing and Julie in marketing for this manufacturer and distributor of MacIntosh-compatible computer hard disk drives and peripherals. They fell in love and knew they were meant to be together. During Corey's first visit to Farmington in September 1993, he told Julie he loved the town and would like to live there some day. Julie's response was that she didn't plan to return to Farmington since she was born and raised there. She felt she had had enough of "small town life" and enjoyed living in a larger city.

After Corey and Julie were married in a quaint chapel in Liberty, MO on March 19, 1994, they settled into married life and started thinking about raising a family. Both agreed that they would rather raise children in Farmington than in Kansas City, so they looked into a move. Julie moved to Farmington in January 1995 and started work as the marketing director for First State Community Bank in Farmington (where she is still employed at the time of this writing). Due to the sudden death of Corey's father, Corey's move to Farmington was delayed until that summer so that he could help his family sort out business matters at the tennis club. When the business was organized, Corey moved to Farmington and went to work as the sales administration manager for Little Tikes Commercial Play Systems in July 1995.

The Powers bought their first home on Michigan Street in December 1995; and their first child, Ian Scot Powers, was born Sept. 20, 1996, in Farmington. After leaving Little Tikes in 1997, Corey worked for Prism Consulting Group, LLC, as a computer consultant for nine months, working on a systems management project in New Jersey. When The Molding Company was opened in Farmington's industrial park, Corey went to work for his friend, Carl Dobrzeniecki, as the company's operations manager. (This is where Corey is employed at the time of this writing.)

The Powers' family attends St. Paul Lutheran Church, where all family members were baptized. The family is expected to increase by one in January 1999, and the addition will complete this branch of the Powers' family tree.

The Powers family was blessed with a beautiful baby girl on Friday, Jan. 22, 1999. Emma Christine was born at 4:19 p.m. She weighed 7 lbs. 5 oz. and was 21" long. Her big brother, Ian, thinks she is pretty neat, and he likes to help take care of her.

PROPES - Margaret Marie Propes arrived in Farmington in 1950 from Albion, IL. She was one of eight children. Her mother was Dora Elizabeth Balding and her father was Joel Carban Balding.

Omer Lee Propes was born at River Aux Vaus and lived there until he was 13 years old. Then he moved to Park Hills (Flat River). Margaret Marie and Omer were married Aug. 8, 1958. There were two children, Larry, who is deceased, and Sherry, who lives in Farmington.

Margaret and Omer Propes

There are eight grandchildren and six great-grandchildren.

Omer is one of five children. His father was Fred Propes and his mother was Margaret Alice Propes. Margaret Marie and Omer both worked at State Hospital No. 4 as psychiatric aides.

Margaret worked 28-1/2 years and Omer worked 29 years for the state. We used to take the children to the hospital swimming pool to swim in the summer. Also we took them to see the outdoor movies in the summer time. *Submitted by Margaret Propes*

PULTZ - When Ed Pultz and Wendy Soderlund moved to Farmington during the summer of 1980, they were not entering unfamiliar land. Ed's great-aunt Bessie had spent summers in the late 1800s in what was to become the Cozean House. His aunt Dorothy Ross Reeves and her husband, Melvin, lived in Farmington from 1946 to 1948, he teaching and coaching at Esther, and they attending the Farmington Presbyterian Church. If Ed was going to attend church, it was going to be Presbyterian. His grandfather was a Presbyterian minister, including a pastorate in Jackson, MO, and so were many of his relatives whose roots went back to Virginia (dad's family) and Missouri in the 1800s (mom's family). Wendy's grandparents were from Sweden; the other side came over on the Mayflower.

Ed, Wendy, Matthew and Alison

So Ed and Wendy, along with 21-month-old, Matthew, moved to 414 Boyce Street where they still live. Alison lived her entire childhood in the same home, with the Stanfields on one side and the Kennons on the other, and gardens behind all three houses.

Wilson-Rozier Park provided a nearby spot for recreation and socializing. Matthew discovered one summer that all kinds of people like to play pick-up basketball: Fish, Mormon missionaries, a mom-daughter duo, and the usual guys. Cross-country bicyclists would spend the night there, enabling Wendy to reminisce about her bicycle touring days.

Matthew and Alison attended Truman Elementary School where they had dedicated teachers and parents who were committed to their education. Before coming to Farmington, Ed had taught in a two-room country school. Wendy was an early childhood educator. They volunteered many hours at the school. Computers were new and Wendy liked to promote their creative uses. When Matthew and Alison were in high school, Ed was elected to the school board and became president the year that a new superintendent, David Cramp, was hired. Ed encouraged efforts to include the community and teachers in open dialog about what was best for children. Matthew went on to college at Rutgers University in New Jersey.

Alison motivated her parents to become involved with the formation of Habitat for Humanity of St. Francois County and then went off to Carleton College in Minnesota. This was not the first start-up project that they had been involved in. Ed, Jerry Sullivan and Terry Atherton, along with Bud Norman, started the Parks Department Soccer League in 1990. Wendy, motivated by the women of the Presbyterian Church, began the Southeast Missouri Family Violence Council in 1994.

Throughout the years Ed practiced law, which included helping out Wendy's causes. He

was city prosecuting attorney and then judge for many years. He represented several local businesses, including First State Community Bank and Inland Energy, Inc., and became very involved in estate planning.

If it included young children and families, Wendy was involved, as director of Window Tree Preschool, starting MAC's child care center and early childhood program, starting US Tool Grinding Child Care Center, owning Wonderland Toys & Books, being a parent educator for Parents As Teachers and working for Head Start in various capacities.

RAGLIN - Charles L. Raglin, born 1886, died 1962, was the superintendent of the Doe Run Schools from 1933-47. Charles was the eldest son of John Criddington Raglin, born 1860, died 1933, and Margaret Ellen Reeves Raglin, born 1864, died 1932, of Greenville, MO. His two younger brothers were John, who died in infancy, and Wilburn Jefferson, born 1889, died 1949.

In 1915 Charles married Catherine White, born 1895, died 1960, and moved his family from Madison County to Doe Run in 1933. He was the new superintendent of schools in Doe Run, as well as teaching business classes. They were blessed with three children: Pearl O.E. "Pat" Raglin, born 1917, died 1996; Charles Marcus, born 1928; and Norma Ruth, born 1930. Pat Raglin married Charles William "Bill" Connelly of Ironton. Their only son, Charles William Jr., was born in 1939 and now lives in Illinois. Marcus married Jeanne Robinson of Farmington and they are the parents of four children: Robyn K., born 1957, married Jack Park and has one son, Lucas, born 1977; Rhett Marcus, born 1959, died 1979; Renee, died at birth; and Rand Charles, born 1973. Marcus and Jeanne live in Salem, IL. Ruth married Joe Williamson of Doe Run. They have three children, all of who live in the Farmington area: Dennis Joe, born 1948, married Linda Black of Farmington and they have one daughter, Christa, born 1971, who married Ceth Jordan; Timothy G., born 1951, is now married to Lisa Romines Davis and they have two sons, Nick and Kory; Susan Renee, born 1959, married Richard "Rick" Pothetos and they have three children: Courtnie Kathleen, born 1979; Natalie Ann, born 1984; and Nicholas Joe, born 1988.

Left to Right: Norma Ruth, Charles Marcus, Pearl (Pat). Bottom: Catherine and Charles (taken in 1946)

Charles Raglin spent most of his life teaching school having begun teaching at age 16. Some of his students were older and larger than he. He was educated at Southeast Missouri State in Cape Girardeau and Washington University in St. Louis, teaching in the winter and going to school in summer. Charles had a strong belief that every child was entitled to the very best education possible. He and Catherine encouraged many young people to stay in school. In addition to his 14 years at Doe Run School, Charles taught in Knob Lick, Caledonia, Greenville, Hermann, Crystal City and Mine LaMott.

Catherine Raglin's sister and brother-in-law, Minnie and Marcus Kirkland, were Farmington business owners during the 1930s and 40s. They owned the Ben Franklin Store until 1947. Marcus Kirkland wrote the book, *Early History of Farmington*, in 1965.

Both Charles and Catherine were dedicated to their family and church, Doe Run First Baptist. He was a deacon, superintendent of the Sunday School and taught a Sunday School class. Catherine sang in the choir, was active in W.M.U. and also taught a Sunday School class. The Raglins later purchased 120 acres on AA Highway, off H Highway. Their daughter, Ruth Williamson, and husband, Joe, along with two of their children, have built homes on the original farmland.

RAGSDALE - William Henry Ragsdale and Luvinia Isabella Porter were married on Valentine's Day at Luvinia's home near Mine La Motte, MO. Luvinia was born June 15, 1876, near Mine La Motte, MO, the daughter of John Porter and Mary Ham Porter. William Henry was born to Anthony Ragsdale and Sarah Elizabeth McDowell, Jan. 1, 1875, at Silver Lake, MO, in Perry County. William Henry's parents both passed away only six months apart by the time he was two years of age. His father had come in from working on the farm and found William Henry's sister, Mary, only 4 years old at the time, holding her dying mother in her arms. William

Luvinia Ragsdale and William Henry Ragsdale in front of the Ragsdale Family Farm home, early 1940s

Henry's father sent the two children across cold snowy fields to their nearest neighbor's house. Mary would pull toddling William Henry out of snowy valleys and ditches. William's father never brought the children home again and died himself six months later. This family found a good Catholic family to raise William Henry. He was raised by John May in Perry County. William Henry had to work for his keep and always related to his own children that if Mr. May felt he had not worked enough, he got no evening meal. His sister, Mary, was also nurtured by a Catholic family who encouraged her to become a nun. She became Sister Mary Dominic of the Ursuline sisters in a convent at Kirkwood, MO. William Henry and Mary also had an older brother, David, and a sister, Matilda Emma, who had already married and lived somewhere in Illinois. They were never able to have contact again.

William Henry began working on his own in 1896 when he left Mr. May's farm being 21 years of age. Mr. May gave him a five-dollar bill and a horse and told him to be on his way. He worked for area farmers making his way to Flat River, MO where he got a job with the St. Joe Lead Mines.

After William Henry and Luvinia were married, they lived in a house in the city of Flat River until they moved to the "Old Merriman Place" as it was always known. It was a big brick house on the St. Louis Road outside Farmington across from what is now Park View Cemetery. He continued working for the mines during this time. In 1907 William moved his family to St. Mary's Road between Coffman and Farmington. They rented the farm from Molly Dalton Helber until 1928 when they finally purchased the 172-acre farm paying $6,000. One small part of that farm was actually in St. Genevieve County. Taxes on that part amounted to $3 per year. The rest of the farm was in St. Francois County. This farm was originally homesteaded by the Marks family in the early years.

William Henry and Luvinia took very few trips. In 1904 William Henry attended the World's Fair in St. Louis along with his brother-in-law, Burl Porter, and Dick Eaten. It is thought they were driven by Irvin Eaten. William purchased a cup there inscribed "To Luvinia." In 1924 William Henry bought his first Model T Ford, a touring car, from St. Francois County Motors, owned by Carlysle Rozier in Farmington. It cost $360. In the early 1930s the family went to St. Joseph, MO to visit Luvinia's brother and his family, Uncle Lee Porter. The family ate their first meal away from home in a restaurant in St. Joseph.

Eight children were born to them. They were William Burle, born Dec. 8, 1895; Mami Irene, born Dec. 8, 1895; Bessie Mae, born March 21, 1903; Ada Estelle, born Feb. 17, 1905; Sylvia Ethel, born Feb. 4, 1907; Melvin Emmett, born March 18, 1910; Marvin Lester, born May 11, 1912; Lillian Delorse, born July 18, 1914, and lived only three weeks. *Submitted by Shirley Ingebritsen, granddaughter.*

RAGSDALE/TOWNSHEND

RAGSDALE/TOWNSHEND - William's father was the youngest son of Lord Townshend of Scotland. Their castle is mentioned in "Lady of the Lake" at Loch Lomond. He was responsible for the Townshend Stamp Act before the Revolutionary war. William came from Scotland, settled in Logan County KY, west of Bowling Green, and owned a large plantation. William's widow, Nancy, and eight children lived with his father.

1) Nancy Brown married Thomas Ragsdale. 2) Elizabeth "Lizzie" married Whitney Sebastian and raised family near Libertyville. 3) Harriet R. married James "Jim" Smith and had two sons, Max and Lee. Max lived below Farmington at Cook's Settlement. 4) Lucy married Ely Welker, 13 children lived on Townshend farm at Libertyville, one son was Lee "Pink" Welker near DeLassus. 5) Will was a captain in the Confederate Army. 6) A daughter. 7) A daughter. 8) George, his oldest son was killed serving in the Confederate Army.

Nancy Brown Townshend was born about 1825 in Kentucky. On Dec. 22, 1840, in Robertson County TN, she married Thomas Ragsdale who was born in Kentucky about 1815. They moved to Cook's Settlement, St. Francois County. Nancy's widowed mother was given negroes and some money by her father-in-law. She and her children moved with Thomas and Nancy to Cook's Settlement where she bought land.

Thomas and Nancy had six children. George W., born 1845, was killed in the Civil War; John E., born 1847; Tom M., born 1850, died 1865 from pneumonia; Sarah Elizabeth, born 1853; William, born 1856, had one son, Benny, who never married and died in a Bismarck nursing home; Nancy, known as Aunt Nin, married John Blake and had two sons, Harry and William.

Sarah Elizabeth Ragsdale, known as Lizzy, married John Warren Hill. Warren and Lizzy had one daughter, Nellie May, born Dec. 22, 1873. John Warren died around 1880 of tuberculosis. Lizzy married William Riley Vineyard, Jan. 5, 1882, in Washington County. They had Mattie, Jim, Ovie and Lawrence. Lizzy was buried in Hickory Grove Cemetery, near Bismarck.

RAY

RAY - James Ward Hall Ray "Wardie" was born 1912 in Livingston, TN, the son of Culton Lee and Frances Ray. He died in 1967. James met Alice Louise Dixon, born 1914, at a carnival in May 1930. They rode a Ferris wheel together then did not see each other again till October. They were

married April 5, 1931. Alice was the daughter of James Allen and Etta (Wyatt) Dixon. They lived at various places in Tennessee. They had four children when they first moved to Missouri in 1943. They had a son, David, then moved back to Tennessee. After the birth of their sixth child they moved back to Missouri and made it their home in 1946.

Front Row: Great-granddaughter, Holly Barton, Janet Ragsdale, Alice Ray, Berta Ray Barton, Joy Ray Hall.. Back Row: Leslie Ray, Frances Ray Hardy, Eugene Ray, Nancy Ray Hall and David Ray

Mr. Ray worked at the Wilkerson Handle Mill in Belleview, MO, later becoming employed by the Iron Mountain Mines. Mr. Ray was in a near death accident on March 10, 1956 and was unable to return to work. After months of recuperating, he received a job with the Farmington State Hospital No. 4, as it was known in 1958, as a night watchman. He moved his wife and the five younger children to Farmington. They bought a house at 919 N. Washington St. Mrs. Ray did baby sitting and hand quilted many quilts for people. She had quilting frames and I, Berta, would help her tack the quilt, and we would have hooks in the ceiling with ropes that were tied to the frames. It was let down in the morning and put back up at night. Mrs. Ray also did ironing for several people.

David set pins at the bowling alley that had four lanes in the basement of Long Memorial Hall. The four girls did babysitting, cleaned houses and car-hopped to help with schooling. They all graduated from Farmington High School: David in 1962, Berta in 1964, Nancy in 1966, Janet in 1969 and Joy in 1970.

David married Linda Pierce in March 1971 and has two children, Brian and Teri.

Berta married Gerald Counts in April 1964 and he was killed in an auto accident in June 1964. She later married Vernon Barton. He had two children, Debra (Smith) and Scott. Together they had two children, Tamara and Douglas.

Nancy married Robert Crawford and had two children, Charles and Denise. After a divorce she married Kenneth Kemp. They divorced and she married Joseph Hall and they had a son, Ryan.

Janet married Garry Odle from Portageville, MO and they had two children, Brian and Deanna.

Joy married Daniel J. Snider, ending in divorce. She later married Thomas J. Hall and has a step-daughter, Shelly.

Mrs. Ray still lives on Washington St. It was a great move for the family. There are friends and family coming by daily to have a cup of coffee in her welcoming home. She still babysits, some are second generations, and she still irons. Her older children are: Leslie Willard, born 1932, married Myrtle Maude Gaston; Etta Frances Daphne, born 1935, married Finis Montel Hardy; Iris Marie, born 1937, married August Queen, and died in 1983 with cancer; Wilburn Eugene, born 1940, married Wanda Black and she died in 1981 with leukemia.

Mrs. Ray now has 24 grandchildren, 32 great-grandchildren and one great-great grandchild. Everyone comes home together the Sunday before Christmas.

REVOIR

REVOIR - Henry Revoir, born in 1862 in Hanover, Germany, came to the US in 1881 at age 19. After two years in Cincinnati, he moved to Iron Mountain, MO, where he had friends. Wilhemenia Koerber, born in 1862 in Hanover, Germany, came to the US in 1882, at age 20, to join her brother in Iron Mountain, MO. In 1884 she married Henry Revoir whom she had known since childhood in Germany.

Mr. and Mrs. Henry Revoir and their children. Front Row: Lena Boswell, Henry Revoir, Mrs. Henry Revoir, Dora Schaefer. Second Row: Ella Goetz, Edna Moscher, Frieda Heinze, Ida Opp. Back Row: Edward Revoir, Fred Revoir. Taken about 1917.

They owned a large farm near Doe Run and had four sons and six daughters, including two sets of twins. Two sons, George and Walter, died in infancy. In 1924 they retired from farming and moved to their home on Middle Street in Farmington. Henry then served as street commissioner for the city. They were devout church members and were married for 47 years. They enjoyed croquet games and family gatherings with their children and grandchildren. Henry Revoir passed away in 1948 at age 85 and Mrs. Revoir passed away in 1931 at age 68.

The Revoir children are:

Ida Revoir married Rev. Max Opp, a Methodist minister who served churches in central Missouri and Illinois. They raised two children, Armel Opp, a veteran of WWII, and Eleanor Opp Robinson. Ida died in 1969 at age 83.

Doretta E. "Dora" Revoir married William Schaefer who owned a farm near Farmington for many years. They raised three children: a stepdaughter, Marie Schaefer, Naomi Schaefer Skinner, who served by working at Small Arms Plant in St. Louis during WWII and Herman Schaefer, a veteran of WWII. They were faithful members of St. Paul Lutheran Church. Dora died in 1968 at age 79.

Carolina "Lena" Revoir married Robert L. Boswell who owned Boswell Hardware Store (now Plummer's) in downtown Farmington. They had a son, Raymond, who died in infancy. Lena had three step-children: Robert K. Boswell, Harry Boswell and Hilda Mae Boswell McHenry. They were faithful members of Carleton Methodist Church. She died in 1974 at age 86.

Edward C. Revoir married Ida Selzer and raised one daughter, Bernice Revoir Kurz. Edward was a well-known businessman in Farmington. In the 1920s he and his brother-in-law, John C. Goetz, owned Fischer Mercantile Store (now Minute-Man Press). He later owned the Plymouth and Chrysler dealership for many years. He and his family were active in St. Paul Lutheran Church. He died in 1986 at age 96.

Ella E. Revoir married John C. Goetz, who served in WWI. He was partners with Ed Revoir in Fischer Mercantile and later a salesman for Kraft Foods. They raised two children, Edward Goetz and Anita Goetz Patt. They were active members of Carleton Methodist Church where Ella enjoyed the Quilting Circle. She died in 1985 at age 93.

Fred L. Revoir married Helen McArthur. They raised three children: Curtis Revoir, a WWII veteran, Gladys Revoir Sigman and Mildred Revoir Lange. Fred was a well-liked businessman who owned the Red and White Grocery Store in downtown Farmington for about 20 years. After retiring he was mayor of the city of Farmington. He was very active in St. Paul Lutheran Church and served on the Stewardship Board of the Missouri Synod. He died in 1963 at age 69.

Frieda M. Revoir married William Hinze who owned a cattle farm near Bismarck. She was well known, having worked in the city light and water office in Farmington for a number of years. They were active members in the Bismarck Methodist Church. Frieda died in 1984 at age 85.

Edna W. Revoir worked in the United Bank of Farmington (now Mercantile) before joining the Women's Army Corp during WWII. Following the war she worked at the Bank of St. Louis. She was active in the Methodist Church and enjoyed singing and drama. She married Walter Mascher. Edna died in 1959 at age 56.

Three of the Revoir's grandchildren reside in Farmington. They are Naomi Schaefer Skinner, Herman Schaefer and Anita Goetz Patt.

RICKARD - The Rickards came from Germany in or around 1712, landing at a New York harbor. Some of the early names were Lodowick, George and Adam, but have some dates starting with *Jacob, born 1794. He married in April 1816 to Nancy Olive, born 1794, died 1859. They had five children: *Jacob, Andrew, Joseph, Elizabeth and Lucinda.

*Jacob was born Sept. 2, 1823, Macon County, WV and later moved to Ste. Genevieve County in 1840. On June 10, 1856, he purchased 83.4 acres at the land office at Jackson, MO, and on Oct. 10, 1856, he purchased 124.53 acres. Both papers were signed by the president of the United States, Franklin Pierce. On July 20, 1873, he donated land, "the south half of ground to be held and used for a common burying ground for the

Jasper Bernus and Julia Marie Rickard

neighborhood forever, The northeast quarter to be used for a Baptist church and religious worship and the northwest quarter held and used for grammar school purpose. If the northeast and northwest quarters shall not be needed for church or school purposed, the title shall revert back to first part and their heirs or assigns." Location is currently Little Vine Church and Cemetery, Ste. Genevieve County. Jacob died Jan. 17, 1909, and is buried next to the church. Several Rickards are buried in the Little Vine Church Cemetery. Jacob was married to Sarah Jane Smith, born Jan. 3, 1830, in Indiana. She came to Missouri in 1842 at the age of 12. Jacob and Sarah had 15 children of their own then took a grandchild at 3 days old, when her mother died. Their children were:

1. William Marian, born Dec. 4, 1846, died May 6, 1927, married Martha Grayson.

2. John W., born July 27, 1850, died Dec. 17, 1929, married Clarinda, then Newberger.

3. Jacob Morgan, born July 28, 1850, died July 13, 1917. He wrote music which is recorded in the Library of Congress. He married Emma Turley.

4. Emily, born Dec. 9, 1851, died Aug. 13, 1879, married Thurman.

5. Mary Elizabeth, born Oct. 24, 1853, died Feb. 29, 1860.

6. Richard, born Feb. 12, 1855, died Feb. 26, 1916, married Roxie Starks.

7. Margaret Caroline, born July 27, 1856, died July 12, 1889, married John Hunt.

8. Grafton A., born Feb. 20, 1858, died Jan. 28, 1950, married Mary A. Lalumondier.

9. Robert Richard. born April 13, 1860, died May 17, 1860.

10. Sarah Hester, born June 4, 1861, died Feb. 2, 1938, married Albert Carlson, then J.T. Dennis.

11. Albert, born June 1, 1863, died June 1, 1863.

12. Newton Leonard, born May 25, 1864, died Dec. 7, 1945, married Margaret A. Cunningham.

13. *Jasper Bernus, born May 24, 1866, died Aug. 7, 1956, married Julia Mary Carron, born May 5, 1875, died April 19, 1947. They were married in Bloomsdale, MO; both are buried in New Calvary Cemetery, Farmington, MO. Jasper was a school teacher, farmer and had a general store in Bloomsdale. They moved to Farmington, F Highway, across from Sand Creek Road. They were married Aug. 24, 1904, and spent their honeymoon at the St. Louis World's Fair. They had seven children:

1. Herbert Jasper, born May 26, 1905, died MIA-Army.

2. Mary Ruth, born Oct. 22, 1906, died July 9, 1907.

3. *Harold Bernus, born Dec. 2, 1907, died June 6, 1960, married Gertie Leota Gregory, born April 4, 1912, died May 15, 1988. Their children were: *Mary Ruth, born March 17, 1932, had three children: Leo Stephen Nicholson, Debra Sue Barton Smith and Scott Allen Barton; Esta Lea, born Jan. 29, 1940, had four children: Robyn Lea Stuart Hall, Gregory Marcus Stephens, Darin Dwayne Stephens, Misty Dawn Cissell.

4. Roscoe Lawrence, born Jan. 26, 1911, died Aug. 10, 1974, married Cellie E. Sherlock, born May 2, 1919, died July 23, 1963. Their children: Rose Mary, Joseph, Clara Jean, Dorothy, Ruth, Martha, James, Carolyn, Bernard and Donna Marie.

5. Marie Rose, born April 6, 1912, married Jack Bunson, no children.

6. Leo Jacob, born Aug. 24, 1914, died Nov. 3, 1979, married Raye Hodges, and had one son, Joe. He then married Edna Ratty.

7. Mildred Agnes, born May 16, 1919, married Vernon Ritter, born Nov. 14, 1911, died Sept. 9, 1997. Their children: William E., Vernon F., Richard L., Mary Ann, Lawrence J., Thomas C., Theresa M., Robert L.

14. Lusetta Jane, born April 12, 1871, died Dec. 15, 1962, married F. Emmett Kerlagon, born March 23, 1869, died March 18, 1919.

15. Stephen Edward, born June 18, 1874, died May 23, 1957, married Mary Hughes.

*denotes direct family line

RICKUS - The history of the Rickus family in Farmington began in 1846 when John and Mimone Rickus, accompanied by a son and a daughter, left their native Prussia and sailed from Hesse, Darmstadt, Germany. They arrived in Farmington on August 12. John was a farmer. They were devout Lutheran; their family members are listed in early records of St. Paul Lutheran Church.

In 1848 the son, Charles Frederick, called "Captain," married Mary Shelton who was born in North Carolina. He was 23 and she 21. Mary was the widow of Elijah Stinnett. They purchased a farm just outside Farmington in the Copenhagen community. (See the Cleve history for Charles Frederick's sister, Louisa.) Except for the time he

served with Company F of the 47th Missouri Volunteers during the Civil War, Charles Frederick, a carpenter by trade, and Mary lived their married life on the family farm. Following his death in 1893, Mary received a pension of $4 per month until her death in 1899.

Archie and Eva Rickus, 1928

George, oldest of their five children, was born in 1849. A farmer, he met Elizabeth Martin a year after her arrival in Farmington from Schleswig-Holstein (Prussia) Germany. They married in 1868. Their children, Louise, Jacob, Charles Frederick, Peter, George and Charles Christian, were also born and raised in the Copenhagen community. A son, John, died at age 1.

The youngest, Charles Christian, was born in 1877 and married Elton Elizabeth Hopkins in 1901. She was the daughter of Jeremiah and Margaret Hopkins. Two of his brothers, Peter and Jacob, married two of Elizabeth's sisters, Anna Mary "Mayme" and Pearl. A meatcutter by trade, Charles Christian operated a butcher shop for several years in the 100 block of E. Columbia St. The fact that Elizabeth was one of the 14 children probably explains her ability to include one or several unexpected guests at any meal time; serving them graciously along with her own rather large family, consisting of Archie, Orville "Jerry", Martin, Charles, Lucille, Alma, Agnes and Robert. A daughter, Lulu Pearl, died as an infant. Elizabeth died in 1959, Charles Christian in 1967.

In 1929 Archie (the oldest) married Eva Frances Smith, daughter of Laiben and Clara "Etta" Woods Smith of Ste. Genevieve County. Archie, a gifted musician (both fiddle and guitar) and an expert carpenter, worked in construction as a plasterer and cement finisher. Also, he operated the farm where they raised the children. Eva's many and varied talents included gourmet cooking (her chicken and dumplings and angel food cake have not been successfully duplicated by her family). Archie died at age 49 in 1952. Eighteen years later Eva married William Thomas. She died in 1978.

Archie and Eva's children Kenneth Bryan, Fay Lee and Margie Louise, all live in and near Farmington. Kenny married Donna Sue Zimmer, daughter of Edward and Della Zimmer, in 1954. Following his elementary and high school education in rural and Farmington schools, his employment included St. Joseph Lead Company and work with his uncle, M.W. Rickus, in the plastering business. He was also a member of the Farmington City Police Department. He served with the US Army Military Police in Europe and later in Fort Ord, CA. Kenny and Donna returned to Missouri in 1958 and for several years owned and operated Kenny's, a restaurant and bar on Highway 32 near Farmington. This was a part of the original "Zimmer Pine View Lakes" property, developed by Ed Zimmer in the 1920s. Kenny retired from McKesson Corp. in 1985. For many years Donna was employed in the offices of Edwards and Plumlee Theaters on Harrison St. She is retired from Presbyterian Manor.

Fay Lee moved to California after graduation from Farmington High School. She married Russell Townsend, a native of North Carolina. They have two children. Russ died in 1988. Fay Lee is employed by First State Community Bank and holds a license with Century 21 Real Estate. Rusty Townsend and his daughter, Beverly, live in Rocklin, CA. Shonna and Linnie Adams and their son, Shane, live in Farmington.

Margie graduated from Farmington High. In 1965 she married Tony Botkin, son of Lowell and Choral Botkin. They have two sons. Anthony served six years in the USMC. He is employed by Washington Inventories and lives in Illinois. Nathan works and resides in St. Louis. Margie is employed by Farmington Cablevision. Tony is retired as co-owner of Botkin Lumber Company.

It is noted that obituaries of Rickus family members in the 1800s and early 1900s consistently portray them as "honest and loyal neighbors," faithful to their families, with strong religious convictions. Perhaps these are the character traits perpetuated by many early settlers throughout this community that contributed to the eventual success and growth of Farmington as we know it today. *Submitted by Donna Zimmer Rickus.*

RICKUS - Martin Ward Rickus was born July 17, 1908, in Farmington to Charles Christian and Elton Elizabeth (Hopkins) Rickus. As a child, he attended a one-room school in Copenhagen. In 1929 he drove Mr. and Mrs. Jeff Counts, Marie, Jeff Jr. and Yalette to Pasadena, CA. The trip, including food, lodging, gas and oil, cost $66. They took along food, including a large country ham. At night they stopped and prepared supper, plus their lunch for the next day. This was eaten along the road.

Left to Right, Back Row: Edward, Don, Marie, Martin and Wendell. Marie and Martin's 65th Wedding Anniversary

While in California Martin found employment with a man named Jack Horner as well as work at the Magic Chef Foundry. In May 1930, he received a telegram from Farmington contractor, Milton Menge, offering a job including training, in the plastering trade at 50 cents an hour. On June 2, at age 20, he and Marie Counts, age 17, were married at a Christian Church in Pasadena. They left immediately to return to Farmington, where they still reside. Traveling in a Ford Roadster, the seven-day trip required 110 gallons of gas and 21 quarts of oil. The young couple began housekeeping in a two-room apartment which they rented for $6 a month. Martin "Bus" worked on some of the new colleges in Columbia, MO, returning to Farmington on Friday nights. When the local Farmington Blues had a game on Sunday night at Wilson Rozier Park, he played and was back in Columbia by 7:00 a.m. on Monday.

Bus entered service in the US Army in 1945. Upon his discharge he and Marie purchased the Fred Heck farm near Copenhagen.

An amusing incident occurred while Marie was helping her dad in his campaign for election to a county office. Her job was to hand out cards to the crowd. During an annual Farm Bureau picnic at Clardy Grove, a lady, who was also passing out cards for her husband, told Marie she had run out and asked to share some of Marie's cards. Later, she ran into her husband and remarked that she was so happy he had hired a girl to help them. She had one card left. Upon checking, he discovered it was his opponent's card!

Marie's many jobs included the position of substitute mail carrier in Routes 1 and 2. When an emergency at the post office required her to work Route 4, she completed the day's mail delivery without an error or a wrong turn. In addition to raising three active sons with their many activities, Marie was employed a total of 27 years at the old Rice Stix Factory.

Donald Jerry, the first son, was born in 1933. Following graduation from Copenhagen Elementary and Farmington High School, he attended Pierce College in Canoga Park, CA. There he lived with his uncle, Jeff Counts Jr., where he also learned the trade of the tile setting. After returning to Farmington he worked for Butterfields Florist. Don and Nora Perry were the parents of three children. Cindy Campbell owns a business in New Port Richey, FL; Martin is a captain in the New Port Richey Police Department; and Michael "Tiger" works in construction.

Wendell Frances "Wink" Rickus graduated from Busiek Elementary and Farmington High School. After serving five years in the Air Force, he became a cement mason. He married Jo Ann (Lore) Meyer. Their daughter, Ann, is married to Todd Carolyn. Their son is Richard Rickus. Wink also has two step-sons, Kenny and Tom Meyer. Wink later married Dorothy Jennings. Wink and Dorothy and her son, Kevin, live in Farmington.

Edward Lee Rickus, born in 1943, graduated from Busiek Elementary, Farmington High School, and Arkansas State University in Jonesboro. At the end of the 1998-99 school year, he plans to retire after 33 years of coaching, teaching and school broadcasting. Ed is married to Rosalea Moore, daughter of Henry and Ruth Moore. They reside in Doniphan, MO. Their daughter, Debra, and husband Anthony Robertson, live in Memphis where she manages a sporting goods store. Their son, James, attends Three Rivers College in Poplar Bluff.

In our lifetime we have seen many changes: a new courthouse, the naming of streets, street cars, good churches and new schools. Proud to be a part of this community.

RICKUS - Robert Lewis was the youngest son of Charles Christian and Elizabeth Elton (Hopkins) Rickus, born in Farmington on Oct. 7, 1921. Siblings included Archie Peter, Orville Glenwood "Jerry", Lulu Pearl, Martin Ward (Bus), Elton Lucille (Nienaber), Charles Otto, Minnie Alma (Simms-Burns) and Agnes Kathryn (Curry).

He married Bernice Elizabeth Barnhart and parented three children: Sandra Sue, Robert Lewis II and Marilyn Beth. He worked construction with a career as a plasterer and cement mason after completing a stay in the US Army during WWII, serving in the European Theater. Among some of his final jobs, before retirement in February 1987, were the brick sidewalks in the downtown Farmington district, Highway 67 South concrete double-lane highway between Farmington and Fredericktown and the Farmington Correctional Center. She was a homemaker and worked as a sales clerk at Shennan's Dress Shop on the courthouse square, L&L Fashions and Debbie's Style Shop after the children were raised.

Sandra Sue, born May 16, 1946, married Robert Pratte, resides in St. Peters and has two sons, Brandon Jonlewis, born Jan. 17, 1978, and Jason Robert, born Dec. 22, 1979. She graduated from Farmington High School in 1964 and worked as a key punch operator at Metropolitan School in St. Louis, O'Fallon Technical School for Computer Programming, worked at St. Regis Paper Company for 15 years, and was then employed at Crider Center in St. Charles for 14 years.

Robert Lewis II, born July 7, 1947, gradu-

ated from Farmington High School in 1965 and attended two years at Arkansas State University, Jonesboro. He served in the US Marine Corps from 1968-1970, obtained a BS degree at Southeast Missouri State University, Cape Girardeau. He has been employed as a teacher, basketball and baseball coach at Bismarck High School and then North County School District, Bonne Terre, MO. He married Rhenda Jane Keay and had one daughter, Rhenda Elizabeth (Moore), born Aug. 10, 1972. He has one grandson, Joshua Paul Moore, born April 21, 1995, who resides in Cape Girardeau.

May 1959, Robert Lewis Rickus Family. Back Row: (L to R) Sandra Sue Rickus, Bernice Elizabeth, Robert Lewis Rickus I, Robert Lewis Rickus II. Front Row: Marilyn Beth Rickus

Marilyn Beth, born Aug. 27, 1952, graduated from Farmington High School in 1970 and Mineral Area College in 1972 with an associate business degree. She was employed by the city of Farmington from 1972-81 and served as city clerk and city treasurer among other positions. She married Scott Lee Lawson and had one daughter, Maridee Beth, born Aug. 22, 1983.

Each child attended St. Paul's Lutheran School. Each family member was confirmed into and attended St. Paul's Lutheran Church. Mr. Rickus passed away April 25, 1996.

RION - John D. Rion was one of the county's leading farmers. He was born March 31, 1878, near Knob Lick, MO, the son of Thomas and Frances (Brewen) Rion and a descendant of French immigrants. John lived all of his life in St. Francois County. He and his wife, Maude (Crawford), raised a family of five boys and five girls.

Mr. Rion was one of the areas most progressive farmers. He had the foresight to see the need for many adventures in the county. Early in 1913 he saw the need for a club for young people so his children and others could belong to something worthwhile. This later grew into the club known as the 4-H Clubs. He became chairman of the first Holstein Calf Club that he helped establish in 1917.

The Rion family at that time was living on the old county farm, located seven miles south of Farmington. With his family growing up, he saw the need to bring the family closer to schools and churches so he bought a large farm two miles north of Farmington on what was the St. Louis road.

John D. Rion

On Nov. 24, 1933, he and five other farmers organized the Production Credit Association. They each invested $5. After about three meetings there were 13 men present who owned stock. On Dec. 2, 1933, Rion was present to receive the charter and the P.C.A. was on its way, an organization to help many farmers. Mr. Rion was president of this organization for 27 years until he retired.

In 1913 he, along with several other men, saw the need for a county agent. They asked for and received one. Mr. Rion was instrumental in organizing the Local Livestock Shipping Association which permitted livestock producers the opportunity to group their shipments to St. Louis markets where they received the benefits of competitive markets. He assisted in getting the Farm Bureau Store which the farmers needed to group together and consolidate their purchasing power in buying feed, grain, fertilizer, etc.

Mr. Rion was president of the Federal Land Bank and was the farm appraiser for the bank in several counties for many years. He was active as a committeeman, delegate and inspector for the government farm program beginning in 1917. He was president of the Farm Bureau Organization, on the local Welfare Organization for several years, and served on the school board for 18 years. He was also instrumental, along with other prominent men, in getting the First State Bank established in 1954.

Mr. Rion passed away Dec. 3, 1965.

RION - Born in Farmington, MO on a farm May 20, 1916, John Milborn "Johnny" Rion grew up with brothers and sisters working the land in St. Francois County with father, John D., and mother, Maude R. (Crawford) Rion.

Ann and Johnny Rion

At the age of 12 he bought a guitar for $3 and shortly was playing at schoolhouses, dances and parties throughout the vicinity. He began writing songs in his teens, sending them to St. Louis entertainers. His songs received extensive air play and were heard on radio almost daily and on CBS coast to coast. By the mid-1940s Cowboy Music World honored him in the Cowboy Songwriter's Honor Roll of writers of over 100 songs along with Jimmie Rodgers, Gene Autry, Jimmy Davis and others. During slack periods on his father's farm, he made various appearances on many radio stations including KMOX's Pappy Cheshire's National Champion Hillbillies, the house band for the "Old Fashion Barn Dance," a national radio show. His song, *Hit the Trail and Ride,* became the show's theme. After becoming a member of a group on radio station KWK in St. Louis for a time, he returned to Farmington to work the farm.

May 11, 1940, Johnny married Ann Winer in Ironton, MO, and they had a daughter, Priscilla, in 1942 and a son, Hugh Daniel, in 1946.

During the 1940s Johnny appeared on radio stations KREI and KFMO, and in 1950 was hired by Carson May Stern Furniture Company in St. Louis to produce shows at WIBV, Belleville, IL and KSTL in St. Louis. He stayed with the company and appeared on many other stations for them until 1966. He also was a featured entertainer on TV station Channel 36. From 1950-58, in addition to his radio career and song writing, he operated the Johnny Rion Hillbilly Park which featured top names from the Grand Ole Opry with

locations in Oakawville, Granite City and Chain of Rocks, IL, as well as St. Louis. On Aug. 18, 1956, Farmington's 152nd Homecoming was designated by the Farmington Chamber of Commerce as Johnny Rion Day and a parade with the guest of honor began the day's festivities.

In 1958 he was ordained as an evangelist at the Dongola, MO Baptist Church and tirelessly traveled to any denomination and hundreds of churches, groups and organizations that called him for the remainder of his days. Among the more than 300 songs that he composed, he recorded four albums of hymns, many of which were original. His music was always an integral part of his ministry which he described as "strictly gospel-the plan of salvation."

Besides his own early recordings released on King and ABC Paramount, his New Life Label contained his later recordings. He also had his songs recorded and released by Ernest Tubb, The Wilburn Brothers, Benny Martin, Johnny Lee Wills, Skeets Yaney with the Four Guy's and many others. His recording of a song written by Reverend John Barton, *The Iron Mountain Baby,* was placed in the archives of the Missouri Historical Society and the Country Music Hall of Fame. Another of his compositions, *That Heaven Bound Train,* a tribute to Hank Williams, was also enshrined in the Hall of Fame at Nashville.

Johnny was also an accomplished sculptor and built model homes. He sculpted busts of country stars and all the presidents through Nixon. Several of his Lincoln sculptures were put on display in the Springfield, IL area. His entirely homemade model replica of the home of country music pioneer, Jimmy Rodgers, remains on display in the Jimmy Rodgers Museum in Meridian, MS. His model replica of the Rhyman Auditorium, home of the original Grand Ole Opry, is on display at the Ernest Tubb Record Shop in Nashville, TN.

During the last 10 years of his life, Johnny and his wife hosted a Cowboy Church Radio Program on station KFMO, Park Hills, MO. To perpetuate the program, Ann continues the Sunday morning program with the help of their son, Danny, which features rebroadcasts of programs of Johnny and Ann.

The world lost Johnny Rion when he passed away at his home Dec. 31, 1996. *Submitted by Dan Rion.*

ROBERTSON - William Abner Robertson, born ca. 1817, South Carolina, died Nov. 30, 1903, Perry County, MO. He arrived in Perry County, MO around 1836-38 with his wife, Jane (Erwin) Robertson, born June 9, 1820, died March 13, 1896, and her parents, James and Rosannah (McKirgan) Erwin. They were the parents of 11 children: James Marion, born Aug. 23, 1837; Eliza Jane, born Dec. 12, 1839; John Thomas, born Sept. 5, 1843; Parthenia Ellen, born Jan. 13, 1846, died 1925; Rosannah Ellen, born Nov. 22, 1849, died Aug. 7, 1923; Nancy A.M., born April 22, 1851; William B., born Sept. 22, 1853; Hannah Eveline, born Feb. 26, 1856; George Washington, born March 23, 1858, died Dec. 21, 1934; Francis Edward, born May 4, 1865; and Joshua A., born Aug. 19, 1862.

Jean Claude Moonier, born Jan. 17, 1813, died Nov. 5, 1902, a native of

George, Henrietta Robertson, Claude and Sarethna Robertson

France. He arrived on the ship, *Old England,* which landed at the port of New Orleans on Oct. 29, 1852. The family immediately departed for Perry County, MO. Adelaide (Crozier) Moonier, his first wife and mother to nine of his 22 children, died on arrival in Perry County, MO in November 1852. On July 12, 1863, Jean Claude married Mary Camille Mejalen, born June 18, 1840, died Jan. 16, 1922. They were the parents of 13 children: Mary Henrietta, born April 21, 1864, died Dec. 20, 1950; Jane, born ca. 1866, married Frank Huber; Louise, born ca 1867, married Thomas Goodwin, F.L., born ca. 1868, died before 1922; Rose, born ca. 1870, married Elmer Clymore; Mary, born ca. 1870, married James Carns; Maryann, born ca. 1872, died Nov. 2, 1890; Henry, born 1874; Edward, born March 25, 1876, died May 28, 1960; Emelia, born March 25, 1878, died May 28, 1959, married John Davis; Sophia; Albert, born Dec. 29, 1880, died Dec. 29, 1923; Elizabeth, born May 18, 1886, died Feb. 20, 1911, married Thomas DeClue.

George Washington Robertson and Mary "Henrietta" Moonier were married in Perry County, MO June 3, 1890. Their children were: Dollie, born Oct. 12, 1890, died Dec. 4, 1974, Farmington, MO, married Joel Laws; Dasie Jane, born Jan. 18, 1897, died Dec. 4, 1970, Farmington, MO, married John F. Schafer; Adele, born Jan. 20, 1899, died April 24, 1978; Doshia Eunice, born Dec. 10, 1900, died Jan. 8, 1937, married Frederick Keel; Claude, born June 21, 1905.

George and Henrietta Robertson moved from Perry County, MO to Farmington, MO about 1909 where they remained for the rest of their lives. George Robertson was a carpenter and broom maker. Henrietta was a devoted mother, grandmother and great-grandmother. She was also known for her abilities with a needle and thread. Several of her handmade quilts survive today. They were members of the Methodist Church in Farmington.

George and Henrietta Robertson are buried at Parkview Cemetery, north of Farmington, adjacent to their daughters, Dollie Laws and Adele Robertson, and close to daughters, Dasie Schafer and Doshia Keet. There are now family members that are fifth generation to the Robertsons who still reside in Farmington (see related Schafer and Hastings family histories). *Submitted by John R. Hastings, written by James D. Hastings.*

ROBINSON - William "Bill" Elbert Robinson was born April 11, 1886, son of Elbert H. and Sarah Permelia King Robinson. Sarah was the daughter of Enoch King, whose tombstone stands alone in a cemetery on Buck Mountain Road near Doe Run. The Robinsons came from Kentucky via Arkansas. Elbert's father, also Elbert H. Robinson, and Dianna Thomas were married in Hardin County, KY on April 25, 1835. The 1850 census of Hardin County lists Elbert as a Cooper. The junior Elbert H. taught school in Randolph County, AR, and then ran a drug store and post office in Syenite, MO, near Knob Lick.

Bill grew up when baseball was truly the great American pastime, and baseball games were played whenever young men could get together. He had a reputation for having a good pitching arm. A St. Francois countian, Barney Pelty, was playing with the St. Louis Browns, and he tried to get Bill to try out for the Browns. Elbert, however, was devoutly religious and opposed to playing on Sunday, so Bill never tried out for the big leagues. A rock chip in a granite quarry struck one eye and ended his pitching career. He attended Southeast Missouri State Teachers College at Cape Girardeau, MO, and worked as a telegrapher before he settled on the farm on Cartee Road in Pendleton Township.

Bill married Rosa Ellen Moore of Bismarck on June 29, 1927. Rosie returned to her birthplace Oct. 7, 1895, when her parents rented it from Bill's father. Rosie was first married to Thomas Walter Pritchett, son of James Thomas and Martha Mitchell Pritchett. Rosie and

William Robinson, Rosa Moore

Walter had one son, Ondis Emmanuel Pritchett, and later divorced. Bill and Rosie were the parents of one son, Billie Lynn Robinson. After retirement from farming, Bill and Rosie moved to Farmington. Rosie attended the Christian Church, Bill the Jehovah's Witnesses. Bill died May 14, 1967; Rosie died Sept. 28, 1981, and both sons died in 1997.

Rosie was the daughter of William James and Rebeckah Ann (Crawford) Moore. The family tradition is that William's parents, John Willis and Mary Jane Watson Moore, traveled from Perry County, IL sometime before 1870, intending to go further west. However, Mary Jane was wounded when she accidentally stumbled over a gun when they camped one night. The family decided to turn back to St. Francois County where there were relatives. Mary Jane died of complications from her wound and is buried in a now unmarked grave near that of Enoch King. William, then a teenager, boarded with the King family. His limited education was furthered by tutoring from another boarder, the teacher at King School. Rebeckah was the daughter of James M. Crawford and Isabel Cartee. Isabel's parents, William and Susannah Cartee, came from South Carolina and settled in St. Francois County in the early 1820s. The Crawfords came from Decatur County, IN about 1840, led by James' father, Rev. William E. Crawford, Sr. *Submitted by Joyce Glasgow.*

ROGERS - The Rogers Family (Floyd, Katherine, Dennis and Andrea) located to Farmington in January 1950. Floyd was assistant manager of the A&P (Atlantic and Pacific Tea Company) Grocery on Columbia Street, where Dicus Drug is now situated. At that time there were seven grocery stores in downtown Farmington, six on Columbia (IGA, Piggly-Wiggly, A&P, Klein's, Boring's and Thal's) and one (Kroger's) on Liberty. Columbia Street had four drug stores (Woods, Lewis, City Drug and Laakman's). Parking for automobiles was on both sides of the street and rear of buildings, while horses and wagons parked in the rear only. Farmington had one policeman who patrolled the streets with a nightstick. Some of the local residents will remember Floyd as winning the Abe Lincoln look-alike contest when Farmington celebrated "Homecoming" in Long Park.

Floyd, who was born and raised in Mine La Motte, served three years in the Army, of which two were in the South Pacific during WWII. Katherine, who was born and raised in Flat River, worked for Southwestern Bell immediately after graduating from high school. They married June 29, 1947, and Dennis was born Oct. 3, 1948, followed by Andrea Oct. 6, 1949, both at St. Mary's Hospital of Ironton. They had three more children: Jane, born Nov. 23, 1955; Cindy, born July 19, 1958; and Kenneth, born April 3, 1962. All five graduated from Farmington Public Schools.

Floyd's maternal great-grandfather, Lewis LaBrot, was born in Paris, France in 1822, and, prior to immigrating to America, was a Trappist Monk. The Labrot family responded to his separation from the Catholic Church by burying him in effigy. He traveled up the Mississippi River to settle in Perry County and married Sarah Shoults in 1842. They had 12 children prior to her death, and Lewis remarried in 1854, to Mary Tucker, with whom he had six more children. He served as a physician at Pilot Knob during the Civil War and passed on vividly detailed stories about bloody, riderless horses returning from battle. He traveled from Womack to Pilot Knob by horse, and on one occasion, had to destroy his steed after it was attacked by a panther. Lewis learned much about the use of medicinal herbs, such as ginseng, golden seal, may apple and calamus root, from Cherokee Indians who were discarded as too sick or too old to withstand the Trail of Tears march. He was also a tailor and his large charcoal pressing iron is still in the family.

Floyd Rogers Family, Christmas 1997

Floyd's paternal great-grandfather, Sam Rogers, was born 1814 in Washington County, TN, and was assumed hanged while trying to protect his family from marauders. He had six children, the youngest of whom was Floyd's grandfather, Franklin. In 1874 Franklin married Jane Johnson of White Water, MO. Her father, Henry Johnson, who was born in 1807, stowed away on a ship from Sweden at age 15. His name was Neigloss; but when he arrived in America and was hired on with a riverboat in New Orleans, he was eventually adopted by the captain, whose name was Johnson. Henry married Judy Hahn, from Holland, and they had nine children.

Katherine's grandfather, Phillip Brenton Cocks, was born in 1861 in Roche Cornwall, England, and immigrated to New Jersey in 1888. He met Moriah Matilda Laakso, from Hauskaa Joulna, Finland, where she was born in 1872. She immigrated to America in 1888, where she met and married Phillip Cocks. They settled in Jacksonville, FL, and had five children, one of whom was Katherine's mother, Esther. Katherine's paternal grandfather, Leo Franklin Smith, was born 1874, and married Katherine Frances Allen. They had two children, Genevieve and Emmett, who was Katherine's father. Lee's first wife died, but he remarried Easter Henkle and they had three more children, Jessie, Bessie and Franklin.

Katherine's father, Emmett Smith, retired from the lead mines in Flat River and farmed near Libertyville with his wife, Esther, until his death in 1974. Esther is 96 years of age and resides in a local nursing home.

Floyd's father, also Floyd, retired from the lead mines of Fredericktown and farmed with his wife, Nettie, until his death in 1955. Nettie's death followed in 1979.

As for Floyd and Katherine's children, after four years in the US Air Force and Vietnam service, Dennis graduated from Mineral Area College (MAC), SEMO State University and St. Louis University Graduate School of Social Work. He works for the Department of Veteran's Affairs Medical Center at Jefferson Barracks. His wife, Ree, graduated from SEMO State University and teaches at St. Joseph's Catholic School. Andrea is a graduate of Farmington High School, is married to Don Lohse, an alumni of SEMO State University, and operates her own computerized medical transcription business in Kirkwood. Jane graduated from MAC dental assistant program and earned a dental hygienist degree from Fresno Municipal College in California. She works out of offices in Farmington and Fredericktown. Cindy attended MAC, SEMO and SIU-Edwardsville, IL. She is married to Mark Wichman, who maintains his family's tradition in automobile sales. Cindy manages the Lighthouse Book Store in Farmington. Kenneth also graduated from MAC, as well as College of the Ozarks at Hollister, MO, as did his wife, Jenny. He manages a Wal-Mart Super Center in Springfield, MO, and can occasionally be lured to Farmington by his mother's potato salad.

Floyd retired from 34 years in the grocery business in 1983, and Katherine still has a reputation as one of the best cooks in the area. They stay busy with their children and nine grandchildren.

ROSS - Doug and Pam Ross became residents of the finest small city in the state of Missouri in July 1965, having previously lived two years in Paris, France, while Doug served as a captain in the US Army Dental Corps. They were married July 28, 1962, in St. Louis and lived there during Doug's last year in Washington University School of Dentistry. Pam worked during that time at the Southwestern Bell downtown office as a cashier and teller. While in Europe, they were fortunate to be able to travel to most of the places tourists generally visit. Four months before Doug's tour of duty was to end, their first child, Kevin Douglas, was born March 27, 1965, with dual French/American citizenship.

Christmas 1995; Left to Right: Corey, Ian, Julie Powers, Kevin Ross, Pam Ross, Scott Ross, Jennifer Ross (and Tobeau), Doug Ross and Bradley Ross

Pamela Jayne Berkley was born in St. Louis June 15, 1944, the second child of Robert Wesley Berkley Sr., a salesman, and Jane Elizabeth (Hunt) Berkley, a clothing designer. Pam's brother, Robert Wesley Berkley Jr. is a paving consultant in St. Louis. Pam's family moved to Iron Mountain when she was 3 years old and lived in "Buford Bottoms." Her brother soon became Doug's best friend and both of them teased Pam incessantly, until Doug and Pam developed a wonderful loving relationship in 1961, while Doug was a junior dental student and Pam was a senior at Arcadia Valley High School. Doug proposed in December 1961, and they were married seven months later. Her "career track" was first as a full-time wife and homemaker for three years, then additionally as a full-time mother to eventually five active, lovable, talented, fun and individually challenging children, each one now fully "grown-up" and on their own. She gave of herself as their parent, friend, conscience, teacher, cook, driver, playmate, confessor, spiritual guide, advisor, confidante, mentor and enforcer of rules and responsibilities. She was their role-model and taught them self-discipline, respect and character. Anyone who knows Pam knows she is a very special and unique person, one who always wears her heart in her smile and on her shoulder. Today those talents and qualities spent during the children's maturation process are being guided as a grandmother and full-time wife and housekeeper again. She truly lives for others, has empathy like an angel, sympathy at the correct times and a shoulder for others to lean on whenever one is needed as unselfishly as one can.

Douglas Kent Ross was born in Ironton Dec. 24, 1938, and delivered by his great-uncle, Dr. Frank Gale, of Bismarck. Doug is the only child of Jewel Gale Ross, postmaster, merchant, inventor and movie exhibitor, and Ethel Hortense (Hall) Ross, postal clerk and merchant. Doug learned the "work ethic" early from both parents who worked 11 hours a day, six days a week, and two hours on Sundays in the Ross Store Company in Iron Mountain. While a young boy, Doug stocked shelves; clerked; delivered groceries, fuel, feed and newspapers; ran a yard and cemetery maintenance service; sold lake building lots; painted; worked in a cafeteria, loading dock and butcher shop and operated heavy equipment in a Del Monte packing plant. He also worked as a real estate research assistant for the I-55 planning in south St. Louis; sold household supplies door-to-door, and held various other jobs before settling into the lifetime career of general family practice dentistry in Farmington at 215 East Columbia Street.

Doug has continued his professional dental education by participating in regular post-graduate programs through the Academy of General Dentistry. In 1973 he earned the AGD Fellowship and in 1990 the AGD Mastership. He has served as a volunteer clinical instructor at Washington University School of Dentistry teaching children's dentistry and periodontics, served in leadership positions in many state and national professional organizations and was awarded the "Missouri Dentist of the Year" by the Missouri Dental Association and the American Dental Association's National Children's Dental Health Month first-place recognition award for nationwide programming in 1986.

Civic and public service activities have always been a way of life for Doug, from many committees at St. Paul Lutheran Church to the Farmington Jaycees, to serving as mayor of Farmington from 1971-73. Some major accomplishments as mayor were creation of the Parks and Recreation Department, one-way street at the Post Office for safe access to the drive-up box, the south waste water treatment plant, creation of a Subdivision Ordinance, the Board of Adjustment activated, the Comprehensive Plan updated, and the past practice of the mayor signing "blank checks" was stopped. An "almost accomplishment" was the City being awarded a special US Civil Service City Administrator Grant for all the costs for three years, with the first quarter's funds in the bank. Farmington was the only city in the entire federal region of six states to receive funds for such a program. The Board of Aldermen refused to accept it and voted that the mayor return the money. After leaving office, time was spent with a group of area leaders to develop the Southeast Missouri Transportation System; those vans and buses with "SMTS" emblazoned on their sides are still carrying southeast Missouri region residents over age 55 and others with special qualifying medical concerns every month to medical appointments, shopping for food and clothing and other general needs to get to important places. The current annual statistics are amazing: 260-280,000 passenger trips over 1,600,000 miles with

82 vehicles and 95 employees in driver, maintenance and administrative positions. Most of his time during the late 1990s has been spent working with the Transportation Committee of the Chamber of Commerce and has resulted in the reactivation of the city's request for a southbound ramp on Highway 32 at US 67, originally made when, as mayor, he approached the state highway department and was told it would be done within 10 years (i.e., 1982; now it appears it will be an actual reality by the year 2000. Further activities have led to the activation of the US 67 Highway Corridor Coalition and the formation of the US 67/I-30 Corridor Coalition with the citizen highway coalition in Arkansas. The goal is to promote and lobby for planning, engineering and actual funding to build US 67 from Little Rock to Festus-Crystal City as Interstate 30. The target goal is completion by the year 2015. Doug will be 77 years old; who knows, it could happen, we'll see.

Kevin Douglas, the oldest Ross child, having renounced his French citizenship, graduated from the University of Missouri at Columbia School of Journalism and the University of Southern California in Los Angeles with a masters degree in film-making. He soon embarked on career development in the arts and entertainment business as a film and video editor in Los Angeles. His work can be seen in such films as: *Lawnmower Man, Speed, Mrs. Doubtfire, Fly Away Home, Miracle on 34th Street, Romy and Michele's High School Reunion* and *The Truman Show*.

Julie Christine Ross was born July 4, 1967, in Fredericktown, studied public relations and marketing at the University of Missouri in Columbia, married Corey Scot Powers, manufacturing operations manager, on March 19, 1994, in Liberty, MO. They both had been living and working in Kansas City; but once Corey became familiar with the qualities of life offered by Farmington and that it was a great place to raise children, he convinced Julie to reconsider her telling her parents upon her graduation in Columbia, "I'm never going to live in Farmington." In January 1995 they moved here, becoming openly active and involved in the heart and soul of the community. Ian Scot Powers came along on Sept. 20, 1996 and another child is due January 1999.

Bradley Kent Ross was born in Farmington on Jan. 30, 1970, studied communications and acting at the University of Missouri in Columbia and soon moved to Los Angeles to develop a career in the arts and entertainment business. His head-shot photography talents can be seen on his web site, www.bkrnhoto.com and in a growing number of Farmington homes from his return trips home. Television and film production and acting credits to date include: *LA Law, Beverly Hills 90210, Budweiser Skunky Beer, Rice Krispies Krispy Treat, And God Spoke, Little Giants, The Sky is Falling,* and a comedy skit on *the Tonight Show* with Jay Leno.

Scott Wesley Ross was born in Farmington on Jan. 24, 1973, studied communications at the University of Missouri in Columbia and soon followed his two older brothers to Los Angeles for his own film industry career as an editor, production assistant and screen writer. His writing is in the development stage while the film production and editing work pays the bills. Specific films to date are: *Ace Ventura: When Nature Calls, Allie & Me, Romy and Michele's High School Reunion* (teamed with his oldest brother Kevin), *Diabolique* and *Simon Birch*.

Jennifer Jayne Ross was born in Farmington Aug. 11, 1974, studied business, communications and computers at Mineral Area College, The University of Missouri at Columbia, Columbia College and Maryville University of St. Louis. After working several years in St. Louis in various work

situations and job descriptions, she has followed her instincts to Chicago where she plans to further develop her career objectives.

All in all, the Doug and Pam Ross family can say their years in Farmington have been full of many memories and experiences, it's been home, it's been a place to come back to after being away, a place truly to be proud of and even boast about to others, truly the finest small city in the state of Missouri!!!

RUEBEL - The Joseph Ruebel family moved to Farmington in 1941 after the completion of the Trimfoot Company's new offices and factory. They purchased a home at 501 North Center Street.

World War II interrupted Mr. Ruebel's career and he served in the U.S. Navy, obtaining the rank of lieutenant commander. In 1946 he resumed his position with Trimfoot, where he was to work until 1977 when he retired as vice-president.

In 1952 the Ruebels moved to 503 West College and lived there until Trimfoot moved their executive offices to St. Louis in 1959. At that time the house was sold to its current owners, the Landrums.

During their years in Farmington, Lenore Ruebel was active in local clubs and civic organizations while Joe Jr. attended the Farmington Public Schools, graduating from the old Farmington High School with the Class of 1959.

In 1989 Joe Jr. and his wife, Joyce, attended his 30th high school class reunion and during their stay became attracted to Farmington in general and one house in particular, 904 W. Columbia St. This property has a long history, being build and added onto over a period of approximately 50 years, beginning with the original part in 1850, the kitchen addition around 1865, and the bedroom wing about 1900. Originally built by the Rudys, it was sold to the Nolands and their daughter, Miss Bessie, lived in the house for many years after her parents died. In 1946 Jones and Geneva Klein bought the house and lived there for approximately 40 years. At one time, Dr. Klein ran a tree nursery there called Picket Fence Nursery. The plantings in the yard reflect his interest in horticulture. When Joe and Joyce Ruebel bought the house, it was in need of restoration and modernization. The work was limited to preserving the antique aspects that had attracted them originally. Four years later, in 1993, they moved into the house.

RYAN - Patricia, born April 8, 1959, in the Bonne Terre Hospital, is the oldest daughter of John and Glenna (Bruce) Ratliff, sister to Marlene (Mrs. David) Womack, granddaughter of Clarine (Sandt) Bruce, the late Carl Bruce, and the late Marvin and Alma (Brown) Ratliff, all of Farmington.

Patricia's father's family hailed from the Ellington, MO and Bunker, MO area before moving to Farmington. They are relatives of William Buford who settled in the Bellevue Valley and Buford Mountain area. Patricia's mother's family emigrated from France in the 19th century, eventually moving to the St. Louis area where the family owned and operated a foundry in downtown

St. Louis at the turn of the century. That is where Mrs. Bruce's multilingual grandfather, Gerhart Sandt, taught English to immigrants that had settled there and wanted to be naturalized.

Kevin and Patricia Ryan

Kevin was born Feb. 17, 1957, in Port Chester, NY and is the fifth of seven children of the late Timothy and Edna (Stone) Ryan. Until 1995, Kevin had lived most of his adult life near the Watertown, NY area, home of his mother's family in the beautiful Thousand Islands region of the St. Lawrence River and Lake Ontario, near the Canadian border.

Kevin's paternal grandparents, the late Timothy and Mary (Jennings) Ryan, hailed from the counties Cork and Mayo of Ireland. It is interesting and maybe a bit of the luck of the Irish that Timothy Ryan arrived at Ellis Island, NY, aboard the *Lusitania*, which had its disastrous ending just a few days later upon its return voyage.

Kevin and Patricia met in 1980 while Kevin was serving with the US Army Security Agency in South Korea. Their friendship continued and the next year as Kevin visited Patricia in Farmington. They corresponded for several years as Patricia continued to live in the Farmington area while working for the Mineral Area Regional Medical Center. Kevin returned to the northern New York area and became employed by the State of New York. Eventually, due to changes in address and time, they lost touch with each other. In July 1994 a very strong premonition prompted Patricia to contact Kevin. Not knowing how to reach Kevin any longer, she searched and finally found Kevin's brother Tim's phone number. Patricia dialed the number and as fate would have it, Kevin was there visiting.

As the time was right, Kevin and Patricia continued to talk and write. Kevin returned to Farmington to visit Patricia where they found that their love had passed the test of time. They were married July 3, 1995, with the Rev. Bernie Crum officiating.

Patricia has two children who both graduated from Farmington High School. Angie is a junior at Truman State University and Shawn who is currently serving with the US Army in Germany with his wife Carrie, who, by the way, is from Northern New York. Kevin also has two children. Travis is a junior in high school and Tarah is a freshman. They reside with Kevin and Patricia during the summer months.

Kevin and Patricia currently reside outside Farmington on Wesley Chapel Road in the old Esther and Emmet Smith house. They are trying to document the history of the property. It is said that a previous owner of the property, William Smith, who was an officer in the Civil War, had moved to this area after the war, from, ironically enough, Watertown, NY.

SAYLOR-COVINGTON - John and Cora Saylor left Livermore, CA in June 1928 and started the long trip to Farmington, MO where they had jobs waiting for them at the Missouri State Mental Hospital. They brought with them their first son, Kenneth Joel, who was only a few weeks old. He

was the first of five boys for them. After Kenneth was Leslie, Earl, Burl and Billy Gene. A girl, Mary Jane, died in infancy. Leslie died in 1996 due to complications from polio as a young man.

Early in life Kenneth was given the nickname of "Sam". In 1950 he met Wilma "Billie" Covington. Billie was the second daughter of Joseph and Hazel Covington. Their first daughter was Nedra. The Covingtons lived in Flat River where Mr. Covington was the district superintendent for Prudential Life Insurance Company. Mr. Covington was well known in the area and in later years he wrote human interest stories for a local newspaper, *The Lead Belt News*. He also was an amateur photographer and built his own darkroom in the basement of their home.

Joe Covington was the only child of William and Mary Ellen (Arenz) Covington. He was born in 1897. On Oct. 24, 1920 he married Hazel Wampler, who was born in 1902, the oldest of five children for Alva and Zoa (Counts) Wampler. Her sisters and brother were: Beulah Howlett, Reva Hall,

Ada Green and Prentice Wampler. Alva Wampler was St. Francois County Assessor for many years.

In 1948, the Covingtons moved into a big two-story house on College Street in Farmington. There Mrs. Covington realized her dream and filled their home with many lovely antiques. Both daughters inherited her love for antiques. Later in life Mr. & Mrs. Covington moved to Hot Springs, AR where Hazel developed her talent as an artist and sold many of her paintings.

After the move to Farmington, Sam and Billie fell in love and planned to be married. However, those plans had to be put on hold as Sam was called to serve his country in Korea. This instilled a patriotism in Sam that stayed with him the rest of his life. He returned home safely, and on Oct. 6, 1951. Sam and Billie were married.

They continued to live in Farmington and had two sons. David Joseph, born in 1959 and Robert John, born in 1961. Both boys went to school in Farmington and excelled in sports, and were very active in the Boy Scouts.

David now lives in Aurora, CO with his wife, Monica, whom he met while working in Venezuela. They have a two- year-old son, David Ricardo. David also has a son, Gregory Joseph, who is 11 years old, and lives in Wyoming.

Robert lives in Wichita, KS. Sam worked for Southwestern Bell Telephone Co. until his death on Oct. 25, 1961. He was 53 years old. Billie still lives in Farmington.

SCANGA - Dennis and his family (wife, Rita, and two daughters, Maria and Katherine) moved to Farmington, MO in the summer of 1994. Dennis was transferred to Farmington by Huffy Bicycles to assist in the establishment of a new manufacturing facility. Prior to this, they had lived in Wapakoneta, OH. Since 1986 where Dennis worked at Huffy's Celina, OH facility. The family had lived in Henderson, KY from 1984 to 1986 where Dennis was employed by Firestone. Before that, the Scanga family had been residents of Pennsylvania. Maria, the older daughter was born in Pennsylvania in September 1982. Katherine was born in Ohio in January 1989.

Both Dennis and Rita were born in 1956, and both were raised in western Pennsylvania. They met at Pennsylvania State University and mar-

ried in 1979 after both graduated with engineering degrees. Dennis went to work for US Steel, and Rita worked for a division of Westinghouse, and later for an electric utility. When the girls were born, Rita worked a variety of part-time positions, and eventually

The Scanga Family

earned teaching certificates in both Ohio and Missouri. While living in Ohio, Dennis earned his MBA from Ashland University.

Dennis' father, Louis Scanga, was born in Lago, Italy in 1928 and immigrated to the US in 1946 when he was 18 years old. His father and older brother had already moved to this country about 10 years before, and found work in the coal mines of Pennsylvania. His father was killed in a mining accident in Climer, PA. Louis settled in Vandergrift, PA and worked for the Pennsylvania Railroad first as a laborer, then as a cook for several years and later as a welder. In 1953 he married Mary Ann Del Vecchio, a native of Vandergrift, whose family had moved to the US around the end of WWI. They owned and operated Del Vecchio's Market, a neighborhood grocery store, since 1926. Louis and Mary Ann have made their home in the large apartment above the grocery store ever since they married. In addition to Dennis, they have one other child, a son, Thomas Anthony Scanga, who still resides in Pennsylvania. Maria and Katherine are the only grandchildren.

Rita's father, Joseph Pelusi, was the first of his family to be born in the US. He was born in St. Louis, MO in October 1919. His father, Massimo Pelusi, and six brothers had come to the US seeking better living conditions several years before. Massimo sent for his wife, Pax Diana, and their daughter, Joseph's older sister, Mary, in 1917. The family settled in St. Louis, where Massimo had found work as a stone mason. His dream, however, was to own a farm, and eventually one of his brothers sent word that a small farm was available in western Pennsylvania. The family moved when Joseph was four. Joseph married Mary Ellen Martsolf in 1949. Mary Ellen's family had lived in that area for several generations. The couple purchased a small farm, and a few years later started a scrap reclamation business. They had four children, Susan Ellen, Keith Joseph, Rita Louise and Steven James. They now have a dozen grandchildren living in Pennsylvania, Texas, France and Japan.

SCHAFER - John F. and Dasie J. (Robertson) Schafer. The Schafer family originated from Poembson, Westphalen, Prussia. John Schafer's grandparents, John (Johann) and Elizabeth (Lueke) Schafer came to America ca. 1853 and settled in Perry County, MO. They were the parents of seven children: Theresa, Catherine, Emily, Mary, Franklin, Matilda and Christene. Elizabeth died in Perry County, MO in 1872. John Schafer later resided in Mine La Motte, MO before moving to Farmington ca. 1890. He died in Farmington on June 6, 1896, and is buried at Calvary Cemetery in Farmington.

Franklin S. Schafer, was born in Perry County, MO Dec. 13, 1862, and died at Doe Run, MO, Jan. 19, 1934. On Jan. 12, 1887, he married Sarah Jane Johnson, born Nov. 16, 1868, and died Sept. 27, 1928, at Fredericktown, MO. Their children were: Emma Elizabeth, born Nov. 19, 1888, died July 10, 1957, married Roy O. Harper and lived her life in Hutchinson, KS; John Franklin, born Aug. 30, 1890, died May 28, 1957; Clarence Edward, born July 5, 1899, died April 7, 1961, married Flossie Mae Simms and lived in Arlington, KS; William Carl, born March 2, 1905, died March 31, 1928; and Daniel Everette, born Dec. 1909, died May 8, 1931. Frank and Sarah Schafer are buried at Parkview Cemetery, north of Farmington with their sons, Carl and Everette.

John F. Schafer, son of Franklin S. Schafer married Dasie Jane Robertson, born Jan. 18, 1897, Perry County, MO, died Dec. 14, 1970, Farmington, MO, daughter of George Washington Robertson, born March 23, 1858, Perry County, MO, died Dec. 21, 1934, Elvins, MO and Mary Henrietta Moonier, born April 21, 1864, Perry County, MO, died Dec. 21, 1934, Lutesville, MO.

The children of John and Dasie Schafer were Viola Lorene, born 1914 and resides in Columbia, MO at this time; and Virginia Lee, born Dec. 20, 1916, Farmington, MO, died Dec. 25, 1996, St. Louis, MO. Lorene Schafer married Charles E. Carnahan, born Sept. 27, 1921, Ellsinore, MO, died November 1994, Columbia, MO, on Oct. 10, 1940, and had one son, Charles Eugene, born 1941, who is a doctor in Columbia, MO, and two grandchildren, Christoper and Libby Carnahan. Virginia Lee Schafer married Harold K. Hastings of Flat River, MO, Oct. 6, 1940 at Farmington, MO (see related history of Harold K. Hastings and Virginia Lee Schafer).

John F. Schafer was a respected business man in Farmington for many years. He was associated with Klein Grocery Co. during the 1930s and 40s before becoming a business partner in that firm into the 1950s with the late Henry Manley also of Farmington. That grocery business operates to this day under different ownership and name. John Schafer worked on several land developments in Farmington that became residential subdivisions along Potosi Street in Farmington: He established the Whistle Vess Soda Bottling Co. in Farmington in the late 1940s, along with the buildings that housed the Rustic Rock Cafe and the City Service Filling Station (operated by Cliff Brewster) at Liberty and Henry Street in Farmington; was a board member of the United Bank of Farmington and several other business ventures in the Farmington area.

Dasie Robertson Schafer spent her life as a devoted wife, mother and grandmother. She worked at the Methodist Church Women's Circle and was well known for her excellent talents as a cook through her church work. John and Dasie Schafer worked hard during the late 1940s and early 1950s to unite two factions of the Methodist Church in Farmington. John Schafer helped to establish the United Methodist Church of Farmington that is now located on North Street.

John and Dasie Schafer are buried at Parkview Cemetery, north of Farmington and would be proud to know that they have produced four generations of Farmington descendants. *Written and submitted by James D. Hastings, St. Louis, MO*

SCHRAMM - Fredrick Schramm was the first-born son of Henry August Schramm and his wife, Philipina Herter, who were German immigrants. Fred was born in a log cabin on the family farm at Miller's Switch in Ste. Genevieve County, MO. He was one of the first children baptized in the Holy Cross Lutheran Church in Ste. Genevieve. Fred learned to work hard on the farm where he lived.

On April 6, 1893, Fred married Carolina Oberbeck, daughter of Henry Oberbeck of Farmington. The young couple moved to St. Louis shortly after their wedding where Fred became a partner in a grocery store and the couple lived upstairs over the store. The children began arriving in rapid succession, Henry in 1894, Alma in 1895 and Walter in 1897.

Concerned for the safety of his family in St. Louis, Fred moved them to Farmington in 1897. He bought an interest in the "Markert Beer, Ice and Bottling Company" on Columbia Street between Main and Middle Streets. Ice for the plant was cut from the Markert's pond in the winter and stored in the ice house insulated with saw dust. A two-story house was built next door for their growing Schramm family: Minnie, 1899; Fred, 1901; Meta, 1903; Herbert, 1906 and Ted in 1907.

Fredrick William Schramm

The profitable business expanded and another facility opened in Elvins. Fred's father Henry Sr. and brother Henry Jr. bought out Mr. Markert's share of the business and the name changed to "Schramm Ice and Bottling Company." All flavors of soda were bottled at the Schramm bottling plant including Whistle and Bubble-Up. With the addition of new technology, an ice plant was added and ice was delivered all over Farmington in horse-drawn wagons. Coal was a factor in running the ice plant; and since the coal had to be stock piled, a home coal delivery business was soon added. Transporting coal to the plant was a major problem and in 1906 the Schramms entered into an agreement with "St. Francois Railroad Company," "Lange and Brother's Manufacturing and Mercantile Company," and "Farmington Milling Company" for construction of railroad tracks from DeLassus to these businesses in Farmington. Fred expanded the business after WWI by adding an ice cream plant and then again in 1921 by adding a creamery. The "Schramm Bottling and Creamery" grew to one of the largest creameries in the area. A cloverleaf was used for its trademark.

Fred took his sons, Fred and Ted, and son-in-law, Charley Braun, in as associates in the Farmington plant while sons, Herbert and Walter, managed another ice plant in Flat River. In 1953, partially due to union trouble, the entire business was sold to "Merchant Dairy" and in 1956 the old ice plant building was destroyed by fire.

Fred retired at his home on Henry Street in Farmington. He was faithful in St. Paul's Lutheran Church and generously shared his good fortune with others.

SCHRAMM - Henry Schramm Sr. was a native of Hannover province of Germany. In 1857 Henry immigrated to Ste. Genevieve County, MO with his father, Friedrich Wilhelm Schramm (a baker), and his mother, Dorothea. The Schramm family, along with several other immigrant families, organized the Holy Cross Lutheran Church in Ste. Genevieve, MO. The family settled on a farm at Miller's Switch in Ste. Genevieve County and erected a log cabin.

In 1864 Henry married Louisa Philipina Herter in New Offenburg. The newlyweds lived with Henry's parents at Miller's Switch until Henry's father died. Henry took over the family farm and the care of his mother. Four children were born in the log cabin: Louise, 1865; Fredrich, 1867; Albert, 1870 and Henry, 1871.

The log cabin became too small for the family; and in 1875 they moved to Farmington where Henry, following in his father's footsteps, opened a bakery. While living in Farmington, three more children were born: Mary, 1875; Emma, 1877 and Henrietta "Yetta" in 1879. The Schramm family became some of the first members of the newly formed St. Paul's Lutheran Church in Farmington.

In 1880 Henry decided farming was more to his liking and moved the family back to Miller's Switch where they built a two-story house that remains standing today. Being an educated, energetic man, Henry was elected to act as the school director of the area. The last of the couple's 12 children born at Miller's Switch were: Emil, 1881; Caroline "Lena," 1883 and Herman, 1886. The family regularly made the three-hour wagon trip to church in Farmington.

In 1895 the family moved to American Bottoms, IL where they operated a truck farm. They would leave as early as 3:00 a.m. to haul a wagon load of cabbage to St. Louis where the whole wagon load would sell for $3. Truck farming was not profitable and in 1900 the family again moved to Farmington where they purchased a farm on Hillsboro Road. By now, the sons were grown and Henry became a partner with his sons, Fred and Henry Jr., in the "Schramm Ice and Cold Storage Company" in Farmington.

Due to falling health, the elderly parents sold the farm in 1917 and purchased a home on Bailey Street across the street from their son, Fred. They were cared for until their death by their four unmarried daughters.

Henry and his wife, Philipina's, home was always a gathering place for friends and neighbors to get together, catch up on the local news, visit, and share mouth-watering meals. They built their life around their religious faith and were known for their friendliness and honesty.

SCHRAMM - Herbert Schramm, born Feb. 10, 1906, was the son of Fred and Caroline Schramm. He lived his whole life in Farmington, growing up next door to his father's bottling and creamery business on East Columbia Street. He would help out in the plant and went to full-time employment after he graduated from Flat River Junior College.

In 1926 Herbert married Cecelia Giessing, born April 17, 1906, the daughter of another Farmington businessman, Charles F. Giessing and his wife, Lydia. Soon after their marriage the couple moved into their home at 407 South Carleton (next door to Cecelia's parents) where they lived their entire married life and raised four children: Chirley, 1929; Charles, 1934; Elaine, 1940 and Mary, 1943.

Herbert and his brother, Walt, took over the management of the "Schramm Ice Plant" in Flat River and remained in this position until the plant was closed in 1946. After working a short time for his father-in-law at the "Farmington Milling Company," Herbert took up employment in the office of "Schramm Grocery Company" in Flat River and also worked as their traveling salesman. In 1961 when the grocery business closed, Herbert became a teller at the "United Bank of Farmington." On April 8, 1965, Herbert died of a sudden heart attack at the young age of 59.

Herbert Henry Schramm 1906-1965

Cecelia (Giessing) Schramm worked at home most of her married life raising their children. When their son went to college, Cecelia went to work at "Revoir's Grocery" in Farmington and later she worked in the cafeteria of the Farmington Middle School until her retirement.

Bottom L-R: Walter Karl, Ruth Schramm, Betty Schramm. Middle L-R: Ted Schramm, Ted Giessing, Herbert and Cecelia, Meta McLarney, Magnon Giessing. Top L-R: Penny Schramm, Raymond Giessing and Arlene Thomasen.

Like their parents and grandparents, Herbert and Cecelia were active members of St. Paul Lutheran Church and in various civic organizations. Herbert served on the Sunday School Board and Board of Elders for the church and was available whenever help was needed. Herbert enjoyed playing croquet, bowling and took up golf in his later years. Cecelia loved flowers, sewing (especially needle point), and cooking. She was a member of the Farmington Garden Club and an active member of her church's Ladies Aide Organization where she helped cook and serve meals, organize bazaars and make quilts.

After Herbert's death, Cecelia remained in her home on South Carleton Street until her health failed and she was forced to sell her home about 1988. Cecelia passed away in 1993. A long-time pet of the family was a turtle named "Poke Along" who was found by their sons, Charles, about 1947 and kept in the basement of their home. When the home was sold in 1988, the contract read that the turtle "Poke Along" was to remain in the basement and be cared for by the new owners.

SCHURTER - The Schurters returned to Farmington in December 1991 when Wayne retired from McDonnell Douglas Corp. (now Boeing Co.) in St. Louis. Phyllis is a native of Farmington and Wayne's family lived here for eight years from 1947-55. Phyllis and Wayne live on West Columbia St. in the house built by Phyllis' parents, Mr. and Mrs. Harvey C. Haile, in 1935. After graduating from Farmington High School, Wayne in 1953 and Phyllis in 1954, they continued their education in Fulton, MO at Westminster College and William Woods College respectively. Phyllis graduated in June 1956 and two weeks later they were married in Farmington. During the summer of 1956 they moved to Chicago where Wayne completed his undergraduate studies in electrical engineering at Illinois Institute of Technology. While Wayne pursued his studies, Phyllis worked as a secretary at J. Walter Thompson Advertising Agency. During this time son Stephen and daughter Laura where born. In June 1959 Wayne graduated, accepted an offer from McDonnell Aircraft Co. and they moved to St. Louis. They lived in the St. Louis area for 32-1/2 years until Wayne retired. A second daughter, Kristen, was born in February 1965. During his career at McDonnell, Wayne worked on the Mercury and Gemini manned space flight programs, the F-4, F-15, F-18 and A-12 aircraft programs and various advanced technology programs. They have three granddaughters, Jessica, Lindsey and Madisen living in St. Louis. Daughters, Laura and Kristen, are deceased.

The Haile family history in St. Francois County and Farmington starts in the late 1700s. The Haile family line in America goes back nine generations to Captain Richard Haile of Essex County, VA in the late 1600s. His descendant, Thomas Haile, moved from Lancaster County, SC to what is now St. Francois County before Missouri became a state. Phyllis' great-grandfather, Thomas Harvey Haile, was born March 15, 1820 in St. Francois County. He was just over 100 years old when he died June 14, 1920. During his long life he was a farmer, county assessor, adventurer and St. Francois County representative in the Missouri General Assembly in 1844. In 1849 he joined the California gold rush and in 1854 he participated in an effort to drive a herd of 900 head cattle to California. In 1866 he married Ann Elizabeth Campbell. Phyllis' grandfather, Oscar L. Haile, was one of five children born to this marriage in August 1864. He owned the Oscar L. Haile Abstract Co. in Farmington.

His home was on West Liberty St. on the east end of what is now the Christopher Chevrolet car lot.

Phyllis' father, Harvey C. Haile, was born March 5, 1896. He was raised in Farmington and attended Farmington High School where he was a member of the football and track teams. These early sports experiences led to a life long interest in sports and coaching young people. During World War I he was a sergeant in the Army, serving in France. He received his college education at Westminster College in Fulton, MO and at Bradley University in Peoria, IL. After college he returned to Farmington High School where over the years he was teacher, football and track coach and principal. Haile Stadium at the current high school is named in his memory. He married Agnes Vincel in July 1928. Her family had moved to Farmington in the early 1900s from southern Illinois. They lived on Middle Street and maintained a farm north of Farmington in the area of the country club on Hillsboro Road. After leaving the public school system, Harvey was the physical education instructor at the St. Joseph Catholic School until 1965. He also wrote a sports column for the Farmington paper and hosted a sports program on KREI for several years.

SCHWARTZ - Mary Agnes Schwartz, who died in 1998, was a well-known employee of State Hospital #4. Of French/German ancestry, her parents, Adam Schwartz and Eulila Rigdon were married in 1908 at River Aux Vases. Adam was employed in agriculture in rural Farmington. Their infant son, Henry Peter, died in 1911.

Adam built (at the intersection of Highway 32 and present Schwartz Road) the so-called "Miller House" which had just four rooms when Mary Agnes was born there in 1912. She was the third child baptized in the new St. Joseph's Church.

Daughter Florence Edna was born on the Harlan Farm (now Harlan Estates) in 1914. From 1922 to 1932 Adam managed the Giessing Farm at the north end of present Schwartz Road. Mary and Florence attended St. Joseph's School, walking the two miles when weather permitted. Later, they drove Mr. Giessing's horse "January" to attend Farmington High.

After graduation, Mary taught at country schools; in February 1939, she was hired at State Hospital #4, working first in the laundry and later at the switchboard. Florence worked for B.T. Gentges at the Farmington Laundry, and for the Roberts', at the *Farmington Press* office. Meanwhile, in spring 1939, the family moved into a solid new house Adam had built on a little acreage purchased from Mr. Harlan.

Misses Mary Schwartz and Florence Schwartz in the early 1940s

During WWII, Charles Gentges wrote home to friends, including Florence Schwartz. Their four-year correspondence ripened into a courtship by mail that continued from the battlefields of Italy. On Oct. 27, 1945, Florence and Charles were married at St. Joseph's; daughter, Mary Elizabeth, was born in 1947. In 1951 the couple went into retailing in central Missouri, first with Western Auto and then with the Ben Franklin franchise. In 1965 they relocated in Colorado, remaining in the variety business until retirement in 1982. Presently, Florence, Charles and daughter, Mary, reside in St. Marys, KS.

Eulila Schwartz died in 1946 and Adam in 1959. Mary remained in the family home and the road was eventually named for her. Having advanced at State Hospital #4, she worked directly under superintendent Dr. Emmett F. Hoctor as registrar in charge of the admitting office, the clerical staff, the switchboard operators and the medical records department, still holding the latter position when she retired at age 70 in 1982. The energetic lady was happiest when she was helping others. In her 43 years at state she had frequently gone quietly beyond her duty to assist fellow workers or patients who would never forget her.

Next, Mary performed a myriad of duties as volunteer secretary at St. Joseph's Church. At age 85 she was still working two days a week, visiting a long list of shut-ins, taking the elderly to Mass, updating the parish history, and also acting as secretary for her rural Wolf Creek Fire Protection District.

When Mary died Oct. 17, 1998, she had lived almost 60 years in the house her dad built just a quarter mile from her birthplace.

SEBASTIAN - James H. Sebastian descended from Lewis Sebastian and Betty Alexander, being born March 5, 1783, in Wilkes County, NC, an illegitimate child. He was indentured to his uncle, Benjamin Sebastian, in November 1800 where he was taught the occupation of farmer and blacksmith. He was a Sebastian by birth and by virtue of his indenture. On May 23, 1805, he and Catharine Wiggins, also of North Carolina, were married. Eight children were born to them, the sixth being William Sebastian, Feb. 10, 1818. William married Julia Ann Miller (reared in Bedford County, KY) on March 25, 1840. William and Julia were parents to seven children, among which was George Whitney Sebastian, born Jan. 5, 1853, in Ste. Genevieve County.

George Whitney married Frances Jane Williams on Dec. 24, 1874. Seven children were born to this union. The fifth child was James Henry

Sebastian, Sept. 18, 1883, who married Sarah Ellen Cowley on Feb. 11, 1917, she being the daughter of Benjamin and Sarah (King) Cowley. She was born July 16, 1896, and expired May 23, 1982. James Henry expired April 13, 1976. James Henry was known as "Tink" and Sarah was called "Duck." Together they had 10 children, Edna, Jane, Helen, Marilyn, James, George, Ben, William, David and Rachel born in 1922 and died in infancy. Ben was born in 1932 and died Feb. 4, 1950, at the age of 17, a result of the ravages of polio. The Sebastians were never a rich family but struggled to raise their family to be upstanding, honorable people. They were a family who moved frequently, but remained mostly in the Farmington area. In later years Sarah worked at Trimfoot Shoe Factory in Farmington and purchased a home in Doe Run, MO. Although the home was small, it was always filled with love and laughter for their children and grandchildren (who were many) and for any friend or acquaintance dropping by. The little house would almost burst its seams on holidays when everyone "came home."

Sebastian Family. J.H. and Sarah Sebastian (sitting). L-R: David, Marilyn, William, Sarah Jane, Helen, George, Edna and James Jr. February 1967

The Sebastian family has been involved in politics through the years, with Earl, brother of James Henry, serving as St. Francois County treasurer for many years and other descendants from the past being involved in state governments. Some family still participate in local political areas.

Daughter Edna married Harold Propst and had children, Mary and Betty.

Daughter Jane (deceased) married Ira Liles and had children, Ronnie Ann and Larry.

Daughter Helen married Hugh Holt and had children: Hugh Jr., Jennifer, Thomas, Michael, Nancy, Joe Tim and Zana (deceased at age 4).

Daughter - Marilyn (deceased) married Harvey Effan, children Terry, Alan, Harvey, Kevin, William, Harlan, and Harleen.

Son James Jr. (deceased) married Evelyn Pierce and had children: Rebecca, Cynthia and Karen.

Son George married Fern Rosener and had children Lida, Judy, George Thomas Jr. and Ben Lee.

Son William (deceased) married Betty Martin and had children, Susan and Sherry.

Son David married Cora Raby Wichman and had children Edward and Diana.

SELF - Prior to the Farmington years: World War II in India a native Kentuckian married to Rosalie Fitzgerald of Flat River, MO in 1951. Three sons: Gerald Lee, James Arleen, Philip Lyle. James deceased at 23 years of age in 1978,

Graduate of Olmstead High School in Kentucky, University of Kentucky 1950. Southern Baptist Seminary 1954, pastored churches in Kentucky from 1953-1958. Taught in Kentucky public schools from 1954-1958.

1958: New arrivals to Farmington - our sons

preschool age. Gerald entered kindergarten first year here. Then James and Philip the succeeding years. Very soon after getting to Farmington we were welcomed by the Welcome Wagon which really set the spirit for the ensuing years.

We appreciate our town very much. We have seen it grow from 40 some hundred to the 12,000 plus. Now it is taking off at a rapid pace. This county seat town is made to order for our entire family.

First there are the churches which seem to work so well together. Our very early experience in Farmington was meeting Brother Loren Jolly at the First Baptist. On the first Sunday here, moved our membership into First Baptist where Rosalie and the boys attended while I was preparing to be pastor at Three Rivers. They then joined me there. (As I type this our dear friend and servant of God, Brother Loren Jolly, lies in state at Taylor's Fu-

James Arlin Self, son of Chester and Rosalie Self

neral home) as we continued to live in this county seat town of St. Francois County.

I discovered it is excellently located for bi-vocational work, both pastoring and teaching school. After almost 6-1/2 years at Three Rivers and teaching both at Graniteville and Leadwood, our home location was working out beautifully. So from 1950-1997 we kept our home on Burks Road even though

we did move to the church field at Iron Mountain for 11 years after new parsonage was built in 1979, until retirement in 1990.

At retirement we found a house in Flat River we liked and moved there until April 1997. We got homesick for Farmington and purchased our home at 612 Carter Street where our family now consists of daughter-in-law, Kymberlie, twin granddaughters, Kathryn and Ann, and Andrea Lee; also daughter-in-law, Melinda, and granddaughter, Courtney Elizabeth, and Chad Philip, our grandson.

There is a choice for the worshipper, we are surrounded by so many churches. I believe every one will find a church to their liking. The Ministerial Alliance work appear to work well together. They are providing many needs for a great number of families going through difficult times.

The schools both public and private offers great choices. Personally speaking I commend the school system which our three boys attended. Rosalie and I were so well pleased with the Farmington Public School System. Good administrative leadership and with many good teachers. With Superintendents P.J. Newell and Ray Henry and teachers that taught our boys: Mrs. Barbara Crow, Olie Goggins, Mrs. Rhodes, Mr. Skinner, Mr. Thomas, Mrs. and Mrs. Wright, Mrs. Detring, Norman Jackson, Mr. Haus to name a few that comes to my mind after the intervening years. Close by there is MAC and SEMO our sons took advantage of their services.

Medical services, two hospitals for our town when it was rather small. Unusual I must say.

Many good doctors and surgeons. How blessed we have been as a family because of the availability of medical help of which we have been the recipients so many times over their 41 years.

A.G. Karraker was our family physician from 1958-1998 until retirement. When Dr. Karraker was not available, Dr. Huckstep and Dr. Carleton were there. The proximity to St. Louis with the many good hospitals has helped so many families. I would be remiss in speaking of medical services in failing to mention one of our very own, Dr. Darrell Griffin. I was his pastor during his high school years. Darrell was a prince of a lad and I had the privilege of baptizing him at the beginning of his Christian pilgrimage in a stream of water near Farmington at Loughboro. Darrell went off to medical school, then if I remember chronologically was married to Jeannie Defrecce then both served as missionaries to Thailand. At first a pediatrician then back to school to be a dermatologist. Speaking of a family town Dr. Griffin has the authority to speak on this subject since he has such a wonderful family.

I will conclude that Farmington has more positives than negatives. One of the great positives was Eddie Klein's Medical Arts Pharmacy where I worked as his billing clerk for 25 years.

SHANNON/QUESNEL - Our story begins in the fall of 1961 during an enrollment at the Flat River Junior College when Homer met Mary. We were married in the spring and Homer signed a teaching contract with the Perry County School District. Afterwards, he began a career with St. Joe Minerals/Doe Run Lead Co. which lasted almost three decades. I spent 10 years in mental health at the Farmington State Hospital and Malcolm Bliss Mental Health before transferring to the Farmington Correctional Center as a special education teacher.

Homer, Mary, Shannon Junior, Marquitte (1977)

In the summer of 1977 we moved into the Wyckcliffe Meadows home where Homer's ancestors, Jesse Washington Sigman and his wife, Nancy Jane Parks, lived during the 1800s. The accompanying picture shows how we looked when we moved here as part of the upward bound generation. Now we find ourselves part of the Senior Citizens Brigade. While living here we raised three children. Scott, who is working towards a degree in psychology at Southeast Missouri State University; Mark is married, has six children and employed by Doe Run Coin Herculleam; Marquitte is named after my mother and has a degree in business administration and is currently employed as store manager for U.S. Cellular.

Homer's hobbies include gardening and raising his two dogs, an Alaskan Malamute and a Great Pyrenees. We have been told that our garden rivals that of my mother's, Opal Quesnel, who resided on West Columbia before her passing. My hobby of genealogy is shared by our youngest granddaughter. We have traced the Sigman line back to Johannes Siegman from Baden, Germany and the Quesnel line back to Paris, France.

SHAW - James and Betty met in early 1995, while Betty was visiting her mother and stepfather, Catherine and Charles Spurgeon, at their winter home in Florida. James was at the time employed with Florida Power and Light as a power plant mechanic, where he had been employed for 14 years. Prior to that he had worked 10 years for Columbus and Southern in his home state of Ohio as a mechanical repairman and powerhouse repairman. Betty has been a registered nurse for 25 years, having worked at Parkland Health Center (formerly Farmington Community Hospital) throughout her career.

James and Betty were married in June 1966 at which time James became a permanent resident of Farmington, after taking early retirement.

James' family originated in England and Switzerland. James was born and raised in Coshocton, OH, the son of Aleytha and Harold Shaw. He was raised on a farm and attended Roscoe Village Schools, where he graduated in 1961. James served a term in the U.S. Navy and was honorably discharged in 1968. He is a certified welder and completed apprenticeships as a mechanical repairman and power house repairman.

James and Betty Shaw

Betty's family history goes back to England and Germany where her parents families immigrated from to settle in this county. Betty was born in Elvins, MO to Catherine and Melvin Short. She was raised in various towns in Texas, Arkansas and Missouri. She finally came "home" to Farmington when her family moved here in the summer of 1960. Betty graduated from Farmington High School in 1961 and has made her home here since. Betty graduated from Mineral Area College in 1973 with an associate of arts degree in nursing. She has gone on to obtain board certification in medical/surgical nursing.

Her mother's family has been residents of Ste. Genevieve for years, with her maternal grandfather, Eugene Steiger, having been born in the Steiger Haus. Her maternal grandmother, Esther Linderer, has been traced back to Baden, Germany.

James and Betty both have been previously married and between them have five children. Betty's two children are Martin "Marty" Beck, an audit assistant for the Missouri State Auditor and in the process of becoming a CPA, and Patti Graham, a cosmetologist who manages The Magic Hare in Farmington. James' children are Glenetta Shaw who lives in California; Rhonda Morrison of Canton, OH who works for Frito-Lay; and Holly Shaw of Bradenton, FL. James and Betty have four grandchildren: Joseph Martinez (Patti's son) of Farmington; Eddie and Kimberly Morrison of Canton, OH; and Kristina of Pearo, FL. *Submitted by Betty Shaw.*

SHELLEY - Ruby Rose Ramsey, born July 14, 1914, moved to Farmington from Wisconsin in May of 1927. The family moved to escape the severely cold winters.

In June of 1934 while serving supper at a thrashing dinner, Ruby met Mr. Nixon Shelley. Ruby must have seen something special in Nixon. They married on October 7 of the same year. Nixon Shelley was born Jan. 14, 1904. The Shelley family was originally from Bonne Terre, MO.

Mr. and Mrs. Shelley chose to live and work on a farm. They had diverse livestock and several types of crops. In September 1941, after renting land, they bought 103 acres of land on Copenhagen Road, south of Farmington.

Shelley Family. 1st Row L- R: Larry Shelley and Dick Shelley. 2nd Row L- R: Bonnie Farrah, Sharon Wien, Ruby Shelley, Connie Weber and NC Shelley. 3rd row L to R: Warren Shelley, Myron Ray Cash, Mike Shelley and Brad Shelley.

Farming usually meant having a larger family, cheap labor. Nixon and Ruby raised 10 children, a son from Nixon's previous marriage, five sons and three daughters of their own, and their oldest grandson. In order according to their age, they are Nixon "NC," Connie, Larry, Bonnie, Warren (Burke), Sharon, Dickie, Michael, Bradford and Myron Ray Cash. Many of the children, along with their families, still live in St. Francois County.

Nixon and Ruby survived many struggles and enjoyed many good moments in life. They put their faith in God when their daughter Connie was badly injured in a car accident in 1956. They celebrated when their son Dickie returned home after serving in Vietnam for he was the only soldier in his platoon to survive an attack.

Nixon and Ruby made the word family more than just a group of people who live together. They made each member feel important by designating responsibilities and giving individual attention as much as possible. One could consider the Shelley family to be closely knitted. This was evident in May of 1977, when Nixon passed away due to a heart attack.

In 1998 Ruby's family consisted of nine children and their spouses, 18 grandchildren, 18 great-grandchildren and more on the way, and a host of extended members. The family can be found having dinner and sharing stories or helping each other at the drop of a hat. Yes, Ruby knew at the age of 20 that her life would be blessed by becoming a Shelley. *Written by Sandy Shelley*

TRADITIONAL DRESS - Time and patience is what it took to make what has become one of our family's traditions. The late Opal Berniece Umfleet Powell crocheted with love and care a baby dress for her oldest daughter to wear on her first birthday. The dress was made with delicate white thread. It has little pink flowers across the chest and pink ribbons gathering the sleeves.

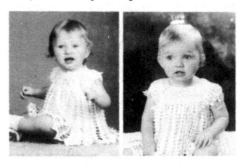
Baby Pictures: Nancy B. Powell and Sandra B. Shelley

Frankie Mae turned 1 year old in 1951. A few years later (1954), the second daughter (Nancy Berniece) wore the same dress on her first birthday. Berniece, as she was called, without knowing had started another tradition.

Nancy cared for the dress as she took it to Germany so that her first daughter and Berniece's first granddaughter could wear it on her first birthday in 1972. Nancy named her little girl Sandra Berniece Shelley after her and her mother. Nancy's other daughters wore the baby dress. Bobbi Shelley Francis wore it in 1974 and Tabetha Harris wore it in 1979. Frankie has one daughter, Crystal Williams Lewis. She wore the dress on her first birthday in 1975.

Berniece Powell's son, Billy has five daughters who all wore the baby dress. Emily Jackson, his oldest daughter wore the dress in 1975. She is a resident of Marschfield, MO. Amanda Powell wore the baby dress in 1983. She lives in Jackson, MS. Renee Hastings' first birthday was in 1985. Andrea Powell wore the dress on her first birthday in 1987. His youngest daughter, Brandi Powell, wore it in 1989.

The dress has now been preserved hoping for a third generation of daughters to look pretty on their birthday and to be told about a very special lady, their Great-Grandmother Powell. *Written by Sandy Shelley*

SHELTON - Felix Theodore Shelton was born Sept. 7, 1936, at Flat River, MO, the son of Felix Abraham and Lena Valeck Shelton. The first ancestor in Missouri was John Bunyan Shelton in Benton, MO in 1853. Two of Ted's great-grandfathers were Civil War veterans in Madison County, John B. Shelton Jr. and Orlando James Denison, who had a saw mill at Marquand. The Shelton Revolutionary War line is documented to the Ralph

Ted and Shirley Shelton

Shelton line in Middlesex County, VA in 1685. The Denison line is documented to Capt. George Denison of Connecticut who was born in 1620.

Shirley Hunt Shelton was born March 9, 1940, at Monsanto, IL, daughter of Samuel Eugene Hunt and Dorothy Rodgers Hunt. Eugene Hunt was the son of Evert and Myrtle Bogard Hunt. He was born July 9, 1913, at Sikeston, MO. The Hunt families immigrated from North Carolina in the early 1700s to Tennessee and Kentucky. Through her maternal line Shirley is a descendant of Revolutionary War veterans, William Addison and wife, Nancy Mobley Addison of South Carolina. James Evan Addison is the Civil War veteran ancestor living in Laclede County, MO after 1880. Susan Henson Addison, wife of Evan, was half Cherokee Indian through her maternal line.

Ted and Shirley were married May 21, 1956, at Edwardsville, IL. They are the parents of four children: Sharon Foard, Karen Smith, USAF Maj. Theodore F. Shelton and USAF Capt. Kenneth A. Shelton. They are the grandparents of 12 grandchildren.

SHINN - Edmond Demmitt Shinn, born Feb. 10, 1874, in Pike County, IL, died in 1952 in Farmington. His father was George Henry Shinn, born 1865 in Illinois and died 1915. He was one of five children. He married Frances Mary Brown in 1901 and they moved to Farmington area in 1912. Ed was a farmer and sold fresh meat and produce, which he transported to the Leadbelt towns by wagon. He later opened a country store with a single hand pump, a Shell gas station located on the site of the Old Plank Road. The Shinns also operated the Chestnut Ridge switchboard for telephone service. They had five children: Edith, Herman, Alfred, Hattie and Ruby.

Back Row: Don, Sandy, Pete, Dennis, Al. Front: Michele, Patrick, Eileen, Hattie, Ann, Patsy (Shinn Family)

Edith Shinn, born 1902 in Marlo, IL, died in 1988. In 1921 she married William Dennis McGuire. They owned a farm on Valley Forge Road and Highway 32. The pine seedlings they planted in the late 30s now stand tall on the property owned by James Womack. Her husband died in 1944 leaving five children: Dennis, Eileen, Donald, Patrick and Michele. She worked for the post office and went to school to train as a practical nurse. She did home nursing and also had a nursing home in her residence on Ste. Genevieve Ave. in Farmington.

Herman Shinn, born 1904 in Pittsfield, IL, married Eula Mae Thompson. He was elected and served as county surveyor for St. Francois County in the late 40s and 50s. They had one son, Allan Dean, who graduated from Farmington High. Herman died in 1975.

Alfred Carl Shinn, born 1906 in Pike County, IL married Ruby Louise Overall of DeLassus. They resided in Alton, IL where he was employed as body shop foreman for Riley Brothers Chevrolet. They had two daughters, Connie and Patricia. Alfred died in 1993. His wife resides in Victoria, TX where Connie lives.

Hattie Eileen Shinn was born 1917 in rural Farmington. She first married Charles Hughes who died ca. 1940. She was co-owner and operator of the Iva Lee Dress Shop on Columbia St. She later married W.W. (Pete) Hutcherson and moved to Saline County, MO. Hattie, now a widow, still resides in Marshall. She and Pete had two children, Robert and Linda.

Ruby May Shinn, born 1919 in rural Farmington, died in 1986. In 1935 she married Ralph Ward, a jeweler and watch repairman. She operated a residential care facility in Farmington. They had three daughters: Sandra, Judy and Priscilla. Judy and Priscilla were Farmington graduates.

SHIRRELL - Noah Ray "Shorty" and Helen (Worley) Shirrell lived more than 52 years together in Farmington until Noah's death on Nov. 27, 1989. Helen still lives in Farmington.

Noah Ray Shirrell was born in Zalma, MO, on April 27, 1912. His parents were Hiram Andrew and Frances (Talley) Shirrell. He and his twin sister, Nora, were the youngest of 12 children. His mother was a twin and she had two sets of twins. Noah's childhood was not an easy one. When he was about 15 years old, his family moved to Brownwood, in southeast Missouri. In 1931 he went to Springfield, MO to work on a farm until 1934. In 1934 he came to Farmington to live with his sister, Delia Aubuchon

and her husband, John Smith Aubuchon. He helped build and worked at Taplin's Cafe and DX Gas Station, located on Ste. Genevieve Avenue where the present Coastal Station is.

Noah met Helen Worley in 1936 while working at Taplin's Cafe. She was working at Rice Stix Shirt Factory in Farmington. They met on a blind date set up by mutual friends, and married on Easter, March 28, 1937, just a year and 10 days after they met.

Helen Melissa Worley was born May 21, 1918, in Esther, MO. Her parents, Albert Lee and Maggie Mae Worley, moved to their farm south of Farmington in 1922. Helen was one of eight children and had a twin brother, Henry, deceased in infancy.

To Noah and Helen three children were born (none twins).

50th wedding anniversary. Noah and Helen Shirrell . Frances, Jim and Helen

Frances Mae (Shirrell) Laney was born April 13, 1938, in Farmington and lived there until 1958, when she moved to St. Louis, MO. She and her husband, David, were married on Oct. 6, 1963. To them, three daughters were born: Andrea Michelle, Suzanne Camille and Jennifer Diane. They have four grandchildren. Frances lives in DeSoto, MO.

Helen Marie (Shirrell) Mattina was born Aug. 13, 1942, and lived in Farmington until 1962 when she moved to St. Louis to live with her sister. Helen married Anthony Mattina in St. Louis on Nov. 30, 1968. They have two sons, Mark and Michael. Mark lives in Farmington and is a member of the Farmington Fire Department. Helen lives in St. Louis County, MO.

James Ray Shirrell, born May 8, 1950, married Bonita Rhodes on Dec. 28, 1974, and has two daughters, Jayme Bonita and Jana Brooke. Jim lives in Sagle, ID.

Noah (known as Shorty to almost everyone) and Helen worked for Trimfoot Shoe Company where Shorty worked for 35 years

Noah and Helen Shirrell , Wedding picture March 28, 1937

and Helen for 32 years. Shorty and Helen were members of pinochle card group for about eight years, where they took turns going to different families' homes, along with the children, for card playing and socializing. Shorty also had a saw sharpening shop in the garage at their home south of town on the old Highway 67 (later known as OO Highway).

Both Noah and Helen had a great interest in gardening and always had a very large garden. Helen always canned and preserved food for the family's use over the winter. Shorty prided himself in growing unique things in his garden, such as loofa sponges, spaghetti squash, foot-long

green beans and many varieties of melons, from super-sized cantaloupe to miniature watermelons.

In the summer many people passing by his house would see him sitting in his lawn chair in his front yard watching his invention (one of many) of his self-propelled lawnmower cutting the grass without his help with a long rope attached to a center stake in the ground that went around and round in circles, getting smaller and smaller as it wound closer to the stake. "I'm not lazy, just saving my energy," he would say.

Helen Shirrell is still living in Farmington where she is active in the First Baptist Church of Farmington. She enjoys ceramics, as well as many other crafts, and has introduced the joy of ceramics to many individuals over the years from small children to residents in local nursing homes and retirement centers. Helen belongs to the St. Francois Arts and Crafts Guild and displays and sells at many craft shows. Her love of travel has taken her to many places throughout the states, Hawaii and Canada.

Throughout the years spent in Farmington, Noah Shirrell made many friends and will also be remembered for his love of his family. He loved to tease his grandchildren and taught them many things about gardening. His many stories or "tall tales" will always be a part of his legacy. *Submitted by Frances (Shirrell) Laney and Helen (Shirrell) Mattina*

SHORT - Michael Short was born Dec. 22, 1819, in Georgia. It is not known who his parents were but he was part Cherokee Indian. He was married to Nancy Ann Raby who was born in 1831 in Georgia. They came to St. Francois County around 1855. They were parents of 10 children:

1) Sarah J. was born in 1850 in Georgia.

2) Malissa A. was born 1852 in Alabama and married Samuel Turpin Feb. 26, 1880 in St. Francois County, MO.

3) John Henry was born March 9, 1855, in Missouri. He died April 26, 1938, and is buried in the Pendleton Cemetery at Doe Run, MO. He married Cordelia Murray Honeycutt July 15, 1880, near Bismarck, MO at the home of D. Matkins. She was born July 4, 1850, and died Feb. 20, 1929, and is buried in the Pendleton Cemetery. She was the daughter of John Murray and the widow of Charles Honeycutt, who she married Aug. 21, 1867, in Montgomery County, IL. They lived in Walnut Ridge, AR and were the parents of Robert, William and Cora Ellen, who was born in Wayne County, MO as they traveled to St. Francois County. Cora Ellen was married to Peter Weiss. John Henry and Cordelia were the parents of Thomas Edward, born Jan. 15, 1882, and died Feb. 21, 1930, and is buried in Parkview Cemetery in Farmington. He married Eva A. Schremp Dec. 22, 1904, and were the parents of six children. Jennie P. was born in June of 1886 and married Fred Giessing. He was the son of John and Johanette Reuter Giessing, the grandson of Charles and Mary Giessing. They had no children. Charles Roy was born Sept. 6, 1894, and died Nov. 14, 1973, in LaPorte, IN. He married Gwinth Hanna Aug. 26, 1915, and they were the parents of five children. He remarried Goldie Fuller and had two more children. He also had two stepchildren.

4) Frances M., born in 1859, died in December of 1933 and is buried in the Woodlawn Cemetery in Leadington, MO. She married Hugh Lovvorn who was born Sept. 4, 1851, and died Oct. 9, 1941. He was the son of John and Lucretia Lovvorn. He was married first to Cynthia Ann Crawford, daughter of Anderson and Mary Crawford. They were parents of six children. He and Frances had one daughter, Cora.

5) Elizabeth was born in 1860 and married

William Samuel Crawford Dec. 29, 1881. He was born in February of 1855 to John and Rebecca Cartee Crawford. They were the parents of Davis F. born in November 1884, died in 1952 and buried in Doe Run Memorial Cemetery. He married Jesse Burch June 6, 1909, and had one daughter Frances. He remarried Mary Alexander in 1938. Jesse Edward, born in 1887, died in 1950 and is buried in Doe Run Cemetery. He married Mary Magdalene Burch and had four children. William Thomas was born in 1897, died in 1943 and married Delia Danielson. Margaret was born in 1883, died in 1962 and is buried in the Knights of Pythias Cemetery in Farmington. She married Zeno Jones and they had four children.

6) Thomas J. was born in 1862, married Mary Jane and they were parents of two children, Venus and Thomas.

7) William P. was born Dec. 11, 1863, died Sept. 1, 1936, married Addie Marie Lands in 1890 and they were the parents of nine children.

8) James H. was born Aug. 11, 1865, died Jan. 6, 1938, married Lettie Hibbits in 1889. They were the parents of James; Olive Gertrude, who married Theodore Perry Schremp, son of Joseph and Frances Ann (French) Schremp; Golda and Mildred. James and Lettie are buried in the Knob Lick Cemetery.

9) Luther Allen was born in 1868, died in 1919 in Pratt, KS and married Sarah Lorene Schremp in 1893, daughter of Joseph and Frances Ann French. She was born in 1873 in Perryville, MO and died in 1957, in Cleveland, OH. They were the parents of six children: Arthur, Lettie Gertrude, Ralph, Sariloa, Frances Elizabeth and Edna.

10) Alfred was born in 1871, died in 1966 and is buried in Bismarck Cemetery. He married Tempie Burch in 1892. She was the daughter of David Burch and was born in 1875 and died in 1959. They were the parents of three children: Effie, Rosa and Clara.

SHUMAKE - Herman Edwin (Cotton) Shumake, Farmington, MO was born Dec. 31, 1929, at Valle Mines, MO, son of the late Charles Henry Shumake and the late Sarah Caroline (Boyd) Shumake. Grandfather late William Gilbert Shumake 1832 and the late Mary A. Jones Eaves; great-grandfather George Washington Shumake 1797 and the late Mary Peyton 1797.

Herman Shumake was united in marriage in 1948 to Norma (Richardson) Shumake. There were four children born of this marriage: Dorothy Marie Cartee, Janet Lynne Wilson, Edwin "Eddie" Lloyd Shumake and the late Gary Gene Shumake.

Ozark Village, trailer court, restaurant, motel, garage

Herman Shumake has seven grandchildren and nine great-grandchildren. He also has three brothers: Henry Lee Shumake (wife, Maxine Pulliam), who resides in Farmington, MO; the late William Raymond Shumake (wife Clarabel Statzell), who resides in Matisse, MO; and the late Robert Charles Shumake of Lithia, FL.

From 1953-1956 he was the pastor of Little

Vine Baptist Church. Herman Shumake received his ordination license Nov. 7, 1954. He was hired as mission pastor for the First Baptist Church in October 1956 and served at Knob Lick, MO for eight years. Then the mission became constituted as a church and he was their pastor for 10 years for a total of 18 years when he resigned. Herman and his family moved to Farmington in 1958.

Left to Right: Henry Lee Shumake, William Ray Shumake, Herman Shumake

His first job in Farmington, 1958-1959, was as a service manager for Oldsmobile; 1960 he opened up Shumake's Safety Service on Washington Street until 1966; 1962 he opened a car lot called Cotton's Used Cars on Harrison Street; 1966 he opened East Side Body Shop at Ste. Genevieve Avenue; 1966 he sold insurance for Missouri National Life Insurance and after four months made general agent; 1966 he was a salesman for Home Improvement House Siding under Monroe Wheeler; 1967-1968 and again from 1971-1972 he was a salesman for American Life and Accident.

In 1968 he received his Notary Public License; 1968-1970, he was a landlord for an apartment house on 104 First Street, Farmington and was also vice president of Lake Lacawana Lake Development. He opened International Leasing and Sales, 1966-1971.

In 1971 he opened Cotton's Auto Repair on North Henry; 1972, opened Cotton's Shell Service on Ste. Genevieve Avenue; and also became agent of Greyhound; 1973 he bought Ozark Village Cafe and later changed the name to Ozark Family Restaurant; also in 1973 he started selling fishing and hunting license which in later years Ozark became the turkey and deer checking station.

From 1973-1974 and again 1976-1985 he was agent for Western Union; 1974 he had a beauty shop called Dots Petite Coiffures inside cafe building; 1975 he became agent of Trailways, which was called Ozark Bus Station; 1975 he made lunches for the St. Francois County Prisoners at the jail; 1976 he bought Ozark Motel and Trailer Park; 1976-1988 he became involved helping the Ministerial Alliance; 1979 he opened Ozark Cab Service; 1981, 1986, 1987 he had a concession stand at the St. Francois County Fair Grounds called the Smoke Wagon.

In 1983 he built a produce stand, and later had auctions; 1983-1984 he let people have flea markets outside on the grounds at the cafe; 1986, he started performing marriages at Farmington Prison; 1986-1987 he gave free Christmas dinner in Ozark Family Restaurant for any one who wanted to come, with the help of friends, family and employees; 1987 received new shuttle vans #3 and #4 for Ozark Shuttle Service; 1987-1988 started having Bluegrass Music inside Ozark Family Restaurant; 1988-1993 and again from 1994 until present day is the pastor of Bible Baptist Church of Brushie.

In 1988 he closed the cafe on lease to Jerry Thorn February 14; Sept. 21, 1989, he opened the Ozark Shuttle Service; 1989-1998 December's Mileage on Van #1 - 624,025 same motor; Jan. 21, 1990, got the cafe back. His daughter, Janet Wilson, managed the restaurant. She changed the name back to Ozark Village Restaurant.

From 1990-1997 he had all kinds of music

inside the restaurant; Nov. 12, 1990, he flew to Washington, DC to give a presentation on the shuttle buses; 1993-1994 was pastor at Sedgeville First Baptist Church; 1994 March, rented antique shop out; 1997 leased the Ozark Village Restaurant. It is now called El Tapatio Mexican Restaurant; 1997 Ozark Shuttle Service Garage, managed by Eddie Shumake.

His house of 37 years on Washington Street where Norma lived burned Jan. 14, 1997.

Herman Shumake is a man who is always there when someone needs a helping hand. He has dedicated his life to hard work and helping others. He has earned the respect of his community. He has a heart of gold. *Submitted by daughter, Janet Wilson*

SIMMS - Harold and Joyce (Laws) Simms were from families near Farmington, MO. Harold was the son of Jesse and Alma (Kollmeyer) Simms, whose farm was on the Old Fredericktown Road. Harold and Joyce raised their family on a 45-acre farm on the same road. Harold and his father worked in a Grade A Dairy business.

L to R: Jesse and Alma Simms, David and Gertrude Laws, Clyde and Betty's Wedding May 23, 1959

Their four children are Ronald and wife, Eva (Harrington) Simms, Farmington, MO; Elizabeth and husband, Clyde Winter, Jackson, MO; Harold Jr. and wife, Connie (McDaniel) Simms, St. Louis, MO; and Sally and husband, Larry Allen, Las Vegas, NV. They have produced nine grandchildren and 11 great-grandchildren.

Harold had a sister, Martha, who married Tilford Thomas Jan. 1, 1940. They were the parents of three sons and one daughter: David and wife, Judy Thomas, Imperial, MO; William and wife, Sharon Thomas, Pevely, MO; Larry and wife, Linda Thomas, Bloomsdale, MO; and Margie and husband, Danny Lindsey, Knob Lick, MO. They had 10 grandchildren and one great-grandchild.

The Laws farm where Joyce was raised is off Highway F near Laws Road. Her parents, David and Gertrude (Yeargain) Laws, lived there about 44 years of their married life.

The Houck Railroad, founded by Louis Houck in 1880 and named Cape Girardeau Railway Co., went through the Laws farm south of Farmington. The name was later changed to Cape Girardeau South Western Railway.

David and Gertrude (Yeargain) Laws were parents of nine children: Ruby and husband, Oscar Feezor (both deceased); Claude (deceased) and wife, Lovell (Thomas) Laws; Mildred and husband, Lynn Hopkins (both deceased); Howard and wife, Lee (Parks) Laws, Blue Springs, MO; Joyce and husband, Harold Simms (deceased), Farmington, MO; Nellie and husband, Eugene Kollmeyer, Farmington, MO; David Jr. (deceased) and wife, Alberta (White) Laws, St. Louis, MO; Charles and wife, Gene (Horton) Laws, Farmington, MO; Joel and wife, Juanita (Stephens) Laws, Fort Worth, TX.

Sons: Howard, David Jr., Charles and Joel Laws and son-in-law, Harold Simms of David and

Gertrude Laws all served their country in WWII and God willingly returned them all safely.

Harold's great-grandfather was Benjamin Simms who married Sarah Yeargain. They were the parents of Calvin Simms and he married Martha Layne. Jesse Simms was their son and he married Alma Kollmeyer. They were Harold's parents.

Alma (Kollmeyer) Simms was one of nine children of John and Elizabeth (Best) Kollmeyer. Her grandparents were Henry and Katherine (Spinhans) Kollmeyer who immigrated to the Copenhagen neighborhood of St. Francois County from Hanover, Germany in the year 1830.

The Laws family immigrated to America from England and Wales in 1600s. Joyce's great-grandparents were Wilson Laws who settled in Wilksboro, NC and wife Margaret (Slate) Laws. Grandparents Joel and Mary (Cunningham) Laws settled in Ste. Genevieve County, MO.

Joyce's maternal grandparents were John and Mary (Simms) Yeargain. Their home, called Valley Forge, was on 32 Highway. There are lots of memories there. Paternal great-grandparents were Patrick and Lucinda (Westover) Yeargain who came over from Wales in the 1800s. Maternal great-grandparents were James and Francis (Walton) Simms. They were married in St. Francois County in 1848 and are buried in Masonic Cemetery in Farmington, MO, as are many relatives.

When Harold and Joyce Simms moved into their first home, Oct. 20, 1940, friends and relatives gave them a house-warming. Harold's Grandmother Kollmeyer gave them a blue and white quilt she had made. It is a cherished possession. *Submitted by Joyce Simms*

SIMMS - Milton C. Simms was born in 1900 on a farm just outside of Farmington, the youngest child of Calvin L. Simms and Martha Layne Simms. He had three brothers and one sister: Frank, John, Ellis and Myrtle (Mrs. Jess) Flanery. He attended Farmington schools and was an outstanding athlete. At age 16 he left to enlist in the Marines in World War I. He served in Germany, France and Belgium. After the war he returned to Farmington and finished high school then attended William Jewell College.

Milton married Vivian "Biddie" Arbuthnot in 1927. He worked as a clerk in the St. Joe mines until he was appointed county clerk by the governor. In 1939 he and his brother, Frank, bought Smith's Cafe and he settled into the restaurant business. After World War II he bought Davis Music Store and the Ozark Village Cafe. He retired in 1963.

Milton and Biddie Simms

In his years of retirement he enjoyed playing golf and traveling. He was treasurer of the Presbyterian Church for many years. He was much respected and loved by his family, one daughter, Babara Simms Hartshorn, and four grandchildren: John David Hartshorn, Milton D. Hartshorn, Nancy Hartshorn Johnson and Susan Hartshorn Eye; also great-grandchildren: Alison Johnson, Roger Johnson, Jessica Hartshorn,

Jonathan Hartshorn and three who missed knowing him: Heather Hartshorn, Molly Eye and Jake Hartshorn. *Submitted by Barbara Hartshorn*

SITZES - Charles Freeman Sitzes Jr. and Wilma Faye (Harvey) Sitzes were married Nov. 20, 1954, living in Bonne Terre until Oct. 1, 1955, when they moved to the Chestnut Ridge area on what is now Dorlac Road, Ste. Genevieve County. They are parents of four children: Janice Ann, Katherine (Loss) deceased, Charles Michael and David Lynn. "Mike" married LinDis Wagenius from Oregon State. They have two daughters, Sierra Faye and Katherine Ann. David married Lori Gibbs from Farmington. They have two sons, Wyatt David and Benjamin Charles.

Charles (known to many as C.F.) was born 1925 in Flat River, MO to Charles Freeman Sr. and Minnie Belle (Brown) Sitzes. Siblings are Patrick, Lorraine (Tauchert), Roderick, Sadie (Jenkins), Betty (Roux) and Rose (Gear). Charles Sr., 1887-1966 and Minnie 1892-1963.

Wilma (known to most as Faye) was born 1930 in Bonne Terre, MO (later moving to Leadwood, MO). was born to Clifton Leroy and Mildred (Hinkle) Harvey. Siblings, Jannette (Cooper) and Annette (Sutton). Clifton 1908-1963 and Mildred 1911-l998.

"C.F." served in the U.S. Army from December 1948 to September 1951. He was employed with the St. Joseph Lead Co. from September 1944 to September 1984.

The Seitz family came from Palatine, Germany to Pennsylvania in 1738, then to present day Lincoln County, NC about 1744. They moved to Madison County, MO around 1916. At that time spelling of the name changed to Sitzes. Charles Sr. and his father, Peter Marshall, came to St. Francois County in the early 1900s. You could say the name Sitzes is a Missouri name.

SKAGGS - Cleo, May 27, 1929, to March 19, 1989, was born in Madison County, MO, the son of William Henry and Ethel V. White Skaggs. He came to Farmington at an early age with his mother and stepfather, Luther M. Francis. He worked at Trimfoot Shoe Company at age 16; was a staff sergeant in Korea in WWII, also drove a bread truck for many years. The Skaggs family came to America in 1700, when it was said James Skaggs, son of Thomas, was born in open waters on a ship from Ireland. James died in Green County, KY

Cleo V. and Verna Mae Johnson Skaggs

in 1798. His grandson, James, died in Madison County, MO in 1832. Cleo spent many of his young years in Higdon, MO and spoke fondly of his grandfather, Columbus Marion "Lum" White, who owned and ran the General Store and Post Office. He had two brothers, Firman T. Skaggs and wife, Mayme Gill Palmer, who resided in Farmington and Virgil A. Skaggs of Cape Girardeau, MO. After Verna Mae's death in 1965, Cleo married Lois Marie Allen Miller. The Skaggs and White families have extensive histories in Madison County, MO.

Verna Mae Johnson was born Aug. 5, 1926, in the Salem area of Ste. Genevieve County, MO. She is most remembered by friends and family for having an extraordinary talent as a seamstress. Her parents were Calvin C. and Mabel M. Mills Johnson. Calvin was born Oct. 9, 1863, in

Richwoods, MO to William Andrew and Amanda Margaret Yates Johnson. Great-grandparents were Calvin and Nancy Bailey Johnson, of Jefferson County, MO. Calvin C. bought a farm in the Salem area in 1907, married Mabel in 1922, raised four daughters and moved to town (Farmington) shortly before his death in 1958. Two of their daughters, Irene (Mrs. Delmar Gillespie), and Ruth (Mrs. Leeman Gallagher), also reside in Farmington. Ruby (Mrs. Leon Wulfers) lives in Crystal City, MO.

Mabel Margaret Mills was born in 1891 in Ste. Genevieve County, MO. Her great-grandparents were Patrick and Catherine Scott Mills who came to the Salem area of Ste. Genevieve County in the 1870s. Patrick and Catherine are buried in the Old Salem Methodist Cemetery. Grandparents were Samuel George and Mary Bryars Cromwell of Clinton, Hickman County, KY. Her parents, Samuel Patrick and Lucy Jane Summers Mills, also had a farm in the Salem, Ste. Genevieve area.

The daughters of Cleo and Verna Mae Skaggs are Sandra Kaye, Mrs. Edward Mackley of Farmington, and Debora Sue, Mrs. George Kenneth Mackley of Boonville, MO. *Submitted by Ed and Sandra Mackley*

SKINNER - Eleanor worked as a hairdresser in the Marionatto Beauty Shop on Columbia Street in Farmington. She married Lynn Meyer whose family owned a large, productive farm outside of Farmington. Lynn was a salesman and later became manager of Boswell Hardware, where he was employed for over 35 years. Eleanor became the co-owner of the Cinderella Beauty Salon, which she operated until her retirement. To their union was born one daughter, Kaye Lynne. Erica Ingracia, born in 1982, was the only child produced by the marriage of Kaye Meyer and James Ingracia. Kaye later married Larry Michael. Lynn and Eleanor are both active members of the Memorial United Methodist Church in Farmington. Lynn was a charter member of the United Memorial Men's Club. Both he and Eleanor are active in the 55 Plus Club. Eleanor served as a past Brownie Scout Leader and is presently a member of the Women's Society.

SKINNER - George has been a common name in the Skinner family. We begin with George Milton Skinner's grandfather, also George Skinner. He was born in 1801 in St. Nicholas, Scotland. His wife was Jane West, born in 1823 in St. Nicholas. The two were married in 1841. They had two sons and five daughters; one of the sons was George M. Skinner Sr., born Dec. 15, 1855, in Aberdeen, Old Machar Scotland. After his father's death, George came with a sister to the US to Massachusetts in 1874, along with some of the Milne (Mell) family. George had worked in the granite quarries in Scotland, so he later moved to the Syenite area in St. Francois County. George met Martha Francis Arnold, who was born in the Possum Hollow area of St. Francois County on Feb. 2, 1862. These two were married in Farmington, MO on Nov. 6, 1882, by the Justice of the Peace, Alvin Rucker. Witnesses were James Low, Emma A. Brady, and Tom Dunaway.

To this union were born eight children: John, born Aug. 20, 1833, died Oct. 13, 1974; George Milton Jr., born Dec. 20, 1884, died Sept. 6, 1953; Bertha (Ragsdale), born Aug. 6, 1887, died May 12, 1943; Maggie (Highley), born Sept. 19, 1889, died Feb. 9, 1920; Sadie (Klob), born May 19, 1892, died March 14, 1972; Thomas, born July 10, 1894, died Nov. 14, 1971; Jessie (Meyer), born Nov. 19, 1899, died April 22, 1989; Roy, born April 16, 1905, died Dec. 12, 1997.

There are a number of granite quarries

around Knob Lick even today, although no longer being used. These granite stones were blasted out and shaped into blocks. A number of streets in St. Louis were paved with them, including south Broadway. The blocks were also used to build houses, churches and schools.

Ella and George Skinner

George Milton Skinner Jr. followed in the footsteps of his father and became a stone mason. A number of buildings are scattered around Farmington, including four in a row near Long Park, the original part of the Church of God on Carleton St., the Church of God in Knob Lick, and the W.L. Johns School. George Skinner was instrumental in laying the stone on most of these structures.

George Milton Skinner Jr. met Ella Sutherland, the daughter of Joshua Sutherland and Tennessee McNiece. Joshua was born Oct. 29, 1859, and died Dec. 31, 1920. Tennessee was born June 5, 1862, and died June 24, 1904. They had four children: Lucretia, Ella, Maude, and Birdie. Ella was born Dec. 30, 1890, and she and George were married April 14, 1910. They lived most of their lives in Knob Lick and on S. Washington St. in Farmington, with some time in St. Louis and Red Granite, WI. George and Ella had seven children: George Dalton, Glenn Allen, Eleanor Loraine, Lloyd Sutherland, Donald Middleton, Clarence Dudley, and Mary Frances.

Dalton was born in Knob Lick Feb. 17, 1911. The family moved to Wisconsin for five years, where Glenn was born Nov. 12, 1912, and Eleanor on Jan. 24, 1915. The family then moved back to St. Louis, where Lloyd was born Sept. 10, 1917. Donald was born May 13, 1923, after a move back to Knob Lick. Returning to St. Louis again, Clarence was born Nov. 26, 1925. Moving to Knob Lick, Mary Frances was born Nov. 14, 1933. Dalton died on Dec. 7, 1919. The remaining four sons all served in WWII. Lloyd was in the 43rd Engrs., Glenn in the Navy, Donald in the Army Air Corps, and Clarence in artillery. Ella continued to change the "star flags" in the window until she had one with all four stars. She thanked God that all four sons returned home safely after the war. George died Sept. 6, 1953; Ella died July 7, 1958; Donald died Nov. 27, 1984; Glenn passed away Nov. 14, 1997; and Lloyd died Feb. 20, 1998.

Members of the Skinner family have lived in this area for over 120 years. George Skinner Jr., his wife Ella, his parents, and two sons, Dalton and Glenn, are all buried in the Knob Lick Cemetery. *Submitted by Jack W. Skinner*

SKINNER - Glenn was born Nov. 12, 1912, in Red Granite, WI. He was the son of George Milton and Ella Sutherland Skinner. Glenn's family returned to Knob Lick, MO, where he spent most of his younger years. He had four brothers and two sisters: Dalton, Eleanor, Lloyd, Donald, Clarence and Mary.

Glenn went through the 10th grade at the Knob Lick School. After school, he began working at odd jobs for farmers. As the Great Depression developed, jobs were hard to find. Once, he traveled to Flat River, climbed into a box car, and rode to Ste. Genevieve to get a job. His favorite pastimes were fishing, hunting and playing baseball. Glenn loved to pitch and played ball for the Brightstone team and the Castor Frogs.

In the early 1930s he met Anna Irene Ward in Knob Lick. Anna was the daughter of Tom and Louzetta Ward. She was born Jan. 26, 1909, near Fredericktown and grew up in Madison County. Anna's aunt had a grocery store in Knob Lick for a while, and Anna went to visit them. After meeting Glenn, she arranged to do some babysitting in Knob Lick to keep the acquaintance alive. There were about four trains each day through Knob Lick, and one was called the "Local." Glenn would ride the "Local" to Fredericktown and then hitchhike the seven miles to where Anna lived. On Sept. 1, 1934, Glen and Anna were married.

They lived for a short time in a cabin on Castor River and then moved to St. Louis. Glenn worked at the Missouri Athletic Club for a while. Their only son, Jack, was born in St. Louis on Nov. 28, 1935.

Glenn and Anna Skinner

Glenn was working at Medhart Manufacturing Co. when Pearl Harbor was bombed. In the spring of 1942, the family moved to Fredericktown. He went to work for the Sinclair Oil Co. until 1954. Glenn has been active in the American Legion during this time and was post commander in 1948. In 1954, he purchased a grocery store, kept it for six months, sold it, and went to work for National Lead Company. He worked there until the mines closed in 1960. He was finally able to get on with the Missouri Conservation Commission, Forestry Div., where he worked until he retired in 1977. He built a forestry tower in Bollinger County in the early 1960s. Glenn was assigned to the Knob Lick tower in 1965, so they moved to a small farm outside Knob Lick. After his retirement, they moved to 506 N. Carleton St. in Farmington. Glenn and Ann were both very active in the Knob Lick Church of God until after his retirement. They then became members of the Nazarene Church in Farmington and took part in the Senior Adult Ministries.

Glenn loved to travel and sightsee. He and his brothers, Lloyd and Dudley, spent many days traveling over St. Francois and surrounding counties. They also traveled to St. Petersburg, FL to visit their brother, Don, until he passed away. Anna loved to cook in her younger days and spent much of her time in helping others.

Anna Skinner died July 6, 1997, and Glenn passed away on Nov. 14, 1997. They are both buried in the Knob Lick Cemetery.

SKINNER - Jack Skinner was born at the Firmin Desloge Hospital in St. Louis on Nov. 28, 1935. He is the son of Glenn and Anna Skinner. Jack lived with his parents in St. Louis until he was five years old. He attended kindergarten and part of the first grade there. In 1942 his folks moved to Fredericktown. Jack attended 12 years of schooling there, graduating in 1954. He was active in the high school band, beginning when he was in the 5th grade. He also played baseball in high school. He was a member of the National Beta Club for three years, vice president of his high school class for three years, and president during his senior year.

After graduation, Jack joined the Army National Guard and worked at Osborne's Clothing Store in Fredericktown. In the fall of 1956, he met Betty Joyce LaChance, the daughter of Orville and Blanche LaChance. She was born Oct. 15, 1938. She attended schools at Knob Lick and Mine La Motte, graduating from Mine La Motte in 1956. Betty worked for the *Democrat News* in Fredericktown.

On Jan. 4, 1958, Jack and Betty were married. They made their home in Fredericktown, and Jack went to work in the laboratory for National Lead Co. in September of 1958. He worked there for three years until the mines closed. On July 6, 1960, their first son, Terry, was born. After the mines closed, the family moved to St. Louis for one year, where Jack worked for Monsanto Chemical Co. In the fall of 1962 he quit and moved to Cape Girardeau. Jack entered SEMO State College in the education program.

Jack and Betty Skinner

Both Jack and Betty worked at Davis Electric during this time. In 1964 the family moved back to Fredericktown. Jack commuted to college at Cape and worked at Madison Memorial Hospital. Betty worked at Dicus Drug Store and Black River Electric until their second son, Christopher, was born on Feb. 6, 1965. In 1971 their third son, Shannon, was born on February 2.

Jack graduated with a BS in education. He did his student teaching at the Farmington Junior High. While there, Dr. Ray Heny, superintendent, signed him to a contract. Jack taught 8th grade Earth Science until 1977 when he went into administration. He received his master's degree in 1975 and retired from the National Guard with 22 years service in 1977. He was in the Middle School administration until 1981 when he returned to the classroom to teach science and work on his specialist degree. In 1989 he returned to the office as the assistant principal at the middle school where he remained until his retirement in 1996. Jack completed the specialist program at the University of Missouri, St. Louis. He also wrote articles for the schools in the *Press Leader* from 1996-1998. He has been associated with the Farmington Schools for 32 years.

Betty worked at Montgomery Ward and Mineral Area College until 1972. She then went to work at Jefferson Elementary School as an aide, later switching to the Washington/Franklin School as secretary. After 22 years with the Farmington School System, she retired in 1994. They have been active members of the Farmington Nazarene Church since 1967.

They have five grandchildren. Terry married Jan VanHerck in 1983. They have one son, Adam. Terry has taught at the Farmington High School since 1985 and Jan has taught kindergarten at Bismarck. Chris married Angie Bullock in 1994. They have two sons: Caleb and Corey. Chris works as a counselor and Angie is a doctor's aide in the Medical Arts Building. Shannon married Jennifer Meinz in 1991, and they have two children, Alicen and Zachery. Shannon spent six years in the Air Force and now works in electrical/air conditioning maintenance for the Farmington Schools. Jennifer works as a computer operator for a local dentist. Since retirement, Jack and Betty have been active in traveling and camping. They continue to live in Farmington.

SKINNER - Lloyd S. Skinner was born Sept. 10, 1917, in St. Louis, MO, the son of George and

Ella (Sutherland) Skinner. He lived for a while in St. Louis and then the family moved to Knob Lick where he attended Knob Lick School. He later moved to St. Louis and worked for the ship yards. He entered the Army in March 1941 and was due to get out in March 1942; but the bombing of Pearl Harbor extended his tour until 1945. He was in the 43rd Engrs. and spent 39 months overseas in and around New Guinea.

After the war, he returned to Farmington where he eventually got into the plumbing business with Boswell's Hardware. He retired from Capital Supply Company and then worked part time for his son-in-law in a cabinet shop. He was a charter member of the VFW Post 5896 and a former member of the Lions Club.

Lloyd married Naomi Schaefer, the daughter of William and Doretta Schaefer of Farmington, on Nov. 7, 1941. They lived on Sixth Street and at different locations on Old Fredericktown Road just outside Farmington. To this union were born three daughters: Sandra (Mrs. David Hoehn), Cheryl (Mrs. Gordon "Rusty" Waibel) and Nancy Wilkinson. Sandra is employed at Ozarks Federal Savings and Loan Association as assistant vice president and David at Little Tikes. Cheryl is a hairdresser and Rusty owns his own business, Creative Cabinetry and More. Nancy is employed at Southeast Missouri Mental

Lloyd and Naomi Skinner

Health Center. David and Sandy have two daughters, Stephanie and Emily. Cheryl and Rusty have one daughter, Amanda Byers. Nancy has one daughter, Kelly (Mrs. Chris Miller). Kelly and Chris have one son, Riley. Naomi worked for many years at Rozier's Clothing Store and now works part-time for Cozean Funeral Home.

Both were active members of St. Paul Lutheran Church. Lloyd served as Sunday School treasurer for several years, was an Elder of the church and a member of the Men's Club. Naomi is a member of the Women's Club, Ladies Aid and Lutheran Women's Missionary League. Lloyd passed away on Feb. 20, 1998. *Submitted by Sandra Hoehn*

SMITH-TAYLOR/SMITH - Madison Roswell Smith was born July 9, 1850, near Glen Allen, MO. His heritage was Dutch-English.

The family came from North Carolina and M.R. attended Central Methodist College. He studied law and was admitted to the bar in 1874. Governor John S. Phelps appointed him prosecuting attorney for Bollinger County in 1878. He was elected to the Missouri Senate in 1884 and served for four years. He declined to run for re-election and moved to Farmington, where he was in law partnership with Wm. R. Taylor. In 1906 he was elected to Congress and served for two years but was defeated for re-election. He was appointed minister to Haiti in 1913. Due to failing health he resigned after two and one half years, returned to Farmington and continued law practice until his death in 1919. In 1881 Madison married Nannie Leech of Cape Girardeau. They had two sons, Melbourne, Taylor and three daughters: Alma, Barbara and Nancy.

Taylor Smith was born Nov. 6, 1891, in Farmington. He attended preparatory school in Spring Hill, TN and Carleton College in Farmington. He served as court reporter for the 27th Judicial Circuit. After years of study he was

admitted to the bar in 1925 and was city attorney for five years. In 1933 he was appointed provisional judge by Gov. Guy B. Park and was elected to a full six year term in November 1934. As circuit judge, he did much to rehabilitate youthful offenders by patroling

Taylor Smith Jr. 1913-1994

them to himself. In 1941 he resumed the practice of law, sharing offices with Raymond S. Roberts. After his son, Taylor Smith Jr., returned from service following WWII, they formed the Smith & Smith Law firm. In 1950 one of their major clients, the National Lead Co., offered Judge Smith the position of general counsel for the Baroid Division in Houston, TX, whereupon Taylor and his wife, Bertha, moved to Houston in 1950. He retired in 1959, moved back to Farmington, resumed the partnership with Taylor Jr. and died after a short illness on July 27, 1960.

Taylor was active in the Presbyterian Church, where he was a deacon and served as treasurer. He was for a number years on the Board of Directors of the Ozarks Federal Savings and Loan.

In the 1920s he was active in the organization of a golf and tennis club on the St. Francois River near DeLassus. This club failed in the depression years when the members were no longer willing or able to pay $15.00 annual membership.

Taylor married Bertha Mitchell, daughter of Mr. and Mrs. J.D. Mitchell. There were three children: Taylor Jr., Betty and Nancy.

Taylor Smith Jr. was born in Farmington March 9, 1914. He attended Westminster College and received his law degree from Washington University. He was an Army veteran of WWII where he was involved with legal matters in the Intelligence Division. Upon his return from WWII, he joined his father in the practice of law. He was involved in numerous civic activities, among them the founding of the Presbyterian Manor and the development of Karsch Boulevard bypass. He was president of the Farmington Chamber of Commerce in 1949 and a member of the Kiwanis Club. He was a long-time chairman of the county Democratic Committee. He served as counsel for the Ozarks Federal Savings and Loan and became its president in the 1970s. Taylor Jr. received the Lifetime Service Award from the Farmington Chamber of Commerce. Steward Landrum Jr. in presenting the award said, "Throughout his life, he has dedicated himself to and worked for the city." He was an elder in the Presbyterian Church. He married Ruth Wilson of Ironton, MO. Ruth was an accomplished musician and was organist at the Presbyterian Church for many years. Taylor and Ruth had two daughters, Mrs. Ellen Bass of St. Louis and Mrs. Martha Fails of Kansas City.

SMITH - Mrs. and Mrs. Robert L. Smith were long-time residents of the Farmington area. They lived on a farm eight miles north of Farmington on Salem Creek for more than 40 years. In 1972 they retired from farming and moved to 521 North Street in Farmington.

Robert married Glenna Woodward in St. Louis on July 13, 1930, and they moved to the Farmington area in 1933. Robert was a full time farmer and raised cattle, hogs and chickens, along with various crops. They were active in the Fairview Baptist Church where Glenna was the adult Sunday School teacher for many years. Robert and Glenna are buried in the Marvin Chapel Cemetery.

The Smiths raised their family on the farm. Richard, born on March 5, 1931, lives in the Ben Nor Apartments. Robert was born on Nov. 7, 1937, and married Connie Powell. They live in Ballwin and have three sons: Robert, Stanley and Alan. Carol was born on April 20, 1943, and married Robert Pennycuick. They live in south St. Louis County and have two daughters, Julie and Jennifer. Rosemary was born on Oct. 1, 1947, and married Charles Oxley. They live in Cape Girardeau and have three children: Melinda, Blaine and Vincent.

Richard, Glenna, Robert L., Robert M., Carol and Rose Mary in July 1968

Robert Lee Smith was born on Aug. 14, 1906, on his family's farm, which was just one mile west of the land he farmed for more than 40 years. His father was William Henry Smith, born 1848, died 1925, and his mother was Mary Elizabeth Mackley, born 1873, died 1948. William bought 240 acres on Three Rivers Creek in about 1870 and built a large frame house for his family. William's obituary was headed "Wealthy Farmer Dies Monday" and this was said to have made his wife very angry. Their other children were Nellie, William, Avah, Willard, Henry, Linn, Claude and Hershel. They all resided in the local area except Hershel, who made a career of the Army.

Robert's grandparents on his father's side were William Westley Smith (born 1820, died 1896) and Eliza Smith (born 1824, died 1897) from Ohio. Both Robert's parents and grandparents are buried in Salem Cemetery. Robert's grandparents lived on an adjacent farm that was settled by Robert's great-grandparents, William W. Smith (born 1767, died 1836) and Elizabeth Smith (born 1782, died 1885) from North Carolina. They lived in a log cabin that sat back in the woods. They are buried in the McHenry Cemetery.

Robert's grandparents on his mother's side were Solomon Mackley (born 1846) and Lucendia Pinkston (born 1848). They lived near and were active in Little Vine Church. Robert's great-grandparents were Jesse Parker Mackley (born 1811, died 1885) and Isabelle Faulkner Mackley (born 1822, died 1906). They were English and came up the river to Ste. Genevieve and then traveled inland by horse and wagon to the Little Vine area.

Robert's wife, Glenna Woodward Smith, was raised in Shannon County of Missouri, and her parents were George W. Woodward (born 1871, died 1968) and Amanda Smith Woodward (born 1865, died 1915). Their other children were Ruth Palmer, Nathal Martin and Hubert Woodward, who all resided in the Farmington area.

Glenna's grandparents on her father's side were Lyman Little Woodward (born 1843, died 1901) and Catherine Fry (born 1853, died 1936). They were both born in Morgan County, OH and were married there. In 1874 they moved to Shannon County and raised their family on a farm.

Glenna's grandparents on her mother's side were Simion Smith (died 1885) and Francis Miner Smith Tripp (born 1852). They also lived in Shannon County.

SPENCER - Remodeling of the Farmington State Hospital in 1958 brought new construction workers into town. Born in Mead, KS Oct. 16, 1908, died Farmington, MO June 24, 1978, Tom Spencer, a pipe-fitter out of St. Louis, worked on the heating and air conditioning units for about six months, boarding with Mrs. Sinclair on the corner of Liberty and A Street and going back to his wife and family in St. Louis on the weekends.

Thanksgiving Dinner at Grandma Spencer's

After the long commute on Sept. 7, 1958, Tom came home Friday night and announced to his family "Pack-Up, we're moving! One-Arm Smitty will bring a trailer tomorrow morning to go to Farmington."

So without warning, Iretta and her girls, Marcia, "Mitzie," Mary, Jeannie, Cheryl and Claudia, with the help of a visiting friend from California, Elsie Sullivan, rolled up their sleeves and began the move.

Tom had arranged to rent the old Mackley house on Patterson that had been vacant for 10 years, promising the proprietor that he'd fix up the old place. The move was unexpected and frightening to the three girls and their mother. School was to start the next day and they had no idea where it was. Jeannie was a beautiful, curvaceous brunette who was encouraged by all who met her at school to try out for majorettes, which she became almost within a week. Cheryl, tall studious and much more shy, also joined majorettes. Claudia, the youngest and more athletic of the girls, was into volleyball and later cheerleading. The young girls were almost instantly the heartbeat of the American teenager at Farmington High in the 50s and 60s. Jeannie was Miss Farmington and Homecoming Queen. Cheryl graduated with honors and scholarship to Cape Girardeau. Claudia was into 4H with her horse and was the Barn Warming Queen.

Iretta was dismayed but determined when she saw the house. It would take a lot of work and love to become a home. She cleaned and painted while Tom cut brush and trees, mowed and plowed. In almost no time the home became a center for the neighborhood to be welcomed and for the older two married daughters and husbands, Mitzie and Bill Detjen and Mary and Frank Voertman, to come home to.

Iretta soon found a job at Lees Grocery Store and then worked at IGA. In 1961 the family bought the Tucker farm on old Colony Church Road. The girls loved the farm, the horses and the opportunity to drive the old Chevy into town to pick up Iretta, who had accepted a job at Medical Arts Clinic as a receptionist where she worked for 37 years. Iretta, a perky, friendly, outgoing person, was perfect for the job and made many lifelong friends.

Tom retired in 1973 and spent his time farming and watching his grandchildren grow. He was saved and accepted Christ at Grace Baptist Church and continued his membership later at Freewill Baptist Church until his sudden death in 1978.

Iretta married her second husband, David Baird, in 1982. David was a painter by trade and they lived out by the airport at the Lazy B Ranch.

They enjoyed their life and many trips to California, Washington, Alaska and many times to Florida. After his death in 1985 Iretta moved to her Center Street house for about a year and then moved to Holiday Park, where she presently resides.

Iretta enjoys her church, Farmington Freewill Baptist, and also sings with the First Baptist Church. She looks forward to many trips with the senior group.

Jeannie married the emminent Farmington lawyer, Clinton Roberts, and they have four children: Cynthia, James and twins, Rebecca and Richard. Cheryl married Patrick Smock and they have four children: Elizabeth, Michael, Patrick and David. Claudia married John "Jack" McCracken and they have three children: Joseph, Jeannie and John. Mary and Mitzie were just married before the family moved in 1958. Mitzie and Bill Detjen have four children: Vickie, Tom, Billy and Lori. Mary and Frank Voertman have four girls: Kim, Kristi, Kathryn and Karah.

The move in 1958 by Tom has been a durable and lasting commitment by the family as Mary and Frank moved to the area in 1965 with their girls and now their three married daughters and four grandchildren live in the area. Mitzie and Bill moved to Farmington in 1975 and reside in the area with son Billy. Cheryl and Claudia live out of state but still call Farmington "home." The ties to Farmington are strong and the family is truly blessed.

STAM - John Henry Ward Stam was born in Farmington, MO on June 8, 1920. He lived in Farmington, MO, worked with his father and brother in farming and trucking business. On October 7, 1939, he married Nellie Irene Howell. During WWII, John served in the U.S. Navy where he was stationed in the Pacific. After the war, John and Nellie made their home in Farmington where he worked for National Lead Company in Fredericktown, MO, and later was employed by the Operating Engineers, Local #513, as a master mechanic until his retirement. Nellie Irene Stam worked as a homemaker, was employed by Farmington Manufacturing Company, and then worked 18 years as a nursing aid at Farmington Community Hospital until her retirement.

John and Nellie had four children: Barbara Joann (b. Jul. 10, 1940); Ruth Evelyn (b. Aug. 14, 1942); John Michael (b. Sep. 15, 1946) (See John and Rita Stam family history); and Susan Lynn (b. July 24, 1953). John and Nellie Stam are deceased and both are buried in Hillview Memorial Gardens, Farmington, MO.

John's father and mother were Edward Stam Jr. (b. Jan. 8, 1892, d. Aug. 29, 1971) and Iva Lois Burgess. His father was a farmer, truck driver and taxi driver.

Of German descent, the first Stams settled in Iron Mountain, MO, where several family members worked for the mining company at Doe Run, MO. John Henry Stam (b. Oct. 8, 1821) m. Mary Callaway Hunt on Feb. 6, 1851, and they had eight children: Thomas Hunt Stam (b. 1851); Lucinda Florance (Stam) Brady (b. 1851); John Henry Stam Jr. (b. 1853); Mary Jane (Laura) (Stam) Burke (b. 1856); Mary C. (Stam) Weber (b. 1858); Lucy Alice Stam (b. 1860); Edward M. Stam (b. 1862); and Henry (Hennie) Hortance Stam (b. 1864). A large portion of land was owned by members of the Stam family, and Thomas Hunt Stam was very active politically, serving as deputy circuit clerk and recorder of deeds. John Henry Stam Jr. was also well known in the community and referred to as "The Professor" even though it has been told that his main interest was raising horses and gambling.

Edward M. Stam, son of John and Mary, married Maggie Blankenship, and they had six

children: Mary Kathaleen (Katherine) (Stam) Defour (b. 1890); Edward M. Stam Jr. (b. 1892); Thomas Hunt Stam Sr. (b. 1894; Bryan Stam (b. 1896); John Harry Stam (b. 1898); and Brad (b. 1901), who died in infancy.

Nellie's father and mother were William Anderson Howell (b. Oct. 10, 1869, d. Sep. 2, 1944) and Cora Lilly Pogue (6/30/1889-02/05/1930) This was a second marriage for both. Mr. Howell came to Missouri from the State of Tennessee. Cora Lilly Pogue's parents were Lilly Johnson Pogue (b. May 27, 1870, d. Apr. 6, 1961)) and William Anderson Pogue (b. Dec. 11, 1860, d. Jan. 24, 1941). *Submitted by Mrs. John Stam, Farmington, MO.*

STAM - John Michael Stam was born at Bonne Terre, MO on Sep. 15, 1946, and has always lived in Farmington, MO. He graduated from Farmington High School in 1964. He has worked for the Missouri State Highway Department, Stupp Brothers Bridge and Iron Company, and has been employed with the St. Louis County Department of Highways and Traffic for 21 years, where he is a survey crew chief. John married Rita Ann Cole on March 25, 1966.

Rita (Cole) Stam (b. May 2, 1947, in Bonne Terre, MO) lived a short time in Flat River and Irondale, MO. She has lived in Farmington, MO since age 5, where she attended school. She graduated from Farmington High School in 1965. She was employed at Trimfoot Shoe Company as a clerical worker while attending Mineral Area College, and since 1967, she has been employed as a legal secretary for David L. Colson. When she started her employment, the firm was Smith & Colson, and it is now Colson, Wagner, Ray & Mackay, L.L.C.

John and Rita have two children: Darren Michael Stam (b. Feb. 9, 1971) and Lori Nicole Stam (b. Jul. 22, 1974). Darren graduated from Farmington High School and the St. Louis College of Pharmacy, St. Louis, MO, with a doctorate in pharmacy. He resides in Arnold, MO and is employed by the St. Louis College of Pharmacy St. Louis, MO. Lori attended Farmington High School and is attending Mineral Area College in preparation for a career in social work. (See John Henry Ward Stam and Nellie Irene (Howell) Stam family history; and Oral Cole and Verna (Clubb) Cole history.) *Submitted by Darren Stam, Arnold, MO.*

STATEN/MATTHEWS - Mary Jean (Staten) Matthews was born in 1912 in Ste. Genevieve, MO to Ella Lajoie, born and reared at Ste. Genevieve, and Dewey Staten, born and reared at Coffman, MO. The family was Catholic. Later Mary Jean and family moved to Coffman. In the spring and summer her father was a farmer and the four winter months he worked at the Lime Kiln in Ste. Genevieve.

Dewey's mother, Mary Jean's grandmother, Comfort Staten,

Mary Jean (Staten) and Lynn Otis "Skip" Matthews

lived to be 103 years old and died at Farmington. She is buried at the New Calvery Cemetery on Hwy. H, Farmington.

At the age of 13, Mary Jean moved to Farmington. She graduated the 8th grade at the Farmington Douglas School in 1926. Her teacher was Ms. Daisy Baker.

Mary Jean did domestic work for the Jim,

George and Walter Morris families. Another family was Carylse Rozier. On April 16, 1932, Mary Jean married Lynn Otis "Skip" Matthews and they had seven children: Betty, Dewey, Bill, Dallas (deceased in 1971), Edward (deceased in 1947), Charles, Gloria (deceased in 1982). Two children still live in Farmington, Dewey and Bill. Dewey retired from the Trimfoot Company and after Bill retired from the Air Force, he too retired from the Trimfoot Company. The deceased children are buried at the Black Masonic Cemetery located on Colony Church Road.

In 1947 Father McKeun was the priest at St. Joseph Catholic Church and Mary Jean was the housekeeper for four years. Father McKeun started the first Farmington school cafeteria at St. Joseph with Mary Jean in charge of operation for 16 years. She also did catering to local clubs and organizations and even traveled to St. Louis. She is a member of St. Joseph Church. Mary Jean was the first black person to work at the Farmington State Hospital #4. She was housekeeper for Dr. E. Hoctor. This position lasted for 20 years.

At the age of 70, she took her grandson, Thomas Frost, age 3, to rear. His mother, Gloria, had passed away. Mary Jean saw that he participated in many childhood activities. Thomas lived with her 16 years. He is now attending Lincoln University in Jefferson City, MO.

Mary Jean and "Skip" have 12 grandchildren and many great-grandchildren. At the age of 86, Mary Jean is enjoying life at her own pace with her hobbies of gardening, reading and sewing.

STEWART - Jesse D. and Marie E. Stewart and four of their children: Bill, Beth, Jo Ellen, and Jeanne moved to Farmington in 1950 from Bonne Terre, MO. A daughter, Carol, and twin sons, Daniel and David, were born after the move to Farmington.

Marie E. Stewart and Jesse D. Stewart

Jesse was born in 1911 in the Methodist parsonage in Bismarck, MO, one of 11 children of the Reverend William Stewart and Mabel Stewart. Marie was born in 1917 in St. Louis, one of seven children of Fred and Helen Marquette.

In the early 1930s, Jesse and his brother Paul, who had learned printing at the Missouri School for the Deaf at Fulton, started the *Bonne Terre Bulletin*, a weekly newspaper.

After Jesse's return from service in the South Pacific in WWII, 1945, he was appointed circuit clerk of St. Francois County and was re-elected five times, serving a total of 21 years. He also was editor and publisher of the *Farmington Press* weekly newspaper. During the 1950s and 1960s, Marie raised the family and assisted in the operation of the newspaper.

In February 1967, Jesse perished in a fire which destroyed the family home at 307 North A Street. He was 55 years of age. Also lost in the fire was his son, David Foard Stewart, age 13.

Marie continued the operation of the *Farmington Press* for six years, selling it in 1973. Marie, a registered nurse, graduated from the Missouri Baptist Hospital School of Nursing in 1939. She worked before and during her marriage at the Bonne Terre Hospital and later at the Southeast Missouri Mental Health Center.

Marie, Jesse and their family were active members in the Memorial United Methodist Church. Jesse's father, William Stewart, was a Methodist minister who served several congregations in St. Louis, Southeast Missouri and was the Protestant chaplain at the State Hospital in Farmington in his later years.

The children of Marie and Jesse Stewart are William F. "Bill" Stewart, who lives in Farmington with his wife, Patricia, and daughter, Sara, a student at Farmington High School. Bill is a certified public accountant and financial planner with an office in Farmington. Bill and Pat have grown children: Cynthia Armano lives in Londonderry, NH, with her husband, John, and children, Adriana and Jeromy; Matthew Stewart, lives in Kirkwood, MO with his wife, Kati, and children, Taylor and Meagan.

Elizabeth Herreid lives in Kirkwood, MO with her husband, David, and son, Todd Blunt. Beth is manager of Corporate Communications at Graybar Electric Company. Her son, Jon Blunt, lives in Dayton, OH.

Jo Ellen Schroeder lives in Cape Girardeau, MO with her husband, Gerald, a retired school teacher.

Mary Jeanne Molleston, a registered nurse, lives in Hattiesburg, MS with her husband, Dr. Michael Molleston. Her children are Tracy Shields, who lives in Kirkwood, MO, with her husband, Norman, and twin sons Brian and Patrick Moriarty, who live in Hattiesburg and St. Louis.

Carol Jane Crites lives in Farmington with her son, Caleb, and teaches art in the Farmington schools. Carol has a daughter, Tara Sukefort, who lives in Springfield, MO, with her husband, Ian. Carol's husband, Eugene Crites, was killed in 1988 in a logging accident.

Daniel Stewart lives in Farmington with Marie and works at the *Farmington Press* and *Daily Journal*.

STEWART - William F. "Bill" and Patricia M. Stewart returned to Farmington in 1986, after having lived in Rock Hill and Webster Groves, MO, for the previous 20 years.

Bill was born in 1942 in Bonne Terre, MO. His family lived in Bonne Terre until 1950, when they moved to Farmington. Pat was born in North Weymouth, MA in 1945. Her father was in the USN submarine service, and the family lived in several locations mainly on the east coast during Pat's school years. Bill is a 1960 graduate of Farmington High School. Pat graduated in 1963 from Warwick High School in Newport News, VA.

Bill is the son of Jesse and Marie Stewart of Farmington. Jesse Stewart died in 1967 in a fire which destroyed the family home and also claimed the life of his 13-year-old son, David. Pat is the daughter of Robert and Virginia McCuley of Orlando, FL.

Jesse Stewart owned and operated the *Farmington Press* weekly newspaper for 17 years, between 1950 and 1967. Bill worked at the paper after school and in the summer starting as a young boy and continuing throughout his high school years. During these years, the *Press* was located originally in the building at 14 West Columbia Street and later moved to the building at 1 West Liberty Street. Jesse Stewart also served as St. Francois County Circuit Clerk from 1945 to 1966.

Bill and Pat met in Virginia while he was in the US Air Force. They married in 1964 and returned to Farmington in the mid-1960s while he attended Mineral Area College for a year. They then moved to the St. Louis area, where he continued school at the University of Missouri, graduating in 1970 with a degree in business. After graduation, Bill worked in St. Louis for a public accounting firm and a banking company. Pat operated the pre-school program for the city of Rock Hill for several years.

Upon their return to Farmington in 1986, Bill began the operation of the accounting, tax and financial planning practice he presently operates at 117 North Washington Street in downtown Farmington. He is a certified public accountant and certified financial planner. Pat works with Bill in the practice, manages rental properties and operates a public records listing service.

Bill has four sisters and one brother: Beth Herreid, of Kirkwood, MO; Jo Ellen Schroeder of Cape Girardeau, MO; Jeanne Molleston of Hattiesburg, MS; Carol Crites of Farmington; Dan Stewart of Farmington. Pat has one brother, Walter McCulley of Roanoke, VA.

Bill and Pat have three children. Cynthia Armano, born in 1965, lives in Londonderry, NH, with her husband, John, daughter, Adriana, and son, Jeromy. Cynthia and John are both doctors of chiropractic. Matthew Stewart, born in 1967, is an electrician and lives in Kirkwood, MO with his wife, Kati, and daughters, Taylor and Meagan. Sara Stewart, born in 1981, lives at home and attends Farmington High School. She will graduate with the Class of 2000. Sara is a pool lifeguard for the city of Farmington.

STRAUGHAN - John Corbin Straughan Sr. was born in Northcumberland, VA in 1781 and died in St. Francois County, MO in 1852. He went to Robertson County, TN sometime prior to 1830 and left between 1840-1850. He was married to Sara Phillips and had eight children, the fifth being John Corbin Straughan II, born in January 1825 in Robertson County, TN.

50th wedding anniversary, Russell and Perle Straughan

John Corbin Straughan II married Caroline K. Holland and their first child, Hiram, was born in 1847 in Tennessee. Hiram later married Ruth Turley. Melissa, born in 1850, married George Miller; William, born in 1851, married Julie Pinkston; Alice, born in 1852; John O., born in 1858, married Sarah Sutherlin; Caroline, born in 1860, married William Silvey; and Jefferson, born in 1861, married Mary McFarland.

Caroline K. Straughan died in 1862. John

Corbin Straughan II, born 1825, died 1891, married Mary Elizabeth Van Swearingen Mentier, born 1838, died 1913, and had 11 children who all stayed and lived in St. Francois and Ste. Genevieve area.

John and Mary's first child, Thomas, was born in 1864 and married Juliette C.; James was born in October 1865 and married Ida Holmes; Alvin was born in 1867 and married Hattie; Penina "Aunt Nine" was born in 1869 and married Ed Brewer; George was born in 1871 and married Burta Havens; twins, Luther and Louella, were born in December 1872 but only Louella "Aunt Lou" lived to adulthood and married Gene Thurman; Maggie was born in 1874; Samuel in 1877; Mary "Aunt Mollie" was born in 1880 and married Ray Turley; Russell was born in May 1883 and married in February 1912 to Lucy Perle Hicks from Byhalia, MS, and I have the honor of having them as my grandparents.

Russell and Perle had three children: Elliott Hicks (1913-1985); James Edward, born 1918 and died at birth; and Harold Albert, born 1922, died 1998.

Russell purchased a small farm in Bonne Terre area about 1909 but wasn't able to make a living off the farm; so after getting married in 1912, he joined his brothers (who were policemen in St. Louis) and became a streetcar conductor. He returned to St. Francois County in 1918 and applied for a job as a rural mail carrier that paid a salary of $1,440 annually. He took the position and purchased a farm on Turley Mill Road, which is still a working farm to this day and is being worked by his grandson, Franklin, the third generation.

Elliott married Faye Maples in July 1934 and from this marriage came three children: Franklin in 1935, Dolores in 1937 and Russell in 1943. Franklin and Russell continue to live in Farmington area and Dolores lives in St. Louis. Harold married Dorothy LaBrot in July 1943 and this union produced three children. Twins Alice and Katherine were born in 1944, Alice died in infancy. Karen was born in 1958. Katherine and Karen continue to live in Farmington area. *Submitted by Dolores Straughan Reason*

STRICKLIN - Just what the doctor ordered. Great neighbors, weather, schools, churches on every corner and a great place to grow up. That is what Janet Lea, daughter of Ray and Shirley Harrington has. She and her brother, Keven Ray, are part of the pattern of growth and stability that Farmington has enjoyed for many years. Janet grew up enjoying the entrepreneurial spirit of her parents.

Rick, Janet, Tiffany, and Kayla Stricklin

Janet went to school in Farmington, graduated Farmington High School then worked after school for her dad, Ray, at Delta Outdoor Advertising. She managed Harrington Dixie Créme Donuts and has worked for Farmington Manufacturing, known today as Thorngate Manufacturing. She has been employed with Medicate Pharmacy for nine years as a pharmacy technician. She is a

steady and conscientious employee who endeavors to make the customers feel at home at the Parkland Hospital Medicate Clinic. Janet met and married her best friend from Rivermines, Richard Stricklin, in 1989. They have two daughters, Tiffany and Kayla, who both attend the Farmington Elementary School System.

Richard Stricklin is a product of the Central School System where he was a star baseball player and was a member of the All-Star baseball team. He is an avid hunter and outdoorsman. He enjoys fishing with his two daughters, Tiffany and Kayla. His parents are Richard and Nancy Stricklin who reside in Kentucky. Rick's dad has retired from the Corvette factory also located in Kentucky. Rick has been employed with Delta Outdoor Advertising for 10 years and Signs Etc. for four years. He has also worked for the Doe Run Company in Herculaneum and is now employed with P.L.C. Electric as a linesman.

The Stricklin Family enjoys living in a small community where they can do many things as a family unit. That's what they call the perfect prescription in Farmington.

SWINK - Emmett D. Swink married Edna B. Bailey, daughter of Rev. James M. Bailey and Annie E. Durson, on June 11, 1917.

After his marriage, Emmett ran a rice plantation in Humphrey, AR for his father. The plantation was sold in 1926, and Emmett purchased a 500 acre farm from John Westover north of Farmington. The farm site was west of Highway 67. He operated this farm and helped his father manage his.

Emmett was known for his soft heart for needy people. One time in the 1930s, a family of 10 moved into a field next to him and was living in a tent. It was minus 20 degrees. Emmett, my dad, told them they could move into a building on his farm, gave them food and hired them so they could buy their own food.

Emmett D. Swink and wife Edna Bailey at the time of marriage (taken at Christian Church parsonage)

One day a "tramp" named Elmer came by and asked for a dime to buy coffee. My dad said he wouldn't give him money but would give him coffee and a meal. Dad asked Elmer if he wanted a job. Elmer ended up working on the farm until he died. Elmer was a Swede that had come to the US four years previously. He could not find a job so he was traveling across the US.

Our home was a gathering place for us kids. There were always games to play; and my mother, Edna, would make popcorn balls, candy or muffins for us to enjoy. Later my father inherited his dad's farm, Oak Grove Farm. This was a large two-story, brick house located across from the old DX Gas Station on old Highway 67.

Emmett and Edna had four children. All four children served in the Armed Services during WWII. James E. Swink was born Aug. 20, 1918, in Farmington. After graduation from Farmington High School, James E. enlisted in the Army and served 30 years in the US Army with action in WWII and in the Korean War. In Seoul, Korea in 1954 he married Ham Soc Ja Anna and they have three children: Linda, Mary Lou and John. The James E. Swink family lives in Orlando, FL.

Edna Mae was born Aug. 19, 1920, in Farmington. After graduating from Farmington

High School, Edna Mae became a registered nurse and served as an Army nurse in Africa. Following the war, she became an anesthetist. For several years she was the head anesthetist at Orange Memorial Hospital in Orlando, FL where she presently lives with her husband, Lee Drury.

John Edward was born Oct. 10, 1921, in Humphrey, AR. More details about John "Johnny" will be given in another entry.

George Earl was born April 13, 1924, in Humphrey, AR. Upon graduation from Farmington High School, George Earl enlisted in the US Air Force. He was a P-47 fighter pilot during WWII. On Christmas Day 1944 George Earl "Porge" was shot down over Germany and taken prisoner. Although Porge was blinded from the crash, he was able to escape from the Germans into Switzerland. Following the war Porge remained in the Air Force. On Aug. 17, 1946, he was on a flight mission over the Bermuda Triangle when his instruments went haywire and he became lost. When his instruments started working again, he was able to contact home base. Two planes joined him to escort him back to the base.

Porge's plane was seen flying into a cloud. This was the last ever seen of him. He was greatly missed by his mother, father and the Swink family.

Emmett D. Swink, died in December 1971. Edna lived for several years after her husband. She was a babysitter and a model grandmother, telling stories and providing valuable advice to her great-grandchildren. She died in March 1984. *Submitted by Edna Mae Drury, daughter*

SWINK - The Swink family history in America begins in 1775 when Wilhelm and Mary Klein Schwink emigrated to Lancaster, PA, from Bavaria, Germany. In the new country his name was Americanized to William Swink.

The old Swink home on Weber Road just west of Maehill Care Center. Part of this sidewalk is still there.

In 1853 one of William's great-grandsons, John Edwin Swink, went with a wagon train to California where he mined and farmed. He married and one of his children born in California was Emmet Edwin Swink. The family returned to a farm near Festus, MO, in 1870.

In 1884 Emmet Edwin married Lillie Drumeller and they moved to a farm near Farmington in 1902. They had nine children, the youngest being Joseph Owen "J.O." Swink.

J.O. Swink was educated in the Farmington Public Schools and attended Flat River Junior College, where he played on their football team. He received his physical education credit by walking to the Junior College from his home via the top of the moun-

J.O. Swink, 1905-1985

tain ridge. Other times he caught the streetcar near his home and rode it to Schramm's Corner in Flat River.

Swink attended Missouri University at Columbia. It took a full day to drive there in his Model-T. He later transferred to the University of Arkansas where he received an LLB degree and was admitted to the Bar in 1929. He served as assistant prosecuting attorney in 1929, probate judge from 1930 to 1942, and then as circuit judge for 24 years.

He also served on the boards of St. Francois County Fair, St. Francois County Savings and Loan, St. Francois County Railroad, and several civic organizations.

In 1935 he married Johanna E. Effrein and they had two children, Joseph Owen Swink Jr., DVM, and Thomas H. Swink.

J.O. Swink had a variety of experiences growing up on the family farm just north of Farmington between what is now Weber Road and Highway 67.

His father was a livestock dealer and had two mule barns in Farmington. He also owned and managed several farms including a plantation in Louisiana. There were times when young J.O. helped out or was sent out by himself to drive herds of cattle or mules from Farmington to the big field south of Ste. Genevieve. If mules were to be taken, he could make the drive in one day, but if he had cattle, it took two days. He would stop midway at Weingarten, corral the herd and his horse, and sleep in a boarding house. The road somewhat followed Highway 32 and parts of the old Plank Road. If one looks closely at the base of the railroad trestle near Highway 32, one can still see a pond made by the county to water livestock on such drives.

One cold winter day on a fast-paced mule drive from a farm near Iron Mountain, J.O. was in the lead when his horse stumbled and went down. He rolled off the horse and crawled to a fence to avoid being trampled by the mules. The horse he was riding was cut up and crippled. J.O. tied the horse tightly to a gentle mule to help in getting it home.

Every fall on the home place he helped his family prepare 100 wagon loads of firewood for heating and cooking in their big brick home. Many times more wood would be needed.

Judge Swink had a keen interest in the people he served. His happiest decisions were granting adoptions to childless couples. His saddest were settling divorce suits between couples married for many years.

He had a love of animals and always kept a good riding horse on his farm. He also had an interest in antique vehicles.

Judge J.O. Swink passed away after a long illness in 1985.

SWINK - Joseph Owen Swink Jr. was born Sept. 11, 1937, graduated from St. Joseph Catholic School, then Farmington Public High School and served in the US Army. He then received a BS and DVM from the University of Missouri at Columbia.

In 1966 he married Mabel M. Reeves and they had three children: Randal Joseph, Bradley Owen and Jody Elizabeth, all of whom still live in the Farmington area.

Joey, as he was known locally since a child, was able to pursue a lifetime love of horses as an occupation.

SWINK - Judge Emmett Edwin Swink was born June 2, 1860 in Tehama County, CA. He moved to his grandfather's home in Missouri in 1870 and later moved with his family to a farm where Festus

is today. On Sept. 17, 1884, he married Lillie E. Drumeller and moved to a farm close to Farmington near Eagle Lake Golf Club. He purchased a farm just north of Farmington which was named Oak Grove Farm. The home included a one-and one-half story house with the kitchen separated from the rest of the house. The house was rebuilt into a large, two-story, brick house with trim surrounding it.

Swink Reunion 1907. Emmett E. Swink family. L-R Back Row: Emmett, Doris, J. Ed, Florence, Ruth. Middle Row: Alma, Grandmother, Grandfather. Front row: Joe, William.

Emmett Edwin was emminent in financial and political affairs. He served as county judge and later as presiding judge of St. Francois County. The governor of Missouri appointed him to the State Board of Agriculture and as a member of the State Fair Board. He later became president of each of these boards. He was a member of the State Highway Commission, presiding on the board and planning for Highways 61, 66 and 67. Before the depression he owned a bank in Farmington and was owner of one of the Farmington's stables.

Aunt Ruth with pony, Aunt Florence on horse, Uncle Ed with pony, Emmett and Alma sitting on steps, Grandmother and Grandfather sitting in lawn chair, c. 1897.

Judge Swink was a mule trader. Each fall he would make a trip through the state purchasing mules. He would go to various stores and branch out buying mules from any farmer who had a mule for sale. He would leave word about mules purchased at the store. One of his sons would follow and pick up the mules. After several weeks, they headed home with 50 to 100 mules. The mules were sent to Ste. Genevieve where Judge Swink owned over 1,000 acres of corn ground. The mules were trained by clearing the ground and pulling up old stumps to make corn fields. The mules were sent by railway cars from DeLassus to Georgia where they were sold to cotton plantations to work the cotton fields.

Judge Swink had four farms where cattle were fed out. Corn had to be fed each day. When ready for market, the cattle were hauled to the home place in Farmington and then driven to DeLassus to be shipped to the stock yards. Grandfather (Judge Swink) had a Ford coupe. He would pick us boys up and place us in gateways

or any place where the cattle might stray while they were being driven to DeLassus.

The corn had to be moved from Ste. Genevieve to the home place by wagon, truck or railroad car. He had a Model T and a Model A truck. He would load the Model T first and then the Model A. The Model A would catch up with the Model T around Weingarten where there was a steep hill. The Model T would be turned around and start backing up the hill with the Model A pushing. This was the only way to get it up the hill. The hill was so steep that going forward the Model T gas tank wouldn't get gas to the engine.

Emmett D. Swink attended Farmington High School and attended the University of Missouri in Columbia (Further information about Emmett will be listed later.)

Doris attended Farmington High School and was a graduate of the University of Missouri. She married Charles Herald. They lived in St. Louis with their two daughters, Gloria and Doris Jean.

William attended Farmington High School. He married Lois A. Westcoat. Bill and Bob were their sons. William was a farmer. Robert died in infancy.

Judge Joseph O. graduated from the University of Arkansas. He was a lawyer, probate judge and circuit court judge. His first marriage was to Lucy Dearing, who died in childbirth. He later married Joanna Effrein and had two sons, Joe and Tom.

Ruth attended Elmwood Seminary (Now this is the Presbyterian Children's Home). Ruth taught school in Desloge and Farmington. She married Lester Clark. *Respectively submitted James E. Swink great-grandson.*

SWINK - John Edwin Swink was born in Franklin County, TN just outside of Nashville on Oct. 27, 1833. At age 3, he moved with his family to Missouri. His dad owned a sawmill and they lived on a farm near Clearwater, MO. At age 20 he left for the Gold Rush in California, where he mined gold for five years. Later he purchased a farm near Red Bluff, CA. It was there that he met and married Maria Louisa Shackelford Waldrop. Maria had an ancestor who married Bettie Washington, sister of George Washington. Another ancestor was the Lewis of the Lewis and Clark Expedition. This ancestor later became governor of the Louisiana Territory with headquarters in St. Louis.

Swink Reunion 1907. John Edwin Swink Family. L-R Back Row: Roy, Byrd, John, Gus, Carrie V. Middle Row: Walter, Grandpa, Grandma, Emmett. Front Row: Lida and Nellie

Maria was born Dec. 6, 1836, in Lincoln County, KY. She and her parents traveled to California by wagon train. Her first marriage was to Bart Walter Waldrop, who died shortly after the marriage. They had one son, Bart Walter Waldrop, born Dec. 9, 1857. He married Rena Vinson and lived in Palestine, TX. Maria's father had a horse and cattle ranch in Sisklyou County, NM.

John Edwin and Maria moved back to Festus, MO, where he managed a dairy and shipped milk to St. Louis. The family were members of the first Protestant Christian Church in the area. In 1902 he sold his farm and moved to Farmington to be with his children. He moved to a farm owned by Dr. Owen Smith. This is now the farm of Chip Peterson's family.

The children of John Edwin and Maria were: Emmett E. born June 2, 1860, in Tehama County, CA. (Further information will be given on Emmett E. in a later article.)

John Lee born Sept. 22, 1862, in Butte County, CA. He married Chessie Jennings and adopted a son, Earl. John Lee was an architect and carpenter, building many houses in St. Louis and Farmington. Some of the large two and three-story homes on Columbia Street were built by John.

Carrie Allen was born Oct. 18, 1866, in Tehama County, CA. She married Joseph E. Clover who was a banker. In Farmington he managed a bank owned by Emmett D. Swink, his brother-in-law. The bank closed during the Depression. Three children were born to the union: Bess, May and George William, who died in infancy.

Robert Augustus was born Sept. 30, 1867, in Ste. Genevieve. He married Mary Adell Ard. Robert was a lawyer and was the author of the Swink Genealogy. He had no children. He moved from Farmington to California.

Nellie Eva was born Aug. 1, 1872. She married Dr. Owen A. Smith. She practiced medicine and surgery and later became an ear, eye and nose specialist in Farmington. Nellie was gifted in music and taught Sunday School in the Farmington Christian Church. They had two children, Laurene and Harry.

Eliza Mae "Lyda" was born April 30, 1876, in Festus. She was a teacher until she married William Fleming. They had one child who died at age 6. They later adopted two children, Mary and Steven.

Sallie Birdie was born Aug. 10, 1878, in Festus. She was a teacher. She married David Carlisle of St. Louis.

Roy Addison was born April 5, 1882, in Festus. His occupation was farming. He married Elizabeth Kohlmier and they had two children, Louise and Lee Roy.

Minnie and George died in infancy.

All of John Edwin Swink's family were members of the Farmington Christian Church.

John Edwin died on Feb. 22, 1915. Submitted by Steve Swink, great-great-grandson.

SWINK - John E. Swink was born Oct. 10, 1921, in Humphrey, AR. At age 5 John's family moved back to Farmington, where he attended first grade at the Annie Loyd Elementary School. John "Johnny" was halfback for the Farmington football team from 1934-1938, playing under Hap Hale. Over the years there has been four generations of Swinks playing football for Farmington High School.

As a child, Johnny was prone to injury. Once he stepped on a nail in the barn lot and was kept in bed for over three weeks due to infection. When recovered, he was in the hay field and stuck a pitch fork prong in the very same place as the nail. One time Johnny was fishing with his brothers. James E. got a bite, yanked the pole back hard, losing the fish, but catching Johnny in the eye with the hook. Johnny was rushed to Dr. Watkins with the hook still in his eye. Dr. Watkins placed him on a stool and told him to open his eye. Johnny was lucky; when he opened his eye, the hook fell out.

Later in high school, Johnny reported that one of his favorite pastimes was to drive the car on the old railroad tracks. His sophomore year in high school he played on the fast-pitch softball team. The team was undefeated. Johnny and a friend coached a girl's softball team that was undefeated. Johnny played baseball for Barton and later for Libertyville Schools.

50th wedding anniversary John and Norma Swink L-R: Lee Ann, Judy, Steve, David, Norma, Johnny

After high school, Johnny attended one year at Flat River Junior College. To get to college he had to hitch hike each day. He was never late.

In January 1941, Johnny joined the Army Air Force and attended Radio Operator and Mechanic School at Scott Field, IL. When he received a weekend pass, Johnny would take a bus from Scott Field to St. Louis, transfer to a trolley car on Broadway and then to a bus which took him to Lemay and Highway 67. From there he would hitch hike to Farmington. While on one of these weekend passes, Johnny says: "Lucky me. I met a beautiful young lady who became my wife."

Upon graduation from Radio School, Johnny was given one  *Norma and John E. Swink* week to travel to Lukefield, AZ. Again Johnny hitch hiked. He was riding with a man from Oklahoma when stopped by the Arizona Highway Patrol. The car had been stolen by the driver. Johnny was cleared but was more careful with whom he would hitch hike.

Johnny was transferred from Lukefield to a new base in Roswell, NM. In June 1942, he got a furlough and hitch-hiked home. There he married his "beautiful, young lady," Norma L. Watson. They lived in Roswell for one year. Their first child, Lee Ann, was born on June 28, 1943. Two days later, Johnny was shipped overseas. He returned when Lee Ann was 18 months old. Lee Ann married Bill Tanner in 1960. Five children were born to the union: Carol Ann, Johnny, Jeannie, Jim and Cathy. In 1987 Lee Ann married Jim Thornton. Lee has worked for many years as an inspector for Amco Oil refinery in Santa Fe, TX.

During WWII, Johnny landed on the beaches of France on D-Day. He served as a radio operator mechanic special duty for the 17th Field Arty. Observation Sqdn. He was stationed in Belgium and was on the border of Germany when shot by a sniper.

Upon return home, Johnny and Norma bought a farm from Dr. Watkins. The farm was close to Libertyville. For several years they managed and operated a dairy farm. John Stephen was born Nov. 10, 1945. Johnny and Norma had been playing cards with friends when Steve decided to arrive. There was no time to get to the

hospital, so Steve was born in Dr. Watkins' office. Steve married Carolyn Scott in 1965. They have four daughters: Christy, Pam, Mary and Amy. Steve has served as a lineman and trouble shooter for Union Electric for 30 years.

In February 1947, Judith Carol was born. She married Larry Whitener in 1966. Judy is a family and consumer sciences teacher for the North County School District. In 1989 she was named Missouri Teacher of the Year and was recognized by Disney in the Salute to the America Teachers. Judy and Larry have three daughters: Debby, Angie, and Elizabeth.

On Friday, Oct. 13, 1950, David Carl was born. David married Traci Bowden. They have two children, Aaron and Jennifer. David is Director of Environmental Health for the city of Spokane, WA

Johnny has always been an avid fan of Farmington athletics. In 1963 when Farmington was playing at North West (no bleachers were available), Johnny was sent back to the home side after receiving a 15 yard penalty for illegal coaching from the sidelines.

Johnny worked as a survey engineer for the State Highway Department for 26 years. He and his wife, Norma still live on the farm near Libertyville. They are both active members of the Libertyville United Methodist Church. Their family includes 14 grandchildren and 18 great-grandchildren.

Johnny is a placid, easy going, compassionate person. He is well liked by all. I am proud that he is my father. *Respectively submitted, Judy Swink Whitener, daughter*

TAYLOR - David, from Desloge, moved to Farmington in 1973, upon graduation from Dallas, TX, Institute of Mortuary Science; after attending MAC 1970-72, David joined the Farmington firm of Miller Funeral Home. Ann, from Flat River, moved to Farmington after graduation from MAC, receiving her degree in Finance from CMSU - Warrensburg and married David in 1976.

David took a leave-of-absence in 1975 from his position in Farmington to work as mortician for the Arabian-American Oil Co. in Dhahran, Saudi Arabia. After marriage and upon retirement as the Aramco mortician, David and Ann moved to Dhahran, Saudi Arabia, where David became mortician for Arabian-American Oil Co. In Arabia, Ann worked in Aramco's Treasury Dept. David and Ann purchased Miller Funeral Home in 1977 and returned to Farmington in 1978. The business name was changed Jan. 1, 1988, to Taylor Funeral Service. David and Ann are the third owners of the funeral business that started in 1881 in Farmington as Neidert Undertaking Co.

David started his mortuary career in Farmington in 1973 and marked his 25th anniversary in 1998. Ann became a licensed funeral director shortly after her return from Arabia. She and David have enjoyed for years the distinction as being active licensees with the most experience and longest service history to Farmingtonians.

In 1990 David and Ann opened the new home of Taylor Funeral Service, Inc. At the time of the opening, this represented the first new and handicapped-accessible, funeral facility in Farmington. Many innovations and improvements were incorporated into this facility to serve Farmingtonians for generations to come.

David's maternal family hails from Mississippi. His paternal family comes from Tennessee and West Virginia. Ann's maternal and paternal family hails from Missouri.

Both Travis and Tracy Taylor were born in Farmington: Travis in 1981 and Tracy in 1982.

The Taylor family belongs to and enjoys the Farmington First Baptist Church. David has served for several years as deacon; 4th grade boys Sunday School teacher and bus driver. Ann has served for several years as a preschool Sunday School teacher, also serving as church treasurer.

David obtained his pilots license at Farmington in 1985 and actively pursues his love of flying. He belongs to several aviation groups and particularly enjoys flying "missions" for AirLifeLine, providing transportation, free of cost, to patients who have both medical and financial difficulties. Some close bonds have been formed with the Taylor family and some of David's regulars as he flies them above the midwest.

David's sister, Sandy, Mrs. Danny Miller, has been an instructor at MAC for years. David's brother, Byron, has lived and worked in Arabia since the mid-70s as a petroleum engineer. David's mom, Rachel Taylor Fieg, lives in Ste. Genevieve.

Ann's brother, Carl, lives in Topeka and is a lawyer and director of Dept. of Economic Development for Kansas Power and Light. Carl previously served as Missouri's economic development director for six years during the Ashcroft governorship. Ann's mother, Lillian Koupal, has resided in Farmington since the early 1980s.

TESSEREAU/BLACK - Harry and Neva moved their family of five, Barbara, Carl Wayne and Joyce Lee to the country in the early part of 1947. They loved living out of town. The family cleared an acre of ground for their yard. There was a drainage ditch dug across the back and it went into a huge wooded area. Country living was just exactly what they wanted. The three children would sneak off to the woods, which was forbidden of course, to play Tarzan by swinging on the huge grapevines and climbing the trees. Their little ventures would always come to light because at least one of them was sure to break out with poison ivy or oak. But they were never to learn; there would always be another time. The family grew to a total of seven. Even though they lived in rural Farmington they were in the Esther School District, so the first three graduated from Esther High School. But when it became cruising time, to Farmington they would go to meet the crowd of teens at "Jack's" to hang out for hours. The two youngest, Michael Glenn and Alice, graduated from Central. At the present time, our little country haven lies directly behind General Custer's Ice Cream parlor on the very busy Highway 67.

Introducing H. Dan Black and wife, Barbara Tessereau Black, their sons, Jonathan Daniel and Joseph Michael, along with Joseph's bride, Sarah Catherine Mackley Black. Also pictured are Dan and Barbara's mothers, Gladys, Mrs. Howard Black of Desloge, MO and Neva, Mrs. Harry Tessereau, of rural Farmington.

As the family grew and the youngsters went their separate ways, Alice to Desloge, Mike to the state of Wisconsin, Joyce to Sullivan, MO, Wayne to Desloge (he passed away on May 3, 1989), and Barb married Howard Daniel Black on Nov. 16, 1962. They rented a few different places lo-

cally during the first few years, but upon Dan's completion of his tour of duty in the military on Oct. 3, 1968, their decision was to make their home in Farmington. After renting for a short time, they bought a small, but nice, two-bedroom house on North Middle Street. That house was made a home but was soon to be outgrown. Jonathan Daniel came along in October 1970. Joseph Michael arrived three years later in August 1973.

Dan and Barb have happily lived most of their married life at 101 Westmoor Dr., Farmington. But time has its way of moving on. Jon still lives in Farmington, but Joseph married Sarah Catherine, daughter of Edward and Sandy Mackley, life-long residents of Farmington, on Oct. 1, 1994. They attended Mineral Area College on theater scholarships. From there they moved to Kirksville, MO. They both graduated from Truman University, each having majored in criminal justice. They are presently making their home in Marietta, GA.

TETLEY - In 1852 John and Elizabeth Babbington Tetley and family left their native home in Derbyshire, England and came to Boston, MA to live. The parents returned to England but six of their children, three boys and three girls, remained in the United States. Frederick, who was born Jan. 28, 1836, in Derbyshire, England, worked as a tailor in Boston until 1857. He then came to St. Louis, where he learned the carpenter's trade. He settled in Bonne Terre in 1876 and married Elizabeth Bland, who was born in Kentucky in 1838. They were the parents of 12 children. Frederick was a dealer in lumber, sash doors, blinds and was a contractor and builder and had a flourishing business. Their children were: Charles, Margaret N., who married Richard Thomas and was the grandmother of Hubert Thomas, Amanda, Richard, Samuel, Mary, Lizzie, Edward and Hattie. Frederick died Jan. 2, 1920, and is buried in the Bonne Terre Cemetery.

John and Robert came to Washington County, MO, and then on to St. Francois County where they settled in Farmington, where they met and married daughters of Wm. J. Gay. The Gay family, William T., his wife Selina Down and four children left Devonshire, England and immigrated to America in 1852, taking passage to Liverpool, landing in New York after a long and dangerous ocean voyage. From there they went to Belevue, OH, where Mrs. Gay's sister lived. After nine years they came to St. Francois County, MO where he purchased a farm. The father followed his trade, making wagons, buggies, plows, grain cradles and all types of farming implements. In 1871 he became the partner of Isenman and from that time this partnership was known as Gay & Isenman. In May 1880 they were burned out with no insurance at a loss of about $6,000. They rebuilt (Jones' Machine Shop building) and continued until the death of William T. Gay in February 1884. William T. and Sam, the two sons, followed their father's trade and began a wagon-making business at Ironton. Sam's son, Dr. Roger Gay, and his two grandsons, Dr. Le Pettit Gay and Dr. George Gay, became well-known physicians in Missouri.

John Tetley, also known as Jack, married Martha Gay and settled on a farm south of Farmington. He was born in 1838, and Martha in 1849. They were listed in the 1870 census with children Elizabeth, born in 1865, and William D. born in 1869. They lived in a lovely farm home at the intersection of highways H and AA. During the time that Sam Hildebrand was so active, it was not unusual for the Jack Tetley's to find his horse in their barn and one of theirs gone, the cot on the porch had been used, food from the kitchen gone, and a piece of money on the table. The Tetleys never did see Sam. Jack and Martha Tetley were the parents of three girls and two boys.

Robert T. Tetley married Ann Gay in 1867. In 1868 they built the Tetley Jewelry Store building, which was also the birthplace and home of all their children. At the death of Robert, his son George continued to operate the jewelry store until his death in 1946. The business was sold, but his grandson, Howard Tetley opened his jewelry store down the street on East Columbia. There has been a Tetley Jewelry Store in Farmington from 1869 to 1977, when Howard sold his store to William Krekeler. Robert was born in 1840 and his wife Ann in 1846. They are in the 1870 census with a son Samuel born in 1870. Henry, the oldest son, was a watchmaker and worked in the store with his father and brother, George. Sam and his brother-in-law, Emil Klein, husband of Elizabeth, operated the Tetley-Klein Lumber Co. for 30 years until the death of Sam.

Sam was appointed the postmaster of Farmington in 1894. He built a lovely home on Patterson St. but the family had to move because the home was not in the city limits. George Clarence and Sam had a hobby of raising cattle.

Elizabeth married Emil Klein, one of the two brothers who founded Klein Grocery Store, now Dugal's.

William moved to St. Louis where he was a jewelry salesman. Clarence, the youngest son, was a dentist and at the time of his death had been a well-known mayor of Farmington. He was instrumental in bringing the Rice Stix factory to Farmington, which was the beginning of the real growth of Farmington.

The Tetleys were always forward looking citizens seeing the needs of the community. Sam operated the first (or close to the first) picture show in the St. Francois County at Flat River over the Neidert Drugstore on West Main St. Dr. Tetley and George Karsch had picture shows here and at Flat River. The Tetleys were the instigators in getting the telephones to the community, the lime kiln at Ste. Genevieve, and the beautification of the city by planting trees and shrubs. They have always worked for the betterment of the Farmington community.

This article was printed in the *Evening Press* March 19, 1979. It was written by Ann Caroline Tetley. She and Roberta were schoolteachers and were the children of Samuel Tetley. They had a brother named Lionel. *Submitted by Howard Tetley*

THOMAS - Hubert Norman Thomas was born July 7, 1882, in Georgetown, CO. He was the son of Richard and Margaret Tetley Thomas, who were born in Cornwall, England. Richard was the son of Stephen Thomas, born Jan. 1, 1811, and Jane Richards, and Stephan's parents were James and Maria Thomas who were born in Redruth, Cornwall, England. Stephen was a miner who was injured in the mines in England. He married Jane Thomas in Aug. 18, 1838. They were the parents of eight children, Moses, born Aug. 5, 1840, and died July 26, 1921, in Mine La Motte, Madison County, MO; Jane, born May 30, 1842; Martin, born Feb. 2, 1844; Mary Ann, born July 1, 1846; Thomas, born March 3, 1848; Stephen, born June 17, 1850; Carrie, born Nov. 3, 1852; Richard, born March 14, 1860, married Margaret N. Tetley; daughter of Frederick and Elizabeth Bland Tetley, and Samuel, born March 14, 1860.

Richard and Margaret came from England to the US in March 1842 on the ship *West Wind*. They arrived in the harbor of New York in June, then sailed up the Hudson River to Albany, where they took the canal to Portsmouth, OH, and from there on the Ohio and Mississippi Rivers to Missouri. They settled at Mine La Motte, in Madison County, where Richard worked as a miner until he died in 1866. Richard and Margaret were the parents of Virginia, born 1880 in Knob Lick; Hubert, born 1882 in Georgetown, CO; Bland, born 1884 in Knob Lick; Gertrude, born 1886 in Knob Lick, MO, Jane, born Georgetown, CO; and Mary, born in Georgetown, CO.

Back Row L-R: Hubert N. Thomas Jr., Clara O'Bannon, Richard F., Mildred Burch, Virginia Edwards, Victor R., Martin B., Tilford W., Marion L. Seated: Essie Mae Parrott, Margrette Logan, Hubert N. Sr., Emily E., Martha Nekola

Hubert Norman Thomas spent most of his first five years on his grandmother Jane Thomas's farm east of Knob Lick. At the age of six the family returned to Georgetown, CO, where he attended 12 years of school and went to work in the mines. He married in 1900 to Emily Elizabeth Schalk, who was born May 19, 1880, in North Platte, NE and died June 27, 1963, in St. Francois County, MO. Her parents were Frederick and Helen Roth Schalk. Hubert and Emily slipped away and married in Denver, without parental consent. He worked about eight months as a miner and then moved to Portland, OR, where he worked different jobs, mostly hauling. Their first six children were born there. They saved enough money to buy his grandmother's farm in Knob Lick, MO, and returned home. Hubert and Emily's children were:

1. Richard, born in 1902 in Portland, OR. He married Hazel Wilkerson and they had a son, Charles. Richard married second Gertrude Robinson, third Dorothy Kessler.

2. Mary Marguerite, born 1904 in Sylvan, OR, married Joseph Richardson.

3. Clara Lucille, born in 1905 in Sylvan, OR, married Park B. O'Bannon. Their children were Martha and Vera.

4. Hubert Norman, born in 1906 in Sylvan, OR, married Elizabeth Woods. Their son was Donald.

5. Virginia Harriet, born 1908 in Sylvan, OR, married William Edwards.

6. Martha Veola, born in 1911, Sylvan, OR, married Roger Nekola.

7. Mildred Emily, born in 1913, Knob Lick, married Perry Burch, the son of Commodore Perry and Emma Carolyn Mund. Perry was born in 1913 and died in 1949. The children were: Perry, Hubert, Jeannie and Linda.

8. Tilford Warren, born in 1917 in Bonne Terre, married Martha Simmons, and were the parents of David, William, Larry and Margaret.

9. Martin Bland, born in 1919 in Libertyville, married Ella Thurman, and had two children, Randall and Mae.

10. Essie, born in 1921 in Knob Lick, married Melvin Parrot. They had five children: Janet, Walter, Nancy, Carol and Darryl.

11. Marion "Tommy," born in 1923 in Knob Lick, married Dorothy Kessler, children were Esther and Marion.

12. Victor Randel, born in 1927 in Knob Lick, married Aug. 10, 1952, Helen G. Williams, who was the daughter of Eugene and Ida Baker Williams. She was born Oct. 2, 1927, and died in 1996. Their children were Susan, born Aug. 22,

1953, and married Darryl Midget. Kathryn Lea, born June 30, 1958, married John May. Their children are John Matthew and Krista Marie. Ann Celeste, born Nov. 17, 1959, married Robert Buchanan. They had one daughter Diana Nicole. Ann married second Tim Barber. They have one son, Clinton Andrew, Jane Elizabeth, born Oct. 16, 1962. She married David Grass, and they have one son Alexander. Victor "Bus" was a mail carrier for many years in Farmington and is retired. He is enjoying his hobbies of bowling and fishing.

Hubert returned to Knob Lick and purchased his grandmother's farm in 1911. He was appointed the postmaster of the Knob Lick Post Office and moved into town. He had a general store in Knob Lick for 25 years and when he retired moved to a farm he purchased on St. Francois River. He spent his next years hunting, fishing, gardening and enjoying his family. They celebrated 54 years of marriage on March 9, 1955. *Submitted by Victor Thomas*

TURLEY - Ralph, Ethel and son Jason, moved to Farmington in 1974. He has been in auto sales in the area since the early 1960s. Ralph was born and reared 10 miles north of Farmington on the family farm that his ancestors purchased from the federal government at a territorial land sale in Jackson, MO in the 1850s. This was located at the edge of Ste. Genevieve County. The family, soon after the purchase, fenced off five acres and gave it to the county for a rural school. Turley

Jason and Melissa (Woodfin) Turley

School, grades one through eight, was in existence until about the early 1960s. Turley Mill Road went from Farmington to a mill that was operated by his ancestors on Terre Bleue Creek, north of Farmington.

Ralph and Ethel were married in 1958 at Fairview Baptist Church. Ethel was born and reared in Bonne Terre, the youngest child of Alfred and Mabel Wigger Dodson. Jason was born Dec. 18, 1969. He married Melissa Woodfin in February 1995. A sister Jodee was born Sept. 18, 1968, and died one day later.

Ralph's father, Bert C., was the son of Ignatius and Eliza A. Thurman Turley.

Ralph and Ethel (Dodson) Turley

The Turley line goes back four generations to Paul Turley of Johnnymore Creek, Fairfax County, VA. Paul was born 1705-1710, and died in 1772. He was a tobacco farmer and a neighbor and friend of George Washington. The Turleys came to Missouri by way of South Carolina and Kentucky. William H. Turley and Martha Miller were married in April 1846, by Justice of the Peace Z. B. Jennings. William and Martha are buried in the Salem Cemetery north of Farmington.

Ralph's mother, Pearl Pig Turley, was the daughter of Reams and Elsie Byington Pigg, born within three miles of the Turley family farm. Pearl's grandmother told her of hearing the cannons at

the Battle of Pilot Knob, during the Civil War. The family was also friends to Sam Hildebrand, who would come to their barn after dark, eat, rest and leave before daybreak.

The Turley farm was sold in 1983, and Bert and Pearl Turley moved to Farmington. Bert passed away in February 1986 at age 84. Pearl passed away in April 1995, at almost 93 years of age.

Bert and Pearl Turley, Bert's parents and brothers are buried at Three Rivers Cemetery, four miles north of Farmington on Highway D. Pearl's parents and brothers are buried in the Pigg Cemetery, 10 miles north of Farmington on Highway C, on the edge of Ste. Genevieve County.

Bert was a farmer most of his life and also worked in the post office in Flat River, where he retired in 1964. He and Pearl had been married and had recently celebrated their 63rd wedding anniversary about two months before his death in February 1986.

The Turleys came to this country in the 1600s from Ireland, Scotland and England.

VALECK - Theodore Franklin Valeck, was born Feb. 22, 1899, at Potosi, MO. He died May 12, 1962, at Farmington, MO. The youngest son of Joseph Walach Jr. and Jennie McClearly, Joseph Jr. was born Sept. 8, 1860, in Bohemia and died May 25, 1916, at Potosi, MO. Jennie was born in June 1867 in MO. Their children were: Mae, born 1883; Joseph D., born 1887; Benjamin, born 1889; Augusta, born 1893; Lena, born 1896; Theodore F., born 1899; and Pearl born 1901.

The grandparents of Theodore were Joseph (Vlilik) Sr. and wife, Barbara. They are in Potosi on the 1870 census with children, Joseph Jr., born 1860; Mary, born 1862; Frank, born 1864; and Augusta, born in 1869. All were born in Bohemia, except Augusta, who was born in Missouri. Joseph Sr. immigrated to work in the lead mines.

Theodore lived his early years in Potosi with foster parents, Bud and Millie Puckett. His mother died early in his life.

On Dec. 18, 1917, Theodore married Josephine DeGonia, daughter of John and Josephine (LaChance) DeGonia. They were the parents of Madelyn, who died in infancy; Lena, born in 1921; Joseph, born in 1923; George, born 1925; Zada, born 1928; and Kenneth, born 1937.

Theodore was interested in automobiles from an early age. He was an automobile salesman all of his life. From 1925-33 he worked for Najim Motor Company at Potosi. In 1928 he won an award for selling the most Chevrolets in 38 counties. In 1937 the Valeck family moved to DeLassus. Theodore worked for Wichman Nash and owned a service station on Ste. Genevieve Avenue, managed by his son-in-law, Abraham Shelton. In 1942, during the war, Theodore was required to work for St. Joe Lead Co., where he was injured in 1944.

All of Theodore's descendants will remember him as a very caring person who shouldered every worry. At the time of his sudden death, Theodore lived on North Long St. in Farmington.

VANDERGRIFF - The Vandergriff family originated in Amsterdam, Holland (The Netherlands). Antonise (Antonius) was the first known ancestor born ca. 1535 in Charlois S. Holland. The first ancestors to come to America were Jacob Van der Grift and his brother Paulus. They settled in (New Amsterdam) presently Manhattan, NY, in 1644. Both Van der Grift brothers were in the employ of the West India Co. Jacob was skipper of the ship

W.C. and Alta Vandergriff

Swol and Paulus was captain of the *Neptune* in 1645 and the *Great Gerrit (Garret)* in 1646.

Willard C. Vandergriff was born on a farm near Farmington Aug. 2, 1915, the youngest of five children of Jesse G. and Margaret (Marshall) Vandergriff. His brothers and sisters are: Alva G., Elmer L., Virgie (Mrs. Charles Princler) and Jessie (Mrs. John Heberlie).

His parents moved from the farm to Farmington in 1922 and resided at 700 N. Washington St. Ironically a Vandergriff has resided on N. Washington St. for over 78 years, however not at the same location. Grandfather Andrew J. Vandergriff was the first in 1920. The Vandergriff resi-

Willard C.Vandergriff

dence at 599 N. Washington St. was a portion of the David Murphy grant dated Dec. 28, 1836.

W.C. first attended North Ward (Annie Lloyd) Elementary School on N. Washington St., then the Farmington Public Schools, graduating in 1933. He received a bachelor of science degree in Civil Engineering from Missouri School of Mines (MSM) - University of Missouri-Rolla (UMR).

Along with millions of his fellow Americans, he served in WWII from 1942-45, first on the Alaska (Alcan) Highway, then he attended Officers Candidate School at Fort Belvoir, VA, and after graduating was posted overseas in India, Burma (Burma Road) and China. He was commanding officer of a engineer service detachment in China.

Returning to Farmington in 1945, he was a partner in the firm of Walther and Vandergriff, consulting engineers, located in the Realty Building at the corner of Columbia and N. Washington streets. At the death of B.F. Walther in 1951, he continued the firm as W.C. Vandergriff, consulting engineer, civil, municipal and environmental, specializing in water systems and treatment plants, sewage systems, occasionally street paving, swimming pools, etc. His work took him to various places, including Louisiana, MO, Cuba, Sullivan, Steelville, YMCA and Boy Scout Camp, Sunnen Lake, Potosi, Bloomfield, Advance, Piedmont, New Madrid, Senath, Ironton, Perryville, the Leadbelt area, plus numerous other cities throughout Southeast Missouri. The firm was dissolved in 1975.

He married Alta M. Jarrette on Oct. 27, 1946, and they were the parents of four children: Camille (stillborn), Edward, Lillith (Vandergriff) Stoessel and Jill (Vandergriff) Haas, two grandchildren, April and David Vandergriff, who reside in Minnesota.

W.C. died in 1992.

VARGO - Michael E. Vargo was born in Bonne Terre on Dec. 21, 1947, to the late Frank and Emma Naeger Vargo. After graduation from Bonne Terre High School in 1966, he enlisted in the Army. Upon his successful tour of duty in Vietnam, he was honorably discharged in May 1969.

On Oct. 10, 1970, Michael E. Vargo and Sharon J. Knittig were united in marriage at St. Joseph's Catholic Church in Farmington. Sharon is the daughter of Frank and Rosemary Knittig, born Sept. 18, 1950, in St. Louis, MO. She is a 1969 graduate of St. Joseph's High School. After their wedding, Michael and Sharon took up residence in Bonne Terre at the family home on Summit St. to care for his mother.

Front Row: Michael Jr., Sharon, Matt. Back Jeremey and Mike Sr. 1994

After training to drive a semi-truck, Michael took a job with Mid-Western Trucking in Fort Scott, KS while still living in Bonne Terre. Then in 1977, he began working at Complete Auto Transit in St. Louis, MO. Sharon began her profession as a lab technologist at the Bonne Terre Hospital shortly after their wedding. Then in 1976, she began working at Mineral Area Osteopathic Hospital.

The first of three sons, Michael E. Jr., was born Nov. 5, 1975, at Bonne Terre Hospital. Not long after, on Aug. 2, 1977, Jeremy L. was also born there.

The second home was in Terrace Gardens on D Highway in Farmington. Moving in 1979 into this tri-level, four-bedroom home on two acres gave the boys plenty of room to run and play. While living there, our third son, Matthew S. was born, on Nov. 17, 1981, at Mineral Area Hospital.

With the closing of the General Motors Car Assembly plant in St. Louis in 1987, Michael transferred to the newly built production plant in Roanoke, IN. One year later, the rest of the family moved to Huntington, just 12 miles from the plant.

Today, Michael Sr. continues to work out of Roanoke and Sharon works at the Huntington Memorial Hospital. Michael Jr., following in his father's trade, drives heavy equipment for a construction company and Jeremy is in the restaurant trade in Fort Wayne, IN. Matthew is a junior at Bishop Dwenger High School in Fort Wayne and looking forward to his graduation in the year 2000. We all still enjoy our visits back to the St. Francois County where most of our families still live.

VOIL - Phillip Voil was born in Tennessee in 1850. In 1898, he married Lucy Ann Watson when she was 15 years old. The couple lived in Arkansas and Illinois before moving to Farmington. The family moved to Farmington in a covered wagon. Along with their three children, Clanzia, Lanskie and Florence, the Voils found shelter in Long Park, as they knew no one in the area. The youngest, Florence, traveled with a broken leg. She later came down with an illness, was attended by Dr. Haw, but died in the winter after arriving in Farmington.

Since the family was so poor, they often had to depend upon the generosity of the local people for food and supplies. However, Phillip and Lucy sometimes had to "fight" for their food. In those days, chickens roamed around the park. Phillip would put a grain of corn on a bent pin, and when the chicken would swallow, he would pull it in. Lucy would then clean the chicken and cook it for dinner for the family. Through all of the hard times, the family grew. They had three more children, Naomi, Leonard and Alma. The family continued to make their home in Farmington. All of the children were educated in the Farmington School District. Leonard, also known as "Zeke," graduated from Farmington High School in 1924.

Lucy Voil and five children. Front row: Leonard "Zeke" Voil, Lucy Voil. Back row left to right: Lanksie, Mrs. W.H. Fortune, Alma - Mrs. W.L. Shoemake, Naomi - Mrs. R.W. Wagoner, Clanzia - Mrs. G.W. Hutchinson.

Mr. Voil worked at many occupations to support his family. He primarily supported his family working as a huckster. Phillip died in 1937 and Lucy died in 1946. The children married and started families of their own. Clanzie married G. W. Hutchinson. Lanskie married Mr. William Fortune. Naomi married Mr. Roy Wagoner. Leonard "Zeke" married a woman from Cape Girardeau, and Alma married Mr. W. L. Shoemake. The Fortune family moved to Seattle, WA, and "Zeke" and his wife made their home in Cape Girardeau, MO.

Two grandchildren, several great-grandchildren, and great-great-grandchildren still reside in Farmington. The two granddaughters that still reside in Farmington have been lifelong residents. They are Florence (Mrs. Melvin Bone) and Alberta "Happy" (Mrs. Arthur "Red" Bone). Many other grandchildren, great-grandchildren and great-great-grandchildren live in different cities throughout the United States.

VIOLA HARTER WADE - I am proud of my heritage. I was born in Elvins, MO, on Oct. 12, 1902, the third child of Frank T. Harter and Cora Counts Harter. My two older brothers were J.C. and Orvall and the three younger brothers were Burl, Emmet and Joseph.

I am a direct descendant of the founding family of Murphy's Settlement or Farmington, the Rev. William Murphy. Rev. William Murphy was married twice. His first wife was Martha Hodges and they were the parents of five children. She died and he later married Sarah Barton.

It is believed

Viola Harter Wade

that Rev. William Murphy emigrated to this country from Ireland. He married Martha Hodges. He was a pioneer; always in pursuit of happiness. While living in North Carolina, William and his brother, Joseph, were baptized at Deep River in 1757. Later, William and his brother were among the first to feel "called to preach" the doctrines of the Baptist denomination. Rev. William Murphy moved to Virginia and then to eastern Tennessee, preaching and farming wherever they were living. His wife, Martha Hodges, died leaving him with five children. Sometime before July 21, 1767, he married Sarah Barton and to this union, six children were born. In 1798, Rev. William Murphy traveled with his three sons, Joseph, William Jr. and David, and a good friend, Silas George, to the Louisiana Territory. Each claimed a 640 acre Spanish Land Grant. The land was blessed with numerous springs and later became known as Farmington, MO.

Joseph Lyde Counts in front of his home on N. Washington, with his peddlers wagon. 1880-1890 circa taken.

William Murphy Jr. served in several arenas during the Revolutionary War. His exploits against British and Tories, and later against the Indians, made him a noted fighter and earned him the nickname of "Big Billy." In 1776 he was a member of Bedford County militia under Capt. Leftridge. In 1777 he served three months in the Henry County militia under Capt. Herston. He rejoined the Bedford militia as a second sergeant.

In 1778 he joined Robert Sevier's company in North Carolina. Later that year, he joined the Regulars in South Carolina and served as first sergeant and later promoted to ensign. In 1780, he served as a sergeant under Gen. John Sevier. Later he volunteered for three months' active duty as a private in Col. Lincoln's Light Horse of Bedford. In June 1781 he served one month in frontier service against the Indians in Virginia and later served against the Cherokees in the Tennessee country. He was allowed a pension on an application executed May 7, 1833, while a resident of St. Francois County, MO.

Elizabeth Murphy Walker

He died on Nov. 10, 1833. His grave is located in a

Mary Miller Counts

small family graveyard, on what is now Jim and Delores Plummer's farm. This farm is part of the original farm of William Murphy Jr. which was obtained from a Spanish Land Grant in 1798. On Flag Day, June 14, 1915, the Daughters of the American Revolution held a ceremony to unveil markers secured from the government to indicate William Murphy's service to his country during the Revolutionary War.

I am a direct descendant from the first marriage through his son, William Jr., married Rachel Henderson. Their fourth child, Elizabeth married Laken Dubart Walker. They had 15 children, the oldest being Martha (my great-grandmother) who married Robert Miller. Laken Dubart Walker was born in North Carolina and came to Missouri in 1803 and was granted a Spanish Land Grant of 640 acres. He married Elizabeth Murphy in 1804. Laken Dubart Walker later became county assessor from 1823-1826. From 1825-

Martha Miller

27, he served as a judge of the county court. He was sheriff from 1828-1833. It was common for elected officials to hold more than one post at a time. In all the years of his residence in St. Francois County he was closely connected with the public interest.

The Walkers were my great-great-grandparents. Martha Walker and Robert Miller had a large family, one of them being Mary who is my grandmother. She was the next to the youngest child. Mary married Joseph Lyde Counts. They had five children; four boys and one girl, Cora. She married Frank T. Harter. My mother, Cora Counts Harter, whose parents were Joseph Lyde Counts and Mary Miller, lived in Ste. Genevieve County. They wanted their children to have an education so they

Cora Counts Harter

moved to Farmington in the early 1880s. My mother attended the South Ward School (now the W.L. Johns School), this being the only public school in Farmington at that time. Cora Counts attended and graduated from the Baptist College in 1892 with a teaching certificate. She taught school for three years in Ste. Genevieve County. She became acquainted with Frank Harter, a farmer, from Coffman. Frank Harter's grandfather, Heinrich Harter, and grandmother, Johanna Gremmig Harter, came to this country in 1843 from Baden, Germany.

My maternal grandfather, Joseph Lyde Counts, and his family lived next to Waide Spring on N. Washington Street. Waide Spring is actually no longer in existence. What the "locals" call Waide Spring is actually Counts Spring. The two spring houses were very close to one another. The Waide and Counts properties joined one another between the two springs. Today, Waide Spring is actually under Maple St. My grandfather built a house at 601 North Washington St. and it is still standing today. My grandfather was a peddler and had a wagon pulled by a horse. He sold vegetables, orchard fruits and dairy products mainly to the people in Flat River because there were no stores and just a few houses located on Federal Hill. He also took orders for clothing and shoes, which were purchased in Farmington and then delivered on the next trip. He was a fine Christian and was a deacon in the Pleasant Hill Baptist Church.

On Nov. 4, 1920, I married Clarence E. Wade. We have always made Farmington our home. He was employed at State Hospital Number 4. About four years later, Clarence went to

work for St. Francois Motor as a mechanic. He proved himself in this position and was promoted to head mechanic. Still exemplifying good work ethics, Mr. Carlyle Rozier, the owner of the business, sent him to Desloge to manage the Ford dealership. Within two years, Clarence had obtained his own Ford dealership, which he opened in Farmington 1941, and retired about 50 years later. He celebrated his 100th birthday on March 19, 1998.

We have five children who are: Edsel, who married Dorothy Mueller; Leroy, who married Patricia Meyer who died in 1985 and later married Sue Hardy Stone; Geraldine, who married Soren Peter Sorenson; Don, who married Anna Jean Welch; and Barbara Ann, who married James Cornelison. We have 21 living grandchildren, one is deceased. We are blessed with 41 great-grandchildren and one great-great-grandchild. We also have four step-grandchildren.

WALKER - Ronald E. Walker and his family (wife, two daughters, Kim and Kelly, and a son, Kevin) moved to Farmington, MO in the summer of 1977. Ron wanted to return to the area where he was born and raised. Ron was born in Leadwood, MO. He wanted to return to a small-town community and his wife was born in Batesville, AR. All three children were born in St. Louis, MO.

Ron's father, William Walker, resided in St. Francois County his entire life. Born June 25, 1892, he worked the mines all of his life and raised his family of six in Leadwood, MO. Ron's mother, Myrtle, was a housewife. Ron's father died Oct 9, 1948, from black lung disease. At the time of his death it was accepted as the killer, and it claimed the lives of many. Ron was the youngest of six. His grandfather would help out after the death of his father. It was a big help to his mother. Grandpa Walker, with his pension check, once a month would buy Three Musketeer candy bars for the children. It was the only candy bar for the month and "a great treat." Most of the siblings reside in St. Francois County today, and Ron's mother, Myrtle Mary Walker, passed away in 1977.

The Walkers built their home on Hollyhock Lane within Holiday Park. Immediately, Ron's yard was one that no one could compete with. It was no time before he was awarded "Yard of the Month" by a community organization. He was also known for the most decorated house on the exterior during Christmas. It is felt by many who resided there at that time, he began the trend; the Christmas spirit was catching. Now if you drive through Holiday Park, the name of the subdivision seems appropriate.

Aside from his finely manicured lawn and his "Kris Kringle Mentality," Ron is a salesman. He sells paper to various companies and businesses in the surrounding counties, Poplar Bluff, Cape Girardeau, Illinois, and the Bootheel. He has been employed by various paper companies but currently works for Nationwide Papers out of St. Louis, MO, serving the same territory. He continues to work but is looking forward to retirement in the future. This will enable him to enjoy golfing, grandkids, and of course "watch out neighborhood," more time for lawn care and Christmas cheer.

Ann Walker came to Farmington, MO after living the city life for a number of years. She began her endeavors as a beautician, a floral designer, not to mention being a part of the local city government as city collector. Ann started her ventures with "a bang." If Ann Walker was in a room, everyone knew it. She was easily accepted by the Farmington workforce and positively contributed to the community and town in everything she did.

Ann began by opening a beauty shop on Washington Street across from Heck's IGA. Hair

Designs was the name of the salon. She owned and operated the shop for four years and then sold the business. The beauty shop still remains in business at a different location. Following that, Ann purchased Butterfield Flowers from Charles Smith in 1982. She then was once again a hairdresser until 1994, working off and on. The political arena called on her at this time and she took over the city collector position for the city of Farmington, fulfilled a four-year term and then decided not to run again. She has since done volunteer work for Parkland Hospital and Children's Haven. She is also active in Nancy Weber Garden Club and member of First Baptist Church in Farmington. Currently, Ann is involved with Dix retail and Christmas with Claudia in Park Hills, MO, not to mention her wonderful grandchildren.

The Walker family included three children: Kim, the oldest, had already graduated high school by the time they moved to Farmington.

She remained in Farmington for five years and then began her career in banking in St. Louis, MO. Kim attended MAC for a semester and then moved to St. Louis in 1998. Currently, she is married, with a daughter, Randi, and a son Koby. She also has three step-sons. She and her husband reside in Farmington. Kim is a "stay-home mom" who takes care of her son and her nephew. Her husband is an RN employed at SMMHC.

Kevin, the only son, graduated from Farmington High School in 1982. He was active in baseball. He played ball in high school and then two years at MAC, as well as the Mineral Area Baseball Association (MABA). Kevin then left Farmington to begin a new life in Kansas City, MO. He is currently employed at Unisource (a paper company), following his father's footsteps as a salesman. He is an avid "Chief's fan. He remained in Kansas City for many years. Kevin would rather be at Arrowhead Stadium - tailgating with his dad than anywhere else.

Kelly, the youngest daughter, graduated from Farmington High School in 1984. She attended college at William Woods in Fulton, MO for two years, with a scholarship in basketball and volley ball. She graduated from Southwest Missouri State University in 1989. She then resided in St. Louis, MO, working with handicapped individuals. She decided to return to the area in 1992, worked for the Division of Family Services, and is currently employed at Southeast Missouri Mental Health Center. She has worked there for the last nine years and maintained concurrent employment at Children's Haven for the past six years. She married Kenny Johns in 1995. Her husband was a high school teacher and coach at that time. He is currently employed with Dix Green House Park Hills, MO. They have a remarkable son, Walker Henry Johns, and are expecting their second child in November 1999. Kenny, the oldest son of Martin and Lois Johns of Farmington, and Kelly plan to remain in Farmington and raise their children in a "small town" valued community. Hopefully, Farmington remains what it is meant to be: "A city of tradition" first and foremost. Progress is inevitable.

WALKER - Bailey Robert Walker and Margaret Grace Ruffin Walker came to Farmington in 1929 from the "bootheel" of Missouri. Bailey was born in Union City, TN, but grew up in Kennett, MO. Margaret was born and reared in Hornersville, MO. She attended Will Mayfield College in Marble Hill, MO and Southwest Missouri State in Springfield. Bailey and Margaret were married in Hornersville in 1928. When they first married, they lived in Sikeston where Bailey was manager of the Kroger Grocery Store. In 1929 they moved to Farmington when Bailey was made supervisor of 16 Kroger stores in the area. The

Kroger Co. had wanted them to live in another town. However, Margaret and Bailey thought Farmington was such a beautiful area with well-kept homes, big trees, good schools and churches and friendly people. They asked Kroger

Margaret and Bailey Walker

Company if they could have permission to live in Farmington and they agreed. They rented an upstairs apartment in the home of Judge Orten located at 510 C. St. Their only child was born there Aug. 21, 1930, and they named her Virginia Nell Walker.

In 1934 Bailey and Jesse Heck, a native of Farmington, opened the IGA store, located on the corner of Columbia and South Henry St. The partnership was continued for some years and then was dissolved. Margaret worked at several jobs, one of which was at Trimfoot Shoe Co. She was employed there for 17 years.

In 1959 Bailey and Margaret bought Smith's New and Used Furniture Store located on the corner of South Jackson and Liberty. They changed the name to Walker's New and Used Furniture. I think that location is now a parking lot. They operated this store until they retired in 1965. Bailey passed away in 1979 and is buried in Kennett, MO. Margaret is now a resident of The Baptist Home in Ironton, MO. They were long-time members of First Baptist Church of Farmington. Margaret taught Sunday School there for many years and was active in the missionary organizations of the church.

Virginia Nell graduated from Farmington High School with the Class of 1948. She went to Southwest Baptist College and Missouri University in Columbia, earning a BS degree in elementary education. She taught school at Brightstone School south of Farmington and also at Norclay Elementary School in north Kansas City, MO. She has a master's degree in religious education from Southern Seminary in Louisville, KY. She met her husband, Paul St. Clair Smith of West Monroe, LA there. They were married in First Baptist Church of Farmington by the pastor, Rev. J. Loren Jolly in 1956. Paul and Virginia served as missionaries of the Southern Baptist Convention for 31 years before retiring to Eufaula, OK in 1996. They served in the countries of Lebanon, Jordan, Morocco and Northern Iraq. They have four grown children, Timothy Walker Smith, Margaret Elizabeth Smith Tarcza, JoNell Smith Hemingway and Kathryn Sue Smith Hollister, and six grandchildren. The grandchildren and great-grandchildren of Bailey and Margaret Walker live in Texas, Kansas and Qatar in the Arabian Gulf.

KEATHLEY-WALLACE-COLEMAN - There were 13 children born to William Tyler and Martha Evaline Lewis Keathley: Della, William Walker, Lucille, Nettie, Lester, Charles Elmer, Clarence, Herschel Fred, Myrene, Lorene, Marshall and two that died in infancy, May and Henry.

Della graduated from the eighth grade at the King School east of Annapolis when they lived on the Brushy Creek farm. She studied penmanship at Ironton on Highway D and at Roberts School east of Des Arc. Her husband, Mr. Arthur Tesreau worked in the shoe factory.

Walker graduated from the eighth grade at the King School, and was a clerk at the Lone Pine Hotel in Ironton, MO. He served in WWII, taking his training at Camp Funston, Fort Leavenworth,

KS. His outfit was ready to ship out for Europe as the war ended. Walker was Superintendent of the Iron County Farm for two years.

Keathley Family. Front row: Clarence, Elmer, William Tyler, Lorene, Martha Evaline, Hershel, Myrene (standing in front). Back row: Lucille, Lester, Walker, Nettie and Della.

Lucille graduated from the eighth grade at the King School. She married Mr. Paul Fanale who worked in a winery in California. Lucille was an excellent cook and worked as a cook in a cafeteria in California. She was also employed in Lasens National Volcanic Park, northern California.

Nettie finished her sophomore year of high school in Ironton and married Eldon Helms. Miss Lester graduated from Ironton High School in 1921, graduated from Stephens College, Columbia, MO, and then received a Masters degree in Elementary Education at the University of Missouri at Columbia. She taught school at Arcadia, Ironton, Cove and Webster Groves, a total of 45 years.

Herschel Fred finished two years at Ironton High School, served apprenticeship with G.A. Buckey, contractor and builder in Ironton. He married Alice Jane Randolph. Herschel was employed as first class carpenter in construction work and later worked 30 years as a finishing contractor in Anchorage, AK.

Lorene graduated from the eighth grade at the elementary school in Ironton. She lived with and helped care for her parents. On March 23, 1993, she completed a perfect Sunday School attendance record of 63 years! She now lives in the Baptist Home, Ironton, MO.

Myrene graduated in 1931 from Ironton High. She played on the girls basketball team. Myrene earned LPN degree in nursing and was employed as administrator and nurse for 18 years in Colonial Nursing Home in Bismarck, MO. Her husband, Bruce Wallace, was employed on the Missouri Pacific Railroad for 32 years, based at Bismarck. Myrene is presently living at the Baptist Home, Ironton, MO.

Myrene and Bruce Wallace had seven children: Elizabeth Ann Jackson, Mary Lou Politte, Helen Lee Coleman, James Bruce, William Lester, David Lenard and Bruce Orville, Jr.(died in infancy).

WALLACE-COLEMAN - Myrene graduated in 1931 from Ironton High School and played on the girls basketball team. She earned LPN degree in nursing and was employed as administrator and nurse for 18 years in the Colonial Nursing Home in Bismarck, MO. Her husband Bruce Wallace was employed on the Missouri Pacific Railroad for 32 years based at Bismarck, MO. Myrene is presently living at the Baptist Home, Ironton, MO. They had seven children: William, James, Elizabeth Ann, Helen Lee, Mary Lu, David and Bruce O. Jr. (died in infancy).

Helen Lee Wallace married James David Coleman in July 1957. James retired in 1997 from Butternut Bread Co. after 30 years. Helen worked at the Bismarck Bank, Bismarck Hardware Store and Bismarck Nutrition Center for many years. They have five children: James Lee, LuAnn

Reese, Martha Jane Frazier, Linda Renee Fisher and Kent Wallace Coleman.

James married Connie Sue (Hadler) and they have three children Mandy, Brandy and Carista; and two grandsons, Joshua and Ryne. Connie owns and operates Connie's Cafe in Bismarck, and James works for Coca Cola Corporation in Farmington.

LuAnn married Joel Reese in 1987 and they have three children: Andrea (Cromer) Hinson, Jeremiah and Spencer; and two grandsons, Jacob and Dylan.

Martha married Scott Frazier and has two children Megan and Jennifer. They live in Florida, where Scott serves in the USAF.

Linda and David Fisher met and married in Springfield, MO. Linda and David moved to Farmington around 1994. They have two children, John David and Tracey. Linda works for Southeast Missouri Mental Health Center in Farmington, MO. David is a manager at JC Penney in Farmington.

Kent Wallace married Bonnie Sue (Asher) on November 11, 1989, and moved to Farmington. Kent works for St. Francois County Ambulance as a paramedic and volunteer fireman for the Farmington Fire Department. Bonnie works for the Farmington Public Library. They have one child, Tyler Preston Coleman, born Dec. 26, 1995, and are expecting their second child in February 2000.

WATSON - Darrell Aubrey Watson and his family, (wife, Dorothy, and two children, Daniel Arthur and Dorene Ann), moved to Farmington, MO from Huntsville, AL, Aug. 31, 1972, retiring after 26 years in the US Army.

Darrell, Dorothy, Daniel and Dorene Watson

Darrell was born in Flat River, (Park Hills), Oct. 3, 1923. He was living there during the time his father, William Albert Watson, was working for the lead mines. During the Depression, (1927-1932) his family moved to DeLassus and lived on a farm. The family returned to Flat River (Park Hills) for the remainder of Darrell's school years. Darrell graduated from Flat River High School, Class of 1942. In February 1943 Darrell was drafted into the Army during WWII. He was discharged in November 1945 and returned to school, attending Flat River Junior College, spring semester 1946-47. In December 1948 Darrell enlisted into the regular Army.

Dorothy was born Oct. 28, 1933, and raised in Brooklyn, NY. She graduated from New Utrecht High School in June 1952. She met and married Darrell in Virginia Beach, VA, Dec. 25, 1960.

Daniel Arthur was born in Brooklyn, NY, July 9, 1961, and Dorene Ann was born in a military hospital Sept. 21, 1963, in Vicenza, Italy. Daniel graduated from Farmington High School in 1979 and Dorene Ann graduated from Farmington High School in 1981.

During the 26 years we have lived in Farmington, Darrell has worked for the Farmington R-7 School District as a bus driver and was employed by the Farmington Post Of-

fice for 12 years. Dorothy is presently employed by the Farmington R-7 School District and has been since 1989-90 school year.

The changes in Farmington during the 26 years we have lived there are the perfect example of a small town growing into the status it is today. Population, industry, churches and schools have all grown.

Gone but not forgotten are the feed mill, grain elevator, where the police station is now, Capital Cafe and its famous round table for coffee and conversation, Rozier's clothing store, and the 5 and 10 Cent Store.

WEBB - "Poe's 'The Pit and The Pendulum' cannot be said to have a theme, but it clearly has an intent. That of evoking very stong feeling of suspense and fear." Charles and Mary Webb are from Bollinger County, MO and had seven children. The children moved to St. Louis, MO. In 1916 Charles Webb was hired by Dr. Overton to clear the timber for railroad ties. Dr. Overton's farm was located on

Vella and Maude Webb c. 1928.

a rural route a few miles from Farmington, MO, which had a new log house with trees on this farm.

The three younger children were born in St. Francois County. The names are listed: Esther R. Webb, Lloyd Webb, Bertha E. Webb, Grace B. Webb, Floyd Levi Webb, Zella Bell Webb, Maude May Webb, Owen W. Webb, Opal B. Webb, Irene Virginia Webb and Everett Charles Webb.

WEBER - John A. Weber was born in Waechterbach, Germany in 1819. He came to America in 1843, landing at Cape Girardeau. He settled in Jackson for the next two years and then moved to Mine La Motte, where he engaged in the jewelry business. He was also interested in the lead mines there.

In 1848 he married Elizabeth Schulte. In 1852 they moved to Farmington where he opened a general merchandise store. He was twice elected to judge of the county commissioners court and was elected first mayor after Farmington became a fourth class city in 1879. He was mayor for four years.

Nan Gardener Weber, 1892-1989

During the Civil War, he was a strong union man and his influence counted for something. Many citizens who were arrested for their Southern sympathies owed much to him for his interference on their behalf.

John A. and Elizabeth lived in a home located where the Long Memorial currently stands. They had one daughter and five sons. One son, Kossuth William, married Anna Claybrook Cayce, a daughter of Milton P. Cayce Sr. In 1877 Kossuth built the home at 513 W. Columbia St., currently owned by Dr. John Fitz. K.W. Weber was reared in the Lutheran Church. His marriage to Anna Cayce resulted in a step towards bringing the German and southern communities closer together.

Kossuth studied law at St. Louis University

and was admitted to the bar in 1876. He served as Deputy US Collector of Revenue for 13 years. In 1899 he was elected mayor but served only a few months before his untimely death in July. K.W. and Anna had two sons, Kossuth Cayce and Frank Schulte.

Kossuth C. graduated from Washington University Law School. In 1910 he was elected probate judge, an office he held for 28 years. He also served as city attorney for several years and was assistant prosecuting attorney. Kossuth was a member of the Board of Directors of the United Bank of Farmington and of the Ozarks Federal Savings and Loan. He was a charter member of the Farmington Kiwanis Club and was president of the St. Francois County Bar Association. In 1916 he married Nan Gardner. They had two sons and a daughter: Kossuth C. Jr., Winston Gardner and Nancy Weber Reed.

Frank Schulte Weber earned his M.D. from Washington University, was on the staff of the Farmington State Mental Hospital and for a number of years had a family practice in Farmington. In 1923 he moved to La Grange, IL where he specialized in eye, ear, nose and throat.

Nan Gardner Weber, 1892-1989, was involved in many human endeavors. She consistently displayed an impressive record for executive leadership in many organizations. She was a woman of tireless energy and a persuasive leader.

She served as co-chair of the St. Francois County "Raise Missouri Out of the Mud" Campaign, 1929-1931. Her slogan "Enjoy do not destroy Missouri's woods and wildflowers" was adopted statewide. She organized the St. Francois County Highway Beautification Committee and was state chairman of conservation and roadside improvement for the Federation of Garden Clubs. She promoted accumulation of hundreds of signatures to fight the politically-oriented State Wildlife Commission. This effort resulted in the creation of the independent Department of Conservation.

She served as state president of the Federation Garden Clubs. Nan organized an early chapter of the Beta Sigma Phi business women's sorority, a group that helped with a National Cancer Crusade that was forerunner of the American Cancer Society. In 1974 Nan was recognized for 40 years of distinguished service by the American Cancer Society.

She gave considerable effort to local endeavors, including the first garden club in Farmington, followed by a number of other clubs in the city. Using cuttings from her own boxwood shrubs, she distributed the shrubs throughout the city. Nan was an accomplished soprano soloist and directed the Presbyterian Choir for 25 years. She helped organize the child welfare organization in the county and was active on the mental health board.

In 1990 Nan was posthumously inducted into the Missouri Conservation Hall of Fame in Jefferson City.

Nan Gardner Weber left a lasting legacy of service to her community.

WEISS - Adam Weiss was born Jan. 25, 1871, in Doe Run, St. Francois County, MO. He was the 10th child of Heinrich and Mary Mueller Weiss, who came from Germany. He married Ida Mae Higbee on March 13, 1898, and they were the parents of 12 children. Ida Mae was born July 10, 1879, in Doe Run and died April 12, 1961. She was the daughter of Henry and Rachel Wood Higbee. Adam lived on property adjoining his father's farm southwest of Doe Run, where they raised their family. Their children were:
1) Stella, born Jan. 31, 1899, and married

Jesse Barnes. He was born in Farmington on Feb. 28, 1894, to George and Amanda Hamm Barnes. He died Oct. 10, 1917, in Elvins, MO. Stella died Oct. 12, 1927, and they are buried in the Weiss Cemetery. They had five children: Alma, Jesse, Merryl, Harold and Hattie.

2) Bessie was born Sept. 29, 1900, in Doe Run, married Freeman Fraizer and had three children: Paul, Russell and Thelma. Bessie died in 1925.

3) Eva was born Sept. 18, 1902, in Doe Run, married Tony Baker in 1920 and had two children, Joslyn and Walter. Eva died April 25, 1980.

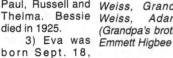
Dorothy Weiss, Aunt Mae Weiss, Nora Weiss, Grandma Weiss, Helen Weiss, Grandpa Peter Weiss, Adam Weiss (Grandpa's brother), Uncle Emmett Higbee

4) Ott was born Oct. 7, 1904, and died in 1969. He married Ethel Hensen and had Debra, Ida May and Curtis.

5) Blanch was born Nov. 6, 1906, and died in 1983. She married Howard Downs in 1927 and had four children: Lowana, Bill, infant unnamed and Darlene.

6) Gilbert was born Feb. 3, 1909. He married in 1937 to Catherine King, born in 1914. She was the daughter of James King and Sallie Goff. They had seven children: Thomas, Melvin, Doris, Sallie, Ronald, Barbara and Phylis.

7) Roy was born Aug. 15, 1911, and died in 1991 in Farmington, MO. He was married to Myra Nichols and had two children, Jerry and Virginia. He married second to Martha Rogers.

8) Marvin was born Oct. 11, 1913, and died June 20, 1982. He married Ellen Moore, the daughter of Oliver Hayden and Martha King Moore, and had four children: Donald, Jack, Mary and Carol.

9) Nora was born Sept. 23, 1916, and married Joseph Edward Williams, the son of Joseph Edward and Josephine Douglas Williams, and had four children: Charles, Shirley, Roger and Duwane.

10) Dorothy was born Sept. 11, 1918. She married Luther Green, the son of William and Lillie Brown Green, and had James, Bill, Patricia and Judy.

11. Earl was born June 14, 1921, and died in 1923. He is buried in the Weiss Cemetery.

12. Helen was born Oct. 21, 1924, and married first Bill Howe and had one daughter, Connie; they divorced and Helen married second William Zimmerman and had daughter, Christine. There are a lot of the family buried in the Weiss Cemetery, which sets on a hill in the country where the Weiss family lived. *Submitted by Helen Zimmerman Doe Run, MO*

WEISS - On Nov. 10, 1854, Henrich Weiss, a native of Hesse Darmstadt, Germany, applied for citizenship of the US of America. "He comes and proves to the satisfaction of the court by oaths of John Hehn and Aaron Isenberg. He has resided in the US at least five years immediately preceding this application during which time he has conducted himself as a man of good moral character, attached to the principles contained in the constitution of the US and well disposed to the good order and happiness of the same and the court moreover, being satisfied that the applicant has taken the preparatory steps required by the laws of the US

concerning the naturalization of foreigners and he declaring here in open court upon oath that he does absolutely renounce and adjure all allegiance and fidelity to enemy, foreign powers, prince, state and whatsoever and particularly to the Prince of Hesson, Darmstadt of whom he was late a subject. Therefore, the said Henry Weiss is admitted as a citizen of the US."

Top Row: Edith, Jesse. Middle Row: Grace, Cora, Peter, Everett. Bottom Row: Robert, Cordelia, Jewell, around the year 1913

Henry was born in 1826 in Hesse Darmstadt, Germany. He died Aug. 13, 1890, in Doe Run, MO as a result of an accident with his team of horses and wagon. He married Elizabeth Mueller, who was born Jan. 29, 1833, in Germany and died Feb. 5, 1874, in Doe Run. They owned land southwest of Doe Run, MO and raised 11 children there. They and several of the Weiss family members are buried in the Weiss Cemetery, which Henry deeded to the Weiss heirs. Their children were:

1) Louisa was born in 1852. She married John Lovvorn and had two children: Margaret and Mary.

2) Henry was born in 1854 and married Clara Kellerman. Their children were: Edward, Anna, Henry, Carrie, William, Pearl, Lille, Josephine, McKinney and Mary Kate.

3) Elizabeth was born in 1855 and married Fred Comber, no children.

4) Mary was born in 1858. She married John Watkins and their children were Fred, Elizabeth, Gertrude, Dora and Robert Charles.

5) William was born in 1860 and died in 1873. When he died, his mother wouldn't let them take him away from the farm, so they buried him on their property and started the Weiss Cemetery.

6) Charles was born in 1862 and married Mary Oelsen. Their children were: Louise, Mary, William, Katie Christian, Frank, Adam, George, Henry and Pete.

7) David was born in 1865 and died young.

8) Caroline was born in 1867 and married John Johnson. They had one daughter, Ethyl who married Ode Williams, son of Francis Marion and Josephine Wright Williams and they were the parents of Alice, Ruth, Lorene, Lesley, Jewell, Dale, Beverly, Marion, Marilyn, Noel and Mavis.

9) Peter was born in 1869 and married Cora Ellen Honeycutt, who was born in 1876 in Wayne County, MO on the way to St. Francois County from Arkansas. Her parents were Charles and Cordelia Murray Honeycutt. Their children were: Edith, born in 1898, died in 1977 and married Alvin Marks; Jesse, born in 1900 and died in 1929. He married Seba Oelsen and their children were Adolph, Firman, Harold and Hilma. Grace, born in 1903, died in 1974. She married William Arnold and had one daughter Barbara Ellen. Everett, born in 1905 and died in 1951. He married Genevieve Johnson and had one daughter, Alice. Cordelia, born in 1908 and died in 1987. She married Leo Forsythe and they had four sons: Theodore, Warren, Dwayne and James. Jewell, born 1910, died

1982, and married Floyd Gilliam. Robert, born in 1913 and died in 1980. He married Ruth King and had nine children: Robert, Virginia, Charles, Norman, Thelma, David, Harold, Donald and Dennis.

10) Adam was born in 1871 and died in 1940. He married Ida Mae Higbee. They raised 12 children: Stella, Bessie, Eva, Otto, Blanch, Gilbert, Roy, Marvin, Nora, Dorothy, Earl and Helen. Adam lived on a farm next to his parents. The Weiss Cemetery is next to his property.

11) Kate was the last child of Heinrich and Mary and was born in 1873. She died young. It was said that Heinrich Weiss stowed away on a ship when he came to America. He had brothers who came and lived in Iron County and Madison County. *Submitted by Theodore Forsythe*

WELLS-WHITE - John William Wells and Addie Belle Sartan were married during the latter part of the 1800s. There were nine children born from this union. There were six boys: William, Roy, Ernest, Wallace, Paul and Joseph. They also had three daughters: Edna, Dottie and Marjorie.

Wells-White Family. Left-Right: Louise, Bonnie, Dorothy, (Charles Warden, Belle's son) Floyd, Belle and Marjorie.

The Wells family owned several farms in Howard County near Boonesboro. One of the main cash crops was tobacco. They raised cattle and bred horses and hunting dogs. They were well known for being avid coon and fox hunters. This was a favorite sport and still is today. Marjorie often spoke of good times as a young girl, of buggies, pretty hats, square dances and basket dinners on the ground. Addie and William Wells were later divorced and neither ever remarried.

James White was orphaned at an early age. He tried for many years to find his family, which he believed were from this area, but with no success. He later married Lenny Mable Beasley and they had five children. There were three sons: Eddie, Thurman and Floyd. They had two daughters, Opal and Marie. They lived in this area for sometime, mainly around Esther, MO, and then they moved to St. Louis while the children were still young. James and Lenny White later divorced. James came back to this area where he met and married his housekeeper, Mandy Brown. Lenny married Bill Speck.

Floyd Preston White, born 1912, and Marjorie Eunice Wells, born 1910, were married in 1931 in Howard County, MO. They settled in Belleflower in Montgomery County, MO. They also lived on what was known as Wild Goose Island on the Missouri River. From this marriage seven children were born. There were two sons, Otis Floyd and Richard Lloyd. Five daughters were also born. Lenny Belle, Marian Adaline, Dorothy Eunice, Bonnie Josephine and Louise Alice. In December 1947 Floyd and Marjorie moved to this area. They bought what was known as the Albright homeplace. The property is about three miles from Knob Lick. The home was a 100 year old two-story log house. It burned in the winter of 1967.

Floyd and Marjorie left for just a short period of time until they could get another place to live in back on the farm. They returned and lived out their remaining years on the place they called home. Floyd passed away Dec. 23, 1974, and Marjorie followed on April 29, 1986. The White Farm is still in the family, and is owned and operated by Otis, the eldest son of Floyd and Marjorie White.

WESTOVER - John Jordan Westover was born in St. Francois County, Nov. 23, 1855, son of Lorenzo and Mary Jane Houk Westover, and grandson of Job and Jane Simms Westover. Job came to Missouri with Moses Austin in the late 1700s and settled first at Potosi and then homesteaded on a land grant signed by President James Monroe in what is now Washington and St. Francois Counties. John Westover was the second generation born in the original home built by his grandfather.

John J. Westover Family, 1909. Front row: Grandson Meredith Westover, John J. and Mattie. Second row: Carrie and Maurice, Paul, Raymond and Mabel. Third row: Anne, Georgia, Mabel, Ellen and Laura.

He was educated by private tutor at home and in 1878 attended Bellevue College at Caledonia, MO, where he met and married Martha Virginia Miller in 1880. Martha "Mattie" was the daughter of Benjamin and Amanda Poe Miller of Cape Girardeau. Benjamin came to Missouri in 1818 from Calvert County, MD, when he was three years old.

John and Mattie established their new home on part of the original Westover Grant. In this home 10 children were born to them: Maurice, Raymond, Edith, Mabel, Emmette, Paul, Anne, Georgia, Laura and Ellen. Edith and Emmette died in infancy and are buried in the Westover Cemetery near Leadwood, MO.

In 1902 the family moved to Farmington, where John continued to farm. The girls attended school at Elmwood Seminary; the boys attended public school. They were active members of the Murphy Long Methodist Church South.

Maurice married Carrie Choate and they had one son, Meredith. Raymond married Mable Lang and they had two sons: Earl and David. Mabel married Walter E. Williams and they had four children: Lawrence, Emmett, Mary Ellen and Eugene. Paul married Rachel Tutor and they had five children: Paul Jr., Tudor, Martha Virginia, Glenn and Harold. Anne never married. Georgia married Henry Nelson McCall and they had twins: Martha and Margaret. Laura never married. Ellen married Dunham B. Dodge, no children.

John Westover died Nov. 8, 1939 at 84, and Mattie died Dec. 2, 1958 at 97. John, Mattie, Maurice, Mabel, Paul, Anne, Georgia and Laura are buried at Parkview Cemetery, Farmington.

WHITE - Marjorie and Floyd White were living in Bellflower, MO, along with their seven children. But Floyd wanted to own some land, and he wanted to live close to the town where he was raised in Esther, MO. He found out about some land available just outside Farmington; so on Dec. 7, 1947, he packed up his wife and children and headed for a new home.

Floyd farmed on his new land along with the help of his wife and seven children:

Marjorie White

Lennie Bell, Marian Adeline, Dorothy Eunice, Bonnie Josephine, Otis Floyd, Louise Alice and Richard Lloyd. Floyd also had to supplement his income by working for several local farmers. Marjorie would take the kids to the store in Knob Lick to get groceries on a wagon, carried by their family horse, who they called Blackjack, and their mule, who they called Andy. Even

Floyd White

though the children had to work hard, they found ways of enjoying themselves, by taking a swim in their pond. The older children left home first, leaving the younger ones to grow up together.

As all the children grew older, they eventually left home. But Floyd and Marjorie still enjoyed visits from their children and their families. Unfortunately, in 1967, their family house burned to the ground but they

Otis White

continued to live on their farm. When Floyd and Marjorie passed away, their son Otis (pictured) acquired the farm. He now enjoys cattle farming on this land and is planning to build a home there.

Fifty-one years later, the White farm still exists. It is a beautiful farm that will hopefully always carry this family name.

WILLIAMS - Ambrose Williams' Genealogy states he lost everything because of the fall of the Continental Dollar; and after first wife Mary Moor died, he married Jane Inman and had several more children. Ambrose was a miller by trade and this was passed down among his children and grandchildren. The old mill at Caplinger Mills, MO was built by his son and grandson but they sold it to the Caplingers from Tennessee. Our Williams ancestors are practically in every county of Missouri, not to mention many other states before and after the westward expansion began. It is said that Ambrose came from Wales with two brothers, John and Harden. Indeed, I believe this to be true because Ambrose has many descendants named Harden Williams.

I am the descendant of John Roy Williams, born in Oklahoma, the son of John Hiram Williams Sr., born in Fannin County, TX, the son of John Hiram Williams Jr., born Fannin County, TX, the son of Thomas Davis Williams, born in Tennessee, the son of John Jefferson Williams who

lived in Liberty Township, St. Francois County, MO. If you have further information on Williams Family, write to Clydene Williams Cannon, 462 Woodrow Ave, Vallejo, CA 94591 (1-707-554-3475)

WILLIAMS - Daniel Williams was born in Davidson County, TN, Dec. 29, 1811, where his father, Lodowick Williams, was listed in the early tax records of 1811. He came to St. Francois County before 1836. On June 22, 1836, he married Sarah Jones, who was born in Ste. Genevieve County, May 26, 1818. She was the daughter of Simon Jones, who died, and she was in the care of John Jones. Richard Jones married them in St. Francois County, MO. Sarah's mother was a Sioux Indian.

Daniel's parents were Lodowick and Susanna Williams, who moved from North Carolina to Davidson County, TN. Several of their children were born in North Carolina and some in Tennessee. They were the parents of 12 sons and one daughter. Six came to St. Francois County during the 1830s. They were Gardner, who married Bedie Calliam; Sarah, who married Solomon Eaves; David, who married Ziba Hailey; Daniel, who married Sarah Jones; James, single; and Wilson, who married Amy Holsted. These are the only known children of Lodowick and Susanna Williams. Wilson and family moved to Cherokee County, KS.

Daniel settled on land, around 1800 acres, on Possum Hollow Road and raised a family of 13 children. He was a justice of the peace and married numerous people, including his brother Wilson, who married Amy Holsted, on March 12, 1840.

This note was left by his granddaughter Addie: "Dad's Father was Daniel Williams. I don't know when he was born or his age. He died in the time of the Civil War. The bushwhackers got after him and he went to Farmington and joined the soldiers where he caught smallpox and died." Pleasent, Addie's father, said Daniel's father died when Daniel was 10 years of age in Tennessee.

In the book *State Wide Missouri Obituaries*, from *The St. Louis Christian Advocate (Methodist)*, published by Mrs. Howard Woodruff, it says "Mother" Williams born in North Carolina in 1767, died 1857 in St. Francois County, MO. This is believed to be the mother of Daniel. Susanna came to St. Francois County, MO with her son David around 1840.

Daniel and Sarah's children were Artimesia J., born 1837, married John W. Griffin, had one son John Wesley; Nancy E., born April 1838, married Hans Jorgensen and had five children; Andrew Jackson, born Oct. 18, 1841, married Nancy Hardesty, no children; Susanna G., born August 1843, married Albert Eaves and had nine children; Washington Lafayette, born Jan. 9, 1844, married Maria Wampler; Rhoda, born March 29, 1845; Daniel Jr., born April 4, 1847; John Franklin, born 1849, married Katherine Ely and had four children.

Thomas Jefferson, born 1851, married Clementine Roe and had eight children. They moved to Cherokee County, KS and raised their family. Francis Marion was born Sept. 8, 1853, and married Missouri Josephine Wright, daughter of Marlin and Margaret Coffelt Wright. They had nine children and lived on Possum Hollow Road by the Old County Farm, then moved to Syenite, then to Doe Run where they died. Pleasant, born Feb. 22, 1855, married Mary Ann Wood; Newton, born in 1857, married Amanda Jane Barnhouse and had six children; Sarah Anne, born Sept. 25, 1860, died in 1918. She married Thomas Merryman and had 10 children.

Daniel died Aug. 17, 1863 and is buried in

the Possum Hollow Cemetery, where several of his children and other family members are buried. This cemetery is located on part of his property. When he died, his widow, Sarah, married Joshua Wood. He died and Sarah lived with her children, dying on Jan. 22, 1911, at the age of 92. She was living with her youngest daughter, Sarah Anne Merryman, and had been blind for sometime. She is probably buried in the Pendleton Cemetery since her family donated the land. *Submitted by Steven Forsythe*

WILLIAMS - Elisha Williams was born in 1836, and came here from Union County, TN. He came to Missouri, first to Ste. Genevieve County, just out of Womack and then to St. Francois County. He traveled with the Acuff family in 1871. It is said that there were several families living near a lake in this area who came from Tennessee. He married Nancy J. Acuff in Tennessee and they had five children. Nancy was born March 22, 1838, in Tennessee and died Nov. 16, 1916, at the home of her daughter Cynthia in Desloge, MO. She is buried in the Knob Lick Cemetery. It is unknown when Eli died, but he was on the 1880 census in Ste. Genevieve County with his wife and four children. Nancy was living in Knob Lick in the 1900 census and was a widow and lived alone. Their children were:

1) Cynthia Elvira, born Sept. 11, 1860, in Union County, TN and died Sept. 6, 1935, in Desloge, MO. She married David Miller Fleming who was born in 1861 and died in 1939. They are buried in the Knob Lick Cemetery. They were the parents of five children, three dying in infancy. Their children are Mary, who was born in 1886 and married George Smith. Mary died in 1926. Maude was born March 14, 1889, and married first a man named Jobe. They had a daughter Jeanette, who married Payton Andrews. Maude married the second time to Jack E. Bell, who was born Oct. 1, 1882, and died Sept. 5, 1945, at Barnes Hospital in St. Louis. He was the son of Capt. Frank and Sarah Bell. He worked for the Kansas City Railroad, was assistant postmaster at Flat River, worked in the National Lead Office and was the superintendent of the County Infirmary in Farmington in 1939, where he and his wife both worked. When Jack died, Maude took over as the superintendent of the infirmary until 1951 when she left and went to California. They were the parents of Frank Fleming and Graham Fulford Bell. The boys lived in San Diego and her daughter lived in St. Louis. She died in California and was brought back to Knob Lick to be buried in the cemetery there.

2) James L. was born in 1868 in Tennessee. He went to Paragould, AR to live. His wife is unknown but they had two daughters, Lottie and Ethel.

3) Melissa "Lizzie," was born in 1871 in Tennessee and died in 1946 in Desloge, MO. She was married to George Faber in 1893. He was the son of George and Louise Lang Faber and was born in 1863 and died in 1936. He was employed by the Desloge Consolidated Lead Co. as a bookkeeper for 30 years. His wife received a letter from Joseph Desloge upon his death. George and Melissa had six children, all but one preceding him in death. George Jr. married Geneva Thurman. Firman Klein, was born in 1905 and died in 1919.

4) Charles E. was born in 1874 in Ste. Genevieve County. He was a minister and moved to Chaffee, MO, where he pastored a church. He married Myrtle Ann Lawrence, who was from Marquand, MO. They had four children, Grace who married Charles Wommer; Claude died in infancy; Hilda married Rufus Heeb, and had three children: Merlin, John and Charles. The fourth child was Lawrence.

5) John was born in 1880 in Ste. Genevieve County and moved to St. Louis.

WILLIAMS - Eugene Williams was born Nov. 18, 1891, near Farmington, MO, to Francis Marion and Missouri Josephine Wright Williams. He married Aug. 17, 1911, Ida Viola Baker, daughter of Lorenzo and Mary Emily Politte Baker. She was married in a double ceremony with her sister Hattie Baker and Charles Clemons. Eugene was a farmer and worked on the railroad which ran Doe Run and Her-culaneum, MO. He then moved to Commerce, OK and became an engineer for the Eagle Pitcher Mining Co. that ran between Miami, OK and Joplin, MO. Ida moved to Farmington, MO after they sold the farm in Doe Run and raised the youngest children. Gene returned to Farmington, where he died in 1975. Ida died 1977 in Farmington, MO.

Ida Viola Baker Williams and Eugene Williams

1) May, born in 1912, Elvins, MO, died 1978, married in 1936 Virgil Burkett from Burkett, TX. Their children: Robert, born in 1937, married Janet Pritchett, daughter Rebecca. William, born in 1938, married Phyllis Hayden, children: Stephen, Cathy and adopted Amy. Rayma, born in 1941, married Bill Golden and had Michael. Betty, born 1943, married Jerry Carter who died in Vietnam, daughter: Jerri. She married second Martin Giger and their children were: Angela, Nancy and Heather.

2) Hazel, born 1914, died in 1989, married in 1934 Harold Chamberlain, their children: Doris Lee born 1935 and died 1938. Donald, born in 1937, married Margaret Marquart (divorced). Their children: Martha, Richard, John, Donna. Darlene, born in 1939, married Ron Burkhart (divorced). Their children: Robin, David, Jeff and Scott. Karolyn, born in 1952, had one son Ben.

3) Lawrence, born 1915, died 1921.

4) Beulah, born in 1918, married in 1937 to Vernon Elser. Their children: Vivian, born in 1939, married Louis Torres, had Lisa and Nina. Second marriage to Robert Maharas, Francis, born in 1941 and Charles, born in 1951. He has a daughter, Krista. Donna, born in 1955 and married Tim.

5) Chester, born in 1920, married Erma Craig, son Terry, second marriage to Louise Province, son Timothy born 1964, married Jamie Ferguson.

6) Helen, born in 1922, died in 1996, married Victor Thomas; children: Susan born 1953, Katheryn, born 1958, married John May, children, Mathew and Christa. Anne, born in 1959, has a daughter Nicole Thomas. Anne married Tim Barber, son Clint. Jane, born in 1962, married David Grass, son Alexander.

7) Melvin, born in 1926, first married Clara Harrington, children: Joanne born 1949, married Richard Fernandez (divorced) children: Daniel, Robin and Amy. Daniel, born in 1951, married Gloria, children, Kellina and Ian. Gary, born in 1958, Mel married second Mary Wyatt. They are working in the ministry at Covenant Life north of Festus.

8) Carl, born 1928, married Jessie Torres, children: Cheryl, born in 1953, married Mr. Lopez, children: Andre, Daniel and Robert; second marriage Bill Brannan (divorced) daughter Christy. Richard, born in 1955, married Linda (divorced), children, Richard and April. Rick has son Mathew.

Roxanne, born in 1957 married David Leon (divorced) and has one son Gabriel. Charmaine, born in 1958, has one daughter, Charmaine, second marriage to Michael Sutphin (divorced) has daughter, Ashley.

9) Laverne, born in 1931, married Theodore Forsythe in 1948, children: Danny born and died 1949, Steven, born 1950, married Gale Centrone, children: Daniel, Katherine and Stephanie. Karen, born 1957, married Terry Pyeatt (divorced), children: Tera and Kirk. Linda, born Jan. 1, 1959 (first baby born in county) married Alan Manning (divorced) her son, Nathaniel Joshua Forsythe born 1990, second marriage Dennis Smith.

Eugene and Ida are buried in the Doe Run Memorial Cemetery at Doe Run, MO, where his parents, brothers, children and grandchildren are buried. *Submitted by Linda Forsythe*

WILLIAMS - When remembering my dad, Eugene Williams, I think of him and his work as a roundhouse foreman, at Doe Run, MO for the Mississippi River and Bonne Terre Railroad, (M.R.&B.T.). It was called Miserable Roads and Bad Tracks by the train crews in the 1920s. I remember him as a hard working and trusted employee, and he did his job without having to have a supervisor to see that his work was done. He was on call day or night, for there were trains running out at all times at the height of the early lead mining business.

His duties were to keep the engines running and maintain the equipment operating at the various places around the yard. He had help from his switchman and helper, John Cromer. The passenger trains were left at the railroad station by their crews; and after the coaches were checked and cleaned, which took 15 to 20 minutes, Dad would get in the cab and John on the front of the engine and take it to the water tank and fill the tank. Then Dad would take it down the track past a switch, which John would turn and then Dad would back the train down the east leg of the triangle and turn around.

I, Chester, born in 1920, when about age six, I used to get to take his dinner bucket to him on Saturday or during school vacation. I would walk down to Antoine's store and going behind it on a path, walked alongside a creek about a hundred yards to a pump station that Dad maintained. I walked up a hill, alongside the water pipe to the railroad yards, where the water tank was located. It was a big tank, up off the ground, and had a big water spout that put water in the engine. At times I was lucky and the engine would be stopped at the tank and I would get to climb aboard the engine and watch Dad operate the levers to make the engine go. After several times of watching, I knew I could operate it too. He introduced me to several of the crew members of the trains, Mr. Pritchett, Mr. Waltman, Al Proffit and John Cromer. Once I saw the engine, with the front of it swung open, and Dad was up in the boiler, beating on the end of a tube, using a swage and a big hammer, trying to stop a water leak in the boiler. He was about as black as coal and wet with sweat. Now days they are welded. He told me to leave the bucket and go home. He was called out at nights to do the same job. The engines didn't operate well with water running into the firebox.

Mother, the jewel of the family, and the kids had passes which let us ride the train free. We used to take rides to Mother's sister, Minnie Chapman's home in Herculaneum and spend the day and then ride the train back to Doe Run. It was a treat to get to do that. We would take the milk run early in the morning and the train would stop often at platforms along the track and I would watch out the window and see the men put the milk cans in a car ahead of the coach we were in.

Late in the afternoon we would return home. I learned the names of the towns at each stop.

As the lead mines slowed, the number of trains which came to Doe Run got less and Dad was transferred to the main yard at Bonne Terre. He worked in the shops and I remember he cut the middle finger knuckle on his right hand with a band saw and he had trouble getting it to heal. At that time he started studying the R.R. Books of Rules for engineers and firemen. Mother would ask him the questions out of the book and he would give her the answers. He finally learned the answers and passed the exam. He got on the extra board, as it was called; and when any fireman was out, he made the run. To start, he was firing the engines on the night runs. At this time the engines had to be fired with a scoop shovel. Coal was scooped from the tinder behind the engine into the fire box. Anytime anyone was out he got the run. Dad also moonlighted as a barber for a while at Bonne Terre.

Dad Eugene Williams Train Doe Run 1910

The family moved to Bonne Terre on a cold snowy day, where we lived for maybe a year. The second house we lived in belonged to a store owner named Kirkpatrick and we lived next to Tessaros. My brother, Mel, cut our youngest brother's finger with a lawnmower and Mother soaked it in kerosene and wrapped it up and it grew back together. Dad was transferred to the Dupo, IL railroad yards, and the family moved back to Doe Run, just before the ninth baby was born. At this time M.R.& B.T. sold to the Missouri Illinois R.R., (Mike & Ike) as it was called. They had a big rally and gave out Mike & Ike buttons. Six months later the Missouri Pacific Railroad bought them out. About 1930 Dad got laid off and came home. He learned a widow, who owned a farm one mile west of Doe Run, wanted to sell her farm, and Dad traded our house in town for it. It had 72 acres and we moved there in 1931. Dad made all kinds of trades to get things we needed to farm and to make a living. He traded for the mule team and a saw rig, which he made a governor for. It was the best and fastest saw rig around.

The house was too small for a family of 10, (we had lost one brother, so we were eight children and two parents) but we managed for a time. The farm had grown up and Dad had to cut the sprouts, as big as three inches, out of the field by himself. I did some of the smaller ones, but Dad cut most of them. We had 40 acres now ready to plow. He worked harder than anyone and the excuse the railroad had for laying him off was that he wasn't well since he had a heart murmur, but it didn't slow him down.

After we got the farm planted, he made a deal for some wooden boxcars at Rivermines and drove up there and took them apart for the lumber, hauling lumber with the team and wagon back to Doe Run. The last trip we made, we had some big timbers on the wagon and the mules couldn't pull them up the hill and we finally dumped them off along the road and I don't remember what-

ever happened to them. They were 1x2x16, as I remember. I remember him tearing down a store building for the lumber in Rivermines, but I wasn't there at the time. He changed our house from an L shape to a bungalow and put two rooms upstairs, mostly of tongue and groove lumber, which helped make our home much bigger. I was helping him one day when I had the mumps and a 2x4 fell on my head and left me in serious condition, and I spent the next week in bed.

Dad bought 160 acres of woodland south of Stono Mountain and we cut wood there. We sold some and traded some for food and clothing to store owners. He traded hay for a 1926 Dodge, four-door sedan and traded it for a Ford pickup one-ton truck to haul wood in. He traded wood for 17 turkeys and traded them for a 1926 Dodge pickup and then sold that. We cut and hauled wood for people in Farmington as well as many others.

Dad was an outstanding farmer and gardener and we had much to eat and sell. The garden had cabbage, lettuce, tomatoes, turnips, carrots, radishes, sweet and Irish potatoes, rutabagas, cantaloupe, watermelons, peas, green beans, pinto beans, corn, okra, blackberries, raspberries and more. He built hot mounds to keep much of the excess in and we had it to use through the winter. We had many fruit trees, and one he had grafted several kinds of fruit on. He, at one time, had 10 beehives supplying honey, which we had to eat and sell, and cattle for milk and butter, hogs and chickens and sorghum molasses, so we had plenty to eat during the time of the Depression. Dad was a hard worker and very resourceful. We weren't rich but we had all we needed.

Dad got the chance to get back into the railroad and went to Cardin, OK to work at the Eagle Pitcher Mining Co. I went to visit him in Miami, where he lived. He got sick one time and I went to bring him home. Dr. Richard Crouch of Farmington, diagnosed him with pernicious anemia, probably saved his life. The doctor in Oklahoma thought he had cancer. Dad finally retired after working as an engineer for about 20 years, and returned to Farmington to live. He began to have strokes and was unable to live alone and stayed with my wife, Louise, and me. He fell while we were at work and we put him into the hospital at Farmington, but he died at the age of 83.

He told me the two engines he had run for the Eagle Pitcher Mining Co. were on display at the Museum of Transportation in Kirkwood. They were #1522 and #1621. He said they are cleaned up and "big 22," as he called it, is being used for shows and tours. A large number of his family, children, grandchildren and great-grandchildren went to see it on a very hot day and really enjoyed the trip. *Written by Chester Williams, 7447 Highway 21, Barnhart, MO*

WILLIAMS - Francis Marion Williams was born near Farmington, MO on the Possum Hollow Road, Sept. 8, 1853. He was the son of Daniel and Sarah Jones Williams. He married Aug. 8, 1888, Missouri Josephine Wright, the daughter of Marlin and Margaret Coffelt Wright. She was born Jan. 18, 1861, in Macon County, KY. The Wright family was living in Perry County, MO in 1870 and in Madison County in 1876. They moved to St. Francois County and lived on Possum Hollow Road, where Josephine met Marion. Marion and Josephine were married and lived next to the Old County Farm, where the children were born. Later they moved to Syenite and then Doe Run, MO. They were the parents of 10 children:

1) George Wright, born Feb. 17, 1889, married Stella Burkett Aug. 4, 1912. She was the daughter of William and Laura Burkett. She was born in Burkett, TX and they moved there to live.

Charles sitting on the lap of Missouri Josephine, behind her is George, Eugene is sitting in the chair, William is standing behind Marion with his hand on his shoulder. The year is around 1896

They had three children: Gilbert, born in 1913, Evelyn, born in 1920 and died in 1951, and Eileen born in 1915.

2) Joseph was born April 16, 1890, and died 1966 in Gillespie, IL. He married Mary Cartee in 1910 and divorced. She was the daughter of Joseph and Sarah Thompson Cartee and was born in Doe Run. They had Thelma, born in 1913 and married in 1928 Lemuel LaRose. Nellie was born in 1915.

3) Eugene, born Nov. 18, 1892, died April 12, 1975, at Farmington, MO. He married Ida Viola Baker in 1911, the daughter of Lorenzo and Mary Emily Politte. She was born Feb. 1, 1892, in Syenite and died Aug. 12, 1977, in Farmington. They were the parents of nine children: Ida May married Virgil Burkett. They had four children: Robert, William, Rayma and Betty. Hazel, born in 1914, married Harold Chamberlain, and had four children: Doris Lee, Donald, Darlene and Karolyn. Lawrence was born in 1915, died in 1921. Beulah, born in 1918 married Vernon Elser and had four children: Vivian married Louis Torres, had two children, married second to Robert Maharas. Francis is unmarried, Charles has a daughter Krista, Donna is married to Tim. Chester was born in 1920 and married first Erma Craig, son Terry, second marriage to Louise Province and had Timothy. Helen, born in 1922, died in 1996, married V.R. Thomas, the son of Hubert and Emily Elizabeth Schalk Thomas. They had four children: Susan, Kathy, Anne and Jane. Melvin, born in 1926 first married Clara Harrington. They had three children: Joanne, Daniel and Gary. Mel married second time Mary Wyatt. They are working in ministry at the Covenant Life Church north of Festus. Carl, born in 1928, married Jessie Torres (divorced) and they had four children: Cheryl, Rick, Roxanne and Charmaine. Laverne, born in 1931, married Theodore Forsythe in 1948 and had four children: Danny, born and died Aug. 30, 1949; Steven, born Dec. 3, 1950; Karen, born April 29, 1957; and Linda, born Jan. 1, 1959, was the first baby of the new year born in St. Francois County.

4) Charles, born July 9, 1893, died March 27, 1953. He served in the Army in WWI.

5) Birdie, born April 13, 1895, died Oct. 6, 1896. Buried Possum Hollow Cemetery.

6) Mary, born Jan. 14, 1897, died Oct. 24, 1974, married Luther Preston. Two children Harold and Belva.

7) Virgil, born Feb. 10, 1899, died Aug. 19, 1907. He is buried in the Possum Hollow Cemetery.

8) Ode, born Sept. 13, 1901, died Nov. 5, 1992, married Ethyl Johnson 1921. Children: Alice, Ruth, Lorene, Lesley, Jewell, Dale, Beverly, Marion, Marilyn, Noel and Mavis.

9) Josephine, born Sept. 12, 1903, died March 15, 1996, married Ben Preston.

10) Vernon, born April 30, 1906, died May

17, 1952, married Naomi Dodson 1931. They had two sons, Cecil and Woodrow.

Francis Marion was a farmer. He died Jan. 8, 1925, at Doe Run, MO and Josephine died Jan. 25, 1937. They are buried in the Doe Run Memorial Cemetery, where a number of their children and grandchildren are buried. *Submitted by Gale Forsythe*

WILLIAMS - Gardner Williams was born in 1806 in North Carolina and was the son of Lodowich and Susanna Williams. He married Bedie Calliam Aug. 4, 1826, in Davidson County, TN. She was born in 1808 in North Carolina. They came to St. Francois County, MO about 1837 and settled in Liberty Township. They were listed in the 1840 census with six children. Gardner was a farmer living in Liberty Township in the 1850 census. Gardner later moved to Pendleton Township and was listed in the 1860 census. After his wife died, he married Catherine Short. She had four children by her marriage to Mr. Short. They came here from Georgia, where Catherine and her children: Julietta, Ruth, Sarah and James Short, were born. Gardner and Bedie had eight children. They moved to Madison County just south of the St. Francois County line, where he died in 1872. He is buried in the Bethany Baptist Church Cemetery on MM Road, which is off Highway 72.

Children of Gardner and Bedie were:

1) Eliza Emeline, born around 1830 in Tennessee, married Jesse H. Bray, Aug. 13, 1846, in St. Francois County, and had one son, Nathaniel born in 1849. She died in childbirth, and Nathaniel and his father were living with Daniel in the 1850 census.

2) Daniel, born in 1832 in Tennessee, married Elizabeth Bennett in 1854 in Doe Run, St. Francois County. She was born in 1831, the daughter of Elisha and Elizabeth Dennis Bennett, who came from Kentucky to Arkansas, then Missouri. Daniel and Elizabeth had four children: Sarah Jane who married John M. Crawford. John Franklin, born in Doe Run, married Emma Lynch. They were the parents of nine children: Joseph Edward, Daisy, Bertha, Carrie, Newton Frank, Roy, Elsie, Cora Begetta, Gladys and Jeremiah. Daniel was a private in the Co. F, 47th Missouri Inf. Vol. and died from typhoid fever in 1865. The company left Cairo, IL for Nashville, TN on the steamer *Minnehaha* a week before Christmas in 1864. The weather was bad and on the way up the Cumberland they hit a snowstorm. He became ill during this time because they had to stand in snow and slush. They also had an outbreak of measles and sickness. Elizabeth died in 1878.

3) Sarah Jane, born in 1835 in Tennessee, married James A. Beard in 1854 and had a son, Gardner, born in 1856. James was born in 1832 in Indiana, the son of Jonathan and Jane Beard. He was in the Civil War in Co. G, 47th MO, Inf. Vol and was a casualty of the Battle at Pilot Knob, MO. He was shot in the head and later died in Climax Springs, MO as a result of the injury, in 1896.

4) Susannah, born in 1836 in Tennessee, married Charles Eaves in 1854, second marriage to John R. Beard in 1864. Their children were Eleanora, Lissi and Madison, who were twins.

5) Frances, born in 1836 in Tennessee, married John Ketchum in 1857 and had four children: Mary, who married John Rambo; Dora Emma married Edward H. Bequette; Elizabeth married George Taylor Bremmer and John Samuel married Minnie Summers.

6) Martha "Patsy," born in 1836 in Missouri, married Samuel White in 1863. He was the son of James E. and Ruth Snow White and was born in 1843 in Missouri. They had four children: Laura, Levi Frank, Virginia Belle; then married Edward

Louis Sebastian and had Mamie, who married George Miller and they had Mable, who married Harvey Reed. The last child of Martha was Julia who married David Inman.

7) Mary Elizabeth, born in 1840 and married William Harrison Higbee, in 1870 in Madison County. They had Phoebe, who married William Walker; and Samuel Bethel, who married Sophia Eleanor Dugal. Their children were Anna, who married Thomas Isabel; Ellery; Aldene, who married Moore Griffin; Arthur and Edward Henry.

8) Betsy, born in 1845, married Andrew McCoy.

Gardner and Catherine's children were:

9) James Morrow, born in 1860 in Madison County, died in 1875.

10) William Penn, born in 1861, died young.

11) Lucinda, born in 1867, married first Robert Sharp and second Charles Weimer. She was born in 1859 in Tennessee. They had no children but adopted Walter Thomas Cartee who was born to Valentine Cartee and Ruth Sort, a half sister to Lucinda. Walter was born in 1890 and died in 1942 in Farmington, MO. He married first Martha Kirstein in 1910 and second Kathleen Lentz. He had three children by first wife and two from second.

12) John Milton Williams, born in 1869 in Madison County, married Sarah Walker in 1889. She was born in 1871 to D.C. and Sarah Kirkpatrick Walker in Madison County, MO. They had seven children born in Madison County; then he went to Montrose, CO, where the family later moved. Their children were John A., who married Anna and had seven children; Nola Lucinda married George Carter; Marcus Antone; Gardner Lee married Lois Books; Annie married Allyn Blunt; Edna married George Dowling; and John Robert, died in infancy. *Submitted by Tera Pyeatt*

WILLIAMS - George Williams was born in Greenbrier County, VA, which is now West Virginia. In 1798 he married Mary Doggett and they moved to St. Francois County before 1830. He bought land one mile south of Bonne Terre, where they lived on the farm. He sold this and moved to Flat River, where there were no houses of any kind at this time, only farms and timber. They were the parents of seven children:

1) James C., born 1822 in Missouri, married Mary Ann Jackson in 1846 who was born in 1820. They had 11 children: Rhoda, William E., George W., John P., Mary Frances, James L., Sarah, Elizabeth, Charles M., Peter T., Barton D. and Anna Rachel.

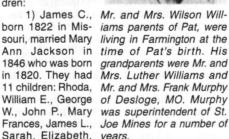

Mr. and Mrs. Wilson Williams parents of Pat, were living in Farmington at the time of Pat's birth. His grandparents were Mr. and Mrs. Luther Williams and Mr. and Mrs. Frank Murphy of Desloge, MO. Murphy was superintendent of St. Joe Mines for a number of years.

2) Asa, born 1824, married Martha Harmon in 1851, children: George, Rachel, Andrew, Lafayette, Andrew, Noah, Nancy, Mary E. and John Harmon.

3) Noah, born 1826, son George A.

4). Sarah, born 1828, married John Massey in 1845, children: Narcissa and Mary.

5) John T., born 1828, died 1908. He is buried in the Masonic Cemetery in Farmington, MO.

6) George McGahan, born in 1831, died

1922. He is buried in the Masonic Cemetery in Farmington, MO. He married Permelia Thomasson in 1857. She was born in 1837, the daughter of Gabriel and Sally Thomasson, died in 1887 and is buried in the Masonic Cemetery. They had seven children: Mary born 1863, married Phil Shaw. George King born in 1864, died 1942, married Barbara Adams, born 1873, died 1942, buried Parkview Cemetery Farmington, MO. John T. born 1867, died 1911, married Amanda Brimm in 1889. She was born 1862, died in 1930 and is buried in Parkview Cemetery. Luther Henry born 1868, died 1940, married Nelly Pearl Moody in 1898. She was born in 1876 died 1940. They are buried in the Parkview Cemetery. They had six children: Gwendoline, Luther, George, Franklin, Mary Lucille, Corine. Martin Windle born 1878 near Goff store in Flat River, married Myrtle Davis, children: Vivian, Maxwell, Katherine Jane born 1880 married Dan O'Sullivan and their children Iva, Lydia, James, Mary Ruth, Gladys, Lucille, Woodrow, Thomas, Mildred and John. The youngest son of George was Noah who was listed in the 1876 census.

7. Rachel, born 1834, married Thomas Murrill, born 1835, and had six children: William Briggs, John, George W., Hardy Thomas, Mary Ann and Sarah. George King Williams was born at the family farm near Bonne Terre in 1864. After working on his father's land in Flat River, helping to clear the timber, he went to work for the St. Joseph Lead Mines underground as a miner. He later worked for the Doe Run Lead Mines, and in 1900 Gov. Dockery appointed him State Mine Inspector and made him in charge of all mines in the state except the coal mines. He and John T. and Luther Henry formed a company called the Williams Bros., which was a general merchandise business.

The first post office was opened there for Flat River with George King as the first postmaster. George King moved to Farmington where he lived until he died in 1942. He married first Alva Nari and had one son, George Naive, and second to Barbara Adams and had Alma, married Albert Holler, and John Richard, married Katherine Orr Nulsen. Luther Henry was among the most prominent financiers of St. Francois County. After receiving his education he went to work in the mines running a diamond drill until age 21, when he went to St. Louis and attended the Bryant and Stratton Commercial College. After finishing, he joined his brothers in forming the business in Flat River which they sold in 1898. Luther entered into the banking business, joining the Miners and Merchants Bank at Flat River and working as a cashier. In 1904 he assisted in organizing the Farmer's Bank in Farmington and was made cashier. He also was director of the Miners Supply Co. at Flat River.

He married in 1898 to Nelly Moody and had eight children. His son, Wilson, born in 1912 in Farmington, married Jean Frances Murphy in 1937. She was born 1914, the daughter of Franklin Murphy and Grace Evelyn Sharp. Wilson worked for Missouri Natural Gas Co. in Farmington and then accepted a position with the Standard Oil Co. of New York, moving to Connecticut. He became the vice president of Gulf Oil Co. in 1947 and later formed his own company, The Warren Petroleum Co. He was on the boards of Westminister College in Fulton, MO and Hampshire College in Massachusetts. He moved to Linville, NC and Jacksonville, FL. He died March 24, 1993, leaving a wife, Jean, and children: Patrick Moody, Wilson Christopher and Katherine.

Patrick, son of Wilson, grew up in Darien, CT. He is active in the field of music as a composer for films, television, records and live performances. He attended Duke University and graduated in 1961 with a BA in history, but music was his first love. He worked in New York, arranging for Bert Bacharach, Steve Lawrence, Eyde Gorme, Dionne Warwick, Mel Torme and others. He and his wife, Catherine, live in Santa Monica, CA and he has been busy in the music industry. They are the parents of Elizabeth, Greer, and Patrick. *Submitted by Laverne Forsythe*

WILLIAMS - George Williams was born in Roanoke County, VA, June 29, 1819. He was the son of William C. and Margaret Bryan Williams. He died March 2, 1906, in Farmington, MO. His father was a native of Virginia, born in 1784, and was of Welsh descent. His parents came from England. William was a contractor by trade, erected the courthouse, jail and other public buildings in Salem. He also was the proprietor of a hotel in that town for several years, was postmaster there, and was also the owner of a large tract of land in Roanoke County. He died in 1852. William C. and Margaret were the parents of 13 children, George, being the eldest. George received his education at Virginia Military Institute, graduating from there in 1843. He then came to Washington Co., MO and began the study of medicine at Potosi. He taught school at Caledonia in 1843-1844 and in 1845 was the professor of mathematics in Potosi Academy. He attended a course of medical lectures at Missouri Medical College in St. Louis, and in the spring of 1846 he located at Valles Mines in St. Francois County and began his practice. At the end of 18 months he returned to college; and in March 1848, he graduated as an M.D. On Nov. 16, 1848, he married Miss Eleanore Catherine Peers, a native of Farmington, who was born Nov. 14, 1826, and is the daughter of John D. and Katherine Cole Peers.

They were the parents of six children:

1) Emma Peers, born Oct. 12, 1849, married Ben Rush Legg June 28, 1880. He died Feb. 25, 1896, in Marietta, GA. Emma died Dec. 25, 1895, in Georgia. They had a daughter Eleanor Williams Legg, born Oct. 17, 1887.

2) John William, born March 26, 1852, married Ella A. Sebastian, daughter of E.C. Sebastian and had a son, Allen. John was a physician in New Mexico. He died Dec. 22, 1928, in El Paso, TX.

3) Katherine Lyle was born June 10, 1855, and married C.F. Mansfield in 1877. They had George Allen and Katherine Peer. Kate died in Tyler, TX.

4) Edward Valintine, born Oct. 31, 1858, and died Dec. 6, 1935. He married Edna Peyton and they had a son, Walter Byron who was a merchant in Springfield, MO.

5) Eleanor Kennett, born Sept. 9, 1861, married G.W. Rutherford in 1884 and had Edna and George.

6) George Benjamin, born July 17, 1864, and died Feb. 10, 1924, married Mattie E. Salvater in 1893. They were the parents of Nellie and Maggie May. George was a medical doctor in Desloge and then at St. Lukes in St. Louis.

7) Maggie died infancy in 1864.

George's wife died in 1874 and he married Sarah Peers, a sister of Eleanor Peers. She died in March 1881 and he married Ellen C. Cole in March 1884, the daughter of Capt. George Cole of Washington County. George W. was one of the leading physicians and surgeons of southeast Missouri, having the largest practice in St. Francois County. George Washington Williams is buried in the Masonic Cemetery in Farmington.

WILLIAMS - John Jefferson Williams was born in 1794 in North Carolina and died intestate before Nov. 12, 1874 at age 80. He was the son of Robert William, born May 7, 1770, NC/VA, died July 5, 1846, El Dorado Springs, MO, and the grandson of Ambrose Williams and Mary Moor born c 1725 in Wales. In 1806 his father moved from North Carolina to South Carolina and then to Warren County and Shelby Counties, TN, where it is thought his mother, Charlotte Scott, died. Between 1828-30 the family moved in mass to Missouri, leaving one son, Harden Williams, in Warren County, TN, which later became DeKalb County.

John Jefferson Williams married Nancy M. Bowles, born 1794 VA, died March 5, 1876, in St. Francois County, while administrator for John's probate. She was the daughter of John M. Bowles and Fanny Bolling; both are buried in DeKalb County, TN. John J. and Nancy M. Bowles Williams had the following children taken from the 1830-60 St. Francois County Census and John's probate record:

1) Lucinda Johnson, deceased by 1874.

2) Charlotta Williams, born Sept. 12, 1820, Tennessee, married Jan. 11, 1837, to Arthur Allen Williams, died before 1874.

3) Thomas Davis "T.D." Williams, born April 27, 1822, Tennessee, married Aug. 2, 1842, in St. Francois County to Hulda Sebastian, daughter of Martin Chandler Sebastian, born 1799 in North Carolina, adopted, and Mourning Smith, born 1800 in North Carolina. "T.D." moved to Fannin County, TX and lived there until the Civil War. He marched to the Battle of Pea Ridge; and upon his return, one child and his wife, Hulda, were dead. He married to Martha Ford and moved to Garfield, Benton County, AR about 1870. He died March 5, 1908, Benton County, AR.

4) John Williams, born July 25, 1825, married Feb. 4, 1847, in St. Francois County to Melinda Jacobs died April 20, 1898, buried Knob Lick Cemetery.

5) Elias Williams, born Nov. 2, 1827, in Tennessee, married April 21, 1850 to Mary Ann Schrum, died Feb. 7, 1892, and buried Knob Lick Cemetery.

6) Ambrose Williams born May 13, 1832, St. Francois County, married Elizabeth Rogers 1859.

7) Sarah Williams, twin, born March 22, 1833, St. Francois County, married John H. White.

8) Lucinda Williams, twin, born March 22, 1833, St. Francois County, married John W. Webb, died May 16, 1919, buried at Knob Lick Cemetery.

9) Frances "Fanny" Williams married April 25, 1837, to Richard Thomason lived in Madison County, MO.

10) Nancy M. Williams, born March 22, 1838, married Sept. 23, 1855, to Asa G.L. Bennett, died Nov. 19, 1916, buried at Knob Lick Cemetery. There is another daughter referred to in the probate, Nancy Hill of Camden, MO. The 1840 Census also shows another daughter Mary "Molly" Cantrell, born 1828 with two grandchildren, Robert and Mary Cantrell.

Our Williams progenitor, Ambrose Williams, who was said to be born in Wales, is somewhat of a mystery. In 1778 he applied for land in Burke County, NC that had a mill pond but never finalized the deeds.

WILLIAMS - Newton Williams, son of Daniel and Sarah Williams, was born in 1857 at Knob Lick, MO. He was married to Amanda Jane Barnhouse on March 25, 1880, at the bride's home in Doe Run by Jeremiah Wood. Amanda was the daughter of Carico J. and Emma Wood Barnhouse. She was born in Ohio on May 29, 1861. Newton and Amanda were parents of six children: Caria E. was born April 1881, and was married April 1904 to Emma Hahn, daughter of Henry Hahn of Pendleton Township. They were married in Farmington by Judge G.O. Nations. Their children were: Paul, John, Fred, Glenda, Lloyd, Walter, Marvin, Ruby, Joe, Jim and Carl.

Walter E. was born April 28, 1883. He was married Sept. 4, 1904, to Rosa Jacobs at Doe Run, by W.E. Ledbetter. Rosa was the daughter of Benjamin F. Jacobs, a grocer, of Pendleton Township. Rosa was born Oct. 1, 1883. They had three children: (Rosa died of appendicitis April 17, 1916). Their children were: Rolla, Roy and Lee (died in infancy). Walter then married Mabel Addie Westover Jan. 1, 1921, in Farmington, MO by C.P. Throgmorten. Mabel was the daughter of John and Martha Virginia Westover. They had four children: Lawrence Gilbert, Emmett Miller, Maurice Eugene and Mary Ellen.

Mary Emma was born in 1885. She married William Matt Golden and they lived in San Francisco, CA. She died of appendicitis Oct. 28, 1917, at 32 years of age, and was buried there.

Amanda Kate was born September 1890. She married Charles P. Mosier of St. Francois County, MO, who was born in 1887. They had one son, Golden Everett Mosier.

Oda Newton was born June 19, 1895. He was married at Farmington on Aug. 1, 1925, to Drusilla McHenry, daughter of Samuel and Armedia McHenry. Oda died Oct. 4, 1930, after being kicked by a mule in the mines. Drusilla died Jan. 19, 1932. They left two children, Leroy and Naomi Jane.

Henry, we have no dates at all, only the name.

WILLIAMS - Pleasant Williams was born Feb. 22, 1855, in Possum Hollow, MO, close to Knob Lick. He died in 1940 and is buried in Knob Lick, MO. He was the son of Daniel and Sarah Jones Williams. He married Mary Ann Wood Oct. 25, 1882. She was born Jan. 22, 1864, in Meigs County, OH and died July 30, 1939. She was the daughter of John and Fedelia Wood. John was the son of Joshua and Sarah Mash Wood, who came to Doe Run, MO with their children from Meigs County, OH. When Sarah Wood died, Joshua married Sarah Jones Williams, who was a widow. Her husband, Daniel, died Aug. 17, 1863, during the Civil War. Pleasant and Mary were the parents of nine children:

1) Bert Edgar was born Aug. 22, 1883, and died in 1981 and is buried in the Knob Lick Cemetery. He married Gertrude Cross who was born May 23, 1885. They had two children, Milton Edgar who was born 1920 and married Ruth Walker; and Wilmetta, who was born Dec. 23, 1917, and married John Murphy in 1940. He was born 1911 and they had Edwin, Ronald and Robert.

Left to right: Pleasant William's family. Nell, Julia, Mae, Adda, John, Jay and Bert.

2) Addie Leah was born March 20, 1885, and died Aug. 10, 1964. She married Charles Medley in 1903. He was born 1879 and died May 22, 1966. He was the son of Harvey and Martha Clark Medley. Their children were Dortha, who was born 1904 and married Adam Ebrecht in 1924. They had three children: Don, Doris and Robert. Oscar Charles was born 1906 and married Margaret Parmeley. They had Charles, who was born in 1927. He married Sarah Posey in 1949 and they had son, Steve and daughter, Robin. Earl Wesley

254

born May 30, 1910, married Cora Mae Wright 1929 and had Paul W., who married Opal Lucille Kinney on Oct. 21, 1948. She was the daughter of Monroe and Opal Canter Kinney. Eugene married Ernestine. Paul William Medley, the third son of Charles and Addie, was born Oct. 22, 1913. He married Agnes Marie Hibbits 1941. Their children are Dale Paul and Frances Jean, who married Larry Ingracia.

3) Thomas Jay was born Jan. 31, 1888, and died in Nebraska. He married Minnie Ina Hibbits in 1910. She was born in 1892 and died in Nebraska. They had one child, Elwood. Thomas married second Lela Mae Rose and they had Everett and Elizabeth. Thomas and Mable were twins.

4) Mable was born Jan. 31, 1888, in Farmington, MO. She married Albert Everingham in 1908 at Knob Lick, MO. She died in 1986 in Nebraska. They were the parents of Eunice, born 1909 and married Herman Boerger; Helen, born in 1911 and married Elmer Swanson; Rachel, born 1915 and married Lawrence Greenfield; Melvin, born 1918 and married Lucille Williams; Paul, born 1920 and married Norma Harrison; Donald, born 1925 and married Lila Rhodes and Estelle, born 1928 and married Dale Black.

5) Julia E. was born in 1890 in Farmington, MO and died 1967 in Caldwell, ID. She married Charles Rogers, who was born 1889 in Champaign, IL. They had a daughter, Julia Mae, who was born in 1915 and married Roy Kapperman.

6) John Milton was born in 1894 in Farmington, MO and died in 1978 in Othello, WA. He married Emma Blanche Anderson in Ainsworth, NE in 1917. Their children were Ann Etta, born in 1922, married Carl Lochmiller; and Alfreida Mae, born in 1924, married Gerald Mahoney.

7) Nellie Maude was born in 1896 in Farmington, MO and died in 1965 in St. Louis, MO. She married Louis Bonk in 1928 in St. Louis. Their children were Helen and Betty.

8) William was born in 1898 and died young.

9) Pleasant was born in 1900 and died young.

Pleasant was a farmer and lived on a farm in Knob Lick, where he raised his family. Several are buried in the Knob Lick Cemetery. *Submitted by Charles Elser*

WILLIAMS - William Browning Williams was born Aug. 18, 1813, in Stonington, CT, and was the son of Robert Williams. He married Mary Hester Cole, who was born Nov. 18, 1823 in Washington County, MO to Philip and Hester Cole. She died Oct. 12, 1896 in Farmington. William died July 2, 1893 in Farmington and is buried in the Murphy Cemetery behind the Christian Science Church on Karsch Blvd. He was a medical doctor. They were the parents of 11 children.

1) George, born April 29, 1841 in Missouri, died May 16, 1859 and is buried in the Murphy Cemetery on Karsch Blvd.

2) Thomas B. was born in 1845 and married Mary Harmon March 18, 1869. She was the daughter of John and Louise Watts Harmon and was born in 1852 and died Sept. 16, 1924 at the home of son John in St. Louis and is buried in Vahalla Cemetery. He died Nov. 30, 1918. They were the parents of Edgar G., born Oct. 6, 1870, died Jan. 1, 1945 in Farmington, married Lucy Alice Cole Nov. 18, 1893, the daughter of Bates and Adaline Blunt Cole in Shirley, MO. They are buried at Parkview Cemetery in Farmington. They had Fanny G., born Sept. 27, 1894, died Oct. 23, 1978, buried at Parkview and Eugene Field, born Jan. 3, 1898, died Jan. 25, 1947, buried at Parkview. He married Freida M. Hicks in 1918 in

St. Louis and they were the parents of Eugene, Donald and Jeanette. Thomas B. was born in 1872 and lived in Colorado Springs, CO. Maude was born in 1876 and married Henry Stahlmon and lived in Cuba, MO and John J. was born in 1879 and lived in University City, MO. They are buried in Knights of Pythias Cemetery.

3) Asa Taylor was born Sept. 17, 1848.

4) Mary Josephine was born June 12, 1850, and married Nov. 3, 1870, Thomas Highley, who was born in 1847. She died Aug. 21, 1932 and is buried in the Murphy Cemetery on Karsch and he died June 7, 1920. They were the parents of Lee, born Dec. 6, 1871, married Olive M. Henderson in 1906. He died in 1940 in Council Bluffs, IA. Tessa, born in 1873, married Val McClanahan. Maurice was born in 1875 and Stella was born in 1877 and married Charles Hopkins. Buried in Knights of Pythias Cemetery.

5) Mary Laura was born Feb. 14, 1852, died Sept. 19, 1924, and married Godfrey Brune Nov. 19, 1873. Their children were: William, Mamie, Ella and Don. They are buried in the Masonic Cemetery.

6) Ellanora was born Dec. 30, 1857, died March 25, 1937, and married George A. McEwen April 13, 1897. He was an M.D., the son of Peter and Mary Anderson McEwen.

7) Georgiana was born Dec. 23, 1859, died May 6, 1936, and married H.B. Ledbetter in December 1884. They were the parents of Mary, Ruben and Frank. They are buried in the Knights of Pythias Cemetery.

8) Lincoln Rufus was born in 1862.

9) John Browning was born Sept. 21, 1864, died Dec. 24, 1925. He married Ida May Moore, Jan. 10, 1890, in Farmington. She was the daughter of Riley and Mary Elizabeth McFarland Moore and was born June 13, 1870, at Loughboro, MO and died Aug. 22, 1960, in Farmington. They are buried at Parkview Cemetery. They were the parents of Bessie Myrtle who was born in 1891 and married Harry Yates in 1911. They lived in Greenfield, IA. James Cole was born in 1892 and married Sallie Amanda Cartwright. They lived in Dallas, TX, Lilly was born in 1894 and died in infancy. Clarence was born in 1895. Robert Moore was born in 1908 and married Margaret Jelly. They lived in Hollywood, CA.

10) Willette was born in 1869.

11) Phillip, have no info.

WILLIAMS - William Carroll Williams was born in Smith Co., TN, near Nashville, on Dec. 28, 1827, to David and Elizabeth Von Hoosier Williams. He married Elizabeth Haze Bennett on April 2, 1850. She was born in 1858 and died at her daughter's home, Mrs. J.F. Lee. She was the daughter of William and Jane Van Atta Bennett, who moved to St. Francois County, MO and lived next to William Carroll and family in the 1860 Census. In June, they started for Missouri and located in St. Francois County, where he purchased 40 acres on the Farmington and Jackson Road. He remained there two years and then bought 200 acres of land about three miles from Libertyville. While his family lived on the farm, he went to an island on the Mississippi River, and by industry and hard work, in six years accumulated enough money to buy the place where his family lived, at cost of $10,500. He bought the mill property at Libertyville, and tearing out the old machinery, replaced it with new. He died Aug. 30, 1886, at the age of 58 and his son, Joseph Carroll, took over running the mill. William Carroll died after being gored by a bull. He was a member of the Methodist Episcopal Church South and steward of the Wesley Chapel congregation. He was one of the most successful farmers in this area. He and his wife were the parents of 12 children: Their children were:

1) Didema, born in 1845, Tennessee, and married Dr. Edward Cozzens. He was born in 1859. She married second W.P. Gibbs. Gracie Cozzens was born in 1888. She is buried with her father in the Harris Cemetery.

2) Mary T. was born in 1852. Mary and Harriett were twins.

3) Harriett, born in 1852 and married first William Webb and second James Leftwich and had one son Franklin Leftwich, born in 1875.

4) William, born in 1855 and died in 1856.

5) John H., born in 1856 and died in 1867.

6) Frances Jane, born in 1858 and married George Whitley Sebastian. He was the son of George W. and Elizabeth Townsend. He was born in 1853 and they had 10 children. First-born son, name unknown; Harriet, born in 1878; Noah, born in 1879; Elizabeth was born in 1881; James Henry, born in 1883 and married Sarah Cowley. They had nine children. Nathaniel Cook, born in 1885 married Victoria Heitman. He died in 1961 at Libertyville, and their children were Carl, Harry, Bernice and Joe. Ena J. was born in 1898, and Pearl, born in 1898, were twins. Vera, born in 1904. Walter, born in 1909.

7) Joseph Carroll, born in 1859 and married first Jennie Price Watts. She was the daughter of Rev. Henry Smith Watts, a minister who was called "Rough & Ready" and was a very well-known and admired man. He married first to Elizabeth Hill and second Mary McFarland. They were the parents of eight children. Jennie, born in 1861, was the seventh child. She and J.C. Williams and had two children. Marvin Carroll, born in 1887 and married Grace Frances Staley. They had a son named Joseph. Henry Paul was born in 1890 and died in 1935. He is buried in the Parkview Cemetery in Farmington. Joseph Carroll married second Ella Black, the daughter of Samuel and Mary Jamieson Black. She was born in Patterson, MO and died at the age of 72 years. Joseph Carroll owned mills in Piedmont, MO and was part owner of one in Irondale, MO. He was the circuit clerk, recorder of deeds, and county sheriff of St. Francois County.

8) An infant daughter was born in 1862 and died in infancy.

9) Sarah Elizabeth, born in 1864 and married Dr. John H. Ferguson. She gave birth to a baby and they both died in childbirth in 1881. Sarah was 16 years of age.

10) Eliza was born in 1866.

11) Laura was born in 1868.

12) Nancy Lillian was born in 1871 and married Frank Lee. They moved to Texas. The obituary of Captain Marvin Williams, son of Joseph Carrol, states, "He was the son of Joseph and Jennie Watts Williams, and was one of the most colorful personages ever born. He passed away in Boise, ID, on Dec. 25, 1952. He was a retired army officer, retiring 16 years ago. He returned to Farmington, MO, and lived 3 or 4 years ago and then went to the state of Oregon and bought property and lived with his only son Joe. He lived past the age of 70 years. His body was returned to Farmington, MO, and was buried in the Parkview Cemetery."

William Carroll was said to have built the house on OO Highway, nine miles south of Farmington, with slave labor. The slaves made the bricks, molded and fired on the property. This 200 acres is now owned by Jerry and Kay Miller, who operate a pick-your-own blueberry farm.

Quite a number of William Carrol's family are buried in the Harris Cemetery located on a farm on OO Highway and Jackson Road. *Submitted by Laverne Forsythe*

WORLEY - Albert Lee Worley and Maggie Mae (Reynolds) Worley came to Farmington, MO in October 1922.

Almost 20 years after his father served as a volunteer infantryman in the Civil War, Albert was born on Nov. 28, 1884, in Wayne County, MO, near Piedmont. He was the son of Andrew and

Albert & Mae Worley, 60th Wedding Anniversary 1966.

Martha (Tinkler) Worley, who were originally from Tennessee. He was one of 10 children (four girls and six boys).

Albert came to Flat River, MO, in 1905 to work in the lead mines. He lived with his brother, Tom, in Desloge, MO. Albert Worley married Maggie Mae Reynolds on July 1, 1906. She was born on May 2, 1889, in Valles Mines, MO, to William and Sophie (Bowen) Reynolds. Her parents moved to Flat River when she was 15 years old. She had two sisters, Bertha Taylor, of Farmington, and Carrie Harris, of Irondale.

Albert & Mae Worley, Wedding Picture 7/1/1906

Albert and Mae Worley moved to Sprott, MO. Near Flat River, they got a railway boxcar and loaded all their belongings in it. Mae and her daughter, Thelma, born in 1908, got on the train while Albert drove the wagon and team of mules to Sprott. Gladys, born in 1910, died in infancy before the move to Sprott. Two children were born, Bernice, born in 1913, and Theron, born in 1915. After several years of very cold winters and dry summers, when the family almost starved, living at times on rabbits and turnips, they moved back to Esther, MO. Albert worked in Federal Hill Lead Mines, going underground this time making $1.25 a day. Albert rode the train back and forth to the lead mine. Twins, Helen and Henry, were born in 1918. Henry died in infancy. Dorothy was born in 1921. About that time, Albert started with a miner's cough and was advised to stop working underground and be in fresh air.

In October 1922, Albert and Mae moved from Esther to a farm southeast of Farmington, MO. While living on the farm, Norma Jean was born in 1928. After the twins were born, making five children in the family, Albert missed having to serve in WWI.

The Worleys and their six living children lived on their farm southeast of Farmington. All the children helped with the farm work while being educated in nearby schools in Libertyville and Farmington.

Eldest daughter, Thelma, married Lester

Price and lived most of her life in St. Louis and the southwest part of Missouri. She is deceased. Bernice married John Cleve and lived on a farm southeast of Farmington near Libertyville. They had one son, Albert, and two daughters, Marjorie and Dorothy.

Theron and wife, Erma Worley, also live on a farm southeast of Farmington. They have three sons: Richard, Eddie and Steve, and two daughters, Faye and Glenda.

Helen married Noah Shirrell and had three children, Frances, Helen Marie and James. They always lived in Farmington.

Dorothy married Mack Brann of St. Louis, MO and had one son, Donald and one daughter, Diane. They lived in St. Louis.

Norma married William Johnson of St. Louis and had two sons, Paul and Wayne. They live in St. Louis.

During the Worley's 63-year marriage, they lived most of those years on their Farmington farm. The original home was a four-room house with a barn by a creek. In 1929, they bought three old houses in Leadwood, tore them down and used the lumber to build a three-bedroom house on their property. After moving into the new house in 1932, the old house was moved with a team of mules closer to the new house, where it continued to be used for churning butter and storing food. They farmed, milked cows, raised chickens and had large gardens. She hatched her baby chicks that they raised. Mae and her daughters sold and delivered butter, eggs and garden produce to residents of Farmington for many years. Albert took special pride in his poppies growing at the edge of the vegetable garden. He also grew peanuts and tobacco (the kids would stem the tobacco, hanging it in the smoke house to dry). This was all done before getting a C. Allys Chalmers tractor in 1944. Fish, especially perch, caught in the creek down by the barn was favorite of Albert's.

In 1924, Albert and Mae became members of the First Baptist Church of Farmington. Both were active members, including teaching Sunday School, until the time of their deaths. Albert was a deacon of the church.

Having large family get-to-gethers for meals and homemade ice cream made with their own fresh cream was a source of pride and joy for the Worleys.

After 63 years of marriage, Mae, at age 80, passed away, leaving Albert to live on the family farm until his death in 1973 at age 88. This lasting marriage produced six children, 15 grandchildren, 30 great-grandchildren, and six great-great-grandchildren, who have fond memories and loving stories to tell about this wonderful couple. *Submitted by Helen (Worley) Shirrell*

WORLEY - Theron Worley was born July 18, 1915, on a farm near Sprott, the son of Albert and May (Reynolds) Worley. The Worley family moved and lived for a time on another farm near Esther, before settling in the Farmington area with Theron and his four sisters when he was seven.

Theron remembers helping his parents with farm chores, including walking behind a horse and plow, "slopping" hogs, milking cows, and cutting wood with big crosscut saws. Theron helped his father build the original Worley farmhouse (on Worley Road south of Highway F) as a young teenager, and he put those skills to work later, when he built the current Worley home in 1949, for his bride.

Erma Horton grew up near Miller's Switch, the daughter of Mack and Opal (Thomas) Horton, and came to the Farmington area to work at the Trimfoot Company in 1943. Erma and Theron met on a blind date with Erma's sister and brother-in-

law and they were married two years later on May 14, 1949.

Theron had purchased 80 acres of property adjoining his father's farm before getting married, and it was here that he, Erma and friends and relatives built their current home and raised their five children: Faye, Richard, Glenda, Eddie and Steve.

Front Row, L-R: Erma Worley, Steve Worley, Glenda Worley Boersig, Theron Worley. Back Row: Faye Worley, Eddie Worley, Richard Worley

Theron worked the farm as a partnership with his father for many years. In 1957, to supplement the family income, Theron went to work for Gifford Lumber Co., helping build homes and traveling St. Francois and Ste. Genevieve counties delivering lumber and supplies to building sites. Theron remembers the terrible tornado and thunderstorm damage of 1957 that struck Desloge. It was a disaster that caused much grief and destruction for many, even as it provided work and income for others.

After six years with Gifford's, Theron went on to work as a hospital attendant with the Farmington State Hospital. While keeping up the expanding family farm and his growing family, Theron continued at the hospital for 17 years, and he retired at age 65, in 1980.

While Theron was off in the fields or at work, Erma was a stay-at-home mom, raising her children, doing volunteer work with the U&I 4-H Club, staying active with the Busiek School PTA and the Clearview Neighbors Extension Club, as well as always being available for friends and neighbors to count on! Theron served for many years on the Busiek School Board of Education, as a deacon in the First Baptist Church and on various committees and Boards with the local MFA and Farm Service organizations.

The Worley home has always been open to family and friends. Many snowy days would find the Worley children and friends playing with their sleds behind the tractor, then into the house for homemade hot chocolate. In the spring you might find them flying kites and on summer days playing in the creek. All five Worley children were active 4-H members and the family has hosted many foreign exchange students through the IFYE (International 4-H Youth Exchange) program, in which Faye was a participant. International 4-H guests at the Worley family home have come from Greece, Japan, Hungary, Wales, Ireland, England, Switzerland and Sweden.

For a time during the 1960s, the Worley home drew people from all across Liberty Township, as the family living room served as the official polling place open for all to trudge through from 6:00 a.m. until 7:00 p.m. on election days. The Worley children soon learned to look forward to those days as a time when they would be rousted from sleep early, mom would prepare homemade sweet rolls, neighbors would visit, and grandpa Worley would spend the day serving as election judge.

The Worley family continues its "open door" policy today, with any number of their 10 grandchildren likely to be underfoot or on the premises at a given time, and a complement of children's spouses, friends and neighbors are likely to be about too!

Theron Worley continues to actively farm what has now grown to 250 acres with sons and grandsons. His chief jobs being helping make hay in the summer and feeding the cattle in the winter. You might find him walking the hills in the springtime hunting mushrooms, or tending a fence row awaiting a deer in the fall. Theron's philosophy is "stay busy, so you don't get stove up!" and Erma is always ready to prepare one of her "quick" meals for family or friends. Besides the joy that all this brings she also enjoys the special times with Theron camping and listening to bluegrass music in the summertime.

WRIGHT - Dale Wright and his family (wife, Denise and three children, Andrea, Aaron and Stephanie) moved to Farmington in the spring of 1979, from Rolla, MO. The move from Rolla was a move home; Dale's parents are Bernice Koester Wright and Bill Wright, who were living in Farmington when Dale and his siblings were born. Bernice grew up in the Koester Springs Valles Mines area; Bill is from Mine LaMotte. Dale's brothers and sisters are Gary, Carol Jenson, Joan Bohn, Ron and Linda Capone.

Joel, Stephanie, Denise, Aaron, Andrea, Dale and Ben.

Dale graduated from Farmington High School in 1969, worked two years as an apprentice carpenter with Paul Hasse and then as an orderly and ambulance driver for Mineral Area Osteopathic Hospital. He graduated from Mineral Area College in May 1973, and a month later married Denise Rowe, also a 1973 graduate of MAC. Denise grew up in the Flat River area and attended Central High School. Her parents are Darrell and Jennell Politte Rowe, who both grew up in the Flat River-Elvins area. Their five children include Denise, twin brother Darrell, Catherine Marler, Randall and Cynthia Minnis.

Dale began work in the warehouse at MAOH. Then in 1974, following the birth of Andrea, he took a job as purchasing director at Phelps County Hospital in Rolla. Aaron was born in 1976 and Stephanie in 1978. After four years at the hospital, Dale took a job in hospital sales that allowed him to move his family back to Farmington. Joel was born in 1982 and Ben in 1989. Dale continued in hospital sales for several years with various companies. He then worked as a marketing director of a group hospital purchasing company. He is currently vice president of sales and marketing for Ni-Med, Inc., based in the Farmington Industrial Park. Denise has been a full-time homemaker, working part-time as a free-lance writer for magazines and newspapers. The family operates an air fragrancing business, Good Scents.

The family hosted two exchange students from Germany, sharing a slice of Farmington and midwestern values. Ancestors from both branches of the family tree came from Germany.

Andrea graduated from the associate degree nursing program at MAC. She is married to Tom Waddell Jr., of Ironton and they have two children, Mary Catherine and Grant. Stephanie attended MAC and currently attends the University of Missouri at Columbia. She is married to Edward Felker of Sikeston. Aaron graduated from MAC and also currently attends Mizzou. *Submitted by Denise Wright*

WRIGHT - Harold C. and Opal Carmen Wright began teaching in the Farmington Public Schools in 1946-1947 school year while living in Esther, MO. They have one son, John Carroll Wright, Sr. Harold taught previously in Washington County.

Opal had taught in Jefferson, Benton and Mississippi Counties. They moved to Farmington in 1951.

Harold is the son of John William Wright and Mary Ethel Phillips Wright of Flat River, MO. Opal is the daughter of Rev. James Carroll Reid and Myrtle Fox Reid.

Harold C. and Opal

Rev. Reid began his Methodist ministry as a circuit rider in Belgrade Circuit in 1905. He and his wife attended Marvin College in Fredericktown, MO.

Harold's ancestors came from England and settled in North Carolina, Macoupin County, IL and Dent County, MO. Opal's ancestors came from Scotland and England and settled in North Carolina and Cape Girardeau and Perry Counties of Missouri. Harold taught eighth grade, senior high industrial arts, was then principal of junior high school (grades 6-7-8) for many years. In honor of his memory and his 30 years of service to the Farmington Public Schools, a 50-dollar Savings Bond is given to a qualifying eighth grade student each spring.

Before going to war, Harold was a member of the Missouri National Guard. Harold was a WWII veteran who fought in the European battles as a member of Co. F, 141st Inf. of the Fighting 36th Texas Div. He won several medals including Infantry Combat Badge and two Bronze Stars. He was a member of VFW Post 5896, the Elks Club and a former member of Rotary. He was past president of several educational organizations, including Southeast Missouri Principals and Southeast Missouri Industrial Arts Teachers. He was a member of Phi Delta Kappa. He retired in 1976 and died Feb. 20, 1998.

Harold and Opal were both graduates of Flat River Junior College, Southeast Missouri State University and received masters degrees from University of Missouri, Columbia. Opal Wright taught grades 6-7-8. She became principal of Washington-Franklin Schools in 1951 and then director of Farmington Elementary Schools including: Douglas, W.L. Johns, Doe Run, Busiek, Washington, Franklin and Jefferson, giving 33 years of service to the Farmington Schools. She and Harold gave a combined 63 years service to Farmington Schools.

Opal is past president of many organizations including Southeast District Teachers Association. She was awarded the high honor by the Missouri State Dept. of Education as Pioneer in Education. She was given an award by the Alumni Association of Southeast Missouri State University for outstanding service to education. Opal was a member of Phi Lamba Theta, Delta Kappa Gamma, Business and Professional Women,

Daughters of the American Revolution (DAR), and Memorial Methodist Church. She retired in 1979 and currently lives in Farmington.

The Wrights' son, John Carroll Wright Sr., graduated from Farmington High School and the University of Missouri, majoring in accounting. He was a member of Kappa Alpha Fraternity. He served in the Missouri National Guard. John is currently a CPA and a partner in the Maloney, Wright and Robbins accounting firm in Farmington. John has three children: John Wright Jr., Susannah Cantrell and Caroline Wright, all of whom are graduates of Farmington High School.

John Carroll Wright Jr., graduated from Mineral Area College with an associate in Business Administration and graduated from Southwest Missouri University with a degree in psychology and biology. He recently graduated from the Ozark School of Nursing. He resides in Springfield, MO, where he is employed by the state of Missouri as a psychiatric nurse.

Dr. Susannah M. Cantrell is married to Robert Wayne Cantrell and they have two daughters, Carmen Ann and Ellen Elizabeth. The Cantrell's live in Farmington. Susannah completed her doctorate in biochemistry in September 1998 from the University of Missouri-Columbia. Susannah received her bachelor degree in biology from Westminster College in Fulton, MO, 1991. She was awarded several academic and athletic scholarships during her undergraduate work. She was a member of the cross-country team and received Athlete of the Year in 1990 from Westminster College. Prior to her graduate work, Susannah worked for the Environmental Protection Agency developing biochemical techniques for rapid and cost-effective identification of hazardous chemicals from soil and water samples. She was invited to give several seminars at International Scientific Conferences including Society of Environmental Toxicology and Chemistry and Marine Environmental Research. Dr. Cantrell is a published author of several scientific manuscripts including two articles in toxicology and applied pharmacology. She is a consultant for SmithKline Beecham Pharmaceuticals and is currently training as a regional medical associate. Robert Cantrell was originally from Chicago and moved to Fulton, MO in 1984, where he worked in the printing industry for 10 years. He graduated with honors from Columbia College in 1997 with a bachelor of science in business administration and was a member of Alpha Chi National Honor Society. He now works for the Western Press.

Caroline Elizabeth Wright completed the training at the School of Cosmetology in Park Hills and is a state licensed cosmetologist. She is now attending Mineral Area College pursuing certification in the nursing program, specialized as a surgical assistant. She and her son, Kristopher Penuel, reside in Farmington.

John Sr. and wife, Rosemary Baker-Wright, are residents of Farmington. She is a certified financial planner with American Express with her office in Farmington. Her son, David, and wife Tricia Ann, live in St. Louis. He is a former teacher and coach of Farmington High School. Presently he is an assistant principal and coach in the Lindbergh School District in St. Louis County. David graduated from the North County High School and Southwest Missouri University, majoring in education. He has a masters degree in business administration from Fontbonne College and a masters degree in education from UMSL. Tricia holds a degree in speech pathology from Fontbonne.

WROBLEWSKI - The Wroblewski family is relatively new to the Farmington area. After hearing of the progressive nature of Farmington and the pro-family atmosphere, Mr. Bruce Wroblewski and his wife, Claire, moved their family of five, in 1994, from Massachusetts to this lovely area.

Bruce attended Springfield Tech Community College, receiving a degree in Liberal Arts. Later he attended Westfield State College, receiving a political science degree. Bruce also ac-

Wroblewski - 1997: Bruce Wroblewski, 42, Louise, 18, Claire Wroblewski, 42, Samantha Wroblewski, 4 and Matthew Wroblewski, 6.

quired his insurance license from Boston University. He sold insurance on the East coast and is presently a student of computer programming.

Claire Wroblewski was educated at Springfield Tech Community College, receiving her associates in criminal justice. Claire also received paralegal and human rights officer training. She is also certified as a CNA, an ACMT and an activities director. Claire worked in the human services field as a direct care giver and human rights advocate in Massachusetts and is currently enjoying being the activities coordinator for Farmington Care Center and St. Francois Manor.

The Wroblewski's have three children, Louise "Ouisie," soon to be 20 years of age, who briefly attended Farmington High. She is currently a student at the University of Massachusetts on a full scholarship majoring in theater and minoring in education. Their son, Matthew, is seven and attends Washington Grade School. Matt has had the great pleasure of discovering all of the many lizards and snakes in the area and has also developed a great love for reading, an interest nurtured by his teacher, Ms. Danieley. Samantha "Sam," age five, their youngest child, enjoys her time spent at Truman Kindergarten. The Wroblewski's are happy to be here in the Farmington area and appreciate their many new friends.

YEARGAIN - Jefferson Donald Yeargain was born and raised on the homestead on Big River and moved to the farm with his father and mother, John Wesley and Mary Elizabeth Simms Yeargain, in 1907. J.D. was born June 30, 1891, and died Feb. 24, 1968. J.D. was married to Pearl Ann Griffin on April 24, 1913, and they both lived on the Forge, where J.D. helped his father John Wesley on the farm.

Donald Yeargain, Reva P., Barney L., Harriet A., Jeff D., Pearl A., Benny B., Betty Lace and Glenwood G.

J.D. and Pearl raised seven children and they are as follows: Glenwood Griffin Yeargain Sr., born Jan. 10, 1914, d. Oct. 25, 1968; Reva Pearl Yeargain, born Jan. 8, 1916, d. Nov. 4, 1996; Donald Jefferson Yeargain, born April 22, 1918,

d. March 23, 1996; Barney Lott Yeargain, born Jan. 10, 1918, d. March 9, 1988; Benny Bernard Yeargain, born Dec. 21, 1921, d. Oct. 19, 1988; Harriet Alice Yeargain, born Oct. 24, 1926; Elizabeth Louise Yeargain "Betty Lou," born March 10, 1928, d. Nov. 2, 1996.

J.D. and Pearl, along with their family, were members of the Murphy Long Memorial Methodists Church - South. The family switched their membership to the Memorial Methodist Church of Farmington when the two Methodist churches consolidated.

A farm was purchased by J.D. and Pearl at 1205 North Washington Street. At that time it was out in the country with fields all around. J.D. went to work for the State Hospital #4 and worked as a farm hand until he retired because of diabetes in the early 1950s. Pearl went to work at Trimfoot Shoe Factory and worked there for many years. As the years went by, Farmington expanded, and the farm was annexed into the city. Eventually the horses, chickens and cows had to be removed from the premises.

J.D. was an excellent croquet player and played croquet with other men around Farmington at different houses. It was not unusual to pass by 1205 North Washington at night and see a croquet field lit up and a game of croquet being played by the family and other guests. There were times of heated debate over the rules and playing of the games; but when the game was over, all arguments were forgotten.

Glenwood was a florist and started the Rhodes Floral Shop until the highway by-pass (Karsh Blvd.) was developed and bought his shop.

Reva worked as a seamstress at the old Rice Stix Factory and Puritan Fashions.

Donald J. worked as a meat cutter for Piggly Wiggly, Powell's Meat Locker and was a concrete finisher during his last years before retirement.

Barney and Benny were two of the family members that went to Los Angeles, CA and lived out their lives.

Harriet worked as a secretary for many years at Rice Stix and Biltwell Factory.

Betty Lou worked as a sales clerk at P.N. Hirsch for many years and then worked for the Trimfoot Shoe Factory until her retirement.

J.D. and Pearl lived on that property until their death and were good neighbors and friends to many people in the Farmington Community. After their death, Reva, Harriet and Betty lived on the same property.

YEARGAIN - John Wesley Yeargain was one of the pioneer citizens of this section of Missouri. John Wesley married Mary Elizabeth Simms in 1907 and moved his family to what was known around the Farmington area as "The Valley Forge." The Forge was a farm south of Farmington on Highway 32 and was the homestead of several generations of Yeargains. John Wesley and Mary Elizabeth had 10 children: Francis Lucinda Yeargain Belnap, Carrie Olive Yeargain Robinson, Lucy Lavinia Yeargain Westover, Ora Amanda Yeargain Branning, Louis Franklin Yeargain, Harriet Martha Yeargain Fry, James Patterson Yeargain, Gertrude Jennie Yeargain Laws, Jefferson Donald Yeargain, Joseph Chesley Yeargain. John was a member of the Murphy Long Memorial Methodist Church-South and of Farmington Lodge 132, AF&AM.

As these children grew up and married, the Forge became a meeting place on Sunday for each of them and their families. Jefferson Donald married Pearl Ann Griffin and they lived and worked on the farm. Pearl would tell how every Saturday she would bake a dozen pies and a half dozen cakes for the visit on Sundays. The Sunday activities included games of baseball in the

barn lot, games of croquet and card games of pinochle. The story has been told by several family members that a man one day approached John Wesley plowing in the field and asked him for a loan to start a funeral home business. John reached into his pocket and gave the man the amount needed and the business was successful. The annual Yeargain Family Reunion still meets once a year in Farmington to commemorate Mary Elizabeth's birthday, the Sunday closest to August 12.

Pictured here is the family of the late Mr. and Mrs. J.W. Yeargain, taken at the "old home place" at Valley Forge east of Farmington in 1910.

Seated: Left to Right: G.P. "Pat" Yeargain, Mrs. J.W. Yeargain, Chesley Yeargain, J.W. Yeargain, Louis Yeargain. Standing, from the left: Mrs. Gertrude Laws, Mrs. Carrie Robinson, Mrs. Lucy Westover, Jeff Yeargain, Mrs. Ora Braning, Mrs. Fannie Belknap and Mrs. Harriett Fry.

J.D. would tell stories his father (John Wesley) passed on to him. One of the stories J.D. heard his father tell was about how the horses were saved during the Civil War. When John Wesley was around 10 years of age, he lived with Andrew Patterson Yeargain on a farm on Big River. During the Civil War, Confederate soldiers would come into the farm. With the farm being located in hilly country, they could hear the soldiers coming and would take the horses about a quarter of a mile away and hide them in a ravine in back of their house. The soldiers were always looking for mounts to steal. J.D. told how his father tied rags and sometimes held their hands over the jaws of the horses so they would not whinny or make noise. J.D. said sometimes they would spend several days down in the ravine in all kinds of weather. When the soldiers left, they would bring the horses back to the barn but were always alert because they knew within a few days the Union soldiers would always come for a visit and the hiding of the horses would be repeated. As far as J.D. knew, Andrew Patterson never lost any horses to soldiers.

Many of the Yeargain ancestors still live in Farmington and are linked to the lives of John Wesley and Mary Elizabeth Simms Yeargain. *This article respectfully submitted Ray L. Yeargain, great-grandson*

ZIMMER - Johann Adam Zimmer was born in Hesse, Darmstadt, Germany, July 18, 1818. He came to America in 1841 and settled in St. Louis. He married Elizabeth Schaub, whom he had met on the same ship coming to America. They had one daughter and three sons. Adam bought a small tract of land, raised fruits and vegetables, and hauled them to Biddle Market. He also cut and hauled wood as he cleared land. He was able to acquire enough land to give farms to each of his children as they married and had families.

Ferdinand L. Zimmer, born July 12, 1855, the youngest of the four children, married Emilie Sahm in St. Louis, MO. They were the parents of 10 children.

Edward Adam Zimmer, sixth child of Ferdinand and Emilie, was born April 22, 1888, in St. Louis. He married Della A. Barnes from Ste. Genevieve County, MO. in 1911. After living in St. Louis and Chicago, they returned to Ste. Genevieve County about 1922 and purchased 160 acres seven miles east of Farmington. This property became known as Zimmer's Pine View Lakes. In 1938, they acquired 120 additional acres. By this time their family included one son and eight daughters.

Goldie (Zimmer) and Elmer Holst lived all of their married life in Bloomsdale. Elmer worked at Pittsburgh Plate Glass in Crystal City, MO. They had two children, Judy and Ed, and four grandchildren. Goldie taught school for over 40 years. Judy Womack teaches Family & Consumer Sciences at Oak Ridge High School near Perryville, MO. Ed works for Bloomsdale Excavating. Goldie and Elmer are deceased.

Back: Goldie Holst, Norma Wilson, Eber Zimmer, Eleanor Huck, JoAnne Henderson, Florence Roth. Front: June Govro, Jean Allen (Twins)

Eleanor (Zimmer) and E.P. Huck resided in Ste. Genevieve and Farmington. They owned several grocery stores and also owned the "Flash" in Ste. Genevieve. Ed died in 1991, and Eleanor resides at Prebyterian Manor in Farmington. They had two children, Nancy and Mike, and eight grandchildren. Nancy and her husband, Dennis Corrington, live in St. Louis, MO. They own two stores and a hotel in Skagway, AK. Mike was killed in a truck accident in 1991. He was the father of three children.

Eber and Alma Zimmer live in Farmington. Eber is retired from Mississippi Lime Co. in Ste. Genevieve. Eber has one son, Jimmie, and four grandchildren who live in Louisiana, and Alma has two daughters and five grandchildren who live in the Farmington area.

Norma (Zimmer) and Woodie Wilson reside in Farmington. Norma retired from First State Community Bank in 1994. Woodie retired from Diesel Power in 1981. They have three children: Kathy, Danny and Ann, and six grandchildren. Kathy, (Mrs. Jack) Neiner is a legal secretary in Fredericktown, MO. Their children are John, Danny and Amy Neiner. Danny Wilson is an accountant for Hutson Furniture in Cape Girardeau, MO. He and his wife, Teri, have one daughter, Andrea. Ann (Mrs. Paul) Mell works for New Era Bank in Farmington, MO. Their children are Katie and Emily, who attend St. Paul Lutheran School in Farmington.

Florence (Zimmer) and Ronnie Roth lived in Bloomsdale and raised four children. Ronnie was a contractor in St. Louis and Florence worked at Ste. Genevieve Memorial Hospital in Ste. Genevieve. Ronnie died in 1991. Their children are Susan, an environmental geologist in Seattle, WA; Kenny, an electronics technician in St. Louis; Mary, (Mrs. Gary) Meadows, who works for Southwestern Bell in St. Louis and Tom, a geological engineer in Atlanta, GA. They have seven children.

June (Zimmer) and Mervyn Burle resided in Weingarten, MO. June worked at Farmington State Hospital, and Mervyn worked for Lead Belt Supply in Farmington. They had three sons. June later married Francis Govro and lived just outside Farmington until her death in 1991. June and Mervyn have seven grandchildren. Her sons, David (and Mikki), Ed and Tim (and Kathy) live in Jefferson City, Ste. Genevieve and Atlanta, GA, respectively.

Jean (Zimmer) and Gene Allen have lived in Farmington for 48 years. Jean was an elementary teacher for 31 years in the public schools. She retired from teaching in 1982. Gene was a mail carrier for the US Post Office and retired in 1984. They have three children. Rebecca Crawford has two children, Adrienne and Jacob Kiesel. She and her husband, Tom, reside in Colorado Springs, CO. Adrienne is a junior in college in Denver, CO and Jake is a senior in high school in Indianapolis, IN. Janie lives in San Jose, CA. She is a regional sales manager for Guidant, Inc. Randy lives in Farmington and owns Hard Rack Restaurant and Billiards in Bonne Terre, MO.

(June and Jean were identical twins. Like many twins, they enjoyed dressing alike and being together. June often related, with amusement, her encounter with Jean's students, who were upset when their "teacher" didn't recognize them when they met her on the street).

Donna (Zimmer) and Kenny Rickus live in Farmington. For several years, in the 50s and 60s, they owned and operated the bar and restaurant on Hwy. 32 east of Farmington known as Kenny's. This was part of the original business started by Ed Zimmer in about 1922. Donna worked at the Presbyterian Manor until her retirement. Kenny was a sales rep for McKesson Corp.

JoAnne (Zimmer) and Homer Henderson have two daughters, Leslie Jones and Sherri Weaver. They all live in the Farmington area. JoAnne has been employed by Farm Equipment Sales for more than 20 years, and Homer is a semi-retired butcher. Leslie is a Title I math teacher in the Central School District. She and Dave have two sons, David and Paul. Sherri and Mike have two children, Charlie and Rebecca. All four attended St. Paul Lutheran School in Farmington.

The children of Ed and Della Zimmer are a close-knit extended family. All nine were confirmed at St. Paul Lutheran Church. Today, the majority of the family living in Farmington remain active in both St. Paul Lutheran Church and school. *Submitted by Jean (Zimmer) Allen*

Late Submission

KARSCH - Karsch is a well-known family name in the history of Farmington, MO. Entering town from the interstate today, you will drive down Karsch Boulevard. The family was especially prominent during the late 1800s and early 1900s. Some of the family remained in the area and a family member founded one of the town cemeteries. The Karsch Family home was a large house built in the Victorian style of the era. It has since been torn down and the land sold.

In the late 1800s Genevieve Lee, a relative of Gen. Robert E. Lee, married one of the Karsch brothers. She gave birth to one child, Eugene

Gene at age 14.

The Karsch home in Farmington.

John Karsch, but died when he was a toddler. Karsch then married Leona (?) in 1901. They had three children in the early 1900s, Ruth Susan, Elizabeth K. and Paul A. Karsch. Leona Karsch raised all four children. In her later years, she resided in the St. Louis area near her two daughters. After her death, she was buried in Parkview Cemetery in Farmington.

Eugene John "Gene" Karsch grew up in Farmington and participated in the local Boy Scouts and achieved the rank of Eagle Scout. After college, Gene left Farmington for Southern Illinois where he settled and later married Jenny Louise Palmer of Sparta, Illinois. They had one daughter, Barbara Lee Karsch born in 1925. At the time of his death in 1952 he was the Executive Vice President of the Sparta State Bank. He is buried in Sparta, Illinois. His daughter Barbara, became a high school teacher. She married and had five children.

Leona, Paul, Bethen and Ruth (in front).

Ruth Susan Karsch became a registered nurse and married Earl Ross "Mac" McAtee. They resided in the St. Louis area. Mac was active during WWII and authored training manuals for the military. In civilian life he was an engineer for the Harry Barrett Equipment Company in St. Louis until his death in 1958 or 1959. Ruth remained in St. Louis until her death in 1983. They are buried in Parkview Cemetery. They had no children.

Barbara Lee Karsch, one year old.

Paul A. Karsch had passed away prior to the death of his older sister Ruth in 1983. He had been married.

Elizabeth K. "Bethen" Karsch left Farmington and married John V. Opie. They resided in the St. Louis area. She and John had one son, David J. Opie. Bethen moved to Canada after the death of her husband in the mid-1980s to be near her son David and his family. *Submitted by Susan Lee Harwood (granddaughter of Gene Karsch).*

City Funny Band in 1903.

Farmington Blues 1937

Highley Stables, 1890, location unknown.

Past meets future, across from courthouse now Mercantile parking lot.

Printed in the USA
CPSIA information can be obtained
at www.ICGtesting.com
JSHW052001150824
68134JS00059B/2706